SERIES FOR SCIENCE AND CULTURE

Making Science Social

THÉOPHRASTE RENAUDOT,
engraved by Michel Lasne.
Courtesy Bibliothèque nationale de France, Paris, 49 B 5343.

Making Science Social

The Conferences of Théophraste Renaudot
1633–1642

Kathleen Wellman

UNIVERSITY OF OKLAHOMA PRESS • NORMAN

ALSO BY KATHLEEN WELLMAN

La Mettrie: Medicine, Philosophy, and Enlightenment (Durham 1992)

Library of Congress Cataloging-in-Publication Data

Wellman, Kathleen Anne, 1951–
    Making science social : the conference of Théophraste Renaudot, 1633–1642/
Kathleen Wellman.
       p. cm. — (Series for science and culture; v. 6)
    Includes bibliographical references and index.
    ISBN 0-8061-3502-6 (hc.: alk. paper)
      1. Science—France—History—17th century. 2. Paris (France)—Intellectual
life—17th century. 3. Renaudot, Théophraste, 1586–1653—Contributions in science. I. Title. II. Series for science and culture; v. 6.

Q127.F8 W45 2003
509.44'09032—dc21   2002029139

Making Science Social: The Conferences of Théophraste Renaudot, 1633–1642
is Volume 6 in the Series for Science and Culture.

1   2   3   4   5   6   7   8   9   10

FOR MY PARENTS,

Art & Mickey Wellman

Contents

Illustrations

Series Editor's Foreword

IN RECENT YEARS, THE STUDY OF SCIENCE, BOTH WITHIN AND OUTSIDE of the academy, has undergone a sea change. Traditional approaches to the history and philosophy of science treated science as an insular set of procedures concerned to reveal fundamental truths or laws of the physical universe. In contrast, the postdisciplinary study of science emphasizes its cultural embeddedness, the ways in which particular laboratories, experiments, instruments, scientists, and procedures are historically and socially situated. Science is no longer a closed system that generates carefully plotted paths proceeding asymptotically towards the truth, but an open system that is everywhere penetrated by contingent and even competing accounts of what constitutes our world. These include—but are by no means limited to—the discourses of race, gender, social class, politics, theology, anthropology, sociology, and literature. In the phrase of Nobel laureate Ilya Prigogine, we have moved from a science of being to a science of becoming. This becoming is the ongoing concern of the volumes in the Series for Science and Culture. Their purpose is to open up possibilities for further inquiries rather than to close off debate.

The members of the editorial board of the series reflect our commitment to reconceiving the structures of knowledge. All are prominent in their fields, although in every case what their "field" is has been redefined, in large measure by their own work. The departmental or program affiliations of these distinguished scholars—Sander Gilman, Donna Haraway, N. Katherine Hayles, Bruno Latour, Richard Lewontin, Michael Morrison, Mark Poster, G. S. Rousseau, and Donald Worster—seem to tell us less about what they do than where, institutionally, they have been. Taken together as a set of strategies for rethinking the relationships between science and culture, their work exemplifies the kind of careful, self-critical scrutiny within fields such as medicine, biology, anthropology, history, physics, and literary criticism that leads us to a recognition of the limits of what and how we have been taught to think. The postdisciplinary aspects of our board members' work stem from their professional expertise within their home disciplines and their willingness to expand their studies to other, seemingly alien fields. In differing ways, their work challenges the basic divisions within western thought between metaphysics and physics, mind and body, form and matter.

Similarly, the volumes we have published in the series reflect crucial changes in the ways we conceive of both science and culture. In an era in which the so-called Science Wars have polarized these allegedly opposing fields of study by caricaturing both camps—"science" and "culture"—as single-minded restatements of invariant beliefs, the studies in the series elevate the level of postdisciplinary discussion by indicating ways in which we can think beyond simplistic modes of attack and defense. All coherence is not gone in a postdisciplinary era, but our conceptions of what counts as coherence, inquiry, and order continue to evolve.

Robert Markley
West Virginia University

Preface

HOWARD SOLOMON, IN HIS BIOGRAPHY OF THÉOPHRASTE RENAUDOT, suggests that "a definitive study of the nine-year career of Renaudot's academy would be, in effect, an analysis of the intellectual world of the mid-seventeenth century."[1] I have taken up his challenge. Using the five volumes of published proceedings, or conferences, produced by this group, I contend that the conferences provide a crucial link in the evolution from Renaissance humanism to the Enlightenment because participants consistently brought science to bear on the rhetorical traditions of Renaissance humanism. Science empowered them to discuss both nature and culture.

The published record of the conferences proved an unwieldy but even more fascinating source than I originally expected, presenting a multifaceted window on the seventeenth century. It offers significant and relevant information on every conceivable seventeenth-century topic (and some inconceivable ones as well). A quick glance at the table of contents of any volume reveals such intriguing titles as "Whether it be best for a state to have slaves," "Of the little hairy girl lately seen in this city," "Of the seat of folly," "Of the origin of winds," and "Whether man or woman be the more noble." Because this source has attracted so little scholarly attention, it has frequently seemed impossible to do justice to its richness. The range, extent, and variety of both the subjects proposed and the kinds of arguments brought to bear make it difficult to grasp the content of the conferences. To console myself I have imagined the challenges faced by scholars who attempted to explicate Montaigne to an audience who had access to neither the text nor other studies of this great figure. How could one present a text as complex as the *Essais* with enough nuance to do it justice and enough simplicity not to overwhelm the reader with so much detail that he or she would simply be better advised just to read the original?

The comparison between Montaigne's *Essais* and these conferences is a fruitful one from several perspectives. Like Montaigne, conferees brought to their discussions vast erudition, but they wore it lightly. They did not use citations extensively or respond directly to other authors. They were beneficiaries of humanism but felt free to use it simply as a frame of reference rather than as an authority. The daunting erudition of the conferees makes any attempt to provide a context for their discussions quite challenging. As seventeenth-century thinkers, they commented both on immediate intellectual antecedents and on works from the ancient past. They reflected on perennial issues found in ancient and Renaissance texts. And despite their criticisms of medieval scholasticism, Aristotle cast a long shadow on their discussion of a wide variety of topics.[2] If the range of material they discuss and their rich and extensive use of a long intellectual past make a thorough contexualization impossible, these very qualities nonetheless allow conferees to convey the richness of their intellectual and cultural world in an engaging format.

The format of the conferences also poses challenges to the scholar. The plethora of topics treated makes it difficult to even determine what kind of study is appropriate. Many aspects present difficulties: the extent of the source (2,550 pages and 460 topics discussed),[3] its format (summaries of speeches delivered by anonymous speakers), and its presentation of information (speeches are simply presented with no attempt to resolve or impose a consensus on the question posed). The structure of the conferences is emphatically anti-scholastic and anti-authoritarian. No speaker is identified, because his status should not shape the public reception of his remarks. Speakers are discouraged from using citations to bolster their remarks. There is an overriding sense that "truth will out," so no attempt is made to force competing remarks into any artificial synthesis. The very aspects that made these conferences so unusual for their day and so attractive for their contemporaries make them challenging for historians to use. It is difficult to present them so that they are accessible to the modern reader and yet reflect accurately the eclectic character of the documents themselves. As a result, historians have found it more fruitful to mine them for quite specific purposes.[4]

One cannot look to any specific conference confident that one can separate the new from the old or the traditional from the progressive.

Such expectations are frustrated by the fact that, for example, when participants argue for progressive or more "modern" scientific views, like heliocentrism, they invoke the most traditional kinds of arguments such as "divinely ordered hierarchy" or biblical examples. Even more striking, participants support traditional scientific positions by appeals to empirical evidence. One conference that might illustrate the challenges of studying these documents, their intrinsic interest, and their use of science is the one dedicated to the topic "Of Bathing."[5] Participants address the topic from a wide range of perspectives: Paracelsian (the benefits of mineral waters), Aristotelian (water is not man's natural element), empirical (those who bathe suffer ill health), or biblical (when God destroyed the earth, he did it with water). But speakers did not present set pieces, arguing for a particular theoretical position. Instead they combined whatever arguments they considered useful and persuasive. Perhaps most disconcerting for the modern reader, of the twelve opinions participants express on the topic of bathing, eight are staunchly opposed to the practice (although this position accurately reflects early modern views).[6]

Despite the rather strange character of these arguments from a modern perspective, they nonetheless indicate a pragmatic approach to this particular topic. They assert that, in general, bathing is contrary to man's nature and detrimental to his health. The conditions of bathing cannot be sufficiently regulated to ensure that it does not produce ill effects such as filling the head with vapors or killing infants in the womb. One speaker, perhaps an early adherent to cost-benefit analysis, notes, "If you add the loss of time to the rich, the charge to the poor, and the inconvenience to all, you will not wonder that most men abstain from them." Virtually every conference presents a similar juxtaposition of science and cultural concerns and offers an engaging glimpse of an earlier time, brought to life by a clever turn of phrase or a glaringly unfamiliar image or argument.

My treatment of this work begins by setting the conferences in the context of academies, scientific societies, and other comparable gatherings of the early modern period, in order to discuss their distinctive character. The first part of this book describes the hopes of their founder, Théophraste Renaudot—the inspiration, facilitator, and guiding spirit behind them. The conferences not only bear his imprint, but his life and career are a good way to set the conferences in a historical context. Renaudot is best known today for the French literary prize, the Renaudot, named after him. In his own day he was both famous and infamous for the medical controversies that swirled around him. His espousal of chemical medicine and his attempts to provide free medical services in Paris brought him into conflict with the Faculty of Medicine of Paris. He was also the founder of the Bureau d'Adresse. The myriad activities undertaken there—conferences, medical consultations, an information and services clearing house, publication of the *Gazette de France*—are a testimony to his creativity and inventiveness and to his unique position in the society of seventeenth-century France.

The rest of this book addresses the substance of the conferences. To impose some order on this chaotic and invaluable source, I have collected the conferences under themes that allow me to treat, in at least glancing fashion, most of the topics discussed. The themes that form the chapters of this study are divided into two topical sets. The first are scientific topics: nature, occult science, science, and medicine. The second are topics treating social issues such as human nature, ethics or social values, politics and economics, and women and the family. These topics cover most of the issues treated in the conferences, while giving the modern reader both a sense of the conferences and an entrée into the culture of the seventeenth century. The content of the conferences allows the reader to reassess the nature and practice of science in the early modern period and to reconsider the connections between science and the development of the social sciences. Finally these conferences suggest new ways to think about the early seventeenth century and its connection to the republic of letters and the French Enlightenment.

Acknowledgments

A PROJECT SO BROAD IN SCOPE AND LONG IN THE MAKING INCURS A great many debts that I am most pleased to acknowledge. I am especially grateful to those friends and colleagues who offered to read and comment on the manuscript. Two of my departmental colleagues, John Mears and James Hopkins, most generously read the first, long, and unwieldy draft and offered both encouragement and suggestions on how to shape the manuscript. Katherine Pandora, Lisa Sarasohn, Robert Schneider, and Elizabeth Williams gave most generously of their time to offer perceptive and encouraging comments on the manuscript at later stages. I appreciate their insights and the opportunity to carry on a dialogue with them.

I would like to recognize the support of the NEH Fellowship for College Teachers, which allowed me to spend an academic year completing the research and beginning to write this project. A Mellon Fellowship at the University of Oklahoma was primarily directed toward a new project on eighteenth-century physiology, but it did allow me to share this work with graduate students and colleagues there. I would like to thank Peter Barker, Gregg Mitman, Jamil Ragep and Ken Taylor for their interest in the project during the year I spent in the History of Science program. I would also like to thank Keith Baker, Allen Debus, and Dena Goodman whose interest, support, and letters of recommendation were critical to procuring successful funding for this work. It has been a keen pleasure to share with Allen Debus our mutual enthusiasm for Renaudot. All of the friends and colleagues with whom I have discussed Renaudot over the years have given me a sense of the virtues of the republic of letters and an appreciation of its merits and significance.

The support of the University Research Council of Southern Methodist University, the Stanton Sharp Fund and the Clements Fund of the history department, allowed me to conduct research in collections at the Newberry Library, the Memorial Library at the University ofWisconsin, the National Library of Medicine, and the Bibliothèque Nationale de France. I would also like to acknowledge the efforts of the interlibrary loan staff at SMU, especially Billie Stovall, for their efforts to facilitate my research. My colleagues in the history department— Jeremy Adams, Peter Bakewell, Jim Breeden, John Chávez, Dennis Cordell, Ed Countryman, Crista DeLuzio, Melissa Dowling, Ken Hamilton, O.T. Hargrave, Jim Hopkins, Tom Knock, Glenn Linden, Alexis McCrossen, John Mears, Don Niewyk, Dan Orlovsky, Michael Provence, Sarah Schneewind, Sherry Smith, and David Weber—have provided a congenial community, fostering research and scholarly discourse. I also appreciate the many ways my work has been facilitated by the staff of the history department—Mildred Pinkston, the administrative assistant, and Brenda Cooper and Julie Stewart, departmental secretaries.

I would also like to thank the staff of the University of Oklahoma Press who have been delightful to work with and who have made the process of transforming a manuscript into a book as painless as possible. I appreciate the professionalism and consideration of my editor, Daniel Simon; his assistant, Karen Weider; the managing editor, Alice Stanton; and the care of my copy editor, Pippa Letsky.

I am grateful for the support of my family. My husband, Dennis Sepper, has shared my preoccupation with the science of the seventeenth century, and over the life of this project, he has been sounding board, critic, and editor. His companionship has made my work that much more enjoyable and my life incomparably richer. My children, Elizabeth and Matthew, were at first bemused by my preoccupation with "anonymous French people," but over the life of this project they too have been captivated by the study of history. My mother, Mickey Wellman, read the manuscript as a nonspecialist reader, so that I might better provide a context for such readers. This book is dedicated to both my parents in grateful acknowledgment of a much larger debt—a lifetime of love and support.

PART I Background

ARMAND-JEAN DU PLESSIS
(Cardinal Richelieu), engraved by Michel Lasne.
Courtesy Bibliothèque Nationale de France, Paris, 90 C 146820.

CHAPTER ONE

The Intellectual Setting

"A Spacious Arena for Your Spirits"

> *"If man is truly said to be a social animal, his soul being the best part of him, then his education can be attained only by conference, which is the commerce of souls."*

THÉOPHRASTE RENAUDOT'S PREFACE TO THE PUBLISHED VOLUME of the first hundred conferences held at the Bureau d'Adresse explicitly heralds their unusual character.[1] The goal of his conferences, Renaudot claims, is to rescue the sciences from scholarly obscurity and to make things intelligible without "the unpleasant and perpetual task of first surmounting the difficulties of exotic words."[2] Like many works written in the period of the scientific revolution, the tenor of the proceedings is deliberately iconoclastic. Participants eschew the authority of established figures except on special occasions,[3] because, as Renaudot proclaims in his preface, "if any man speaks reason, it ought to suffice without another's authority to recommend it." Authority, he insists, except for the laws of the prince, "should exert no force over free souls." To avoid the divisiveness of rival schools of thought, no moderator resolves differences of opinion; instead the issue is left to the judgment of the reader, all speakers remain anonymous, and natural speech rather than rhetoric is used.[4]

In "these assemblies of learned people, curious about the sciences and the arts," Renaudot notes, "all were received to give their advice or to listen to that of others on the subject proposed." He extols the manifest utility of the conferences: "The young will fashion themselves,[5] the old will refresh their memory, the learned will make themselves admired, others will learn there, and all will encounter an honest diversion." This startlingly progressive claim asserts that the value of the conferences did not depend on the cultivation of a specialized knowledge or information privileged by discipline or by audience. Instead, Renaudot emphasizes the inherent benefit of knowledge to all, regardless of social status or level of expertise. He heralds the conferences as a "true academy" because there "one brings to light precepts demonstrated in shadow," offering a forum for many learned people "who have not had until now any place in this kingdom." He insists:

> The innocence of this exercise is remarkable: because, not only is slander and back-biting banished from it, but also, from fear of irritating spirits easily heated by the issues of religion, one leaves to the Sorbonne all that concerns religion. The mysteries of the affairs of state, belonging also to the nature of things divine, of which those who speak of it the best speak of it the least, those [mysteries] we send back to the councils of state from where they come. All the rest here is presented to all to serve as a spacious arena for your spirits.[6]

The claim of innocence is common to many innovative activities in the early modern period. Other scientific institutions like the Royal Society sought protection by claiming "innocence." Individuals, too (most notably René Descartes), justified their endeavors by insisting that they posed no threat to the established religious or social order. The stricture against discussing religion and politics was also characteristic of seventeenth-century salons and academies.[7]

Conference, in this context, is a seventeenth-century usage meaning "a comparison or collation of views, a bringing together of ideas with the purpose of making a complete description of the subject of discussion."[8] Initially the term referred to a gathering of people treating a subject in common. Later in the seventeenth century, it took on a more structured sense and came to mean a discourse where one publicly treated an intellectual topic.[9]

The most vivid impression conveyed by Renaudot's conferences is the vast array of topics and the variety of opinions expressed on each, revealing, as one commentator has remarked, an "impatient curiosity, a naive appetite for science, an intellectual pantagruelism."[10] The range of topics indicates, as Simone Mazauric has suggestively remarked, "a Baroque sensibility" or "a cabinet of curiosities."[11] The conferences were deliberately designed to be thoroughly eclectic, open to any topic or, as Renaudot put it, "all that which fell under the commerce of men."[12] They were held every Monday afternoon, from two to four, from 1633 until 1642, and they were attended by a room-capacity crowd of about one hundred people.[13] The topic for the week was determined at the previous meeting. Renaudot published reports of these conferences each week from 1634 to 1641; his son published the conferences of 1642 (in 1655). Renaudot noted at the beginning of publication that "the resolution of the last conference had been henceforth to print the material, which might be proposed, and the opinions upon them, which might merit attention, and thus to speak of the most beautiful things which are found in the sciences."[14] The reports were printed each week on inexpensive paper to foster wide dissemination and were collected into sets of one hundred in expensive leatherbound volumes. Both the popular and the more expensive forms were printed at the Bureau and provide distinctive examples of the collected mémoirs of early scientific societies.[15] The first two hundred conferences were translated into English in an elegant two-volume set in 1664. Individual conferences were often pirated, translated into other languages, and reprinted throughout the seventeenth century, attesting to their continuing popular appeal.[16]

Renaudot left a direct indication of what he intended the conferences to accomplish. A speaker in the conference on "Whether the conference is the most instructive way to teach,"[17] held in 1641, the eighth year of the nine-year history of the group, cites the great utility of this form of instruction in a way that is entirely in keeping with Renaudot's own aspirations. The principal speaker on this occasion was very likely Renaudot himself, since he not only reiterates fundamental points Renaudot makes elsewhere[18] but also explicitly defends the conferences and cites the benefits of their publication. He argues that the longevity of this form of intellectual exchange evinces its utility, "as it is impossible that an institution should last so long if it had not proved highly beneficial." Publication made the conferences even more useful: "It has been found good not only to record on paper so many fine thoughts, a part of which would have escaped the memory of hearers, but also to print and publish them . . . with a popularity known to all." He singles out the conferences as the only institution he developed "which has had neither contradictors nor opposition."

He explicitly identifies the conferences as a new intellectual forum that allows the expression of new ideas by those barred from traditional assemblies. This was an open venue for those who would not have been welcome in the salon or the academy. The setting was congenial, wonderfully ecumenical, and intellectually accessible; it offered participants an opportunity to discuss a wide variety of topics of intrinsic interest. As Renaudot notes, "Indeed it may well boast of having given publicity to several wits and having produced others who had previously held themselves hidden and buried in the dust of the schools." The conferences then provide a new public space that he defines as "between the pulpit and the bar." Like "the public declamations of old," he contends, this space provides a setting "for those, fresh from school, who are incapable of the life of the court and of other places where they must appear." Renaudot thus envisions the conferences as a kind of civic training ground for public discourse, especially for those as yet unskilled in the arts of verbal expression. Those who may move on to the more demanding forum of the court, bar, or pulpit can hone their oratorical and analytic skills in the hospitable setting of the conferences.

Renaudot also defines a new philosophy of education that rejects scholasticism in style and substance. He condemns "the stubborn humor that Scholars ordinarily contract in dispute, where they learn never to yield," as a "most disobliging quality," completely inappropriate to intellectual discussion. Renaudot emphasizes reason as the definitive human characteristic and advocates its unfettered exercise. He bemoans the constraints on free expression of the schools (meaning scholastic universities) and more conventional academies. Because both of these are more concerned with social status and formulaic expressions, they have impeded the emergence of knowledge. He offers an alternative that is open, progressive, and disseminated through print "to announce to succeeding ages the happiness and felicity of ours." The conferences offer education through open intellectual exchange, an education that in turn fosters further exchange. They grow out of Renaudot's conviction that great things could be accomplished only if people were brought into fruitful contact with each other, a conviction that lies behind all the activities of the Bureau.

Renaudot's conferences offered to the seventeenth-century participant a forum that was as open and as egalitarian as any in the early modern period. They were also by their stated intention both progressive and, despite claims of innocence, subversive, at least intellectually. For the modern reader, it is quite striking that so early in the seventeenth century we have such a fully articulated model of Habermas's public sphere.[19] That is to say, Renaudot's group offers an early model of the public exercise of reason by a group of private individuals whose critical acumen comes to focus on broad issues of public concern, including the state itself, in the interest of the common good. The term *public sphere* is most effectively deployed to describe the culture of the Enlightenment.[20] But the connection between the conferences and the Enlightenment is not just of form but also of substance. By applying science as a decisive standard, especially as opposed to theology, conferees explored issues from many of the same perspectives as the encyclopedists did, defined many of the same epistemological stances, and worked toward creating the social sciences.

The conferences are not only significant steps in cultural and institutional trends that burgeoned in the eighteenth century. They are also important documents for our understanding of the seventeenth century. These open, uncensored meetings took place with the active support of Richelieu in the early period of consolidation of political power in the hands of a central government, a form of government later termed absolutism. They also provided a context of thorough and intensive scientific discussion on the eve of the scientific revolution. This study of the content of the conferences affords the reader an opportunity to reevaluate the character of seventeenth-century culture, the nature of seventeenth-century sciences, the role of science in the development of the social sciences, and the connection of seventeenth-century culture to the Enlightenment.

📖

The hopes that Renaudot had for his conferences—as accessible to a wide public for cultivating useful knowledge in a public setting—mark him as a man of progressive ideas. He sought to implement these ideas in what were called his "inventions"—the Bureau d'Adresse, medical consultations, the first dispensary and public chemical laboratory, various publishing ventures, and a forum for popularizing science in the conferences.[21] Born in Poitou to a successful bourgeois family in 1585, Renaudot pursued a medical career, receiving a medical degree from Montpellier in 1606. He traveled in Italy and studied with surgeons before returning to Loudun to practice medicine. His ideas for poor relief brought him to the attention of Père Joseph and Cardinal Richelieu. Richelieu's support took him to Paris where, after protracted legal battles, he was finally authorized to pursue his inventions. Richelieu's support led to a number of titles, offices, and royal decrees endorsing his controversial endeavors, but Renaudot could maintain these activities only with the support of Richelieu and Louis XIII. With their deaths in 1642 and 1643 respectively, those whom Renaudot's activities had thwarted, especially the Faculty of Medicine, launched a campaign against him that shut down most of his activities. Although the regent, Anne of Austria, supported the Faculty of Medicine against Renaudot, she continued to use him as royal publicist in his capacity as publisher of the *Gazette de France*. When Renaudot died in 1653, his extensive influence had been almost completely curtailed.

Renaudot is a striking character because of his unusual ability to maneuver successfully within the stratified society of the ancien régime. Always on the fringes of elite society he nonetheless carved out a highly successful if unconventional career. For example, in his medical practice and education, Renaudot always worked outside the established order, taking an unlikely path to success as a physician. Because he considered the practice of surgery and surgical education important to medical practice, he went so far as to enroll in the surgical Collège de Saint-Côme after he received his medical degree from Montpellier.[22] He dedicated his practice, in large part, to the medical relief of the indigent. But his unconventional activities were not restricted to medicine. He came up with novel ways to deal with France's social and economic problems at a time when Richelieu, his influential patron, was interested in reform. He operated a clearinghouse to bring many kinds of people and diverse sources of information to his Bureau. (The ways in which Renaudot's concerns shaped the conferences themselves will be treated in the next chapter.)

Throughout his career, Renaudot proudly touted the great utility of the conferences. Despite his sanguine sense that they alone of all his activities were universally appreciated, they have had a surprisingly checkered historical reputation. In the seventeenth century, most commentators affirmed Renaudot's positive appraisal. His most vociferous critics, notably the members of the Faculty of Medicine, considered them unequivocally credible. Even in the heat of dispute over contested authority, Faculty polemics did not condemn the conferences.[23]

Despite their seventeenth-century credibility, the eclectic, nonsystematic, and unconventional nature of the conferences has often opened them to disparaging comments, to charges that they catered to riffraff and wastrels or that they were not sufficiently intellectual. The most concerted criticism of Renaudot's group has been inferred by historians from characters in seventeenth-century novels. In the *Roman bourgeois*, Antoine Furetière describes a character as a "fine gallant . . . [who] was also a barrister, one who wore his robe and bonnet . . . never made a plea. . . . In the afternoons he used to go the conferences at the Office of Address . . . and to all the other public games and amusements that cost nothing."[24] Gideon Tallemant des Reaux, in his biographical vignettes of seventeenth-century figures, used the playwright La Calprenède's attendance at the conferences to cast aspersions on him, saying that "although he played the man of rank, he was long one of the buttresses of the Bureau d'Adresse."[25] These few characterizations have been the chief sources in the historical interpretation of the value, or lack thereof, of the conferences. They suggest that those who participated were ne'er-do-wells looking for something to do and that the conferences were the preferred venue of intellectual parvenus. Scholars who have studied the conferences as stopping points on the way to more "scientific" science have taken these derogatory characterizations as indicative of their overall value.

There are several reasons to reassess these facile dismissals. Did all new academic institutions face similarly critical assessments by contemporaries simply because they were new, different, and violated conventional academic norms? Ishmeal Boulliau's criticisms of the Académie des Sciences make some of those of Renaudot's gatherings look mild. Charles Sorel, in his history of the Académie Française, notes that it, like the conferences, provoked criticism because of hatred for their protector, Richelieu. As he points out, "acts against the projects and persons he favored are a good way to discharge anger."[26]

These two examples of institutions that subsequently gained credibility, although they were disparaged initially, suggest that they overcame charges of dilettantism or political bias largely because of their long histories. Their histories allowed them to outlast their early critics and to evolve in ways that conformed to or even shaped standard notions of culture or science. In other words, other groups that "practiced" science in much the same way as Renaudot's group did were transformed into more conventional societies in part because they lasted longer than the nine years of the conferences. As a result, historians have not used the "science" of the 1630s to discredit these other groups. Ultimately, the "proof" of their scientific value has been their subsequent history.

Sorel, official historian of the reign of Louis XIII, maintains that Renaudot's conferences should not be despised, neither because Renaudot was an *intendant* nor because there was so much varied activity and so much clutter that his house resembled a second hand store. Sometimes, Sorel insists, it was "a true house of philosophy," and the variety of activities there made it "a model of our civilization and a mirror of human life." He summarizes the contribution of the conferences by saying that "this assembly has had something of excellence beyond many others," and in the books of the proceedings one finds "many beautiful curiosities."[27] "Beautiful curiosities" is sometimes construed as an indictment of Renaudot's conferences. However, it is more appropriate to see this characterization as an endorsement, especially since it reflects the same general tone as Sorel's defense of the much more prestigious Académie Française.[28] In the context of the assiduous pursuit of wonders of nature, a hallmark of early modern science, perhaps best epitomized by Solomon's House in Francis Bacon's *New Atlantis,* "beautiful curiosities" might well be construed as praise of scientific enterprise. Recent biographers of Renaudot have also evaluated the conferences more positively. Jeanne Mauret cites their duration of more than nine years as testimony to their success and notes that "The same public, which went to the Hôtel de Bourgogne to applaud the Cid and Horace, came to the Bureau passionately interested in the range of topics discussed there."[29]

Harcourt Brown suggests several contextual reasons why some classical writers might have discounted the conferences. Renaudot not only suffered from a lack of high social standing, he had also managed to alienate powerful individuals and groups. Through his medical activities, he aroused the opposition of the polemicist par excellence, Guy Patin, and of the Faculty of Medicine. Through his activities as a journalist, he antagonized Gabriel Naudé and other members of the Cabinet Dupuy by rivaling their publishing ventures, and he challenged the privileges of printers. His influential neighbors, inconvenienced by the bustle of activities at the Bureau, were disgruntled enough to file suits against the clinic Renaudot proposed to build on the banks of the Seine. All these groups—neighbors, journalists, and physicians—strongly resented the special privileges Renaudot was able to gain for his endeavors. Perhaps most significantly, many of his activities—the *monts-de-piété,* an employment exchange, free medical consultations, a secondhand shop, classified advertisements—dealt with the down-and-out.[30] As Solomon puts it, "Renaudot's house on the Rue Calandre hardly breathed the sweet air of Parnassus."[31] Criticisms of Renaudot have become attached to the conférences themselves, despite the fact that they were generally well regarded by his contemporaries.

Although their luster has dimmed in some later discussions, the conferences were not only well regarded in their day, but they also had significant seventeenth-century diffusion and direct descendants. In

England they inspired intellectuals such as Samuel Hartlib and John Comenius and in France provided a model for other groups of intellectuals, as in the conferences of Jean de Soudier de Richesource and Pierre Bourdelot.[32] The printed conferences were widely diffused in England. They were translated and published individually and in collections of four or five. A translation of the first two hundred conferences appeared in 1664–1665 under the title, *A General Collection of Discourses of the Virtuosi of France*. The translator's preface to the second volume notes that these discourses "are extremely well fitted both for instruction and pleasure, they handle weighty questions with great facility; and what would be a load in the ordinary mode of writing thereupon, is here as fully and substantially delivered, and yet with exceeding elegance and perspicuity." The preface to the second volume heralds the "good reception of a volume of the like conferences," and the editor offers assurance "that the readers will not find themselves worse entertained at the second course than they were at the first." He praises the conferences as "the production of an assembly of the choicest wits in France" and acknowledges their relevance; they treat "subjects as are most inquired into at this time by the curious of our own nation."[33]

How were the conferences conducted? They began when all were seated in the great hall of the Bureau. In the initial format, the first hour was dedicated to a general topic, the second to a more specific one, and the third to inventions, such as "a microscope that made a flea appear as big as a mouse."[34] After the first few weeks, the inventions were no longer reported in the proceedings, though there is some anecdotal evidence that they continued.[35] Although they were originally given in paired sets, with one conference described as general and the other particular, for the modern reader the distinction seems to be that the first is dedicated to science and the other to more traditional rhetorical topics.[36] However one describes the distinction, the conferences demonstrate a great deal of crossing of arguments and evidence. Some "scientific" topics like "Of the little hairy girl" seem more like rhetorical topics, and the rhetorical topics like "Whether men ought to have many wives or women many husbands" are supported almost entirely by scientific arguments.[37] The participants in both kinds of discussions were probably the same, since the paired topics were discussed the same afternoon. Both kinds of conferences used the same standards of evidence and argumentation. Thus "science," very broadly construed, provided demonstrable evidence and standards of judgment rooted in empirical observation regardless of the topic under discussion. After the first one hundred meetings, over the course of about two years, it must have become clear that participants were trying to cover too much ground in one afternoon, so from this point on only one topic per week was discussed.

Many scholars have tried to determine who among the noteworthy members of the seventeenth-century community of scholars might have attended Renaudot's conferences. It is conventional to claim that important international scholars such as Jean-Baptiste Morin, Tommaso Campanella, and Etienne de Claves attended.[38] With most such claims about specific participants, one can trace them back to late nineteenth or early twentieth-century secondary sources, which invariably make the claims without attribution.[39] The best evidence is found in internal references in correspondence where one correspondent mentions attending a conference or describes someone else as attending. Laurence Brockliss and Colin Jones have recently raised the veil of secrecy over the participants by establishing, on the basis of the letters of Guy Patin, that the Montpellier graduate and Protestant Isaac Cattier attended. John Headley maintains that Campanella participated and found solace from his troubles there, and Mazauric has shown that Morin attended.[40] Most scholars assume that significant numbers of professionals such as doctors and lawyers participated because of the high incidence of medical topics discussed, because several conferences were specifically directed to comparisons between medicine and law, and because Renaudot's medical activities took place on the same site. Other historians have suggested that women attended. Although it is true that gender relations seem to be a fundamental concern of many of the conferences, there is no conclusive evidence that women attended. The fact that several conferences preface remarks by saying "if the ladies were here to defend themselves" suggests that they did not (although Renaudot's preface encourages men or women to present the results of their experiments in the third hour of the conferences).[41] The Bureau also attracted, as contemporary critics often pointed out, a number of dilettantes or virtuosi, as they were sometimes called, men of rank, leisure, and wealth.[42] It was, whatever the specific membership, an unusually open group in the context of seventeenth-century French academies.

The conferences are a compelling reflection of popular science. Even those historians most critical of their content nonetheless acknowledge that they occupy a distinctive niche in our knowledge of scientific culture. They illuminate a cultural level below the most elite level.[43] As Solomon has noted, "under the best of circumstances, pure scholarship and mass audiences do not mix; under the stultifying pressure of seventeenth-century Parisian social and intellectual pretension, the gap remained nearly unbridgeable, except for Renaudot."[44] Although the conferences were initially open to all, later, the size of the room, which could hold only about one hundred people, led to the restriction of admission to, as Renaudot put it, those of "a certain quality."[45]

The conferences have a highly unusual format because Renaudot deliberately did not reveal the identity of any speaker;[46] he did not want the reputation of a speaker to prejudice any readers. He did not intend to privilege any individual's contribution or to impose a kind of censorship or de facto ordering of the speeches of participants. This policy also served pragmatic purposes. As Sutton notes, "much of what the Bureau's guests said had dangerous implications; anonymity protected the verbal jousters from possible embarrassment, harassment, or worse."[47] Protected anonymity, at least in the printed form of the remarks, might have emboldened some to speak who might not have found their voice if intellectual authority and social preeminence were recognized. The policy of anonymity also betokens an unusual attitude toward knowledge, which is reflected in the content of the conferences as well. Not dependent on the reputation of the proponent, knowledge must win adherents on its own merits in the court of public opinion.

This explicit strategy says something important about Renaudot's intentions and his attitudes toward knowledge and fame, but it has frustrated historians. Although we know that one hundred people filled the room set aside for this purpose, we do not know who they were. We can determine that some people attended regularly because some speakers refer back to earlier conferences.[48] The historian has no sense of the speaker or his reputation and little indication of the impact or credibility of any particular point of view. There is no way to determine who or even what sort of person held any particular opinion. Even more disturbing for the historian who might like to explore the distinctive treatment of any topic at the Bureau is that there is no way to determine which approaches to specific issues were more persuasive than others. Members frequently respond to each other's remarks, but it is not always clear which arguments carry the day.

The printed format of each conference also presents difficulties. Each individual conference begins with "the first speaker said," whose remarks range from a half to several full folio pages, then speeches follow, given by one to eleven successive speakers.[49] The method of presentation—no set number of speakers and no moderator—does not afford a specific mechanism whereby one speaker can respond to another, though inevitably one speaker will frequently follow up on remarks made by another. Because these conferences are reduced to transcribed reports for publication in proceedings, they are essentially minutes of the meetings. One cannot know to what degree the speech was structured to meet the demands of publication, or if Renaudot exercised any editorial control after the speech was given. Two facts suggest that the speeches were not substantially edited after they were delivered: they were printed on inexpensive paper for mass distribution the same week they were given, and the length of the speeches is such that they would likely have filled the hour (reading them aloud supports this conclusion). The brief exposition and the deliberate policy of not citing sources also make it difficult for the modern reader to situate arguments in their seventeenth-century context or, without seventeenth-century erudition, to categorically separate the original from the derivative.

There are other considerable difficulties in dealing with individual conferences. Frequently the first speaker's approach to a topic is particularly jarring. One might assume that the first speaker would take the most obvious, direct, and conventional approach (and this is indeed frequently the case), but often he deflects discussion from the obvious into quite unusual avenues. This dissonance raises the question as to whether what is an unfamiliar approach by modern standards was conventional in the seventeenth century, or whether the speaker was a crank, or whether (as is sometimes the case in faculty meetings, for instance) the first speaker was using the stated topic of discussion to further his agenda no matter what the topic might be. Sometimes it is difficult for the other speakers to return to the topic or for the reader to perceive any relationship between the proposed topic and the first speech. However, the very chaos of material vividly illuminates what issues are contested, what aspects of topics are controversial and why, and the conceivable range of opinion on a given topic. In fact, one of the more useful as well as more disconcerting facets of these conferences is the completely unexpected approach taken by speakers to some topics.

Despite these difficulties, the conferences are much too rich a source to neglect. A diverse set of opinions presented by anonymous speakers on a wide range of topics affords the historian certain advantages for investigating science and culture in early modern France. The opinions presented are diverse; each conference lays out from two to twelve opinions on a given issue. Renaudot specifically advocated the "conference" as a forum that lays out multiple arguments, letting them stand on their own with no commentary except the response of critics within the conference itself. Because the conferences brought together people interested in new ideas who found the universities and academies stagnant, conservative, and unresponsive to popular concerns (especially those dealing with recent scientific information and issues), they provided a broader, more freewheeling, and more contemporary approach to issues than did the academic establishment. The most intriguing conferences are those that deal with commonplace topics on which every opinion expressed is strikingly foreign to modern sensibilities. Those conferences afford the kind of "opacity" that Robert Darnton has suggested presents the most effective means of entry into a culture remote in time from our own.[50]

These documents are consequently a compelling source for understanding the culture of early modern France. In her study of feminine "versions and subversions" of Cartesian discourse, Erica Harth, as she looks to novels for representations of Cartesianism, laments, "We would like to know what people may actually have said in the salons and academies."[51] Renaudot's conferences tell us, to the degree that any extant source can. It is of course legitimate to wonder how accurately and how thoroughly remarks were transcribed and to what degree they were self-censored by what Alain Viala calls "euphemization," the use of code or allusion to evade authority.[52] But certain factors suggest the accuracy of these documents as reflections of what was said; the conferences were public, the remarks were printed at the *Maison du Coq*, Renaudot's establishment,[53] and were widely disseminated almost immediately.

The conferences are important not only for their close relation to the spoken word, but also because they took place during a crucial time for French culture and thus allowed speakers to reflect self-consciously on the evolutions occurring within that culture. They are positioned to examine and to expose critical changes in the intellectual traditions of the time. In particular, they provide convincing evidence of the trans-mutation of humanism into science. Although participants were much indebted to the humanist tradition, they deployed that tradition to their own ends and so contributed to the demise of humanist methods of analysis. They agreed with humanists in their disparagement of the scholastic tradition. Renaudot abhorred what he called "the Scholastic rod of magisterial authority, to which the humor of our nation adapts itself less than any other." He extolled the conference as a unique means to erode such authority because "daily experience shows us that there is nothing more harmful to learning than to prevent the truth." Since the truth "appears chiefly in the opposition of contraries," the confer-ence was the ideal method to attain it.[54] Although humanism had offered a way to undermine medieval scholasticism, by the seventeenth century it seemed to many thinkers fraught with the same kinds of problems posed by scholasticism. It relied too heavily on authorities and offered an array of competing authorities without any way to adju-dicate between them. Seventeenth-century thinkers ultimately became dissatisfied with appeals to authority or to ancient texts. Philology and textual exegesis no longer seemed to offer productive methods to explore the natural or the social world. The members of Renaudot's group reexamined traditional questions with a new approach: they invoked the authority of science. Thus they afford a crucial view of the transformation of humanist culture in light of science. They built on a tradition but gave it a distinctive cast by adapting it to their own ends. By treating both rhetorical and scientific topics with the same evidence, vocabulary, and methodology, Renaudot's group suggests the importance of rhetoric to science and the applicability of science to the complete spectrum of topics.[55] Conferees treat issues common to Renaissance humanism but from the perspective of science, filtering rhetorical and civic concerns through the prism of science.

These conferences also provide an important perspective from which to understand science in the seventeenth century. I use the term *science* deliberately as the term most appropriately applied to the discussion of natural phenomena by conferees, despite its anachronistic character. The term did not take on its modern connotations until the nineteenth century in English. "Les sciences" in French referred to knowledge in general and gradually evolved to take on more specialized meanings. (And there are intimations of this evolution to a more modern meaning within the conferences.) The term that can be applied most appropriately and without anachronism to early modern natural investigations is *natural philosophy*. When early modern thinkers explored, studied, or theorized about the natural world, they were in pursuit of a new philosophy to replace Aristotelian philosophy. Some were dissatisfied with Aristotelian explanations of particular phenomena. Others hoped for an all-encompassing Christian philosophy. When mechanism was recognized by the end of the seventeenth-century as having produced a successful replacement for Aristotelian philosophy, it was heralded not as science but as the new "mechanical philosophy." Well into the eighteenth century, those figures we identify most with the progress of science—Robert Boyle, John Locke, Isaac Newton, and so on—considered themselves natural philosophers and deemed their investigations natural philosophy.

I have chosen to use the term *science* rather than *natural philosophy* for several important reasons. *Science* is the term we consistently apply to characterize ancient Greek and Roman, as well as medieval Arabic and Western investigations of nature. This use, though equally anachronistic, is considered unobjectionable, probably because there is no expectation that such remote investigations of nature will correspond to our own. It is in treating the period of the scientific revolution that historians insist on excluding the term *science* from what they do not recognize as modern. My use of the term asserts that *science* is at least as appropriate as when applied to earlier periods. My use also explicitly objects to the narrowing of notions of seventeenth-century science to what we are most comfortable with as opposed to the full range of investigations of nature.[56]

For these participants, science was an inclusive method, which could be broadly applied as a method of cultural analysis, rather than a technical skill based on narrow "expertise." Renaudot's group made a commitment to the dissemination of knowledge, which clearly challenged the old and, by implication, privileged new information. The conferences also afford an extensive demonstration of the character of seventeenth-century scientific discussion, which distinguishes them from comparable sixteenth-century gatherings. This group was overtly opposed to religious explanations (though participants sometimes gave them), disinclined to credit tradition and authority, and inclined to favor the experiential, the pragmatic, and the demonstrable. Participants were acutely aware that science gave them a new authority to wield against old authorities and to privilege their arguments. This "scientific perspective" was brought to bear on issues that would previously have been treated rhetorically, theologically, or metaphysically. The cultivation of science is proclaimed as progressive and utilitarian, but there is no emphasis on science as a key to moral regeneration as in many earlier academies. Science is not tied to religious goals, millenarian movements, or mystical quests for *pansophia*.[57] The secularism of these conferences is striking.

Renaudot's conferences reveal an unusually independent perspective. Part of the reason they warrant reexamination is that they seem curiously out of place in the conventional understanding of the culture of seventeenth-century France. The reformist agenda of Renaudot and the particular fusion of humanism and science of the conferences did not conform to the new mechanical science of the scientific revolution, nor did the fluidity of the form and content of the conferences conform to the rigidity of absolutist culture, best epitomized by the court of Louis XIV. The conferees' use of science—and indeed of all intellectual authority—was fluid. Science was neither narrowly defined by a single theoretical commitment, like mechanism, nor circumscribed within state institutions. As a result, participants shared some of the faults of Enlightenment philosophes: that is to say, they were quite unsystematic in their discussion; they played fast and loose with tradition; and the documentary evidence they have left is somewhat inconsistent. But absolutism—as the quest to centralize the government under the control of the monarchy is conventionally called—was not yet as rigid as it would become under Louis XIV, so it exercised less effective control over artistic and scientific institutions than it would later.[58] Even in this early period, Richelieu exercised considerable control over cultural institutions, as his intervention in the early Académie Française demonstrates. The case of Renaudot offers a problematic counterexample to the way in which Richelieu's control over cultural institutions is generally described. Renaudot was in an ambiguous position vis-à-vis Richelieu; he was a client, and he most clearly carried out Richelieu's wishes as editor of the *Gazette de France*. However, conferees seem quite uninhibited in making their arguments, even on social and political topics. The case of Renaudot suggests that, in the interest of the development of French culture, Richelieu tolerated some more independent cultural institutions.[59] Paradoxically, Richelieu's endorsement allowed Renaudot's group more autonomy and opportunities for independent and free inquiry, even of controversial topics, than comparable groups.

The conferences also set forth a different understanding of encyclopedic knowledge than what was characteristic of the sixteenth century. Renaudot's conferees do not assume there is a mystical key that will unite all knowledge. Instead they have a sense that comparison and presentation will allow them to reach a conclusion and to make comprehensive claims without resorting to mysticism. Nor do they see knowledge as gained by the compilation of apt quotations, a method Ann Blair describes as a "notebook method."[60] The conferences are explicitly encyclopedic, not in the sense of an organized and comprehensive presentation, but in the variety of opinion expressed on any given topic, a range designed to present complete knowledge. Renaudot did not feel compelled to proselytize for specific views or overtly direct the presentation of ideas. Thus the nature of knowledge in the conferences is encyclopedic more in the sense of the eighteenth-century *grande encyclopédie* of the enlightenment than in the sense of sixteenth-century *pansophia*. The conferences aim both to present ideas as thoroughly as possible and to indicate the current state of knowledge. They are epistemologically modest and anti-authoritarian; they present as many views as possible with the clear sense that truth will emerge through a comparison of ideas. For this to occur there must be widespread discussion and dissemination of divergent views by a wide variety of individuals. There is no need to impose consensus. Instead the conferences implicitly appeal both to the ultimately self-evident quality of truth and to the ability of the individual to judge the value of the information presented to him. This implicit faith in human reason prefigures Descartes's appeal to common sense as available to all and the foundation of the scientific method in his *Discourse on Method*.

Because the conferences provide such a palpable demonstration of connections between science and broader cultural issues, they evince an important step in the development of the social analysis toward the social sciences of the Enlightenment. They explicitly show how nature (although there is wide disagreement among participants as to what this term actually means) can be used as an inclusive category to unite science and culture. Participants, much like the later philosophes, use science to sustain social analyses of ethics, politics, commerce, and gender roles. They also share epistemological perspectives. While science is fundamental to both groups, neither has a coherent or uniform notion of science or its social ramifications. Both groups understand knowledge as polyvalent and thus the social analyses that depend on it vary widely. Both groups are optimistic that their analyses will produce practical and useful knowledge—a fitting legacy to posterity.

CHAPTER TWO

The Context of the Conferences and the Career of Their Sponsor

THE CONFERENCES BEGAN ONLY AFTER LOUIS XIII WAS FIRMLY established as king and after Richelieu was secure in his position as minister. It must have seemed to many in the 1630s, among them Renaudot and his conferees, that France was poised for great political and economic development. Political peace and security had been hard won after decades of religious war pitting Catholic against Huguenot (the French Calvinists), and noble factions against the crown, from 1562 to 1589. Louis XIII had managed to quell the nobility's opposition and to reduce the political factionalism that had characterized the regency of his mother, Marie de Medici, after the death of his father, Henry IV, in 1610. Such a long period of political instability had had a devastating effect on the French economy. Peace, with a new monarch on the throne supported by a strong and able minister, gave some the sense that the problems facing France could be ameliorated if they were addressed by men of intelligence and goodwill. The negative effects of Richelieu's involvement in the Thirty Years' War on such plans for economic expansion had not yet been felt. Still less could one have imagined the disastrous economic impact of France's militaristic pursuit of international hegemony far beyond the limits of its citizens to pay.[1] But in the 1630s, it must have seemed not only possible but even likely that thoughtful, critical analyses like those conducted at the Bureau would be productive.

The years of Renaudot's conferences also saw productivity in the arts and letters and the burgeoning of new forms of intellectual life in the academies and the salon. But this was not yet the period of the golden age of French classicism and the apogee of French artistic influence under Louis XIV, when the arts, richly supported by royal revenue, were marshaled to support the Sun King and hence could criticize only obliquely. In the 1630s the arts and other forms of culture were less well supported but somewhat more independent.

This independence is also reflected in a new intellectual spirit in the 1630s. The response of many intellectuals to the political chaos of the decades of religious wars and the crisis of belief produced by a divided Christendom in the aftermath of the Protestant reformation was to call all knowledge into question. Montaigne and his contemporaries advised intellectuals to flee the chaos of politics and to cultivate the life of the scholar. Renaudot's conferences took place at a time when many intellectuals were intent on rescuing knowledge from skepticism. Conferees rejected any notion that the contemplative life was the ideal and instead advocated constructive political and social engagement. A renewed confidence in science could provide a new foundation for certain knowledge, and such a quest fueled many of the new academies. Social hierarchy, patronage, and state sponsorship shaped the practice of these academies. We know with historical hindsight that the centralization of political power would become stultifying. We know that royal or ministerial sponsorship of the arts and sciences not only fostered but also inhibited their development. We, as a result, bring to our investigations of the work of such academies a cautious skepticism—in stark contrast to the ebullient confidence and optimism with which Renaudot and his participants embraced the conferences.

THE LEGACY OF THE ACADEMIES

Although Renaudot loudly proclaimed the conferences as original, they actually emerged from the rich cultural context of the early modern academy. While they do indeed represent a distinctive intellectual institution, they must properly be understood within the context of other contemporary academic institutions. Their intellectual antecedents in the Renaissance must also be acknowledged.

Given the integral connection between the university and medieval culture, particularly as reflected in scholasticism, it is not surprising that the Renaissance looked to another kind of institution—the academy—as a more compelling model of intellectual life. Italian humanists invoked the classical antecedents of the academy, the *exhedre* of Plato and the *lyceum* of Aristotle.[2] Italian academies were specifically indebted to Plato, and Platonism found a congenial home in the Florentine academy of Ficino and Pico.[3] Renaissance academies successfully evaded the clerical control and Aristotelian dominance of the universities and responded to the social and intellectual concerns of Renaissance elites.

There is a direct connection between Italian humanism and the idealization of the conference as a method of intellectual exchange. Giovanni Botero, a Renaissance humanist who wrote primarily on law and politics, specifically proclaimed the value of conferences and made some suggestions on how to profit from attending them. Since conferences offer an opportunity to converse with men of diverse abilities and occupations, Botero recommended that one "frequent the company of experts, so that by noting their observations and suiting them to particular judgment, you may discern the difference between art and nature, experience and learning."[4] Whether or not Renaudot came into contact with the writings of Botero in his travels in Italy, he shared many assumptions about the possibilities for fruitful intellectual exchange offered by the conference format.

The influence of Italian academies on the development of academic traditions in France is unmistakable. Attempts by French kings to emulate the Platonic academy in the late sixteenth century were fruitful. Catherine de Medici was interested in furthering the intellectual traditions of her illustrious Medici antecedents and sought to extend to France the Platonic model of the Medicean academy. Neoplatonism influenced the Pléiade, an informal academy that was the model and immediate precursor of the officially instituted academies such as the

Académie Royale de Poésie et de Musique established by Catherine's sons, Charles IX and Henry III. Although these academies reflected the interests of their royal patrons, sometimes they incorporated discussions that were wide-ranging, especially if music was a focus since, in a neoplatonic framework, music entailed encyclopedic scope.[5] An early sixteenth-century academy under the direction of Jean-Antoine de Baif was both an academy and a music conservatory and was shaped by an implicit agenda of moral reform. It inspired Nicolas Colletet, Marin Mersenne, and other prominent seventeenth-century intellectuals, by offering a model of the heights to which an academy could aspire, that is to say, no less than universal knowledge and moral regeneration.[6]

The Palace Academy provides an interesting example of both the character of a sixteenth-century academy and its evolution. With the support of the royal family, members of this group—the first in France to be designated an academy—met in the Louvre from 1570 until about 1584. Initially their interests focused on rhetorical topics like beauty, love, and the merits of the *vita contemplativa*, but in later years the group focused on religious topics, especially in response to the Catholic reformation and Henry III's exposure to Saint Charles Borromeo, one of the leaders of that reform movement. Like other sixteenth-century academies, the Palace Academy had broader scope than a specific artform or discipline and understood its mission to be broadly directed toward moral regeneration. The connection of these academies to science is less obvious, because science, in these fora, is best understood as hermetic knowledge cultivated to produce the moral regeneration of the practitioner. As academies focused on religious issues or moral regeneration in the face of growing religious fragmentation, science became tied more directly to a mystical understanding of a world soul that could readily transcend the religious divisions of the reformation.[7]

After the demise of the Palace Academy, a host of institutions provided fora for intellectuals to circumvent the constraints, in terms of both membership and topics of discussion, of more traditional academies. Neither these groups nor the more conventional academies of the period have been much studied, and few have been considered very significant, partly because of the general decline of academies at the turn of the century. The last years of the Valois kings were not marked by intellectual or scientific vitality, and Henry IV and his court did not revitalize intellectual pursuits.[8]

The first seventeenth-century attempt to revive a court academy occurred in 1612 when the tutor to Louis XIII, David Rivault de Flurance, set out the following design: "The academy is to meet on certain days for debate, and, after the debates, if any member has composed a song or a madrigal, it may be performed." The subjects for discussions were "not to be directly concerned with theology, but may be on any other subject, philosophy, humanity, poetry, the mechanical arts, history." Written records of speeches were to be kept and given to the secretary "with a view to possible publication." The connection of the academy to moral regeneration was made explicit by the stipulation that "on the first Thursday in each month, one of the officers shall read an exhortation to piety, recommending the academicians to live life as men of honor and good Christians."[9] In his introductory discourse (apparently the first and last in this short-lived academy), Flurance argued for its utility. Although Renaudot later used almost the same terms in the preface to the first volume of the conferences, his group offered no performances and rejected the pietism of Flurance's group. There is an even greater distance between the interests of the two organizers than might be apparent. To gain support for his academy, Flurance argued for its practical benefits, although he himself was most interested in its mystical ends. Renaudot, on the other hand, never advocated a mystical sense of science but was genuinely interested in the practical results it embodied.

Specifically important as background to Renaudot's conferences was the circle of Pierre, Scévole de Sainte-Marthe, a humanist intellectual and local luminary in Loudun. Renaudot's friendship with Sainte-Marthe, who not only attended but also wrote the history of Henry III's Palace Academy, gave him a direct connection to the academies of the late sixteenth century.[10] Through his attendance at Saint-Marthe's circle, Renaudot was able to draw on a rich heritage of academies in France, absorbing firsthand the tradition of humanism and hospitality.

Thus, while Renaudot himself signaled the novelty of his conferences, he was nonetheless generally indebted to the academic culture of the Renaissance and specifically indebted to Montaigne, his acknowledged source of inspiration. Montaigne's statement of the value of the conference is indeed illuminating: "The most fruitful and natural exercise of our spirit is, in my opinion, the conference. . . . The study of books is a languid and cold movement which does not have the heat which the conference teaches and exercises in a blow."[11]

Renaudot's conferences were likewise intended to provide a revitalized forum for intellectual life, but he was also able to build and capitalize on the sixteenth-century attack on scholasticism. In 1551 Peter Ramus spearheaded an attack on the rigid scholasticism of the university and offered an alternative humanist curriculum at the Collège de France. Ramus realized, as Renaudot did later, that one way to subvert an established educational institution was to set up a parallel institution, especially if the new institution was directed to a broader public than the one supplanted.[12] Reliance on patronage, the creation of a new institution, a broader, more inclusive constituency, and an appeal to utility characterized both the Collège de France and Renaudot's conferences.

Renaudot's gatherings incorporated some of the crucial social benefits of Renaissance academies; they too fostered intellectual autonomy and appealed to a broad range of intellectuals and new professionals. Their open character meant that Renaudot's gatherings could influence a diverse section of the population; in particular, they offered some opportunity to mold an emerging elite—nobles of the robe, bureaucrats, professionals, financiers, and so on (to give a general sense of where participants were drawn from rather than any explicit identification of membership, social class, or profession). Open to individuals of different status and occupations, the conferences also allowed social mixing to initiate the young, the inexperienced, and some of the disenfranchised into the exchange of ideas.

In the seventeenth century, academies evolved in significant new directions, only some of which were followed by Renaudot's group. In general, membership in these groups was defined more by a specialized interest tied to more rigid organization—a change, Robert Mandrou claimed, from a republic of letters to a republic of savants.[13] Indeed, Renaudot's group evolved from a private gathering of friends and acquaintances *chez lui* from 1631 to 1633, to a group with a regular schedule and a larger venue after 1633, and thus embodied the pattern of the organization of more specialized groups. But Renaudot's group did not narrow the scope of investigation into a specialized area of interest or to a restricted membership.

Generally speaking, seventeenth-century academies were both more pragmatic in spirit and more avowedly progressive than their sixteenth-century counterparts. A focus on science broadened their appeal and meant that their sponsors and proponents felt less compelled to justify them; the advantages science seemed to embody were sufficient justification.[14] Frances Yates traced a decisive shift in the intellectual character of the academy from the mystical neoplatonic understanding of science of the sixteenth century to the mathematical and mechanical interests of the new sciences of the seventeenth century. She singled out Marin Mersenne as the individual, and his circle as the group, that most vividly demonstrate this shift.

Despite his own interests and reputation in the scientific sphere, Mersenne reverted to a Renaissance tradition in the form and content of his academy. He himself had extensive contact with the earlier academies, believed in the religious and mystical effects of "ancient music," and was most eager that the musical experiments of Baif's academy should be continued.[15] He also emphasized the benefits to be gained through a full exploration of themes of neoplatonic humanism, such as the Christianization of pagan myths.[16] He hoped for the unification of Christendom through the universal harmony of music. In terms of organization and support for the academy, Mersenne looked to the court for both patrons and members.[17] The group he gathered around him was very small (about seven members) and very exclusive both socially and intellectually. Only after the conferences had ended did Mersenne publish the works of mechanical philosophy that cemented his reputation in the history of science.[18] But if Mersenne incorporates both the sixteenth- and the seventeenth-century evolution of the academy, Renaudot decisively represents the seventeenth-century.

While sixteenth-century groups often focused on literary topics, the early seventeenth century saw the rise of groups more inclined toward philosophical or natural philosophical topics. These groups also allowed the expression of less orthodox views, largely because they engaged in philosophical or scientific speculation. As Luce Giard notes, they could entertain "minority views like those of the Platonists and the skeptics, or heterodox ideas such as the new astronomy."[19] The extent and variety of scientific discussion in Renaudot's conferences attests to these new interests and reflects this evolution of intellectual life. The conferences, like other intellectual gatherings in seventeenth-century France, offered an attractive alternative to the university.

Many seventeenth-century intellectuals chafed within the confines of the French university system, which was subject to perennial criticisms for its rigidity. It was denounced as too wedded to Aristotelianism and too resistant to innovation in texts, ideas, and practices.[20] Reform efforts continued to reflect old weaknesses rather than to effect revitalization. Innovative fora for discussion such as Renaudot's conferences offered greater accessibility, a less structured framework, and a more flexible and unconventional approach to ideas. Entertainment was an added attraction of this educational experience.

Because his group does convincingly reflect these shifts in intellectual activities and interests, Renaudot's conferences would probably have been much more readily integrated into the history of science if he had been a central figure in the scientific networks of the seventeenth century. But Renaudot was outside them. Many of these networks were maintained through the correspondence of intellectuals, many of whom were clerics, well connected to each other and blessed with the leisure to pursue scholarship. Although Renaudot was not a figure in the prominent Gassendi-Mersenne-Peiresc network that was so influential in the science of seventeenth-century France, he did have tangential relationships with many important contemporaries.[21]

Renaudot would probably not have been able to penetrate the Cabinet Dupuy, an influential private academy begun when Jacques-Auguste de Thou, the author of an important history of France and a man with wide-ranging interests, surrounded himself with like-minded friends in an informal intellectual circle, called the Cabinet de Thou. After his death in 1617, the group was reorganized around the brothers Jacques and Pierre Dupuy.[22] Membership was narrowly restricted to men of high birth; the practicing barrister or physician was unable to penetrate their circle.[23] Intent on cloaking its discussions in complete privacy, the Cabinet followed an elitist academic tradition by jealously resisting any who would bring the glare of public attention upon it.[24] Renaudot's group can be compared to the Cabinet Dupuy because of the range of topics discussed, but it was not similarly restricted and was unique in bridging the gap between elite scholarship and a mass audience.

Renaudot may have had some direct contact with Nicholas-Claude Fabri de Peiresc, another important figure in the tradition of seventeenth-century private academies. Peiresc's range of interests—which included antiquity, certain aspects of nature, and the practical arts—made him a model of the virtuoso of the latter part of the century.[25] His correspondence, particularly his communication with the Dupuy brothers, is an important source of information about seventeenth-century intellectual life. But the only direct reference to Renaudot in Peiresc's correspondence is his negative response to Renaudot's offer to publish his letters.[26]

A comparison between the interests of Peiresc and Renaudot is revealing because it attests to two very different models of early seventeenth-century intellectual life. As Peter Miller shows, Peiresc and his interests are central to the seventeenth century but his particular approach consigned him quickly to oblivion. Peiresc was interested in a vast array of material but took an antiquarian approach to all knowledge that was completely out of favor by mid century. He failed to publish at a time when publication became essential to the dissemination of knowledge.[27] Renaudot on the other hand was an impresario of publication, making sure that his efforts and activities received notice in the printed word. Even if his conferees would later debate the value of the spoken word as opposed to the written, Renaudot's own career recognized the value of not only the printed word but also its role in promotion of his ideas and activities. Renaudot, unlike Peiresc, was intensely interested in the practical application of knowledge. Whereas Peiresc was marked decisively by his interest in the past, Renaudot looked to the future. With such dramatically different notions of the role of an intellectual, it is not surprising that the two did not have much contact.

Another connection between Renaudot and this prominent network might have been through Tommaso Campanella, who both had access to the highest intellectual circles in France and likely attended the conferences. Campanella was an extraordinary figure, and he might throw some light on the conferences, if, indeed, such an unconventional individual with such unconventional views was welcome there. Campanella is well known for his defense of Galileo, which was written from a Neapolitan jail cell and extolled both Copernican astronomy and freedom of inquiry. But this was not the first time he had suffered for challenging orthodoxy. In 1595, the Holy Office detained him for two years because he attacked Aristotle. In 1599, charged with conspiracy to overthrow the Spanish government and establish a communistic commonwealth, he was tried before an ecclesiastical court, tortured by a civil tribunal, and finally sentenced to life imprisonment. He did not improve his situation by publishing his defense of Galileo in 1622.[28] On 15 May 1626, after twenty-seven years of confinement, he was paroled to the Holy Office and in 1629 granted complete liberty. Even under these extremely adverse conditions, he produced voluminous works, exploring hermeticism, magic, astrology, and other topics brought to the forefront of intellectual discussion by the discovery of hermetic texts.[29] When in 1634 it appeared that he might be implicated in another Calabrian conspiracy, the Spanish monarchy, which ruled the Kingdom of Naples, sought his extradition from Rome. With the aid of Cardinal Barberini and the French ambassador, Campanella fled to the court of Louis XIII. In Paris he was enthusiastically received by the king, who saw the sheltering of Campanella as part of his anti-Spanish foreign policy, recently demonstrated by his entrance into the Thirty Years' War on the side of the Protestants and against the Hapsburgs. Campanella, clearly understanding his role as a pawn in power politics, composed a dedicatory preface to Louis XIII in which he praised him as the "right arm of God"—a title prized by the king of Spain. After spending five years in peace supported by Richelieu, who gave him a pension of three thousand livres, he died in 1639 at the Dominican convent of Saint Honoré in Paris.[30]

Campanella was initially very hospitably received by Peiresc, who sought to ease his way into French society and provided him with introductions to Mersenne, Gassendi, and others.[31] But, as John Headley so vividly documents, Campanella—a peasant friar with a narrow experience of the world, great confidence in the value of his own ideas, but very little tolerance for those of others—soon wore out his welcome in the elite circles of intellectual Paris. He did not disguise his horror of Gassendi's epicureanism, and Mersenne and others considered his appeals to pantheism and magic retrograde.[32] He may then have turned to the conferences in hopes of greater appreciation of his ideas. But although the Bureau addressed some topics related to Campanella's interests, they did not generally take positions he would have found congenial.[33] Even if Campanella did participate in the conferences, the religious mysticism that characterizes his scientific utopia *The City of the Sun* and much of his work is completely foreign to Renaudot's conferences, although some of the more radical political ideas expressed and the defenses of astrology presented may well indicate Campanella's participation. It is interesting, given the general notion that absolutism quashed freedom of expression, that Richelieu would have brought the notorious freethinker to Paris.[34]

Despite these tantalizing connections to prominent figures of the scientific revolution in France, Renaudot remains on the fringes of the scientific community. The kind of academy he sponsored—unorthodox in form and composition and eclectic in interest and approach—was soon displaced by the appropriation of the academic tradition by the state. Louis XIII and his ministers promoted state sponsored institutions for the benefits they expected them to produce. But under the aegis of the state, the academic tradition was fundamentally altered; French intellectuals thrived, but in much more circumscribed directions and conditions. Scholars have focused their attention on the two state-sponsored institutions, the Académie des Sciences and the Académie Française.[35] Neither of these institutions treated the broad range of issues or implemented an encyclopedic approach to knowledge that characterized both the early academic tradition and Renaudot's conferences.

The Académie Française neither incorporated hopes for *pansophia* or *renovatio* nor had the popular, public character of the earlier seventeenth-century academies. Instead it explicitly and narrowly focused on the French language and relevant specific projects, such as the creation of rules of grammar and the composition of a definitive dictionary of the French language.[36] And it was as elitist as any Renaissance academy; its constitution specified rigid strictures governing membership and restricted all discussions to members. The most critical difference between the Académie Française and Renaudot's groups was the scope of inquiry: a narrow focus on grammar and language versus a myriad of topics.

Because the establishment of state-controlled academies has decisively shaped the scholarly study of science in France, earlier groups are studied simply as forerunners to the prestigious Académie des Sciences, which scholars have recognized as *the* appropriate vehicle for the dissemination of science in France. Largely because of Bernard de Fontenelle's influential thesis that only with the lavish support of the state could professional science flourish, and because of the central and privileged position of the Académie des Sciences, the format and substance of earlier scientific groups have been neglected. Other groups are rarely considered to have any intrinsic merit of their own and are usually treated as indicative of a much less developed science or as relatively insignificant footnotes in the history of scientific institutions.[37] Although the history of institutions came to prominence in historiography as a way to expand the purview of the history of science beyond the narrow confines of the histories of great men, this method too can be unduly narrow. In England, largely because the roots of the Royal Society are unclear, a wide swath of possible antecedents has been investigated. Less prestigious and more popular scientific institutions have been studied for their possible connections to the Royal Society.[38] In the case of France, the Académie des Sciences has been the almost exclusive focus for discussion of early modern science.

Given the highly structured and state-orchestrated shape of post-1635 state-sponsored science in France, Renaudot's conferences provide an intriguing example of a much more open academy, which avoided the rigidity and to some degree the constraints on expression of opinion of more orthodox and state-formed academies. One question to consider is why Richelieu might have allowed Renaudot such comparatively free rein in view of the tight control he exercised over so many other institutions. One possible explanation is that Renaudot's activities worked to undermine certain groups whose authority Richelieu too was interested in weakening. Renaudot's group challenged established authorities—the nobility, privileged academic institutions, and the Faculty of Medicine. These were groups discomfited by Richelieu's seizure of power and vociferous in their objections to him. Richelieu might have suspected, with good reason, that some positions taken by conference participants might well challenge the traditional privileges of the nobility. He might also have appreciated Renaudot's attack on the Faculty of Medicine and his attempt to set up a rival medical faculty as a way to cut the power of the Faculty and by implication the university. Renaudot's medical facility could be construed as a new medical institution that would owe its existence to royal authority. Perhaps most compelling, from Richelieu's point of view, might have been that the discussions of Renaudot's group offered the hope of pragmatic, utilitarian solutions to social problems. In any case, Richelieu's support of both Campanella and Renaudot betokens greater flexibility and openness than is usually associated with intellectual issues in the ancien régime. The range of issues addressed and the sometimes heterodox approach taken to them in Renaudot's conferences suggests that, despite Richelieu's repression of some French cultural institutions, he allowed this group considerable freedom of expression. Renaudot's career is illuminating as an example of the possibilities open to a creative, unconventional man of ideas despite the constraints of the hierarchical culture of seventeenth-century France.

"A SINCERE FRIEND OF PROGRESS AND A TRULY LIBERAL SPIRIT"

Despite this biographer's laudatory assessment of him, Renaudot is not widely acknowledged as a significant seventeenth-century figure.[39] He is perhaps best known for the annual literary prize the Renaudot, or for the establishment in France of the *monts-de-piété* (pawnshops that essentially functioned as a low-interest loan program for the poor by allowing the poor to pawn their goods in exchange for revenue for subsistence). The bit of glory that adheres to his name across the ages is not sufficient recognition of this innovative and entrepreneurial spirit, a man of such wide-ranging interests and pursuits that he seems rather out of his time in the seventeenth century.[40]

Although his wide-ranging activities were controversial in his own day and have provoked historical controversy as well, Renaudot is only recently finding a place in historical literature. Until the late nineteenth century, he was virtually imperceptible in the historical record, despite the range of institutions he created, the offices he held, and the highly visible character of his works and his battles.[41] More recent scholars have produced widely divergent assessments of him. In Solomon's study of his career, Renaudot is a prescient social observer, adept at assessing the needs of contemporary France and well able to implement practical, effective reforms. Solomon depicts Renaudot as a medical reformer persecuted by the conservative and vindictive Faculty of Medicine and as a thinker ahead of his time in understanding the need for educational reform and for providing a popular forum for science. In Sutton's study of early modern scientific culture, Renaudot's conferences are used as an example of what science should not be. Renaudot himself is depicted as a dilettante opportunist who recognized and exploited every coming trend for his personal and professional gain. Sutton characterizes Renaudot's career as "the story of the most improbable accretion of power, wealth, responsibility, and the enmity of all traditional sources of authority in Paris."[42] Who was the man behind these conflicting interpretations?

Renaudot's accomplishments are all the more impressive since his background would not have singled him out for success. He, like the conferences he sponsored, was criticized for not having a sufficiently high social tone. His parents were successful members of the bourgeoisie, affluent enough to secure a good education for their son, but they were Protestant and from Loudun, in Poitou, a cultural backwater with a tainted history in the wars of religion.[43] After acquiring a conventional grounding in the classics, Renaudot chose to pursue a medical career. Like some of his contemporaries from Loudun, he went to Montpellier to pursue medical training because Montpellier tolerated Protestants. (The Faculty of Medicine of Paris, on the other hand, required its students to swear not only that they were loyal Catholics but also that they would faithfully attend Faculty masses.)[44] The Faculty of Montpellier afforded provincial Protestants not only religious toleration but also an education that was less tradition bound and more open to medical innovation. So tightly connected was the Faculty of Medicine of Paris to Catholicism and traditional ideas and Montpellier to Protestantism and innovation that any seventeenth-century medical innovation could be denounced as tainted with religious nonconformism.

After receiving his medical degree, Renaudot spent some time traveling in Italy.[45] These travels may well have fostered some of his innovations. His plans for the alleviation of the plight of the poor were likely sparked by his exposure to the *monts-de-piété* in Italy. He then pursued a course of study with the surgeons of the Collège de St. Côme. Renaudot's heterodoxy in turning to the surgeons for medical expertise later became one of the principal charges in the Faculty of Medicine's polemical denunciations of him. Despite the outrage such studies provoked among physicians, there were good reasons for him to study with the surgeons: they opposed systematic adherence to Aristotle and Galen, as had his Montpellier professors, and they placed a priority on experience.

In 1611 Renaudot returned to Loudun to begin his medical career. He also pursued an interest in botany, collecting and recording his findings in a number of "anatomies," studies of the structure and form of organic beings. These were published and heralded by contemporaries as innovative, although no copies have survived.[46] He also published a discourse favorably assessing the merits of a remedy called *polychréton*, another term for the controversial chemical remedy antimony.[47] This text would have identified him as a proponent of chemical remedies and thus further made him anathema to the Faculty of Medicine, which took a rigid stance against adding any chemical to the conventional pharmacopoeia. He also began to investigate the causes and remedies for poverty in Loudun. These very early ventures point to the interests that shaped Renaudot's entire public career. He was interested in avant-garde medicine and science, in disseminating new knowledge, and in implementing poor relief.

His interest in poor relief launched his public career. His early treatise on the topic brought him to the attention of Père Joseph, who introduced him to Richelieu, then the bishop of nearby Luçon, as someone capable of bringing to successful completion "the most important affairs."[48] This introduction would subsequently produce a mutually beneficial relationship between Richelieu and Renaudot and eventually take Renaudot to Paris. However, from 1611 to 1625, Renaudot was primarily in Loudun, where he practiced medicine and was associated with the influential figures and significant events in the region. There he associated with Urban Grandier, a Catholic bishop who tolerated Protestants and who attained enduring fame for his role in the legal process against the Ursulines featured in Aldous Huxley's *The Devils of Loudun*.[49] Renaudot wrote his first treatise on the poor and dedicated it to his friend Sainte-Marthe whose circle might well have inspired his conferences.[50]

Renaudot's interest in poor relief was a response to a growing crisis. The assassination of Henry IV in 1610 produced a series of insurrections by the feudal nobility, which exacerbated poverty in the provinces, so much so that Richelieu, a deputy to the Estates General of 1614, complained, "we are all beggars in this country of Luçon."[51] In 1618, Père Joseph sent Renaudot with his *Traité des pauvres* to Paris, where it was so well received that it procured for him the title *commissaire général des pauvres*. But, because the death of Henry IV had also made the conditions of life more difficult for Protestants, the situation was not conducive to Renaudot's pursuing his career prospects in Paris. He returned to Loudun, where he remained until 1629. Conditions became more difficult for him in his hometown as well, for the period after 1614 saw a change in the governance of the province from Protestant to Catholic, heightening religious tensions.[52] In 1628, no doubt urged by his influential sponsors and in the interest of smoothing his path in Paris, Renaudot and his children converted to Catholicism, although his wife remained Protestant.[53]

The region of Poitou was also embroiled in the political factionalism of the early seventeenth century. It was perceived as a rebellious province, likely to be swayed to support the feudal nobility against the crown.[54] During the wars of religion, it was predominantly Protestant and loyal to Henry of Navarre (later Henry IV) against the crown. After the assasination of Henry IV in 1610, Poitou once again was tied to royal opposition led by the Prince of Condé. Renaudot was present during the five-month period when the treaty between the Prince of Condé and Louis XIII was negotiated, and he came to know both Richelieu and Condé well. But when the peace between the crown and the nobles failed, Richelieu fell into disgrace. This setback for Richelieu probably explains why, even with the cardinal's backing, Renaudot's entrance into public life was neither easy nor uncontested. Even though his first public title as *commissaire général des pauvres*[55] was endorsed by many official pronouncements, these were not sufficient authorization to allow him to assume the office.[56] Not until 9 August 1629 did Parlement confirm his titles and offices. The final confirmation was due in part to his conversion to Catholicism and more decisively to Richelieu's definitive rise to power. Renaudot expressed relief when the "long succession of years required for the solid perfection of a durable work" finally came to fruition.[57]

Renaudot exercised an important public role throughout the 1630s and early 1640s, in three specific areas, poor relief, medical practice, and publishing. By discussing these three specific areas, we can glean the outlines of Renaudot's biography and some of his central concerns that are also addressed in the conferences.

THE BUREAU D'ADRESSE AND POOR RELIEF

The Bureau d'Adresse, Renaudot's personal brainchild, was the umbrella institution under which most of his other interests were subsumed. All of his concerns—medical, scientific, and academic—were shaped by his fundamental notion that bringing people into contact with one another would facilitate effective operation within the public sphere and enhance the order and efficiency of society. He considered participation in the civic sphere to be both a fundamental responsibility and an essential part of the human soul. He cited a litany of things that went wrong in contemporary society because people who should be brought together for their mutual benefit and that of the state were not. Most of the things he enumerated have to do with missed commercial and employment opportunities. Renaudot explicitly cited as his inspiration one of Montaigne's essays, which suggested that certain villages with specific needs should be so designated and that the citizens of those villages should register with an officer of the crown, appointed to coordinate an effort to meet these needs.[58] Renaudot may have also been responding to more contemporary calls for the implementation of a bureau, such as Isaac de Laffemas's impassioned plea for "the invention of public offices" as "a preservative against the ruin of our commerce."[59]

Another important source for contemporary thinking about the problems of poor relief—*De l'assistance aux pauvres* (1525), written by the Spanish humanist Juan Luis Vives—may have also influenced Renaudot. Although Vives is usually appreciated for his contribution to Renaissance ideas about education, he was provoked by the spectacle of the indigent classes to write a lengthy treatise on poor relief. Like Renaudot, Vives was drawn to the issue because charity is required of the Christian and essential to the well-being of cities "to make of them a place where goods are given or received, where, by mutual help, charity and the solidarity of men are augmented."[60]

France offered concrete models of charitable practice. Renaudot's poor relief efforts took place during the full flowering of the Catholic reformation in France. This renewal of Catholic zeal saw the creation of new forms of religious life, especially those devoted to the practice of charity. For example, Louise de Marillac founded the Daughters of Charity with the support of another of Richelieu's clients, Vincent de Paul, best known for his efforts on behalf of the sick and the poor.[61]

The practice of charity extolled by Vives and practiced by de Paul also animated Renaudot's Bureau. A royal declaration authorizing the Bureau spelled out some of the things it was intended to do. It would provide care for the poor, in part, "because charity is agreeable to God." The efforts of the Bureau to provide health care would also prevent mendicancy. At the Bureau, the declaration noted, "the unhealthy poor receive counsel and assistance in their illnesses and inconveniences by the charity of physicians, surgeons, and apothecaries who assemble to this end." To make sure that Renaudot was able to continue to offer these treatments, the king noted that "we have permitted the said Renaudot to hold *chez lui* the said furnaces and to carry out all sorts of chemical operations, which pertain to medicine alone."[62] The Bureau also sold "the services of notaries, apothecaries, masters of all arts and trades." It provided information about lessons, real estate listings, and experimental medical treatments and tracked down elusive information about deaths, marriages, changes of address, and missing persons. The royal declaration cited approvingly the fundamental precept of the Bureau: "this office will harm no one and will benefit each."[63]

Renaudot himself elaborated on his intentions for the Bureau in an article in the *Mercure françois*, in which he laid out its benefits and defended it against naysayers. He acknowledged that his challenge was to "make the public taste the benefits it will derive, nothing more innocent, but of great benefit . . . as one augments and facilitates there the commerce of all." The Bureau was not just a site for buying and selling, but also a place where those who needed housing and jobs could meet those who had them to offer. Facilitating the public good required that those who had money and power be brought into contact with those who had skills and talents. Open from eight to eleven in the morning and from two to five in the afternoon, this institution, like the others he established, "remake themselves daily to the contentment of the public"; he justified the Bureau by appealing explicitly to utility, novelty, social improvement, and posterity.[64]

Renaudot also presented pragmatic and epistemological rationales for the Bureau. Pragmatically, the Bureau brought together people interested in the public good to address common needs they recognized. This was necessary because "many conditions, arts, and different professions, which constitute the cities and states like the many parts and members of a great body," were "often estranged or distanced, often unknown, and almost infinite in their number." But Renaudot also had a keen sense of the intellectual possibilities of bringing people together, a sensibility best demonstrated by the conferences he hosted. Thus, he also made an epistemological claim for the establishment of the Bureau. Sounding like a prescient Lockean, Renaudot pointed out that because "one's spirits are limited by one's body, admitting nothing *chez soi* except by the organ of senses," the conferences might enhance one's experience, in the Lockean sense of providing the key to knowledge. As he put it, "the perfection of our society seems to lack some public place, . . . assembling so many detached pieces, furnishing general notice to our intellect, species to the memory, and objects to the will."[65] Renaudot believed that a collective endeavor like the conferences could overcome the limits of the individual mind and expand the utilitarian possibilities of intellectual endeavors.

Renaudot not only was a proponent of commercial development but also recognized some of the problems that the burgeoning commercial development of the early seventeenth century had created. He sought, through the Bureau, to ameliorate the dislocations caused by what many had considered a "disorder" resulting from the "blind conduct of fortune." Renaudot suggested that the Bureau would redress the impotence associated with the perception that a vast proportion of human affairs are simply due to chance instead of "choice, one of the most excellent powers of the soul." He concludes with an optimistic assessment of what the Bureau could accomplish: "I claim to remedy, my reader, by the establishment of the Bureau of Adresses and of Encounters, all the inconveniences of life."[66]

Renaudot railed against those who opposed the Bureau: "no one can doubt that this will be good for commerce or that an increase in commerce will benefit the kingdom, especially the poor, which is the object of my labors and the most agreeable end to which I have ever dedicated myself." To silence his critics, Renaudot noted that the Bureau posed no threat but only opportunities, since "each is permitted to use it for what seems to him good or not to use it."[67] The wondrous opportunities available at the Bureau were bruited in advertisements published by Renaudot himself, which claimed that at the Bureau one might "sell, buy, rent, exchange, let, borrow, learn [or] teach practically whatever one wanted."[68] The activities at the Bureau captured the popular imagination. During Carnival in 1631, a ballet debuted that was a collection of pieces, half-sung, half-danced, a kind of review with all the newsworthy events of the year depicted on stage. One of these pieces portrayed the Bureau, Renaudot, and his clients.[69]

Renaudot also piqued the interest of other seventeenth-century innovators and reformers. They saw in the Bureau a rare example of an institution responsive to a commercial revolution that could create a new social and economic order. The claims made for the Bureau attracted attention abroad; Englishmen were greatly intrigued by it. In 1638, just a year after Renaudot's *Discours sur l'Utilité des Bureaux d'adresse* outlining the purpose of the Bureau and the services it would provide was printed in the *Mercure françois*,[70] Captain Robert Innes established an "Office of Intelligence under Letters Patentes" from Charles I.[71] Hartlib, who was interested both in the advancement of knowledge and in its use for social amelioration, asked friends in Paris to send him information about Renaudot's Bureau and for copies of Renaudot's *Renouvellement des Bureaux d'Adresse*.[72] Hartlib's own *A Further Discoverie of the Office of Publick Addresse for Accommodations* argued all of Renaudot's fundamental points, emphasizing as well the innocence of his inventions. Like Renaudot, he was concerned to classify the poor, especially to separate those who could work from those who could not. He suggested workhouses and deportation to the colonies of those for whom no domestic employment could be found. But unlike Renaudot, he explicitly connected poor relief to Protestant ecumenism and millenarianism;[73] he hoped to re-create the Kingdom of God on earth. In his Utopian text *Macaria*, he described a society intended, as he wrote to Robert Boyle, to propagate religion and to reform the world.[74] The educational reformer Comenius also expressed his interest in Renaudot's Bureau and lamented his ignorance of French, which kept him from reading about it himself.[75] Henry More, the noted Cambridge Platonist, was also keenly interested in Renaudot's institutions.

Although Parliament did not support Hartlib's petition to establish a bureau, his friends John Dury and Henry Robinson enthusiastically promoted the plan. Numerous schemes for "Offices of Intelligence" and "Places of Encounters" were discussed. In 1650 Hartlib's proposals were finally implemented by Henry Robinson in an Office of Addresses.[76] Like Renaudot, Robinson expressed exasperation that so many were reduced to beggary simply because those who needed laborers could not find those who needed jobs. Like Renaudot's Bureau, Robinson's Office was dedicated to poor relief and offered the same range of services. Renaudot's English contemporaries were quick to appreciate the way the French innovator had brought humanitarian concern to bear on economic realities in a way that was both visionary and practical. As these English enthusiasts acknowledged, the greatest benefits of the Bureau were its efforts to provide poor relief.[77] This concern motivated Renaudot's entire public career.

Renaudot argued that in French villages political privilege was gained through public service and civic-mindedness, but the reverse was true in Paris, where the pursuit of individual glory and wealth conveyed political privilege. Renaudot attempted, through his institutions, to remake public culture. He argued for civic charity as the foundation of public life and for public responsibility to aid the unfortunate members of society. When he went to Paris after his medical education in Montpellier, he was struck by the numbers of indigent who, dislocated by the wars of religion, had come to the capital where, completely without resources or health care, they were reduced to begging.[78] Much of Renaudot's career was directed toward ameliorating their plight.

The French monarchy had adopted legislation to contend with the problem of the indigent. With increasing numbers of poor, especially urban poor, the French classified them into two groups, those who were able but unemployed, "les valides," and those who were sick poor, "les invalides." Although most charitable activity was carried out under the aegis of religious orders, the government had established in each province, by decrees promulgated from 1552 to 1555, *bureaux de charité* to deal with the unemployed poor. Hôtel Dieu, the hospital of the poor, became less capable of treating or contending with the poor who were sick or otherwise unable to work. In 1612 poor houses were created to "enclose" them. But in 1618, when the government had to put down several revolts by "mendicants valides" (healthy beggars), its plans for "enclosure" were abandoned. Although several other hospitals, like La Pitié and De la Miséricorde, were founded, poor relief in Paris proved quite inadequate to treat the large numbers of needy.

Letters-patent of 1612 authorizing Renaudot's appointment as *commissaire général des pauvres* enthusiastically endorsed his projects for poor relief and gave him broad powers. He was entitled to "put into practice and establish all other inventions and means uncovered by him for the use of the healthy poor and for the treatment of the sick poor, and generally all that will be useful and convenient to the regulation of said poor."[79]

Throughout his career, Renaudot was a forceful advocate for the poor. In arguing for his free medical consultations, which also provided free medications, Renaudot maintained that, for the sick poor, medication must be considered equivalent to nourishment.[80] His Bureau, he claimed, put the poor into contact with those who were rich enough to have something they wanted to sell and who might also be able to provide employment or housing. Moreover, despite his stated refusal to address questions of politics and religion in the conferences, Renaudot proclaimed the integral relationship between the concerns of the state and the religious mandate to practice charity. He noted that the affairs of the state are always joined to those of religion, for zeal for the good of the state and the practice of charity are inseparable. Since, he claimed, all professions are destined for the care of men, he hoped that others would join his endeavor: "I hold out one of my hands to the sick and, with the other, invite all those who can aid me in this charitable project."[81]

Renaudot attempted to replicate in France the *monts-de-piété*, a religious institution that functioned as a pawnshop, which he might have seen on his travels in Italy.[82] The Franciscans, well aware that the financial problems of people on the margins were exacerbated by the usurious rates charged by moneylenders, established these institutions where those who needed a small short-term loan could obtain it in exchange for small goods left as a pledge. Supported by voluntary contributions and gifts, the *monts-de-piété* were originally able to lend money without interest but later were forced to charge a small percentage. Founded first in Orvieto in 1463, they spread rapidly throughout Italy and were operated by either religious orders or lay confraternities.[83] By a decree of 27 March 1637, Louis XIII authorized Renaudot to lend "to all those who have furniture and goods to liquidate to pay their debts."[84] The *monts-de-piété* were just one of the many practical solutions Renaudot implemented in order to address widely recognized problems of his day, especially those of the poor.

BATTLE WITH THE FACULTY OF MEDICINE

Renaudot's medical services to the poor aroused intense opposition largely because the Faculty of Medicine of Paris perceived them as a direct threat. The Faculty was not able to prevail against Renaudot as long as Richelieu was in power and Louis XIII on the throne. However, they worked assiduously to overturn his medical endeavors and were successful as soon as Renaudot was bereft of these patrons.

Renaudot's medical innovations are impressive. At the Bureau he operated furnaces, a laboratory, a dispensary, and a clinic. Both the extent of his medical endeavors and their official sponsorship by powerful patrons led the Faculty to perceive Renaudot as a threat. But the most serious threat he posed was that he assembled all of the elements necessary to establish a faculty to rival the Faculty itself. Renaudot's medical practitioners at the Bureau consisted of non-Paris-trained physicians, licensed and certified to practice in Paris by virtue of their affiliation with the Bureau. His teaching staff consisted of physicians who discussed new medical theories, particularly the chemical topics spurned by Parisian doctors, in the weekly conferences. They demonstrated the practical application of these theories in equally public consultations. Renaudot had established chemical laboratories to produce the drugs his doctors and apothecaries were dispensing. Moreover, the public consultations were in fact teaching clinics, providing practical knowledge, which the Faculty did not. Thus his clinic not only provided an important service to the poor but also contributed to the development of clinical medicine in France.

These activities aroused the Faculty of Medicine to great ire. There were many specific grounds for the antagonism between Renaudot and the Faculty. Renaudot's medical degree was from Montpellier, an institution fundamentally at odds with the Faculty of Medicine. The Faculties of Paris and Montpellier had a contentious history in the seventeenth century.[85] While the Faculty of Montpellier sponsored chemical medicines, accepting antimony, opium, laudanum and quinine as effective additions to the pharmacopoeia, the Faculty of Paris denounced as poisoners physicians who used these new treatments. While the Faculty of Montpellier was open to innovation, the Faculty of Paris had a well-deserved reputation for conservative, text-based education, which defended the traditional, ancient medicine of Hippocrates and Galen against innovations, all of which it considered, by definition, pernicious.

One striking example of these propensities was the response of the Faculty of Paris to Harvey's discovery of the circulation of the blood.

Instead of conceding that Galen had been wrong about certain fundamentals of the physiology of the heart, they defended him. One of their
most prominent members, Jean Riolan, mounted a prolonged and vehement defense of Galen, which became more firmly entrenched over
time.[86] Guy Patin, who became the chief Faculty polemicist against
Renaudot, was an adamant proponent of Galenic medicine. He claimed
that the new discoveries merely restored what the ancients already
knew. Extremely conservative in medical terms, he anathematized the
drugs imported from the Arabs.[87] Temperamentally, Patin was
extremely combative and more than willing to take on anyone he saw
as a threat to the medical status quo.[88] His goal was to preserve and
extend the privilege and authority of the Faculty of Medicine of Paris.[89]
He could not fail to make Renaudot a target of his polemics.

Renaudot's practice of chemical medicine provoked great hostility,
not only because of the Faculty's long-standing opposition to chemical
remedies but also because of a very recent setback suffered by the opponents of chemical medicine. In 1638 Hardouin St. Jacques, dean of the
Faculty, had finally forced the acceptance of antimony on to the
approved list of Faculty medications. Guy Patin was more than willing
to reopen the issue using Renaudot as a foil.

The animus between Renaudot and the Faculty did not simply rest
on the fact that he, by virtue of his education and his medical interests,
represented everything that was anathema to them, however. He also
challenged their privileged position in medical practice in Paris.
Renaudot opened his house to free medical consultations, at first, in
1631, on Tuesdays from two to four,[90] and by 25 July 1641, the Bureau
expanded medical consultations to every day of the week.[91] Not only
were chemical remedies produced on Renaudot's property, his physicians also prescribed to apothecaries in Latin, a language that had been
reserved to physicians. Conceding such status to apothecaries undermined the existing medical hierarchy. Renaudot's sponsorship of
apothecaries was especially problematic because it usurped the surveillance of medical practices by the Faculty.[92]

It became increasingly obvious that Renaudot could easily assemble
both a teaching corps and an eager group of students from those who
staffed the clinics and attended the conferences at the Bureau. The

prospect of such an innovative and independent system of medical education was especially attractive to those persecuted by the Faculty and those who found its methods stifling. Renaudot's Bureau thus attracted staff from the medically disenfranchised, especially physicians from the University of Montpellier.[93] He also had the active support of the surgeons and apothecaries, "none among them who would not voluntarily offer to contribute his efforts and industry" to the Bureau, he noted.[94] The Faculty of Paris could extract similar cooperation only through the pressure of formalized right.

At the time of Richelieu's death, Renaudot was pursuing other medical agendas that would have further eroded the power and authority of the medical faculty. An intriguing idea, which might ultimately have reshaped the medical profession, was Renaudot's plan to send to rural doctors and patients in remote areas a questionnaire to be filled out and submitted for diagnosis by mail.[95] As his operations extended throughout the realm, the Faculty began to fear that he wished to establish national licensing standards at their obvious expense.[96]

The most serious challenge to the Faculty was Renaudot's plan, supported by Richelieu and Louis XIII, to create a hospital in Paris staffed by his physicians, all volunteers, entirely independent of the Faculty. Renaudot planned to build, on a piece of prime real estate along the Seine, a facility where fifteen or twenty doctors could more efficiently treat the large crowd who came for medical treatment to his multi-functional residence, particularly those who needed longer-term care.[97] He was poised— with a new faculty, a clinic, and the right to build a hospital adjacent to the Bureau—to implement a medical establishment to rival the Faculty of Medicine.[98]

The Faculty was not passive in the face of this threat. Intent on subverting Renaudot's medical activities, it mounted an all-out pamphlet and litigation war. On 2 September 1640, Renaudot had received the letters-patent authorizing the charitable consultations. On 22 October the Faculty cited as a precedent a decree of 1598 whereby the Parlement of Paris expressly forbade all empirics and all those not authorized by the Faculty to practice medicine in Paris.[99] They chose, as was their habit, to argue on the basis of legal precedent. University of Paris medical candidates were granted a license to teach and practice medicine *hic et orbi* (in Paris and the world), a privilege of which they were inordinately proud and jealous. They defended this privilege in the narrowest spirit and inevitably contested any challenge to their authority in interminable lawsuits before Parlement.[100] The Faculty consistently claimed that, no matter what documents, titles, or specific exemptions Renaudot had procured, these were not sufficient to license his medical practice in Paris.

Renaudot expressed umbrage at being challenged in this way. He listed his credentials: a doctor for thirty-six years, a *médecin ordinaire du roi* for twenty-nine years, the *commissaire général des pauvres* for twenty-three, *maistre et intendant général des Bureaux d'Adresse* for fourteen; and he had royal letters authorizing charitable consultations and the preparation of remedies. But as far as the Faculty was concerned, Renaudot was a renegade whose medical achievements flouted professional standards and conventional routes to advancement. The Faculty wrote to the *Prévôt de Paris* demanding an interdiction of the charitable consultations, which they said were "a lie to cover up" Renaudot's "frenetic desire to enrich himself." The Faculty listed specific reasons to oppose any medical practice at the Bureau. First and most important, the Faculty was and must remain in charge of all medical education; second, the Bureau was undignified and its lack of dignity discredited the practice of medicine; third, Renaudot was ignorant of medicine. Indeed, the Faculty asked disingenuously, "with all of his activities, how could he possibly keep up with medical developments?" Finally, they claimed that Renaudot simply used the guise of charity to contravene the laws and that, in his practice of medicine, he was both an empiric and a charlatan.[101]

Renaudot defended himself in a *Mémoire au conseil du roi*. He not only asserted general principles such as the value of innovation, he also responded directly to specific arguments of the Faculty. He described the nature of the charitable consultations to demonstrate that they in no way impeded the practice of medicine by the Faculty. The Faculty could not seriously claim to be defending the liberty of physicians, he claimed, since all of his physicians practiced at the Bureau voluntarily. The quality of medical practice at the Bureau could not be deficient as the Faculty suggested, since the charitable consultations had been in effect for ten years without any complaints from patients. Moreover, unlike the services recently inaugurated by the Faculty, the services and the medications at the Bureau were free to the needy.

Richelieu, who had affected disinterest up to this point, called Renaudot and Guillaume Duval, the dean of the Faculty, before him. Legend has it that his charge to the Faculty was "Do better than M. Renaudot, Messieurs." Parlement ordered the Faculty to establish medical clinics and dispensaries but the pamphlet war continued.[102] The Faculty mobilized some of its most powerful members—including Michel de la Vigne, René Moreau, Jean Riolan the Younger and Patin— to write tracts excoriating Renaudot.

After the deaths of Richelieu and the king, the Faculty was positioned to proceed against Renaudot even more aggressively. They took the issue of Renaudot's practice of medicine to the Queen regent, Anne of Austria, and submitted a pamphlet contending that Renaudot's service to the poor was illusory, that he was disloyal to the royal family, and, perhaps most to the point, that such issues would be better left to Parlement.[103] Renaudot responded with a direct appeal to Anne of Austria, beseeching her to allow him to carry through on the project Louis XIII had authorized. He pointed out that he had acted as *commissaire général des pauvres* for twenty-five years and procured gratis both the services of twenty doctors and ingredients for medicaments for the poor. More than twenty thousand people had already sought medical care at the Bureau, demonstrating a clear need for his services.[104] He argued vociferously that a great therapeutic benefit would accrue from a move to a more permanent site for treatment, because, without such recourse to medical treatment, the sick poor would become more seriously ill.

Anne of Austria did not respond to his pleas, however, and the arguments of the Faculty prevailed. They brought a case against Renaudot in which they accused him of practicing illegally, and they argued for a prohibition against his consultations and medical treatment of the poor. The Faculty also charged that the use of furnaces at the Bureau, which obviously sanctioned chemical medicine, impeded the rights of apothecaries.[105] (This was an ironic stance for the Faculty to take, since the apothecaries actually sided with Renaudot as a fellow proponent of the chemical remedies that were crucial to their practice.)[106] On 19 December 1643, the court condemned all of Renaudot's activities and ordered that they cease immediately. The act was registered in Parlement on 1 March 1644, despite Renaudot's appeal.[107]

Patin rejoiced that Renaudot had "folded his baggage" and left the scene once his powerful supporters had died. But Patin was not content with having brought Renaudot's public career to an end; he worked to humiliate him further. The personal and contentious nature of the dispute is indicated by the fact that Patin had one of his students sustain a thesis, "*Est-ne tous homo a natura morbus?*" This thesis, an inside joke at the expense of Renaudot's syphilitic nose, was reprinted in six editions. The balance of power in the quest for medical influence in Paris had shifted so thoroughly that the Faculty was even able to prevent Renaudot's sons, Isaac and Eusèbe, from receiving their medical degrees even though they had successfully completed the degree requirements. Although the Parlement of Paris ordered that their degrees be granted in a decree of 1642, the Faculty did not comply with the order until 1648, after Renaudot's sons had renounced, in an oath taken before the Faculty, all their father's institutions.[108]

The institutions Renaudot had worked so hard to establish could not endure without his active guidance and the protection afforded by the patronage of Richelieu and Louis XIII. These institutions are nonetheless impressive in their own right and of interest to this study because they demonstrate the spirit behind Renaudot's institutions in general and the conferences in particular. Renaudot's challenge to the medical establishment raised issues of medical hierarchy, professional organization, and authority, illuminating his understanding of the nature of medicine.

Not only was Renaudot firmly committed to the dissemination of medical practices and treatment, he cast his crusade in publicly acceptable modes and thus was able to combat the Faculty effectively. First of all, he responded aggressively to all attacks and cast his medical endeavors in the unexceptional guise of charity. Indeed, he claimed in outrage, it was difficult to believe that the doctors could attack charity. He insisted that, because illness is one of the most pressing afflictions of mankind for which God created medicine, every avenue for treatment should be open.[109]

Another fundamental feature of Renaudot's endeavors was his appeal to innovation. He both voiced the suspicion that too many things were opposed simply because they were new and insisted vehemently that the new could well serve the public good.[110] Renaudot's appeal to innovation was reflected in his own career; his medicine, his journalism, his academy, the *monts-de-piété*, all violated established institutions and were effective largely because he successfully circumvented the traditional restrictions on these activities. Despite his appeal to the new, he was immeasurably aided in these endeavors by perhaps the most traditional means of career advancement in the ancien régime, patronage.

PATRONAGE AND PROPAGANDA

The immediate demise of Renaudot's institutions and his precipitous fall from grace after the deaths of Richelieu and Louis XIII attest to the significance of patronage. Throughout his career, Renaudot was fortunate in those who chose to support him. His first patron was Père Joseph, who was drawn to Renaudot because of his activities on behalf of the poor and because of his efforts to reconcile Catholics and Protestants in Loudun.[111] Impressed by the views Renaudot expressed in his *Traité des pauvres*, Père Joseph extolled Renaudot's social ideas to Richelieu. In 1612, Père Joseph procured for him the title *médecin ordinaire du roi*, which allowed Renaudot to practice medicine in Paris without credentials from the Faculty of Medicine of Paris.[112] Renaudot remained on friendly terms with Père Joseph all of his life. In fact, Père Joseph had him called to his bedside as his physician in his last illness.[113]

Significant patrons fostered Renaudot's career at every step, but he benefited most directly from the active support of Richelieu. The relationship between Renaudot and Richelieu, as well as that between Renaudot and Père Joseph, clearly exemplifies the patron-client relationship in early modern France. As a patron, Richelieu provided job opportunities, offices, and protection to Renaudot; as a client, Renaudot was a loyal subordinate. Another role Renaudot played in the power relationship was that of broker, or one who brings "people and opportunities together to facilitate the use of power and the distribution of resources."[114] The Bureau could be understood as an attempt to apply the practice of brokerage in an unusually comprehensive fashion. Richelieu both benefited from and deployed the crucial components of patron-client relationships, such as "kinship, friendship, common geographical origins and patronage" to increase his own power and his access into court circles.[115] Richelieu cultivated both Parisian and provincial client networks, and Renaudot is an apt example of Richelieu's sponsorship of provincial talent. Because of Renaudot's interests and abilities, Richelieu brought him to Paris where he functioned as a client. Although the difficulty in bringing him to Paris reflects Richelieu's initial weakness as a patron, the flourishing of Renaudot's activities in the 1630s attests to his growing political power.

Patronage was necessary, but it is not sufficient to explain Renaudot's success. Significant too is his extraordinary and inventive manipulation of the conventional routes to success and personal advancement in the ancien régime. But there is no doubt that Richelieu significantly advanced Renaudot's endeavors. The history of this particular patron-client relationship developed over time and was based on shared local concerns and shared interests in economic and political reform. Each party to the relationship could effectively exploit many specific situations. For example, Renaudot received the permission to print the *Mercure françois* because Richelieu was particularly interested in manipulating public opinion in favor of his foreign policies. But with the *Mercure françois,* as with all of his other ventures, Renaudot made it work to his advantage. For example, he used it to publish those royal decrees that sanctioned his activities, and to comment on and to publicize the affairs of the Bureau.[116]

Although patronage sustained all of his activities, Renaudot also provided important benefits to his patrons, Richelieu and Louis XIII, especially a forum for their interests in his publishing ventures, the *Mercure françois* and the *Gazette de France.*[117] The *Mercure françois* first appeared in 1614 and offered a hodgepodge of official and semi-official documents that had appeared during the year—brief accounts of events judged important, commentary on the life of the king and his court, pieces praising the king, and reports of military events and treaties. This periodical continued throughout the reign of Louis XIII. From 1624 Père Joseph exercised editorial control to make sure the pieces most favorable to the crown were inserted. In 1638 Renaudot succeeded him as editor until the Fronde in 1648. Because it offered a retrospective on past events instead of actually reporting the news, the *Mercure françois* could not effectively quash rumors. So the *Gazette de France* was established for this purpose and to mold public opinion more effectively in support of the crown.

Renaudot offers an explanatory preface to the *Gazette*, justifying its publication in terms of its manifest public utility, a rationale he cites for virtually all of his activities. Not reticent about asserting its explicit political purpose, he notes, it "will impede many false noises, which often ignite movements, and [thus] undermine seditions."[118] Furthermore, all groups will benefit by reading his *Gazette*. By familiarity with it, a merchant will know better than to try to sell goods in a town under siege, and a soldier will not seek employment in a country where there is no war. (This claim seems rather disingenuous; it assumes a high degree of literacy, and surely a newspaper would not be the most likely source of information for such groups.) He points out that it is difficult to provide the appropriate range of information in light of his broad readership of army officers, lawyers, the devout, and interested members of the court.[119]

The *Gazette de France* best indicates the symbiotic relationship between Richelieu and Renaudot. It was created because Richelieu and the king both recognized that this could be a useful vehicle with which to attack their enemies and to justify the policies of the regime. Renaudot had the skills of a publicist, and the large crowds at the Bureau served as sources of information and as an audience for the publications. Renaudot said that, when he came to Paris for the first time, he was struck by the great number of "small, folded, printed sheets, sold under the name news at hand, that one reads avidly."[120] And, remarkable in his ability to understand the power of publicity, he "soon had twenty writers occupied all day in gathering the stories, true or false, of the numerous visitors to the Maison du grand-coq."[121]

The initial idea for such a journal may have come from Père Joseph, who had noticed the role that journals were playing in other countries, especially in border areas, in maintaining support for the Thirty Years' War. Richelieu, too, recognized the potential of these publications for justifying the policies and actions of the king and his minister and responding to their critics.[122] He thus counted on the *Gazette* to shape and direct public opinion. Such a mobilization of public opinion to gain support for the policies of the state became crucial during the 1630s because of the controversial, pro-Protestant, anti-Hapsburg foreign policy Richelieu pursued in the Thirty Years War. Richelieu's alliance with the Protestants caused much opposition at home and led him to repress all opposition. The *Gazette* was designed to dissipate the threats produced by an unstable political situation, to gain support for the monarchy, and to reduce threat of civil war by quelling discontent with a foreign policy that had led to an unpopular involvement in a foreign war.[123]

There is no doubt that the *Gazette* served the function of royal propaganda or that Renaudot used it as an important source of publicity for his own concerns.[124] Although the *Gazette* is both acclaimed for its role in the development of the French press and disparaged for its role in royal propaganda, perhaps a dispassionate overview of the first volume can give some indication of its content and tone. There are some signs of propaganda. An article of 13 December 1631 praises Cardinal Richelieu as the figure responsible for the full flowering of theology, so much so that he is appropriately considered the second founder of the Sorbonne. On 7 May 1632 the *Gazette* reported an exhortation by the pope to all the Christian princes to resist the efforts of Cardinal Borgia and his "sectateurs." Richelieu overtly acknowledged the propagandistic quality of the journal when he wrote, in one of his letters to the king, that he had just dropped a word to Renaudot to make sure that a specific interpretation of an event designed to quell public complaints got into the *Gazette*. The king himself occasionally wrote for the *Gazette*; he reported on war, publicized royal entertainments, diverted blame from his errant brother to Gaston's followers, and methodically kept Queen Anne's name out of the public eye. At one point he suggested to Richelieu, "I think it would be a good thing to print in the *Gazette* the news [of the Spanish governor of Perpignan being caught reconnoitering on French soil] . . . it will show everyone that they are the aggressors against us."[125]

Propagandistic, jingoistic, and self-serving, the *Gazette* certainly is. On the other hand, it offered engaging information and some news, such as reports from the front and glimpses of elite culture and the court, that would be of intrinsic interest to seventeenth-century court and royalty watchers. It reported newsworthy events such as the execution of the Maréschal de Marillac (10 May 1632) and reproduced the discourse of the king of Sweden to the court. Obituary notices of members of the nobility were prominent. Many issues were specifically dedicated to "Nouvelles Ordinaires de divers endroits," which offered reports of news, high culture events, and prominent personalities from foreign courts and capitals. Reports of monsters and tragedies, such as the beast who ate fifteen people, were occasionally featured.[126]

Despite the failure of Anne of Austria to support him in his battle with the Faculty of Medicine, Renaudot was called back into service as propagandist during the Fronde. He went with the royal family to St. Germain-en-Laye where he continued to produce the *Gazette*. His sons remained in Paris to publish another journal also designed to further the interests of the monarchy.[127]

Renaudot carved out a successful, unconventional career within the constraints of ancien régime society. He benefited from traditional routes to advancement such as patronage networks, but he was also an adept self-promoter. He concentrated on spreading the news about the great number who flocked to the Bureau and the great events that transpired there. He provided services that the notables would require and seek, such as an information clearinghouse and an office for the placement of domestics, and equipped with their addresses, he conveyed that information to them. Renaudot's flouting of convention produced a great deal of opposition, but the conferences themselves were generally exempt from this opposition. If the *Gazette* provided political reporting along pro-monarchical lines, the conferences worked against the restriction of opinion implicit in propaganda, by opening up every topic explored.

PART II Science

Mandragora mas.
Mandragore.

MANDRAGORE MAS
(The Mandrake), engraved by Abraham Brosse.
Courtesy Bibliothèque nationale de France, Paris, 63 C 20687.

Introduction

WHEN JEAN LE ROND D' ALEMBERT WROTE THE *PRELIMINARY DISCOURSE*
to the *Encyclopédie* of the eighteenth century, he not only set out the
ideological agenda of the Enlightenment but also, in a very real sense,
defined the shape of the history of science. He begins his account of
the development of the sciences by saying, "the history of the sciences
is naturally bound up with that of the small number of great geniuses
whose works have helped to spread enlightenment among men," and
so too the history of science focuses much of its attention around its
heroic figures. The period just before the scientific revolution was, in
d' Alembert's account, hamstrung both by the mindless appreciation
of ancient texts, "devoured indiscriminately," and by "theological
despotism," which held sway over the understanding of the natural
world. These blindfolds would eventualy be cast off due to the efforts
of those "who prepared from afar the light, which gradually, by imperceptible degrees, would illuminate the world." D' Alembert even singles
out those who have formed ever after the pantheon of early modern
science—Bacon, Descartes, Newton, and Locke for science within a
philosophic tradition, and others whose more specific scientific work
"lifted, so to speak, a corner of the veil that concealed truth from us,"
figures such as Galileo, Harvey, and Huyghens.

D' Alembert's polemical panegyric to science has had a great influence on the standard understanding of the scientific revolution that
persists to our day. For d' Alembert, Francis Bacon defined the scientific method, and he was profuse in praising Bacon's works, "everything, even their titles, proclaims the man of genius, the mind that sees
things in the large view. He collects facts, he compares experiments and
points out a large number to be made." D' Alembert appreciated
Descartes primarily for "the application he was able to make of algebra
to geometry, one of the grandest and most fortunate ideas that the
human mind has ever had. It will always be the key to the most
profound investigations, not only in sublime geometry, but also in all

the physico-mathematical sciences." But Descartes's philosophical audacity led him to overextend his conclusions beyond demonstration to forge a system. This unwarranted systematization required the corrective of Newton, who would, in d' Alembert's words, give "philosophy a form, which apparently it is to keep." Newton was the "great genius" who "saw that is was time to banish conjectures and vague hypotheses from physics." Locke then endowed metaphysics with the clarity of Newtonian physics by writing "the experimental physics of the soul."[1]

This telling of the tale—a story of isolated geniuses remaking knowledge, which leads only slowly to enlightenment and progress—is one that prevailed unchallenged and unexpanded in the history of science. This positivistic account still holds pride of place in textbook accounts and still shapes our notions of what is considered unquestionably appropriate to the history of science. The historical profession continues to privilege works that reflect this view. The science of the early modern period is still more credible the closer it hews to astronomy, physics, and mathematics—the sciences that count in the standard telling of the tale. There is no doubt that a study of one of these heroes, or of physics or astronomy, is central to the scientific revolution.

The development of the history of science as a discipline is in many ways the story of a successive broadening of the historical perspective on science. That broadening first questioned the lone genius characterization of the central figures of the scientific revolution. Scholars have studied their debts to earlier tradition—noting, for example, the influence of the scholastic tradition on Galileo and Descartes. Science has been set in broader institutional and cultural settings; the Royal Society, the Académie des Sciences, universities, and provincial academies have been studied for their role in the development and promulgation of science.[2] Studies of medieval science called into question d' Alembert's unambiguous statement that Bacon was "born in the most profound night."[3] Scholars have established the centrality and vitality of the old or Aristotelian science and its centrality to the development of the new.[4] Renaissance neoplatonism and hermeticism are now recognized as much more intellectually vital and scientifically significant than d' Alembert's cavalier dismissal of the Renaissance as merely the uncritical absorption of the classics would suggest. Studies of science in the early modern period now recognize the influence of such unconventional figures as Marsilio Ficino, Theophrastus Paracelsus, Jean-Baptiste van Helmont, and others neglected by the standard accounts. Even the heroic figures were decisively shaped by the hermetic tradition, alchemy, and neoplatonism. The influence of alchemy on Isaac Newton and Robert Boyle has been well studied but remains controversial, in part because the cultivation of less orthodox science by our most revered heroes most seriously calls into question the positivist account.

There has been a growing recognition of the sterility of d' Alembert's definitive account and an increase in scholarly assaults on the narrowness of that interpretation. Many have worked to broaden the scope of the history of science beyond the heroic figures and the physical sciences. The history of science has become more inclusive, particularly in response to issues raised by social and cultural historians. Historians have documented alternative approaches to science, such as natural history and the secrets and wonders of nature, and alternative aspects of scientific practices, such as patronage and the domestic setting of science.[5] Renaudot's conferences can be readily integrated into this more inclusive and expansive historiography of early modern science.

Most discussions of seventeenth-century science fail to include Renaudot's conferences; and when they are recognized, the recognition is cursory or disparaging. The dismissals are based on certain suppositions about what is significant to the history of science, suppositions that are increasingly being called into question by those seeking to broaden the discussion of early modern science—but not so consistently as to rehabilitate a group like Renaudot's. The first supposition is that science must be discussed in terms of the paradigmatic revolution of the seventeenth century (largely confined to astronomy and physics), and therefore, scientific discussion is significant only insofar as it prefigures this development. The second is that his group does not merit inclusion in the story of the development of science during the scientific revolution because it can be dismissed as a society of dilettantes. This last raises a number of considerations about what factors, entirely extraneous to the content of a text, serve to heighten or diminish its credibility within the history of science.

Renaudot himself defined his conferences and those who assembled for them in ways that have made it possible for historians of science not to take them seriously. First of all, early modern groups clearly benefit from a policy of social exclusivity. Such groups are best constituted if they allow only members who are essentially full-time, practicing scientists. This practice became more common in later seventeenth-century academies and corresponds better to modern notions of the pursuit of science and the careers appropriate to those who foster it. Renaudot, however, admitted all comers, until the size of the room required that attendance be restricted to one hundred members "of a certain quality."[6] This restriction, which really went against Renaudot's own sense of the necessity for the widespread, public dissemination of knowledge, was insufficient to protect the group from charges of dilettantism. Because these gatherings were not sufficiently restricted, they were, according to some critics, déclassé, the venue of the social parvenu.

Any seventeenth-century group that can claim as participants the likes of Gassendi, Descartes, or Mersenne has enhanced credibility derived from its illustrious members. While many scholars have suggested that some influential figures, such as Campanella and de Claves, attended the conferences, it is difficult to find supporting evidence.[7] (It is significant to note that all studies of the Bureau cite these specific possible participants in order to claim some credibility for the group.) Furthermore, Renaudot—frustrating scholars in the very formulation of his conferences—insisted upon anonymity so that no opinion could prevail on the basis of reputation as opposed to solid analysis. Instead of privileging the accomplishment of any individual, Renaudot had a collective, civic approach to knowledge and its dissemination. He advocated the disinterested pursuit of knowledge motivated not by self-interest but instead by public utility, and he cited the civic responsibility of intellectuals to make private knowledge public. Much of the history of science, on the other hand, has been written to demonstrate the role of the scientific genius in furthering the cause of science. If Renaudot had been willing to proclaim the merits of the conferences at the Bureau based on the reputation of the members he could proudly tout, or if obscure members later became prominent, its proceedings would not only have been considered more significant, simply by virtue of association, but they would also have been well studied to trace the intellectual development of their noteworthy participants.

Although Renaudot saw the "conference" as an ideal vehicle for the dissemination of knowledge, and he published the proceedings in collections of one hundred to further disseminate that knowledge, his group would probably have been more credible if it had met in secret and never published the proceedings. With publication, every bizarre idea, every inconclusive discussion, every uncritical use of evidence is laid bare. Without published proceedings, historians can assume much more sophisticated levels of discussion. Secret meetings with no written records can also be assumed to reflect the highest denominator, that is to say, the level of accomplishment of the most distinguished members of the group. (It probably redounds to the credit of the Académie des Sciences that the transcriptions of its early meetings have been lost.)[8]

The short nine-year history of Renaudot's group has also worked against its inclusion in the history of science. Other seventeenth-century groups such as the early Royal Society produced documents very like those of the Bureau, both in terms of the topics discussed and the eclectic approach to them. However, those groups evolved later in directions that fit our notions of science. Because of its short duration, Renaudot's group does not reflect such an evolution. It is clearly possible that its evolution might not have been in a direction the profession would have credited. Nonetheless, a more protracted history would make it easier to determine how the participants' approach to science evolved and what kind of cultural influence this group exerted.

Another distinctly French notion of the history of science, the so-called Fontenelle thesis, has also militated against the inclusion of the conferences in the heroic story of the rise of science. This thesis claims that in France, science depended on extensive subsidization by the crown. Since the gathering at Renaudot's establishment[9] is neither restricted in membership nor sustained by government funding, it does not meet the criterion for inclusion in French science. Even if it had an explicit scientific agenda, it did not have enough money or royal support to effectively carry it out.[10] Renaudot's group did benefit from

Richelieu's unofficial protection of Renaudot's activities, but the group had neither the advantages nor the disadvantages of state-sponsored science.

Although many contemporary scientific groups were the inspiration of a single individual, this is a risky way to win acceptance into the annals of the history of science for several reasons. First, the group might too narrowly reflect the interests of its sponsor or organizer. (This is not a problem for Renaudot's group since their interests were wonderfully eclectic.) Second, an individual is much more vulnerable to the vicissitudes of fortune. Renaudot's group and virtually all of his activities ceased immediately upon the deaths of Richelieu and Louis XIII, who had allowed him to maneuver in such a highly effective way that his activities flourished despite the constraints of the old regime. Without their support, Renaudot could not keep the Bureau in operation. Thus Renaudot's notion of his group as inclusive, meeting publicly, privileging no participant, under the aegis of an individual, and without state support are all external features that have dimmed the posthumous reputation of the group.

The intellectual content of the conferences has been even more problematic to recent historians than the social composition of the group. Because Renaudot's conferences paired rhetorical and scientific topics, they have been dismissed as "bad science" and "old rhetoric." The rhetorical topics are sometimes characterized as mere rehashes of humanist conventions. As a result they have not been studied, even though they in fact demonstrate an interesting application of science to conventional rhetorical themes and can be used to explore the connections between rhetoric and science, a preoccupation of recent historiography.[11] But the mere fact that Renaudot's group did not restrict itself to scientific topics made it unlikely to garner attention. Historians of science are much more likely to acknowledge an institution as worthy of study if that institution identifies itself as an academy of science and focuses solely on clearly scientific topics. Renaudot's group attended *conferences,* and the proceedings were published in *recueils,* or collections of one hundred. Neither the character of the group nor the nature of its publications fits a model that makes their relevance to the history of science obvious.

Despite their extensive treatment of scientific topics and the existence of published proceedings, the little attention they have received has been largely negative; the conferences are generally discussed in terms of what they are not—not mechanistic, not systematic. Historians of science find no coherent, consistent position that can be heralded as signaling scientific progress on any topic. In fact, the most serious failing of Renaudot's group, in terms of the content of the conferences, is the failure to espouse a consistent philosophical point of view that would allow the group to be appropriately located in the great paradigm shift of the seventeenth century. The best-case scenario for a seventeenth-century group is to espouse early the philosophical position that will prevail—in this case, mechanism. If his group had espoused mechanism in the 1630s, Renaudot might have challenged Robert Boyle and the Royal Society for hegemony in the annals of the history of science. Bourdelot's Académie of the 1660s and 1670s has found greater favor in the history of science because its members worked within a mechanical consensus.

The presentism of the history of science has eroded to a sufficient degree that less clearly positivist elements in early modern science have gained a foothold both in the historiography and in our notions of science. Even textbook treatments now interrupt the triumphalist march of Copernicus, Kepler, Galileo, and Newton with awkward asides to Neoplatonism or even Paracelsianism. But even if mechanism is no longer the only acceptable science, historians appreciate consistency. Thus, if his group could have been clearly identified with a consistent philosophy, even an unconventional one, Renaudot might have attained some preeminence in recent historiography. But the conferences spectacularly fail to espouse any particular philosophy. There are occasional references to mechanism, but also to Aristotelian explanations and Paracelsian positions. Members make arguments based on appeals to direct observation, on authority, on analogy. Although the sometimes mind-boggling eclecticism of Renaudot's conferences certainly makes it difficult to include them in a narrative of scientific progress, the process of competition and accommodation of ideas in gatherings like these tells us a great deal about the process of the evolution of scientific ideas.[12]

Renaudot's conferences also make a significant contribution to the new, more inclusive historiography of the history of science. Although these discussions treated scientific issues in ways that are rarely incorporated into a modern understanding of science or the scientific revolution, they nonetheless allowed conferees to confidently assess their world. This confidence is based largely on their exploration of those sciences that are not considered central to the scientific revolution—the natural sciences, those sciences that would not even take on their modern names, geology and biology, until the early nineteenth century. Participants also relied heavily on medicine, a particularly "unscientific" science from a modern perspective. They offer a different perspective on what kinds of knowledge were important and useful. I want to use the discussion of the sciences by Renaudot's conferees to suggest that the natural sciences, even if they were not the basis for a "revolution," were historically significant. The natural sciences provided a foundation for the social sciences and, perhaps more surprising, a way to explore the epistemological issues of the scientific revolution.

The content of the conferences must also be assessed on its own terms, not as a system manqué. Although the notion of "science" the conferences reveal is problematic for us and defies easy categorization, the very things that make it difficult for us also made it attractive to those who attended them. The conferences present a different view of the "scientist" and the range of his activities. Although we presuppose a chasm between the arts and the sciences, these participants used the same methods of analysis and discussion to treat fevers, the philosopher's stone, commercial agendas, and family relationships.

The conferences offer a more characteristic sense of the science of the day than our conventional accounts presuppose. The fact that the opinions expressed are not organized into a coherent system does not mean that the treatment of science by conferees should be dismissed.[13] Many ways of thinking that are jarringly unfamiliar to modern readers compete in this marketplace of scientific ideas. But because participants were committed to the evaluation of claims by staunchly empirical and skeptical standards, the conferences demonstrate that attitudes essential to the epistemology of the scientific revolution could develop in unorthodox forums independently of the new mechanical philosophy. As a result Renaudot's group has much to tell us about science in the seventeenth century, particularly about the transmission of science to a popular audience. The conferences are strikingly effective documents for elucidating the range and nature of scientific opinion. They manifest in a concrete way that scientific opinion was in a period of tremendous flux. They also attest to public interest and set up an important source for the subsequent popular success of science.

The fact that Renaudot's conferences have so rarely been considered for their role in the history of science raises several questions: Are our definitions of science unduly restricted or inordinately presentist, particularly in evaluating the early modern period? What might inclusion of a group like Renaudot's add to the history of science? Is the history of science, especially when dealing with the hallmark event of the scientific revolution, still too whiggish to integrate Renaudot's conferences into the saga of early modern science?[14]

This section of the book explores the extensive discussion of the natural world that took place in the conferences held at the Bureau. Chapter Three begins with the understanding of nature that characterized these discussions and with their treatment of occult topics. Although the latter might seem a strange way to approach questions of early modern science, indeed an approach that might from the outset seek to undermine the credibility I seek for science at the Bureau, their treatment of nature and occult topics lays bare their understanding of nature and science.

CHAPTER THREE

Talismans, Incubi, Divination, and the Book of M★

Nature and the Occult

These figures act, as they say, either upon men's minds, as to cause one to be loved or honored . . . or upon their bodies, as to cure them.

S O CONTENDS THE FIRST SPEAKER IN A CONFERENCE CONVENED ON 7 April 1636, to discuss "Of Talismans."[1] He defines them as nothing but "images in relief, or engraved upon medals or rings, ordinarily of metal on precious stones, in the shape of men or animals." Produced under specific constellations, these images are powerful because they retain the influence of that constellation. Thus he assumes not only that the macrocosm-microcosm relationship—that is to say, a relationship between the unchanging heavens and specific, transitory, earthly phenomena—exists and is efficacious, but also that its power can be captured in objects.

Other speakers, too, cite the fundamental relationship between the macrocosm and the microcosm as *the* most compelling support for talismans and the most appropriate way to approach the hidden forces of nature, or the occult. As one speaker puts it, "The knowledge of these sympathetic correspondences is the true magic . . . the highest point of human knowledge, marrying heaven with earth"; its opposite, "black magic, is detestable, shameful and ridiculous." Another points out that talismans have concrete practical uses, such as "the magnetic cure of wounds, by applying the medicine to the weapon that did the hurt or to the bloody shirt."[2] As this example attests, when participants discuss any occult topic, they align their belief in a particular occult phenomenon with their overall understanding of nature and marshal empirical evidence to support their positions.

Other speakers want to demystify talismans. One insists that they are "natural agents . . . by occult and sympathetic virtues, which cause many strange effects, which the ignorant vulgar incongruously ascribe to magic or spells." Although he is careful to distinguish his understanding of the issue from that of the vulgar, he does not doubt the efficacy of talismans. He cites historical evidence, such as the idols of the pagans and Paracelsus's talismans against the plague, which "render their effects as common, as their existence [is] certain."[3] But, he insists, the learned understand that talismans work by natural principles and only the vulgar, who do not understand the operations of nature, consider them magical. Another speaker presents an analogy he finds so compelling that he assumes there can be no effective rebuttal: "It is not necessary to seek reason and authorities to prove talismans, either in art or nature; since man himself may be seen to be *the* talisman and perfection of God's works." His ultimate point is the query "Isn't this soul in its immortality a talisman of His divinity?"[4]

For other participants, the topic of talismans raises epistemological issues. Some attack the skeptics, objecting to those "who impugn the truth of things, under pretext that they do not fall under our reason." Instead of relying on puny reason, a speaker urges one to "witness what is seen in all the admirable works of nature and art, in the magnetic cure of wounds and of diseases by amulets." Others take a more skeptical stance, insisting, for example, that "occult" phenomena must act in accord with our understanding of causation. One speaker vehemently contends that *none* of the supposed connections between talismans and their effects can be sustained. Remedies cure not by resemblance but by virtue of the properties inherent to them. A talisman can neither act through its own power nor act on the will, nor is there any connection to the stars.

This brief overview of one specific conference on an occult topic not only concretely demonstrates the range of responses to a particular topic but also casts into high relief some of the themes that recur in discussions of other occult topics I will explore in greater detail. These are: (1) the connection between occult topics and a general understanding of nature; (2) the problems of definition posed by occult topics; (3) the grounds on which occult phenomena are understood, accepted, or doubted; (4) and finally, what their understanding of nature, vividly reflected in participants' attempts to deal with occult topics, tell us about science at the Bureau. This chapter will discuss a number of conferences under the category "occult" not because the participants themselves define the topics this way, but because at least one speaker on the subject believes that the topic under consideration operates by hidden or occult means (although frequently at least one speaker on each of these topics contests the characterization).

Participants discussed a wide range of phenomena that operated in ways they could only with difficulty incorporate into an understanding of the usual operations of nature. Participants raised questions about the existence and appearance of bizarre entities like the unicorn and the philosopher's stone, and they assessed the merits or lack thereof of occult practices and texts. It is not surprising that Renaudot's group should dedicate a number of conferences to occult topics.[5] Although foreign to our notions of science, such topics were integral to seventeenth-century discussions of nature. Because they lay bare some of its fundamental epistemological problems, such topics also preoccupied the heroic figures of the scientific revolution.[6]

The conferences on nature and occult topics specifically highlight the debates over natural magic and the question of whether the macrocosm-microcosm relationship was a valid way to understand the universe and man's role in it. Because the macrocosm-microcosm is found in Aristotle's *Physics*, it might be considered simply as part of conventional scholastic science. In the Renaissance, however, it became a crucial point of opposition to scholasticism; it was much more central to the neoplatonic and cabalistic texts, which were an important part of the Renaissance revival of the ancients, than it had been to the Aristotelians. The revival of these texts made debates over the macrocosm-microcosm as central to the culture of the seventeenth century as those over innovations such as heliocentrism or the circulatory system with which we are more familiar. A number of issues and events served to make the occult topical.

The ideas of Paracelsus can be used as a lens through which to examine the influence of the occult in the early modern period. Born in 1493, in Einsiedeln near Zurich, the self-named "greater than Celsus," was an unconventional figure in a period populated by larger-than-life individuals. Like his contemporaries, Luther and Erasmus, Paracelsus sought religious renewal and reform. Like other Renaissance humanists, he used neoplatonic and hermetic texts to critique Aristotle and to suggest an alternative account of nature. He advanced a three-element theory (salt, sulfur, and mercury) to rival Aristotle's four-element theory (earth, air, fire, and water), which opened a large chink in Aristotelian science and allowed his followers to chip away at its authority.

By providing an alternative, fundamental science of matter, Paracelsus exerted an influence in most areas of science but especially in chemistry and medicine. His science was predicated on three chemicals, and he understood the world as a chemical laboratory. Rejecting Galen's humors as an explanation of health and disease, he instead posited "disease seeds," which grew in organs of the body just as mineral seeds grew in the earth. The macrocosm-microcosm, which united man and nature and provided an integrated basis for science and religion, was central to Paracelsian science.[7] It also supported Paracelsus's belief in action at a distance (the Aristotelians insisted on direct contact). This belief put Paracelsus in the center of a number of issues central to the early seventeenth century. Action at a distance authorized astral influences or astrology, which was an influential part of the occult sciences and unified both elite and popular science.[8] It also offered a theoretical foundation for the phenomenon of magnetism made popular by William Gilbert's *De Magnete* (1600). It was central to the medical debate over weapon-salve, the practice of applying salve to the weapon as a way to cure the wound it inflicted.

Paracelsian ideas came to the fore in a number of other contexts as well. Scientific utopias such as Bacon's *New Atlantis,* Johan Andreae's *Christianopolis,* and Campanella's *The City of the Sun* emphasized (as Paracelsus had done earlier) science as a route to religious and moral renovation. Paris was set abuzz by the appearance of the Rosicrucian texts, the *Fama Fraternitas* (1614) and the *Confessio* (1615), which used Paracelsus as the basis for their calls to reform science, education, and medicine and announced an upcoming visit of the Rosicrucians to Paris in 1623. These texts told the tale of the successful quest for new learning through travel to learned communities of the East, such as Damascus and Fez, by the leader of a new order, Christian Rosenkreuz. His followers sent out an appeal for like-minded individuals to join their quest for new learning that rejected Aristotle and Galen and emphasized instead the connection between God and nature and medicine as a basis for this new knowledge. These calls went out all over Europe and attracted many eager recruits ready to join a movement, which then failed to materialize. (Johan Andreae may well have been the author of the anonymous Rosicrucian texts.)

But Paracelsian ideas did not simply have mystical appeal. They were influential enough to attract increasingly credible adherents. Many of the most prominent figures of the scientific revolution took them seriously enough to debate them.[9] In 1623, a widely publicized debate over alchemy took place in Paris. Mersenne argued the value of mathematics over chemistry as a way to understand the world. He mobilized Pierre Gassendi to participate in the debate, and Gassendi denounced alchemy as dangerous to religion. The work of Jean-Baptiste van Helmont built upon many of Paracelsus's ideas but also made them more intellectually credible by making them less mystical and by connecting them to experimentalism. He insisted that the macrocosm-microcosm was neither magical nor divine but simply natural. When he debated the Jesuits over weapon-salve, he made the strategic mistake of comparing the action of the salve to the effects of relics. Nonetheless, because van Helmont's work seemed promising as a scientific alternative to mechanism, it inspired many prominent figures of the scientific revolution, especially those interested in chemistry, like Boyle, Newton, Walter Charlton, and Thomas Willis.

Given the fact that the conferees addressed such a broad swath of intellectual issues, it would be surprising indeed if they did not treat occult phenomena. They were committed to wide-ranging discussion of cutting-edge intellectual issues, and many contemporary concerns were rooted in the hermetic tradition. They presented themselves as bound by the highest standards of skepticism and empirical judgment, stances they employ in treating the occult.

When conferees grappled with occult phenomena, they tried to rationalize them by applying their fundamental beliefs about nature to them. Even the most casual perusal of early modern texts suggests that *nature* functioned as the critical term defining the relationship of human beings to their world. But between the early modern view of nature and our own lies the intellectual chasm and historiographical minefield of the scientific revolution.[10] The basic conception of nature has functioned in the history of science as the acid test of the evolution from pre-modern to modern, a mechanical view of nature heralding the modern. The work of Allen Debus, Betty Jo Dobbs, Lawrence Principe and others has shaken our faith in positivistic accounts of this development.[11] Extensive exposure to the virtues of Paracelsus, van Helmont, Robert Fludd, John Dee, and other less conventional scientific figures has made clear both that the transition from early modern to mechanical views of nature was less than clear-cut and that there was extensive and empirically grounded opposition to a mechanical view of nature throughout the early modern period.[12] The fundamental influence of hermeticism and alchemy on the heroic figures of the scientific revolution such as Newton and Boyle has also complicated the picture. Some more polemical studies have attacked the scientific revolution as the source of an approach to nature that produced environmental disaster; that is to say, the mechanical philosophy is charged with condoning man's rapacious exploitation of the earth's natural resources.[13] Because Renaudot's conferences comment extensively on nature, they provide a particularly useful source for examining what nature meant in the early seventeenth century. Because their treatment of these issues is so eclectic, they, too, call for a reappraisal of the remnants of positivism in the history of science.

UNDERSTANDING NATURE

Before examining what makes the participants' use of nature significant to the transformation of their worldview, it is important to point to what unites them in their understanding of nature, for this understanding shapes their approach to the specific topics. First, conferees appeal to nature to explain the limitations of human beings. While man may be, according to some speakers, at the apogee of creation, he is humbled before nature. Although limited by nature, man must nonetheless look to nature as a source of knowledge, especially through the investigation of similarities and other bases of comparison that allow him to know nature. Explicitly religious topics are taboo, so nature is the ultimate abstraction that grounds discussion of natural phenomena. In other words, nature substitutes for God as the explanation of natural phenomena. Second, in the context of this study, "nature" is a term that charts a transition from a rhetorical approach to a number of topics to a scientific one that can then easily be applied to society. Third, "nature" is the defining term for the epistemology of science because participants assume that nature means us to know. They assume that their knowledge of nature gives them a critical sensibility from which to assess both popular beliefs and received opinion. Thus they are both confident in their ability to know and critical and skeptical in weighing specifics.

When Renaudot's group gathered to discuss a wide array of topics, they invoked "nature" as a fundamental term of authority or explanation. Premises sharply different from modern scientific attitudes shape their discussion of nature. They take as a given man's limited ability to probe certain questions. For example, to try to understand the nature of light is a misbegotten enterprise because, as one speaker puts it, "Light is a form, to seek the cause of light is to seek the reason of forms which is not known to us."[14] Just as God is incomprehensible because of his grandeur, so too, matter is comprehensible because of its baseness.[15] Instead of investigating the secrets of nature, one commentator suggests, we are fit to simply admire them. He charges that "those who give reasons are not less ignorant but more vain."[16] One speaker, discussing how minerals grow, claims that all of nature's works are occult or hidden from us.[17]

Paradoxically, even if the human understanding of nature must be acknowledged as incomplete, participants insist they can know fundamental things about it because nature operates consistently. For example, nature acts according to the standards of propriety.[18] Participants, of course, define the qualities that reflect propriety and apply them to nature.[19] They assume that the propriety that characterizes the operations of nature extends to nature's effects on man; man is the direct beneficiary of what speakers consistently refer to as the "propriety of nature." Thus nature does not allow man to seek the unattainable, such as perpetual motion or the philosopher's stone. So, some speakers argue, because men seek them, they must exist.[20] Nature has also given man what he needs; for example, "hearing is given to man to facilitate his natural desire to understand the thoughts of his species."[21] The pervasive and compelling analogy between natural and human operations is one of the significant means nature provides to obtain knowledge. Although speakers acknowledge that nature supersedes human operations, they also assume that its operations are analogous to those undertaken by human beings.[22] The analogy works both ways: Nature's operations apply to man in a less grand fashion, but what man can do, nature must also be able to accomplish to a more admirable degree.[23] Because he is a part of nature, man can accomplish things that mirror the much greater activities of nature. But paradoxically, the activities of nature also conform to human notions of the fitting. Thus for some speakers, all facets of nature from the heavens to the simplest creatures are connected by the relationship between the macrocosm and the microcosm, a notion one speaker succinctly expresses as, "Superior bodies act on inferior, and all motions here below proceed from those of the celestial."[24] Speakers frequently make that fundamental relationship carry the weight of the conclusions they draw. Thus one contends that, because there is perpetual motion in the heavens, perpetual motion is possible on earth, but it must be circular. Another cites lightning and thunder as celestial activities analogous to the generation of metals in the earth. Yet another sees divination as possible because of the close connection between superior and inferior.[25]

Regardless of the position of the speaker on the scale from Aristotelianism to mechanism and regardless of how avant-garde or retrograde the topic of discussion, speakers bring these deeply held but almost contradictory presuppositions to bear. Instead of assuming that all will be revealed through the application of science and technology, speakers invariably either begin with or fall back to a position of epistemological modesty; that is to say, fundamental knowledge about the operations of nature is and will remain unknowable. Equally important, they also assume that nature and man are related in a variety of ways, but that those ways are consistent and predictable, and thus nature provides a means to knowledge. Although these principles might be considered contradictory, they are also analogous to the epistemological position taken by the philosophes of the French Enlightenment—that ultimate knowledge of the physical world cannot be gained, so we must direct our attention to that which is under our purview or "all that man can know of man."[26] Unlike the philosophes, however, these conferees do not direct their optimism about what man can know solely to the social realm. They instead maintain that nature intends man to know a great deal about it and that man has the means to do so. (Despite their expressions of epistemological modesty, the philosophes also directed their attention, with considerable confidence, to nature.)

Certainly the use of analogies—in particular, the all-embracing macrocosm-microcosm analogy—might well be considered typical of much writing about nature in the early modern period. How those analogies are used and the results they produce in the conferences are worth noting. First, they allow participants to address a broad range of topics with quite considerable confidence. Second, participants demonstrate consistent skepticism; they seem imbued with a sense that they are the advocates of a new standard of evidence. Several conferences explicitly contend that maxims (that is, popular sayings) are dangerous to health because they encourage self-diagnosis and thus keep people from seeking medical care. Other speakers dismiss reports of monsters as apocryphal or the result of misguided credulity.[27] Participants assume a gap between the ways that the popular classes and the elite approach these issues. For example, one speaker explicitly denounces the claim that the anger of God against certain men causes their wives to bring forth monsters as simply the misguided opinion of the vulgar.[28] However they, too, are more credulous of reports of unusual phenomena from exotic locations like the New World.[29] But references to monsters or irregularities of nature are made only occasionally.[30] The predominant sense in the conferences is that any reported "freaks of nature" must be examined in terms of the regular, more significant operations of nature. In fact, all reports of monsters are discounted to some degree. Participants routinely speculate about the effects of the imagination on those individuals who claim to have seen them. One speaker on the subject of fables categorically asserts that monsters are offensive to human reason.[31]

A speaker in a conference on the subject of incubi and succubae exemplifies the attitude of conferees on occult topics when he says, "Two sorts of people err in this matter, the superstitious and ignorant vulgar who attribute everything to miracles done either by saints or devils, and the atheists and libertines who believe neither the one nor the other. Physicians take the middle way, distinguishing what is fit to be attributed to nature and her ordinary motions from what is super-natural."[32] Clearly, conferees identified with the physicians, presenting themselves as skeptical and critical students of natural phenomena. This middle way between credulity and complete skepticism might be said to encapsulate the participants' sense of their place along a spectrum of scientific opinion.

Another fundamental belief shared by participants, that nature presents an ordered hierarchy they can know from top to bottom, reinforces skepticism about unusual phenomena. They saw a natural hierarchy reflected in the order of the heavens and in the great chain of being, which connected each creature to the creature above and below it in this natural hierarchy. And the heavens were connected to the earth through the macrocosm-microcosm relationship, where the earth reflected some sign of the heavens. As one speaker puts it, nature "observes such an order that she always begins with the most simple and never passes from one extremity to another without a medium."[33]

Despite their shared consensus that nature is ordered, participants presume that the order itself is based on a variety of principles. Nature, some consider, keeps order by the opposition of contraries, a battle of forces in opposition. As one describes the application of this principle to human beings, "life lasts only so long as the natural heat acts upon the radical moisture, when their combat is ended, man must necessarily die."[34] Another understanding of nature sees that order as produced by a progressive ordering of raw materials, a process of refinement from undifferentiated matter to matter under a particular form.[35] One speaker defines generation and growth as fundamental natural processes accomplished by the separation of the humors by heat, the crucial agent of nature.[36]

Whatever principles are seen as fundamental, all of the conferences that address natural phenomena are preoccupied with the question of order in nature; but even a fundamental belief about order in nature does not reflect certainty about its operations. This lack of certainty leads some speakers to draw strikingly inconclusive generalizations. As one concludes, there are three kinds of events in nature, things that always happen, things that sometimes happen, and things that rarely happen.[37] But if the operations of nature are unclear, speakers nonetheless assume that her intent is clear because nature acts in the best interests of the creatures of the earth. For example, nature has given animals attributes that suit their needs; as a result, a creature grows "until the body has attained the proportion and stature requisite to its functions."[38] The instinct for self-preservation most strikingly indicates the care nature takes of her creatures.[39] Belief in the beneficent teleology of nature is so pervasive that it is used to sustain arguments the modern reader finds distinctly peculiar. Even smallpox, one speaker argues, indicates nature's favor: "Those that are taken with this disease are usually the most healthy, and of a sanguine constitution, which is the most laudable."[40] Nature is regarded as beneficent regardless of one's view of the basic principles of nature. If nature operates through an ongoing battle of contraries, those contraries ultimately work in man's interest; it sets bodies "on such an edge that they become so much more active."[41]

In striking opposition to this view of the ordered beneficent nature, a dissenting view occasionally emerges, which sees nature as less transparent, less predictable. The most extreme statement of this kind assigns to nature an almost malign character. "There are certain secrets in nature dreadful to human reason, incredible, according to the principles of art and of our knowledge. That nature is the great Circe, the grand sorceress." The speaker hastens to qualify this statement; "it is not to be imagined that nature is so cruel a stepmother, but that ... remedies may come from the same hand that caused the disease."[42] Thus even when proclaiming the Circe-like quality of nature, participants assume that, although nature is difficult to know, she nonetheless provides antidotes for any ill effects she may have produced. In a peculiar turn of argument, the very incomprehensibility of nature suggests beneficence. Nature may be capricious, but even that quality seems to work for man's benefit, "for though nature loves change (of which she is the principle), yet it is only that of generation or of changing a lesser into a more noble substance."[43] Although they generally assume, regardless of the ordering concept, that the operations of nature demonstrate a beneficent order, these speakers claim to be taking a consistently critical stance. The notion that nature acts according to an order, no matter what the ordering principle is, gives participants grounds for skepticism about phenomena that violate the order they assume.

Although these rather arbitrary applications of "nature" and inconsistent definitions might strike the modern reader as divorced from science, nonetheless, to early modern intellectuals such assertions could have the persuasive ring of the modern. Francis Bacon heralded Bernardino Telesio as the "first of the moderns," and Telesio's use of nature in his "Of the nature of things" (1565) resembles that of Renaudot's conferees. Ignorance of nature, Telesio maintained, was due to the uncritical reliance on the authority of the ancients; knowledge would be gained through impartial observation whereby nature will "announce herself." Like the Paris conferees, he sought a unifying principle as a way to understand nature and deduced, like some of them, that "the nature of things" was, fundamentally, the conflict of hot versus cold.[44]

What do these views of nature ultimately give to the conference participants? These remarks suggest that without a mathematical or mechanical worldview, participants are perfectly able to consider nature, study it, and claim to understand it. Their understanding, nebulous as it might seem to us, nonetheless assures them that they are critical enough not to be misled by the irrational and secure in their confidence in the order and uniformity of nature. Armed with both skepticism and a firm belief in the uniformity of nature, conferees approach nature with the same confidence characteristic of prominent proponents of the scientific revolution, even those natural phenomena that pose great difficulty because they deal with the hidden operations of nature or the occult.

UNDERSTANDING THE OCCULT

Even more than conventional topics, occult topics require clarification and definition as a way for speakers to gain control over them, since they are by their very nature elusive. Even if a conference begins with a relatively clear exposition, subsequent speakers frequently offer emendations that obscure the issue.[45] (Ultimately some conferences on occult topics degenerate into sessions that look like definition by committee.) Definitions allow participants to discriminate "true manifestations from delusions," to confine the influence of practitioners of the occult as narrowly as possible, to discuss belief in the occult in terms of human psychology, and ultimately, to demystify the hidden. Speakers are not simply skeptical; they also conscientiously winnow out the unacceptable from the acceptable.

Even those who concede some legitimacy for occult practitioners (sorcerers, for example) circumscribe their activities so they fit into ways of discussing the natural rather than the occult. For example, in "Of divination,"[46] a speaker insists that they are talking neither about medical diagnosis based on the reading of symptoms in the sense of Hippocrates' *Prognostics* nor about reading perfectly obvious and consistent natural signs, like the prediction of rain based on seeing a rainbow. Instead, he says, "if, not knowing a prisoner nor his affairs, I foretell that he will be set free or not; that an unknown person will be married and how many children he will have, or such other things which have no necessary, or even contingent causes known to me; this is properly to divine." He concludes, "Therefore all your soothsayers, augurs, sorcerers, fortune-tellers, and the like, are but so many impostors." For him, any claim to divination is fraudulent. Another speaker classifies the "occult" out of consideration by removing from discussion divination caused by God or the devil. These, he says are not therefore properly divination. He then focuses solely on natural divining by drops of oil, looking glasses, crystal cylinders, enchanted rings, entrails of beast, amniotic fluid, and so on.

Although definitions serve many important functions, they do not always offer satisfactory solutions to the intellectual complexities of occult topics. Some, frustrated by the difficulties involved in discussing these kinds of topics, adopt strongly skeptical positions. The question "Of sympathy or antipathy"[47] raises, for at least one speaker, fundamental doubts about our ability to know; "to speak truth, all these effects are no more known to us than their causes . . . both . . . impenetrable to human wit." Another speaker goes further, suggesting that "it is more fit to admire these secret motions . . . than to seek the true cause of them unprofitably." Occult topics, for entirely understandable reasons, produce frustration. Participants are not as able to address them with the confidence they demonstrate in discussing more demonstrable topics. Nonetheless, such topics are, at least in part, the intellectual coin of the realm.

The occult is much more prominently integrated into early seventeenth-century culture than the modern reader might expect. Just to note several important figures who were central to the development of occult philosophy in the early modern period and who would have been familiar to speakers at the Bureau, we should mention François Rabelais, Jean Bodin, James I of England, and the poets of the Pléiade. The theological warfare, especially the discussions of witchcraft, revolved explicitly around magic and superstition.

Conferees are well aware that arguments made in support of the occult require strong substantiation, but they demonstrate conflicting notions as to what counts as compelling evidence. Some evidence is drawn from the historical record. A speaker on the topic of the philosopher's stone cites its historical witnesses, such as Hermes Trismegistus, Johann Glauber, and Raymond Lull.[48] Although some willingly discount a source or its application to a particular issue, others contend that it would be unwarranted hubris to dismiss the entire historical record. One speaker is unwilling to dismiss accounts of the ghost of Brutus or the scriptural accounts of the return of "Samuel, Moses, and Elias." As one participant put it, "it is presumption to disbelieve all antiquity."[49]

How should one evaluate evidence? What are the limits to human certitude about evidence? Although many conferees take critical positions in discussing occult topics, others express concern that skepticism has perhaps gone too far. They espouse a constructive skepticism of the kind associated with contemporary thinkers such as Mersenne and Gassendi.[50] For example, one of them counsels moderation in either accepting or rejecting satyrs,[51] because "it is easier to overthrow than to establish a truth when the question is about a thing apparently repugnant to reason, which many times does not agree with our own experience."

When participants discuss occult phenomena that are widely believed to exist, they take a number of different positions. While a few are disconcertingly credulous, most recast the topic in more credible, naturalistic terms. Their goal seems to be to rationalize and naturalize the occult. The conference on "Incubi and succubae,"[52] for example, uses the topic to explore the physiology of belief in occult phenomena. One speaker points to diseased states as the cause, that is, one believes in incubi and succubae because of the impeded movement of spirits through the brain. Another explores a range of physiological conditions that might cause one to believe in the incubus. "When respiration . . . is impeded, we imagine we have a load lying on our breasts. . . . And because the brain is involved in the incubus, all the animal functions are hurt, imagination depraved, sensation obstructed, motion impeded." He also describes the effects of diseased states on the imagination. "Though the cause of this disorder is within us, nevertheless, the distempered person believes that somebody is about to strangle him by outward violence, which the depraved imagination thinks about rather than about internal causes." In this case as in many others, the reasonable man or the physician is able to distinguish the cause. But "depraved imagination" misleads "the vulgar, who charge these effects to evil spirits, instead of imputing them to the malignity of a vapor or some phlegmatic and gross humor oppressing the stomach." A legitimate treatment of some occult phenomena requires medical expertise, because physicians can distinguish "what is fit to be attributed to nature and her ordinary motions from what is supernatural." However, as one speaker cautions on the topic of the mandrake,[53] that intriguing plant whose roots suggest the human form and that some believed grew from human seed spilled on the ground, the association of certain occult phenomena with the vulgar has led to an unwarranted dismissal of them. Unfortunately, as a result of the superstitions of the vulgar, it is less likely that the mandrake, despite its beneficial medicinal properties, will be used, because "mountebanks have by their frauds and tricks brought people to believe their strange stories of it, even that it eats like a man and performs his other natural functions."

On the topic "Of the unicorn,"[54] the first speaker assumes that, because so many written sources deny its existence, belief in it is simply a popular error. He does not find it credible that the Romans who "were very careful to delight their people with spectacles of the rarest beasts, would have forgot to show them unicorns, if there had been any." However, he is refuted by a speaker who claims that negative arguments are not sufficient to discredit an occult phenomenon or an occult practitioner. While it is fairly common to argue against certain phenomena because the vulgar believe in them, one speaker reverses this argument. He insists that the unicorn must have existed, because so many influential people have put unicorns to so many uses. "It is not credible that Clement VII, Paul III, and diverse others would have taken this animal for their arms, if there were no such animal; nor are popes so lacking in understanding that Julius II would have bought a fragment of it for twelve thousand crowns." The appeal to social evidence—that is to say, the argument that because influential figures believe in a phenomenon it must therefore exist—is highly unusual in these conferences. It is an interesting reversal of the much more common argument that might be summarized as "the vulgar believe it, therefore it is not credible."

Occult phenomena, more than more conventional topics, require conferees to consider which authorities are relevant, to distinguish the uninformed beliefs of the vulgar from the educated understanding of the learned, and to determine which popular beliefs are credible. While a few insist on professional status and education as necessary criteria for discussing occult topics or performing occult practices, most speakers do not suggest that training in arcane knowledge or apprenticeship to an occult practitioner is either necessary or advisable. Instead they attempt to determine the philosophical grounds on which occult phenomena are to be accepted or rejected. In other words, they take on fundamental epistemological issues. Some participants object to rationalist dismissals of occult phenomena. (It is interesting that in many conferences on the occult, empiricism functions as a way to undermine too great an emphasis on reason.) Other speakers substantiate their definitions by direct appeals to empiricism. Magnetism, for example, provides an important empirical demonstration of the application of sympathy. But empirical evidence does not necessarily clarify these issues because speakers are unable to adjudicate between contradictory claims based on equally probable or improbable empirical evidence.

Empirical evidence is not universally hailed. One speaker insists that to believe only what we see is to be "too sensual," especially since the evidence from estimable ancient sources, like Aristotle and Plato, confirms that spirits exist.[55] "Too sensual," in this case, connotes too great an insistence on the primacy of one's own experience over the authority of the ancients. (This term, which reoccurs quite frequently, is usually invoked as a staunch critique of excessive reliance on empiricism or the evidence of the senses.) Certain kinds of empirical evidence are harshly castigated. The empirical evidence cited for the existence of the unicorn is, according to one speaker, "equivocal, incredible, and ridiculous," and the "trials of empirics are even more ridiculous." He concludes that "these numerous contradictions, impossibilities, and uncertainties make me conclude this story of the unicorn is a mere unicorn."[56]

A speaker, who also criticizes too great a reliance on empirical evidence, suggests that, in maintaining that incubi and succubae exist, he is carving out a moderate position.[57] "As it is too gross to recur to supernatural causes, when natural ones are evident; so it is *too sensual* to seek the reason of everything in nature and to ascribe to mere phlegm and distempered fantasy the coitions of demons with men" (my emphasis). To support his argument with evidence he finds compelling, he cites testimonies of direct confrontations with devils; especially credible are those from exotic locales such as Peru and Turkey.[58] He offers several arguments about how the propagation of devils might rationally take place. They might well, for instance, "borrow some human seed and transport it almost instantly so as to preserve its spirits from evaporation." Just "as the devil performs the natural actions of animals by supernatural means, . . . so he may make a perfect animal without observing the conditions of ordinary agents." This speaker supports his argument from contradictory perspectives. He offers empirical evidence to explain the propagation of incubi by devils. He then advances his own rationalistic explanation, enumerating the possible natural processes that might explain the phenomenon. But ultimately he insists natural processes do not bind devils. This conference highlights just one of the many difficulties involved in defining or categorizing the conferences as subscribing to a specific philosophical school or defining a consistent scientific or epistemological position. Participants use whatever arguments make their case or whatever they conceive as the most persuasive response to another speaker. Although some herald empirical evidence as decisive, others recognize it as problematic, especially "the tricks of empirics" or reports from afar.

NATURE AND THE OCCULT

Those participants who firmly believe in occult phenomena do so in part because they are able to reconcile that belief with an understanding of nature. Often the correspondence between a particular occult phenomenon and their understanding of nature is based on their presuppositions about nature, which we do not necessarily share, presuppositions such as the presumed existence of the devil, a commitment to Paracelsian matter theory, or a belief in the hierarchy of nature. While these might seem jarringly unscientific nowadays, beliefs such as these do not in any way distinguish conferees from universally heralded figures of the scientific revolution such as Bacon, Boyle, or Newton.[59] It may be difficult for the modern reader to credit, but it is undeniable on the basis of textual evidence that views of nature based largely on analogic relationships, like the macrocosm-microcosm, remain persuasive explanatory tools throughout the seventeenth century. And they remain persuasive to the great figures of the scientific revolution who are all too often assumed to have completely forsaken earlier ways of seeing and describing nature.

In addressing occult topics, conferees directly confront their presuppositions about things that they believe are or are not restricted to operating within natural bounds and also insist on uniform and universal operation of nature (although they are not agreed on what those operations might be). Thus they circumscribe, to whatever degree possible, the occult within the operations of nature. One speaker integrates the philosopher's stone into a Paracelsian understanding of nature; "salt is its matter, and motion its fire."[60] When discussing sympathy and antipathy, speakers situate the topic within a broader framework of how nature functions. They assume, for example, that all creatures seek self-preservation, using both manifest and occult qualities, by, as one speaker puts it, "adhering to what was conducible to it and avoiding the contrary."[61] A speaker dismisses satyrs as fabulous because of his understanding of nature; because humans have a rational soul, which the speaker claims is indivisible, it cannot be shared with a goat.[62] But some speakers protest these efforts to demystify nature or force it into a mold that conforms to human reason. While acknowledging that phenomena like the unicorn seem to contravene human reason, one speaker nonetheless claims that to doubt its existence calls the "power of nature" into question. This insistence on powers of nature beyond human reason is an unusual position for speakers to take. They are much more prone to argue that nature is indeed accessible to reason and knowable by many means, including the empirical study of the signatures or signs nature has left as clues for the learned to decode.

In a discussion "Of the mandrake,"[63] the first speaker states, "Nature has (instead of the instinct bestowed on other animals to guide them to their good) given man reason, whereby he may proceed from things known to things unknown; so besides the manifest and occult qualities of plants, from which their uses may be inferred, she has marked those which are most useful to us with certain signs and characters." Although he accepts the signature theory as a given and the mandrake as the most thoroughgoing example, he is critical of the overextended application of signature theory. The mandrake is such an inclusive signature, encompassing the whole man, that it has been too broadly and too uncritically construed. It has not been well understood or described by the learned, "leaving the vulgar the liberty to attribute supernatural virtues to it." While this speaker would restrict conclusions drawn from the signature of the mandrake to its natural properties, he nonetheless relishes telling the tales of the power of the mandrake from various histories.

Another participant offers logical reasons why it is possible that a plant like the mandrake could grow from human sperm on the ground. Because man is composed largely of "niter, . . . which as a salt is not lost by death," he believes it possible "that from fertile soil, a plant . . . should arise out of it." However, he is careful to qualify his belief. It can be maintained *only if* the experiments reported can be replicated, to demonstrate "that the salts of rosemary, sage, mint, . . . being extracted according to art and frozen in a glass, exhibit the image of those plants, and, if sown in well-prepared earth, produce the plants of same species." Another speaker insists that a creature like the mandrake can readily be integrated into an understanding of nature;

> since there are middle natures composed of two extremes, as your zoophytes between plants and animals, to wit, sponges and coral; between brute and man, the ape; between the soul and the body of man, his spirits: why may there not be something of a middle nature between man and plant, to wit, mandrake, a man in external shape, and a plant in effect and internal form?

Thus, he suggests, although creatures that fall between our categories may be difficult to incorporate, it is not impossible to reconcile them with the more regular behavior of nature. The mandrake allows participants to explore a number of interesting points. How can one use the evidence from experiments on other plants to draw conclusions about a plant supposedly derived from man? Since we know there are intermediate creatures, why rule out the possibility of the existence of a creature between man and plant? And ultimately, how do we know nature, and how can we draw legitimate conclusions about natural phenomena?[64]

Although nature provides an ordered spectacle, some speakers see a fissure in their worldview between nature and art.[65] The distinction between art and nature is based on one Aristotle drew in his *Physics* between those things constituted by nature, which have a principle of motion and stability, and those things created by art, which have "no innate impulse to change."[66] A conference on "Whether a piece of iron laid upon the cask prevents thunder from marring wine contained within it, and why?"[67] most explicitly addresses the relationship between nature and art. A speaker contends that "the operations of nature are not like those of art, her ways and contrivances are more obscure and the causes of things are occult." He cites some obvious examples of the occult operations of nature: "The lodestone draws iron even though no body of air or smoke can be perceived issuing out of the lodestone; and magnetic balsam, or weapon-salve, cures a wounded person, though at a great distance." But the operations of art are as readily apparent "as those of a clock," while those of nature are less so; "art goes to work publicly and before the senses, and nature does her business within doors and secretly." At least as far as this conference is concerned, mechanism would have more in common with mere art, whereas nature, as less apparent, would be considered more difficult to know than simple mechanical processes.

When they turn to the quest for a perpetual motion machine,[68] participants also rely on the distinctions between art and nature. Because they believe that art can but imperfectly mirror nature, it cannot produce such a machine since there is not one in nature. The only natural phenomenon that might encourage one to imagine a perpetual motion machine is the lodestone, which attracts on one side and repels on the other, and "by continuing this little motion (which would be of no great benefit), it might render the same perpetual." Another insists that, far from being useless, a perpetual motion machine "would be one of the greatest helps that art could afford man, to ease him in his labors." However he does not believe it will be constructed because "there is in all arts something of impossibility." One of the fundamental disagreements between participants about the technological implementation of their understanding of nature is whether what they imagine can be implemented—and how close they think "art," or what human beings produce, can come to nature.

The question of the philosopher's stone[69] also raises the question of the relationship between art and nature, because its existence would suggest that art could surpass nature, although one speaker asserts that drawing out gold from base metals would be but a pale reflection of the vast accomplishments of nature. He suggests that knowledge of the occult is vouchsafed to man by nature, as a kind of knowledge that demonstrates nature's power without encroaching upon it. Another speaker insists, since nature gives us no desire in vain (another fundamental presupposition about nature that was well rooted in the classical tradition), the search for the philosopher's stone must be productive. Just as mathematicians have, by their quest to square the circle, arrived at the knowledge of many things that were unknown to them, so too, (he argues), though the chemists have not discovered the philosopher's stone, they have nonetheless uncovered admirable secrets in vegetables, animals, and minerals. Pursuit of occult knowledge provides a productive research agenda, because nature does not allow man to seek in vain. Once the claim is made that, although man may not find what he is seeking, he will make discoveries that are useful and productive, then "science," broadly construed as any systematic investigation, is guaranteed to be productive and utilitarian.

The relationship between nature and the occult works both ways: Speakers use their understanding of nature to refute or to corroborate occult phenomena, and the arguments they use for or against a specific occult phenomenon ultimately support their understanding of nature. Despite the difficulties involved in defining and applying these qualities, speakers find such topics particularly engaging and a constructive way to understand and describe natural processes such as generation, growth, and survival.

An interesting facet of their discussion of the occult is their understanding that one way to deal with such topics is to separate the question of whether occult phenomena exist from the question of why people believe they do. Some speakers suggest that the lure of the occult is rooted in human nature. On the question "Whether there be any art of divination,"[70] a speaker notes, man alone understands time and "thus his ardent desire to predict." Others contend that people believe in occult phenomena for various psychological reasons: some see spirits but only because they are "prone to acquiesce in their own imagination, misguided by the passions of fear, hope, love, and desire, especially children and women who are more susceptible to all impressions." Thus some, because of the weakness of their minds, are prone to believe in the occult. Another speaker is more harshly critical: "some jugglers pass for sorcerers among the vulgar." Another points out that apparitions are caused when a soul is in pain because of present or future evil, perhaps because of an unfulfilled vow. (This point clearly suggests an understanding of the effect of guilt on the imagination.) Another explains that jealousy makes some credulous. For example, "when a private person arrives to great honor or estate suddenly, though it be by his merit, most people, the poorest of whom account themselves worthy of the same fortune, attribute such extraordinary progress to the devil."[71] It is interesting that the gullible, the guilty, and the jealous, identified in these conferences as those most likely to believe in the occult, are recognized in recent, sophisticated scholarly treatments as the principal players in the drama of the early modern witchcraft trials.[72]

The conferences belong within a tradition of writings that clearly articulate attitudes which make it possible to question the presuppositions fueling the witchcraft persecutions and ultimately to develop alternative views. By insisting that all occult phenomena be studied naturalistically rather than spiritually, conferees participate in the rationalization of the occult. They develop attitudes critical to the demise of witchcraft. They are not wedded to the scholastic sources identified with witchcraft. They distinguish their approach from the credulity of the "vulgar"; they are more critical and less gullible. They consistently seek natural explanations rather than supernatural ones for occult phenomena.[73]

PHENOMENA OF OCCULT AND POPULAR SCIENCE

Although concern with the monstrous and the bizarre is much less common to the conferences than to many other contemporary sources, there are a few discussions of strange popular phenomena. One such case is "Of two monstrous brothers, living in the same body, which are to be seen in this city."[74] All monsters, the first speaker insists, are produced by the anger of God "since the Scripture threatens to cause the wives of those whom God intends to punish to bring forth monsters." His position demonstrates once again that the occult or the monstrous—phenomena that defy participants' efforts to rationally circumscribe nature—are most likely to cause speakers to resort to religious explanations. The second speaker quarrels with the first, expressing an attitude that better reflects the general perspective of the conferences. Just "as it is impious not to ascribe the natural actions on earth to heaven," so it seems to him "superstitious to attribute the same to the Supreme Author, without seeking out the means by which he produces them."

Although it is perhaps extreme to suggest that explaining a natural phenomenon by recourse to God is impious, it is characteristic of the general position of conferees to assume that natural phenomena are appropriately addressed by recourse only to nature. The speaker is thus suggesting a natural cause, which "does not diminish the omnipotence of the Divine Majesty" but, on the contrary, "renders it more visible and palpable to our senses; just as the ministers, ambassadors, and military people employed by a great King for the putting of his command in execution, are no disparagement to his Grandeur." (This is an argument for both natural causes and the value of ministers and thus perhaps a less than subtle recognition of the value of Richelieu's sponsorship.) Instead of assuming that divine wrath was the cause of monsters, he suggests that monsters are caused by too great a "quantity of the geniture, being too much for the making of one child, and too little for the finishing of the two," or the malformation produced "by some fall or blow that happened when the parts of the embryos began to be distinguished and separated one from the other." Under such circumstances, he recognizes that ordinarily a spontaneous abortion would occur. A monstrous birth occurs when the abortion fails to take place. Another speaker characterizes the two brothers as "one of the most notable errors of nature that have appeared in this age" and suggests as an explanation "some extraordinary conjunction of the stars happening at the time of his conception." A speaker contends that conjoined twins do not qualify as monsters. Another subscribes to the Platonic definition of monstrous: "whenever virtue or nature exceeds its ordinary rules, the result is monstrous." Except for the evil influence of a particular star, the explanations given by the speakers relate to quite specific problems in the formation of the fetus. Monsters, in the view of most participants, involve an excess of generative material. While monstrous births were traditionally considered individual anomalies and therefore portents, participants integrate them into natural processes, an approach that was not common until the eighteenth century.[75]

For conferees, the issue of monsters raises questions Europeans faced in incorporating anything exotic into their culture. Did this creature have two souls, one in each of its bodies? Is it a monster in the civil sense or is it, as one speaker puts it, "able to make a will, inherit, contract, and to do all other civil actions?"

Having discussed monsters generally just the previous week, speakers address the specific case "Of the little hairy girl lately seen in this city."[76] The first asserts "this German girl, born at Augsburg, called Barbara Ursine . . . is no monster." Excessive hairiness is an ordinary effect of nature with many natural causes such as excessive internal heat. Thus "some notable warriors and pirates [obviously endowed with excessive heat] have had hairy hearts." Another significant cause, according to this speaker, is the maternal imagination during conception "when the embryo, being like wax, is capable of every impression." He then cites the example from Hippocrates (the example most frequently cited whenever maternal imagination is mentioned) who "saved the honor and life of a princess who had brought forth an Ethiopian, through the too attentive minding of the picture of a Moor hanging at the foot of her bed." A speaker cites more contemporary cases of "a woman in our time [who] brought forth a child like a frog, by having held a frog in her hand." Another expands the definition of *monster* as anything against the intention of "universal nature, which could not design any profit from a bearded woman." Thus he concludes, "the girl must be termed a monster." He agrees with the previous speaker that it may be caused by the imagination of the mother, which many times "hinders the formative virtue from doing what it designs." For the next speaker this girl can only be considered a monster, if the term is so broadly construed as to "comprehend everything that is contrary to the intention of the agent or is extraordinary." In this sense, "Aristotle calls a woman a monster and a fault of nature."

But this definition of a monster, he suggests, is too broad to be useful. Furthermore, we share hairiness with this creature, who simply has a greater quantity of hair produced by "extreme moisture, and moderate coldness."

Another conference is dedicated to a topic of great contemporary interest and one that, throughout the early modern period, united elite and popular science, the question "Of judicial astrology,"[77] by which the conferees mean consulting the stars to make predictions about earthly events. A speaker questions the premise of judicial astrology, asking, "why should we seek in heaven the causes of accidents which befall us, if we find them on earth?" Another supports its predictive power. Because "everything here below suffers mutation, and nothing is able to change itself," he concludes: "consequently the heavens, which are the sole bodies that do not suffer change, must be the cause of all mutation." Since it is inflicted on the earth, change must be effected by the heavens. Despite the outrageous claims made on behalf of astrology, such as "the impostures, which are affirmed by casters of nativities," these abuses "can no more prejudice or disparage judiciary astrology, than mountebanks do medicine." One must distinguish between the competent and fraudulent practitioner. The existence of the latter, he insists, does not call into question the former.

Another speaker quarrels with the belief that underlies astrology, because, he insists, "every effect follows the nature of its cause, and therefore the actions and inclination of the soul cannot be ascribed to a corporeal cause, like the stars." He refuses to acknowledge any causal role for the stars: "I acknowledge but two virtues in the heavens, motion and light, by which alone, and not by influences of occult qualities they produce corporeal effects." As a result, human agency cannot be influenced by the stars. The next speaker is even more dubious about using astrology to make predictions. He does not object to the premises of astrology but is not persuaded that measurements will ever be accurate enough "for the making of a sure and certain art grounded upon many repeated experiments." The extremely rapid and violent turning of the heavens does not allow the determination of the precise minute of a nativity, and the vast number of stars and the seven planets allow one to make "conjunctions and combinations to infinity, which surpasses the comprehension of human wit."

A participant considers that the involvement of God in his creation ("having from all eternity numbered the hair of our heads") attests to divine foreknowledge. He makes a fundamental connection between divine foreknowledge and astrology: God "established an order for them in the heavens, disposing the course, aspects, and various influences of the stars, to draw out of nothing those accidents at the time that they are to happen to men . . . confirmed by the exact and admirable correspondence." He does concede that astrology is difficult "since the faculties and qualities of the stars are not perfectly known to us," but no less true. An analogy allows him to appreciate astrology; "it is like a great book printed in Hebrew cast aside and slighted by the ignorant and admired by the more intelligent." Astrology is thus a difficult method of obtaining scientific knowledge, reserved to the diligent and educated—like, as his reference to Hebrew suggests, knowledge of the cabala.

The last to address the subject claims that "three sorts of persons err touching the credit which is to be given astrological predictions. Some believe them not at all, others believe them too little, and others too much." And he attempts to moderate the beliefs of all three. Even the most skeptical, "cannot deny that the stars are universal causes of sublunary effects." They must therefore "confess that . . . any natural effects may be foreseen and foretold from them." Those who believe "too little in the stars" must concede "that the stars act upon the elements and mixed bodies," for even "every peasant knows" about the "many particular effects of the moon." Those who believe too little sometimes insist that the soul of man is free and therefore not subject to celestial influences, "yet it is no greater absurdity to say that the soul is subject to the Stars than to say, with Aristotle and Galen, that it is subject to the temperament of the body." But those who insist on too great a control for the stars ultimately deny free will.

Although they consider sophisticated methods of divining, like judicial astrology, with some skepticism, when they turn their attention to more popular forms of divination, such as "Of prognostication or presaging by certain animals,"[78] participants are much more dubious. The first speaker acknowledges that any attempt to read the future is very appealing, "because this knowledge of things to come would rid him [man] of the two most violent passions that perplex him, fear and hope." Because of the lure of control over the unknown, man has created distinct arts of prediction, which "attract the admiration and consequently the money of credulous persons." Despite this hard-headed assessment, he nonetheless holds out some hope for the validity of divination because "there seems to be a correspondence and connection between present and future things as there is between the past and the present." The second speaker points to the human body itself as a tool of divining the weather. There are "persons so regular in the constitution of their bodies, that they will tell you, beforehand, better than any almanac, by a toothache, a migraine, or sciatica." This ability is, he notes, "commonly attributed to the rarefaction or condensation of the peccant humors in their bodies." Another speaker limits the extent of divination, suggesting that "did we know all the internal or external characters of animals, we might by their motion and disposition obtain some knowledge of that of their star, and from it draw conjectures about the future." Without such complete information, divination is dubious. As the final speaker concludes, one cannot prognosticate about men because their conduct is "varied by a thousand businesses, imaginings and troubles, and especially by their free will."

It is important to recognize the distance conferees put between themselves and their remarks about divining by animals. In the case of divining by the stars or judicial astrology, some speakers express skepticism, but it is clear that, despite their doubts, judicial astrology has more claim to credibility than more popular methods. Divining by animals, some contend, is a practice that preys on the gullible.

The practice of sleepwalking provokes considerable speculation.[79] The first speaker claims that this phenomenon affects the animal faculties and yet seems in some way to be against nature, because "to move when we should rest is against nature." He suggests as a cause "the thick and tenacious vapors seizing upon the brain, and obstructing its outlets." This explanation persuades him, "since the smoke of tobacco is sometimes kept in our bodies two whole days, the same may happen to the gross and viscous vapors raised from the humors or aliments." Another, more intrigued by the fact that sleepwalkers perform their activities "better and with more courage in the night than in the day," suggests that, when they are "awake, they have reason, which contradicts their imagination and appetite." The next speaker concurs, saying, "if men left themselves to be conducted by their natural inclination without making so many reviews and reflections upon what they do, their actions would be much better and surer." The sleeper, without the inhibiting factors of reason and self-awareness, acts more boldly. Another speaker demurs, insisting that when a man is awake his actions are more vigorous and "all his senses [are] strengthened by the concourse of the spirits" despite the fact that men seem stronger while sleepwalking. To explain this phenomenon, he resorts to a disconcerting explanation: "Some spirits, good or bad, whether such as they call aerial hobgoblins or others, insinuate themselves into the body, as into a ship whose pilot is asleep, and govern and guide it at pleasure."

The previous speaker to the contrary, most participants approach occult topics from a skeptical perspective, although their efforts at demystification and rational clarification are more likely to be tentative if the topic resonates within the Christian tradition. Despite the claim in Renaudot's preface to the collection that religion will not be discussed in the conferences, religious arguments are invoked, if infrequently. (Religious topics are not proposed, and if a topic veers from the natural to the theological, speakers will object. However, scriptural citations are sometimes made, and scriptural examples form part of the "historical" evidence.) Religion is more likely to be raised in discussing occult topics, especially those that bear on Christian beliefs. For example, one participant suggests that the cabala, an occult philosophy developed by some Jewish rabbis and based on a mystical interpretation of scripture, should be esteemed especially for "the hieroglyphical and mysterious namers of God and angels that it contains."[80] If the cabala can be associated with divine power, how can its powers be questioned? Or, if "black magic can do wonders by the help of malignant spirits, why not the cabala, with more reason, by means of the names of God?"[81] This reverential treatment is quite foreign to the general spirit of the conferences. By this statement, the speaker not only casts a religious reverence over the topic, but also effectively cuts off subsequent discussion of this topic—as if, once a topic is linked to orthodoxy, speakers are unwilling to pick up the conversational thread.[82]

On the topic of sorcery,[83] many participants assume that sorcerers require the cooperation of the devil, which further entails God's consent, since "without [it] not one hair falls from our heads." Although the actions of the individual sorcerer are grounded in a compact with the devil, speakers insist, his work uses only commonplace items that have no special power in themselves. Others note that the effects attributed to sorcery are illusory, produced when the devil "makes use of delusions to cover his impotence, making appear what is not and hindering perception of what really is."[84] For this speaker, the powers of the devil do not extend to power over nature but only to alter human perception.

To question the power of the devil would obviously undermine conventional religious beliefs. Participants were certainly aware that Giulio Vanini's naturalistic pantheism, deemed a threat to the Church's teaching on demons and miracles, had led to his burning at the stake in 1619 at Toulouse. Perhaps as a result of the dangers of challenging those views, most speakers are unwilling to deny the existence of sorcerers, but they are willing to curtail their influence. One speaker claims "that the power of evil spirits, whose instruments sorcerers are, is so limited that they cannot either create or annihilate a straw, much less produce any substantial form, or cause the real descent of the moon, or hinder the motion of the stars, as heathen antiquity stupidly believed." Despite this rather scathing critique of the credulity of others, he concedes that sorcerers do have power over earthly things; "they are able to move all sublunary things; so they cause earthquakes, the devil either congregating exhalations into its hollowness or agitating the air within."[85] The devil, in this account, is able to mobilize the powers of nature.

Occult topics are treated much more critically and skeptically when they are not part of the Christian tradition. For example, metempsychosis (the belief in the transmigration of souls)[86] is described as a "heathen" belief, and conferees directly question whether such beliefs can be sustained through reason. Without the constraints of the Christian tradition, they feel free to assert the necessity of "free and open" inquiry, insisting that "there is nothing that more enriches the field of philosophy than liberty of reasoning." One speaker insists that "the heathen, guided only by the light of nature," has no reason to "maintain this extravagance." Another cites metempsychosis as a logical impossibility. "It is impossible for one and the same thing that has been to be again new." For him, the notion of the body as a reflection of the soul makes it impossible for the soul to move to another body, which would not reflect it.

This conference raises, in a way that is fairly consistent in the treatment of occult topics, questions of what kinds of arguments and evidence can be brought to bear to sustain or refute occult phenomena. However, it is significant that metempsychosis is denounced on logical grounds. In light of our understanding of the epistemological evolution of the scientific revolution, it is rather peculiar to note that "new" ways of arguing are used most frequently to bolster the existence of the occult, and conventional arguments are used more frequently to doubt or discredit occult phenomena. In other words, syllogism, analogy, or the most traditional kinds of arguments refute phenomena considered mystical or bizarre. In contrast, mystical or occult topics are frequently supported by appeals to specific historical cases or medical reports. In supporting the occult, speakers are particularly inclined to provide empirical substantiation, which ranges from personal experience to anecdotal evidence, to examples from ancient sources. Citing ancient examples is not considered to be invoking authority but instead is presented as the careful use of evidence drawn from specific cases in ancient sources. Thus, these examples are considered credible counters to an excessive reliance on reason.

A discussion of the existence of the satyr more than amply demonstrates this case. The first speaker on "Of satyrs"[87] points out that there are no rational grounds on which to accept the existence of a satyr, because "those that have most exactly examined the power of nature, find the mixture of these species impossible." The next counsels moderation in either accepting or rejecting its existence because "it is as dangerous to conclude what we have not seen is impossible as to be credulous about everything. But when reason and the authority experience carries with it are on the same side, our incredulity has no excuse. Now the case of satyrs is such, for they may well be as produced by the mixture of the seeds of two species, as mules are." Such things are evidently possible since we have the "daily examples" of the mother's imagination imprinting "change of figure in a child's body." There are also credible if ambiguous testimonies, such as that of Saint Hieronymous who described the satyr who appeared to Saint Paul the hermit. Thus the speaker concludes that "to doubt the existence of satyrs after so many testimonies is to ascribe too much to our own senses and too little to the witness of the ancients."

Another view of nature that exerts some influence on the conferees is that of the Paracelsians, an interest reflected in a number of conferences dedicated to Paracelsian themes such as the power of sympathy, the quintessence, the philosopher's stone, the Fraternity of the Rosy Cross, and the weapon-salve controversy. Since the conferences treat a fairly inclusive range of contemporary issues, one would expect Paracelsian topics to be addressed. In fact, Paracelsus gave many of the occult topics discussed in this chapter a new currency. Conferees also employ Paracelsian terms. Some analyze dreams as signatures; others insist the senses tell us that most bodies are reducible to salt, sulfur, and mercury; and many speakers take for granted a macrocosm-microcosm relationship. Because Renaudot himself was a practitioner of chemical medicine, which Paracelsus had advocated, it is not surprising that his rather unconventional gatherings attracted other Paracelsians.

The conference "What Paracelsus meant by the Book of M*"[88] offers a final, illuminating example of the treatment of the occult in these conferences. By raising questions about the appropriate language for science and issues of secrecy and obfuscation, this conference highlights an important theme of the conferences in general. Both the preface to the collected conferences and the general statements speakers make about language insist on the value of clear expression and the open dissemination of science. In response to this concern, participants indicate both positive and negative assessments of Paracelsus and the Paracelsians. Sympathetic with Paracelsian critiques of existing knowledge, they disparage the arcane language and the deliberate obfuscation of Paracelsian texts. They appreciate the reformist endeavors they associate with the new chemical philosophy but are discomfited by the mystical overtones. In essence, they put their stamp of approval on a kind of sanitized Paracelsianism.

The first speaker suggests that the *M* stands for *mundus* (the world), "that great book open to all that are minded to read it." Although he criticizes the obscure language of Paracelsus, he is sympathetic to Paracelsus's claim that the book of nature should replace all other sorts of books. "For almost all books being false copies of this book of the world, it is no wonder if book-doctors are most commonly ignorant of things whose solid contemplation produces satisfaction in the informed intellect." He attacks knowledge that is too theoretical, too remote from nature, too intellectual, as "fancies" that cannot be implemented, and he sees in Paracelsus an important counterweight to these kinds of knowledge.

The next speaker attacks the *Book of M* as an assault on medicine. The *M* must, he insists, stand for "magic"; Paracelsus must be a practitioner of magic because of the chemical cures he advocates. Anyone who would presume to overthrow the art and tradition of medicine must inevitably act with the help of either God or the devil. For this speaker, the unorthodox treatments Paracelsus suggests can only be the result of diabolical magic. Speakers are quite critical of claims made for magic, but nonetheless, any concerted attack on magic elicits a defense that carves out some acceptable arena for its practice. One speaker distinguishes between types of magic—natural, which is commendable, "to wit, true and natural magic, such as was professed by the Magi," and black magic, "no more deserving that name, than empirics and quacks do that of physicians." He acknowledges natural magic as a specialized knowledge, available only to the learned.[89]

Another speaker suggests that *M* is a talismanic figure that Rosicrucians use to recognize one another.[90] The next dismisses "secrets" as mere absurdities and indicts "authors who puzzle their readers' minds with such figures." They "are as culpable as those are commendable, who feed them with true and social demonstrations." He ridicules the pretensions and obscurantism of the Paracelsians; "whereas we thought that this M signified Mons, we now see that it signifies no more than Mus; according to the ancient fable of the laboring mountains, out of which . . . issued forth nothing but a mouse." He attacks any cult of secret knowledge. But the speaker who most vigorously defends Paracelsus directly challenges this argument. He deliberately defends obscure language, saying "that high mysteries have always been veiled under contemptible and oftentimes ridiculous figures; as if the wisdom of the more sublime spirits are meant to mock those of the vulgar, who judge of things only by appearance." Because there are many cases of medical treatments that do not reveal any clear affinities between cause and effect, "Why then may not the same reality be admitted between these characters and the effects claimed by those brothers of the Rosie-Cros?"

The very name Paracelsus flags concern with the occult and highlights some of the divisions of opinion speakers reveal when they discuss occult topics. Since the topic is so open-ended (that is to say, what did Paracelsus mean by "M" in the Book of M?), it leaves participants full range to insert whatever word beginning with the letter "M" they associate with Paracelsus. Obviously, they must first decide on whether "M" should carry a positive or negative association. Then, if the word is one like *magic*, it raises further questions about what magic is, the relationship between claims to magical knowledge and the practice of magic, and whether it has positive or negative connotations. This conference vividly demonstrates the division between proponents of clear public expression of knowledge and proponents of knowledge as the hidden and deliberately obscured realm of the special practitioner.

📖

Examining the treatment of nature and the occult in these conferences is revealing. First, and perhaps most striking, the discussion is quite deliberately restrained. There are no gory details and almost no reveling in the bizarre. The conferences do not counsel awe before the wonders of nature, a phenomenon that Daston and Park have richly documented for this period.[91] They do not emphasize the bizarre, the monstrous, or even curious phenomena. Participants do not look to occult phenomena as signs of demonic magic or use them to predict the future or the Second Coming. Instead they address these phenomena from the highest possible intellectual level. They are, in effect, engaged in an effort to normalize and rationalize the occult, a process more usually ascribed to the eighteenth century than to the early seventeenth century. Second, they are acutely aware of the difficulties involved in treating these issues: they require definition, a restraining of the topic within appropriate parameters. As a result, occult topics consistently illuminate epistemological issues, in particular questions of what standards of evidence should be argued for and how far one should go in insisting on the value of one kind of evidence over another. Ironically, because these topics consider occult or hidden qualities, they offer a clearer indication of what counts as evidence than do some discussions of more conventional topics. (Occult qualities, like many of the claims of the new mechanical science, contravene sensory evidence.) These topics offer oblique recognition of the damper religion put on scientific discussion. Although they approach occult topics from a number of different scientific traditions, participants do not generally offer set pieces, for example, the speech of an Aristotelian challenged by a Paracelsian. Instead (and this has proved frustrating for those who have worked on the science in the conferences), these speakers invoke tradition as they see fit, borrowing freely without regard for theoretical consistency. Because participants meld together pieces of various traditions irrespective of the internal logic of the theory and because they use whatever pieces of the theory seem persuasive, the conferences substantiate a more complicated and diverse evolution of scientific opinion within the scientific revolution than the mere replacement of an Aristotelian understanding of science with a new mechanical worldview.

How do participants contribute to contemporary discussion of occult phenomena? They are not interested in preserving knowledge of the occult as arcane but rather in the public dissemination of all knowledge. They reject the tradition of the specialized, privileged knowledge of the magi. As a result, they are not especially interested in astrology or numerology. Insofar as they discuss such practices, it is not to advocate them but rather to critically assess them. In fact, one might claim that they are as critical in their assessments of Paracelsian ideas as they are of Aristotelian notions. One very decisive break with the tradition of the occult and of natural magic is that participants do not attempt to unify religion and nature. The fact that they pay fairly scrupulous attention to the directive not to discuss religious topics means that, even if individual participants might have a more mystical approach, the quest for knowledge as a route to God is quite strikingly absent from the conferences. Thus they do not reflect the integration of religion and natural magic so characteristic of the sixteenth and early seventeenth-century philosophical and scientific writings. Nor do they reflect the natural philosophy tradition that was particularly strong in seventeenth-century England and characteristic of the works of major figures of the scientific revolution, like Boyle; they do not argue for science or knowledge of nature as a way to know God. Although these conferences (as we will see) privilege medicine as a particularly important science, they neither canonize the moral or religious character of the physician, nor make him analogous to the priest as Paracelsus did. Although some participants describe the operations of nature in Paracelsian terms, they use the same methods of argumentation and the same standards of evidence as proponents of more conventional views. They too are predominantly concerned with the order and beneficence of nature. All participants suggest that their arguments are empirically sound, based on direct observation. Discussion of "occult" phenomena, which might most reasonably reflect "pre-modern" attitudes toward nature, is instead as rigorously rational as the specific topic allows.

These conferences, occurring just before the widespread acceptance of mechanism, ought to allow one to examine the transition from the pre-mechanical to the mechanical view of nature—or at least so historians of science have supposed. If one assumes that the scientific revolution occurred as Aristotelian science was replaced by the new mechanical philosophy, one cannot plot the position of the participants in Renaudot's conferences in this evolution. Scholars looking for evidence of a sharp break between early views of nature, ranging from the classical to the hermetic, and the emerging mechanical philosophy find no evidence for this thesis in the conferences. The conferences indicate only occasionally the tangential familiarity of the participants with the mechanical philosophy. They occasionally use mechanical analogies; they discuss atoms and Galileo's astronomical findings. But this is not (to the detriment of its subsequent historical reputation) a group that espoused the mechanical philosophy of nature. Some might then expect the conferences to reflect the pre-mechanical understanding of nature, with a female earth, revered as both nurturer and chaotic principle in an animistic universe. However, the conferences neither depict a feminine earth (although "nature" is a feminine word in French and thus the pronoun referent is "she") nor show a marked reverence for the earth. Those speakers who emphasize the mysteriousness of nature are more exasperated than reverent. There is also no sense that the earth is alive, although generation is considered to be the most important natural process. An animistic sensibility seems surprisingly absent, even in the discussion of Paracelsian topics. In fact, in the conferences, discussion of Paracelsian topics seems considerably more abstract and less mysterious than earlier Paracelsian works.

When conferees present a view of nature, it is neither magical nor mechanical. They have rejected the mystical but they have not embraced the mechanical or the mathematical as a way to understand nature. The question they grapple with is not whether to submit to unknown natural processes or to subjugate nature by force, but rather to assess the degree to which nature can be known. In essence, participants discuss how occult or opaque nature's methods are. The discussion of nature in the conferences suggests that an organic view of nature as vitalistic, mysterious, and revered had broken down well before the seventeenth century, or at least that such attitudes had little appeal for the members of Renaudot's group. Nature instead is shaped to human reason and invoked as an abstract ordering principle. "Nature" was also a fluid term, not firmly attached to any specific scientific paradigm. Although conferees portrayed and understood the term "nature" in widely varying ways, this understanding gave them great confidence that they could not only understand a myriad of natural phenomena but also address even those that seemed occult and apply that understanding to man's benefit.

The views conferees express about nature defy easy classification. Their appeals to empiricism and the confidence with which they assess nature make it difficult to posit an "epistemic break" à la Michel Foucault, between old science and new.[92] They not only present instead a great fluidity in views of nature but also suggest that, as participants addressed scientific topics from a great variety of stances, they develop ways of talking about nature that become significant in the development and promulgation of the new science. For example, although participants do not, except for the rare mechanical analogy, discuss nature in mechanical terms, they nonetheless conceive of it in abstract terms. It seems reasonable to suggest that an understanding of nature as abstract but ordered and good might well have laid the foundation for the success of the mechanical philosophy. In other words, perhaps the erosion through abstraction of a personified nature prepared the way for a mechanical worldview. As part of this process, nature as a source of nurture and chaos has been rationalized into a principle of order and beneficence. An ordered and beneficent nature is in conformity with and is susceptible to rational investigation by human beings, a compelling basis on which to project improvement for human society. The discussion of nature or science without recourse to God, which characterizes the conferences, might have also made acceptable mechanism's propensity to do the same. Conferees present all opinions in a public setting and in print, defining new fora for the diffusion of science. The most vivid impression conveyed by any specific conference is of an open-minded eclecticism. Individuals present their views in quest of a sustainable foundation for scientific knowledge. There is great openness toward a philosophical foundation for understanding nature, without any overt desire to impose a distinct philosophical view.

Occult topics challenge participants to reconcile a number of contradictory elements in their worldview—demonstrable evidence and traditional beliefs, the scientific and the religious, experience and reason or logic, nature and the devil. These topics also challenge modern historians to expand notions of "science" to include such discussions, and to reappraise the scientific revolution by acknowledging the fundamental significance of the occult within groups like the one that met at the Bureau. However unorthodox their form and conclusions might appear in the positivist story of the scientific revolution, these conferences evaluate traditional knowledge in light of science. The speakers' thoughtful assessments of the complications inherent to discussions of occult topics make these conferences particularly revealing documents in our attempt to understand the role of the occult in the culture and science of the seventeenth century.

CHAPTER FOUR

"Whether the Heavens be Liquid or Solid"

Science at the Bureau

O<small>N 26 JUNE 1634 THE GROUP ASSEMBLED AT THE BUREAU</small> wondered "Whether the heavens be solid or liquid,"[1] a topic that highlights important issues for the more conventional discussion of the scientific revolution. It both signals the challenge to Aristotle posed by the new astronomy and casts into high relief the epistemological issue of how and to what degree our senses should be trusted. The first speaker takes a rather indirect approach to the topic, beginning by disallowing the evidence of the senses. He points to a host of circumstances under which the evidence of sight is problematic: Things that are too close appear larger than they are; things remote appear smaller. Shapes too are misperceived; "we are apt to mistake a square tower to be round, one color for another, nothing for a body, a tree for a living creature, a beast for a man, one face for another." Our sight is even more unreliable and fails more frequently and "with more reason, in diaphanous and transparent bodies, such as light, fire, air, water, glass." He concludes, "when the proportion requisite to the necessary distance between the sense and its object fails either in excess or defect, there is no more credit to be given to sense." In response to this unreliability, he does not advocate complete skepticism about the senses but instead concludes that other senses can compensate for misinformation produced by one sense. By introducing the senses into a discussion of the nature of the heavens, he seems to digress from the topic of the conference, but his point is that on the topic of the heavens any misimpression of sight cannot be corrected by the other senses. He must therefore rely on a kind of rationalism based on logic to conclude, "the heavens are neither solid nor liquid." If they were solid, they would be dry, and if liquid, wet. But these qualities depend on the elements, and "the heavens not being composed of the elements cannot partake of their qualities." Because he accepts the fundamental Aristotelian understanding that the heavens are qualitatively different from the sublunary world, elements do not apply to the heavens. He juxtaposes the old and the new. Clearly conversant with the epistemological problems of the new science, he is nonetheless wedded to a fundamentally Aristotelian view of the universe.

The next speaker argues that when the senses are found wanting, one turns to reason (a quasi-Cartesian argument). Although the senses cannot, for the reasons given, be considered relevant to discussions of the heavens, reason supports a mathematical physics that unites the heavens and the earth under the same laws. One would expect this speaker, having made this point, to be a staunch proponent of the new sciences, believing with Galileo in the motion of the earth. Instead, reason sanctions the Aristotelian worldview and "requires that there be some solid surface, serving as a boundary and limit to the elements." Without such a demarcation between the heavens and the earth, the heavens would "exhale and evaporate their more subtle parts into the air," and "the air would exhale its vapors into the heavens; and fire . . . would mingle itself with the substance of the heavens." Without this boundary, the heavens "would no longer be pure and free from corruption." He thus insists on the fundamental hierarchy of Aristotelian cosmology. He cites examples of what would occur if the heavens were not solid; meteors would disrupt the planets, the stars would come closer to each other, and planetary motion would not be regular.

We are unable to consider this question because puny human reason cannot know the mind of God, the next speaker asserts. Thus we cannot imagine any relationship between creator and creature except for the relationship we have with the things we make. Those who maintain that the heavens must be solid restrict God to human ways of keeping things together, which is to affix a solid to a solid. This perspective constrains the power of God, who could just as easily "have appointed a law to the stars to move regularly in a liquid space (as fishes do in the water), even in a vacuum (if there were any in nature), as to have riveted and fixed them to some solid body." Some might object that a liquid heaven does not correspond to scriptural descriptions of the nature of heaven. (Terms like the "throne of God" or the "firmament" suggest solidity.) This speaker proposes that, because scripture describes things only as they seem, it is not to be interpreted literally. He cites the example from Genesis "where the sun and the moon are styled the two great lights of heaven, not because they are so in reality, but because they appear so." The most conclusive evidence for the liquidity of the heavens, in his opinion, "is that comets have often been above some planets, which could not be, were the heavens solid." He presents a number of opinions that, although almost contradictory, all challenge the traditional Aristotelian universe. He also raises a number of problematic epistemological positions. If "the mind of God" is the determinant of nature, what can human beings know of it? But he also concludes that scripture is neither the authoritative key to nature nor to be understood literally.

The new astronomical evidence complicates any simplistic notion of planetary motion. "For astronomers observing that the planets not only go from east to west by their diurnal motion, common to all the celestial bodies, but also have a particular one of their own . . . [and] observing the planets to be sometimes nearer, and sometimes further off from the earth, they assigned them another sphere, called an eccentric." Conferees hesitate to consider the new science as conclusive against either other evidence or fundamental presuppositions about the heavens. They are aware of new findings and theories but are more inclined to adapt them to their conventional understanding of how the universe operates. As a speaker asks, "What needs this multiplication of spheres?" since God has appointed every star to its course. Epicycles, these irregular motions of planets, are not significant enough grounds to overturn established wisdom. They are simply anomalies, their relationship to ordinary phenomena of nature so out of the ordinary that they might be considered analogous to monsters.

What does this conference with its panoply of views concerning the heavens offer as a way to understand seventeenth-century science? As one of the topics addressed by members of Renaudot's group that is most directly relevant to the conventional telling of the story of the scientific revolution, it demonstrates a confrontation between Aristotelian cosmology and that of Copernicus. It sets out some unexpected arguments in support of both the old and the new and adapts the old to the new and vice versa. It also reveals the role that fundamental suppositions about nature play in discussions of specific topics and how empirical evidence is used and weighed against rational arguments.

This conference also lays out some of the important themes of scientific discussion at the Bureau. It both reveals the importance of Aristotle to all scientific discussion and exposes challenges to conventional Aristotelian wisdom. It shows that participants understood the epistemological implications of the new astronomy as well as related questions that the new astronomy placed directly in the intellectual foreground. The participants' use of an Aristotelian legacy was neither deferential nor systematic. They treated topics and epistemological issues central to the new science, issues that were accommodated into more conventional ways of understanding. Although mathematics and physics are more usually cited as the significant sciences of the scientific revolution, Renaudot's conferences focused on those sciences that were forerunners to the natural sciences, such as geology. Because they were based on empirical observation, participants believed, these sciences offered ways to know nature and would yield useful knowledge.[2]

THE USE AND ABUSE OF AN ARISTOTELIAN LEGACY

A number of the earliest topics in the nine-year history of the conferences treat the fundamentals of Aristotelian science, such as the four elements, and some of them (like the one that introduces this chapter) challenge him. The treatment of these issues, at the very beginning of the conferences, suggests that participants both wanted to establish some essential terms and to orient themselves vis-à-vis Aristotle, the most prominent intellectual authority of the seventeenth century. These conferences are perhaps among the least intrinsically interesting of the collection, as speakers grapple with the existing definitions and try to say something interesting about fire, air, earth, water, and other standard terms of Aristotelian science. These initial conferences are confused and confusing, but they clearly demonstrate the erosion of Aristotelianism.

The issue of how these participants use Aristotle is central to determining their place in the scientific revolution. Presumably, if they were expositors of Aristotle, they would be adherents of the old, and if they were staunch proponents of Copernicus or Galileo or precocious advocates of mechanism, they would belong with the new. Insofar as historians have discussed the science of these conferences, this has been the approach taken. However, as the work of Charles Schmitt in particular has demonstrated, such a dichotomy distorts both Aristotelianism and science. The early modern period offered multiple versions of Aristotelianism, some of which were quite critical and adapted to new scientific discoveries. To portray mechanism as the vanquisher of Aristotle asserts too simplistic an understanding of the rich, complex intellectual tradition of the seventeenth century to do the period justice.

When conferees turn their attention to such conventional Aristotelian topics as causation, they are neither orthodox nor consistent expositors of his philosophy. (This is not to say that Aristotle is not the most important intellectual source for them, whether they are discussing scientific or moral and political concerns.)[3] My purpose here is to cite some of the earliest conferences in order to consider how participants used and abused Aristotle and what role his science plays in the discussions.[4] For example, a speaker in "Of causes in general"[5] argues against the degradation of the term *cause* to mean simply "reason" and instead insists on a more orthodox definition as "that which produces an effect" and the four Aristotelian causes of "matter, form, the agent, and its end." The next speaker challenges this Aristotelian definition by opening up the categories, insisting that causes must be treated "according to the diversity of the sciences"—a good

Aristotelian principle! Another even more overtly challenges Aristotelian causation, dismissing all four notions of causation on logical grounds: "Matter and form being parts of the whole cannot be causes thereof; because then they would be causes of themselves; which is absurd." This conference is a striking demonstration that participants were not wedded to conventional Aristotelian definitions of even the most fundamental terms.

The discussion of the common terms like "causes" as Aristotelian, neoplatonic, or even mystical gives some indication as to why, in assessing the science of these particular conferences, the posthumous reputation of the group might well have been different if conferees had presented more orthodox opinions. But this suggests that the interest of the historian of science in telling a story of credible science is at odds with the interest of the historian in using these documents to investigate the culture of science. Although these Aristotelian topics are maddeningly inconclusive, they reveal the basic suppositions held by an educated group below the level of the great scientists of the day. Imagine the results if a modern, university-educated group—with a few scientists specialized in nonbiological fields, and others with enough interest to attend a scientific discussion—was assembled to discuss a topic of contemporary interest like the gene. What might the published proceedings of such a group tell us about the nature and penetration of scientific understanding or the culture of science in the early twenty-first century?

The discussion of causes provoked conferees to propose "Of first matter"[6] for the following week. Abstract topics like this one require them to consider how we know. A speaker attempts to diffuse empirical doubts about the existence of first matter by claiming "We would be too sensual as philosophers, if we believed nothing but what we see." First matter, he claims, is the subject of all substantial forms and exists before and after corruption. That which our senses perceive as enclosed in a particular form is second matter. Another speaker concurs that first matter, as the common subject of all mutation, must exist as a logical necessity. Another rejects a reliance on categories of logic and returns to the "sensual" perspective dismissed by the first speaker. To know what first matter is, one should "proceed by way of the senses, and then examine whether reason can correct what they have dictated to us." The evidence of our senses, he claims, supports a chemical understanding of nature; "mixed bodies are resolved into salt, sulfur, and mercury." Because "the chemists affirm that these three bodies cannot be reduced into any other matter," they must be first matter. The initial discussions of this topic juxtapose Aristotelian reliance on authorities and logic with Paracelsian experience and chemical principles.

Once specific elements have been identified as first matter, subsequent speakers challenge those opinions by advocating more conventional views of the primary elements, identifying one Aristotelian element or another (air, earth, fire, or water) with first matter. But all attempts to equate any of the Aristotelian elements with first matter are challenged. The topic "Of first matter" raises serious epistemological problems about what the world is made of and how we know it. Participants wonder: Must all particulars, like forms of matter, be categorized under a universal concept, like first matter, even if it cannot be perceived? Should one rely on reason or logic or appeal instead to the senses? Should the fundamental terms of nature be defined according to the authority of Aristotle or the newer competing views of the chemists? Or are there ways to combine or reconcile these views? A fundamental confusion about the relationship of first matter to any other kind of matter shapes the discussion. These issues become no clearer as participants discuss the four elements themselves.

The first speaker on "Of fire"[7] uses astronomy and optics to argue specifically that the first fire cannot be below the moon, "for if it were, the refraction, or parallax caused by it would cause the stars to be seen in another place and of different magnitudes than they are." He cites an experiment from optics as evidence: "By the experiment of a piece of money put into a basin which we behold not, by reason of the imposition of its sides; and yet it appears when you put water into the vessel." He points out logical reasons why earthly fires cannot be first or elemental fire: first, as an accident, fire can be neither an element nor a substance; second, we are composed of things that preserve us, but "there is no animal that lives of fire." He concludes that if any fire enters into "the composition of mixed bodies, it is only the heat of the sun that quickens and animates all things." Another speaker agrees that "fire is but an accidental form," but he insists that, since "it never enters into the composition of natural things," it cannot meet the Aristotelian criteria for an element. Other speakers take more conventional approaches. One argues the importance of fire because of its central role in ancient philosophy. As he notes, "Fire is a most perfect element, hot and dry, according to Aristotle, the most perfect form and activity of all the elements, according to Plato, the principal instrument of nature, and, according to Empedocles, the Father of things."[8] Another cites the sun, as "the element of fire, from whence all other fires come," and fire as "the cause of all generation." Others challenge Aristotle by relocating fire from its Aristotelian position in the heavens. One places it below ground because of the evidence of volcanoes. Another places it both above and below ground and even suggests that it could move into the regions of the planets in the form of comets. For these speakers, then, logic and the evidence of experience allow them to suggest alternatives to the Aristotelian system. Only one speaker makes the case for the conventional Aristotelian point of view. Maintaining with Aristotle that fire could not be part of the heavens because they are immutable, he "denied that the sun can be the element of fire," for the sun "is a celestial and incorruptible body."

Sutton uses this particular conference to claim that Renaudot and his colleagues were more concerned with logic than with Aristotle. Thus they lost sight of orthodox Aristotelianism and were left only with logical formulations without connection to the physical world or to the elegance of the Aristotelian understanding of the cosmos. They had, as he puts it, "rendered Aristotle's description of the physical world suspect at best."[9] But speakers feel free to discount the authority of Aristotle and to use experience or other theories as the grounds on which to challenge him. It might well be the case that there is only one Aristotelian speech on the topic of fire because it seemed the most conventional and least interesting. What do participants offer in its stead? True, they try to determine by logic a consistent definition of an element. By locating fire beyond the moon, the first speaker more sharply differentiates the macrocosm from its pale reflection below. Others too, in keeping with the significance of the sun in the hermetic tradition, sharply distinguish between it and earthly fires. One speaker cites the Paracelsian notion of fire at the center of the earth, while others invoke observations, experiments, and ancient sources. Their use of the term *fire,* unconventional and inconsistent though it is, might have seemed creative and liberating.

Conferees are no more consistent in considering the other elements. Some speakers point out their challenges to Aristotle. A speaker on "Of the air"[10] notes that he is taking an unusual approach to the topic; he "thought fit to step aside, a little out of the ordinary way." His intention is "not so much to impugn the maxims of the school [meaning medieval scholasticism], as to clear them." If air is cold and moist, it would be the same as water, and therefore he asks, "What else are those vapors which are drawn up from the water . . . and those which arise in an alembic, or from boiling water, if we do not call them air? Now those vapors are nothing but water rarified and subtilized by heat." Another speaker refutes him, "since all alteration is made between two different things, water and air, transmuting one into another, as it has been said, they cannot be the same." A participant shifts the discussion to focus on the qualities of air. Based on his experience, he concludes, "air is cold and dry, because it freezes the earth and water." One speaker explicitly challenges the ancients, who "believed the air supremely moist and moderately hot," to support the moderns, who "affirm with more probability that the air is cold." Once again, a fundamental Aristotelian term has been subjected to inconclusive and contradictory speculation, which does not necessarily offer a compelling alternative view but does, by offering an array of alternatives, undermine the authority of Aristotle.

Although the discussion "Of water"[11] begins with an attempt at universal definition, it quickly evolves to an emphasis on the particular. One speaker admits confusion, noting that water has many properties, producing "so many varieties in color, taste, odor . . . it seems to surpass ordinary ratiocination." As just one example of a specific property of water, he cites "a certain river in Sicily, the water whereof cannot be brought to mingle with wine, unless it be drawn by a chaste and continent woman." The many qualities of water cause him to question whether a single definition is possible.

In "Of the earth,"[12] a participant defines it as "a simple body, cold and dry, the basis of nature." Another concludes that earth is clearly a mixed body "from its coldness and its dryness." Yet another says it cannot be an element, because it is also moist or, in other words, contains the element of water. One speaker redirects the discussion away from the elemental quality of earth to offer instead proofs of the roundness of the earth. Another makes a distinction between astronomical and actual "roundness," or between theoretical knowledge (mathematically useful) and empirical evidence. The empirical evidence of the roundness of the earth, he asserts, was vouchsafed by Jean de Betancourt, a Norman explorer. In their discussion of these elements, conferees not only undermine Aristotelian definitions with endless complications and caveats but also introduce specific natural phenomena as telling counterexamples.

In addition to the four Aristotelian elements, participants consider "Of quintessence,"[13] or the fifth essence. Their discussion of quintessence both adds a Paracelsian term to the orthodox Aristotelian four-element theory and transforms the Aristotelian fifth element of the heavens into a more prosaic entity.[14] A speaker first defines it as the highest good for each thing and then attempts to determine it. For man, it is his mind, "the purer part of him, . . . among metals, it prefers gold." Another speaker has a more occult explanation, saying that the *quintessence* is the role that the heavens play as universal agents on earth. "The stars produce metals even in the center of the earth."

As we saw was common in considering occult topics, one speaker denounces the very consideration of the topic by his contemporaries as "the humor of unsettled heads, instead of cultivating the precepts of antiquity, to go about to fabricate new." Not dissuaded, the next connects the quintessence to the beliefs of the chemists. "The chemical quintessence is an ethereal, celestial, and most subtle substance, composed of the salt, sulfur, and mercury of bodies dissolved, stripped of all their elementary qualities, corruptible and mortal, united to a spiritual body, or corporeal spirit, which is the medium and bond uniting bodies and spirits in nature." A final commentator wants to allow the quintessence as crucial to defining chemical properties, but his definition robs it of any occult qualities. It is "nothing else but these elements [salt, sulfur, and mercury] pure and refined, and consequently no more a quintessence than all mixed bodies are with regard to the elements of which they consist." Quintessence thus is a touchstone for chemical issues, and as such, it can be attached to a range of opinions about natural phenomena from mystical to thoroughly rationalistic.

Anyone who looks to these conferences as an example of the Aristotelian paradigm, before the assault of mathematical physics upon it, might be horrified to find such a garbled and mangled Aristotelianism. But this is to assume that conferees intended to present Aristotelianism and that Aristotelianism unaltered is *the* pre-mechanical science. If we do not subscribe to these presuppositions, we can see how this garbled Aristotelianism might have been productive. What have participants introduced to challenge Aristotle? They have cited their experience and directly refuted Aristotelian premises. Their attitude toward the ancients is not constrained by undue deference. They have a clear sense that their opinions can be advanced with a credibility equal to that of Aristotle and that their experience can challenge his authority. When they address the elements (the most conventional topics in the conferences), it is clearest how they respond to their Aristotelian inheritance. These conferences demonstrate in a concrete way the erosion of Aristotelianism in the early seventeenth century. Participants generally use Aristotelian language without adhering to his science. Terminology unfettered to a systematic science is a good way to understand what the erosion of Aristotelianism meant, however. As Sutton notes, "While the language of Aristotelian nature philosophy recurred throughout the decade, there is no sense in which the straightforward Aristotelian system described the physical world in which the speakers lived."[15] The conferees' use of Aristotelian language thus demonstrates an effective adaptation of Aristotle to new concerns. They do not hesitate to disagree with him or to challenge his premises. It is not that they simply got him wrong. Instead they present an array of positions on all topics—an array demonstrating the chaotic, competitive sense of science that predominates in these discussions.[16] Participants and readers of the published proceedings might well have been pleased to find so many kinds of evidence and arguments marshaled for their edification. The presentation of so many points of view might well have enthralled the listeners and readers, offering an array of intriguing and unconventional ways to understand the world.

What might participants or readers have found inspiring or rewarding about these early conferences? First, they might well have appreciated the attacks on Aristotelianism. Any such attack, after all, would have been a hallmark of virtually any claim to be avant-garde in the seventeenth century. Second, the discussion of these topics effectively empowers the individual to try to bring them under some sort of theoretical control. There is no orthodox opinion to which one must conform. Sutton notes with dismay, but participants might have seen as liberating, "the rarest of natural phenomena, the most abstruse of purported theoretical developments, the subtlest bit of logic; each could tear down the centuries old Aristotelian cosmology."[17] Their cavalier treatment makes an important point about the breakdown of Aristotelianism before there was a well-defined replacement—that is to say, Aristotelian science was no longer treated as authoritative or as a coherent, persuasive system.

Such unorthodox discussions of Aristotelian elements are, Schmitt notes, common to a host of individual treatises written about them in the seventeenth century, which were "Aristotelian, semi-Aristotelian, and non-Aristotelian." In these works, "Aristotle was tempered by atomism, Platonism, alchemy, and much else."[18] The comments on elements and other fundamental Aristotelian concepts provide a concrete demonstration of the use and abuse of Aristotle. Although they do not offer a view that can be correlated to the new science, they do show what kinds of evidence could be brought to bear on Aristotelian themes. The discussions are frequently inconsistent and incoherent. In their defense, this incoherence is deliberate and cultivated. Renaudot advocated the presentation of as many views as possible to allow for the emergence of truth. He rejected the imposition of consensus or synthesis and recognized that the conferences were going against the grain of conventional scientific opinion. He responded to those who expected his group to hew to an Aristotelian line: "It may be that some would have preferred that we had not allowed any opinion to be put forward contrary to that held by the School. That, however, seems to be repugnant to the freedom of our understanding, which would lose its name if it remained entirely enslaved to the rod of magisterial authority."[19]

By fostering so many diverse ideas, each conference demonstrates the many grounds for the critique of Aristotle and the many Aristotelian residues in the presentation of arguments. These discussions thoroughly document the penetration of Aristotelian terms into general parlance for discussing almost all topics, but particularly those associated with science. But the terms are turned against Aristotle and his authority is eroded, perhaps as effectively as by the more direct broadsides launched by Bacon, Galileo, and Descartes. Harcourt Brown, for example, cites the arguments made by conferees against scholasticism that espoused, at least in terms of attitude, a kind of Cartesian skepticism. He notes that scholastic syllogism and metaphysical disputation rooted in Aristotelianism would not facilitate the practical ends sought by Renaudot. These conferences, much broader in constituency, are not intended to resolve narrow sectarian disputes. Their approach is more inclusive and more democratic.[20]

What do conferees suggest in place of Aristotelianism? They do not advocate a replacement paradigm. Instead they use his terms in ways that subvert him; they offer different definitions based on antithetical positions, from Platonic to Paracelsian; they present specific observations, particularly their own observations, as telling, perhaps even telling enough to call into question the master. (Francis Bacon too wanted to fill terms with new meaning—in an ordered way.) It is clear that, probably because most participants were familiar with Aristotle (the greater the education the greater their exposure), they oriented the initial conferences around fundamental terms of Aristotelian science, but in a way that challenged it.

Perhaps because they are so rooted in the tradition, the conferences on Aristotelian topics do not have the engaging character or the sharp disagreements that characterize subsequent conferences, concerned with the epistemology of the new science or with specific phenomena, which suggests that topics identified with the new science provoked greater interest on the part of some conferees. If their discussion has consistently called Aristotelian physics into question, can one conclude that the conferences have paved the way for the acceptance of new scientific views, particularly the mechanical sciences? By laying out opposing views, the conferences not only demonstrate that Aristotelianism had suffered enough of an assault that it was no longer compelling but also that science has a burden to persuade. And guided by these critical perspectives, conferences examined issues of the new philosophy and science.

TOPICS OF THE NEW SCIENCE

Speakers are acutely aware that the terms of discussion of many issues are changing. Some of them express consternation about these changes; others readily adapt to the new. Regardless of their personal response, they could not, given their interest in science, fail to be aware of the new science, admittedly still in its earliest stages, especially as embodied by both the views and tribulations of Galileo. A conference on "If it is better to follow common opinions than paradoxes"[21] offers an argument for the authority of traditional opinion and a clear exposition of some issues people faced as they contemplated new ideas. Heliocentrism lurks just below the surface as the most obvious paradox.

The first speaker begins with the statement that "just as the large roads are more sure than small paths, so too, common opinions are always more certain." Common opinions are those held in esteem by the public and followed as precedent by the courts. On the other hand, ambitious spirits, who want to be renowned for being outside the common opinion, produce paradoxes. Those inclined to paradoxical opinions are contrary, he asserts, like those who insist on eating fish when they are far away from the sea. Paradox is the source of schisms, heresies, quarrels, factions, and the ruin of philosophy. Paradoxes sometimes even dispute the evidence of the senses. "Thus Copernicus, instead of enriching the inventions of Ptolemy, who wanted the sun immobile and the earth the center of the world, made all turn around it and thus made almost all phenomena reasonable." He acknowledges Copernicus's accomplishments, comparing them to "an extraordinary sauce," but he nonetheless insists to the contrary, that the senses, which support Ptolemy, are the true judges, the most faithful witnesses of truth that we can know, and that the effect of such unpalatable fare as Copernicanism is indigestion. The next speaker is even more appreciative of the value of old opinions. Old opinions offer the advantages of "universal opinions," which can be known by all. They are better because "the repose and the satisfaction of the understanding proceeds from a truth known." Thus old opinions are those "that universal reason has received and that usage has confirmed by many examples and practices of centuries passed." New opinions produced in an instant are like "monsters that have nothing agreeable in their novelty." Those who espouse new opinions are like those who change their hats or beards simply to be distinctive. For these two commentators, common opinions have the stamp of approval of both reason and sensory evidence, while paradoxical opinions are simply changes in intellectual fashion.

The next speaker addresses this issue from a perspective of particular interest for historians of science. One should, he suggests, subscribe only to the opinion of the learned, who have opinions entirely separated from those of the people, "especially in astronomy and physics." The distinction between the opinions of the people and the learned are clearest in response to the new astronomy: "According to the learned, the smallest star one sees is larger than the earth, while the vulgar believe the sun is the size of cheese and the moon even smaller. . . . In physics, the same sun that the vulgar deem hot is demonstrated to have no elementary quality; the people call and consider a bottle empty, and philosophy shows that there is no vacuum." All these opinions of the learned, he notes, are paradoxes to the vulgar. The fact that relatively few people hold learned opinions enhances their credibility, because there are many more "pagans, idolaters, Turks, and heretics than true Catholics" and "a great many more ignorant men than men capable of judging the truth of things." Pointing to an evolution in scientific thinking, he notes that "all that today pass for rules of the mind" were at one time considered paradoxes. Sometimes the paradoxical opinion of a single man, preserved by his followers, will come to be recognized as true.

Despite the obvious unease produced by new or paradoxical opinions, the conferences could not fail to treat issues of cosmology and astronomy. If participants had taken a consistently progressive position they might well have figured more prominently in the history of science, but their discussion is disconcertingly inconsistent, even though some use the new astronomy to challenge Aristotelian cosmology. The orthodox cosmology of the seventeenth century, rooted in Aristotle, was hierarchically ordered and man-centered. The sublunary region was the area of change in which the four elements combined to form minerals, plants, and animals. The world of the heavens beyond the moon was unchanging, with spheres ascending from planets to the rotating sphere of the heavens, to the sphere of fixed stars, constellations, and finally to heaven. But this order was obviously challenged by the heliocentric hypothesis of Copernicus, which had been put on firmer, more empirical grounds by the findings of Galileo. This view, by having earth and the other planets revolving around the sun, blurred the distinction between the heavens and the earth. Galileo's *Dialogue concerning the Two World Systems* made this topic relevant.

The condemnation of Galileo had not yet been promulgated when participants considered "Of the motion, or rest of the earth"[22] on 24 October 1633. Although a conferee initially suggests that there is equal weight on both sides of the topic, he nonetheless argues for the immobility of the earth, basing his remarks primarily on a sense of what is befitting. He acknowledges that "this question has been in debate for more than two thousand years" but maintains that the most common opinion is that of Aristotle, Ptolemy, and Tycho Brahe "that the earth is unmovable." Although he bolsters his argument by noting its conformity with great authorities, his "proofs" are based on a different kind of argument—evidence rooted in argument from analogy between the heavens and his understanding of the operations of nature. For example, the simplicity and the gravity of the earth require that it be both central and immobile. His observations, such as the fact that the stars are always of the same magnitude, also support his claim. He insists that the heliocentric hypothesis is both illogical and counter to observation. It is illogical because simple bodies "have but one sole and simple motion . . . wherefore the earth having, by reason of its gravity, a direct perpendicular motion of its own, cannot also have a circular one." Heliocentrism runs counter to our observations because, "if the earth moved, then a stone thrown upward would fall to earth at some distance from the one who threw it." He thus reiterates one of the key arguments of Jean Buridan, a fourteenth-century thinker, to support the revolution of the heavens as more likely than that of the earth. But the speaker goes further, heightening the dramatic potential of such arguments: If the earth moved, a cannonball fired from west to east would not go as far as one fired from east to west; the clouds would always move in the same direction and at a much more rapid speed than they do; and cities and buildings would shatter, because they could not hold together in the face of such continuous rapid movement. Another participant offers scriptural reasons for believing that the earth does not move; God created a firm and stable earth and a sun that rises and sets, and thus Joshua's stilling of the sun was a great miracle.

The next speaker does not follow up on the religious argument but offers a point-by-point refutation of the scientific claims. He cites those who agree with him "that the opinion of Copernicus is the more probable." Such views were held in the past by "Orpheus, Thales, Aristarchus, and Philolaus" and by "Kepler, Longomontanus, Origanus, and diverse others of our times." He accepts the legitimacy of the claim that the noblest body must occupy the noblest space and thus asserts that "the middle, the most noble place, is therefore due to the most noble body of the world . . . the sun." He connects the evidence of both Harvey and Copernicus to assert "it is no more necessary that the heart be seated in the middle of man, than that the sun be placed in the middle of the universe." The uniformity of nature supports heliocentrism because "the circular motion of the planets around the sun seems to argue that the earth does the same." He suggests that there is logic and propriety in the earth's seeking the sun, because it needs "light, heat, and influence" rather than the sun seeking what it does not need. "Rest and immobility, a nobler condition than motion, ought to belong to the visible image of the deity, the sun, which in that regard has been adored by sundry nations." This speaker reverses traditional analogies to support heliocentrism;[23] he presents a vivid example of couching the new in terms used to sustain the old.

He then offers empirical evidence. It is not impossible, he notes, that a heavy object could continue in motion, like a stone on a sling. Experiments on the lodestone suggest evidence analogous to that of the motion of the earth; "if both the direct and the circular motion be found in the lodestone, which tends by its gravity to the center and moves circularly by its magnetic virtue, the same cannot be conceived impossible in the earth." Ultimately he praises the mathematical simplicity of the Copernican system, which does away with "a multitude of imaginary orbs in the heavens." This speaker thus both responds to the arguments from analogy and offers empirical evidence as well. This conference demonstrates that participants were well able to articulate the parameters of the early seventeenth-century debate on Galileo in an unconstrained way. This proponent of Galileo refuses to engage the religious arguments, perhaps because he is abiding by the injunction of the preface to avoid religion or because he does not consider it central to the discussion, which he can address more effectively by reversing conventional analogies and providing empirical support.

The potentially dangerous interplay between religion and science became explicit six months later, when news of Galileo's condemnation and abjuration reached Paris.[24] The news cast a deep pall over scientific inquiry in France. Descartes felt compelled to suppress publication of the *Traité du monde* and to argue that science posed no threat to orthodoxy. Mersenne maintained in his *Questions théologiques* that there was not enough evidence to prove that the earth moved.[25] Renaudot might have felt vulnerable because of his recent conversion to Catholicism. He responded to the threat by reporting on the condemnation of Galileo in the *Gazette de France* and recanting the favorable commentary Galilean science had received in his conferences.[26] But Renaudot was less vulnerable than one might assume. He was protected by Richelieu, whose foreign policy sanctioned a Protestant alliance to defeat the Hapsburgs. This policy not only suggested a religious view more audacious than heliocentrism, it also put France at diplomatic odds with the Vatican. For whatever reason, caution did not characterize subsequent discussion at the Bureau. Renaudot's conferences avoided dangerous astronomical topics for less than six months. On 29 May 1634 the group discussed comets. They raised other controversial topics, such as the one that introduces this chapter and "Whether the heavens are moved by Intelligences." Many remarks on topics remote from astronomy simply take heliocentrism as a given. And, despite Renaudot's recantation, the controversial conference appeared in all subsequent reprintings.

On the question "Of comets,"[27] a speaker raises a question central to the new sciences, that is to say, whether the evidence of our senses conforms to astronomy. He points out that "the deceitfulness of our senses" makes it difficult to understand the nature of comets. After all, he says, "who would not believe that the moon and other planets have a true light, were it not for the reasons of astronomy?" Nonetheless, in doubtful matters, he reflects, it is best to adhere to the conventional opinion, "which holds a comet to be a hot and dry exhalation inflamed in the highest region of the air"—an opinion derived from Aristotle's *Meteorologica*.

The next speaker refutes this opinion, since he does not believe that the former explanation of comets is physically possible. "There is little probability that matter so thin and subtle . . . can burn for several months . . . for the sustenance of so great a flame," such as the comet that appeared "in this city in November 1618, [and] occupied forty degrees of the firmament." These challenges to Aristotle do not go unanswered. Despite his recognition of fundamental points of the new science, a speaker maintains the fundamental Aristotelian distinction between heavenly and earthly things, "for the heavens being incorruptible, it is impossible to fancy any corruption in them."[28] He acknowledges some changes in the heavens as a result of new astronomical evidence: "The apogees and perigees of the planets, which are the points of their greatest and least distance from the earth, are . . . changed more than twenty-six degrees since Ptolemy's time." But he insists that "this permutation of place induces no mutation of substance." He thus incorporates new astronomical information but is unwilling to have it overturn his worldview.

Other participants express ideas that fueled early modern discussions of the nature of comets.[29] One insists that a comet is simply a star that moves and thus is sometimes invisible to us. Another considers it an optical illusion "produced by the darting of sunbeams through an exhalation." Speakers thus challenge or support Ptolemaic astronomy but then present speculative arguments about the import of comets. One claims that, because comets are simply the results of a peculiar reflection of light, they cannot be portentous. Others insist that comets "always presage strange events." One correlates historically significant events with their appearance and observes that, of "sixty-six comets that have appeared since the resurrection of our Savior, there is not one that has not been immediately followed by some disorder or division in the Church, caused by persecutions, schisms, or heresies." Another speaker correlates the size of the comet to the significance of the event it foretells and offers signs whereby its projected impact can be read. For example, "The sign of the zodiac in which the comet appears designates the country it threatens." A final speaker unites the two strands of interpretation: comets are portents precisely because they are not just signs but also natural causes of "dearth and famines, wars and sedition, burning fever and other diseases, by the inflammation they impress upon the airs and, by it, upon all other bodies."[30]

Participants also raised points more central to astronomical discussions, such as the explicitly Galilean topic "Concerning the spots on the sun and the moon."[31] A speaker suggests that spots might result from the transits of little planets, like the ones that revolve around Jupiter. Only one speaker maintains the immutability of the heavens; he insists that any alleged spot must reside in the eye of the beholder or close at hand (a thinly veiled attack on the telescope). Another responds with a speech that Sutton heralds as "the most successful scientific argument the Bureau ever saw."[32] The speaker points out that one does not need to rely on the telescope to determine spots on the moon. Instead, if one simply pierces a piece of paper with a small hole to admit a ray of light, spots can be seen projected on a piece of paper that intercepts the ray and displays the moon's image. Since these spots are stationary and do not progress across the face of the moon, they cannot be remote from the moon's surface; atmospheric phenomena form and dissipate but the spots on the moon do not. The presentation is a clear, cogent exposition, effectively integrating experimental findings. Another speaker is so inspired by the spots on the moon that he suggests the moon is just like the earth; just as we can see the moon's irregularities on its surface so would the earth appear from the moon. He further embellishes his account; the moon might have valleys and lakes or even be populated.[33]

Participants also discuss topics provoked by the seventeenth-century revival of atomism, which made the vacuum a subject of intense scientific speculation. Discussions of the vacuum bring to the fore different notions of matter. The question is not simply whether a vacuum exists but what its existence or non-existence entails for an understanding of matter, and thus it was a topic of passionate interest in learned circles in the first half of the seventeenth century. Prominent figures took various positions: Galileo attributed the vacuum to a certain resistance to matter; Mersenne reported results of experiments on the vacuum, with less enthusiasm than he generally accorded new findings; and Descartes denied it.[34] An initial speaker in the conference "Of vacuity"[35] cites ancient sources of atomistic philosophy, Democritus and Leucippus in particular, but repudiates them; "these opinions being antiquated, I adhere to the common one, which admits no vacuum at all." (Perhaps he considered it rhetorically or strategically important to show familiarity with these sources.) The next speaker argues in favor of the existence of a vacuum, basing his remarks on the atomic understanding of matter, although he seems almost resentful of the difficulties this entails as an explanatory system: "To say that bodies give way one to another is to increase the difficulty instead of resolving it; for the body that gives place to another must displace a third, and this a fourth, and so to infinity." Another's explanation combines chemical processes with atomism to prove the existence of the vacuum "by condensation and rarefaction." When condensation occurs, "a body is reduced into a lesser extent, and its parts approach nearer," and then "either these parts penetrate one another, or else there is some void space."

One speaker argues against a vacuum by insisting that unity is fundamental to any understanding of nature: "all things find their good and conservation in unity, as they do their ruin in disunion," and unity entails contiguous matter. A more persuasive argument for him is that, "if there were a vacuum in the world, the heavens could not transmit their influences into the elements and their compounds." If there were a vacuum, the causal connections between the heavens and the earth would be broken. Another participant suggests that a vacuum allows medicine to be productive. "What makes the effects of blood-letting and purgation so sensible, but this very flight of vacuum?" The next offers a compromise position, making it a question of degree, which is to say, "small, interspersed inanities may be between the particles of the elements and compounds, like the pores of our bodies," but a large space or vacuum is not possible. A final speaker suggests that a vacuum can be produced by a kind of coercion, a violation of nature. "Nature does what she can to hinder a vacuum, yet suffers one when she is forced to it." (This is the only reference to such a sense of nature that can be found in these conferences.) It is interesting that it is not man but rather natural processes that inflict violence on nature.[36]

Although conferees touch on matter and motion, issues common to the revival of atomism and to the new mechanical philosophy, they do not treat these topics extensively. There are only five of these topics in the conferences. As Sutton notes, only one speaker—on the topic of "Whether or not of two bodies of different weight, one descends more rapidly and why?"—takes an avant-garde position, one that heralds the new science, when he asserts that bodies of the same shape and material, no matter what their size and weight, fall at the same rate.[37]

What do these conferences have to say about issues central to the new science? They demonstrate something important about its reception. Some participants were effective advocates for the new, and others made what contemporaries considered the most reputable arguments for the old. Their discussions show (and this should not be at all surprising) that in the 1630s and early 1640s mechanism was not firmly accepted.[38] It was only over the course of the period in which the conferences occurred that the first fundamental works of mechanical philosophy began to appear.[39] Although the issues of the new astronomy are often cast in terms of the trial of Galileo, in these conferences religious arguments are neither prominent nor decisive; such arguments and references are few. The preponderant and compelling arguments are naturalistic. The conferences, while they can not be aligned with the rise of the mechanical sciences, nonetheless demonstrate familiarity with and receptivity to new ideas. It is impossible to draw any conclusions about what this group might have reflected had it persisted over the course of Renaudot's life. Its early history tantalizingly suggests that it might well have provided a compelling case of the mutual accommodation of the old science to the new, especially since the group, so committed to a thorough presentation of knowledge, did in fact present a popularized version of the most contemporary information.

EPISTEMOLOGICAL ISSUES AND SCIENCE

It is worth remembering that, although the triumphalist account of the scientific revolution emphasizes the discoveries of great heroes, especially in astronomy and physics, the scientific revolution is also integrally connected to intensive philosophical and epistemological explorations. This speculation is largely a response to the predominant intellectual crisis of the day.[40] Religious dissension in the wake of the Reformation shattered a belief in one truth. Skeptics responded by calling into question our ability to know and act effectively. The challenge of the new science was, in part, to respond to the contested state of knowledge. Descartes, most notably, sought to reserve an area of "clear and distinct ideas" from doubt.

Renaudot's conferees raise important epistemological topics, many of them tied to the new science. A conference on "What sect of philosophers should most be followed"[41] indicates a thorough knowledge of the epistemological issues raised by the new science and addresses practical implications associated with various philosophical positions. It positively appraises the prospects for knowledge and endorses science as a means to knowledge. This conference is one of the longest in the collection, and the remarks are so extensive that they could not possibly have been delivered in a two-hour time frame.[42] The unusual length suggests both that participants were keenly concerned with these philosophical issues and that this debate over rival philosophical schools was hotly contested.

One speaker distinguishes between skepticism and science to offer a compelling endorsement of science. He claims that the two most important philosophical sects incorporate all others: "One is the Pyrrhonian [skeptic] who doubts all things and says that there is no science." The skeptics base their understanding on the received maxim "there is nothing in the understanding that has not passed by the senses, and the senses being deceivers, all of our knowledge is necessarily such." Members of the other sect are "those who are neither in doubt nor in perfect certitude, but in the search for the truth that they believe they can find." This is the proper approach to knowledge, although we do not know the essence of things, "which still to us is often hidden." He insists against the skeptics that "they must avow there is a science of something." Although doubt can be the basis of knowledge, he urges us to move beyond doubt; we cannot fail to recognize either that the senses provide knowledge of our existence or that they are the foundation of all action based on the knowledge of existence of other things. For him, as for Descartes, God plays an important metaphysical role, and an awareness of oneself is also a crucial basis of knowledge. One must recognize the work of the scientist, because "work is the element of great souls, action is a mark of immortality." For him, the fact that skeptics assert the futility of human action is most troubling: "A science that always keeps the spirit elevated is preferable to that which makes a good agent lazy and which impoverishes him while persuading him that he has enough riches." Activity and the pursuit of knowledge not only define the human being and give meaning to human life, they also yield useful knowledge: "Astrologers attempt to discover new stars, as chemists research new secrets and as doctors do new remedies. Philosophers find new opinions every day, and finally each dreams to discover that which is still hidden." Ultimately, those who pursue the truth are much closer to it than those who, for whatever reason, flee it. For this speaker, the impetus to science decisively defeats the skeptics.

In a conference on "Whence diversity of opinion proceeds,"[43] participants deal with the role of the senses in acquiring knowledge, a fundamental epistemological problem raised by the new science. Some insist that opinions depend on the impressions made on the senses; others consider the state of the senses themselves ("the necessity that mediums be well disposed") more essential. One important question asked in this conference is, If we are dependent on the senses for knowledge, do we all experience what we sense in the same way? The initial commentator offers a host of explanations for the diversity of opinion—some organic, some occupational, some rooted in the soul. He raises a number of interesting issues, but ultimately his speech is inconclusive. He insists that the differences between the senses of different individuals create different sense perceptions; thus "two eyes are not perfectly alike; . . . the same thing appears divers according to the diversity of those that judge of it." Judgment depends on the evidence of the senses, "since the intellect judges things, according to the report of the outward senses." Despite individual differences in sense organs, the judgments of the senses produce a great conformity of opinion. "These senses and their mediums, being well disposed, agree all in their reports, the whiteness of this paper, the blackness of this ink, and the truth of all other objects being faithfully represented to us." But this consensus breaks down on more complex issues. As he puts it, "why should not all men who hear one and the same proposition, and the reasons whereby it is backed and opposed, make the same judgment for or against it, without being divided, as they are, into several opinions?" The causes for divisions, he suggests, are both physiological and sociological. In the first case, "dispositions and habitudes of the organs . . . render the soul's operations different." In the second, each listener hears according to his estate; the scholar might quibble whereas the peasant might be overwhelmed.

The next speaker accepts the Aristotelian dictum "nothing is in the intellect but was before in the senses," but he seems dissatisfied with its implications. He notes that "many times the intellect is so prepossessed with prejudice that all supervening reasons signify nothing; and when some passion, as love or hatred, biases it, there is no room for equal consideration." Ultimately he is forced to modify his reliance on Aristotle; "this variety of judgment proceeds not only from the diversity of the species introduced by the common sense into the intellect, but from the different connections the intellect draws from those species." Even if, as he might in theory maintain, there is nothing in the intellect that was not first in the senses, nonetheless, the intellect itself plays a significant role in shaping the evidence of those sensations. Indeed the intellect exercises its influence to such a degree that it can almost disregard the evidence of the senses.

In the conference considering "What is truth,"[44] a speaker, who says the topic might be too bold, concludes that we come to truth "by means of a faculty of our soul that conceives, understands, and reasons on all things." But since there is nothing in the understanding "that has not first passed by the senses," knowledge about things is similar to "images imprinted in the fantasy." Truth then is an accord between the faculty of knowing and the object known. However, he asserts, truth "is more truly in the faculty that knows and judges . . . than it is in the things themselves." The next speaker breaks the question down; there are two kinds of truths. The first is the simple apprehension of the thing. The other truth is of understanding, produced by a faithful rapport between the understanding and the thing known.

Another conference asks "Whether species or things are the objects of the senses,"[45] a topic invoking the debates of the Middle Ages between the nominalists and the realists. The first speaker insists that one should not deviate from the common and received opinion that "sensation occurs with the introduction of species into the organs of our senses." This is proved by the fact that one cannot speak of a stone or a horse, unless it is already "in the head" by way of the internal senses. He considers questions of perceptions highly complicated, because each external sense depends more or less on material conditions of the sense.[46] The next two speakers seem to argue against "species" in favor of simpler, more scientific analyses. One objects that some philosophers have imitated astronomers who, "to facilitate, for us, the science of heavenly bodies, have feigned circles, poles, and so on, which are not really in the sky." So too, some philosophers have used the word *species*, but because they multiplied terms without adding anything to our understanding of sensation, these terms have only raised more doubts. The next speaker says that those who contend that vision is made by the emission of visual rays and not by the reception of the objects or its image in the eye have effectively refuted the notion of "species." Another participant objects to quibbling over words, insisting that "there can be no internal sensation without a connection between the external sense and the *sensorium commune;* . . . The connection between them cannot be the thing itself, just as the letters I trace are not the things they signify but only their signs." Thus, whether one calls them "signs, phantasms, or species," it is by their means that the faculties of the soul exercise themselves.

If we are to know, knowledge must in some fundamental sense be tied to the senses. Virtually every epistemological topic cites the Aristotelian dictum that everything that is in the intellect was first in the senses. Since the senses are so central to knowledge and to its acquisition, and so rooted in seventeenth-century epistemological debates, it is not surprising that they should be extensively discussed in the conferences. A specific conference is dedicated to each of the five senses. In order to set up the rationale for the discussion, speakers assert the importance or unique qualities associated with each particular sense discussed. For example, several conferees discussing "Of touch"[47] assert its importance because it is the foundation of the other senses— or because, unlike the other senses, it is diffused throughout the body or because it distinguishes man from lower creatures. Another speaker touts sight as the most essential to philosophizing, since "it is by sight that we have cognition of all the goodly objects of the world . . . it discerns as far as the stars of the firmament."[48] Others are quick to dismiss statements about the distinctiveness of any particular sense.

Arguments lauding a particular sense are generally rooted in a notion of a hierarchy of nature. The more restricted the sense to creatures further up the scale of being, the more it is to be venerated, according to some speakers. Touch is therefore low in the hierarchy, according to a speaker who points out that a tactile quality is the sole sense of many animals, especially zoophytes or plant-animals such as sponges, coral, and all kind of oysters.[49] Some assume the functioning of the sense corresponds not only to an anthropocentric ordering of the world, but also to God's design for the universe. The following description of the eye is both anthropocentric and invokes the argument from design: "The eye, so regarded by nature that she has fortified it on all sides for its safety . . . is the instrument of most exact knowledge and so serves not only the body but the soul."[50]

While conferees assess the senses according to hierarchy, God's design, and other ways of understanding nature that seem quite foreign to us, they also focus on the physiological functioning of each sense. One speaker suggests that sound cannot be understood solely as the action of "spirits" as some have argued. Instead sound "presupposes in the bodies collided together, hardness, smoothness, and such other secondary qualities, without which the collision of bodies is not audible."[51]

In "Of smelling"[52] a conferee claims that, because odors are "introduced by the nose through the spongy bone into the mammillary process, which are appendices of the brain," smelling is thus "more particular to the brain than any other sense." Another speaker discusses some of the ways that odors are conveyed. When the source is remote, it is conveyed by species: "Thus the species of the odor of a worm hanging upon the hook so exquisitely penetrates the water, that the fish, though very remote, instantly goes to it." When participants discuss the functioning of the senses, they distinguish between data proximate to the sense itself and that which must be transmitted over distance. Hearing is the most problematic sense, because sounds "are the least material qualities of all."[53]

Participants also offer empirical evidence about the functioning of the senses. In "Of taste,"[54] a speaker notes that the tip of the tongue perceives tastes more accurately because of the nerves destined for tasting. The connection between hearing and speaking is empirically demonstrated "because of the straight connection of the auditory nerve with the root of the tongue." As a result, those born deaf are also dumb. Odors are especially powerful, for experience demonstrates that the womb moves in response to good and bad smells, either because the womb "has a particular sympathy with the brain, the conservatory of the spirits, or because the contraction of the nerves is caused when a displeasing odor drives the spirits downwards."[55]

Most discussions of the senses describe physiological processes with supporting empirical evidence. But sometimes conferees describe the functioning of a sense in atomistic terms, as the result of the movement of particles, or even in mechanistic terms, as the result of matter in motion. One speaker describes hearing as the result of local motion; "by friction attenuating the parts, it generates heat, and by the meeting of two bodies, it makes sound." For another speaker, sound is produced by "the body striking, the body struck, and the medium resounding." The same process produces human language, "which is formed by collision of the air in the lungs against the larynx, the palate, and the teeth."[56]

A speaker on sight makes a point of great relevance to the epistemological concerns of the scientific revolution. He dismisses the significance of optical illusions as a repudiation of sight. He insists that "if the sight happens to be deceived, as when we judge the moon greater in the horizon by reason of the vapors of the earth than when it is at the meridians; or when a straight stick seems crooked in the water; the same eye, which is deceived, finds its own error by comparison with other objects." He rescues the senses from the attack of the skeptics much in the way Descartes did, saying "so the sense cannot be said altogether faulty since it discerns its fault."[57]

A conference on "Of the visible species"[58] is about how we see. A speaker argues that "the visible species are a reflection of light, which is various according to the different color and figure of the objects . . . species being received by the spirits, are by them carried to the *sensorium commune* and the imagination." There the intellect forms "like to itself, which are more spiritual and incorporeal." Another speaker objects that any theory of visible species poses acute problems, such as "how those of each different object in the same place can fill it all." Other speakers attempt to describe just how visible species work. "Although objects send their images toward the sight, yet the eye emits the most subtle and active spirits to receive them." Thus to sharpen our visual perception, "we contract our eyes, or shut one of them so that the visual beams may be more strengthened by being more united." Participants cite empirical evidence of these emissions. One notes, "if sight were performed without any emission, the basilisk should not kill by its aspect; . . . women should not infect looking glasses at certain times."[59] In trying to explain how one sees, participants invoke arguments ranging from scholastic philosophy, to empirical examples, to the effects of the evil eye. One speaker finds it entirely improbable and illogical that the eye should emit spirits. It cannot be an incorporeal substance, "for then a man should emit his soul. . . . Nor can it be a body, for no body is moved in an instant." How, he wonders, could such a quantity of spirits be produced so as to reach so far as to allow us to see the heavenly bodies?

The topic "Whether colors are real"[60] is interesting for its implications regarding the new sciences for the understanding of perception. A speaker lays out the difficulties in treating the topic; "nothing is so manifest to the senses as color, nothing so obscure to the understanding." At issue is "whether it has a real existence or whether it only appears such according as bodies variously receive the light." Conventional wisdom suggests that colors are in the object, but the new science says that they are a refraction of light. Regardless of the epistemological issues involved, another insists on the Aristotelian point that "the object of vision is color; the organ is the eye; the medium is a diaphanous body illuminated. Provided these three are correctly disposed . . . all men will necessarily behold colors as they are, and always alike, which would not be so if they were imaginary, or fortuitous." Thus, differences of perception are due to differences in either the organ or the medium. One speaker insists that colors, like other secondary qualities, have a real existence, since they arise from the mixture of moist and dry, caused by heat and determined by cold. The next directly refutes him, flatly asserting that "colors cannot proceed from the . . . mixture of the four first qualities." Despite the diverse perspectives they bring to bear on the epistemological issues associated with sensation, conferees were vitally concerned with the issues central to early modern philosophical discussions. They focus explicitly on the crucial issues of the scientific revolution: what we can know, how we can know it, the surety of sensory knowledge, and of the role of science in the acquisition of knowledge.

INVESTIGATING THE EARTH: AN EMPIRICAL SCIENCE

By the end of the seventeenth century, the victory of mechanism, the geometric method, and the mathematization of both nature and science could be confidently propounded by expositors of science like Bernard de Fontenelle.[61] With victory declared, the sciences of physics, mathematics, and mechanics flourished and captured the popular imagination. Although Renaudot's conferences took place before the definitive success of mechanism, their significance to the history of science would seem to depend on a premature appreciation of the new philosophy. Although participants took cognizance of new developments in science and philosophy, they were not consistent proponents of the new. In fact, they were much more interested in the natural sciences (the study of the earth and its creatures), the sciences that did not experience a revolution until the nineteenth century. But only a highly selective reading of the historical past would allow one to conclude that this interest was unique to Renaudot's conferees or that such interest evaporated in the face of the mechanical philosophy. Many of their contemporaries were quite interested in the actual as opposed to the mathematical exploration of the world and in the discussion of specific phenomena—Robert Hooke, van Helmont, Robert Fludd, and Descartes, to name just a few. Although the natural sciences are not central to narratives of the scientific revolution, they were nonetheless a significant part of contemporary scientific discussion. If there was a science that particularly captured the attention of Renaudot's group, it was discussions of the earth, or topics that would eventually emerge as the science of geology.

Why was there renewed interest in geology in the early modern period? The humanists had revived early writings about the earth, those of Pliny in particular, and had begun to investigate the natural rather than the mystical properties of minerals. The humanist Ulisse Aldrovandi coined the term *geologia*. The discovery of the New World provoked interest in exploration, some of which focused on different mineral and rock formations and other geological comparisons between the old and the new worlds. States also sought to increase their wealth by mining. Paracelsians, with their understanding of the universe as chemical and of changes as rooted in chemical processes, obviously fostered interest in chemical exploration of minerals. For these reasons and because of the Paracelsian sympathies of Renaudot and some of his fellow physicians, a significant number of discrete conferences are dedicated to geological topics.

When participants turned their attention to natural phenomena, they were acutely interested in those questions that would form the basis of the geological sciences. They proposed topics that allowed them to address all of the key geological topics of the seventeenth century, questions about the earth that had been central from the time of Aristotle but were once again topical, such as how are minerals, metals, springs, and mountains formed? How can one explain earthquakes and the differences between kinds of minerals? Conferees drew on a rich tradition of ancient writings about the earth and incorporated new humanist writings and controversial sources such as alchemical texts. They were neither bound by the sources nor consistent in their approach.

For example, most speakers agree that minerals grow within the earth, but they offer many different explanations as to why this occurs. If they believe that minerals grow, they must then explain how their original formation in nature occurred and how that development has continued. Most of them accept the Aristotelian explanation that the sun's rays cause the earth to give off exhalations. If those exhalations are moist, they form clouds; if they are dry, they might cause thunder or condense and form stones or minerals. Some of these exhalations penetrate into the earth's interior where they form stones if they mix with earth but metals if they mix with water.

Some participants also bring alchemical explanations to bear, however. The alchemists emphasized the role of the great fire at the center of the earth that gave off dense clouds of metal-producing vapors. The molten rock and ash of volcanoes most effectively demonstrate this process. More recent texts, such as that of Agricola, were more skeptical about the existence of a subterranean fire.

The specific arguments made by participants about the growth of minerals vary according to the evidence and sources they can bring to bear.[62] Some explanations point to empirical evidence such as the accounts of those who have worked in exhausted mines and return to find more metal. The growth of minerals, some suggest, is most fittingly related to an understanding of much more basic processes, such as life itself. Participants further acknowledge that it is very difficult to understand these issues because natural processes are occult. However, because they are consistent throughout nature, these processes can be productively explored. As one speaker puts it, life in man "consists but in one sole action, to wit, that of heat upon humidity," and plants too have cavities, "which heat attracts into them." Because these same natural processes apply to the growth of minerals, "we may observe these tokens of life in the production of minerals." But he concedes, this argument cannot be demonstrated; "because all nature's works are occult, and the instrument she uses [natural heat] is imperceptible, it is no wonder that it is hard to know truly how minerals hidden in the earth grow." The next speaker agrees that this analogy is an effective way to deal with what cannot be observed. Another concurs that heat affects minerals, but, since minerals show no signs of the internal processes of life such as "nutrition, equal and uniform augmentation in all their parts," he concludes, "the bark, roots, and veins attributed to them have nothing but the shape of those things." Thus the analogy between the growth of living things and the growth of minerals is unpersuasive. This position refutes that of Cardano, who argued that minerals closely resembled plants and animals (complete with digestive organs), and of Claves (who, scholars believe, attended the conferences), who argued that the generation and nutrition of stones could be demonstrated.[63] Ultimately, conferees who address geological topics are interested in testing their general sense of the operations of nature against specific geological manifestations. Because the growth of minerals is unobservable, it promotes the same kinds of skeptical responses that occult topics elicit.

A conference on a very similar topic, "Of the generation of metals,"[64] produces a much less skeptical response. It allows participants to bring to bear a number of suppositions about the organization of nature and about the relationship between kinds of metals. The first speaker defines a metal as "a mineral, solid, opaque, heavy, malleable, ductile, and sounding body, . . . compounded by either nature, art, or chance," offering his audience many different ways to understand both metals and their manufacture. He claims that there are seven kinds of metals, corresponding to seven planets and making metal a concrete demonstration of the macrocosm-microcosm relationship. He also describes the growth of metals in terms of Aristotelian causation. "Their general efficient cause is heaven, by its motion and influences producing heat, which attenuates and concocts the said exhalation, which is afterward condensed by cold." Such a wide range of definitions makes metals relevant to a host of scientific positions. This malleability of defining terms might explain the great attraction of geological topics for conferees.

The second speaker distinguishes between the initial generation of metals at the beginning of the world (in mines from which they were extracted by Tubalcain) and their subsequent generation "by the afflux of suitable matter, which is a metallic juice formed of humidity, not simply aqueous (for then heat should evaporate instead of concocting it), but viscous, unctuous, and somewhat terrestrial." He directly correlates his understanding of metals with that of the chemists. The chemists "compound them [metals] of sulfur and mercury; sulfur, holding the place of the male seed, and mercury, which is more crude and aqueous, that of the maternal blood." Because the sulfur or mercury of the chemists renders metals malleable, it is comparable to the "viscous, unctuous, and somewhat terrestrial" quality he has described. He points to some of the advantages of a chemical analysis of minerals, which allows the chemists to proclaim "the easy transmutation of one into another; imperfect metals differing only in certain accidental degrees from gold and silver, which they may be turned into after refining by nature or art." He suggests that "the opinion of some moderns," who consider "the earth a great magnet," supports transmutation, since "the power of heat in the bowels of the earth" formed all metals, from the least perfect, iron, to the most perfect, gold. Despite some reliance on Aristotelian terminology, he essentially subscribes to a chemical understanding of the production of metals and their subsequent transmutation, ultimately, into gold.[65]

While conceding that transmutation is possible, the next speaker insists there can be no common source of all minerals: "the different properties of metals plainly argue the diversity of their species." He considers the chemists' claim—that, because nature tends toward perfection, it always makes gold—to be a misunderstanding of what a tendency to perfection entails. Nature's intention is "not to reduce everything to one most perfect species, as all metals to gold; but to make a most perfect individual in every species." Furthermore, the world "would have been very defective, if nature had made only gold, which may be better spared than iron and steel." Indeed, if nature intended to transmute all metals into gold, it "should be more plentiful than iron and lead; since wise and potent nature seldom fails of her intentions."

Another speaker disputes the conclusions drawn from chemistry. He insists that transmutation does not prove all metals are derived from the same species, since "change of species being very ordinary and as easily made in crucibles as in mines." Nor should transmutation be considered an alchemical skill; "nothing else being necessary but to open the bodies of the metals, and set at liberty what is in some most active and in others more susceptible to the forms you would introduce." He points out that, although the chemists agree that the components of metals are salt, sulfur, and mercury, they disagree as to the relationship between the three elements and in describing the differences between kinds of metals.

It is important to note that, in all of the discussion of the growth of minerals, the speakers espouse some of the chemists' views, although some are skeptical about some specific chemical beliefs, like transmutation. Despite a general adherence to a chemical understanding, conferees also appeal to more orthodox sources such as Aristotle or Anaxagoras. Some criticize traditional sources on the basis of logical consistency. Conferees appreciate some aspects of what the chemists offer as a way to understand the earth, but they also object to the rigid imposition of a system on nature.

When they consider the topic of earthquakes, participants rely on common empirical information about the phenomenon. They recognize that earthquakes are more pronounced in certain locations and that they are marked by fissures in the surface of the earth and elevation or subsidence of mountain surfaces. They are accompanied by rumbling noises, great sea waves, and hot or cold exhalations from the earth. (This last quality leads participants to associate earthquakes with volcanoes.) Because earthquakes are such impressive events, they are generally described as "elemental forces of nature" and are treated as the results of the activity of a specific element.[66] Geological phenomena like earthquakes impress on conferees the limits of their understanding, and this recognition may also underlie their desire to present this material so extensively to their auditors and readers. In the case "Of the earthquake,"[67] the first speaker finds that the phenomenon challenges his understanding of nature because "irregular motions are as strange as regular are agreeable." This unease is magnified when irregularity characterizes those "bodies designated to rest, as the earth is, being the immovable center about which the whole fabric of the world is turned." Despite his sense that earthquakes violate the stolidity of the earth, he notes that there is historical evidence of "every age having experiences of earthquakes." Just as his view of the earth has been shaken (both literally and figuratively), so too, the new sciences have forced him to emend at least partially his view of the heavens. As he puts it, "though the whole heaven cannot rest, any more than the whole earth move, yet the parts of them may."

Another speaker assumes on the basis of accounts by Aristotle, Pliny, and geographers that new islands appear as a result of earthquakes. He cites the common belief about the cause of earthquakes as "a dry exhalation, which makes a concussion in the belly of the earth . . . when it cannot otherwise get free from its confinement." Another commentator complicates the discussion, pointing to the various causes of earthquakes as "either divine, or astrological, or physical." In some cases, the cause is "the will of God, who often thereby manifests to men his justice and power." The astrological causes are "the malignant influences of Jupiter and Mars." Although he cites these causes, he does not subscribe to either of them: "the first are too general," and the second "are very uncertain, being built for the most part, upon false principles." He also doubts explanations that "suppose the earth a great animal, whose tremors are made in the same manner as those which befall other animals." Instead he concurs "with Democritus that torrents of rain coming to fill the concavities of the earth by their impetuousness delve out the other waters, and that, upon their motion and swaying from one side to another, . . . these torrents drive out the winds impetuously . . . and agitate the earth until it sends some issue."

Another speaker disagrees, "since if it were so, then the whole earth should tremble at the same time, which is contrary to experience." If water caused earthquakes, "regions and whole countries" would "cleave and crackle" like the earth in a drought. Instead he contends that a body as ponderous as the earth must be moved by "the most active of all agents, which is fire." The magnitude of the earthquake depends on the character of the fire; "if it be nitrous, they are very violent . . . [if] bituminous, the tremors are moderate." This speaker thus relies on both Anaxagoras's belief in the centrality of fire and Cardano's specific description of the qualities of that fire.

The next speaker claims to draw no conclusions about the earth's motion but suggests instead an analogy as a way to understand earthquakes. "Without determining the famous question of the earth's motion (it may be said that it moves about the heavens as a stone in a circle), it would have the same tremors and titubations as those which astronomers attributed to the bodies of planets, besides the regular motions of their spheres." He thus makes earthquakes part of the "regular motion" of the earth. Through the safe qualifier of an analogy, he describes the earth as one of the planets.

Volcanoes too are difficult to make sense of as the first speaker in "Of volcanoes or subterranean fires"[68] concedes: "subterranean fires are no less manifest than their cause is unknown." He also points out that investigating volcanoes has proved dangerous, having occasioned the death of Pliny. Thus, although "the artifice of man has indeed excavated the entrails of the earth," he has not been able to investigate volcanic fire, "which like a savage beast, devours everything it meets." A speaker supports the understanding of the Pythagoreans on fire against the Aristotelians, suggesting "that fire being the principal agent of nature, necessary to all sorts of generations . . . is likewise found everywhere, especially in the earth." He also describes fire in Paracelsian terms: "the matter of all fire is any oily, fat, and aerious body." Two kinds of subterranean fires, sulfurous and bituminous, produce volcanoes.[69]

Another speaker copes with limited knowledge about volcanoes by resorting to an analogy; both the earth and the air operate in an analogous manner in the three distinct regions defined by differences in temperature, which produce different kinds of exhalations. In the second region of the earth, these exhalations "meet with cold spaces, which being for the most part hollow or cavernous, and stored with sulfur, bitumen, and other fat earths, become inflamed by the anti-peristasis of cold and the proximity of those materials." The oils of the earth feed the fire and thus explain the ongoing nature of volcanic activity. His sense of the unity of natural operations leads him to dismiss other prominent explanations for persistent volcanic action, such as "combustible matter in the bellies of mountains," or "an inextinguishable fire, or perpetual light." These kinds of explanations, he contends, presume that nature acts inconsistently, irrationally, or in ways that do not correspond to human understanding. Instead, he insists, even though nature's means are beyond those of art, they are nonetheless, analogous and thus comprehensible. The operations of nature in volcanoes can be compared to other natural actions, and the legitimacy of the comparison allows participants to bring empirical evidence to bear. For example, the volcano's "activity is sufficient to attract or fetch in its sulfurous food, which being only an excrement of the earth, and like the soot of our chimneys, is found everywhere, but especially in mines."[70]

A number of conferences treat the geological material of the earth. "On the origin of precious stones"[71] distinguishes between common stones and precious stones. Many participants assume that nature takes greater care with those things we value. Although all stones "are compounded of the four elements, chiefly of water and earth, but diversely proportioned and elaborated, . . . precious stones have more of water and less of earth, both very pure and simple . . . and exactly mixed by heat . . . to a most perfect degree." Since the product of this process is extraordinary, one speaker supposes that it must be produced "by help of that universal spirit, with which the earth and whole world is filled." Another speaker refines this discussion, adding a Paracelsian element, "a certain lapidisic [stony] juice supplying the place of seed and often observed dropping down from rocks." This theory of lapidifying juice drew on Agricola's *De re metallica,* which posited a kind of fluid circulating through the earth's crust; under certain circumstances this fluid could turn other substances into stone.[72] According to this speaker, if this lapidisic juice is "thick and viscous," it produces common stones, "if subtle and pure, the precious." Thus while the initial speaker suggests that nature takes special care with precious stones, most insist that, although they have extraordinary qualities and value, precious stones are produced by ordinary natural processes. A speaker asserts that "Nature (when she designs to enclose her majesty in the luster of the most glittering jewels) is nothing else but humidity condensed by cold."

Another speaker objects, pointing out that if cold produced precious metals they could not be found in warm locations. As a result, we must look for something in them other than cold water. He lays out a kind of research agenda that might accurately determine the character of precious stones. "We must examine the principles of bodies most akin to them as alum and glass, which by their splendor and consistency most resemble precious stones." Indian glass, because of its close resemblance to precious stones, can tell us something about them. It "has no other principles but a spirit mingled with much salt and some little of earth, which are united by the activity of heat, and condensed." Despite his commitment to a comparative investigation, he concludes that "divers species are made according to the different impressions of heaven or the place of their generation." A final speaker offers an even more mystical explanation: "It is most probable that in the beginning there were species of stones of all sorts . . . that have continually generated the like, determining fit matter by the emission of a certain vapor or spirit, impregnated with the character of their species during its union with their substance." Precious stones prove an interesting topic for conferees because virtually every speaker assumes that "preciousness" resides in the stone itself. As a result, they must discuss the natural process that produces the clarity of these stones as in some way distinct from the process that creates more ordinary stones.

When participants turn their attention to the question "On the origin of mountains,"[73] they consider a topic on which ancient writings were less extensive than most of the geological topics they consider. (The topic preoccupied other early modern thinkers such as Leonardo da Vinci and Nicolaus Steno, who studied the erosion of mountains.) Perhaps because this topic had fewer ancient antecedents, conferees quite uncharacteristically move beyond natural explanation and invoke the argument from design. Because God created the world in perfection, "it was requisite there should be plains, mountains, and valleys upon the earth, without which agreeable variety, there would be no proportion to its parts." The speaker uses Galileo's discovery of the unevenness of the surface of the moon both to assert his support for Galileo and to argue that such mountains belong to the notion of perfection. These mountains, he insists, "cannot reasonably be attributed to any cause but His primary construction." This is a clever way to reconcile Galileo's discovery of mountains on the moon with the traditional notion of the perfect spheres of heaven. The speaker simply changes the notion of perfection to one of proportion—valleys and mountains are necessary for proportion and therefore for perfection.

This sleight of argument does not fool the next speaker who insists that the proportions of the heavens and earth are "sufficiently manifested in the correspondence of the four elements with the heavens" and does not include craggy mountains. God's work demonstrates "the prejudice for perfection that is found in the spherical figure." These perfect spheres obviously do not have mountains disrupting their spherical shapes. When "it was time to render the earth habitable to animals,"

God created valleys with their inevitable by-products, mountains. (This speaker may be suggesting an allegorical reading of the creation account, because surely God would not have created the world as a perfect sphere on the first day and then as craggy, imperfect, but suitable for human habitation a mere six days later!)

Subsequent speakers suggest naturalistic explanations for the existence of mountains. One notes that, although some were undoubtedly part of the initial creation, others have been formed over the course of time "partly by rains and torrents, partly by winds and earthquakes." Another suggests that waters from the seas "impetuously entering into the caverns of the earth go winding along there till they find resistance, whereby their violence redoubled makes the earth rise in some places and so forms mountains." Another finds this explanation plausible and elaborates on it. "It is easy to conceive how waters running underground make breaches and abysses"; things that might seem prodigious are simply a matter of scale. Another speaker cites Copernicus's notion of the movement of the earth around the sun to suggest "that the several concussions it receives from that motion may possibly elevate one place and debase another."

When conferees raise the question of "Why a needle touched by a lodestone turns toward the north,"[74] they deal with a specific mineral, but they also have to contend with the mysticism generally associated with the lodestone: Anaxagoras described it as living; Pliny maintained that it had miraculous powers; Cardano emphasized (as he did other stones) its need for nutrition. As is their wont generally, conferees seek to assess mystical claims critically. One agrees with those who explain the phenomena by suggesting that, under the north pole, there is an island of Ilva with mountains of lodestones, which "diffuse their virtue over the whole earth, and so draw all lodestones and whatever iron is rubbed with them toward themselves." Another contends that, instead, this motion "ought rather to be ascribed to something in heaven, because in ships that approach that island of lodestone, the needle still tends toward the north, and not toward that island." Others relate the movement of needles toward the lodestone to the common phenomenon of sympathy: "The female palm bends toward the male, straw moves to amber. All flowers, and particularly the marigold and sunflower, incline toward the sun, the lodestone toward the iron." In other words, given our knowledge of sympathy at work in the universe, the action of the lodestone is not surprising. Another suggests that, because the lodestone is dry, it seeks the north as the "center of all waters." Another shares Cardano's opinion "that stones are animated, and consequently, that the soul of the lodestone carries it to search for its food and its good," that is to say, the iron filings that nourish it.[75] These explanations amply demonstrate the difficulties involved in explaining attraction. These are the same kinds of comparisons that will be used to discuss Newtonian gravity some fifty years later. But as a final speaker points out, all of the arguments advanced by previous speakers "leave many difficulties to be resolved." To cite the heavens as the cause does not make it less obscure, and "the terms of sympathy and antipathy differ not much from those who profess naked ignorance." Although conferees seek to rationalize the phenomenon, their position is similar to that suggested by d'Alembert in the *Preliminary Discourse* when he concedes that magnetism may remain unknown or occult.[76]

Participants generally adhere to the prohibition against introducing religion into the conferences, but the more abstract the topic, the more likely it is to provoke a religious response. A question such as "Whether the world grows old"[77] might look like a question of cosmology, but it raises the topical, religious issue of using the Bible to establish the age of the earth. Thus a participant questions the entire discussion, on the basis of the Bible, "since the end of the world is to be supernatural, it shall not proceed from old age." Other speakers treat the question more naturalistically. One draws a fundamental distinction: if by "world" is meant "all the inferior bodies contained under the concave of the moon, it is certain that it changes," but if "world" includes the heavens, it cannot grow old, "for the heavens are not altered." He considers the aging of the sublunary world likely and the result of natural processes, which he explains in the following way: "it is impossible that the elements acting so powerfully one against another by their contrary qualities would not be weakened and their activities impaired." From the world he extrapolates to man's position. As all things in the world have become more susceptible to decay, man's position too is more vulnerable. Because both we and the food we eat suffer this augmenting decay, we are much shorter-lived than our forefathers. Our declining life span reflects the degeneration of the earth. "Our fathers of old . . . in the flower of the world's age . . . lived almost a thousand years . . . but at present few attain to eighty." This decline, he insists, has had social ramifications. It is reflected in the decline of the "virtues and arts," in the "depravation of manners," and in the proliferation of "laws and ordinances." One speaker is sharply skeptical of the accounts of the great age attained by men in earlier ages. He doubts that men lived as long as they do in the present century, and if they did, their long life "may be attributed to a special privilege of God." Another speaker also disputes this sense of decay of the world and makes a most positive statement about the future: "the world is so far from growing worse, that on the contrary it becomes more perfect."

A conference on the topic "Of the flowing and ebbing of the sea"[78] adopts an unusual format in that participants ask related questions, which others respond to in the course of the conference. The first speaker asks "whether there be any other cause of this flux than the heaping together of the waters from the beginning under the equinox?" The next speaker responds that "the moon indeed makes the flux and reflux of the sea greater or less . . . because being at the full she causes a rarefaction of its waters," but then he asks, "why also does not she move the other seas, and all sorts of waters, as well as the ocean?" Another posits a separation of the waters of the sea, "one earthy, thick, and vaporous, which contains the salted, the other thin, sweet, and vaporous." He also answers the question "Why have not lakes also an ebbing and flowing?" It is, he explains, because their waters, "being more thin, let pass those vapors which the sun has stirred." For another speaker, this system of flux and reflux resonates within the human body "by the motion of reciprocation, called the pulse, consisting of a diastole and a systole (or dilation and contraction), caused by the vital faculty of the heart, the fountain of heat." This is an interesting parallel between the tides and the circulatory system. He subscribes to circulation because he also believes, as did Descartes and many of his contemporaries, that the heart is the source of natural heat. He concludes that the heart must act on the body as the sun does on the water of the seas.

Conferees treat a question that had preoccupied the earliest writings on the nature of the earth, that is to say, Where do springs come from? Most sources, including scriptural sources, claim that streams come from great reservoirs within the earth. Aristotle offered three concrete possibilities: rainwater that has penetrated the earth's crust, or water that has formed within the earth either by the condensation of air or from the condensation of vapors rising from the surface of the earth. The water that does not form into reservoirs is held in the mountains like a sponge. Bernard Palissy's work of 1580, *Discours Admirable de la Nature des Eaux et fontaines,* might well have provided a topical source for participants when they considered "Of the origin of fountains"[79] (by which speakers mean "springs"). The first speaker contends that "all rivers go into the sea, but the sea is not thereby increased." The seas do not rise because "the gravity of the earth, always inclining toward its own center, bears upon the sea, and pressing upon the water, causes it to rise up into the veins and passages of the earth." Another speaker offers two other explanations. The first, based on his understanding of nature, asserts "that the waters are carried upward by the virtue of the celestial bodies." If this explanation is not persuasive, he suggests that we might ascribe "this effect to God . . . [who] caused the water in the beginning to ascend to the highest places." It is interesting that he first explains the phenomenon by the effects of the heavens on the earth, and he suggests the argument from design only if his first explanation fails to persuade.

Geological topics, like other kinds of scientific discussions, allow speakers to present various ideas, to juxtapose them against each other, to call into question or even winnow out certain kinds of arguments (the vulgar, the astrological, and so on). But what is missing is in many ways as interesting as what is presented on these topics. Participants do occasionally insert arguments based on the argument from design, but these are rare and are not especially significant in structuring their understanding of nature or geological phenomena. Geological topics are the most likely to elicit this argument, which is understandable because such topics more clearly deal with the formation and configuration of the world. When conferees consider the rationale for metals, streams, or other basic configurations of the world, they look to God. His intention to provide for his creatures, especially man, sometimes shapes the explanations they offer. However, it is significant that the argument from design is less prominent, even in geological topics, than was common to works of the early modern period; it is mentioned in these contexts but does not shape geological speculation.

Many contemporary texts describe the operations of the earth in more mystical terms, explicitly connecting the explorations of the earth to a quest for salvation. For example, Samuel Ward compared the effects of the lodestone to the effects of ministers in their quest to gain souls for Christ and claimed that the power of the lodestone is a reflection of Christ's goodwill toward man.[80] It is significant that this sense is entirely lacking in the conferences. They also do not reflect contemporary attempts to use geological evidence to support biblical chronology; when conferees discuss the age of the world, Aristotle rather than the Bible is the important source. They do not, as so many of their contemporaries did, anchor their geological theories with biblical evidence or present evidence to conform to the Bible. Although they use concrete information derived from the newer work of chemists on the nature of the earth, they nowhere propose a mystical chemical creation account, which was so common to chemical texts. It is noteworthy that there is no discussion of mythology, only one brief discussion of the age of the earth, and participants avoid becoming embroiled in the theological quagmire provoked by fossils. In these respects, the conferees foreshadow the positions of eighteenth-century thinkers such as Nicolas Demarest, who insisted on separating the geological and theological.[81]

But why did the conferences focus so extensively on geological topics? What does this emphasis allow us to conclude about their notions of science? Geological topics offer participants ways to present knowledge that they must have found particularly attractive. These topics afford more opportunity both to provide specific information and to use more recent views and texts to challenge ancient authorities. Conferees assert opinions of their own or of an iconoclast such as Paracelsus to quarrel with venerable figures such as Aristotle or Pythagoras. They clearly have the sense that the new sciences have opened up questions about the earth. They are better able to see, apparently, the possibilities offered by the new science for criticisms of particulars rather than for wholesale rejection of the old and replacement with something new.[82] Participants expand the kinds of arguments used and the kinds of evidence deemed valuable. On geological topics, it is vividly clear that not only is there no desire to impose a consensus but there is also a very real sense that there are no definitive answers to these questions. Many of these topics do not provoke contention; there are too many possibilities for one to be challenged directly by another.

The interest in geology, like the interest in occult topics, reflects a willingness by most speakers to suggest possibility rather than certainty. They are, in other words, comfortable with ambiguity. They are especially interested in the areas of scientific discussion where certainty does not seem possible. They are not distressed by relative claims to knowledge or by multiple explanations of the same phenomenon—this is indicated not simply by multiple speeches on each topic, but also within the speeches of individuals. These discussions offer a position of epistemological modesty, an overt recognition of the limits of human knowledge, limits that make it appropriate to acknowledge the relative, but at the same time limits that are not so restrictive they force a retreat into skepticism. Although such skills gave participants a way to address natural phenomena, they do not produce what we consider the modern form of the science of geology or of biology or offer a new paradigm to unseat Aristotle.

Frequently, because the late seventeenth century is read backward and Newtonian science and its reception is heralded as paradigmatic, our notion of significant science is restricted to the physical sciences, mathematics, and astronomy. These sciences demonstrate dramatic developments and more readily support the argument that the mechanistic paradigm replaced the Aristotelian. But questions of the day were just as focused on the "life sciences" and the geological sciences where the shifts of opinion are less compelling and thus less well incorporated into the history of science. The conferences show such a pronounced interest in the life sciences that perhaps some of our suppositions about the prevailing character of seventeenth-century science should be revised.

By the mid–seventeenth century Aristotle could no longer be acknowledged as the "master of those who know." Some of his fundamental teachings on form, matter, motion, and the void had been called into question by d'Alembert's heroic triumvirate of Bacon, Galileo and Descartes. The view of science enshrined by these three and others used mathematics as a foundation for understanding the universe and applied experimental and observational methods much more extensively than Aristotle had. But, as Charles Schmitt has emphasized, it was unusual for early modern thinkers to completely divorce their understanding from that of Aristotle, and historians of science have been much too inclined to accept such claims uncritically, taking them at face value. Recent studies by historians and philosophers of science have documented the pervasive Aristotelian influences on defining figures of the scientific revolution, even those who most vigorously distinguished themselves from him.[83] Schmitt himself has documented the widely diverse "Aristotelianisms" of the Renaissance, which extend well into the eighteenth century.[84] Despite the critiques of Aristotle with which we are so familiar, Aristotelianism could continue to exert influence because it was so eclectic that it could readily incorporate the new, as its early modern commentators demonstrated. For example, during the Renaissance, Platonism and the hermetic tradition were adapted to Aristotle by many commentators.[85] The Jesuits, who as the preeminent educators at the secondary level may have influenced the young Descartes's view of the world, also effectively combined Aristotelianism with mathematics and modern science.[86] Some historians have blamed or praised Renaudot's conferences because they do or do not reflect coherent Aristotelianism. Given the plurality of "Aristotelianisms" of the Renaissance (a plurality even more marked in the sixteenth and seventeenth centuries because of the proliferation of printing), consistent Aristotelianism seems an inappropriate expectation for an eclectic seventeenth-century group.[87]

So what role do these conferences play in the story of the scientific revolution? First of all, they address in a concrete way the legacy of Aristotle and provide a telling case study of how his influence continued to be both incorporated and eroded. In these conferences, Aristotelian terminology was used, but it no longer had the systematic coherence of scholasticism. Words were no longer used with fidelity to their Aristotelian context. Second, the conferences treat a number of scientific and philosophical topics that are of central concern to the scientific revolution. As such they tell us something about how those issues were perceived by those who were receptive to but not innovators in that tradition, how individuals meshed the new with the old and how they argued for the new. The conferences thus serve as important documents indicating the penetration and diffusion of the new science. Finally, participants were acutely interested in the sciences most directly related to observation, like geology. Geological discussion relied on observation and demonstrated an attempt to apply critical reason to conflicting accounts. Participants attempted to subject observation to rational analysis.

Because the history of science has privileged astronomy and physics as the keys to its positivist and theoretical accounts of the scientific revolution, the biological and natural sciences do not play much of a role in the saga. As Schmitt has pointed out, the role of Aristotle in the scientific revolution would be far different if the biological sciences were seen as central. This would mean, for example, that William Harvey, the heroic figure of early modern biology, would have to play a larger role, and he was deeply indebted to Aristotle and effusive in appreciation of him. Such an approach to the scientific revolution would better explain or incorporate the interest in the occult and the so-called pseudo-sciences that was prevalent as "modern" science took hold.[88]

Although Renaudot's conferees consider topics drawn from new astronomical discoveries and from issues of perception raised by the new science, they do not subscribe to any standard modern notion of the scientific method. Although the hour following their two-hour discussion was dedicated to the discussion of experiments, these were considered much less significant than the discussion of the topic before the group. (The experiment itself is only mentioned for the first few conferences.) Members of the group do occasionally refer to a specific experiment, but it is not reported as definitive. Participants do not spell out the circumstances or suggest that through testing and independent corroboration an experiment could become definitive. Instead, when a speaker cites a specific experiment, it retains its early association with experience. Experiments are not privileged as a different or more compelling kind of experience or data; experimental results are reported as equivalent to any other kind of experience or the remarks of any other speaker.

Although conferees disparaged scholasticism, just like any other group that wanted to identify itself with the forces of progress, nonetheless some of the topics raised were conventional thesis questions treated in scholastic *disputationes* by degree aspirants in philosophy, theology, or medicine. Participants could also have seen their use of the form of a university defense as innovative. From a modern perspective, however, the form seems mired in the past. Many of the arguments made by individual speakers reflect some version of Aristotle and do not look forward to Descartes or Boyle. Although they make some nods to atomism or mechanism, participants are equally likely to point to the innovations of Paracelsus. Despite their own confidence in the innovation of their discussions, it is difficult to claim the conferences for the new science, as we understand it. Participants did not particularly appreciate experiments or mathematics; they did not replace old views of nature with mechanism. But this does not separate them from their contemporaries.

The historiography of early modern science has been characterized by contentious battles over the legitimate topics for inclusion—over what, in essence, is admissible in the telling of the tale. The earliest and most conventional accounts are positivistic and highly selective. They focus on heroic figures and practices and perspectives that most clearly conform to the later understanding of science. Such accounts pluck Copernicus, Galileo, and Newton from their historical contexts in order to raise them to the status of pre-modern geniuses and thus to read a modern scientific sensibility backward—to find in the past an emphasis on the mathematical, the measurable, the experimental, and other hallmarks of modern science. The historiography of the history of science has been not simply positivistic but also driven by theory-centered accounts, which presuppose that the history of science is the history of the competition of theories with the inevitable triumph of the true theory. Renaudot's conferences suggest a more complex story of the evolution of scientific ideas.

Recent studies have challenged earlier accounts by placing the heroic figures in their historical contexts, not to debunk them but to demonstrate the ways in which science is embedded in culture. Since the early modern period is the beginning of a three-century-long evolution (it is of course strange to use the abrupt cataclysmic term "revolution" to describe this long period of change in the understanding of how to study nature), historians of science have tended to concentrate on this period. They have found much in the study of nature by seventeenth-century figures that does not seem modern. Many of the profound influences on these great figures of modern science, such as hermeticism and alchemy, were clearly "unscientific" by modern lights. These myriad ways of approaching nature have inevitably provoked interest from those who want to expand the notion of science to more accurately reflect the variety of early modern culture, but they have received some resistance from scholars who want to include only what seems entirely modern.[89] The fundamental question raised by this difference of perspective is, If one restricts the notion of science to its narrowed or modern connotation, can one write a history of early modern science? Can one reasonably consider any early modern figure as fulfilling a narrow notion of science?

The treatment of Aristotle in the conferences, the exploration of topics of the new science and its epistemological implications, and especially the interest of conferees in the sciences such as geology that are rooted in observation, all urge us to see the conferences as helping both to broaden our understanding of science in the early seventeenth century and to redefine where its center lay. This broader understanding of science must focus explicitly on the natural sciences, sciences in which observation counts more than experiment and critical analysis more than theoretical application and deduction. Without such broadening and redefinition, we would continue to interpret who the central figures and what the central sciences of the early modern period were in a way that is more congenial to us than perhaps to those who lived then. At the center of early modern science we would continue to place what looks most like us.

As the preceding discussion of science in the conferences amply demonstrates, Renaudot's conferences belong in the historiographical debate. Of course, the narrower the notion of science, the less appropriate it is to include Renaudot's group in that history. If one insists on the specialized character of the scientist as a professional, as an experimenter, as a member of a scientific academy, then the members of Renaudot's group (although some were practicing physicians or significant scientific thinkers) should not be included. If one insists that science in the early modern period entails adherence to mechanism, an emphasis on measurement and mathematics, and a cultivation of the experiment[90] to the exclusion of other early modern approaches to nature such as hermeticism, alchemy, and Paracelsianism, then the conferences have only the slightest relevance to the history of science.

Renaudot's group does meet other notions of what "science" entails, however. In their basic attitudes toward the nature of science and scientific knowledge, the conferees can be appropriately associated with the scientific revolution. If the scientific revolution privileges "science" as providing a unique perspective from which to describe "how things really are,"[91] then Renaudot's conferences did make an important contribution, privileging science as a way to know not only nature but also society. In this respect Renaudot's conferences in fact look beyond the scientific revolution.

Much seventeenth-century discussion privileged mathematics and physics as a persuasive solution to the crisis of knowledge provoked by skepticism. But if it were necessary to name a single science that best reflects the approach of conferees, that science would not be physics or mathematics, the hallmark sciences of the new science. It might be geology, the concern of a number of conferences, but more likely it would be medicine. Medicine, because of the utilitarian benefits it afforded, served as the model for science in the conferences.

CHAPTER FIVE

Of Physiognomy, Smallpox, and the Bezoard

Health, Disease, and Medical Therapy

W HEN RENAUDOT'S GROUP GATHERED TO DISCUSS TOPICS OF general concern, medicine was consistently cited as a crucial area of investigation; it could most immediately ameliorate the human condition.[1] Perhaps this opinion was so frequently expressed because some of the participants were reform-minded physicians who staffed Renaudot's clinics. But medicine was a difficult discipline to grapple with in the seventeenth century, as speakers readily acknowledge. For one thing, it was virtually all-encompassing. In this sense, speakers were carrying through on a notion of medicine that goes back to the Roman physician Galen (129–200 A.D.).[2] One participant in the conference "On life"[3] characterized the range of medicine's mission as "to govern nature." He noted that it was also difficult to classify and categorize medical phenomena, and most important, medicine had life and death ramifications. He warns that in medicine, maxims *must not* be formed for, "in medicine as in law, no two cases are the same." Conferees acknowledge, as do modern historians, that seventeenth-century medicine is characterized by theoretical disputes, incoherent method, lack of practical application, and limited claims to knowledge. They frankly admit that medicine, in the quest for effective treatments, offers bizarre ingredients that are inexplicably effective. "Indeed," one speaker notes, "if you take away all cures wrought by occult and inexplicable means, there will be nothing admirable in Physick."[4]

Problematic as it is in these conferences, medicine is illuminating for several reasons. First and most generally, medical analysis is applied to a broad array of issues in an eclectic and nondogmatic fashion and explicitly invokes the highest empirical standards. Second, the conferences themselves were designed to be reformist and thus open to more unconventional medical opinion. Third, because the conferences were not exclusively medical, they provide a good way to look at the cultural role that medicine played, especially how it informed other opinions, values, and social issues. Fourth, since the conferences occupy a specific cultural niche (that is, because participants were the educated but not exclusively the academically educated), they can tell us about the extent of medical knowledge available below the highest professional and educational level. (To the degree that the opinions expressed are those of professional physicians, they are outside the Paris Faculty of Medicine.) Another significant factor in the medical import of the conferences is Renaudot's interest in innovative medical practice. Most important for this study, medicine offers a paradigmatic science that can be applied productively to social issues.

While the central role of medicine in a series of conferences open to all topics might be unexpected, science was clearly of great interest to the layman in the seventeenth century, and medicine was the science most accessible to him.[5] Educated laymen would have been generally familiar with the humoral theory of Galen (the four humors of black bile, yellow bile, phlegm, and blood) as a way of understanding health, disease, individual disposition, and intelligence. Hippocratic medicine also enjoyed new currency in the seventeenth century.[6] It offered a commonsense view of medicine; it was predicated on concern with the environment and diet, questions the layman might weigh just as successfully as the professional. The layman shared with the physician an understanding of medicine as loosely attached to humoral theory and supported by encyclopedic information derived from the arts, sciences, and curiosities. Medicine had not made a decisive break from its past by the seventeenth century. Because there had been no medical revolution, no crucial new developments isolated the layman from the professional practitioner. The common currency of medical information, medicaments, and reasoning explains in part the vehemence with which the medical establishment defended its prerogatives and the obscurantism to which some medical practitioners resorted, even though it subjected them to devastating ridicule by critics like Molière. But, as a result of a shared perspective, no chasm of information or education would compel the layman to silence on medical topics, even in the presence of medical professionals.

Medical theory was not an irrelevant abstraction for the layman but instead directly relevant to his everyday experience. From the mid-sixteenth century on, a number of physicians, able to take advantage of the printing press and the market for medical information, sought to disseminate their work to a wider audience by writing in the vernacular and by offering self-medication texts for the layman.[7] Physicians recognized, as did their contemporaries in religion and other kinds of controlled knowledge, that the printing press was inherently subversive. It could be used to undermine the authority of Galen, or, as Ambroise Paré, the prominent sixteenth-century surgeon, had, to argue for the surgeons against the authority of the doctors.[8] Medicine was a common intellectual coin of the realm. Medical vocabulary infiltrated common parlance and medical metaphors were common analogies in social and political theories. Medicine was also the focus of the ever-present concerns with health and morbidity. Given the permeation of medicine in the culture of early modern France, it is perhaps not surprising that these participants reveal sophisticated knowledge in debates about the underlying premises of medicine, the nature of various diseases, and appropriate therapies. It seems highly likely, given Renaudot's iconoclastic refusal to privilege authorities, that both layman and physician spoke on medical topics.

Although some medical topics proposed for discussion strike the modern reader as peculiar, they generally correspond to the kinds of theses medical students were expected to defend. Some seventeenth-century thesis topics include: "Was the cure of Tobias by the gall of fish natural?"; "Is it beneficial to health to get drunk once a month?"; "Are beautiful women more apt to bear children?"; "What do you think of the saying *in vino veritas?*"[9] Renaudot's nemesis, Guy Patin, defended the following thesis topics before the Faculty of Medicine just before the conferences began. "Is the transformation of a woman into a man impossible?" "Are baths useful in uteromania?" (He answered both of these in the affirmative.) Topics such as these might strike us as peculiar, but they presumably allowed the medical faculty to determine something significant about the candidates' level of education. Similar topics also allowed conferees to present their views on health, disease, and medical treatment. However, the use of these topics in Renaudot's conferences can be distinguished from their use by the Faculty in several significant respects. First, ironically, many of Renaudot's conferences are much more narrowly directed to specific diseases than was characteristic of medical theses. Second, medical theses, in keeping with the emphasis of medical education in seventeenth-century Paris, treat topics by expounding on the ancient texts.[10] Renaudot's conferees do not rely on the presentation of arguments from the ancients, although the medicine of Hippocrates and Galen is critical background to their medical discussions.

From the Middle Ages onward, the dominant concepts of health and disease were derived from the ancients, and especially from the works of Galen, who fused the philosophy of Aristotle with Hippocrates' observations into a rational system of treating disease. Galen's understanding of health and disease as fundamentally connected to the balance of the humors was pervasive and tied together the worlds of elite and popular medicine. As Brockliss and Jones repeatedly emphasize in their study of medicine in early modern France, Galenism was a "critical, dynamic, and plastic medical philosophy," well able to incorporate new ideas.[11]

What did Galenism mean in the seventeenth century? Physicians were indebted to fundamental Aristotelian premises that all things are composed of matter and form and that there was a radical distinction to be drawn between lunary and sublunary bodies. On earth, bodies were unstable and variable. The heavens were filled with changeless bodies. All earthly things were composed of the four elements of earth, air, water, and fire in varying proportions. The human body could be understood in the same terms. It too was unstable, composed of the four humors or bodily fluids. But the application of Aristotle was exceedingly flexible, even in discussing Aristotelian terms. It was even more flexible as applied to concrete discussions of health and disease. But physicians generally rejected Galen's materialism by emphasizing with Aristotle that the soul was the form of the body; it directed the whole and was responsible for the critical functions of growth, nutrition, sensation, and thought. Galenic physiology emphasized the centrality of the liver for the creation of blood at the expense of Aristotle's emphasis on the heart. In light of this understanding of the human body, physiological differences between individuals were rooted in the preponderance of one fluid over another. Generally women were colder and moister than men. Climate was important, and the French were considered fortunate to live in the temperate zone, which was ideal in terms of body moisture.

Despite their familiarity with medical language, theories, and epistemology, and their confidence that these were meaningful ways to understand health and disease, conferees dealt with medical phenomena they frequently found difficult to explain. Just to point to several examples that produced widely varied conjectures, the connection between music and the bite of the tarantula and the magnetic cure of disease were acknowledged as difficult to determine. When confronted with these problematic relationships, participants brought a rationalist perspective to bear. They dismissed some arguments as illegitimate, pointing to them as the refuge of those who were not sufficiently skeptical or those who were inclined to rely on God as the ultimate explanation. Just as they did in discussing scientific topics, participants consistently distinguished between their own rational and empirical arguments and the opinions of the vulgar, based on ignorance, superstition, and credulity.

The explicit injunction at the outset of the conferences that each would speak on his own authority was generally adhered to in the medical conferences. This adherence is striking since medicine remained the science most wedded to authorities. The fact that participants did not use them extensively attests to their commitment to avoid the invocation of authority as much as possible. To the extent that they violate this injunction, they cite ancient authorities often to challenge them. When the topics refer to occult qualities, like the efficacy of amulets or talismans, participants draw examples from the works of Renaissance humanists such as Ficino and Pico della Mirandola.[12] When a speaker seeks to classify phenomena, Aristotle is likely to be his source of choice, although sometimes Plato is invoked to counter Aristotelian classifications.[13] On very rare occasions, a speaker refers to a modern work on a certain subject,[14] but he is always careful to refrain from mentioning the author's name (although it is clear from the way the remarks are made that the source would be known to the audience). This explicit avoidance of contemporary references indicates a serious effort to conform to the specified dictates of the preface that the conferences will not be used to aggrandize the opinions of any particular individual and that an opinion will not be considered as having greater authority by virtue of the person who holds it.

As a general rule, speakers invoke authorities most extensively when the topics are especially abstract, such as "Of life" or "Of death."[15] On such topics, perhaps because they are disinclined to use their own authority to define such ineffable abstractions, virtually all speakers begin with a definition derived from a citation. Cited figures include not only the most prominent and usual ancient sources such as Galen, Hippocrates, and Plato but also medieval thinkers like Avicenna, Thomas Aquinas, and Albert the Great. The phrase "if one believes" often prefaces a citation and perhaps most succinctly characterizes the attitude of participants toward authorities. (For example, in a conference "Of Bleeding,"[16] one speaker notes that blood is the site of the soul, "if one believes Galen.") Authorities are also regularly pitted against each other in order to discount the value of all such arguments. The almost irreverent use of authorities is just one manifestation of an attitude that characterizes most participants' remarks; they see themselves as critics of received opinion, hardheaded empiricists in their evaluation of evidence, and representatives of avant-garde opinion. Their frequent skeptical pronouncements best document these attitudes.

Because conferees believed that medicine was not only the most essential but also the most problematic field of investigation, they felt bound to maintain a critical sensibility. Certain tenets of medical theory warrant harsh criticism. For example, some speakers contend that temperament theory has long been recognized as being too simplistic.[17] Others rule out entire areas of investigation; physiognomy is sharply repudiated as a completely groundless basis of analysis.[18] One speaker scathingly dismisses the magnetic cure of disease, claiming that there is no reason to resort to "superstitious remedies."[19]

As part of their growing skepticism, participants distance themselves from what they see as misbegotten popular beliefs by dismissing them as fabulous. For instance, one speaker begins a conference on bleeding[20] with the rather disconcerting remark that the invention of bleeding is fabulously attributed to sea horses with too much blood, who rubbed against the rocks to make themselves bleed and then stanched the flow of blood with lemon. As the initial remark on the subject of bleeding, this example bears a particular burden. Associating it with popular opinion or legend as opposed to more learned opinion initially discredits the topic and sets a tone whereby other examples of this sort are less likely to be raised as credible by subsequent speakers. In contrast to this sort of nonsense, the speaker notes, physicians have correctly credited Galen with the invention of this singular remedy.

Although the generally skeptical tenor of the conferences is appealing, sometimes the critical perspective produces conclusions that jar the modern reader. For example, in a conference on sleepwalking,[21] one conferee derides the arguments developed by several previous speakers that airy spirits are responsible for sleepwalking because, he insists, these spirits are completely undemonstrable. But the solution he proposes to the vexing question of how to explain sleepwalking is strikingly at odds with his rigorous empiricism. He insists that, because there are cases of individual sleepers walking upside down on rafters and because no spirits could be that airy, the explanation is, of course, hobgoblins. Although the implications of a skeptical stance are not always persuasive from a modern perspective, skepticism is nonetheless important to the way in which participants structure their remarks; they rule out or avoid as much as possible discussion of the divine. They also narrow the focus to deliberately eschew authorities, the simplistic, and the popular. This epistemological modesty—both in terms of how topics should be discussed and what can be known—ties the approach to knowledge taken by these participants to the scientific revolution and suggests a legacy of gatherings of this kind to the Enlightenment.

UNDERSTANDING HEALTH AND DISEASE

The underlying suppositions about nature, such as its propriety and beneficence and the applicability of macrocosm-microcosm analysis, which participants bring to bear on other scientific topics, also color observations about health and disease. Diagnostic techniques are often rooted in a basic appreciation of correspondence theory. Participants' remarks about medical conditions and treatments are shaped by a general, but somewhat critical, notion of a correspondence between parts of the natural world. For example, the first speaker "On physiognomy" begins by noting that the intentions of the soul are most visible in "the countenance and . . . the eye seems to be the most faithful messenger of it." The second contends that physiognomy "is grounded upon the correspondence of the soul with the body. . . . If the body be sick, the soul is altered in its operations, as we see in high fevers."[22] Although some speakers make skeptical remarks about analogies based on correspondences, others continue to use analogies as an epistemologically compelling way to formulate arguments. Correspondences, they suggest, can be the basis of reasonable conjecture for diagnosis and treatment, but they are neither sufficient nor infallible.[23]

One reason for the prominence of medicine in the conferences is the vast extent of its domain. For example, a speaker, weighing the merits of chemical medicines, asserts that all the bodies below the moon have been created for the health of man; thus physicians judge the full range of nature's bounty as food, medication, or poison.[24] Participants are empowered by their understanding of nature. They believe that the natural world is created for man's benefit, that he is able to use his reason to understand nature, and that understanding is essential to his ability to direct nature to the interests of man. In the case of medicine, man's ability to manipulate the natural environment means that he can neutralize the harmful effects of some substances and thus render them innocuous or even beneficial to man. This sense of control does not depend on the control of the world as machine of the scientific revolution, but rather on an understanding of fundamental relationships like that of the macrocosm-microcosm.[25]

Conferees thoroughly discuss medical issues, specifically conditions of health, disease, preventive care, and treatment. This discussion suggests that either the level of medical information in the general population was quite high or that, as most scholars have assumed, a considerable number of physicians attended the conferences. The content of the medical discussion also indicates a high degree of self-medication by people at the social and educational level of these participants; many of the discussions of health and disease are directed toward prescriptive medical therapy of the sort that, if the symptoms are X, then do Y.

It might seem strange to us that there should be so much public dissemination of medical treatments. Many conferences expressly urge caution about the conditions under which treatments should be undertaken and issue many caveats about who should not be treated in a particular manner and about the improper preparation of medications. Perhaps participants consider all the warnings sufficient to curtail problematic treatment. But they also discuss diseases and treatment in a way clearly meant to diffuse medical information. Renaudot, acutely sensitive to the great need for medical services especially in rural areas, disseminated a questionnaire to rural physicians to be used as a basis for diagnosis. And he fought to make medical services more accessible to greater numbers. His entire medical career worked against the stranglehold of the Faculty of Paris. Because he advocated chemical medicine, which the Faculty certainly did not want promulgated, he favored the dissemination of knowledge as a way to effect reform. He and other participants might have felt that the dissemination of medical information, including therapeutic advice, was inherently laudable. These conferences thus prefigure the encylopedists in their efforts to make previously restricted information public.

Despite their intent to inform the public, speakers also grapple with a number of fundamental epistemological problems inherent to contemporary medicine, such as the basic question of the degree of certainty to which one can aspire. They regularly exhort their fellows to avoid generalizations, noting that "the more a man knows, the more he finds himself deterred from establishing maxims."[26] One speaker counters that "as there is but one straight line, and an infinite number of crooked, so too there is but one right manner of acting and infinite oblique . . . [in the treatment of] ephemera, fevers, and frenzies."[27] Speakers call for the highest critical standards when deciding what kinds of evidence to admit; physicians must "make a certain judgment upon external signs" and "heed must be taken that they be natural." (Several others find Galenic medicine too narrow a basis for medical analysis.)[28]

The conferences raise several interesting questions not only about the extent and certainty of medical knowledge but also the ways of presenting medical arguments. In discussing "Whether every disease has a specific remedy"[29] one speaker warns against the too broad categorization of remedies. Another complains that, although the axioms of medical practice may be persuasive, "when these rules come to be applied to practice, everyone confesses that he finds them not wholly correspondent to what he expected." This quote is a heartfelt acknowledgment of the difficulties medical practitioners face when they try to apply theoretical descriptions of diseases to the manifestations they confront. Another conferee points out the grave difficulties involved in determining the appropriate remedy, difficulties compounded because the efficacy of some remedies depends on their manifest qualities and others on their occult qualities.

This argument raises an epistemological dilemma for these participants. If the virtue or efficacy of certain medications is rooted in what cannot be seen, the hidden qualities of medications, then the value of empirical evidence is called into question. As one speaker puts it, "physick, invented at first by use and experience, has nothing to do with reasoning about things which fall manifestly under our senses, but only about those which surpass their comprehension." For most participants, the evidence of the senses is the foundation of medicine—but when experiences are "confirmed by reason," the grounds for certainty are even greater. One speaker insists that, "When reason seems repugnant to experience, we must rather hold to experience, provided it be established upon many observations. . . . It is better in this case to rely upon the testimony of the senses destitute of reason, than to adhere to reason, contradicted by experience." The difficulty of determining specific remedies exacerbates these problems. Because experience shows us that there are specific remedies for some diseases, a speaker concludes that there must be specifics for all diseases, "but they are unknown to us by reason of their multitude. And who is he that can know the virtues and properties of everything which is in the world?"

Conferees are generally optimistic about prospects for medical knowledge but pessimistic about specific cases. They believe that the failure to identify a specific remedy for each disease is simply the result of incomplete knowledge. However, when a speaker wants to argue for empiricism or a rational approach to medicine, he is stymied by grave difficulties in defining, explaining, or even classifying certain phenomena. For the historian, the issues that are most problematic for these participants are the most revealing; where participants are not able to come to certain conclusions, they are most willing to reveal areas of ignorance that illuminate their understanding of medicine. For example, those who discuss "ringing in the ears"[30] contend that common opinion and ancient superstition have obscured this topic. A participant notes that because hearing is the sense that disciplines or organizes the others, the ancients superstitiously considered ringing an important indication of the future. He notes with dismay that support for this superstition persists to his day. Resorting to these kinds of arguments based on sympathy, according to the next speaker, goes too far; it proves "something obscure by something that is even more so." Thus those who hear ringing and believe it comes from the outside are instead afflicted with a diseased organ, which "communicates its disorder to the imagination." Another speaker offers the explanation most focused on physiological phenomena; he insists that the cause is "a brain, weak and ill disposed, which engenders so many evil humors that they exit by the ears." Thus it is absurd to cite any evidence on this question except that drawn from medical practice, especially since those left untreated "are frequently menaced by deafness." This speaker denounces common opinion, insisting that only medicine can accurately assess this issue. He shares with other conferees the belief that, because they are at a critical distance from received opinion, they are well placed to adjudicate between common and elite opinion or ancient and modern opinion.

A conference "Of the diverse terms of pregnancy of women and why infants are more likely to live at seven months than at eight"[31] is set in motion to contend "scientifically" with a commonplace of seventeenth-century opinion, that is to say, the belief that infants survive if they are born in the seventh or the ninth month but not if they are born in the eighth. It too is an interesting example of the use of rival theories and authorities, highlighting differences of opinion between astrologers and physicians. According to the astrologers, "infants live at seven months and not at eight because, in the first place, delivery takes place when the moon, which is favorable to deliveries, predominates." Infants born at eight months die because of the dominance of Saturn, the planet that is the enemy of life. The evidence for these opinions is found in the astrological texts of the Chaldeans, Cicero, and Plutarch. But physicians, a speaker notes, rely on more credible evidence from thinkers like Aristotle, who claimed that lateness or earliness depends on the hardness or softness of the matrix (an early term for the cervix), and Hippocrates, who asserted that women with more blood deliver earlier. The speaker asserts the validity of empirically grounded methods of the ancients (such as Aristotle and Hippocrates) over those of astrologers. Modern physicians (the speaker's terms) have sought firmer empirical grounds by looking for connections between the complexions of the parents or the principles of generation, specifically to the temperament of the mother and the degree of heat involved. More recent views are more directly connected to the opinion of the medical profession and thus more credible, this speaker suggests.

Another speaker offers a kind of logical explanation for the failure to thrive of babies born at eight months. "The child, being too feeble before the seventh month, tries to leave at that time, and if his effort is then useless, but he nonetheless comes to leave the following month, which is the eighth; he cannot live because of his weakness, caused by continuous labor. If instead he rests during the eighth month, he is vigorous enough in the ninth."

Another makes the kinds of objections to the formulation of the question that a twentieth-first-century reader is pleased to see. He says there is no reason why infants live at seven months and not at eight. Because the time of gestation is not certain, one cannot even determine the age of the infant, and as a result, "it would be better to attribute the slowness or acceleration of delivery as the key to life to the principles of generation alone." Other factors that need to be taken into account are the good or bad habits of the parents, the weakness or strength of the mother and the child, the nourishment of mother and child, and the various accidents that happen during pregnancy. By enumerating so many factors, he acknowledges the limits of current knowledge. However, other speakers are clearly discomfited by these appeals to such wide parameters of medical explanation. A final speaker dissents from the previous medical explanation: he reasserts the value of the astrologers by arguing that, "since birth is a kind of crisis, it is best connected to numbers and to the planets rather than to other causes." He bemoans the fact that his fellow participants do not rely sufficiently on authorities.

Seventeenth-century medical discussions are complicated by under-lying presuppositions about health that, although frequently foreign to the modern reader, are nonetheless invoked as givens meant to carry an argument. The following are some of the guiding presuppositions that shape an understanding of health in the conferences and are often cited as clinching arguments: Nature has a preference for rest over activity; whatever is being discussed behaves the way it does because it seeks to avoid creating a vacuum; health is determined by the vigor of the formative virtue (the strength of the creature as a result of its initial creation); and vital heat is the crucial agent that allows the body to perform its functions.[32] The crucial determinants of health are myriad and none seems entirely obvious, easy to classify, or decisively persuasive. For the modern interpreter, the factors that participants recognize as crucial determinants of health are not at all obvious. For example, Aristotelian elements play an important role in evaluating health. But one of the problems involved in insisting that health is due to a proper balance between two antithetical elements, hot and dry versus cold and humid, is that there is no compelling way to determine what has which quality, particularly when one is describing internal organs. Although frequently invoked, these suppositions cannot prove decisive; the same evidence can be arrayed to support antithetical arguments. For instance, one speaker says the brain is by nature hot; another says it is by nature cold. (In this conference, the compromise position contends that both excessive cold and heat of the brain produce illness.)[33]

Several conferences, like that on cure by contraries, demonstrate the role of competing medical paradigms in arguing the most compelling prerequisites for health. Some of the possible paradigms include a marriage of heat and moisture, the "contemperation" of the four humors, or a fixed volatile salt. Participants consider the possibility of cure by contraries[34] in its broadest dimensions and from different points of view. The first speaker notes that the efficacy of any remedy depends on its ability to prolong life, but, he notes with discouragement, medicine will not be credited. "Let a man, by good order, or the use of remedies, live as long as he will, it will not be believed that his life has been prolonged, but on the contrary, that his hour has not yet come." The next concurs that the question is unknowable because life depends upon an amount of heat and moisture predetermined at birth, so that although medicine may teach one to husband this heat and moisture, it "cannot produce it anew." A speaker proposes a geometrical analogy: "life is a straight line; the accidents, which disturb it and at length bring death, constitute another." These participants have quite contradictory notions of the determinants of health and the ability of the physician to affect them. Although some are quite skeptical about whether medicine has any impact on this process, a final speaker cites the efficacy of medicine: "it were a strange thing if human art could repair all other defects of the body and mind, excepting that for which there is most need and all ages have complained, the brevity of life . . . physick would seem useless without this."

Many speakers insist on moisture as the precondition of health.[35] A speaker on the topic "Which is most healthful, moisture or dryness?"[36] lists a catalog of reasons to favor moisture: "Thales affirmed water as the principle of all things. . . . The spring, the most healthful and agreeable of all seasons, is moist. . . . Moisture is also the cause of plumpness and beauty, which is never found in a lean face and a dry body."

Hippocrates too proclaimed the spring, the warm, moist season, as the healthiest. Another speaker makes the most striking claim for the importance of moisture: "death and old age, which leads to it, is nothing but a desiccation." Other speakers cite vital heat as the most significant factor in the preservation of health and the effective functioning of all faculties; we have less vital heat and function less effectively as we age.

Conferees also recognize the effect of the imagination on health. In "If the imagination can produce and cure illnesses,"[37] one speaker notes that "Aristotle based his physiognomy on the grand liaison and sympathy of the soul with the body." To affect the body, the soul "does not employ a more efficacious instrument than the imagination." Although some speakers discount the correspondence theory, for others the relationship between body and mind substantiates it. A strong imagination can push spirits because they are airy and very hot by nature and exert a great influence on the humors. The most persuasive evidence of the role of the imagination, consistently cited by speakers, is the power the mother's imagination exerts over the fetus. But several speakers dispute the imagination's role in causing disease. One insists that the imagination does not act directly on the body but only on the sensitive appetite. Prefiguring modern physicians like Oliver Sacks, some assert that those who are sick by imagination must be cured by imagination.[38] They cite such cases. A man who thought he had no head was persuaded that he did only when he was made to wear a lead bonnet, whereupon he complained that his head hurt. Or the man who was afraid to urinate because he believed he would create a universal deluge was cured when his peasants cried "fire" and begged him to extinguish it with urine. Or the man who refused to eat because he believed he was dead was persuaded to eat again by a nephew who said he too was dead but nonetheless proceeded to eat a meal.[39]

If imbalance or deficiency produces disease, then health requires the maintenance of a balance. So too, if imagination can cause disease, then it can be mobilized to effect cures. Perhaps because speakers lack specific information about crucial considerations for health and disease (contagion in particular), medical discussions depend to a large degree on the application of logic, and speakers rely on their general presuppositions about nature. Although this period of scientific innovation is generally assumed to entail the application of mechanism to medicine, Renaudot's conferences occur before the widespread acceptance of mechanism. Indeed, they rarely invoke mechanism as a way to understand the functioning of the body, and when they do, it is simply as a rhetorical or stylistic device—an analogy or metaphor. (The following is a rare mechanical comparison: "Illness proceeds from the least defect . . . like [a defect in] the least tooth of the wheel of a clock.")[40] Both nature and the imagination offer important explanatory tools in cases where there is no clear reason for continued good health or its breakdown. The two categories might be considered analogous to modern discussions of the role of genetic inheritance (to the degree that specific genetic factors remain unmapped) and the effect of "disposition" or mood on disease.

The "Galenic gospel" not only maintained that a balance of humors was necessary for health and the disruption of that balance a cause for disease, it also acknowledged that natural temperament could be disturbed by an external cause, also producing disease. Heredity, a wound that might introduce a poisonous element, an epidemic disease, all are possible causes of an unnatural qualitative change to the body. There are also the six Galenic non-naturals—air, food and drink, exercise and rest, sleep and wakefulness, bodily evacuation, and the passions of the soul—all of which have to be managed for health.[41] Discussions of specific diseases and therapies apply these presuppositions in a more concrete and practical manner, but they are even more problematic than general discussions of health, because there is no underlying consensus on the causes of disease. As with most conference topics, a lack of consensus provokes rather than inhibits discussion of fundamental issues such as the causes, the nature, and the most appropriate classification of diseases. Even though participants disagree on which qualities are to be balanced, when they discuss the specific symptoms of disease, they are nonetheless willing to entertain many diverse explanations simultaneously. When confronted with specific problems, theoretical principles give way to therapeutic hopes.

Many discussions of disease begin with the cause, the first known example, an authoritative source on that disease, or a general description of the disease. Subsequent speakers quarrel with these perspectives or refine the definitions. They point out inconsistencies in the initial presentation or in the descriptions of the manifestations of the disease. They explain away the inconsistencies by further redefinition. This frequently paves the way for subsequent discussions, which focus on anomalous cases or specific treatments.

Certain problematic diseases vividly illuminate notions of causation of disease because participants suggest multiple explanations.[42] So, for example, birth, contagion, or defect, one suggests, might equally well cause a disease like leprosy. Participants place disease on a continuum, for instance, a waning of vital heat from life to sleep to death. Discussions of disease reveal inconsistencies and confusion, especially since the notion of contagion is not clearly understood. One speaker says diseases like smallpox are caused by something in the air. Another disagrees because, if that were the case, it would spread like the plague. (It is not clear whether speakers consider smallpox to be much less virulent or whether the historical memory of the plague is so strong that no other disease seems as fearsome.) Participants have a general sense of the spread of disease through "miasmas" or exhalants of bad air but no clear or consistent notion of contagion. These general notions are probably rooted in their understanding of Hippocrates' environmental medicine. A more contemporary source—Fracastro's *On Contagion* (1546), which argued that "seeds" propagated diseases—is not represented.

The conference on epilepsy[43] vividly demonstrates the wide range of possible explanations for a single disease. The first speaker ruefully acknowledges that, although epilepsy is a disease well known since antiquity, nonetheless "the vulgar maxim that a disease thoroughly known is half cured is not always true." He defines it as "the cessation of sensory and voluntary motions, accompanied by convulsion," and acknowledges the implacability of this disease in the face of medical treatment. "Neither of its fundamental causes, the remote cause of the position of the stars at birth and its proximate cause of a vapor or humor pricking the brain, is really susceptible to medical treatment." The second speaker notes that, as distinct from medical opinion, the vulgar believe there is something divine about the disease, "since nothing amazes us more than sudden uncomprehended alterations." One speaker asserts that it is caused by an "abundance of gross humors" whose flow becomes obstructed. The next objects that "a gross humor cannot be the cause of those quick and violent motions of the epilepsy." Because autopsies reveal that "no such gross obstructive matter is found in the brain of those who die of this malady, but only some traces or signs of some malignant vapor or acrimonious humor," he concludes that its cause must be "some biting and very subtle matter."

Two distinct kinds of arguments are used here. One is a kind of logic based on the movements of fluids through the body, that is, sudden movements cannot be caused by a gross humor, which is the kind of argument mechanist physicians might make. The second is based on crucial empirical evidence, autopsies of the brain, that reveal no such gross humor. Another participant offers an explanation that relies on chemistry: "There is a special occult quality of the humors particularly disposing one to this disease; the chemists call it a mercurial vapor." The difficulties involved in describing epilepsy are so extensive that participants suggest explanations across the spectrum of medical opinion, and no speaker insists that his explanation is comprehensive. While many topics provoke sharp controversies, these problematic diseases do not allow participants to weigh the relative value of opinions based on a clear standard of evidence. Thus one speaker rarely refutes another. Instead they present the view they favor, without insisting on it to the exclusion of other opinions.

The conference on gout[44] also reveals important ways to understand diseases. A speaker defines gout as "the general name of all of the pains of the joints caused by fluxion . . . but which differ according to the diverse connections of bones and according to the parts they afflict." He contends that diseases have to be discussed in terms of all their variables, not simply causes and effects, but also location. Another speaker suggests four variables to consider, "the matter which flows, the place it comes from, the road by which it passes, and the parts on which it falls." One speaker directs our attention to issues outside the medical dimensions of the disease. He notes, for example, that those afflicted by the disease can console themselves with the fact that it is caused by the strength of the parts that produced the humors. The idea that disease is the badge of a great strength is indeed a strange one, but it also suggests an almost modern understanding of the ferocious growth of some cells, like cancer cells, at the expense of others. So too, gout is caused by great vigor in the humors that produce it.

Participants also try to classify diseases in order to better understand them and in the hope that classification might promote more effective treatment. A specific conference classifies diseases according to the point in the course of the disease where the crisis occurs.[45] (This was an attractive way to consider disease, since the most marked symptom of many diseases was a fever, and the spiking of the fever before it broke defined the crisis.) One speaker expresses his frustration; there are so many different types of crises—perfect crises, less than perfect crises, and different symptoms for each kind—that such classifications are diagnostically useless. Nonetheless, another proceeds to classify them up to twenty-day intervals.[46]

Despite the fact that fever is the most prominent symptom of many diseases, it is largely inexplicable in terms of seventeenth-century medicine.[47] Participants thus use many kinds of analogies to explain it. For instance, fever can be a fire kindled in the heart. (This claim might well be influenced by the prominent analogy of heart as furnace in mechanical philosophy.) The waxing and waning of heightened temperature provoke a comparison to the motion of the sea. Another speaker suggests the model of tyranny as an explanation for fevers, that is, fever occurs when a specific humor refuses to obey the laws of nature and acts as a tyrant over others.

The possibility of a new disease called into question fundamental presuppositions because the early moderns generally adhered both to ancient sources and to an unchanging universe.[48] Thus smallpox occasions much discussion about its advent.[49] Since it too was manifested by pox, smallpox *(la petite vérole)* was considered related to the pox, the venereal disease syphilis *(la grande vérole)*, which had come to Europe from the Americas with Columbus's soldiers. Participants contributed to the contemporary debate over whether the disease was transported from the New World to the Old or whether it had existed from biblical times.[50] One participant considers smallpox the result of sin, by which he means that the causes have always existed, but the conditions that make them possible exist only at certain times in response to great sinfulness. Thus he is able to reconcile an unchanging universe with the relatively new appearance of this disease. Another argues for the ancient origins of smallpox, pointing out that Hippocrates mentioned red, round pustules. This speaker strongly disagrees that smallpox could be the result of the perpetuation of pernicious and venomous matter by nature over many years. Such a claim "would be to accuse nature of weakness or imprudence, which being all good, wise, and powerful, has nothing so much at heart as to purify the body."

Clearly a problem for these speakers is the fact that the disease seems so nearly universal. How then can one avoid accusing nature? This speaker reflects the general sensibility of conferees that the actions of nature are constant and beneficent. (Its constancy suggests to them a basis for amelioration of the human condition as well.) Nor can the disease be caused by malign air, as Jean Fernel suggested (a rare reference to a modern author).[51] "Otherwise, smallpox would make itself popular like the plague and other contagious maladies and would attack all men indifferently, without exempting those who have been one time attacked." (The speaker thus denies airborne contagion but acknowledges the immunity conferred by a previous case of smallpox.) The period of the conferences was marked by waves of plague (both 1636 and 1638 were plague years in Paris),[52] and this phenomenon might have made it more difficult to come to a consensus about contagion. When participants discussed contagion, they compared all other diseases to the plague, to conclude that the others were not in fact spread by contagion. But the prevalence of the disease led them to wonder why such diseases should be so nearly universal. One speaker suggests that small pox is so prevalent because "smallpox, most physicians agree, is an ebullition of some venomous matter contracted by each of us in his mother's womb, by impurity of the menstrual blood retained during the time of breeding."

The discussion of the causes of smallpox highlights some of the difficulties involved in considering particular diseases.[53] A speaker says that where one sees a common effect, one should assign the same cause, so that smallpox and the pox are not different except that one is produced by a more subtle blood and the other by one that is more *gross*. He cites as causes (1) corruption caused by the mother's menstrual blood (therefore everyone should be purged once) and (2) natural heat, which pushes out impurities. When a speaker says that as original sin is to the soul so smallpox seems to be to the body, he supports the religious analogy with empirical evidence. Because the disease so often attacks children who have committed no fault and who should be strong as "they are closer to the principles of their birth," he concludes that smallpox comes from the vice of the parents.

Some diseases almost defy explanation. For example, the topic "How those who are bitten by a tarantula are cured by the sound of a musical instrument"[54] is problematic because of the great variety of responses to the venom and because of the relationship of those bitten to music. Speakers concur that the bite infects the nerves and the infection goes to the brain. As one points out, "this venosity so accommodates itself to the inclination of those who are attacked" that it is difficult to generalize about its manifestations. Another speaker is incredulous that the ancients ignored the connection between this venom and music. This obvious connection, proved by everyday experience, is so firmly rooted that, in some cases, the afflicted must have several hours of music per day for many years as a remedy. Another notes that the ignorant are likely to look for evidence of the hand of God when there are obviously natural causes such as the conformity between musical sounds and the venom of the tarantula. (He does not develop the specifics of that conformity.)

Many of these conferences use arguments that we might well consider to be in conflict. For example, in "If scrofula can be cured by the touch of a seventh son and why,"[55] the first speaker identifies this disease as common to many glandular sites in the body (something he professes to know from autopsies of people with this disease). He also contends that since it is endemic among certain groups in the Alps and Pyrenees, it is a hereditary disease. His point thus far seems clear and empirically based. However, to explain the efficacy of the touch of a king or a seventh son in the cure of scrofula, he resorts to different kinds of arguments. These exceptional curative powers must be a free gift of God, but the power of the seventh son is not surprising given the importance of the number seven to Platonists. Their appreciation corresponds to empirical observations that all important developmental steps in human life take place in multiples of seven, "teeth at seven months, fourteen months first steps, language at twenty-one months, seven years old another set of teeth, fourteen puberty, growth till twenty-one, vigor till forty-nine." The next speaker objects that, if the seventh son has this power because of the increased strength of generative semen, then surely this power would be even greater with successive sons. Thus, he insists, one must look to God rather than to nature for the explanation of the power of the seventh son. (This is clearly an example of critical thinking based on a quasi-empirical perspective, but once again the conclusion is a bit unexpected.) Participants bring empirical evidence to bear and express skepticism about popular beliefs, and as on most questions of this kind, they both credit and disparage ancient sources and popular opinion.

Conferees try to determine what it is about man that makes him disease-ridden. In discussing "If man is the most unhealthy of all the animals and why,"[56] the first speaker defines an illness as a disposition that violates nature, wounding its function and impeding its actions. He notes that animals, too, have proclivities to certain diseases and suggests that, in general, human beings are the most temperate and best-ordered of creatures, "because humans are destined for the greatest actions." But with "the least occasion they lose their just proportion." Human beings, he suggests, are more sophisticated and thus more easily deranged. Others find man's greater propensity to disease attributable to such qualities as his greater perfectibility and the wider range of activities undertaken by him.[57]

ISSUES OF MEDICAL PRACTICE

Despite the invocation of medical authorities on occasion and the formulation of medical positions that are loosely based on medical theories (whether Galenic, Aristotelian, or Paracelsian), the conferences are also pervaded by challenges to authority. Some speakers pronounce Galen's cure for leprosy less efficacious than the mercury advocated by Paracelsus and dismiss the humoral system as an inadequate explanation of epilepsy (which Galen's critics explain as the result of spices or fevers).[58] But despite criticisms of Galen, humoral medicine is very much in evidence. By the seventeenth century, invoking humoral medicine is less adherence to Galenism than acknowledgment of its usefulness in explaining disease. Under this rubric, entirely different notions of the cause of a disease and widely divergent views of the appropriate treatment could be subsumed. Thus, although participants feel free to disagree with Galen, Galenism conforms well to the general character of medical discussion of the conferences.

When a Galenic explanation is advanced to explain a particular disease, this view is frequently challenged directly by a Paracelsian interpretation. Paracelsus advocated direct study of nature but according to certain underlying suppositions. He placed a great deal of significance on the macrocosm-microcosm analogy and claimed that three elements—salt, sulfur, and mercury—were the key components of the natural world. His notion of the treatment of disease did not involve rectifying imbalances. Instead, disease involved a poisonous external force that destroyed the *archeus* (the indwelling spirit) associated with each organ. For Paracelsus, cure was effected by treatment with similars rather than with contraries à la Galen; the study of nature would yield plants, animals, and minerals that corresponded to some aspect of the afflicted organ. The curative power of this similar could be made available for therapy through distillation and other chemical processes that released occult qualities in remedies. Because these hidden qualities could be unleashed to treat diseases, Paracelsus was much more optimistic about the potential for medical treatment. He also used many poisonous remedies such as mercury, antimony, and arsenic because like cured like and because diseases were poisons that had to be eradicated. Paracelsians also advocated cures by mineral waters.

A number of conferences dealt explicitly with issues raised by the Paracelsian assault on Galenic medicine; participants frequently emphasized minerals and chemicals in healing. When they addressed the topic "Of mineral waters,"[59] they generally concurred with the Paracelsians that mineral waters offered therapeutic benefits, but there was much discussion as to why. Some speakers point out that minerals produce a drying effect, and thus they "heal ulcers and dry up scabs and pustules." Some point to the ability of minerals to penetrate and attenuate, provoking urine and sweat, cleansing the kidneys and bladder. Others cite their coldness as their medicinal property, and thus "they cause shivering at midsummer, correct the heat of the liver and kidneys." One speaker extols their beneficial effect on virtually every kind of disease. In the case of diseases of obstruction, they "penetrate and, like a torrent, open not only the great passages, but also the small veins."

Some discussions of disease bring Galenic and Paracelsian views into direct conflict. For example, in discussing gout,[60] the Galenic proponent described it as the result of the acrimony produced by a corrosive, mordant humor. The Paracelsian countered that the disease was caused by salts "derived from the Alembic of the Earth," which accumulate because they "are not convertible to our substance."

That is not to suggest that Paracelsus had eclipsed Galen.[61] Some participants in the conferences were clearly ambivalent about Paracelsus. In fact, denunciations of Paracelsus are among the most vehement statements in the conferences. (The vehemence demonstrates powerfully that adherence to a chemical position was not a necessary precondition for participation in the conferences or for discussion of medical topics, even though Renaudot himself was an advocate of chemical medicine.) One critic of Paracelsus noted that there had always been irregular, extravagant, and incapable spirits who blamed their failure to learn on their professors.[62] (Paracelsus had, to his credit or damnation, flamboyantly rejected his education by burning his books.) Although the name Paracelsus elicits negative remarks, Paracelsian analyses of diseases and methods of treatment are sufficiently acceptable to be cited to challenge Galen's. Some speakers approve of Paracelsus's emphasis on signatures as the basis for effective practice. Others praise the chemists for going beyond the prejudices of the vulgar, who are concerned only with the obvious or the "manifest qualities." Chemists, unlike more conventional physicians, rely on "many excellent secrets, whose effects seem miraculous and as such surpass those of ordinary remedies."[63]

The following supposition allows many conferees to include chemicals in the pharmacopoeia: Treatment is conditioned by what is sought. If one is seeking to do the least harm, then one should use those remedies that are most like the human body, and therefore the most conventional remedies are to be preferred, that is to say, Galenic remedies. If one is seeking dramatic results, one should use chemical remedies.

Given the controversy surrounding Renaudot's career, provoked in part by his acceptance of chemical remedies, it seems strange that the division of opinion on these issues is not wider. Instead there is a high degree of consensus on when chemical remedies are appropriate and what the risks are. Those who support chemical remedies acknowledge the risks involved, and those who oppose them acknowledge when their use might be appropriate.

In a conference "If it is good to use chemical remedies,"[64] the first speaker provides the rationale for their inclusion: all that is created below the moon is designed for man's use, so chemical remedies are explicitly intended to "void harmful humors or make them harmless." Some participants defend chemical remedies by minimizing the differences between them and other medications. Such attempts to blur distinctions, however, provoke both sharp critiques and staunch defenses of chemical remedies. A speaker asserts that the benefits of remedies are derived from their resemblance to us, and since chemical remedies resemble us least, they necessarily are the least efficacious. Also, chemicals are dry and therefore the enemy of natural heat, which is humid and benign. But, he concedes, chemicals can be used against virulent diseases because they are stronger medicaments. Another speaker is unequivocal in his endorsement of chemical remedies: the mark of a good remedy is that it acts "promptly, surely, and with pleasure," and in these respects, chemical remedies are often to be preferred over others as "sure in the despoiling of impurities and malign qualities."

Chemical remedies also bring into high relief the problem of the preparation and regulation of medication.[65] Because vulgar practitioners do not take sufficient care in preparing medication, those remedies that are "mixed, dead, corrupted, and deprived of radical humidity" can cause adverse effects. Nonetheless, chemistry offers hope to those who have not been cured by conventional remedies. "Chemistry is a new world discovered only recently, not the less rare and admirable than the others, although it be as carefully cultivated and drawn from the hands of barbers." Thus chemical medicines require greater caution because they are new, virulent, and drawn from socially or professionally suspect sources.

In the conference "Of the principles of chemistry," the first speaker presents the Paracelsian case at great length. He defines chemistry as explicitly medical; that is to say, chemistry equals the art of drawing out principles and properties in order to prepare medications. The principles of chemistry entail a different method of treating disease: "to build, it must destroy." Other speakers deny the centrality of chemistry to medicine. They see the benefits of chemistry as just incidental by-products of the alchemist's quest for the philosopher's stone and thus presumably incidental rather than essential to the pursuit of medicine. However, for all participants, chemistry derives its credibility from its association with medicine.

The discussion of Paracelsian medicine raised many therapeutic issues, and participants address many of the same issues in the context of conventional Galenic medicine as well. If health and disease are difficult to determine, therapeutic prescriptions are no easier. Most early modern physicians prescribed by taking into consideration a wide range of factors, among them the heavens, the season, the habits of the individual, and most of all his temperament.[66] Cure was attained by removing the pathological quality from the affected part. Restoration of the natural state could be achieved by following the golden rule of Galenic therapeutics: curing by opposites. To make sure not to over-correct an imbalance, a small quantity of a remedy was used initially, with stronger remedies only if the early treatments failed.[67] Many medical discussions focus on the role of the diet as the first and most common part of medical treatment.[68] One important question that participants consistently grapple with is the nature of the correlation between the disease and the remedy.[69] What is it about the remedy that produces the cure? (If the speakers making these pronouncements are not all doctors, they show an incredible willingness to practice medicine without a license.) Discussions of the treatment of disease assume that the physiology of the individual is fundamental.[70] Although resemblance is frequently the key to therapy, the specific case is inevitably complicated by the physiology of the patient. For example, the discussion "If wine aids or impedes digestion and why"[71] becomes endlessly complicated as speakers discuss the complex relationship between wines and stomachs, both of which differ from individual to individual and from wine to wine. Brockliss and Jones have noted that medical practitioners could reconcile the parameters of individual constitutions with their belief in their ability to treat disease. Even though they considered each disease unique and dependent on the temperament, they could relate individual diseases to patterns so that "symptomatically similar complaints were expected to respond to a particular albeit flexible, pattern of treatment."[72] Whether the approach to therapy is Galenic, chemical, or a combination (and it is important to recognize the syncretic quality as characteristic of the conferences in general, and in the medical conferences in particular), recommendations are cautious or framed by extensive caveats.

Speakers understand that substances have different effects under different conditions. For example, in "Of drunkenness,"[73] they contend that certain substances, like wine, are beneficial if used in a measured fashion. Even though wine can act as the best kind of food and medication, consumed in excess it produces "evils without number like paralysis, epilepsy, convulsions, and it produces evils in the soul . . . and impedes its beautiful functions of intellect and will." However, another speaker notes the social uses of drink as "the antidote with which working people alleviate their pains."

Conferees are not only familiar with the diverse range of general issues of health, disease, and therapy, they are also well acquainted with topical issues such as chemical remedies and the weapon-salve treatment. The weapon-salve theory contended that wounds were cured by treating the weapon that inflicted them, demonstrating the effects of the occult quality of action at a distance. The conference "Of the magnetic cure of diseases"[74] draws the connection between magnetism and the weapon-salve treatment of diseases because both phenomena demonstrate the efficacy of action at a distance. This conference is a measured and critical discussion of this specific topic and indicates some more general issues of medical therapy. The first speaker exclaims, "how many authors report that wounds have been cured by the sole application of a certain unguent . . . to the instrument or offensive weapon that made it!" So widely accepted is this relationship that it has become a commonplace "that it is ordinary for the peasants of his (the Emperor Maximilian's) country to cure wounds in their feet, by sticking the nails or thorns that made them in lard or bacon grease." He continues by describing the actual salve, which bears a disconcerting resemblance to "eye of newt" brews,[75] but cautions that this recipe "is not to be practiced in wounds of the arteries, heart, liver, and brain; because it would be to no purpose." He cites the obvious reasons for its success as "the sympathy that there is between the blood issued from the wound and remaining on the weapon and that which is left in the wounded body, so that the one communicates to the other what good or evil it receives." This speaker, as a proponent of the weapon-salve treatment, touts empirical evidence, cautiously excludes certain cases, and has a theoretical grounding rooted in a correspondence theory of nature. Another speaker expands the notion of sympathy to insist that "the weapon-salve has such sympathy with the constellation that is to cure the wound, that by its magnetic virtue, it attracts its influence from heaven and reunites it . . . to the instrument that made the wound, communicating its healing virtue to the same." It is interesting that the opinions expressed are nearly universally positive. Only one participant rebuts claims made for cure by weapon-salve, but he does so most effectively. First, he refutes the erroneous attribution of "the cure of disease to sympathy, to the power of character, words, images, numbers, celestial figures, and such other things that have no activity at all." Second, he insists that "there is no need to resort to these superstitious remedies, since nature, of her own accord, heals wounds, provided they be not in the noble parts and kept clean from impurities." Finally, cures that seem extraordinary are, simply, "the effects of the strength of the mind, which is such that, where it believes anything firmly, it operates on what it believes."[76]

Bloodletting, one of the most common seventeenth-century treatments, was especially controversial. Phlebotomy, the practice of drawing blood by slitting a vein below a ligature, was the conventional remedy for serious disease.[77] Proponents of bloodletting explicitly identify themselves as physicians, a rare practice in the conferences and a clear appeal to professional authority. It suggests that physicians defended bloodletting as an issue on which their expertise ought to carry some weight against the challenges of nonprofessionals. Others express caveats, noting that Galen and the Greeks knew it should be used rarely on children younger than fourteen. Another speaker notes circumstances under which he finds bleeding to be completely inadvisable; when good fluid would be voided or when the impurity is rooted in the very habitude of the body.[78] For the most successful results, the physician should first discern which vein best corresponds to the replete humor; one should also consider the specific disease being treated and "the strength, temper, age, and sex of the particular patient."[79] The doubts of conferees about the efficacy of bloodletting were quite similar to those expressed, over the course of the seventeenth century, especially by members of the Montpellier faculty.[80]

In reading medical discussions of the past, it is difficult not to cheer for the critics of outmoded practices like bloodletting and to look for and extol signs of medical progress, in other words to read the present into the past. This propensity can only get the historian into trouble in general and in discussing the conferences in particular. On many occasions, the participants most wedded to Galenism support blood letting with empirical evidence, and those most critical of Galenic medicine base their criticism on positions that scarcely herald the coming of modern medicine. In a discussion of contagion, a thoughtful commentator notes the circumstances to be avoided if one is to curtail the spread of disease, but his ultimate conclusion is that the stars are the cause of disease.[81] Some of those who criticize humoral theory replace it with the equally vague "venomous spirits." It is disconcerting to get to the end of a critical and well-developed discussion of antidotes to various poisons and find that, in the final analysis, the commentator advocates amulets as the best treatment. Another speaker notes that, although comets are not really portents, nevertheless, one should be thoroughly aware of the signs, colors, intensity, and time of the comet in case one wishes to hazard a prediction. Staunch criticism of popular beliefs or superstitions and an insistence on empirical evidence—positions that underlie medical discussions in the conferences—do not necessarily produce results that inspire confidence in the modern reader.

Conferences dedicated to specific remedies provoke sharply different assessments of their efficacy. Perhaps the most cynical remark about medicine is that made by the second speaker in a conference "Of Bezoard."[82] Bezoard, a stone formed in the gastrointestinal tract of various animals (especially goats, llamas, and antelopes) was so highly regarded as a universal antidote to poison that it was frequently given as a gift to kings.[83] Although long known in the East, its discovery in Peru by Petro de Osma in 1586 had heightened Western interest. The cynic launched a stinging attack on such remedies: "Those who wish to acquire a reputation in medicine, seeing more illness indomitable to common remedy, so as not to appear lazy or to have their art or their ignorance impugned, . . . propose the use of remedies so rare and so difficult to find that one cannot discover their imposture."[84] A proponent of the remedy rebuts him, saying that those who disparage it do so because it does not act by manifest qualities; he advocates instead recourse to experience and authorities. He notes that, although the ancients were unfamiliar with this remedy, Arab sources confirm "that this stone is a powerful antidote against all venom and bites of poisonous animals."

Medical literature of this period relies for its therapeutic prescriptions on a mixture of humoral medicine and occult operations of nature. Drugs had to be prepared carefully; one had to make sure that the ingredients, especially exotic ones, were authentic. They took the form of pills or potions, enemas or poultices. Many diseases called for purgatives after bleeding to rid the body of disease. Drugs themselves were complicated mixtures of animal, plant, and mineral preparations concocted according to complicated recipes. Although it might seem quite admirable that there are challenges to the efficacy of remedies like bezoard, it is important to acknowledge that the standard pharmacopoeia included ingredients we would find disconcerting. For example, Jean Riolan's popular pharmacopoeia published in 1608 and 1637 included scorpions, frogs and vipers, body parts such as the human skull, the heart of a deer, tusks of elephants, and substances like the fat of pigs, the marrow of calves, and the excrement of various animals.[85] These remedies sanctioned popular practices by giving them a theoretical foundation. In response to the obvious question as to why anyone would assent to such remedies, historians speculate that they "worked." The very naming or diagnosing of a disease gave some assurance to the patients and perhaps produced a therapeutic benefit analogous to a placebo effect. With a name attached to a disease, perhaps the early modern patient could feel more confident that his ailment might find remedy.[86]

It is quite interesting that the tenor of the conferences on medical therapy seems so universally optimistic, especially since the Galenists were therapeutic pessimists, expecting failure from treatment no matter how extensive or heroic the efforts of the physician. Much medical literature concentrated on ways to avoid disease because prospects for treatment were so limited. Many physicians emphasized that life is a process of moving toward death, a sentiment occasionally reflected in the conferences. Much medical literature also emphasized that, although the patient was responsible for his own health, ultimately it was in God's hands.[87] Conferees had good reason to share in these low expectations. They too expressed frustration over the difficulties in diagnosing and treating disease. They too had to contend with the dilemma of the role of the individual constitution and the variable manifestations of a disease. Nonetheless they were remarkably confident, perhaps because of their growing sense of the social significance of medical practice.

The conferences made significant claims for the medical profession, which are most emphatically expressed as a rivalry between doctors and lawyers as to which profession is most beneficial to a state. This topic is a set piece of rhetorical debate from the Renaissance onward, and in that debate medicine was on the defensive. In the hierarchy of early modern professions, the physician occupied a social and cultural position inferior to that of the cleric or the magistrate. Physicians were neither cerebral nor influential enough to rise in stature.[88] Within the context of the conferences, the discussion of this issue suggests that a significant proportion of the participants belonged to the legal and medical professions, particularly given the probable participation of physicians attached to Renaudot's clinics and the likely social and economic composition of this group. The medical conferences also assess the relative strengths of both the medical and legal professions in the broader social sphere. The fact that doctors see their power as threatened by lawyers indicates an increase in the power of the judiciary—and of lawyers in general (participants express quite a bit of concern over increased legalism in seventeenth-century France)—and suggests their disgruntlement with medicine's social position below that of theology or law. Other speakers, probably lawyers, are intent on demoting medicine to a lower place in the social and intellectual hierarchy.

Those who assert the legitimacy of medicine do so in terms of the social benefits it produces.[89] When conferees discuss social issues, they frequently assume that a good is greater the more common it is. The underlying analogy is that the more widely a good is extended, the more closely it resembles the goods that God has given to man. This assumption plays a prominent role in social analysis at the Bureau and provides a rationale for the social agenda of increased access to social and medical services, which Renaudot fosters.

Medicine chez Renaudot suggests a much more open view about the range of possibilities for good medical practice. Renaudot did not believe it should be restricted to university-educated practitioners. His medical ecumenism was reflected in the incorporation of the surgeons and apothecaries into his medical consultation. He also sought to disseminate good medical practice by circulating a form that allowed patients to mark the location of their symptoms and return the form to the Bureau for a diagnosis.

The conference "What is the most necessary to the state and more noble, medicine or jurisprudence"[90] tackles the issue of the relative value of the two professions head-on. Although many of these conferences begin with statements by the first few participants expressing antithetical views, which are then moderated by subsequent speakers, this conference presents clear-cut dichotomies. One staunch claim is that medicine deals with defects of the body and law with defects of the spirit, and since spirit is higher than the body, law is the more valuable profession. Because health applies to both beasts and men but the law applies only to men, medicine must occupy a lower role in a traditional hierarchy. Another claim for the superiority of law is made on epistemological grounds: medicine deals with mere sensory knowledge, while law deals with the elevated domain of intellectual knowledge. (The relatively low position of the body vis-à-vis the soul was the rationale for the position of medicine below theology and law in the university.)[91] Another argument uses a scientific analogy: just as nature abhors a vacuum, so too jurisprudence functions to fill the vacuum that would otherwise exist in social life. Religion too supports the importance of law; jurisprudence is derived from the Garden of Eden as the knowledge of good and evil. Surely claims to a connection between paradise and the legal profession make it likely that lawyers participated in these conferences!

These arguments do not pass unchallenged. Some speakers assert that the earlier development of medicine makes its claims over jurisprudence unassailable, for medicine is derived from the tree of life itself and is, therefore, prior to knowledge of good and evil. Medicine is founded on nature, which is infallible, whereas jurisprudence has no foundation other than "the will and fantasy of men, which changes with time, place, and person." Furthermore, states can exist with crime and without law but cannot exist without health. Medicine is useful not only to the body but also to the soul.

Issues of professionalism also focus on the question of public versus private good. For example, one speaker argues that jurisprudence carries advantages over medicine, "because of the greater utility it carries to a state, in delivering it from the greater quantity of evils." He argues that medicine benefits private individuals, but jurisprudence benefits the public, and therefore it is a greater good. Jurisprudence seeks to resolve lawsuits, sedition, wars, and other evils, "which being public are much more important than those to which medicine is attached." Jurisprudence is so important because its end is "the purpose of all states . . . but the end of medicine is simply the body of each private person." (It is important to note that, just as in conferences on more clearly political topics, the good of the public is explicitly identified with the preservation of the state.)

When conferees raised medical questions, frequently they were assessing issues of topical concern. For example, over the course of the sixteenth and seventeenth centuries the medical community was organized into three distinct branches under the control of the physicians. Physicians could claim that their text-based education gave them superiority over the apothecaries and surgeons, who had an education based on apprenticeship. In a conference entitled, "If more harm or good has come from the three-part division of medicine into physicians, surgeons, and apothecaries,"[92] the first speaker tries to persuade his audience that the issues involving the medical profession are of vital concern to them; the public must be well informed so that, as patients, they can make choices. This topic was directly relevant to Renaudot's operations, where doctors worked very closely with apothecaries, and chemical remedies were prepared in furnaces on the premises. One speaker contends that the gravity of these issues leads him to support the status quo because "there is no reason to trouble civil society, which subsists principally by mutual support of the *corps*" (meaning the division of medicine into physicians, surgeons, and apothecaries as distinctly constituted bodies). Another speaker notes that in the past all three medical functions were undertaken by a single person who was not part of a single well-defined profession. For example, priests of Egypt made medical information available, the Greeks authorized medicine by religion, and Hippocrates too practiced all three parts of medicine together. Medicine continued that way until the time of Galen. Then a pernicious development occurred. Physicians, behaving like the "children of those who have amassed goods by means of commerce," wished "to avoid the pain and retain the honor and the profit." As a result they "reserved for them-selves the sole authority and the power to order." They left the onerous task to others—"the choice, dispensation, preparation and composition of medications" to the apothecaries and "the operations of the hand" to the surgeons. (The correlation between professional privilege and unearned economic advantage foreshadows the philosophes' concerted attack on privilege.) He thus denounces the division in practice as simply a convenience for physicians; they retain the authority and avoid the unpleasant tasks associated with the practice of medicine. The divi-sion of faculties is thus completely unwarranted—"to divide them is to wish to separate the liver, the heart, and the brain of the same man"— and has produced a detrimental effect on public health. "Theory never being as well known as practice, it is not a marvel that from this disunion have come so many ignorant empirics." But another conferee objects that to insist a doctor carry out the work of surgeons and apothecaries makes "the general of an army both give the orders and carry out the functions of a simple soldier."

Perhaps in deference to the professions of other participants or to avoid counterproductive recriminations, several speakers claim that they will not deal with professional abuses but will only discuss the professions as they should be practiced. However, one with a more jaundiced view objects that he is unwilling to consider the professions detached from the question of corruption. He insists that within a given state a large number of doctors is a sign of sickness and a large number of lawyers is a sign of corruption. Therefore, both doctors and lawyers are equally useless to the state, "which without them would be deprived of the wicked and the miserable. Lawyers contribute to the ruin of the states, just as physicians ruin health." The following speaker concurs in the disparagement of the lawyers but is interested in salvaging physicians from disparagement, "as it is more necessary to live, and to live in health than to live in society or with riches which are the things that rule jurisprudence."

📖

What can these conferences tell us about the nature and role of medicine in the seventeenth century? Although we do not know much about the participants, some of what we do know makes them especially interesting sources for medical opinion. They are well enough informed to present health, disease, and therapy in their full diverse complexity. They are also well acquainted with topical issues such as debates over chemical remedies and the weapon-salve issue. These participants straddle the private and professional divide. They speak for the medical profession against the legal profession, but they do not speak with the voice of the Faculty of Paris. They attempt to speak for the public interest and insist that effective treatment is integrally tied to the dissemination of information. They are well aware of the difficulties involved in categorizing diseases or in describing the range of manifestations of disease under a theoretical rubric; this chaos of opinion and practice empowers them and endows them with confidence. Unlike the Faculty of Medicine, conferees were predisposed to reform. To the degree that they represent a consistent body of medical opinion, physicians who attended the conferences were probably from Montpellier because those physicians staffed Renaudot's clinics. They were less conservative in general and more open to chemical remedies than physicians educated in Paris. Renaudot defended chemical remedies, and since he no doubt had an influence on the composition of the group, his concerns must have lent a medically avant-garde character to the conferences.[93] Nonetheless, medicine as discussed there is not exclusively or even preponderantly chemical. Instead it is almost bewilderingly eclectic. Speakers invoke Aristotelian, Galenic, and Platonic principles, empirical evidence, and even popular beliefs to explain medical phenomena. Medicine at the conferences cannot simply be reduced to an example of the chemical polemic of the mid–seventeenth century.

Of all the sciences of the early modern period, medicine would seem to be the science most rooted in common experiences and thus most accessible to the educated. It would also seem to be the science most tied to pragmatic concerns and most likely to produce utilitarian benefits. The hopes embodied in medicine were common to seventeenth-century scientific reformers. Medicine was central to Francis Bacon's advocacy of science and technology, to Paracelsus's vision of the reform of science, and to Descartes's expectations of the results of the new science. For Renaudot's group, medicine not only exemplified the expected benefits to be derived from science, it also offered a model for the nature and practice of science.

It is easy to disparage the state of medicine in the early modern period, and it has not been conventional to portray the era as innovative, much less revolutionary. When one imagines the sufferings of those subjected to medical practice, it is hard to be as optimistic as the conferees were about the prospects for medicine. However, the sense of medicine as the model of science that characterizes the conferences was common to Paracelsus and to Francis Bacon. If medicine were not the paradigmatic science for Descartes, it would nonetheless best demonstrate the utilitarian benefit of the new science. So medicine was a reasonable choice for conferees to pin their hopes on for the benefits of science. After all, it was medicine, not astronomy or mechanics, that most clearly held out the hope for the immediate improvement of the human condition.

What scientific method did medicine suggest to conferees? Can that method be correlated in any meaningful sense with the scientific revolution? First of all, the fact that medicine was so broadly inclusive and so readily inclined to adopt new approaches and incorporate new information (at least outside academic medicine) was very appealing. As such it could readily seem to be an avant-garde science. Its approach had always been eclectic, and it was not hampered by the hegemony of a single authoritative figure. It had always been staunchly rooted in the authority of experience and of the individual practitioner. Medical practitioners might well have wondered what was novel about calls for empiricism in the scientific revolution. They could certainly have seen themselves in the forefront of such practice. They could also have pointed with pride to the stringent, critical standards that characterized their discussions of medical phenomena; they were quite conscientious in winnowing out the extraneous, the superstitious, and the "vulgar" from the evidence they considered. They were also critical of "received opinion" no matter how venerable the source, a stance derived from their general skepticism. But while that skepticism made them critical, it did not subvert all knowledge. Instead they were quite confident of their ability to gain information about the nature and treatment of disease. To analyze health and disease they relied on rational deductions, and their fundamental suppositions about nature gave form to those deductions. They used empirical observations, case studies, or the opinions of other medical figures as they saw fit, confident that, despite the challenges of a specific case or a particular disease, their methods would produce real improvements in the condition of individuals and, ultimately, in the conditions of health for human beings in general.

This confidence does not mean they were unaware of the pitfalls of medical practice. They understood that treatment was hampered by the parameters of the individual constitution, new manifestations of disease, and attempts to determine the most effective remedy from a myriad of possibilities. So although they were confident and optimistic about the science of medicine and the methods they employed, they were also quite modest in the epistemological claims they drew from medicine. Because its potential benefits were clear, they believed medical knowledge should be disseminated to as wide a public as possible and that the public must be involved in their own health. These notions suggest that conferees had some legitimate grounds to consider medicine a paradigmatic science. They also allowed conferees to investigate the social sphere and to suggest that the science of medicine provided a model for social science. Clearly the opinions presented in these conferences are not forward-looking enough or far enough ahead of conventional wisdom as to be heralded as significant forerunners to modern medicine. Nonetheless they do define attitudes broadly characteristic of the Enlightenment as an intellectual movement, such as limited skepticism, humanitarianism, utilitarianism, and optimism about the efficacy of science.[94] These attitudes suggest that the conferences can justifiably be seen as a seventeenth-century foreshadowing of the Enlightenment.

Yet it is not surprising that a connection between the conferences and the Enlightenment has not been drawn. The conferences themselves are little read by historians, and the roots of Enlightenment are usually sought in the works of English scientists and metaphysicians rather than in documents of French popular science and culture. Much of the literature in the history of medicine is shaped by English language scholarship, which has used early modern England as a template and thus understood the impetus to medical reform as tied to the religious and political reforms of the Puritan revolution. Renaudot's conferences provide a significantly different perspective. The conferences took place in a context closer to the norm for much of continental Europe, that is, in a traditional monarchy. Historians have been inclined to discount seventeenth-century continental European texts as irrelevant, and those of France in particular, perhaps because they cannot be tied to the progressive political development of a constitutional monarchy or to the rise of religious toleration. This neglect has meant that historians have not generally acknowledged the significance of French medical attitudes to the development of the Enlightenment; but, because texts like Renaudot's detach medicine from theology and millenarianism, these connections can be more readily drawn than to their English counterparts.

Another important cause for neglect is that seventeenth-century medical literature is full of bizarre discussions, and, except for William Harvey, there are few bright spots that allow the easy integration of seventeenth-century medicine into a progressive history of science.

However, some of the attitudes expressed by conferees, especially on medical topics, are important to the development of the Enlightenment. Medical discussion fosters ways of presenting the body that resonate in later materialist texts. For example, in the conferences the connection and mutual influence of the body and the soul is a given (without discussion as to whether it is a theologically orthodox position). Men and animals are deemed comparable; one finds virtually no sign of the dualism of Descartes, and there are very few cautious exceptions drawn for the soul. Several important methodological positions emerge that connect this mid-seventeenth-century work with the methodology of the later Enlightenment. Participants take a position of epistemological modesty on some questions. For example, it is commonplace to say that the cause of the union of the soul and the body is unknown.[95] A speaker begins a discussion of "How long a man may continue without eating" by exempting miracles and the will of God from discussions of medical issues, but he further notes that, although miracles are beyond our ken, God "does not forbid our inquiring into natural causes."[96] This confidence that scientific investigations are not at odds with religion will find much more developed expression in the natural philosophy of later thinkers such as Robert Boyle, who try to reconcile the mechanical sciences with divine providence. Renaudot and other conferees also clearly believe that the dissemination of medical information, including therapeutic advice, is inherently laudable. For them knowledge is public and open, not the privileged, private knowledge of the academies. Furthermore, in disputes arising between arguments based on reason and those based on experience, participants universally insist that reason must yield to experience, provided that the experience is based on many discrete observations.

It goes against the conventional discussion of the progress of the scientific revolution to point to medicine as a source of confident assessment of the potential of science. But as Brockliss and Jones have documented, one could reasonably be much more optimistic about prospects for medicine and general well-being once the plague was a less prominent disease. The confidence of conferees in the efficacy and benefit of medicine can be construed, in part, as a response to the positive effect exerted by the control of the plague on the culture at large. But Renaudot's conferees are even more optimistic about medicine than even such a significant development might warrant. Just as the philosophes' expectations about medicine were so essential to what Peter Gay called the "recovery of nerve" that propelled the Enlightenment, so too, for conferees, medicine was a great source of confidence about human prospects.[97] Renaudot's medical interests can be directly correlated to Enlightenment hopes for medicine. He argued for a virtual right to medical care and against any monopoly of medical knowledge. His conferences disseminated medical information and asserted the centrality of medicine to a range of intellectual and social issues. The explicit use of science by Renaudot's group to analyze society underscores their affinities with the philosophes. They, like the philosophes, saw science, especially medicine, as a crucial source of social rehabilitation. They took the perspectives they gleaned from medicine and applied them to a broad array of social issues.[98]

PART **III** From Science
to Human Science

THE PROFESSIONS: BLEEDING.

Courtesy Bibliothèque nationale de France, Paris, 51 C 6955.

Introduction

A SPEAKER ON THE TOPIC OF INCUBI AND SUCCUBAE SUCCINCTLY
expresses the approach that conferees took to a wide range of subjects
when he claims that one should look to the physician because he avoids
the pitfalls of the ignorant and the freethinker, the one too credulous,
the other too skeptical. Physicians distinguish "what is fit to be attributed to nature";[1] they both understand nature and exercise a judicious
method. By emulating the physician, participants believe they too can
gain knowledge. Their understanding of nature in the face of staggering
diversity and complexity makes them confident that nature is ordered.
In light of this ordered disorder, one speaker asserts, one can do no
better than to lay out the contradiction of opinions, just as the conferences have done, for human "understanding has no better means to
obtain truth than by contrariety of opinions; for identity is as disagree-
able to the mind as it is to nature."[2]

When Renaudot's conferees consider questions that are not clearly
scientific, such as cultural, political, and economic issues, they employ
the perspective of the physician; they are neither credulous nor skeptical, and they believe that laying out different views will lead to truth.
They not only take the approach but also a great deal of the substance
of their discussion from their understanding of nature and science. It
is a commonplace of our notion of the scientific revolution that mechanism was necessary to the development of the social sciences. We
assume that its widespread ready application to natural phenomena
also made it an appropriate analogy and method for understanding the
social. This application of science to the social, it is generally assumed,
occurred after the thorough penetration of the scientific revolution into
the culture at large in the late eighteenth century. But these conferences demonstrate that a "science" or an approach to nature little
affected by mechanism could also be deployed as a persuasive basis of
social analysis long before the development of Enlightenment social
science.

One likely reason that the conferences have not been incorporated into histories of science in the early modern period is that they develop a view of the authority of science and of the scientist that works against the modern notion of the professional scientist. They offer no hegemonic view of what counts. They are willing to offer competing views, so that while they appreciate the value of knowledge of nature, they are not willing to assert with authority the importance of any single view. They believe, as do more conventional scientists, that knowledge of nature is empowering, but they advocate the widespread dissemination of knowledge rather than the concentration of specialized knowledge in the hands of professionals. Science is empowering for these participants just as it is for mechanists and other seventeenth-century champions of science, but they have different conceptions of how to wield that power and to whom it should extend.

Neither Renaudot's conferees nor the intended readers for their published accounts are restricted to the professional or to the privileged. They offer a strikingly different model of the practice of science. They depict an understanding of science as a community event directed toward the exposure of truth through open discussion. The effort is collaborative and does not exalt the accomplishment of the individual. The cultivation of knowledge then rests on an emerging consensus rather than on the work of any individual and an understanding of the practice of science as cooperative rather than competitive. Speakers are anonymous so that the conclusions a reader might draw from diverse views could not be distorted by the reputation of any individual speaker. Their notion of truth does not, as Steven Shapin documented for seventeenth-century England, depend on social status; the word of a gentleman does not entail truth.[3] Instead the opinion of an individual must bear the scrutiny of public discussion and print.

The notion of scientific writing itself is richly descriptive, perhaps one might say anecdotal. Little attempt is made to force description into abstraction. Unlike the more rigidly professionalized groups we usually associate with the rise of modern science, Renaudot's group is much more open in terms of both participation and the eclecticism of the ideas entertained in the forum of the conferences. Despite the diversity of views presented there, the conferences bespeak an appreciation of the value of science (particularly in the loose sense of the study of nature) as the basis of a shared culture.

The model offered by the conferences does not correspond to what will later be associated with the culture of science, that is, the individualistic, technically trained scientist, master of a discipline, who could refer with authority to the dictates of "science" as opposed to ignorance of the general population about specialized fields. Instead the model of science the conferences present is expansive. It opens science and medicine up to all educated men (and potentially women as well). It is not restricted to the possessors of a traditional education but, rather, contends that all who are educated can participate in the conferences and all who are literate can benefit from them. The understanding of both science and the nature of its authority evinced by Renaudot's conferees proved short-lived, however. It was undermined by a notion of science as the preserve of the professional and a narrowed notion of the academy. Nonetheless, because of their expansive and inclusive treatment of science, the conferences foster the development of the human sciences. More than our conventional, restrictive sense of science, they provide an example of a direct connection to the development of the social sciences.

How might their attitudes toward nature, especially as applied to difficult questions of occult phenomena, have empowered conferees to weigh social issues? Even if (as we have seen) participants use nature as an abstraction whose fundamental operations they categorize under a variety of organizing principles, nature is no less effective as the principle guiding social and cultural concerns. Nature provides such a malleable category of analysis that, indeed, participants invoke it on virtually every topic. Specifically, nature shapes discussions of human nature, social relations, politics, economics, and the rhetorically inflammatory "woman" question (themes that will be developed in the rest of this book and that form the substance of the human sciences of the eighteenth century).

The connections between science and social analysis are perhaps clearest in the ways participants use "nature" to address the social. Because "nature" imparted authority to discussions of human nature, it can then be legitimately invoked to comment on society. Participants express no dissonance between nature and culture (at least, culture understood as social organization). They assume that nature both provides a fundamental principle for society and the state and is directly concerned in making sure the affairs of state function well. Nature offers assurance that her gifts are apportioned to further the interests of society. For example, a speaker defines health as "a disposition, according to nature, which renders a man capable of performing the offices of life aright."[4] Nature, recognizing the fundamentally social character of human beings, gave man speech because society is in "no way imaginable without it."[5] In fact, nature suggests a rationale for public life; as a speaker citing the vacuum confidently proclaimed, since *"all things quit their particular interest for that of the public,* undoubtedly, there is no such thing as vacuum in nature" (my italics).[6] Just as participants assume that analogies from macrocosm to microcosm and from microcosm to macrocosm are equally compelling, so too they consider analogies from nature to society and from society to nature as equally persuasive; both, they assume, accurately describe the relationship. Not only does nature sanction society, but also natural principles, like order and harmony pervade the universe, human beings, and human society. Because the same principles characterize nature and society, "he that lives long can learn nothing new in the world, which is but a revolution and repetition of the same effects produced always by the same causes; not only in nature . . . but even in affairs of state and private matters."[7]

Nature, as benevolent and ordered, provides a useful analogy for discussing the hierarchical arrangement of society and for sanctioning specific social policies. As a speaker on the topic "Why men love to command more than to obey"[8] puts it: "nature has established this law, that inferior things ought to obey superior, the less worthy the more worthy, so that obedience and command are the different consonances that compose the harmony of the world." Social roles also have a physiological basis: "those who lead are called by the philosopher, lords and masters of nature, having an heroic spirit and [being] capable of governing not only themselves but others as well; their bodies being usually weak and delicate, hair fine, skin smooth and thin. Others are servants by nature, being strong and sturdy, fit to carry burdens, to undergo labor." Nature even sanctions slavery. "Servitude may be termed natural, being founded by the inequality of the abilities of men; some being born with organs so nimble and pliant, that their mind acts almost divinely; others are so dull, that the soul seems mired in dirt."[9]

Their understanding of nature endowed these participants with such extraordinary confidence that on questions assessing the ancients versus the moderns, they invariably argue that nature supports the moderns or, at least, equally favored the ancients and the moderns. "For nature being still as wise and powerful as any previous time, and the universal causes being the same, their operations must also be as perfect, and their effects as excellent in these days as they have been in any."[10] Human beings benefit from nature's consistency. "As for our minds, they are so far from being impaired, that they improve more and more in accurateness and being of the same nature with those of the ancients, have such an advantage beyond them, as a pigmy has upon the shoulders of a giant."[11] Thus conferees were, with few exceptions, outspoken in their expectations of social amelioration through science.

The principles whereby nature is understood vary widely, but speakers are strikingly similar in their general expectations concerning nature and the legitimacy that comparisons to nature confer on social analysis. Confidence in the order and beneficence of nature carry over into expressions of confidence in the order and legitimacy of social structures, institutions, and policies. Some historians suggest that the absolutist state of seventeenth-century France favored or even required the manipulative power of a mechanical understanding of nature.[12] However, these conferences suggest that, although the contemporary understanding of nature endowed an unassailable legitimacy on some existing social structures, it authorized the reform of others. Thus neither the establishment of absolutism nor the critical evaluation of seventeenth-century political institutions depended on a mechanical view of nature. Instead, the conferences demonstrate that pre-mechanist science provided conferees with intellectual resources flexible enough to both affirm and critique the social and cultural reality they confronted. They did not need to wait for the full-blown scientific revolution to apply their understanding of nature to cultural institutions. Although their discussions of nature in general and its more specific relationship to the culture of early modern France are sometimes almost chaotically eclectic, this very eclecticism bespeaks openness, flexibility, and confidence. This flexibility affords participants a tool for social analysis that they find adaptable, useful, and compelling enough to make assertions about their world.

Although this invocation of nature might seem quaint or might read rather quaintly, it is not merely a backward-looking way to sustain an argument that is indefensible from a modern viewpoint. Anchoring an argument about the social order in assumptions about nature is almost an identifying characteristic of the French Enlightenment. To cite one of a myriad of possible examples, when d'Alembert points to the solitary geniuses who have produced science, he says, "nature is always the same."[13] Conferees, unlike some philosophes, do not discuss laws of nature. They do not have a single notion of nature that they can apply to all of society as an organizing principle. Their use of nature might seem more jarring than that of some Enlightenment texts because it does not invoke a unifying principle; instead its contribution is rather inchoate, the search for a new standard of order. The conferences never offer a single authoritative perspective, so their discussion inevitably fails to produce unity. Thus the application of nature to society by philosophes is more constrained and uniform than that of Renaudot's conferees who, by contrast, are less concerned to force nature to conform to abstract laws. They also share with the philosophes the assumption of both the unity and the simplicity of nature (whether or not it is Cartesian). They, no more than the philosophes, saw these assumptions as being in conflict with their professed interest in empiricism. However, just as the philosophes are imbued with unshakable beliefs that their understanding of a simple and unified nature will both allow them to analyze society and lead to progress, so too conferees believe that nature is ordered, knowable, and directly relevant to analytical and critical discussions of society.

The notion of "science" as revealed by these conferences is problematic from a perspective more than three centuries removed from these discussions. But the very things that make this particular understanding of science problematic from a modern, positivist, and theory-centered point of view perhaps also served to make it attractive to those who attended the conferences. Because science offered an inclusive method rather than mere technical expertise, it could be broadly applied to analyze culture. This attitude toward science suggests that Renaudot's group made a more significant contribution to the early seventeenth century than is generally recognized.

First of all, he and his colleagues afford a crucial view of the transformation of humanist culture in light of science. Like other humanists, Renaudot abhorred scholasticism and extolled the conference as a unique means to erode such authority, because "daily experience shows us that there is nothing more harmful to learning than to prevent the truth, which appears chiefly in the opposition of contraries."[14] He invoked, as a model for his loosely structured gathering, the sixteenth-century republic of letters, but he extended the scope of discussion beyond its literary concerns.[15] By treating both rhetorical and scientific topics with the same kinds of evidence, vocabulary, and methodology, Renaudot's group highlighted the importance of rhetoric to science and the applicability of science to a broad range of issues. The conferences treat issues common to Renaissance humanism but from the perspective of science, filtering rhetorical and civic concerns through the prism of science. The appeal to the standards of science frequently makes the perspective of speakers seem modern, even when the content of the speeches often does not.

Second, conferees extend the realm of science, asserting a new secular ethics and a pragmatic approach to knowledge. Their reflections on nature lead them to an understanding of human behavior, including ethical behavior, as embedded in human physiology. They use physiology and medicine to understand all human behavior, including moral and social behavior, amplifying the right and the role of science to comment on moral and social issues. Their use of physiology reflects a concern to categorize human nature more extensively and more broadly than might have seemed possible with an abstract, philosophical definition of human nature. Science thus challenges scholasticism and metaphysics as a way to understand human psychology.

Perhaps participants use physiology so consistently because it seems concrete and particular. Based on a consensus of opinion corroborated by empirical evidence, it offers a way to move from abstract to practical knowledge. In this period, when science was neither compartmentalized into various disciplines nor isolated from the humanities, it provided a new empirical approach to issues that formerly would have been treated theologically or metaphysically. And participants extended that approach along a broad front. Although we presuppose a chasm between the two cultures of the arts and the sciences, these participants used exactly the same scientific and empirical methods of analysis and discussion to treat fevers, philosophers' stones, commercial agendas, and family relationships.

The conferences are fundamentally shaped by several attitudes that allow them to comment on the social. In particular they assert that empirical evidence weighs against arguments from authority even on ethical questions. As a result, they turn science into a powerful method of analysis for discussing and shaping the social values that they believe should characterize seventeenth-century France. The science they practice provides some specific rationales for social commentary. First, by his wisdom the man of reason, perhaps best embodied in the physician, is able to assess the proper, and therefore virtuous, course of action. Second, social problems are understood according to the medical analogy with disease, so they are to be dealt with pragmatically and according to the evidence of science. (This does not mean that consensus or uniformity of opinion is any more characteristic of discussions of social topics than it is of scientific ones.) It seems both unusual and quite modern that participants should so frequently invoke science to suggest solutions to social problems and to provide the basis for governmental policies.

Participants share several fundamental presuppositions that foster this approach. First, they believe that society is natural and therefore its policies should reflect nature. Second, they consider the health of society in general and specific states in particular as in some ways akin to the health of an individual and governed by the same practices; thus the knowledge and authority of the physician is important. Finally, they consider that to determine effective policies, one must understand the motives of the citizens of the state, and motivations can be understood in physiological terms. (Subsequent chapters explore how these ideas about nature and science are applied to more specifically social topics.)

Perhaps unexpectedly, given the scientific content of the conferences, they can also be used to sustain a broader argument that attitudes of vital importance to the promulgation of the new science developed independently of the mechanical revolution. Even if these texts cannot be neatly correlated to the paradigm shift that still dominates the historiography of science, conferees announce a number of attitudes that are critical to the success of science. First, they explicitly divorce science and religion. Renaudot's preface to the collection of the first hundred conferences specifically and overtly opposes religious topics, and participants rarely invoke religious explanations. No doubt the intent is to avoid the shoals of theological disputation, but the effect is to present science unfettered by dogma. Second, participants are also disinclined to credit tradition and authority, they discourage citation as a way to shore up argument. They do, however, consistently appeal to the empirical and the practical as new standards for evidence. They claim to exercise the most stringent critical stance. Conscious that science affords them a new standard from which to judge and against which the old can be winnowed out, they also understand that science offers a means of social analysis with practical implications and utilitarian benefits that they eagerly apply and disseminate.[16]

CHAPTER SIX

Souls, Passions, Learning, and Language

Human Nature, Human Knowledge

W HEN SPEAKERS DISCUSS "OF INTELLECT,"[1] THEY FIRST REFER TO the Aristotelian categories of the rational, animal, and vegetative souls, but the real question they focus on is the connection between body and soul, obviously one of great importance within the theological tradition of the Christian West. This issue would be central to all philosophical discussions in the aftermath of Descartes's separation of body and soul and mind and matter, announced in the 1637 publication of the *Discourse on Method*. Conferees grappled with the problematic parameters of these issues both before and after Descartes made this one of the central elements of contemporary philosophical discussion. Some speakers treat such topics within the general parameters of the theological tradition, but most (as in scientific topics) try to keep the discussion within the natural; in this case, they attempt to naturalize the soul. For example, when the first speaker explains how one could have ideas separate from the senses, he claims that, although the intellect is a faculty of the soul, it is categorically different from other faculties because it must operate free from the sense organs. Some have even thought, he notes, that God performs human intellectual actions, because the operations of the intellect seem so far beyond the range of sensible faculties. Although he does not deny the "divine" character of thought, he is uncomfortable with divine agency. Nonetheless, he insists that "intellection" cannot be the product of the senses, because "that which is sensible and material, remaining such, cannot act upon what is spiritual and immaterial," thus espousing the neoplatonic view that the two are separate. Because of his adherence to a theological understanding of the soul, he is backed into a rather nebulous position on the intellect. He, like many of his contemporaries, is left in a quandary about the connections between the intellect and the senses and the body and soul—critical questions of seventeenth-century philosophy.

For another speaker, the intellect integrates man into the great chain of being and mediates between the body and soul or, as he puts it, "the intellect is to the soul as the soul is to the body, which it perfects." The soul, as the apogee in the human hierarchy, is the essential link unifying man and uniting him through analogous operations to nature and to heaven. This faculty is "Jacob's ladder, which reaches from earth to heaven, by which the angels, that is, the species and most spiritual notions, ascend to the heaven of man, which is his brain, to inform him, and cause the *spiritus* to descend from there to put into practice the excellent inventions of the understanding." The soul also explains the occult knowledge of the cognoscenti and the Magi, for "God has given to all men ratiocinating, but not understanding, which he proposes to reward his favorites." For these speakers, the quasi-divine nature of intellection raises questions about man's relationship to God and the rest of creation.

The next speaker begins with an essentially Cartesian position, arguing for a complete separation of body and soul. (The view that the intellect is immaterial, immortal, and entirely distinct from matter is a fundamental position in Cartesian philosophy but it also characterizes neoplatonism.) When he develops the epistemological implications of this separation, they are dramatically different from those of Descartes and more in keeping with neoplatonists. He contends that the soul, as separated from the body, "has nothing to do with sensitive knowledge," and is exempt "from the demands of the sensitive appetite." Like Descartes, for this speaker, thought is the characteristic of the soul. Because thought, unburdened by the senses, is so illuminating, his understanding of thought resembles Cartesian clear and distinct ideas. However, for him, the knowledge available to this separated soul not only has a different character, it is also more limited than for a soul united to the body. The soul connected to the body, he insists, has greater access to knowledge, because "entangled in the body, it receives some impressions resulting from the parts, humors, and spirits destined to its service." In contrast to Descartes, this speaker greatly appreciates the value of sensory knowledge and suggests that the experience of the soul enmeshed in the body is far richer than that of the soul detached from the body. It is striking how many ideas conferees share with Descartes, although they frequently deploy them to different ends. Other speakers on the topic of the intellect emphasize the control of the body, specifically the temperament, over the soul. This influence is demonstrated by the fact that the behavior of human beings changes with age, so that "children cannot perform the functions of the reasonable soul, because they are of a hot and moist temper, inapt for the actions of the understanding."

As this conference demonstrates, conferees did not hesitate to explore the most central, but also the most difficult and controversial, questions of seventeenth-century philosophy, epistemology and, ultimately, the new science. They used science (particularly medicine and physiology) to weigh conventional views of human nature, especially in debates over the passions. Conferees were also acutely interested in the pragmatic application of their epistemological concerns. Thus they considered at length what kinds of knowledge people can and should acquire, how they can most effectively convey it to each other, and how it can effect social change.

SOULS AND BODIES

Despite the inherently controversial nature of topics that explore the relationship between souls and bodies, conferees raise them repeatedly.[2] In considering the question "At what time the rational soul is infused,"[3] the first speaker asserts that it is infused when the body is created, "as religion obliges us to believe." He tries to determine, based on observation, when a human being is sufficiently developed to take on a rational soul. He modifies the conventional view based on Aristotle (who on the question of the infusion of soul received the imprimatur of Thomas Aquinas)[4] that the soul must await a time until "the conformation of the parts is finished, which is the thirtieth day for boys and the forty-second for girls, whose less hearty and more watery materials require a longer time for conformation of their spermatic parts." Without blanching in the face of his refutation of what he saw as Aristotelian and Thomistic orthodoxy, he concludes, only later "when the organization of the parts is perfected, to wit, about the third or fourth month," the inferior, vegetative soul "gives place upon the arrival of the reasonable soul."

The next speaker agrees that only after the body is virtually completely formed is the reasonable soul, as the end point of human development, infused. Because the soul, by its nature, cannot have anything in common with the corruptible body, it cannot depend on matter at all. He concludes that the soul is most probably infused the third day after conception, "at which time the actions of life appear in nutrition, growth, alteration, and configuration of the parts," activities that demonstrate the existence of the soul. Paradoxically, for him, although no property is shared between soul and body, the soul is both the principle of activity and contained in matter. The next speaker agrees and contends that the soul cannot be separated from the body no matter how severe the circumstances. Even under the most adverse circumstances, such as "apoplexy, which abolishes all the noble dispositions," the soul remains united to the body. Thus the fetus must have a soul from the time of conception. What is significant about these obviously inconclusive treatments of theologically charged topics is that participants, except for the formula "as religion obliges us to believe," treat these questions from a perspective that might be defined as the logical deductions from their understanding of the nature of life, substantiated by specific observations.

Other topics that would not seem directly relevant to the relationship between body and soul nonetheless have this question as their fundamental concern. For example, in discussing "Where do good and bad gestures, good grace and grimaces come from,"[5] the first speaker claims that the soul infuses the body like metal in a mold, but he describes the effects of physiology on behavior as so comprehensive that there is virtually no role for the soul. For him, the soul "exercises its functions according to diversity of organs and temperaments."[6]

On the question "If the evils of the spirit are greater than those of the body,"[7] a speaker points to examples (such as the man awaiting execution whose hair turned white overnight) to demonstrate the great evils of the spirit. Another insists that the spirit is affected only by means of the body, but he nonetheless maintains that "bodies feel only by the faculties of the soul that give them sentiment." For another, the passions of "fear, love, envy, ambition, jealousy" demonstrate that it is impossible to separate soul from body, because we know the soul only through body. A final speaker insists that the solution to this question depends on the distinction between spirits and temperaments—spirits act independently of the body, but temperament has a direct effect upon it. The inconsistent positions conferees express on these questions attest to a dilemma that preoccupied many more distinguished contemporary philosophers: not simply the relationship between body and soul but more specifically the complex relationship between the two in human action. This conference highlights differences of opinion about the relative influence of the body on the soul, but most participants discuss the soul in terms of the body.

A speaker on the topic "If the beauty of the body is indicative of the bounty and beauty of the spirit"[8] assumes the integral connection between body and soul. Because the soul provides the form of the body and the body is the guide to the soul, he assumes that physiognomy is a reasonable guide to character. Another speaker objects that, in the interests of justice (nature would not be so unjust as to give all her gifts to the same individual), there can be no relationship between beauty of the body and beauty of the soul. His opinion, he claims, is borne out by experience: the most twisted vines bear the sweetest grapes. Although, as this final speaker points out, the authorities are in conflict,[9] most participants are inclined to see an inverse relationship between good character and good looks, reflecting the view that equity requires the diffusion of nature's gifts. As we have seen, physiognomy was a controversial medical topic. Some extolled it as a diagnostic tool, some tied it to human character, and still others discounted it entirely.

Questions about the relationship between the body and the soul are perhaps too inherently controversial for participants to push their conclusions as far as they might like. They take a conference on the famous Aristotelian maxim "there is nothing in the intellect that has not been in the senses"[10] as an opportunity, not to discuss the epistemology of the scientific revolution (although this maxim raises those issues in other conferences, as we have seen) but to address instead questions of human nature. A speaker suggests that knowledge is built from sensations and can be acquired when the senses have developed sufficiently. The development of the senses is necessary for the requisite proportion between the senses and their object. Because the intellect must accommodate itself to the body, the intellect is never a blank slate but develops its capacity for knowledge as the body develops. The connection between bodily and mental states is critical, for "if the eye were angry, it could not be a judge of colors, any more than a tongue charged with bile could [judge] flavors."

Another speaker foreshadows a Pascalian view of human nature, or perhaps draws from the same Augustinian well. Man, he contends, is suspended between the animal and the divine, "resembling angel and beast." This intermediate position has led some to concur with Aristotle that there is nothing in the intellect that has not first passed by the senses, because association with matter taints all human operations. However, he insists that "there is nothing in our spirit that has had commerce with the senses," because spiritual power "should not be attached to this heavy mass." Reason must be acknowledged as decisively different from the instinct of beasts; beasts experience "that which is sensible," but the "soul is above all sentiments." This radical separation is necessary; "reason and liberty are not organic principles, they do not depend on organs." Although he takes what seems to be a Platonic or Cartesian position on the separation of body and soul, his conception of that separation seems rooted in the theological. To unify the body and soul, he insists, is "to shock notably the immortality of the soul," for the soul "flies more freely the more that it is distant from the earth."

The next speaker disputes the radical separation, for even "our most delicate thoughts" are tied to material images, and thus they are not entirely spiritual. The actions of the soul cannot be divorced from matter, for as he puts it, "if the soul as reasonable informs the body, as the greater part of philosophers maintain, it is necessary that all the acts of reason depend as much on the mass as on a spiritual principle." Furthermore the radical separation leads to dangerous positions, such as "the error of those who believe that our soul is attached to the body only by assistance, as a sailor is united to his boat." Such a separation, he insists, also refutes common experiential evidence derived from case studies of mental illnesses. Another speaker carves out a middle position between two extremes. Although he concedes that it is certainly possible that "the greater part of our intelligence is joined to the operations of the fantasy" (in other words, connected to the body through the imagination), we know certain things independently of the senses. For example, we know "the thing purely possible," which has never been in nature and thus "never touched the senses," and we have knowledge of God and the angels without the senses.

The last two speakers call into question this speaker's argument; he has, by their lights, put into play issues that should have no role in this forum. By raising a merely possible phenomenon, he has made the topic one that is not appropriate to a conference, since discussions must focus on real phenomena. (Even when they discussed topics like unicorns, they attempted to establish evidence for or against the existence of such phenomena.) They both vigorously object that the topic is a religious one and therefore should not be discussed.

In a conference on "If the human spirit is limited in its operations and why,"[11] a speaker proclaims that there can be no reason to consider the spirit of man limited, since it ranges freely from the center of the earth to the firmament. Man's memory allows him to "make an infinite number of connections," and his inventions imitate "the operations of the creator." Since theologians and metaphysicians agree that man is the image of God, man must not be limited, "our spirit being created to know the creator and the creator being infinite." He approaches Cartesian dualism but casts the argument in religious terms. While the first speaker notes all the attributes of the spirit but disparages those of the body, the second emphasizes the limits the body imposes on the spirit. The soul must accommodate itself to "the operations of external senses, which are limited, and so limit the soul that she ceases to see as soon as the body does not have eyes any more." Internal senses also limit the body so that, for example, inflammation of the brain membrane produces delirium.

In considering the relationship between body and soul, many speakers raise issues that preoccupied Descartes at roughly the same time.[12] These issues, so central to the preeminent philosophical works of the early modern period, are deeply rooted in fundamental epistemological questions. To a degree we perhaps rarely appreciate, they form the basis of seventeenth-century discussions of philosophical topics by those (such as Renaudot's conferees) who have made a limited impression on the historical record. Although they raise controversial points and play with interesting ideas, speakers are unwilling or incapable of forming these into a coherent system. Theirs is an exercise that addresses specific questions from whatever perspective the individual wants to take. Looking for adherence to a specific or consistent philosophical position or methodological research program in the conferences, as some historians of science have, has been futile. What is significant about the conferences is their range and their level of engagement rather than their systematic character. These topics impinge on theology and demonstrate participants' preoccupation with ideas that had controversial implications. But conferees take an important and distinctive approach to these topics; in essence, they naturalize and physicalize the soul—an approach that encroaches on conventional theological and metaphysical treatments of it. They then extend this approach into discussions of human nature.

THE PHYSIOLOGY OF HUMAN NATURE

When participants raise questions about human nature, they frequently cast them as traditional rhetorical themes about virtues and vices, but they also apply whatever scientific information they have at their disposal. That science shapes discussions of ethical issues should not be surprising, given the dominance of science as a crucial standard of evidence and certainty in these conferences and the increased cultural expectations imposed on science. However, the connections between science and ethical discussions are striking for a number of reasons. Participants correlate human behavior, from the simplest to the most complex, to a general understanding of the operations of nature.[13] They assert the significance of physiology to any discussion of human motivation or ability. They take it as a given that the soul depends on the body or, as one speaker puts it, that "its operations . . . are different according to the divers structure of the organs."[14] As the discussion of epistemological issues reveals, some participants grapple with Cartesian-like dualism; however, when they discuss human nature they integrate the soul into the body. Probably because the body is more susceptible to analysis, the soul is frequently discussed in terms of the body.

As a way to analyze human nature, speakers consistently draw analogies between emotions and scientific processes. For example, friendship joins two parties in the same way that like seeks like or, as another speaker puts it, nature unites matter and form.[15] The passions are to the soul as disease is to the body.[16] Ambition begets a "hypertrophic thirst of the soul, which all the waters of the world cannot allay," while "zeal for one's own opinion" is the result of the antipathy of diverse humors.[17] Human discontent is explained by man's position within the macrocosm-microcosm. Since the heavens are in continual motion, man, as the noblest part of the inferior world, "cannot be at rest."[18] This analogy is interesting because it first redefines the Aristotelian notion of fixed stars as a source not of stability but of agitation. The use of analogies in these cases suggests a greater prescriptive authority than analogies usually exert in the conferences. But whether these particular analogies are genuinely explanatory or simply a persuasive rhetorical stratagem, they demonstrate that physiology enjoys a privileged position in explaining human character; it clearly explains the physical manifestations of the emotions.[19]

Conferees apply their understanding of nature to human beings with contradictory conclusions; some speakers assert a positive view of man's abilities and accomplishments, whereas others use nature to explain human failing. But on both sides of the issue, the understanding of nature provides crucial evidence for their positions. For example, a speaker on "Why no one is content with his condition" suggests that the restlessness of men corresponds to the constant transitions in nature.[20] Another compares the variety of nature with the vicissitudes of fortune. But, according to him, variety is entirely arbitrary; thus nature's favors do not reflect merit or acknowledge the efforts of the individual: "We see many persons enriched without performance of any service, . . . hated by those they love, and loved by those they hate. For all of which we must either assign some cause, or confess that there is no other cause of it but hap or mishap, which they call fortune."[21] This is an interesting juxtaposition of arguments about the effects of nature. Nature is the agent responsible for human characteristics and fortune, but although nature and human nature are in conformity, nature and civil society are fundamentally out of sync.

The use of nature allowed speakers to explore the physiological basis of emotions. "Nature" was also equivalent to fate or the indifference of the universe to the individual. To some degree, the very inclusion of the vagaries of physiology and the myriad of scientific influences on an individual's character introduces some relativity into discussion of human actions, including moral actions. If conferees discuss the emotions and the passions primarily in physiological terms, it is a short step to take for them to argue that physiology influences our ability to behave morally. One speaker spells out this connection forcefully: "We must not seek the cause of our vicious inclination other than within ourselves; it being derived from the structure and composition of our bodies." The effect of the body on our ability to practice virtue is decisive; "poor virtue meets with nothing in us but opposition; the stomach, the intestines, and all natural parts revolt against temperance and continence: the choleric humor fights against clemency."[22]

Participants also understand pleasure and pain, the fundamental principles of a utilitarian ethos, primarily in terms of their physiological effects. One speaker notes, "Pleasure and joy produce the same effects, . . . namely, too great a dilation of the spirits."[23] Another speaker traces in vivid terms the physiological effects of the passions; "they make the body suffer and cause an alteration in the heart and pulse." The passions have clear physiological correlates. "Those that aim at pleasure, enervate contraction, because they dilate the spirits; . . . those that relate to sadness diminish dilation." Each passion has a distinct physiological process as its material cause; anger, for example, is "an ebullition of the blood."[24] The ways participants describe physiological causes and emotional effects seem close to a process one might want to consider automatic or mechanical. They carefully describe the passions as specific physiological responses, which, because they are "automatic" effects of a particular cause, are predictable, measurable, and modifiable. When historians of science look for the influence of mechanism on medicine, they look for descriptions of physiological processes in terms of machines. However, in the rather broader sense of a mechanical philosophy that understands nature as following clear laws with predictable, quantifiable results, at least some discussion of the passions by conferees is mechanical.

There are compelling reasons for participants to use physiology to discuss the emotions. Physiology is flexible enough to advance plausible arguments, both positive and negative, about the ultimate value of any specific passion, and, the connection between physiology and passion is not so hard and fast that competing notions of the connection cannot be offered. Questions touching the physiology of the passions also frequently appeal to the authority of individual experience.

Participants bring some rather novel perspectives to bear on traditional ethical and social issues in part because they feel quite comfortable extending the right and role of science to comment on them. They consider physiology to be the crucial determinant of human motivations and abilities, and they detail the effects of specific substances on human character. Physiology offers them an opportunity to come to terms with human nature and to categorize human behavior with a greater degree of theoretical control than might be possible with the abstract view of human nature that characterizes most philosophical discussion. They instead suggest the cultural relativism of virtue and vice and assume that the passions manifest themselves differently in people of different temperaments.

No matter what the topic, science offers these participants an opportunity to explore issues from many perspectives, providing a flexible tool and a method of analysis and explanation. When they apply science and scientific arguments and examples, they find medicine and physiology particularly useful because the arguments and the evidence are both malleable and socially useful and appropriate. Conferees can use physiology not only to relativize issues like the passions but also to question absolute values associated with the classical tradition.

UNDERMINING ABSOLUTES

When conferees address what might be considered transcendent values, they are inclined to challenge conventions, to break down universals, and to advocate social and cultural relativism. The very format of the conferences, which asserts that the way to truth is to lay out antithetical views, demonstrates an inherent relativism, which is most apparent in conferences that consider abstract ideals. For example, a conference on beauty[25] pits the classical appreciation of beauty against newer and more relativistic attitudes. Although the first speaker places beauty among the great transcendents such as goodness and truth, he immediately undermines its transcendent character by saying that each kind of thing has its own standards of beauty.[26] Another speaker, even more effectively undermining the notion of universals, asserts that beauty is imaginary and thus "has more to do with the fantasy than with nature." Ultimately, he insists, beauty is a judgment about what pleases us. A final speaker who argues for absolute, transcendent beauty challenges these proponents of the relative. He insists on the connection between the ideal and the natural and cites Plato, who says that beauty is produced when form predominates over matter, and Aristotle, who will not allow perfect happiness without the beauty of the body. This speaker immediately undermines his own argument, pointing out that the appreciation of beauty is cultural: "White is esteemed among northern nations because there issues out of white bodies a certain brightness or light agreeable to the eyes of those people. But the same color loses that pre-eminence proportionally as one approaches the south." This conference deals with the one topic most frequently invoked in the Western tradition to present universals, and, although some speakers want to invoke them, even they erode the universal by rooting beauty in time, place, and culture. Whenever participants apply abstract qualities to human beings, they immediately introduce the relative, the customary, and the evidence of experience.

Participants also discuss specific virtues in both physiological and cultural terms. In a conference entitled "Of courage,"[27] one speaker emphasizes, as many participants do, the integral relationship between virtue and physiology. He says that, since courage is found in all stations of life, it must "proceed from the fitting and well-proportioned temper and structure of the heart and arteries." Some arguments for a hereditary monarchy are based on a physiological notion of virtues such as courage. One speaker, who claims that courage is generally found in the nobility, qualifies this claim, noting that "there seem to be some intervals in illustrious families proceeding from malignant influences." Nonetheless, courage in noble families is due to the resemblance of children to their ancestors, in mind and body, "eagles never producing doves, nor doves eagles."

In a conference on "If courage is natural or acquired,"[28] a speaker notes that fear of danger is natural and that there is no true courage without knowledge of danger. He cites, as do most of the speakers on this topic, the courage of the French soldier. Another participant argues that, if courage could be acquired through instruction, everyone trained the same way would be courageous, but the differences between people with the same training are so significant that for some courage must be as natural as "the structure of parts of bodies, the temperament of humors." Furthermore (and this consideration seems to weigh heavily with several of the speakers), the assumption of a natural predisposition to courage and presumably other virtues is the basis of the inherited nobility: "The infant ordinarily holds to the habits of bodies and temperaments of their mothers and fathers, from which comes that courage which seems to come from race, that which makes possible our nobility." However, as this speaker notes, "at all times, instruction serves to greatly perfect nature . . . but art can do nothing without nature."

This topic was of sufficient interest that conferees raised it again in the form of the question "If courage comes from nature or from institution,"[29] where a conferee addresses the question through the story of an infant raised by wolves. Tales of this sort were fascinating and offered examples relevant to many philosophical issues.[30] In this version of the story, the child rejoined the human community when men attacked the wolves and took him alive. The child retained his ability to relate to wild animals for several years and ultimately died fighting in a war. The point of this story is that the infant would not have been so courageous had he not learned courage from the wolves. The Spartans also provided a model of the way to inculcate courage, exposing their young warriors to ferocious dogs. To avoid anything that could dissipate courage (love of gold, for example), they prohibited foreign merchants. When the Romans wanted to control a people, they deliberately cultivated those arts that would make them weaker; they made them learn music and forbade them war exercises. In other words, avoidance of the arts and exposure to ferocity foster courage. For the next speaker, temperament or nature as opposed to nurture produces courageous actions: "Because art cannot have privileges greater than those of nature, it is thus impossible to change nature." Another speaker relies on empirical evidence from medicine to demonstrate that courage can be fostered. All physicians agree that "complexions change one to another, according to the usage of six things they call the non-naturals." Thus with diet and other therapeutic measures one can change temperaments so much so that an individual "will not only quit his phlegmatic temperament, but will become bilious, and as courageous as he was formerly a poltroon." This malleability of temperaments leads the speaker to the following pragmatic conclusion: if courage were natural and not susceptible to nurture, it would be wrong to punish cowardice.

A conference on "Whether virtue consists in mediocrity"[31] questions another classical ideal, the mean as the root of virtue. The first speaker supports the classical view that the via media is the route to virtue because everything destitute of reason is carried to extremes, and extremes are everywhere found to be vicious. He cites two extremes, both vicious: the prodigal and the miser. "The prodigal by doing good to others, does hurt to himself; the miser does no good to others and much less to himself." Rashness and cowardice are two extremes, "but valor, holding a mean between both, prevents them." For another speaker, the mean suggests mediocrity, which he harshly castigates as the refuge of small-minded and irresolute souls. These fence-sitters "keep themselves indifferent to any choice; and so long as they do so, they show their want of masculine virtue." Mediocrity must be abhorred. Indifferent friends "God will spew out of His mouth, they being, in truth, no better than hypocrites." Charity, justice, and valor ought to be extreme. Mediocrity thus poses a serious threat to society: "If you have to deal with a priest about a case of conscience, is anything more insupportable than to find an unresolved mind? The same may be said of an ambiguous lawyer and physician, who send back their clients and patients more dissatisfied than they came." This conference reveals a conflict between those who are committed to an ideal (and thus insist on either the via media or extremes as the sources of virtue) and those who look at the circumstantial evidence of specific cases in which mediocrity may be not only undesirable but positively abhorrent.

In general, the discussion of virtues assaults classical ideals as too remote from contemporary experience, which for some conferees supports a more nuanced view. They use the classics, but the weight of the classical tradition is no longer a heavy burden forcing them to shape their thought around its contours. The specific evidence to challenge classical abstractions is drawn from science, particularly medical and physiological opinion. When they consider the fundamental question of whether human behavior can be socially modified, participants tend to be both impressed by the sway of nature and optimistic about what rational and empirical assessment, so characteristic of medical analysis, can add to the discussion of social issues.

THE PASSIONS

The passions even more directly connect medicine to social analysis. The passions had a long-standing connection to medicine because certain mental conditions, most notably melancholia, were traditionally under the purview of medical treatment. Because the passions were also discussed in the context of the Christian tradition (sin was rooted in the passions), they were a specific focus of theological discussion.[32] Renaudot's conferees generally reject the association between the passions and theology; they instead alter the nature of the discussion by placing the passions firmly in the medical realm. As the terms of the argument become less religious, the discussion of the passions grows less controversial. If they were treated primarily as medical phenomena, the passions could, ironically, be seen as both more universal and more particular—universal as common to all human bodies, particular as characteristic of an individual physiological constitution. In the medical tradition, treatment of ills of the passions is based less on the assumption that self-control is the solution and more on specific therapeutic recommendations.

When philosophers focused on the passions, they compared them to reason to the detriment of the passions—reason was active, the passions passive; reason was rooted in the intellect, the passions were dependent on the body and occupied uneasy terrain between the body and the intellect. When philosophers raised moral questions, the ability of the individual to control the passions through the will became crucial. As Stephen Gaukroger has noted, in the early modern period the imperative to self-control was broadened and connected to mastery of nature; in essence, the passions, as the Stoics had claimed, provided false judgments, and therefore failure to master them stood in the way of knowledge and science. The passions then were antithetical, even hostile, to the rational mathematical sciences. Thus, largely because of contemporary concern that they stood to frustrate the rational efforts of science, the passions provoked a vast literature in the seventeenth century.[33]

Conferees were less inclined than some of their contemporaries to focus on the problematic nature of the passions. Instead they consider that the passions can be most appropriately addressed by incorporating them into a broad discussion of human physiology. They employ what had always been a part of the discussion of the passions, that is, an emphasis on their physiological dimensions. Their appreciation for this approach is much more positive than that of many of their contemporaries, probably because of their adherence to medicine. Because they are aware that understanding the passions physiologically allows for broad social commentary, conferees make a distinctive contribution to the seventeenth-century debate on the passions.[34] Although they generally agree that the passions have physiological causes and effects ("a passion is an irregular motion of the sensitive appetite"),[35] they disagree over whether the passions are forces for good or ill. Some take the conventional approach and argue that it is only by taming the passions that man can act morally. For example, on the question "Whether it is better to be without the passions than to moderate them,"[36] one speaker claims that "the true moral wisdom of man, considered alone, consists in taming his passions and subjecting them to the command of reason." Others claim that through the passions men "degrade themselves below beasts." One speaker drew a medical analogy: "What a disease is to the body, whose actions it hurts, so are the passions to the soul." Because the passions are akin to disease, "to ask whether the soul is happiest without passion, is to question whether the body is most at ease without sickness." Others suggest that reason serves "to moderate them and hinder the disorder caused by them in the sensitive appetite." One speaker makes a staunch case for the passions. Without them "there would be no virtues, for the passions are the objects of virtues; thus temperance moderates pleasure and pain, fortitude regulates boldness and fear." Furthermore the passions preserve the animal, because pleasure incites animals to feed and reproduce. This conference comes to an inconclusive end, when the final speaker concludes, "we quit our passions, but they quit us not."

Even though some participants appreciate the Stoic criticism of the passions, many assess stoicism critically. Although one speaker in "Of the apathy of the Stoics"[37] acknowledges that the Stoics rightly consider the passions as a source of vice and seek to cure vices at their source, he takes issue with the social implications of stoicism. To go too far down that path, he claims, reduces humans to the level of stones and discounting the passions can also have ill effects. For example, a child who cannot be motivated by appeals to passions, such as fear, will be incorrigible, and an incorrigible child will be a "pest to the state when he is grown." (This makes an interesting point about the relationship between philosophy and politics.) Even such a model Stoic as Seneca professed his love for a woman when he lay dying, conclusively demonstrating that even the most stoical cannot manage it all the time. Scorn for the passions, some speakers suggest, makes human beings unnatural, and the unnatural child becomes the unnatural citizen.

Discussions of the passions are an important barometer of social attitudes. The conference "Which is most powerful, hope or fear"[38] indicates the wide variety of issues the human passions raise and the ways in which scientific and social issues impinge on each other. A speaker describes fear as of two sorts; filial, which is mixed with proper respect, and servile, which arises only from anticipating punishment. Because fear has these two distinct manifestations, it is an emotion that can be manipulated effectively to produce desired social ends. Fear is a universal motivator because, although only the good feel hope, both the good and the bad feel fear. Thus no state "encourages virtue to hope for anything, but all infuse an abhorrence of crimes with the fear of punishments."[39] For some speakers, if the passions are physiological, they are then part of lower animal functions. While the manipulation of the passions might make for the good of the state, social policies based on fear might put our claims to rationality at risk.[40]

While conferees discuss specific passions in physiological terms, they also want to determine not simply whether a specific passion is good or bad, or even whether it is good or bad for the individual, but whether it is beneficial or harmful to society. A telling example is the conference dedicated to the topic of envy.[41] The first speaker begins with an unflinching denunciation of envy; "it is no wonder man is so miserable, since not only the evil but also the good of others renders him equally unhappy." He describes the ignoble antecedents of envy: "Pride is the mother of it, self-love the father, treachery, dissimulation, detraction and ruin its daughters." The next speaker contends that, while other vices have some ameliorating aspect (covetousness, for example, can produce public benefits), envy has no positive features; it is the "sworn enemy of mankind for the envious looks only askance upon the prosperity of others, the thought of which incessantly gnaws his heart." Envy, like other passions, has serious physiological manifestations, consuming its practitioner "by drying up the blood in his veins." Another speaker objects that envy has some utility, for the competition motivated by envy fuels the interests of the state in a number of ways; it causes artists to try to outdo one another, and states to try to limit "the grandeur of neighboring states." Others note that actions motivated by envy have produced unintended but beneficial effects on society. Some Romans, motivated by envy, tried to blemish Cato's reputation by calling him before the senate forty-six times, but this only made him more famous. "And the poison that it [envy] made Socrates drink, killed his body indeed, but rendered his memory immortal."

Some speakers thus suggest that the ultimate outcome of an action must be taken into account before indicting the passion that produced it. Others insist that no good can come from such a malign influence. One said, "it is such an irregular passion that it seems to aim at subverting the established order of nature and making other laws after its own fancy, a monster composed of all of the vicious passions."[42] Several participants express concern that any given passion, especially one as malign as envy, undermines reason and works against man's better nature. The passions that have an entire conference dedicated to them are those with compelling social implications.[43] Envy, for example, is so topical because the social dislocation caused by the rise of new elites elicits it.

Although religious issues are not central to these conferences, traditional theological arguments combine with Stoic sensibilities to shape some discussion of the passions, largely because the passions are deemed so fundamental to human nature, and in particular, to any notion of sin. For conferees, the passions function largely as a physiological phenomenon with social implications. For virtue to flourish, the passions need to be controlled or at least understood. Some of those who seek to constrain the passions work within the Stoic tradition. Others use physiology as a less-value-laden descriptive tool and as a way to appeal to empirical evidence. Much discussion of the passions asserts that society should neutralize the evils in human behavior by turning the passions to good purpose and that, in effect, the interests of the state can be attained by manipulating the passions to this end. Speakers go to considerable lengths to find some socially or politically redeeming facet of specific passions that otherwise might be denounced. They are much less interested in condemning the passions than in assessing them in terms of their effects. Whether a quality is praiseworthy is relative to its effect, especially on the public sphere. The relativism of the conferences, particularly the sense that good frequently comes out of evil, is based on fairly widespread optimism. There are many ways for participants to positively construe the passions. For example, because we share with animals appetites that foster self-preservation, some of the passions, like anger, contribute to self-preservation and thus must be acknowledged as a gift of nature.

A conference "Of shame"[44] makes the general relativism of the conferences explicit by claiming that the passions are evil or good under different circumstances. It is, a speaker contends, important to particularize discussion of specific passions, like anger or shame, because they have different effects depending on the situation. For example, shame must be recognized as a distinct manifestation of grief. Grief over evil in another provokes our compassion, but if the evil is in us "and apprehended as prejudicial to our honor, it causes shame." Ultimately, shame occurs when we fall short of our end, which is the exercise of the will and the understanding "and so being less than men: but (as Plato said) monsters of nature." Although this speaker describes shame in universal terms ("Some things are of themselves shameful, because they are vicious"), another points out the relativity of the situations that produce it. Some things are shameful only in certain times and places "to which the customs of each country, for the most part, give law."

Discussions of specific passions emphasize the cultural relativism associated with the manifestations and assessments of these sentiments. For example, a speaker on jealousy claims that this passion depends on the climates, "northern people being very little subject to it; whereas those in the South cannot hear a mass or a sermon, without a wall between the men and the women."[45] Even virtue and vice vary by nationality. On the question "Which is the greatest vice," a conferee notes that "in Sparta it was no crime to steal, and some northern nations are undecided about drunkenness."[46]

Participants, probably because of their interest in medicine, consistently acknowledge that the physiological constitution of the individual complicates discussion of the passions even more. If the passions are physiologically based, they are also individualistic because they are directly subject to the components of an individual physiological constitution. Society then can be criticized for unreasonably inhibiting the individual. This understanding of the passions provokes some arguments for tolerance. For example, a speaker on the topic "What is the greatest delight of man" remarks that "the same thing may cause joy to one imagination and repugnance to another as many different humors and inclinations as there are, so different will the judgments be upon this question." Another speaker follows up on this point to argue against prohibiting what gives one joy as "a kind of inhumanity."[47]

Whether deliberately or unintentionally, participants promote relativism and individualism and thus adumbrate positions from which to criticize existing social institutions: relativism because, if no abstraction warrants universal acceptance, then one concedes at the outset that there are no absolutes; individualism because there is no reason to impede the individual, if allowing him to follow his natural proclivities does no harm. Nevertheless, all discussions of the passions, even in their physiological dimensions, are dedicated at least implicitly toward altering human behavior. The conferences that explore human motivation try to get at the root of what will produce virtuous behavior. Because the passions can be discussed in terms of utilitarian ends, they implicitly contribute to the discussion of politics and economics.

The conferences can be understood as part of the rich political and philosophical discussion of the passions in the seventeenth century. By the seventeenth century, the tradition which argued that virtue could be produced by manipulating vice to serve the interests of the state was well established. Montaigne was one of the most effective promulgators of this position.[48] But unlike Montaigne, conferees do not offer the *politique* solution of a public morality that accommodates itself to political realities and a private morality concerned with the cultivation of private virtue.

Any number of significant thinkers of the seventeenth century (Descartes, Gassendi, and Pierre Charron, among others) address the passions in a concerted fashion. Descartes wrote *The Passions of the Soul* long after the conferences,[49] and Gassendi's Christianized epicureanism was both controversial and in its philosophical and linguistic complexity beyond the realm of general popular discussion. Charron's *Of Wisdome* was more accessible and an especially influential seventeenth-century treatment of the passions. He presented two distinct views of them. The first invoked the classical ideal of the wise man who is able to discipline his passions through the exercise of reason. But Charron offered an alternative model for the man who was not a sage. Unable to control himself, he must be controlled by outside forces, for he cannot be constrained to virtue through his desire to be thought well of by others.[50] Renaudot's conferences do posit a distinction between the views of the educated and those of the vulgar, which occasionally extends to their ability to understand political realities. However, perhaps due to the social openness of the conferences, they do not sharply divide society between the wise and the ignorant. The vision of culture they offer is much more homogeneous. It is most striking that they do not propose different standards of morality for elites and non-elites.

It is instructive to compare briefly the moral guidance offered by Charron's text with that conveyed in the conferences. Conferees accept a hierarchical notion of the human being, which places the soul above the body, but they disagree with Charron about other crucial characteristics of the passions. Charron proclaims "the soul is as a little God, the body as a beast, as a dunghill." The conferences are much less inclined to posit a dichotomy between soul and body, according to which the soul is the source of good and the body unmitigated evil. Charron insists that because the spirit of man is dangerous, "especially if it be quick and vigorous," it "must be bridled." He acknowledges no socially ameliorating aspect of the passions and is unstinting in his denunciation of them. For him, covetousness is a "gangrene in the soul." Revenge is a "cowardly and effeminate passion," characteristic of the weakest minds (those of women and children, for example). Man is, in Charron's assessment, "vain, feeble, frail, inconstant in good" but "strong, constant, and hardened in misery."[51] This pessimistic view of man is strikingly absent from the much more optimistic, measured, and pragmatic assessment of human nature and human passions in the conferences.

Discussions of the passions and human nature are not any more likely to produce a consensus of opinion than any other topic treated. But it is interesting, given the broad range of issues the passions provoked in seventeenth-century philosophical and scientific discussion, that participants chose to emphasize particular strands. First, they are much more likely to assume that the passions serve positive functions, and thus less likely to treat them as entirely negative in their impact on reason or behavior. Second, they emphasize particular manifestations of the passions and treat them therapeutically. Finally, when participants consider the moral and epistemological issues associated with the passions, they focus more on pragmatic than on theoretical concerns.

THE SOCIAL RAMIFICATIONS OF KNOWLEDGE

The conference on "From where diversity of opinion comes"[52] is one of many that treat the social ramifications of how knowledge is conveyed. It explicitly addresses the problematic epistemological and social issues raised by the reformation and wars of religion. Why couldn't there be a consensus of opinion? Why couldn't people hear the same speech and have the same assessment of it? One can sense a desire for consensus, a hope that a biblical passage, for instance, might produce the same understanding among all those who hear it. One speaker cites a fundamental reason that people respond differently to the same text or speech. "To what shall we ascribe it except to the soul alone, that some men are naturally so given to devotion, that in an affair wherein religion is never so little concerned they account nothing equitable against Ecclesiastics; and, in the meantime, there are others to whom whatever this sort of people propose is suspect." No wonder that religious issues have proved divisive.

Another speaker attempts to understand this dilemma by drawing a crucial distinction between responses to issues that involve practical opinion and those concerned with speculation. Practical opinions "follow the temperament and conformation of organs." For example, "the melancholy man, who fears even imaginary dangers, cannot be persuaded to prefer trading at sea over trading on land, but is always prepared to risk nothing." Things that pertain directly to us are speculative, and on speculative topics, individuals are less constrained by their temperaments or physiological predispositions. Their lack of restraint is the result of "the vanity and ambition of the human mind, which judges itself to be as capable and sufficient as any other." On speculative topics all love "liberty, which seems disparaged by consenting to an opinion advanced by another." Thus speculative topics such as religion, philosophy, and science inevitably provoke great disagreements. "We see Scotus, disagreeing with Saint Thomas, as Paracelsus does in physick with Galen, Copernicus with Ptolemy in Mathematics,

Raymond Lully and Ramus in Scholastic philosophy with Aristotle."[53] One speaker privileges mathematics as the only speculative kind of knowledge immune from divided opinion.

In general, the conferences focus considerable attention on epistemological issues, especially those associated with science. It is a mistake to dismiss these discussions as mere rhetorical flourishes designed to attest to the intellectual prowess of the speakers.[54] Instead conferees seek to explore and understand the philosophical implications of the epistemological topics. The conference format encouraged them to be self-aware and self-critical about their own endeavors, even asking such questions as whether the conference was an effective way to learn. The conferees constantly recur to three questions: Is knowledge valuable? How should it be acquired? And what social benefits does it have?

A speaker on the topic "Why all men naturally desire knowledge"[55] begins by asking if indeed it is true that they do. He makes the obvious argument that there cannot be a natural desire for knowledge because so few pursue it. "In a school of five hundred scholars you shall scarce find fifty that have profited well from learning." Another returns the topic to its Aristotelian premises, claiming that each learns according to his abilities. Several speakers see the quest for knowledge as spiritual, insisting that ultimately the "natural quest for knowledge is rooted in man's desire to know his creator." One speaker extols knowledge as the means to honor, prerogative, and pleasure.

A conference that asks "If man can have too much knowledge"[56] is particularly significant because some speakers connect the term *les sciences* to a modern understanding of the sciences. Speakers claim, for example, that "les sciences" allow man to penetrate the inner realm of the earth and to envision imaginary space. Such knowledge is gained by the ascent of the intellect to a truth manifested by demonstration. This use of the term documents an evolution from "les sciences" as knowledge in general to "les sciences" as the specific study of nature. On the topic itself, the first speaker suggests that this is a rather absurd subject for a conference, since it is akin to asking if a man can see too clearly. He enumerates some of the more significant benefits of knowledge: it perfects the understanding; it helps discern good from evil (thus demons tempt men with the promise of wisdom because it is our greatest good); and the more enlightened a man is the closer to the angels and more remote from the beasts he is. He then describes the process whereby truth is known as the acquiescence of the intellect to a truth that demonstration teaches it; inquietude comes from a lack of demonstration. Not only does this notion of the assent of the intellect when confronted by or persuaded by demonstration seem Cartesian, it also suggests a position on knowledge that is fundamentally hostile to skepticism. The speaker attacks the claim that we can know too much by vehemently asserting, "no one will say that we can know too much about God or the things that concern our health." To excuse their own ignorance, the credulous have called into question all knowledge. This speaker is vehement in refuting any notion that knowledge is dangerous to faith; too little knowledge about faith is dangerous because doubts come from ignorance.

Except for a caveat about religious knowledge, the next speaker violently disagrees with the first and insists that we can indeed know too much. Just as too much light makes it impossible to see, so too much knowledge distorts judgment. Judgment, he insists, is clearest without too much knowledge. The quest for knowledge is also physically debilitating and indicates human vanity, mere curiosity. He contends that, "in civil society, great learning is not only useless but often harmful and always suspect." Because of his distrust of learning, he maintains that "one should much prefer to deal with a good bourgeois of no or mediocre learning than with refined and subtle spirits," for well-educated spirits are not conducive to the harmony of the state. It is the great wise men who "become heretics and who meddle in the affairs of others, . . . who rebel against common views by their own opinions, undermining the union of spirits, which is the condition most essential to maintain a state in peace." He is not only deeply suspicious of intellectual endeavors but also concerned that those who pursue knowledge pose grave dangers to society.

For the next speaker, only *demi-savants* or the half-educated are dangerous. The ancients, he points out, rightly understood that only the wise can rule and form happy states, and he insists that the benefits of knowledge are obvious and overwhelming. Without knowledge, armies run in terror during eclipses (an example that suggests this speaker's appreciation for the value of the new astronomy). Knowledge delivers people from the worship of idols, distinguishes the gentleman of the court from the peasant, and makes all human beings aware of their imperfections, because perfection is found only in God. This conference demonstrates a division between speakers along an intellectual fault line—proponents of learning versus advocates of untutored common sense.

It might seem surprising that these gatherings, which met for nine years to discuss intellectual topics, should have so many speakers taking an anti-intellectual stance. One thing that makes this collection interesting is that speakers even question the proclaimed mission of the conferences themselves. On the question "Which is the most given to vice, the ignorant or savant,"[57] a speaker makes the case for ignorance as a moral and social advantage. Because he believes that innocence exists only without knowledge of good and evil, he considers ignorance beneficial. It produces chastity in villages as opposed to the refined license of the court (not even the discourse of courtesans can have an impact on the virtuous country folk, he claims); ignorance is less likely than learning to lead to sin. The next speaker vehemently refutes the first. In either theological or philosophical terms, ignorance is always associated with sin; all knowledge leads to God whereas ignorance always leads away from Him, and all states give privileges to the learned. Another speaker extols the advantages of ignorance. Science engenders an attitude of scorn and complacency as opposed to the humility fostered by ignorance. Those who claim to know often perpetuate chicanery and heresy whereas the vulgar and ignorant are the true voice of the people. Furthermore, knowledge produces unruly women who dominate their husbands. This whole conference, essentially a dispute between the new and the old, raises many significant cultural anxieties, and (as is frequently the case) the anxieties focus, in part, on gender issues.

Participants confront head-on the social ramifications of knowledge and its pursuits, asking whether knowledge fosters progress or foments social instability. They recognize that privileging particular kinds of knowledge or its possessors has an impact on the social order, that it can in essence produce new social structures. Either explicitly or implicitly, an appeal to anything new raises fears about its impact on tradition, religion, and gender relations. When they discuss the effect of knowledge on religion, most speakers insist that knowledge cannot have a deleterious effect on faith. Yet the conferences can also sometimes exhibit a dichotomy between a Cartesian and a Pascalian vision of human possibility (to use later terms). Some speakers share Descartes's confidence in the power of human reason. Others, perhaps influenced by the Augustinian view of man so pronounced in Pascal, emphasize its futility.

Several other conferences also reveal an acute awareness of the power of knowledge to effect social change. For some speakers, this power is grounds for hope and optimism; for others, any change is fraught with danger. This difference of perspective comes to the fore in the discussion of inventions.[58] One speaker praises them as "the epitome of the arts and sciences," because they "produce greater facility in human actions." Inventors, who "excel in imagination, spirit, and judgment," are praiseworthy "as good citizens who contribute their industry to public well-being." Another finds it strange that inventors languish in obscurity when they should be celebrated. Some acknowledge the rarity of inventiveness, for inventors have not only particular faculties of the soul but also unique ways of understanding, so that they "know some subjects that are mysteries for the others."

For another speaker, a fascination with invention is the hallmark of a society entirely too impressed with the new. Old institutions, old ways, and even old inventions are of greater utility and founded on surer principles than new ones. The old should not be disdained, and innovation should not be extolled for its own sake. Inventions, founded on the new, are imperfect and weak, even in their principles. He points to the many social settings where the old is preferable to the new. "Isn't an old captain and an experienced general of an army preferable to a new one who would have to think of the most beautiful invention to attack his enemy?" Similarly, wouldn't one prefer to follow the maxims of an old theologian and the remedies of an old surgeon or doctor rather than "to follow the fantasies of a new dogmatizer?" For this speaker, "old" suggests "experienced" as opposed to "untried."

A conference on "Whether it were better to know all that men know or all that they don't know"[59] assesses the current state of knowledge.

A speaker is skeptical about both the present and the future prospects of knowledge. He claims there is "no science without demonstration" and that there are very few demonstrations in any discipline. He points to a kind of infinite regress of this lack of knowledge. Disciplines are themselves based on principles that are not demonstrated. Therefore, he concludes, "it follows that there is no science and that we know but one thing with Pythagoras, to wit, that we know nothing." The more one studies theology, medicine, and law, the more one becomes aware of disagreements, contrary precedents and prescriptions. The confused and contested state of every discipline makes it "easy to conceive that there are infinite secrets (such as the philosopher's stone, the quadrature of the circle, the fountain without end, and many other things whereof we have only confused notions)." The pursuit of "secrets," then, according to him, is a desire to deal with the seeming impossibility of certain knowledge. Although he casts doubt on the possibility of any knowledge, he recognizes that the prospect of knowing what others do not has a certain allure.

Another speaker contends that those who seek secrets have met with nothing but smoke. He admonishes that instead of fruitlessly pursuing secrets one should appreciate the current state of knowledge. "In the liberal sciences, is it possible to read, write, and speak in either prose or verse better than men do at present? Can the demonstrations of mathematics become more certain in time than they are now? . . . Can the laws be better understood than they are?" In sum, one should be well pleased to know what men now know.

When conferees address what kinds of knowledge one should seek, they express a strong preference for utility. In a conference on "Whether it is best to know a little of everything or one thing exactly,"[60] a speaker suggests that knowledge is akin to riches; it must be not only preserved and enjoyed but also "brought into the light and put in practice." This, he insists, is "better done by him who understands but one thing perfectly." Another speaker takes an equivocal position, noting that "it is better to know a little of everything than one thing alone," but from a more practical point of view he notes that "he who applies himself to many sciences never succeeds well in them, but loses himself in their labyrinth." For another, it is a great mistake to restrict the quest for knowledge, "the understanding being a most subtle fire, a spirit always indefatigably moving . . . it is too great an injustice to retrench its inheritance, to clip its wings, and confine it to one object." One speaker cites the great practical benefits that have accrued from dividing knowledge into disciplines and disciplines into subdisciplines. The division of the medical profession into physicians, surgeons, and apothecaries entails that "each of them would attain a more perfect knowledge of his subject." Outstanding success is associated with effort in a specific field rather than in dilettantism. This speaker extols prominent examples his readers would have all recognized: "Plato . . . applied himself only to metaphysics, Socrates to morality, Democritus to natural philosophy, Archimedes to mathematics." And as a counterexample, he notes, "Erasmus would have been greater, if he had been contented to be less."

A number of conferences deal with specific kinds of knowledge, and they are assessed in terms of their practical benefits. For example, on "Whether poetry is useful,"[61] one speaker, censorious toward poetry on grounds that it is frivolous and morally suspect, asserts instead a commercial ethos. He notes that "Plato and sundry other politicians accounted poetry not only so useless, but so hurtful to their commonwealth that they utterly banished it." Generally poetry does not tend toward productive knowledge as "verses are more proper for loose loves than the sciences." Furthermore, one cannot make a living through poetry. A final speaker vehemently refutes all of the preceding arguments. To renounce poetry is to reject a significant part of what it is to be human. Poetry has important social implications; because it "has such power over men's minds. . . . The gods of antiquity affected to deliver their oracles in verse; and so did legislators their laws, to render them more venerable." Poetry has an important ethical dimension; it praises virtue and immortalizes heroic actions. Poetry also serves several important practical functions; it aids "the memory . . . and serves for a guide and introducer to great personages." Ultimately, even poetry is condemned or praised for its practical benefits.

A conference dedicated to the question "Whether music does more harm than good"[62] also looks at the value of an art in terms of its social implications. The first speaker cites its beneficial uses. "It cures some diseases (such as the bite of the tarantula and melancholy) and assuages the raving of demonics . . . it both honors the Gods and inspires the troops in battle." Another speaker highlights the deleterious effects of music; it "makes men effeminate, excites [them] to filthy pleasures, and blinds the eyes of the understanding." Once again, conferees make their positive or negative arguments by appealing to social utility.

Even the more banal topics raise interesting questions about the nature of knowledge and its effective acquisition. To understand how knowledge is acquired, participants use a physiological understanding of human beings and their mental capacities. In a conference dedicated to the topic "Which is the better time to study, the evening or the morning,"[63] a speaker favors study in the evening for medical reasons (because in the morning, arteries, interstices of muscles, and the ventricles of the brain are full of excrement, whereas in the evening, they are full of good humors). His specific advice is to go to sleep late and get up late, a far cry from the "early to bed early to rise" maxim associated with the glories of rural life. One should, in fact, follow the practices of courtesans, "who know better than anyone how to preserve their beauty, which is inseparable from the health of the body." Another disagrees, insisting that morning is a better time because "the soul must be empty before we try to fill it with new impressions." Nighttime study disrupts digestion by "calling the spirits, which should digest the food, from the stomach to the brain," and thus those who study at night suffer from incomplete sanguification. One speaker takes the approach of the practicing physician, insisting that one must consider the distinctive physiology of the individual.

The question of physiology is also integral to discussion of the topic "Which is the most necessary to acquire the disciplines, great spirit or great work."[64] A speaker touts the value of work and suggests that the spirit of man is esteemed according to the difficulty of the accomplishment. Thus David's battles with the Philistines are appreciated, and (with a clever slip from the biblical David to Michelangelo's) works in marble are greatly admired. Another claims rather dishearteningly that spirit is necessary for science, and without a sufficient quantity of spirit, our efforts are in vain. This argument has immediate practical implications because, if their children have insufficient "spirit," parents misdirect them to careers in which they cannot succeed. "From which comes so many complaints of fathers and mothers, who having the means and the ambition to push their children into letters and sciences, see finally all their youth and the money they have spent to have them instructed, consumed without effect." Subsequent speakers refine the question. One notes that clearly both spirit and effort are required, and this question can be judged empirically by the proportion "of men who have compensated for their little spirit by an invincible assiduousness." Another refocuses the question, claiming that the problem is "just as Tacitus said of his time, not due to a lack of spirit but due to the laziness of children and the negligence of masters." Ultimately the question focuses on the measures one can take to ensure that education will be effective. Similarly, when participants wonder "Who are the most ingenious in the world?"[65] they are interested in determining what temperaments and what climates foster this quality.

Not only do some members of Renaudot's group doubt the value of knowledge, those who tout it rarely consider it valuable for its own sake. They consistently assess specific disciplines for their contribution to social utility. Science provides critical evidence of the utility of various kinds of knowledge and is a great source of optimism about human potential.

PRESENTING KNOWLEDGE

It is not surprising, given that these conferences were presented publicly and their proceedings printed, that conferees were preoccupied with how to present knowledge effectively. The topic "Whether it is better to speak well or to write well"[66] was of great contemporary interest. The conventional wisdom of the day favored the spoken word,[67] and indeed, the first speaker subscribes to this view, saying, "writing itself has not much force, unless it be animated by speech." He cites the great benefits of "speech, which protects innocence, accuses crimes, appeases popular tumults and seditions, inflames courage, excites to virtue, dissuades from vice, and gives praise to God and virtuous men." Again, it is the social utility of speech that establishes its value. Another speaker puzzles over the question of why an individual seems to either speak or write well, but not both. Nonetheless he too believes that oratory has a much more pronounced effect than the written word, for "the father of Roman eloquence (Cicero) overswayed the mind of Caesar, and Demosthenes all Greece." Another speaker cites the limited diffusion of the written word; writing "cannot be comprehended by more than one or two people at a time; whereas the voice reaches to many thousands together." Even though the published proceedings allow them to present their thoughts in both written and spoken form, participants extolled the efficacy of the spoken word, because they believed it had a greater effect and a broader diffusion. Several speakers praise writing because it "refines and polishes our conceptions, which otherwise escape from great persons but ill digested," and because it endures, good writing "has great weight with posterity." One argues for writing on the basis of human distinctiveness; animals have some form of "speech" but only humans write. This division of opinion places these participants at the point of transition from a culture of humanist rhetoric to the culture of the book.[68]

The first speaker on the topic "Of eloquence"[69] extols its efficacy in politics. Eloquence has gained important positions for its practitioners, notably Demosthenes and Cicero, and adherents for political regimes. Conquerors "employ so many orators to justify their exploits and make their government acceptable." But religious division poses the greatest dangers to a state, and eloquence plays a crucial role in gaining adherents to religion, for "if the inward part be not won, people pay with nothing but countenances, like bad servants." This speaker evinces a humanistic understanding of the integration of rhetoric and religion, that is to say, rhetoric effectively exercises moral suasion, moving the will to practice Christian virtues.[70] Another speaker argues that eloquence cannot be taken seriously for several reasons: "it is a woman's virtue to talk," and "truth ought to be unadorned." Underlying this disagreement is a cultural divide between the plain speaking associated with traditional society and the rhetorical flourishes of elite circles. For those who extol simple speech, not only did Renaissance rhetoric distort traditional values but it also upset social and political hierarchy by arguing the legitimacy of emotional persuasion. Equally problematic for some conferees is that, if rhetoric can alter and shape politics and religion, it demonstrates that they are modifiable, whereas the most conservative position argues the immutability of the political and religious order.[71]

Conferees share with other early modern philosophers and political theorists a preoccupation with language. A conference entitled "If the French language is sufficient for learning all of the sciences"[72] raises questions central to royal attempts from the time of Henry IV to unify France through the use of the vernacular.[73] Given that the conferences themselves utilize the vernacular and that Louis XIII supported it, one might expect participants to advocate French as the language of science. But conferees take equivocal positions. They understand themselves to be part of a civilization that is Western and derived from the ancients. Thus a speaker distinguishes two kinds of languages: mother tongues (Hebrew, Greek, and Latin) and imperfect languages that depend on these mother tongues. French is a derivative language and thus a defective tool for learning the sciences. Its inadequacies are demonstrated by the fact that French is in transition, changing from year to year in its use of words, definitions, and aphorisms. "When the understanding finds the truth of a principle of demonstration in a science, it rests in perfect contentment," whereas French "always has new inquietude in words and their properties." The fact that French must borrow from Latin and Greek demonstrates that it is not sufficient for understanding the sciences. For him, science requires a static language but also one that is universal, and such a language is Latin.

The second speaker takes a more pragmatic position, arguing that languages are learned from books, and just as the Romans learned from the Greeks, so too the French have learned from both the Greeks and the Romans. Since there are many more books in Latin and Greek, French is not yet sufficient to learn all of the sciences. And even when there are more translations, French will still not be sufficient, because "these are only small rivulets drawn from the great source, which finds itself in the original languages." His bias in favor of original as opposed to derivative works characterizes most of these speeches. Some participants suggest that science or knowledge is most appropriately considered a process of rediscovery in ancient texts. Others emphasize that a more nearly universal language will provide a more effective means to disseminate knowledge, because "all the sciences and the universal language should be connected to the unity that one notices in an encyclopedia."

One speaker is more skeptical about the reverence due to ancient languages. He says there are two kinds of signs, one derived from nature and the other from human invention. Since only the language of Adam corresponded directly to nature, all other languages are derivative. He is also critical of the efforts of cabalist scholars to trace the connections between languages, like their attempt to connect the words *Jehovah* and *God,* asking, "who does not see the absurdity of this convention?" It is, he asserts, difficult enough to learn the sciences with existing languages without adding the imaginary language of the cabalists. A final speaker argues that because all languages represent things by signs, it is a matter of indifference which language is used. In fact, French is becoming the richest language because of its appropriation of words from so many other languages. To persist in the use of ancient languages is a pedantic vanity. This conference divides participants with respect to the humanist tradition. Most of them look back to the ancient languages and to some degree to ancient texts for illumination, but others doubt the value of adhering to old languages in the face of the accessibility and adaptability of French.

This conference also illuminates certain attitudes about the sciences. Because participants contend that the sciences aim at repose of the intellect through assent to demonstration, they believe that science requires a clear and certain use of language, much like the arguments Descartes makes. This conference also suggests that the cabalists have opened up discussion of the origin of language, the history of language, and the connections between languages. Those participants who uncritically accept Adam's assigning of names as the original source do not contribute to the development of an anthropology of language. Others clearly understand modern languages as transitory, evolving, and embedded in history. Those who argue for the intrinsic value of the French language share the concern of many contemporaries, especially those associated with the formation of the Académie Française, who want to give French the clarity, the certainty, and the prestige of the ancient languages.[74] One speaker suggests that the unity of the sciences requires an encyclopedia. Those who argue for Latin might seem reactionary in light of both the effort of the crown to use the French language as a foundation for national unity and Renaudot's own espousal of the vernacular as the appropriate language for the conferences. But their commitment to Latin also reflects their appreciation of it as the universal scientific language.

Although the first speaker on the question "Of the diversity of languages"[75] notes that there are two conflicting scriptural sources on this question, he nonetheless begins by asserting, "here we only adore Mysteries but fathom them not; *we seek the natural causes of the variety of speech*" (my emphasis). This is one of the many clear cases where conferees rule out religious evidence and sources. The origin of language will not be discussed in the context of the tower of Babel or Adam's naming of creatures but instead will be investigated naturalistically. Understanding natural language involves a discussion of both physiological organs and customary practice. (The connection between physiology and social practice is central to participants' discussion of social and political issues.) As an explanation of the origin of language, he suggests that "the variety alone of the organs seems sufficient to diversify speech." Those nations whose windpipes were freer easily retained the Hebrew aspirations, if indeed (the speaker qualifies his remark) Hebrew is assumed to be the original language. Subsequently languages evolved because of distance from the center of the original language and because conquest imposed one language on another, which created a third.

Another speaker insists that one must also address the essence of language, which is "the means our mind makes use of to conceive the species or images of things." Language represents things as truthfully as there is a correlation between the idea and the object. Thus he assumes that language allows expression of the common and universal human experience, so that "when the conditions are right, it cannot be but all persons of the world must agree in one and the same judgment, and all say, for example, that this rose is red." Certain things are universally recognized, and those words convey that meaning regardless of the differences in language, "for every one knows a circle, a triangle and a square, although each nation calls it something different." This speaker makes several crucial points. He takes the connection between words and things as a given and concludes that, although words may differ, certain geometrical "conceptions" are universals, much on the order of Cartesian innate ideas.

Conferees raise questions about language acquisition, such as "Whether men, not having learned of others, would frame language to themselves."[76] They assume that nature gave animals voice for communication, a voice "distinguished into as many tones and accents as they have different passions and necessities." Believing in the hierarchy of nature with man at the apogee, the speaker insists that "it is not credible that she [nature] has provided worse for man, what was more necessary to him." Because man is more subject to the passions and has greater needs, he requires the support of society. Thus, the speaker insists, it is inconceivable that nature would not provide language for a social animal, since society is "in no way imaginable without speech." Thus children "frame to themselves [language], as soon as the moisture of their brain and organs serving speech, being dried by age, permitted free motion to their tongue."[77] Language is the natural product of human conceptualization, "for the mind of man, being active, incessantly conceives; his greatest pleasure is in communicating those conceptions." The next speaker returns to more limited ramifications of the question, claiming that, "speech being only an imitation, he who would never hear another speak could never speak himself." Thus he says those who are born deaf are always dumb, even though "they have all the organs fit for formation of speech." Another concurs that a person born deaf would not form a language, because "the species of voice cannot be introduced into the understanding but by some outward sense."

Questions of language are fundamentally rooted in debates about knowledge. In the conference "If one should write as one pronounces or follow ancient and common orthography"[78] a speaker maintains that conservatism is the proper approach to all issues of theory and practice.[79] He points out that it is "fitting to begin the four hundredth conference and a new volume of collected conferences with learning to read and write well" and extols the wisdom of ancient "graybeards" as opposed to the novelties favored by the young. According to him, there are many areas in which change is dangerous; "there is always more peril to removing ancient institutions and derogating a custom, than to holding to the practice of them." Change is particularly dangerous and destructive under certain circumstances. "One never changes the theology of the state without war; in medicine except at the expense of the sick poor; nor in the palace without endangering the multitude." Although he is generally opposed to change, he concedes that, if there are changes to language, the usage of the people must dictate them. When changes are mandated, they serve only to make language incomprehensible, with dire consequences. "The change of the letters, which are the foundation and the base of all the disciplines and affairs between men, under the appearance of an uncertain profit, will bring to them a certain confusion and irreparable loss."

Although this speaker insists on preserving languages and takes a conservative stance against an absolutist imposition of new standards for language, he has great affinity with the agenda of the encyclopedists more than one hundred years later. Both recognize that language is culturally constructed and that the shaping of language carries a political agenda. This topic also raises the question of the relationship between what is good and what is customary. The development of medicine makes a case for progress and innovation. As one speaker says, those who want to close the door on invention have "always been judged uncivil," for they are "spirits jealous and envious of the ornament of their century." He argues for innovations, saying "things are not good because they are customary, but rather become good because they are customary." Even in the most traditional realms, he points out, there have been significant innovations. Without theological innovation, we would not have the work of the doctors of the Church, and "medicine is marvelously illustrated by new observations and enriched by the remedies unknown to our ancestors."

📖

When participants discuss human nature and human knowledge, this discussion is shaped by certain presuppositions. First, they believe that their understanding of nature applies to human beings and, to a lesser degree, to society. As a result they attempt to understand human behavior through what they understand of nature, especially physiology.

Their use of physiology reflects a concern to categorize human nature more extensively and more broadly than might seem possible with an abstract, philosophical definition of human nature. Many arguments rely on scientific analogies or physiological evidence that implicitly challenge an abstract, static notion of human nature. Their use of science, particularly medicine and physiology, also challenges scholasticism and metaphysics as a way to understand human psychology. Perhaps they use physiology so consistently because it seems concrete. When participants attempt to understand vice and virtue in physiological terms, they are trying to develop a quasi-scientific understanding of them.

Based on opinions that could be corroborated by empirical evidence, science thus construed offered a way to move from the abstract to the practical. Because science was loosely defined and incorporated into many different approaches to nature in the early seventeenth century and because it was not compartmentalized into various disciplines or isolated from the humanities, it could provide a new empirical approach to issues that formerly might have been treated theologically or metaphysically. This kind of scientific argumentation was also more accessible to a wider range of people; it required a less systematic education because, to a certain degree (a degree disturbing to the modern reader), one person's opinion was as good as any other's.

Participants are concerned with the value of knowledge in general and of certain arts in particular. Although some of them are quite scornful of theoretical knowledge, most extol the utilitarian benefits of knowledge. Although a few speakers make profoundly skeptical speeches, those who do are consistently rebutted. Most speakers are quite optimistic as they look to the state of knowledge in their day. Although some quite vehemently denounce the socially detrimental effects of knowledge and tout the social advantages of ignorance, most participants are confident both of the utility of knowledge and of their ability to know. Science is the light that vanquishes the darkness of both ignorance and skepticism. Because they emphasize the practical benefits of knowledge, participants address a number of fairly specific questions about the acquisition of knowledge. They wonder how to get results (especially intellectual results), what kinds of temperament produces intellectual accomplishments, what conditions maximize intellectual productivity. They focus on the social ramifications of knowledge and its acquisition, and thus they treat intellectual issues in a context of social interaction and in terms of social benefits.

Conferences on human nature, particularly the relationship between body and soul, reveal an uncharacteristic concern with the religious ramifications of participants' positions. Yet speakers, even those most disquieted by the unorthodox opinions of other speakers, reject the argument that religion requires the cultivation of ignorance. Debates about knowledge reveal considerable unease on the part of some speakers concerning the impact of innovations, especially in the social sphere.

It would of course be anachronistic to contend that, simply because they apply nature to social concerns, these conferences are significant texts in the development of the social sciences. This term is defined so decisively by its nineteenth-century usage that any application of it to the seventeenth or the eighteenth centuries would be inappropriate. Nonetheless, the relationships drawn between human nature and science, particularly medicine and physiology, connect Renaudot's conferences to the discussion of these issues in the Enlightenment. Historians have generally recognized the significance of these kinds of discussion (although Renaudot's group has not received much attention), but also wish to avoid the anachronistic connotations of "social science," so they have coined the term *human sciences* as a more appropriate way to characterize such discussions. The human sciences are usually considered in the context of the embryonic social sciences of the Enlightenment.[80] Although Enlightenment thinkers, like Montesquieu, carried out much more extensive investigations on issues such as the relationship between the environment and customs or the development of language, for instance, conferees evince the same interests as the philosophes in a science of man. Both frequently relied on medical commonplaces to explore the relationship between the parameters of human nature and environmental factors.[81] Both used human nature as if it were a self-evident basis on which to found moral arguments, whether of a Christian or a secular variety.[82] Many prominent eighteenth-century writers also used "nature" in the ways the conferees do, as a vague but crucial determinant of both human nature and human society.

The use of scientific knowledge, rather than religious dogma or historical learning, allowed participants to comment on a range of social topics that form the human sciences in the eighteenth century. As a result, one can draw clear comparisons between the discussion of these issues by Renaudot's group and those of the philosophes. For both, these concerns were at least partially rooted in Galenic medicine and in a revival of Hippocrates. Thus both groups demonstrate a renewed interest in the connections between physiology and the environment as determinants of human behavior and society. The integration of man and nature shaped tentative forays into "the human sciences" and ultimately paved the way for the development of the social sciences. This transition from an ambiguous nature to human nature suggests further evidence of an evolution from Christian culture to secular culture.[83] *Human nature* became a useful term, providing, as it did for Renaudot's conferees, a unifying basis for the discussion of topics such as ethics, politics, and education. For the conferees, as well as for the philosophes, the connection between an understanding of nature, human nature, and a description of moral behavior afforded the foundation on which to construct social values.

CHAPTER SEVEN

Covetousness, Friendship, and Interest

Ethics and Practical Wisdom

I N A CONFERENCE ON "WHICH IS THE LEAST BLAMABLE, COVETOUSNESS OR profligacy,"[1] the first speaker strongly makes the case for covetousness. It is not, he concedes, that covetousness is an unproblematic good, but it does more good than prodigality. Covetousness "looks at its own profit and takes care for its own benefit, and the preservation of its dependents; so that it exercises at least the first fundamental of charity, which is to do well to those who are nearest us." He recasts a number of traditional ethical themes; "the good" is explicitly reinterpreted to mean the interest of society or the state, and "charity" is construed to mean taking care of one's own. Because it thwarts these goods, prodigality is to be abhorred; it "ruins and perverts the laws of nature, leading a man to the destruction of his relatives and the undoing of himself." The law, recognizing the ills wrought by them, has "enacted penalties against prodigals, depriving them of the administration of their own estates; and the most sacred edicts of our kings aim at the correcting of the luxury of prodigality."

When participants address questions of the ethical values of society, they often assume that the law stands as the best reflection of what is right or in the best interests of the community. Many arguments consider the good of the community as the determinant of right action. The speaker remarks that, whereas prodigality "causes the downfall and destruction of the most illustrious houses," covetousness "seems rather to have built them." The success of the covetous in providing for their families demonstrates their value to both their families and their communities, and by implication their moral worth. By concentrating wealth in private hands, which this speaker considers to be a positive good, covetousness also increases the economic health of the state.

Another speaker is somewhat more equivocal on the topic. Instead of looking to the state for moral standards, he connects the practices of the state to laws of nature. Nature does not provide as clear a basis for analysis as the state afforded the previous speaker, but because natural analogies suggest that both covetousness and prodigality are perverse, he would "drive out of a well-policed state the covetous and no less the prodigal." The covetous violate his sense that the goods of nature should be accessible to those who need them. Yet he considers prodigality more pernicious, because "the covetous raises an estate which many times serves to educate and support better men than themselves." Ultimately conferees suggest that the ends produced (though not the ends sought) by covetousness are justifiable as being in the interest of the state, while the prodigal gains nothing for himself, his offspring, or his state. Conferees also appeal to the empirical evidence that fathers do not in fact urge their sons to feats of profligacy. This empirical evidence proves more persuasive than traditional moral principles.

Given the fact that participants set themselves the task of adjudicating between two rather undesirable traits, it is revealing that no speaker finds covetousness more reprehensible than profligacy. They apply many of the same criteria and arguments that they used to discuss scientific topics. For example, many assume that nature provides compelling analogies for social processes and that specific cases provide telling evidence. The conferences discussed in this chapter focus explicitly on issues of moral philosophy, especially participants' opinions on the values necessary and appropriate to society.[2] In general, when they address moral issues, their position is relativistic, adaptable, and pragmatic; they eschew the stoic and the absolute. Some of the points raised in this particular conference on avarice and profligacy are surprising because of both the hardheaded pragmatism and the clear secularism they demonstrate. Speakers neither assert the necessity of Christian charity nor demonstrate concern with the deadly sin of greed. This conference provides a revealing example of the interests of the state as a determinant of moral value. It also demonstrates the preoccupation of participants with ethical issues and their social ramifications and provides evidence of the social tensions provoked largely by the imponderables of economic change.

This chapter will explore how conferees assess questions of social values and practice. As their discussion of covetousness reveals, conferees frequently take positions strikingly removed from more conventional moral discussions within the Christian or Stoic tradition. They are, as in their scientific discussions, comfortable with ambiguity. They do not force social practices to conform to moral precepts, largely because they recognize that a changing society and economy make these difficult to define or apply. Instead of relying on traditional values, they look to science as a way to understand human beings and to evaluate social practices. They explicitly consider these questions using pragmatic standards of feasibility and utility.

SOCIAL PRACTICES

Participants not only discuss virtue in the abstract (as noted in the previous chapter), but they are also keenly interested in evaluating specific kinds of behavior. The topics they propose are those they see as controversial; thus their discussion reveals the fault lines in contemporary opinion and suggests that notions of appropriate behavior were in a state of flux. One such topic is "Whether it is permissible for one to commend himself."[3] The first speaker classifies people according to three kinds of practices:

The first prize and respect themselves so highly . . . they catch cold with too much speaking of themselves bare-headed. The second, having heard that glory is a shadow that follows those that flee it, affect blame with such palpable design that it is plainly seen they fall down only to be lifted up. . . . The third observing how odious self-praise is to the entire world, never attribute any to themselves.

Although all of these responses, he suggests, are inappropriate, they reveal the difficulty of striking the right note. One speaker contends that we find self-praise so odious because we resent seeing someone advanced over us (since we always consider ourselves worthy of praise) or seeing a man "make himself judge in his own cause." Another finds self-praise less reprehensible; "he who commends himself is not to blame, provided he say nothing but what is true." Another concurs, alleging "that a wise man may commend himself without blame, since he is so impartial [presumably a quality implicit to wisdom] that he does not consider himself as himself, but as he would another man." A speaker considers self-praise legitimate in certain situations, such as "to oppose to the contempt, or detraction of our enemies." Even such a model of holiness as Saint Paul "boasted that he was noble and a citizen of Rome, that he had studied much, and that God had imparted to him his highest mysteries."

Participants point to the specific social conditions that make credible an action or practice that might generally be considered reprehensible. While they indict self-promotion, they also recognize the social purposes served by having one's accomplishments recognized. The issue is more complex in a large urban setting where it is difficult to be known for one's deeds. Their discussion of social values and behavior conveys a sense that social relations have become more difficult to assess by the standards of a rigid or abstract moral tradition. They are perhaps also responding to the intense preoccupation of their contemporaries with issues of precedence and privilege.[4]

The social relationship that provokes the most discussion is friendship. There is a general discussion "Of friendship"[5] and four other conferences dedicated to the obligations associated with friendship. Although this topic reworks classical and humanist conventions, participants make minor but significant modifications to old tropes in order to accommodate them to contemporary concerns.[6] Conventional topics allow them to confront the differences between conventions and the ways they actually experience the world.

One of the conferees' most significant early modern sources on friendship was Montaigne's essay "Of Friendship." Those speakers who emphasize the exclusive, unique relationship of one individual with another are drawing on a tradition that was vividly and lyrically depicted by Montaigne in his appreciation of Etienne de la Boétie. For Montaigne, friendship is an extremely rare gift, so intense that it can involve only two human beings at a time, because it is a complete fusion of two souls. His idealization of friendship, based on an ancient Stoic notion, is at the heart of the conference on the topic "If it is better to be content with one friend than to have many."[7] The arguments for one friend highlight the intensity of the relationship, and the arguments for many friends emphasize sociability. All the speakers laud friendship as the foundation of the civil state. For one, even though he argues for the most exclusive notion of friendship, man is nothing as much as he is sociable and that sociability is founded on nature. Drawing on the classical tradition, the speaker cites friendship as a foundation of sociability and thus of civil society. According to him, Aristotle correctly argued that the laws of justice are more durable if they are founded on the laws of friendship rather than on "a pure liberty of will, without other obligation." He cites the striking benefits of friendship for civil life; it renders force useless and the rigor of law superfluous. Despite his appreciation of the civic role of friendship, he endorses an intense, exclusive notion of friendship reminiscent of Montaigne. He describes friendship as a perfect union of heart and soul.

The second speaker expresses a more cynical view. The idealized relationship described by some speakers cannot exist for long because no one is without defect. Over time a coldness of spirit will arise inevitably, leading to a split between friends. Therefore, he suggests, a friendship among three is best so that the third can always reconcile the other two. Another speaker argues from a psychological perspective. Because friendship is a natural inclination, rooted in the will, it can be extended to many, although some are more limited in their affections.[8] He cites Cicero as the source for his pragmatic approach to friendship as founded on conversation, and the best conversations take place among those who eat and drink together. Another participant follows up on this theme; since friendship is rooted in conversation, it requires many friends and produces three kinds of goods: "the useful, the agreeable, and the *honnête*."[9]

Other discussions of friendship consider the impact of the actions of a friend. To the question "Which is more unbearable, the offenses of a friend or of an enemy,"[10] most conferees respond that the injuries produced by friends are much more serious because of the impact they have on us. One contends that each of us finds it intolerable when our judgment is exposed as lacking. The betrayal of a friend throws the will into a violent contest between what it desires and what it abhors. He cites the powerful examples of the betrayals of Judas and Brutus, the abandonment of Medea by Jason, and the violation of hospitality by Paris when he carried off Helen. Another notes that the law takes this greater offense into account by punishing murder by an acquaintance or theft by a domestic more severely than crimes committed by strangers.

Speakers address both the ideal and the pragmatic ramifications of friendship. They are indebted to Montaigne for the idealism; for the pragmatism they follow Cicero. Invoking Aristotle's dictum "friendship also seems to hold states together," they discuss the civic ramifications of friendship.[11] Although they agree with Aristotle that friendship and sociability are fundamental to the state, participants are more inclined to treat the issue pragmatically, especially since friendship reflects and affects changing social and economic circumstances. For example, when they discuss "If friendship is more durable between equals or unequals,"[12] the first speaker is somewhat unclear on the very subject he is addressing. His ambivalence is the result of the virtual impossibility of guaranteeing that, in the new and transitory world of commerce, relationships will ever remain equal. He expands on the ancient definition of friendship as born of abundance on the part of one and need on the part of the other to conclude that the relationship must inherently be one of inequality. Inequality creates conditions where "we are willing to procure good for ourselves or for others." A friendship of unequals is thus stable, whereas equals jockey for position, seeking the things that will put one individual above another.[13] But without an ability to predict the future (and the notion of the future seems to be an economic one), there can be no continued expectation of equality, so friendship rooted in equality is unlikely to persist.[14]

Another speaker makes the case for friendship among equals. He cites a satiric poet's example of a friend who begins to sweat as soon as his friend says he is hot.[15] This sympathy is physiologically based; the two friends are made of the same elements and together form a mixed body. Although this speaker proclaims psychological affinity as a source of friendship, he also sees social equality as essential to friendship. One makes friends with those of equal social standing, and "the shepherdess will ally more often and more durably with a shepherd than with a courtier and the lady of the court more often with a gallant than with a shepherd."[16]

These discussions of social relationships reflect tension between the abstract and the concrete, the ideal and the real, the theoretical and the pragmatic. This conference demonstrates a great awareness of social fluidity and reflects considerable insecurity, resulting most significantly from economic changes that cannot be predicted. These changes produce inequities of wealth and status and seem to call into question any number of the moral certainties of the day. Conferees who use friendship as the basis for civil society describe it as the grease of social exchange rather than as the intense, exclusive relationship that characterized some earlier notions of friendship—though some hark back to this ideal. They are interested in combining notions of friendship with those of civil society and public responsibility. Such a fusion would create something like a continuum between intimate human contact and public conduct. It would not require, à la Montaigne, a separation of the motives attached to unique friends and the less idealistic rationalization of interests associated with public life.[17]

If participants acknowledge friendship as the glue that binds the members of civil society to one another, custom is the source of many of its practices. They both weigh its general role in society and discuss specific customary practices. In "Of custom,"[18] the first speaker begins with the premise that "right is divided into written and not written; the former is the law, the second is custom, which is right used for a long time."[19] Conferees suggest that custom is "better" than law, because it has stood the test of time and thus better conforms to the interests of the people. They acknowledge custom as the foundation of all kinds of practice. It gives nations their identity, for "variety of custom makes some nations prefer a supercilious gravity; others, familiarity and courtesy; some are commendable for sobriety, others are notorious for drunkenness." In brief, the speaker concludes, "we are civil or uncivil, good or bad, foolish or wise, or anything else, according to custom." In many seventeenth-century texts, custom is frequently discussed not only as the accumulated, unwritten wisdom of a culture but also as the equivalent of all of one's experiences, much in the way that the sensationalist followers of John Locke use the term *education*.[20] Since conferees were interested in disseminating information and shaping opinion, education was crucial to their concerns; thus when they address the significance of custom, they are both assessing culture and weighing in on educational issues.

The next speaker refutes laudatory claims made for custom; he sees it instead as a force that works against reason and is therefore ultimately destructive. "Custom bears such a sway over all the actions of men, that it renders all things familiar to them," and the familiar blinds judgment. Custom distorts the will, which "finds itself more inclined to acquaintances than to the unknown but more accomplished person." For this speaker, custom is a force for unreflecting conservatism: those who argue its merits will always extol the familiar above the new. Because it impedes judgment, custom is a function of prejudice, not reason. He articulates the criticisms, which become so much more concerted in the Enlightenment; because custom works against reason, it is a force for ignorance. He also intimates that custom, or the familiarity it produces, is the foundation of unwarranted social preferment. Conferees (as we will have occasion to note on other topics) do not use these criticisms to develop the full-blown attack on institutions that characterizes the Enlightenment, nor do they develop a consistent position. They do not make the case, argued by some philosophes, that custom is an entirely negative social force.[21]

The next speaker moderates the claim that custom exerts a negative impact on human conduct. He claims instead that, because the roots of custom are not as deep as those of nature, its ill effects can be more readily overcome than proclivities rooted in nature. "It is easier to reclaim one who is vicious by custom than by nature." The effects of education then must be imposed on nature, for "philosophy masks rather than amends nature" and "custom is easily altered by a good resolution." His point is to suggest that any faults induced by custom can be eradicated more readily than those that are innate. But he suggests almost a physiological determinism to describe the control exercised by temperament. For example, "You will see sanguine humors that cannot counterfeit sadness even in matters that require it most." By raising the question of the strength of custom in light of the effects of a physiological constitution, some speakers assert the irremediability of a natural predisposition, issues that become much more common to discussions during the Enlightenment, particularly by the materialists.[22]

Others point to custom as almost akin to social determinism; they tout custom as the root of all civilized behavior and the source of social stability. As one puts it, "we are beholden to custom that everyone abides his own condition"; it is, for example, due to custom that "seamen abide the sea." For him, custom is the crucial factor in social conduct. It "exercises dominion over ceremonies and civilities," and citing Seneca, he claims that "we govern ourselves not by reason but by custom, accounting that most honest which is most practiced." Custom then, for good or ill, is the foundation of the social, political, and cultural practices of every community. However, because custom enshrines the values of a community, those values are relative. They are established through time-honored practice.

Participants also consider the merits of customary social practices. One of the initial ways to define a topic is scientifically, no doubt to endow the topic with enhanced credibility. For example, dancing is first described in physiological terms:[23] "the soul, being moved, stirs up the spirits, the humors and the parts, and constrains them to follow their bent and motion." Such practices, though customary, are rooted in human physiology; they have a disproportionately great effect because they depend on human nature rather than on particular social and political organizations. As such, they can be used as part of medical therapy. Understood as part of motion, dancing can be used as a way to regulate the body and to integrate the body and soul.

Although dancing is praised, the wearing of masks provokes a stringently critical response. In "Of masks and if it is permitted to disguise oneself,"[24] the first speaker understands that the topic ultimately has more to do with reversing gender roles (an important feature of the early modern festival tradition) than with the actual wearing of masks. He notes that the custom must be very old, since God gave his people the injunction "that man may not take on the clothes of the woman," which is the way in which masks are most often used. Saint Jerome advises men to avoid women who wear male clothes or cut their hair or in other ways reject nature.[25] In the spring, the Romans were allowed to wear flour masks or to represent any person they wished no matter how grossly, which proves, as far as this speaker is concerned, that wearing masks is a sin of vice and hypocrisy, which God rightly forbids. Masks are also akin to makeup, which Seneca outlawed as something that no decent woman would wear. Why would anyone wear makeup except to disguise her wicked intentions? Although Roman customs are often praised, in this case Rome is identified as pagan, and Christian prohibitions are decisive. Underlying this discussion of masks are concerns with gender roles, specifically men representing themselves as women and women misrepresenting themselves with makeup.[26] Masks flag the social dangers of deception, and ultimately the discussion focuses on the question of when, if ever, deception is acceptable.[27]

The next speaker points out all the laudable reasons to disguise oneself. In times of war, one disguises oneself to keep from being recognized by the enemy. When traveling, the rich often disguise themselves as poor to avoid highway criminals. In the courtroom, we can see that lawyers speak masked. He then boldly states, "Even theologians and physicians are not exempt from it; they are garbed in a certain way in order to make themselves agreeable to their penitents and their patients." And, he concludes, to blame masks is to blame all of human society, because, "as Augustus said in dying, life is nothing but a comedy where each plays his roles under a mask." He objects that the prohibition of makeup is too severe; women who wear it do so "to conserve and illustrate their beauty, which is . . . their principal recommendation to men."

This conference, like most discussions of specific customs, suggests that there are two sensibilities in conflict, one a kind of Puritanism, the other a more liberal perspective. One might be tempted to see in them a battle between aristocratic and bourgeois values, between urban and rural, or Huguenot and Catholic,[28] but it would be difficult to assign these attitudes to specific seventeenth-century groups. As Jonathon Dewald's study shows, the nobility were able to adapt to changing social mores. The fact that the Jansenist moralist Pierre Nicole was a key figure in supporting a new ethos of economic realism against more traditional arguments points out the difficulty involved in dividing economic positions on religious grounds.[29] So while these conferences demonstrate contested values, the divisions do not neatly fall out according to rank, economic status, or class divisions.

If these attitudes cannot readily be assigned to specific social or religious groups, the conferences nonetheless consistently reflect this division of opinion. In "Of fables and if they convey more evil than good,"[30] the first speaker takes a harsh stance, contending that the lie is a bad flower of rhetoric, as Aristotle says, and that the liar is always worthy of blame. Even more reprehensible is "he who covers and disguises his lie under the appearance of a true-seeming story that is avidly received by our intellect." Since fables are egregious forms of lies, they are to our understanding as monsters are to nature. He develops the implications of his analysis: "Only ignorant children can receive pleasure in hearing fables, but even they might find that their tabula rasa has been corrupted by fables." Although "many great persons" think it a great educational innovation to imprint fables on the minds of children, they are leading children away from truth. "It is like using the debauched to instruct boys and girls in chastity or leaving clothes to be bleached at the collier." The next speaker makes the positive case for fables as intellectual restoratives for those individuals tired by their quest for truth. Fables provide important community services; they are a source of recreation and a method of instruction.

One social practice that provokes a lot of discussion is dueling. In the early seventeenth century, this practice was not merely a question of custom but one fraught with political overtones. Dueling became extremely common in the sixteenth century and persisted, despite a ban issued by the Council of Trent and many laws passed against it. In 1626 Louis XIII again banned dueling with strict penalties for any violation. Challenging someone to a duel could lead to loss of property and banishment, and participating in a duel could lead to loss of noble status or death. When the Count of Bouteville, the victor of twenty-two duels, staged another to protest the law, he was executed even though he was a member of the powerful Montmorency family and despite the pleas for clemency of the Duke of Montmorency and the Prince of Condé. Reflecting the ambivalence of his age, Richelieu, although he abhorred duels (his father had killed a man in one and his brother had died in another), could not resist expressing sympathy for the gallant nobleman. This sobering example put a temporary halt to dueling. But by 1634 Louis XIII complained that the law was being ignored. Recognizing the futility of punishing so many violators, he pardoned them in 1638 and again in 1640.[31] Against this backdrop of laws ineffectively enforced, conferees discussed dueling at great length.

In "Of the point of honor"[32] (the point of honor is defined as that which a man will be provoked to defend), a participant indicts dueling as blatant disregard for the law; many who are reluctant to go into battle do not hesitate to disobey the injunctions and prohibitions of God and men by dueling and acting as seconds for their friends. The principal cause, he claims, is the fear of being held in contempt, a contempt prejudicial to one's fortune, "which we know, in these days, depends upon our reputation." So, despite his arguments against it he concludes, "the point of honor is not so little real as is imagined, since it has an influence not only upon a man's honor, but likewise upon his goods and life." "Honor" has pragmatic ramifications, which makes its defense understandable, although hardly commendable, since dueling reflects a blatant disregard for the legal prohibition.

The next speaker heightens the expedient sense of virtue by making a telling distinction between honesty and honor. An honest man has virtue, but "to be a man of honor, besides that, the world must know that we possess it and give us the reputation of being virtuous." Honor rests on reputation, and he insists, "it is stupidity not to care what opinion men have of us." Another draws a sharper distinction between honor and the point of honor to note the complete relativity of what will provoke a man to defend "a point of honor." While honor is the praise that men give us because of our virtuous actions, the point of honor "is that conceit which our mind proposes and forms to itself of that opinion." As such, "it is pure imagination, which alters according to the diversity of times, places, and persons." This ambiguous assessment of the value of the defense of honor is just one of the many points at which social considerations have an impact on ethical topics. While all conferees laud honor, they also recognize to a greater or lesser degree the dissonance between honor and the point of honor. For some, the point of honor is mere conceit and its defense legally and morally problematic. On the other hand, most also realistically acknowledge that theirs is a society built on reputation, and each man must take care to preserve his.

When the topic "If it is permitted to die for a friend"[33] is raised, participants consider dueling because it is the prevalent social practice that makes the ultimate sacrifice conceivable. One speaker asserts one's right to die for a friend for several reasons: a friend is another one of ourselves, and God has ordained that we love one another as we love ourselves. As one can expose one's life to preserve one's own honor, so one can do likewise for the honor of a friend. The next disagrees with this argument because of his understanding of both nature and friendship. Both nature and art seek perfection, which cannot entail the destruction of their work, and the purpose of friendship is to make life sweeter, not to live less and die sooner. He also distinguishes sharply between obligation to the state and to our friends. We owe our goods to our magistrates and above all our prince, and for them we are required to expose our lives. The obligation one has to an individual friend is of a much lower order, however. Only those who confuse these distinct kinds of obligation defend dueling. Although duelists vaunt their protection of the lives of their friends, instead they live "enveloped in a veritable infamy, natural and civil, temporal and eternal." Another speaker both discourages dueling and extols friendship. Although one should not refuse to a friend anything in one's power, nonetheless friendship entails greater virtue than can be found in those who contravene the laws of their prince "with gaiety of heart, like the duelists."

The issue of dueling is also raised by the topic "Whether pardon is better than revenge."[34] A speaker insists that to fail to take revenge is fundamentally unjust and indicates civic irresponsibility. But when revenge extends to dueling, the pursuit of private vengeance perpetuates gross civil irresponsibility. "He who takes satisfaction . . . cannot more palpably declare the ill opinion he has of the laws under which he lives." This disregard opens "so wide a door to our duels and encounters, as can hardly be shut at this day by many ordinances and edicts." Another speaker makes a rare invocation of the *politique* distinction between what is appropriate for the public person and for the private individual, "because it is as dangerous for a public person to be gentle and merciful, as it is commendable in a private person." But even for public persons, dueling is a special case where laws exist to restrain retribution. Thus those who duel "must conclude that they abandon solid honor, to follow its shadow; since the honorable and the just are inseparable." And *just* must mean adherence to the law.[35]

In their discussion of ethical concerns of public life, conferees address not only pressing topics like dueling, but also perennial issues such as the merits of the contemplative life versus those of the active life. This topic took on new prominence when Italian humanists questioned the medieval idealization of the monastic life. Some participants emphasize the value of the active life because it allows not only the practice of charity but also the cultivation of the civic sphere. Conferees consider the issue not just from the perspective of the individual, as would be conventional, but also from the perspective of society. On the topic "Which is to be preferred, company or solitude,"[36] the first speaker considers the question settled and unworthy of discussion. He expresses his exasperation, saying, "it is henceforth lawful to doubt of everything, since a problem is made of an axiom." The answer is obvious; solitude, he insists, is antithetical to man's inherent sociability. In solitude, "not only speech, courtesy, and civility, but all sciences and arts, indeed, almost all virtues become useless to him." Without a life in society, man puts "on bestial properties, such as silence, rudeness, ignorance, and in a word, brutality itself." As a result, solitary persons are called by the vulgar werewolves, the enemies of men. Although he is "likely to think he is thinking great thoughts," the solitary man "is in fact constructing castles in the air." On the other hand, the man of sociable humor is pleasing and agreeable, and "all good things" such as "balls, comedies, revels, feasts, and all ceremonies both civil and ecclesiastical," take place in society. These social activities well reflect the "goods" of the new society. "Wherefore if you take away company, you at the same time deprive men of all the means of employing the goods that they have gotten by their labors." The final point is clearly meant to be the clinching argument: man on his own needs nothing to cover his nakedness "whereas the magnificence of Courts is the most glorious token of the splendor of the state." This speaker extols not only sociability but also the economy and social structure created and maintained by sociability.

Another participant defends solitude. The perfection of Christian life is found in meditation. Solitude allows us to avoid many kinds of sin. (We are left only with sins of thought.) Company thwarts many of the great pleasures of life, such as reading, meditation, and contemplation. Solitude is necessary to cultivate great thoughts and develop skills in all disciplines; "not only the speculative sciences are best polished by it, but also the civil and popular, such as eloquence and poetry." It is interesting that solitude is extolled not for its own sake but as preparation for scholarship and productive social roles. Another speaker, citing Aristotle, distinguishes between two kinds of solitary men, those who are above the rest of mankind, such as the heroes and demigods of antiquity, and "the other sort [who] are below men, and avoid conversation." While he makes a special case exempting heroes, he scorns those who eschew sociability. Speakers generally consider the contemplative life valuable only as a preparation for more public roles, and for the most part, they acknowledge sociability as an unquestioned good.

Those participants who assert the value of sociability as the foundation for virtue may well be drawing on neoplatonism, particularly in its distinctively French form, which sanctioned sociability even in its more ethically problematic manifestations such as the pursuit of luxury. Because this neoplatonism was not antithetical to life in this world and sanctioned life in the court and the city, it could seek purely secular ends such as "happiness, friendship, pleasure."[37] Their discussions of customary practices demonstrate that participants consider sociability fundamental but are also concerned about changes in social mores, especially those affecting social distinctions. Ultimately their discussion of customs exposes tensions between new and old social attitudes.

VALUES AND THE STATE

Many conferences take positions supported by scientific analogies and physiological evidence that are meant to challenge (at least implicitly) abstract, static notions of human nature and virtue and vice. These attacks on abstraction might have been motivated by a desire to respond more effectively to a rapidly changing social and political situation. Other conferences forcefully address issues that would reasonably have been of direct concern to the sorts of professionals, scientists, and dilettantes in attendance. They also reflect the new attitudes toward the acquisition of wealth and its social ramifications that were being articulated in the seventeenth century. These new attitudes were largely a response to the changing commercial economy and to the challenge posed to a traditional feudal aristocracy by the rise of the *noblesse de la robe* (the new nobility created through the sale of bureaucratic offices) and the growing influence of commercial elites. Despite the legitimate resistance of historians to extending the term *bourgeois* back to the seventeenth century, discussions at the Bureau afford new perspectives that, at the very least, were shaped by the interests of the professional classes.[38] Conferees only rarely voice views that represent any of the groups associated with a feudal order. They frequently address issues associated with changing economic and social mores, often from the perspective of a new commercialism.

One of the critical changes of values during the early modern period, most thoroughly documented by Albert Hirschman, is the notion of interest, which he traces from Saint Augustine through the commercial ethos of the seventeenth century.[39] This term, "interest," commonly added to discussions of the passions, brought the perspective of the individual to bear on moral abstractions. Although Saint Augustine denounced lust for money, power, and sex, he opened the door to making the pursuit of personal interest acceptable. He conceded some value to the civic virtue of the Romans, which included consideration of the interest of the community, and suggested that interest might allow one vice to check another. When the civil strife produced by religious division in the reformation vividly demonstrated the inability of both reason and religion to control the passions, some thinkers (John Calvin and Thomas Hobbes, for example) responded by putting the passions under the control of the state. However, if the passions are denounced as inherently destructive and reason as consistently unreliable, there is little ground for optimism about human prospects. Interest, Hirschman claims, provided a solution; it rehabilitated the passion of self-interest by rationalizing it. Reason could then be deemed more efficacious because it worked with rather than against the passions. Interest thus proved to be a useful socioethical concept. It not only offered prospects for rationalizing the passions but also responded to the increasing complexity of social analysis, providing some basis for predictability and rationality on which a social order might be constructed. It also offered a basis for understanding human motivation: the individual could indeed confidently assess his interest because "interest will not lie to him or deceive him." Those associated with commerce pursued their interests (sometimes termed "soft" as in *doux commerce*), but those interests were not destructive of the social order, at least as compared to the pursuits of the aristocracy, whose military exploits were shaped by violent passions. Interest was, of course, not completely unproblematic as a basis for society, since political and social issues invariably produced opposing interests.[40]

The conferences reflect this new positive sense of interest.[41] Participants define interest as the result of an antipathy of humors. One speaker, like Saint Augustine, insists that interest might act as a laudable rein on the passions. Another defines interest as both good and natural. Participants also acknowledge that, although all men can judge their interests accurately, interest as a basis for society does not always provide a clear guide. Any situation can produce conflicting claims, even on the individual's sense of his own interest. For example:

> Now a man who has judged and given his advice, . . . seeing that advice rejected, falls into a *double interest,* one arising from the charitable inclinations that he has for the good of the one who consulted him, . . . the other being his own proper interest, for the slighting of his advice is tacit to accusing him of failing in a thing essential to his end and to calling him a monster, or fault of nature. (My emphasis)[42]

Participants not only regard interest favorably as a force that rationalizes and legitimates the passions; they also acknowledge its ties to both nature and human nature. But if the pursuit of interest is legitimate, then inevitably, monolithic notions of virtue and vice are undermined, which further opens up the possibility of moral relativism. The empirical and scientific evidence participants bring to bear also fosters relativism. Any number of discussions of specific kinds of behavior conclude with the remark that the conditions are relative to the times or to the character or customs of a people, and thus no definitive position can be taken.[43]

A discussion of "Which is most in esteem, knowledge or virtue,"[44] brings to the fore the relativism implicit in a notion of virtue as shaped by interest. One conferee explicitly says that this question must be addressed in light of social considerations. Because virtue bears no correspondence to fortune or status, he disparages it in favor of knowledge, which has the advantage of greater social exclusivity. As he puts it, "that which makes virtue less prized is that it falls upon all sorts of conditions and sexes; a poor man and a poor woman exercise no less virtue in supporting their misery with constancy than a great captain in overcoming his enemy." He forthrightly claims that virtue does not lead to wealth or fortune, "for what man can promise himself that when he labors he will infallibly become rich, that when he fights he will be victorious, that when he serves he will be acceptable?"[45]

Another speaker returns to more conventional grounds and offers a response that seems naively idealistic compared to the others. He concludes that knowledge is inferior because it is merely "a means to the end, which is virtue." The next speaker immediately returns to the social dimension of the topic, explicitly rejecting the claims of the idealistic speaker and insisting that such a topic must be evaluated in light of its social impact. Virtue, he notes, is most necessary to the state, "which rather resembles a cavern of robbers or wild beasts when virtue is banished." On the other hand, "whole states and kingdoms very easily and many times profitably dispense with knowledge. And the gross ignorance of the ancients did not prevent them from leaving flourishing states." On ethical topics, the successful argument seems to be the one that makes the best claim to support the interest of society or the advancement of the individual within society. Notably lacking is any discussion of the pursuit of virtue for its own sake.

If a pronounced feature of bourgeois life is disparagement of the culture of the nobility, these conferences are distinctly bourgeois. They forthrightly charge that the court and the manners of the court have produced a degeneration of French culture.[46] However, all speakers are willing to separate the king and his ministers from this malign influence, perhaps in deference to the support of Louis XIII and Richelieu for Renaudot's efforts or perhaps because they saw hopes for reform in central control by a monarchy. Their criticism of the court does not necessarily entail any desire to overturn the established order. Conferees demonstrate considerable concern to establish a natural basis for hierarchy and to prove that any challenge to a natural hierarchy is illegitimate, dangerous, and unnatural. Thus they analyze forces of human motivation in terms of their impact on social hierarchy. For example, a speaker distinguishes appropriate from inappropriate ambition;[47] the former "is bounded within the limits of each condition, whereby every one desires to become perfect of each condition," but the latter "is that thing which carries us to honors that greatly exceed the bounds of our condition." Like the conservatism evident in discussing similar topics, "inappropriate" ambition is dangerous to the state "because it causes great confusion in men's minds and consequently in states. For what is more absurd, than for a citizen to act a gentleman, or a gentleman a prince?"[48]

Participants frequently turn their attention to problems of poverty, perhaps because they are concerned with social instability. As with many other subjects, the conferences reflect contemporary issues. Over the course of the seventeenth century, urban poverty became a more pressing concern to the state. The seventeenth century was a period of demographic crisis; the death rate was higher than the birthrate. The crisis was caused by disease, famine, and war, and for about 50 percent of the population it led to chronic, grinding, unrelenting poverty. These conditions led many to flee the country for the cities. Contemporaries estimate that during the regency of Marie de Medici some forty thousand beggars filled the streets, doorways, churches, and hospitals of Paris, giving the city the appearance, some complained, of an indigent hostel.[49] There were so many who were so miserable that they posed a threat to public order, health, and hygiene. Under these circumstances, it is not surprising that the early years of the seventeenth century experienced severe famine (1629), followed by particularly serious outbreaks of the plague (1631).[50]

Conferees, like many of their contemporaries, take the problem of poor relief seriously. In their discussions, they contest a traditional sense of poverty as tied to Christian virtue with a new notion of wealth as connected to virtue. Some conferences discuss poverty in abstract terms. For example, a speaker on the question "Which condition is most expedient for the acquisition of wisdom, riches or honor?" [51] argues that wisdom comes with poverty because nature is egalitarian, and presumably she would not give both wealth and wisdom to the same individual (although it is a rather strange view for a modern to entertain that wealth should be considered a gift of nature, but since wealth would ordinarily be tied to birth, it is not an unreasonable argument). Another connection between knowledge and poverty, which speakers seem to find persuasive, is that knowledge is produced by necessity, the mother of invention. The poor are also more likely to be virtuous. As this speaker notes, "it is observed that rich nations, and those who live on good soil, are the most vicious, lazy, and dull, but those who are on poor land are ordinarily more virtuous and addicted to industry."[52] Another speaker agrees that poverty indeed fosters creativity, but he seems concerned that this quest will also encourage a foolhardy willingness to divest one's goods or to disrupt the political order. He points out that the difficulties of the poor "make them despise all the rigors of laws and often abandons them to rage and despair." Poverty is inherently disruptive: "Hence not only mutinies, seditions, and revolts are commonly made by the poor and miserable, lovers of innovation, wherein they are sure to lose nothing and may possibly gain, but they also are almost the sole authors of theft, murders, and sacrileges." There is no doubt for these conferees that poverty is more likely to lead to all sorts of creativity including the cultivation of wisdom. However, they neither idealize poverty (in the monastic tradition, for example) nor are they unaware that the discontents of poverty might undermine the stability of the state. They understand that, although wealth may lead to the undesirable personal qualities mentioned above, interest in one's goods tends to make one attached to the status quo.

The problem of poor relief both cries out for pragmatic solution and was a fundamental concern of conferees. It was a long-standing personal interest of Renaudot's, and the Bureau actively sought to ameliorate the plight of the urban poor. Just as Renaudot's Bureau drew on Juan Luis Vives's work on poor relief, so too the treatment of poor relief in the conferences shares Vives's concerns. Vives was motivated, in part, by the conviction (consistently demonstrated by Renaudot's conferees) that "the study of the sciences is as useful morally as materially." Poor relief for both Vives and the conferees is a topic that impinges on political and economic issues of the early modern period. Just as some conferees do, Vives argues that poverty poses a real danger to the republic. He notes, "in a republic, one does not despise the weakest and the poorest without danger for the powerful."[53] Furthermore, civil wars are caused by those who have so little they are less interested in preserving what they have than in destroying what others have, and as a result of civil war, the maladies of the poor are transmitted to many others. But Vives, like some participants, is not content to simply discuss the issue of the poor in general terms. Beginning with the remark that it is absurd to find so many mendicants in Christian cities, he has a number of concrete recommendations to make. Magistrates should visit every house and note the conditions; vagabonds should give their names and the reasons they were forced to beg; the sick should go before commissioners assisted by physicians. Workshops should be opened to instruct the poor in trades. The sick and the mentally ill should be investigated to see if they are capable of any sort of work. Information on the poor—their ages and conditions of health, for example—should be compiled. Vives points to the great advantages that will accrue to cities that pursue creative methods of poor relief. There will be less crime, greater harmony, and not so much division between rich and poor. Arguments about the need to redress poverty and the benefits of such plans are also made by Renaudot's group, but they do not share the more conventional attitude, which Vives emphasizes, that poverty is to be supported with patience and welcomed as a gift from God.[54] Although participants concede that poverty may be more likely than wealth to lead to virtue, they are more concerned with poverty as a social ill.

Many speakers focus on ways to effectively organize poor relief, that is, they want to identify the cause of the problem, categorize the poor, and then resolve the problem they pose for the state.[55] The moral issues are of less concern to them than the concrete bureaucratic ones. They see the poor as a dangerous source of political instability. One speaker delivers a diatribe against the poor who are physically fit but do not work. He maintains that the public must remedy their sloth because its effect is akin to that of a paralytic member on the human body. He suggests work in the galleys as a prudent solution to the problem of the able-bodied poor. Another speaker argues strongly for poor relief based on scientific analogies, such as the ways nature compensates for dearth: "The soul immediately sends an affluence of blood and spirits to a wounded part; the principles of nature, no matter how simple they are, cannot endure privation, which is the image of poverty." Another speaker suggests that to deal with the poor, "we must imitate the physician, assuage the most urgent symptoms, and remove the concomitant cause yet not forgetting the antecedent or the general remedies." In more concrete terms, he suggests, each of "the robust poor must be sent to the place of his birth, classified by sex, age, and ability, and given a trade." Those who cannot be trained in a trade should be put to public works, and the old should care for children.

A long discussion of the *monts-de-piété* (the pawnshops set up for poor relief)[56] begins with the premise that to get men to give freely to the poor would require an entirely different human nature. Given this unlikely transformation, a commentator cites both natural and civic reasons why one must make provisions for the poor. "The harmony of a society ceases when some one part is swelled beyond measure, then will the others pine and languish." He defines three kinds of charity to ascertain what is attainable, (1) giving, (2) lending freely, (3) lending with a moderate degree of profit. Another speaker picks up this point to suggest that only the latter is really attainable. "Unless a New World were framed and every particular person inspired with charity toward his neighbor equal to the love that he bears to himself, it is impossible to bring men to lend freely one to another." In discussing poor relief, participants formulate their reform proposals under the constraints of what they see as the limited malleability of human nature; they are interested in proposing reforms that are feasible. They also take a "no nonsense" approach to social problems, insisting that they must be dealt with pragmatically and according to the evidence of science, regardless of what one might want to suggest about the moral principles involved. Social problems, they assert, must be dealt with in the same way that physicians deal with disease.

⌘

When conferees address social issues, they share a perhaps unexpected kinship with their unofficial patron, Richelieu. He too produced a collection of discourses on moral topics. Although his *Emblema Anima* is concerned with some of the same topics (such as the passions, poverty, and education), the tone is quite different. His discourses frequently express moralistic platitudes. For example, after defining poverty as twofold—a lack of necessities and lack of what is desired for pleasure—he advises: "If you will live according to nature, you will never be poor, if according to opinion never rich: nature desires little, opinion much." [57] His discourses also reflect a rather dour moralism that is entirely foreign to the conferences, and unlike conferees, he vehemently insists on the fundamental role of religion in all things.[58] Richelieu's text is much more consistently stoical than the conferences; he advises that one draw good from evil and look to the ancients for models of those who suffered adversity. It is ironic, given his own career, that Richelieu is also much more opposed to ambition than are the conferees. But he does share some of the basic attitudes that characterized Renaudot's conferences; for example, he too insists on the importance and moral value of a commitment to civil life. As he puts it, "Truly man is not borne to live idly, but rather . . . he must *confer,* and attribute his whole travail and pain to the conduct and conservation of that civic society and condition in which he is placed."[59]

This sense of civic responsibility is one of the fundamental tenets that participants in Renaudot's group bring to bear on the discussion of social and ethical issues. Civic responsibility shapes discussions of specific topics like dueling, wearing masks, and the problem of the urban poor. A fluctuating economy and social structure make it particularly difficult for these participants, so many of whom are so interested in the pragmatic, to come up with definitive moral prescriptions. The attitudes they have developed in discussing other kinds of topics hold sway here as well. Their perspectives on ethical matters are quite strikingly remote from the Christian tradition. A new pragmatism, especially in acknowledgment of the particular and the circumstantial, separates the positions taken by the conferees from the classical and the Stoic moral traditions as well. As they did in discussing topics of the natural world, participants bring empirical evidence and individual experience to bear. They assume that their understanding of nature can be readily imposed on the social order.

The question remains as to why science is so frequently invoked in ethical arguments. Perhaps it fills a void left by the decline of other ways of dealing with these issues. As with discussions of the passions and other aspects of human nature and human behavior, physiology is a useful kind of analogy, which seems to exercise some prescriptive weight in clinching an argument. Empirical evidence weighs against arguments from authority even on ethical questions, and science is considered a powerful method of analysis, which can appropriately be brought to bear to discuss and to shape the social values that should characterize seventeenth-century France. Science and its application to social issues also open up new possibilities for making arguments and adducing evidence. An intellectual climate, which exposes and fosters a wide variety of opinions on virtually all issues, contributes to a relativistic approach, especially when the traditional, authoritative opinions are consistently called into question. In these discussions, appeals to nature offer a disinterested empirical approach. In confronting a world in which it is not clear what the standards are or should be, or what will remain and what will prove transitory, appeals to nature offer some claim to certainty.

Because science was of keen interest to many participants, they used scientific analogies and arguments as the crucial points in ethical arguments to both challenge and sustain conventional ideas. In essence, conferees amplified the right and the role of science to comment on moral and social issues. Some scholars have claimed that mechanism gave early modern Europeans the confidence to believe one could not only manipulate nature but also control the passions.[60] Conferees did not wait for mechanism, however. Without it they still approached nature with confidence, and without it they confidently applied physiology to understand the passions and themselves. It is true that the science they used may not have given them as unambiguous an ideology for social analysis as mechanism later would, and their invocation of science might seem inconclusive to modern readers. Nonetheless, their concerted application of even nebulous scientific knowledge to social issues might well have prepared the way for later uses of science in social analysis.

What is distinctive about the kinds of ethical and social arguments conferees make? They are almost universally concerned with practical solutions to concrete problems. On social issues, they express clear impatience with abstractions. For example, they do not simply discuss poverty in the abstract but, rather, propose concrete solutions to existing social problems. Their discussion of social values also suggests the greater attractions of morally ambiguous positions in the interests of personal success or social stability. Because they are impatient with absolutes, they take the approach to issues of an impartial physician in search of effective therapy. Their arguments are much more forthright and explicit when affairs of state or concrete issues of public policy are involved than when they treat abstract issues.

These conferences also deal directly with the issues of special concern to the sort of professionals and virtuosi who attended them. Participants seem to presume, in a way that might be at odds with emerging absolutism, that the culture of the court and the nobility are extraneous and irrelevant—an attitude with affinities to Richelieu's promotion of the nobles of the robe at the expense of the traditional nobility. Conferees are concerned with social hierarchy. Although they would like to see a hierarchy based on nature, they also believe that any change or challenge to hierarchy is both ill-advised and dangerous. They take a relativistic stance on the corresponding moral issues and believe that virtue and vice are relative to situations. They recognize with perfect clarity that virtue does not guarantee success, and this fact, for some, makes the pursuit of virtue a less pressing concern.

As a result of the turmoil of the religious wars, French moral theorists of the late sixteenth and early seventeenth centuries developed two moral positions, one for private life and the other for public life. Many scholars of French political theory see this as the response of elites to the emergence of absolutism and contend that there is no rival political theory because bourgeois intellectuals subscribed completely to the moral and political views of elites.[61] There were, however, exceptions such as the Huguenot political theorist Louis Turquet de Mayerne, who did indeed speak for a bourgeois ethics and who might have influenced those gathering at Renaudot's Bureau.[62] Renaudot's conferees define another significant exception, and it is important that it was a *group* that cultivated a practical ethos. Their treatment of social and moral issues point to an alternative to the bifurcated vision of the conduct of a moral life. Renaudot's conferees nowhere subscribe to the ethos of a divided morality—a life of predominantly Stoic virtue at home and expedient disengagement in public. Instead they advocate civic responsibility. They also promote the values of public accomplishment, particularly in commercial and professional ventures, and in activities to promote the common good. They draw clear connections between the development of thinking about the passions and the interests and *raison d'état;* they apply the idea of interest to the development of the state.[63] While the seventeenth century saw concerted debate on the issue of private versus public utility, Renaudot's group decisively blurred the distinction by insisting on the universality of public good. The group's very existence suggests public engagement as a moral value, but its commitment to a civic communitarian culture is most thoroughly developed when it addresses political and economic topics.[64]

The treatment of social issues by conferees supports some broader conclusions as well. First, participants are consistently concerned with social problems. Second, when they propose solutions, these are generally institutional, bureaucratic, or governmental; they advocate the intervention of the state to address social issues and moderate social problems. In general, the sway of the classical tradition and the Stoic and Christian moral traditions lost ground in moral discussions. Participants assume that science and medicine provide important evidence and means of analysis with clear ramifications for social policies. The attitudes developed in the conferences, which here seem strikingly progressive or anachronistically secular, became commonplaces in the moral analysis of the Enlightenment. By the eighteenth century, the passions will once again be rehabilitated; they improve a world governed solely by private interests and can be made to work in the interests of society. Bernard de Mandeville most strikingly asserts that the pursuit of luxury can promote the interests of the state, and Adam Smith develops a vocabulary of advantage and interest to displace that of passion and vice.[65]

Much discussion of the changing ethos of the early modern period has focused on elite social groups as they wielded language to consolidate their political power—whether Norbert Elias's study of the evolution from *courtoisie* to *civilité* or Jorge Arditi's recent study of etiquette as defining eighteenth-century aristocrats.[66] The conferences represent a distinct and alternative point of view; they may be legitimately seen as an attempt to apply science as a universal social solvent rather than as the perspective of a distinct emerging elite. Elias insists that what was necessary for the emergence of the bourgeoisie was the practice of equality in an intimate setting. This setting allowed the bourgeoisie to exercise reason in a focused milieu before they turned their critical attention to established power. It is worth applying this notion to the conferences. Although short-lived, they indisputably offered just such a venue for the nourishing of social analysis and criticism.

CHAPTER EIGHT

Of Censorship, Sedition, and Luxury

Politics and Economics

I N A CONFERENCE ENTITLED "IF CENSORSHIP IS NECESSARY TO A STATE,"[1] participants disagree vehemently about the use of censors. The first speaker praises the censors of Rome, who regulated the duty of the citizens, made each aware of his obligations, and registered his goods. He compares their actions to the effects of drugs that evacuate bad humors. "One cannot govern a state in peace without it any more than one can conserve a body in health with the rebellion of one humor imperiously controlling all the others." Thus the best legislators have considered their ordinances useless without a censor to enforce them. "Without the censor to cauterize and to cut the corrupt parts of the state, one will always only with difficulty make a distinction between the virtuous and the vicious." Without censors, it will be difficult to praise or punish, "the two pivots of civil society." The purpose of censorship "is the equality of all the citizens by harmonic proportion to give birth to a union capable of binding them in peace and amity."

The second speaker gives a more nuanced depiction of censorship. Censorship is more useful the more democratic the state. Where command is divided, many lords presume that they "themselves can govern their appetites," and as a result, they are less fearful of the severity of the laws than they should be. Thus there is greater need for a censor. But in a monarchy where the king rules alone, there are laws to punish crimes and thus less need for the censor. The speaker draws a medical analogy to suggest the limited, beneficial impact of censorship: "the censor only stops the bad actions as flies do on wounds" (revealing the limits of both medical analogy and practice, even though putting maggots on dead flesh has come back into medical practice).[2] Thus censorship can only expose the negative, or, as the speaker more elegantly suggests, "censorship is like a painter, who can well represent the wrinkles and defects of a face, but can never begin to express the graces that make the flaws bearable." According to him, the republican form of government requires surveillance of the individual, but because monarchy more severely prescribes liberty of the individual, censorship becomes unnecessary. Yet he also condemns it, because censorship violates spaces that are appropriately private. "The custom of houses separated by walls and covered in roofs would be useless, if domestic spies, suborned to this end, made manifest what should be hidden." These two analogies suggest that censorship is misdirected, ineffective, and ultimately against the interest of the state. Most problematic of all, a censor contravenes the very notion of limited government. If censors are accepted, there are no logical limits to their role. "The riots of a husband and his wife will not be exempt, the chastisement of a valet will be considered inappropriate." There will be no separation between surveillance of the public and the private spheres.

For another participant, since censorship is built on the premise that vice is more common than virtue, it seems to grant license to vice by placing it in the foreground of the public's perception of the state and its citizens. If vice is perceived as common, it is more likely to be tolerated. He suggests the following medical analogy to argue against censorship: "some medicines move the bad humors but are not strong enough to evacuate them." As in medicine, "it is more expedient to remove nothing from the patient if it is not completely evacuated; the same applies to a state." As his parting shot, he notes that "censorship does not differ from the Inquisition" and wonders, "would it be well received from a nation, which has never had a taste of this rigor?" The next speakers qualify the preceding arguments: The censors of Rome did not simply constrain manners, they also registered goods to control the pursuit of luxury; in France, sumptuary laws are unnecessary because avarice is more common than prodigality. The interests and power of families control the acquisition of wealth and make censorship impossible and unnecessary in contemporary France. Another speaker ruefully sees censorship as the only defense against the distortions produced in the state by flattery. "They have planted censorship in some states like gardeners plant onions near roses, to attract all the *mauvais suc* from the earth to fortify the odor of the roses."

The conference on censorship reveals an unexpectedly high degree of sophistication in talking about political issues. The use of historical examples seems particularly critical; the advantages and disadvantages inherent in the adoption of any state policy are forthrightly expressed; the degree of genuine difference of opinion is striking; and, much more than is characteristic of other conferences, these topics depict a rather jaded view of human nature. Medical analogies to the state are pervasive and provide an effective way to rhetorically manipulate questions about the state.

The discussion of censorship reveals distinctions in the speakers' understanding of the state and the connections they see between censorship and political institutions. Although no speaker offers unadulterated praise of censorship, some suggest that even in its faulty manifestations censorship can inculcate positive values in citizens. The topic also raises the question of the classical legacy and the degree to which that legacy is relevant to discussions of contemporary French politics. It addresses the limits and legitimacy of the exercise of political power and invokes comparisons between the household and the state as a staple of political analysis. It also addresses questions about human nature and the appropriate form of government for diverse peoples, themes that become mainstays of Enlightenment political discussion. These are some of the central issues Renaudot's conferees return to in their discussions of political topics.

Renaudot's group officially subscribed to the restrictions on discussion he expressed in his preface, "to avoid matters of religion and affairs of state."[3] Nonetheless, participants move well beyond abstract generalizations about ideal states into more direct discussions of specific policies that would be appropriate to the French state. Given Renaudot's reputation as the royal propagandist par excellence as the publisher of the *Gazette de France*, one would perhaps expect political remarks to bolster the interests of the monarch uncritically. One might assume that participants would adhere to the directives for political discussion that Richelieu himself laid out in *The Art of pleasing in conversation*. "When we are pleased to discourse on the State under which we live, we should never extend our conjectures too far, nor affect to appear too penetrating. You know nothing does more to contribute to the happy success of an enterprise, than the secrecy observed therein."[4] However, the treatment of political issues by conferees is more explicit and unconventional than one might expect, given Renaudot's position and dependence on patronage.[5]

Although participants frequently violated the prohibition on political discussion, their predominant concern was not politics; fewer than 40 of the 460 distinct topics explicitly address politics. Nonetheless, they make a distinct contribution to seventeenth-century discussion of political and economic issues. As might be expected, they discuss political issues within the context of monarchy—their contribution to that discussion focuses on the responsibility of the king for the well-being of the community and for the economic development of the country. To a degree not characteristic of their discussion of other kinds of topics, participants shape their discussion around the contours of humanist texts but use them to assert an ethos of public engagement. In politics as in medicine conferees look to the practical and the useful. They weigh in on the contemporary debate between the ancients and the moderns, which came to the foreground later in the seventeenth century, generally on the side of the moderns. Participants are eager to discuss the nature of the state; they assess the changes occurring in it and consider specific issues of state policy such as sedition and censorship. When they turn their attention to economy their concern with specific policies is even more evident; they apply mercantilist theory to economic topics and to concrete proposals for economic reform. Somewhat surprisingly, they also assess domestic relations within the household in political terms.

ASSESSING POLITICS

Much discussion of political theory in the early modern period has been directed toward tracing the political roots of democracy. As such, the concerns of thinkers associated with the development of a centralized monarchy have not generally been deemed significant. In a significant study that sought to redress this neglect, Nannerl Keohane points out that the Anglo-American tradition of political theory focuses on two specific assumptions: (1) that for power not to be abused it must be checked and divided; (2) that the rights of individuals are the basic elements to be safeguarded by the state.[6] Neither of these principles was central to the French tradition. His countrymen took Bodin's claim that sovereignty is indivisible as axiomatic, and Frenchmen were more concerned with interests than with rights. As a result, seventeenth-century French political philosophy has not generally been considered significant to the progressive evolution of political thought. However, it has become clear that seventeenth-century French political theory fostered a concern with limited power and the development of rights, which ultimately bore fruit in the Enlightenment.[7]

The wars of religion in France raised questions that were central to political discussion. Was customary law made by the king or by the people? Who, if anyone, had the power to make new laws? Was the king himself originally chosen by the people and thus legitimated by their prior authorization? Or was this authority superior to any popular will? What was the historical basis for the Estates General, and how much independent power could it claim?[8] These questions and their treatment by political writers such as Huguenot political theorist Philippe Duplessis-Mornay[9] were often intended to establish a theoretical foundation for a new kind of political authority that would allow for political opposition rooted in religion. Although religious freedom legitimated political dissent, it also allied religious and political extremism; in Catholic France, political opposition was identified with heresy.[10] With the end of the religious wars and the fervent desire for political stability, it is not surprising that virtually all seventeenth-century French political theorists were proponents of greater centralization under a monarch. Their support was based on dramatically different understandings of the monarchy, however. Some saw the king as having absolute power subject only to divine law; others considered the king bound by fundamental law. Absolutism itself can be construed in dramatically different ways, each of which understands the relationship of the monarch to the nation and its history quite differently. In one view, the absolutist state is a new manifestation of a feudal state, supporting a besieged feudal aristocracy.[11] In another, the absolutist state is the ally of emerging capitalism, protecting bourgeois interests against those of a feudal aristocracy. Some see the absolutist state as the adjudicator between the competing interests of the old, feudal aristocracy and the ascendant elites—nobles of the robe, bureaucrats, financiers, and an emerging bourgeoisie.[12]

Absolutist political theorists sought support for an all-powerful monarch from various strands of the philosophical tradition. Guillaume Budé, for example, invoked the legitimacy of Plato's philosopher-king. Bodin transformed Budé's heroic monarch into a legislator king, although the actual exercise of sovereignty that he envisioned allowed for a shift of power between the king and his administrators according to their abilities. While the king created a community and affirmed the classical values of harmony and justice as the foundation of the state, the royal administrators allowed the cultivation of "private" interest in the public sphere, a pronounced feature of the modern state.[13] In this way, the philosopher-king was adapted to an increasingly commercial society.

Those who believed that the monarch was bound by "fundamental law" saw that law as represented by competing groups within the state. Some influential sixteenth-century theorists felt that they had to explain the basis for competition. For example, Philippe de Commynes identified a natural impulse to power and domination, and Claude de Seyssel applied a theory of harmony of four humors to the state.[14] Just as in the body, if one humor becomes too dominant, the entire body is destroyed, so too if one component of the state becomes too powerful, the health of the whole is jeopardized. For Seyssel, because the liberty of the king is limited by "good laws and ordinances and by the multitude and great authority of officers," a king cannot easily act against the good of his subjects.[15] Should a king be malevolent, Seyssel's political theory envisioned three bridles—religion, justice, and the police—as checks on royal authority. Competing interests thus legitimated the monarchy by making an abuse of power impossible. This cursory account signals some of the significant permutations in views of royal power and governance in early modern France. These different approaches to absolutism developed over the course of the seventeenth century as political theorists grappled with an evolving monarchy and with the legacy of political instability inherited from the wars of religion.

THE PARAMETERS OF POLITICAL ANALYSIS

What do the discussions of political topics by Renaudot's conferees contribute to these political debates? First, as all other seventeenth-century French political writing, their discussions implicitly endorse a central government under a monarch, although, within the constraints of absolutist political theory, participants take surprisingly progressive positions. Some believe that political progress could be attained most effectively through the rule of a monarch responsive to public needs. Concern with the well-being of the public offers participants a fundamental principle in light of which they can argue for the reform of monarchy or critique specific political practices. To the degree that they endorse absolutism, they focus on absolutism as a vehicle for advancing a commercial economy. They are quite willing to address the role of the nobility and to make arguments to curtail its role. They take monarchy for granted and do not advance arguments about the relationship between the monarch and other groups as the source of the law. In effect, they endorse an increase in the role of the monarchy at the expense of traditional orders. Because they insist on the responsibility of the monarch for the well-being of his kingdom and its citizens, they also see him as a source of progress. They define the tyrant, much in the way that Italian humanists like Bartolo de Sassoferrato[16] and Protestant political theorists like Duplessis-Mornay did: a ruler is illegitimate if he is not concerned with the common good. Instead of asserting the importance of traditional constitutional powers of the monarch, conferees assume explicitly that rather general constraints, such as a concern for the common good and the health and well-being of the state, bind the monarch and legitimate his exercise of power.

Although participants claim to address political issues de novo, in fact, like other political thinkers of the seventeenth century, they both respond to a rich humanistic tradition and draw on the legacy of Greek and Roman literature to shape their political writing. Just as the humanists did, they look past the Middle Ages to affirm their connection to the ancients. Participants deem themselves heirs to the culture of humanism. They share with civic humanists an appreciation of the active life in the public sphere but also feel well positioned to evaluate that legacy critically. It might well be objected that by the seventeenth century humanism had become a rather arid kind of investigation. In fact, humanist philology provoked the same kinds of attacks on its aridity, verbiage, and irrelevance as had characterized its own critiques of scholasticism.[17] Conferees (as in their assessments of the natural world) reject humanism as too bound to textual authorities. But in addressing political issues, they found it harder to cast off the weight of ancient texts transmitted through the Renaissance, particularly Aristotle's *Politics,* Plato's *Republic,* and Cicero's *Orations*—texts that define political discussion in the West. Nonetheless, participants revitalize issues of humanist discussion, both in light of science and because, some of them contend, new social and political situations require new perspectives. They reshape their humanist inheritance to their own concerns, adapting classical texts to some contemporary issues and dismissing them as irrelevant to others.[18]

Renaudot's group revives a culture of humanism in part by recombining it with an ethos of public engagement. Perhaps because this group feels newly empowered, they express great optimism about prospects for change and little of the alienation that characterized the response of French humanists to the wars of religion. But in order to develop an ethos of involvement in civic life, the Frenchman of the seventeenth century had to reject some strains of his intellectual heritage that strongly advised against such involvement. This attitude, best conveyed by Montaigne, suggested resignation as the appropriate response to an untenable political situation. By advocating outward attention to public duties (despite his scorn for politics as corrupt) and the cultivation of the private pleasures of scholarship and friendship, Montaigne articulated an attitude that was common in the prominent strain of humanism in France, known as the Stoic revival.[19] At the end of his *Politics,* Julius Lipsius, an influential figure in this tradition, advises "the honest man to sit still during civil war and not take either side." This political situation, in which "the leaders, under the pretext of the public profit, each strive for their private authority," is not worthy of the attention of intellectuals.[20] The *libertins* of the seventeenth century took seriously the Epicurean counsel to avoid the business of the world. They conformed to that advice as much as possible but found their true pleasures in scholarship and the company of friends.[21]

Participants in these conferences do not have as jaundiced a view of politics as the neostoics or the *libertins;* they do not separate the realms of action and contemplation but rather argue the pragmatic, active implications of their discussions. In the tradition of civic humanism, they consider examples drawn from the classics relevant to their political situation. They apply the model of the Roman republic directly to contemporary France.[22] The Greeks also provide important models. Plato, in particular, is a fundamental source for commenting on political issues, and the French are often compared to the Greeks. (For example, speakers assert that similarly variable climates have produced two peoples of a volatile character who have achieved distinction in the arts.)[23] Political discussions invoke not only ancient works and models but also more contemporary humanist works. One conference is dedicated to the issue of whether goods should be held in common, a legacy from both Plato's *Republic* and the more recent Christian republic of More's *Utopia.* In several conferences, the Christian humanism of *Utopia* and the realpolitik of Machiavelli's *Prince* are two pivots around which political opinion swirls. Machiavelli also lurks behind questions of ends and means and the uses of cruelty and kindness.[24]

Participants raise a number of specific questions that respond directly to the discussions of contemporary writers such as the political philosopher Jean Bodin and the economic theorist Antoine de Montchrétien. Bodin, in his *Six Books of the Republic,* treats a number of fundamental political issues that are subsequently raised as the topics of specific conferences; for example, why there are so many lawsuits, why the French are so inconstant, what causes seditions, and whether kingdoms have natural causes.[25] The very topics they treat indicate that conferees were well acquainted with the general texts and issues of political thought in the seventeenth century. Although they do not subscribe to all of the conservative implications of Bodin's arguments, they are nonetheless aware of his position on the issues that they discuss, and he plays a significant role in these questions about the character of the French.

One conference offers a revealing demonstration of the explicit use of a humanist legacy, as it addresses the question of whether death is preferable to dishonor,[26] which the speaker defines as civil death, that is, banishment from Rome. In this discussion, Rome both stands for Paris and epitomizes classical civilization, without specifying the type of regime, republic or empire. In other words, one can cite Rome without necessarily supporting a republic, with its implicit rejection of absolutism, or an empire, with its tacit endorsement. The first speaker insists that civil death deprives one of the greatest good, which is honor. The actions of soldiers indicate that civil death is more abhorrent than natural death, and more pragmatically, a man without honor or the means to regain it cannot hold any office. This is the sort of statement one might expect both from the perspective of political expediency and from a thorough, if unrealistic, identification of the French state with the Roman republic. However, the critical response of the second speaker much more effectively illustrates the general character of the adaptation of a humanistic legacy to the particulars of seventeenth-century France. He pokes holes in the previous argument by noting the relativity of honor; "what is honest in one place is dishonest in another, which is seen in the diverse customs and manners." The banished can be reinstated, as Cicero was, but the dead cannot be brought back to life. Furthermore, since the banished is almost always a wise man who is not persuaded of his guilt, he does not really experience any real dishonor, and "his spirit is in repose amid the tempest that agitates others." Ultimately, participants assert the power of nature over art, and thus death, as opposed to civil death, is to be abhorred, "since civil deaths are artifices and inventions of legislators to astound men without making them die." While life is an absolute good, esteem is merely a "good that is a fantasy and fleeting." Although he, like most who invoke a humanist legacy, takes note of ancient sources and examples, the speaker neither idealizes the past nor accepts it as the crucial factor in addressing contemporary issues. Participants generally demonstrate a hardheaded pragmatism and insist on a realistic assessment of both the French situation and the constraints of human nature. This particular speaker weighs the question of public values and service versus private values. Most noteworthy, he endorses neither a self-sacrificing ethos nor a sublimation of the interests of the individual to the interests of the state—at least not to the point of considering civil death a greater evil than natural death.

When conferees gauge their strengths and weaknesses or measure their accomplishments against those of an earlier age, they are not generally discomfited by the legacy of the ancients but instead critically empowered by it. In a rather abstract discussion in a conference "Of the end of things,"[27] a speaker assesses contemporary history and insists that "what is said of the miseries of this world is not to be taken absolutely; the barbarousness of past ages is not to be compared with the politeness and learning of this age." For a speaker on the topic of "Whether the world grows old,"[28] a positive assessment of the state of the world could be made if France were a republic: "Were we in those commonwealths." This suggests both that in commonwealths people express their true opinion and that such a body would invariably assess the state of the world optimistically. Participants' confidence in the present derives largely from their understanding of the operations of nature, which suggest continuity rather than decline. Some speakers suggest that the question is best understood as a difference between the psychologies of the old and the young. In other words, they see the practice of bemoaning the decline of civilization as the ageless sport of an older generation looking with trepidation upon the young. Another speaker makes a modern retort to these lamentations. Such complaints have been made since the time of Seneca, but "the quality of 'spirits' has not diminished since then." Although his spirited defense of modernity is engaging, he resorts to traditional misogyny to clinch his argument; the source of any weakness of "spirits" is the depravity produced by the Fall, amply reflected by "the weakness of the spirit of a man who lets himself be governed by his wife."

Only one speaker argues that there has been a consistent decline since the time of the creation of man.[29] His argument, too, is based on what he understands of science, although the decisive evidence for his argument is cultural. "Just as a stone has less force the further it is from the hand that threw it, so too," he notes, "human beings are less perfect the further they get from their source and principle." This decadence is especially marked in our bodies. It is less apparent in our minds because we are able to take advantage of the good foundation of earlier centuries. Nonetheless, he notes, "there have not appeared in the last centuries any who can equal these great men of antiquity."

The staunchest arguments that human beings have not declined and that the accomplishments of the ancients are not beyond the aspirations of the moderns are made on grounds of the constancy of nature. As one speaker notes in the same conference on the quality of men, there is no reason to believe that there has been a decline, "because *God, nature,* and *art* are the three agents of the world that produce all effects both then and now" (my emphasis). The first two agents are constant: "God does not create souls with fewer advantages and grace than earlier. Nature and secondary causes do not contribute less than earlier times." The only possible source of decline would then be in the quality of the human mind, but since "the spirit depends on the body now and as it always has, and the bodies being as well disposed as they have ever been, the spirits should be as perfect."

Another speaker claims that the entire issue of the ancients versus the moderns is the result of familiarity breeding contempt; for "it is only rarity, which gives the price to things." There have never been so many doctors, regents, and professors as today. In past centuries, a man who knew a few words of Latin passed as a great scholar; today it "is a language almost as common everywhere as originally." While this speaker is surely overconfident in his assessment of the extent of the dissemination of humanist culture and learning, he also points with satisfaction to the great number of recent inventions such as the cannon, the printing press, and Galileo's telescope.

THE STATE IN THEORY AND PRACTICE

Perhaps because of the political instability produced by the wars of religion, participants grapple with fundamental questions about the state—such as how changes occur in them.[30] Sometimes they address these issues from perspectives we might consider unusual, but which are central to seventeenth-century political philosophy. For example, when they ask "If the changes in states have natural causes?"[31] the first speaker shifts the focus of the question by wondering whether changes in the state are caused by God. He believes that it is essential to determine at the outset the relationship between God and politics, or (as he casts it) to explore the extent of free will and the realm of human ambition in political events. He contends that the intellect invariably seeks to know not only the causes but also whether those causes are natural, supernatural, or contingent. This investigation of "natural" causes provides a way for the speaker to justify political inquiry. Changes in natural bodies offer the crucial analogy; states are natural because they are composed of individuals with bodies, and therefore, "it would be ridiculous to say that the causes of changes for persons are natural, but those for the states they compose are not." Furthermore, the only incontrovertible knowledge we gain from medicine is that our bodies change, and as natural bodies change, so do political bodies. "Natural change" as attested to by the evidence of science thus endorses political change.

Another speaker, who argues that God controls the political order, relies on more traditional arguments. He challenges these scientific analogies with scriptural evidence that God's will directs the change of scepters. His arguments restrict individual freedom to a degree other speakers find unacceptable, however. One proffers a compromise. He acknowledges that, although God is, of course, the supreme cause of the birth, conservation, and destruction of states, He does not prevent the operation of the "subaltern causes." These causes depend on the will of human beings, which is free. If human beings or changes in states were entirely dependent on destiny, there would be no free will, which would, of course, be an impossible position to take in the face of Catholic theology. This argument, which suggests a scholastic synthesis of antithetical arguments and uses a theological tenet as crucial, is unusual in the conferences. But for this speaker "free will" also entails a republic as the form of government consonant with our nature; thus, "in the administration of Republics, He [God] let the greater part of things to chance, in order to occupy the industry of men according to their will." For some speakers, the fact that God allows us free will in the conduct of our lives endorses a republic, because it is the form of government that allows the greatest exercise of freedom and produces the greatest rewards for human industry.[32] Although a discussion of free will as the basis of a philosophy of the state might seem a rather reactionary approach, it nonetheless allows some speakers to develop an avant-garde position.

Some of the most controversial political topics address property relations. In fact, one of the things that give these conferences such a distinctively modern flavor is their preoccupation with economic issues. In discussing "On the community of goods,"[33] the first speaker vehemently insists on the importance of the city and suggests with Plato that the harmony of cities depends on goods held in common. He makes the crucial point that society is fundamentally shaped by its economic structure. He invokes an analogy frequently used to argue for poor relief: "the greatest goods are communicated to many"—things such as sunlight and the beauty of the earth, which God has given to all.

The second speaker distinguishes between those goods that are better for being widely disseminated and those that become devalued by their greater diffusion. The virtues and the sciences, for instance, become more excellent the more they are communicated and taught, but gifts of fortune like honors, riches, women, and material possessions diminish in value to the extent that they are commonly held. He concedes that the community of goods is founded in nature, where all was common at the beginning, and that goods became particular due to avarice alone. Nonetheless, "in all times, it is entirely contrary to the happiness of a city, which is not only a society of men, but of many men, different in condition, of which the lowliest are usually the most necessary to a state." Although this speaker suggests that nature provides a model at variance with that of society, he nonetheless provides an analogy from nature to justify this discrepancy of conditions. "Just as in nature there is nothing more beautiful than diversity, it is the same in the diverse conditions of the inhabitants of the city." He contends that, although Plato and Socrates desired that children be held in common, adopting this policy would have disastrous effects on the society. "It would impede generation, fathers would not recognize their children and vice versa; and consequently there would be neither paternal love, nor filial nor conjugal love, which are the most secure foundations for human society. Incest and parricides would often be committed." This speaker reveals a rather Machiavellian notion that, although the political theories of Plato and Aristotle might well describe an ideal, their application is at best impractical and, in fact, frequently disastrous. He also offers what seems a strikingly "modern" response to the communism of Plato. Inequity may be unnatural, but it is absolutely necessary to society. Anything held in common becomes valueless in the civic sphere. Rewards and hierarchies, as reflected in differential ownership of goods, produce the best order. These speakers immediately hone in on the most inflammatory tenet of communist texts, the sharing of women and children.

Only one speaker wants to implement Plato's *Republic,* which, he says, created a city "more venerable than formidable and less rich than just." He concludes that we cannot overestimate the significance of a community of goods since it furthers our path to contemplation. As is clear from other contemporary texts, this topic was central to the concerns of many sixteenth- and seventeenth-century political writers. Obviously the issue came to the fore through the rediscovery of Plato, and it also resonated with the Protestant emphasis on the simplicity of early Christianity. Conferees grapple with economic issues, acutely aware of the increasingly evident wealth in French society and the concomitant discrepancy between rich and poor. More's *Utopia* drew a sharp distinction between the cultivation of wealth and the practice of Christianity. Other Utopian literature, including *The City of the Sun* by Campanella, maintained that holding goods in common was essential to an idealized restructuring of the community.[34]

A confrontation between the Christian humanism of More's *Utopia* and the realpolitik of Machiavelli's *Prince* takes place in a conference entitled "If it is easier to make one obey by kindness or by fear."[35] Although participants bring a weighty legacy of humanist political philosophy to the fore, most speakers support Machiavellian realpolitik. One acknowledges that only "if men let themselves be led by the movement of reason rather than their passions, would it be easy to make them obey by kindness rather than by fear." He concludes, however, that political and household relationships are based on what the inferior owes the superior, demands that can be best effected through force. Another speaker concurs; only poets have imagined societies constructed without laws and discipline, "assembled by agreeable and melodious concerts, but these are fables." Instead, he suggests, one could consider as a philosophical principle that things are preserved by the same principles whereby they are established, and therefore, states *could be* governed well by kindness, if they had been established by kindness. He makes the obvious argument, richly illustrated with scriptural examples, that most states are established by force. Since fear is felt by both the wicked and the virtuous, it is the most effective way to deter all from vice. Another speaker agrees that in political circumstances, force is the best method, although it depends on the character of those who command and obey. Family relations, which he suggests are also about power, should be moderated by kindness. This remark might well have suggested the topic for a few subsequent conferences on closely related topics and invokes what most speakers seem to accept, that the family is a political unit and family relations are about power.

Given the stated injunction against such explorations, participants are surprisingly eager to discuss not just general notions of political order but also specific issues of state policy. Opinion divides along two visions of the state. One is progressive and rejoices in the economic development of France; the other resists devolution away from a traditional monarchy and aristocracy and warns of the vices associated with economic development. These conflicting views come into play in addressing such topics as censorship, the causes of sedition, and whether one should take part in a civil war—questions of obvious immediate relevance in the period following the wars of religion.

When participants turn their attention to the topic of sedition, they are probably indebted to recent French writers on the topic, Bodin and Gabriel Naudé, for example. Bodin specifically raised the question as to whether the prince should take sides in a civil war and identifies great discrepancies of wealth as the root of this form of political instability. As a result, Bodin cited Thomas More's claim "that the only way of safety for an estate, is when men live in common, which cannot be where there is any property."[36] In his *Considérations politiques sur les coups d'estats,* Naudé forthrightly considered under what circumstances a coup was warranted. Although this controversial text was produced in only twelve copies, it nonetheless horrified many of his contemporaries that his prime example of a justifiable coup was the massacre of Saint Bartholomew's Day.[37]

The topic of sedition[38] was not simply one of scholarly interest. All the participants would have been aware of recent events that had nearly produced coups or had led to civil war. Marie de Medici faced the continuous opposition of the nobility during her regency. They mobilized against her in 1612. In 1614 the Prince of Condé made a bid for power that could have precipitated a civil war; the nobles did force the queen to call the Estates General into session to deal with their grievances. In 1617 the nobles had begun to raise troops against her minister Concini. By 1619 Marie was leading the opposition to her son, and by 1624 Louis had resolved to lead troops against his mother. All these threats of civil war were averted, but sedition would have been highly topical.

When conferees address the topic of sedition, they are initially concerned with how political opposition develops. They take the responsibility of the prince for political dissent as a given; an outbreak does not occur under the leadership of prudent and restrained rulers. But, one speaker insists, citizens can be provoked: "when superiors consider only their simple interest, without regard for that of the people they command, oppression makes them [the people] first utter injurious words against the government until, finally, the least movement can push them to a violent uprising." Even if the cause of sedition is the fault of the prince, several groups are likely to exploit these "public troubles" for their own ends, to wit, the ambitious, the miserable, and the guilty, all of whom see any change, even instability, as being in their interest.

Another speaker distributes blame for provoking sedition by identifying its three principal causes: the sovereign who oppresses, because oppression invariably touches on the most sensitive issues such as "immunities, privileges, and religion"; the people who foment revolution "by their luxury, laziness, ambition, and avarice"; and particular events that spark revolt, such as the continuation of war or the interruption of commerce. Another speaker addresses revolution from the perspective of the psychology of the poor. Elites persuade the people to join them by presenting the revolution as being in their best interests. Since the two most general causes of revolution are fear and hope, rulers must "reward well the good and punish exemplarily the wicked to prevent it."

Although most discussions about involvement in civil wars are written from the perspective of the state, a conference asking, "Is it more expedient in a civil war to remain neutral or to take part?"[39] raises the question of political unrest from the point of view of the citizen. A speaker evades the question by denouncing civil war as the most detestable of wars: it is much more difficult to end, and its end does not produce peace; it is brought about by force of arms and provoked by the ambitious who then remain in power. The next speaker forthrightly maintains that all citizens must take a position, because if one does not try to halt a civil war, one is lazy and indifferent, qualities completely incompatible with good citizenship. Only one speaker condones neutrality, it "being most expedient to be simply a spectator rather than to make himself an actor in a bad play."[40]

Several conferences address the future of the state, revealing a conflict between traditional forms of monarchy and the emerging wealth and concentration of authority of the French state. A conference entitled "Which science is the most necessary to a state"[41] raises themes closely related to the debates over the value of knowledge, although it specifically treats the implications for the state. A speaker insists that the most knowledgeable citizens are the most useful to the state. With wise ministers and counselors, the state can avoid the perils that menace it. Another speaker challenges him, saying that to answer the question one must weigh whether learning is advantageous for subjects or sovereigns. He contends that learning has turned Frenchmen and their monarchs away from their traditional greatness. He catalogs examples of the pernicious effects of learning on the state, noting that one of France's greatest rulers, Louis XI, knew only five words of

Latin. The Turks continue to advance because they banished printing to prevent the spread of learning. The sciences are directly destructive of the character of citizens. Learning "inflates those who are learned; it makes them presumptuous and consequently refractory and disobedient to the laws of the prince, which is the seed of sedition, the worst evil of a state." Learning fosters laziness, which is pernicious to states. That is why the Goths did not burn Roman libraries: they were sure that learning would make the Romans lazy and susceptible to defeat. Studies indubitably take one away from productive activities like agriculture and commerce and "effeminize" body and soul, the body by reducing its strength due to lack of exercise and the spirit by presenting it with an array of ways to acquire goods and honors.

This speech is both a vehement denunciation of the values of learning and a thoroughgoing indictment of the changes of seventeenth-century social structure that had directed France away from its feudal and agrarian past. The argument hopes to bolster a traditional political and economic order by maintaining that the strength of the state rests on a staunch military culture. Learning poses a danger to the state because it misdirects the attention of the aristocracy away from military exploits, and that of citizens away from traditional agrarian occupations. Learning, whether a speaker argues for or against it, represents the new social order as opposed to a more traditional one.

These conferences change the grounds on which arguments are made and the very nature of the discussion of many political issues. Although the roots of democracy cannot be uncovered at the Bureau, as historians might wish, nonetheless a number of political issues are illuminated. Participants take a hardheaded and pragmatic approach to political issues, which are not discussed in terms of any ideal. Instead they present clearheaded discussions of the causes of dissent and changes of regime. They identify the underlying cause of political strife as an abuse of power, particularly on the part of rulers, who confuse their narrow self-interest with the interest of the state. This confusion produces a fundamental failure to implement the common good. Conferees understand the competing interests of different groups and the interrelationships between them. They reveal a fairly sophisticated understanding of political rebellion and crowd psychology. They emphasize the responsibility of the monarch to seek the common good, to allow for personal liberty, to reward the good and punish the wicked, though these categories—goodness, wickedness, and personal liberty—remain disturbingly amorphous. So many of these abstract concepts are not clearly defined that these political discussions can seem naively optimistic on the one hand or pragmatic and critical on the other.

Several conferences move beyond general discussion of the nature and character of the state to consider specific policies that states might adopt. These conferences cannot be construed as plans for policy in part because each topic raises controversial responses, at least one of which usually questions the wisdom of carrying out the action at all. Such discussions should instead be understood as debates about the value to the state of pursuing specific policies. For example, in "How to make a place populated,"[42] the first speaker notes that the way for states to establish a reputation is to build cities. To attract people to these new cities, one must appeal to the body or the soul. Since there are more sensualists than intellectuals, the speaker asserts, it is most important to appeal to "physical commodity" and thus to build near sources of food and water and fertile land. This speaker uses his sense of human nature to refute various scientific views. Men live in cities, he contends, "because man [is] in himself a political animal" not because of "the fortuitous concourse of atoms, as Epicurus contends." His idea of the inherent sociability of human beings is designed to discredit any atomist notion of social formation by chance. (He may also be expressing some frustration with the regular use of scientific arguments and analogies to describe the political.) Reflecting contemporary discussion of the origin of society, this speaker insists that societies form because of "their natural inclination to conserve themselves" against savage beasts and their enemies.

Another speaker notes that frontier towns are hard to populate because it is difficult to develop agriculture and manufacturing. But since people are often willing to relocate to improve their conditions of life, one should also appeal to the spirit to motivate people to relocate. For example, religion requires pilgrimages, offerings, and devotions, and the new cities should offer these. Academies and universities, libraries, and laboratories also offer incentives to intellectuals. One speaker makes a strong case for increasing the population of cities: "The force of states consists in the number of men." That is why, he points out, those legislators who have limited the number of inhabitants have sometimes lost their republics, because they could be defeated in a single battle. On the contrary, Rome flourished when it was most heavily populated, and the Romans enacted legislation to encourage population growth such as "rigorous laws against celibacy and privileges given to those who have several children."[43] Subsequent speakers doubt the wisdom of attempting to increase population at all. One notes that "wise legislators like Solon and Lycurgus limited the number of inhabitants in their towns; new buildings are often prohibited in Lisbon, Naples, and Paris; and many nations discharge their people to colonies." This discussion suggests a wider division of opinion than is characteristic of early modern discussions of population. Mercantilists generally saw population as an essential component of national wealth, and by the eighteenth century, the philosophes pronounced increasing population as a key measure of political and economic health.

Participants also consider several specific policy issues that are acutely relevant to actual political events. Spanish troops moved into the interior of France in the summer of 1636, threatening Paris itself. This event is reflected in a conference "If it is better to guard the frontier or carry the war to the enemy."[44] It sets the terms of the discussion by claiming that war has peace as its end, so whatever leads best to that end is most desirable. Since soldiers defend most vigorously the place they live, the frontier should be guarded. The next speaker weighs both sides of the issue. It is always more "convenient, useful, and glorious" to attack the enemy on his own territory than to wait for him on yours. It is also easier to defend one's country by creating a diversion in enemy territory rather than by awaiting the ravages that inevitably accompany war in one's own country. Furthermore, war carried on in a foreign country is almost entirely self-sustaining, "because the soldier who can live there at his discretion and enrich himself by pillaging conquered places, is less of a burden to his prince and his country." The Romans provide a telling example; they were always victorious outside Italy but were often beaten at home. A great and powerful prince will be sure to push back his enemy from his own territory.

Another speaker, eager to move beyond general principles and to focus on specifics, insists that strategy depends on the conditions of the state, specifically the security of borders, and the character of internal politics must be considered. He offers a cynical assessment of the social aspects of warfare: "Foreign war serves as an asylum for bad citizens and those who fear the chastisement of their crimes: Thus it purges and bleeds the body of the state." But ultimately the French should always favor aggressive warfare because of the "ardor and impetuousness" of their national character. Speakers consider "temperament" a crucial component for understanding the individual, and the "temperament" of its citizens defines "national character."

THE ECONOMY IN THEORY AND PRACTICE

Topical and pragmatic concerns also predominate when conferees turn their attention to economic issues. They both understand economics as integral to the policies of the state and assert a natural basis of economic activities; that is to say, "nature has given us a desire for what we don't have." A conference on the topic of "Whether exchange is more convenient than buying and selling"[45] argues by analogy to number theory that just as unity or one is the first number, so too initially goods were held in common. A speaker acknowledges, however, that the word *mine* is more compelling than *ours,* since "even monks take it for a mortification and children cry when anything proper to them is taken from them." Thus the phenomenon of holding goods in common is relatively short-lived in human history. Other speakers assume the "naturalness" of rights of property, a belief that is challenged by those who assert the "community of goods."

Conferees are responding to a sense of economic crisis, which they see reflected in the increasing number of poor and the growing discrepancy between the wealthy and the poor. They might well have been acutely sensitive to these issues because of Renaudot's position as *intendant des pauvres* and the conditions they would have observed at the Bureau and his medical clinics.[46] In economic discussions there are two poles around which arguments swirl. Some speakers object to new economic developments and insist on the validity of an ancient and venerable feudal tradition; others assert the advantages of the new over the old and advance mercantilist claims for the economic agenda of the state.[47]

When conferees consider the economy, they work within a tradition of mercantilist writing. Despite the preeminence of mercantilism in the seventeenth century, modern economists sometimes treat it with a rather bemused puzzlement. They find the emphasis of mercantilists on balance of trade simplistic and the obsession with precious metals as a source of wealth naïve. But modern disparagement fails to acknowledge the important steps taken in economic analysis by mercantilists or the connections between mercantilism and the more accepted and even venerated tradition of laissez-faire economics of the modern period.

For seventeenth-century thinkers, mercantilism had the great attraction of providing a rational basis for analysis of the state. Mercantilists attempted to understand the economy as a system—local, national, and global. They proposed policies for states to implement in order to alter economic developments in their favor. Their systematic analysis of the economy was based on principles they considered fundamental. Mercantilism is generally understood as an economic philosophy that saw the state as the repository of both politics and economics, but it also sanctioned specific policies in light of the general understanding of the economy. It emphasized the importance of precious metals to the economy and extolled industry at the expense of agriculture. Mercantilists were greatly preoccupied with foreign trade as a source of wealth and, in the eighteenth century, emphasized a dense population as an element of national strength. They saw the state as the agent capable of implementing economic goals. Three specific hallmarks of mercantilism were (1) great attention to commerce, (2) cultivation of a favorable balance of trade, and (3) prohibition of duties and monopolies.[48] Even if modern economists find these principles crude, at the time they gave adherents of mercantilism the beginnings of a comprehensive economic theory. Implicit in that system was the possibility of rational analysis, productive intervention, and control over processes previously considered incomprehensible or beyond man's control. These attitudes are roughly the same as those that characterize both practitioners of the new sciences and participants in Renaudot's conferences. The prospects for a degree of control and for improvement in material conditions empowered intellectuals and contributed to their growing sense of optimism about their time and their own participation in positive economic changes.

There are a number of texts within this tradition from the early seventeenth century that discuss economic plans for France, particularly for the cultivation of new industry. These texts provide the background and context for the discussion of economic issues at the Bureau. Isaac de Laffemas recognized the need to put the national economy first. He deliberately focused on measures that would strengthen the economy of France at the expense of other economies. He typified the general approach of the early mercantilists and raised most of their specific concerns. He worried about the flow of gold and silver out of the country; he disapproved of imported luxuries and emphasized keeping raw materials at home for French manufacturers; and he made concrete suggestions for putting the poor to work, reducing vagrancy and laziness, and controlling and encouraging internal trade. In his *Histoire du commerce de France,* he praises the king for "always putting as his first intention to favor what is useful and necessary to his people," and the Assembly of Notables of 1596, without which "the mechanical sciences would be dead, buried in ignorance." Although wise ministers can play important roles in economic development, only the king can effect sufficient reform "to cut out the gangrenous portions of commercial abuse before they infect the entire body." Laffemas insists on the importance of maintaining economic order. Previous failures to do so have forced some workers to change the type of work they do to have any hope of profit, and others to flee to some better-regulated country.[49]

Although French writers praised the economic steps taken by Henry IV and his minister Sully, Henry IV's death coupled with the attendant political disruption of the regency of Marie de Medici curtailed economic development. Other states, also wedded to a mercantilist notion of the economy, sought to further weaken France by imposing excessive duties on French products. To respond to these concerns, Montchrétien, another influential figure who explored the relationship between the economy and the state, published his *Traicté de l'oeconomie politique.* He, like Laffemas, is an important representative of the period of economists of the state, beginning with Henri IV and ending with Colbert. Born in 1586, Montchrétien attended the Collège de Caen and had an early career as a poet and playwright. But he fell afoul of the new regulations on dueling. After unsuccessfully pleading his case to Henry IV, he fled to England to escape hanging. He returned to France an economist, passionately interested in the economic reform of his country. He had been impressed by the development of industries in England and the Netherlands, some of which were French industries exported to England with an exodus of the Huguenots. His ambition was to establish workshops like those he had seen abroad. He visited both commercial towns and industrial cities and studied their economic organization "in their smallest details." He hoped that the French would rival the English and the Dutch in the manufacture of fine textiles and praised the king's plans for new manufacture, especially of textiles. He wanted to see animal husbandry fostered and expressed concern that the overregulation of the wine industry was detrimental.[50]

Although the commercial developments he cites seem more potential than actual, Montchrétien is full of praise for France's commercial prospects. He insists that France is a country capable of feeding and clothing an infinite number of inhabitants. His optimistic assessment of the future of France revolves around both the character of the French and the natural resources of the country. He connects political liberty and effective economic development, arguing that from antiquity France has been the true domicile of liberty and was the first country to abolish servitude. Although optimistic about France's commercial potential, Montchrétien bemoans its neglect of economic development, a neglect that proved detrimental to the public well-being.[51]

Although Montchrétien, like most of the economic reformers of the early seventeenth century, believed that economic growth and development would benefit the country, he was also concerned that some of the economic power of the state be directed toward ameliorating conditions for the poor. His text explicitly charged that an emphasis on the contemplative life is detrimental to the republic.[52] Instead the individual should participate in activities that further the economic development of France.

Ultimately Montchrétien threw in his lot with the Huguenot party and was killed as an armed participant in a Huguenot uprising in Normandy. Contemporary documents denounce him as "a wicked adventurer, a dualist, and counterfeiter."[53] It is ironic that Richelieu, a key figure in the suppression of the Huguenot uprising, was also a deputy of the clergy to the Estates General of 1614, which convened in large part to deal with the economic issues raised by Montchrétien's treatise. Richelieu was greatly influenced by Montchrétien's ideas, an influence reflected both in the economic maxims spelled out in his *Political Testament* and in the economic policies he pursued.[54]

Richelieu's rise to prominence in the French state was due in part to the positions he held, many of which were influential in shaping the political economy. After serving as a representative of the clergy in the meeting of the Estates General of 1614,[55] he was appointed chief minister in 1624 to succeed La Vieuville, who had been finance minister. As a result, the chief minister's position incorporated a concern with finances. Early in 1626, Richelieu was appointed *grand maistre surintendant général du commerce et de la navigation,* a position that gave him control of the navy and shipping. In this capacity, he wrote a memorandum for the Assembly of Notables arguing the need to protect trade with a navy.[56] He initiated policies designed to reorganize naval administration, to foster recruiting for the navy, to refurbish ports, and to build war ships.[57] These specific policies were part of Richelieu's ambitious plans for economic reform. He hoped to restore stability to the king's finances and to create the first budgetary surplus since Sully's ministry by curtailing expenditure and redistributing taxes. But his economic goals were compromised by his foreign policy interests. The military expenditures precipitated by France's involvement in the Thirty Years' War both heightened Richelieu's concern with the economy and made his plans for reform impossible.[58] France's involvement required a sharp increase in war expenditure, from sixteen million livres in 1620, to thirty-three million in 1635 and thirty-eight million in 1640. Such increases required concomitant increases in revenues collected in taxes.[59] Against this backdrop of innovative economic ideas combined with severe economic constraints produced by military expenditures, conferees turned their attention to the economy.

ECONOMICS AT THE BUREAU

The conference "Which is more harmful to the state, laziness or luxury"[60] brings economic issues to the fore. The first speaker claims that laziness is the root of all evils. He notes that, as physicians tell us, laziness creates a vacuum that allows diseases to enter the body. The measures nature takes to prevent a vacuum "ought to serve as a warning to men of the lengths to which they should go to avoid laziness." To counter the dire effects of laziness, the speaker offers a trickle-down theory of the value of luxury. The rich enrich others by employing them. If one were to banish luxury, one would banish most of what we call the arts. Scorn for luxuries disparages the gifts of a provident nature; "Nature having produced all these gentlenesses to divert us from the cradle to the grave and to soften the chagrins that accompany the course of our lives." Besides, the failure to pursue luxury is fundamentally at odds with the passion that carries men to the aggrandizement of states, which is to say, "the desire for what they do not have." As a case in point, he cites the savages of the New World who have not advanced since their beginnings because they wished for nothing. Furthermore, those who attack luxury and allow only what is purely necessary are forced to discredit gold and silver, which are essential to the maintenance and defense of states. On the other hand, he notes, no country has had the luxury of present-day France, which conclusively proves that "luxury is not the vice most dangerous to the state."

The next speaker uses another natural analogy to argue the reverse. Movement is to luxury as rest is to laziness. Just as nature favors rest, so too laziness is less dangerous to states, because luxury "always makes its subjects innovators and agitators of this public repose." He points to three great evils associated with the pursuit of luxury: First, the subjects of the nation are impoverished. Second, Frenchmen who import luxury goods enrich other states by adding to their stores of gold and silver. Finally and most detrimental, because the human understanding knows nothing except through the external senses, luxury encourages some to "let themselves be easily persuaded that he who is fashionably dressed is a man of merit." Another conferee counters that the difference in the punishments ordained for offenses best indicates their relative harm to the state. While the greatest punishment for luxury has been a fine, Saint Paul condemned do-nothings to die of hunger, saying that those who do not work should not eat. In other words, the pursuit of luxury works against laziness, which is a much greater evil.

On this topic, participants are well aware of mercantilist writers on the economy and the state. Those arguing for luxury invoke Montchrétien's distinctive contribution to economic discussion, that is to say, the notion that avarice makes a positive contribution to the well-being of the state.[61] The concern that the pursuit of luxury will remove vital gold from the state coffers and thus weaken its position vis-à-vis other states is a commonplace of mercantilists writers who draw on Bodin's extensive discussion of this point. For most participants, nature provides an essential way to understand the economy, and the economy is construed as vital to society and the state. When the advocate of luxury expresses concern that those who attack luxury also attack gold, the very foundation of the economic health of the state, he is implicitly referring to texts such as More's *Utopia,* which argue that goods should be held in common and cite the folly of valuing shiny metals like gold.

When participants turned to economic issues, they were acting on, Richelieu's interests (as indeed they were commissioned to do). Richelieu requested that the Bureau consider the economic situation of France over the summer of 1638. There were compelling reasons for them to consider these issues. First, French economic writers turned their attention to the growing commercial states, especially the Netherlands, and argued that the governments of these countries fostered economic development. These writers recognized that the economy was a crucial component of state policy. The growing hegemony of the Dutch in Atlantic trade was of great concern to France in the early seventeenth century. Second, participants were uneasy because of shifts in the character of economic activity. When historians look back to the period of the 1630s and 1640s, they still debate the character of political economy at the time. For some, the early seventeenth century belongs to a period of economic expansion, and France is properly understood as a constitutional monarchy committed to a rational state directed toward economic expansion. For others, this is a period of monarchical consolidation characterized by economic contraction and great political unease. Just as the historical interpretations of this period remain contested, so too participants in Renaudot's conferences reflect the same conflict between unease and optimism.[62]

The connection between the mercantilists' vision of the economy and the discussion of economic interests at the Bureau is fairly straightforward. Barthélemy de Laffemas, controller-general of commerce for Henry IV, made an impassioned plea for establishing public offices to facilitate commerce as a "preservative against the ruin of our commerce."[63] Mercantilists assumed that economic interests of the monarch and the people were the same, both rooted in increased productivity. Because the wealth of the prince and his kingdom depended on economic growth, mercantilist writers addressed the questions of how to economically motivate the people. As a result, they too were interested in issues that shaped ethical discussions at the Bureau, such as how to motivate people, and the impact of ambition and covetousness. Mercantilists were more likely than conferees to see these qualities as economically beneficial rather than ethically problematic. Mercantilists were inclined, as were conferees, to see the state as an agent effectively directing economic policies. Early economic theorists Bodin and Sully both proposed strict taxes on exports of raw materials and on imports of finished goods, to protect national resources, encourage local manufacture, and bring revenue to the crown.[64] Montchrétien believed that "wise nature" requires the aid of human authority to turn the pursuit of profit to public advantage. He argued that such aid should come from a powerful government, operating according to the same principles as nature herself; that is, recognizing the centrality of the "bait of honor and the lure of profit" in human life and making sure that these motives are encouraged, given free scope, and properly rewarded. Montchrétien described the human understanding as "a tabula rasa on which can be imprinted socially useful motives and goals as easily as slothful ones."[65] While conferees were clearly in favor of economic expansion, they were (perhaps because they treated a broader array of topics than simply economic issues) much more aware that the values tied to economic development might be ethically or socially problematic.

Conferees turned their attention to a number of specific economic topics. For example, the question of "Whether commerce derogates from nobility"[66] is hotly contested. (This was the practice in France whereby a nobleman lost his noble title if he pursued commercial ventures.) A speaker takes a strong stand against the derogation from nobility through the pursuit of commerce; he insists that only "do-nothings" criticize industry. He cites as misplaced delicacy the belief that the nobility should either remain poor or live as thieves; the dignity of a title, after all, is not worthwhile if one is condemned to starve. In addition, the evils of primogeniture,[67] particularly its disastrous effects on daughters, will be avoided if the nobility is allowed to pursue commerce. Although some ancient legislators disdained commerce, this speaker concludes that men are made more prudent "by the knowledge of the customs of several peoples." This knowledge of other cultures, he presumes, will inevitably lead to an increased respect for commerce. The next speaker, a proponent of the traditional social order, expresses concern that the quest for gain will distract the nobility from the defense of the state.[68] Furthermore, merchants are so tainted with dishonesty that God even forbade his people to have a merchant among them. Another speaker reassesses the traditional praise for the *vita contemplativa* to argue instead that the contemplative are a drain on society. A good political leader attracts those who can contribute most to the well-being of the state by all sorts of honors and privileges. Merchants must be acknowledged as individuals invaluable to the state, for without their trade many areas would be poor. He recognizes (as did other seventeenth-century thinkers) that rulers have to offer incentives to foster economic activity.[69] He also refutes historical objections to commerce, noting that although God forbade his people to trade to isolate them from idolatrous peoples, "we should no more take this as significant for us than abstinence from pork."

In discussing economic issues, conferees are not only discomfited by the conflict between the traditional feudal class and the new mercantilist economy but also between the ideal and the pragmatic. In "What gives the price to things,"[70] the first speaker begins by saying that the price of things is real or imaginary, depending on whether the thing is "honest, useful, or agreeable."[71] These values, speakers suggest, correspond to the way prices are set. However, they are also forced to confront the arbitrariness with which value is assigned, an arbitrariness that contradicts the rational abstractions some want to apply. Although this first speaker points to a logic behind pricing ("the greater degree of good found in the thing, the more it is esteemed"), he also raises the problematic question of whether, since some pricing is determined by whimsy, there is any possibility of rational ordering. He cites, as a revealing example, "the low hats with a large brim that were much esteemed thirty years ago [but] are today ridiculous and of no value." But, he nonetheless maintains, the true and solid foundation of the prices of things is their goodness. The value of things, he seems to suggest, is rooted in a kind of natural hierarchy, that is to say, we consider command better than obedience and, therefore, venerate things according to their rank. He suggests that a striking distortion of this natural order has appeared because of the practice of buying offices. Despite this anomaly, he believes that the purpose of an object determines its value, so that "the inventions harmful to the public will never be esteemed as much as those who establish those things that are useful and pious." He is intent on emphasizing that the way prices are set should reflect abstract principles. Despite some qualms and some examples that belie his thesis, pricing, he insists, is rational and thus reinforces the civic and the utilitarian.

The second speaker, considerably disgruntled, notes that the ways prices are in fact determined suggest a joke of nature.[72] For example, gold has not always been as highly esteemed as silver, although, he insists, both are equally perfect. He disparages "the stones, pearls, and the other superfluities of men, which only their fantasies have drawn from the scorn in which nature left them, hidden in the caverns of the earth and in the depths of the sea." Another claims forthrightly that imagination sets the price of things in this world; things are good or bad, vile or excellent, according to whether one approves or rejects them. As a case in point, he notes that people value precious stones more than medicinal plants. This kind of arbitrary valuation occurs because "they have gained the credit and opinion of men, which pleases itself to esteem or disdain a thing, according to its diverse appearance or to the variety of the season and the inclination of the country." This arbitrary valuation "proves then that most things of this world have two faces; if they are considered well in one fashion, you will find them good, and regarded them from another bias, they will appear bad. From this comes so many diverse laws and customs."

A speaker points to some more modern economic considerations as important to setting prices. The goodness of the item, he insists, is the true cause that one values something. Another is its availability. Something that is forbidden, rare, or difficult to possess has a higher price, although he concedes that values are determined in part by entirely arbitrary forces. "The judgment of a noble, a wise person, or another person of merit" will affect the price of an item. Our inclination to prize one thing over another can be entirely irrational. This conference seems to indicate a breakdown of rational analysis and a recognition that arbitrary values influence the economy.

A series of special sessions was held over the August vacation in 1638, entitled "Touching on the means of reestablishing commerce"[73] and undertaken at the behest of Richelieu. They include speeches ranging from high-flown panegyrics to commerce to hardheaded proposals for specific economic policies. The initial remarks justify the entire endeavor by promoting commerce as the source of the riches of the state and the chief of all political enterprises. "It gives states what they do not have, gets rid of surpluses, and serves as the wet-nurse to the arts and manufacture." A participant extols commerce as the source of the state's riches and as the chief of all political enterprises. It "furnishes the palaces of princes, provides provisions for soldiers, lawyers with litigants, sentences, and decrees, the tables of all with food-stuffs and spices, physicians with most of their pharmacopoeia, books to the learned, and even incense to God."[74] Commerce not only provides "goods" for the individual, it also enhances those of the culture. Conferees express concern that France is falling behind other countries because it does not cultivate trade sufficiently. The value of commerce, a speaker insists, is demonstrated by destitute towns without trade as compared to those enriched by it, like those of Italy and England. The Netherlands provide the most striking example: their success can be attributed entirely to trade, since "their air, sea, and water is all bad and unhealthy."

Participants are unstinting in their advocacy of commerce and the benefits that will accrue through its cultivation, but they are more ambivalent about the agent of commerce, the merchant. They return repeatedly to the issue of his problematic social position. One speaker points out that, despite a reputation for dishonesty, to succeed a merchant must be a person of good faith selling a known commodity at a fixed price. Another deals head-on with the question of the honesty of merchants: "I would say only that those who scorn the merchant as they would something vile and abject, are more worthy of pity for their gross error. . . . Do they think the great Romans less praiseworthy for the trade they brought to so many states?" A speaker distinguishes between two kinds of merchants, those who are content with a reasonable profit over the long term as opposed to those who are willing to gouge their customers for a onetime, quick profit. Another praises the merchant by pointing out the distinction between the nobleman who has lost his status through trade and one who retains his high social status; "the assiduous merchant will build his house, the gentleman will destroy it." The good legislator, he insists, must authorize what is most useful to the state. Thus the merchant must be favored with marks of esteem that will attract the young to commerce. Merchants, he laments, have more incentives to direct their sons into careers that are socially prestigious but less useful to the state.

Participants also propose specific measures that must be taken to further commerce. Because commerce requires good faith, fraud and the falsification of goods must be prohibited, and money, especially its weight and value, has to be firmly established "so that each knows what he has." Roads must be safe. To deal immediately with the threats posed to the security of local trade, one speaker suggests that each neighborhood should have an exact record of who lives in each house, each street should have bright lights, and guards should be provided for those who must transact business at night. Measures must be taken to counteract the dearth of insurance companies, the lack of vehicles for travel, and the threat of brigands and pirates. States must negotiate advantageous tariff agreements, such as those currently being pursued with the king of Poland. Participants suggest that, as a first step toward resolving many of the economic problems under discussion, a census should be taken to ascertain their extent so that they might be addressed more effectively. These calls for census also suggest a quantitative, mathematical approach or "scientific" approach to economic problems.

Commercial ventures, they suggest, should be reorganized into companies because "they can do more than an individual, they spread the risk around, they can draw on the experience of many and the strengths of different temperaments." A conferee points out that other venerable professions like the clergy and physicians have benefited from a corporate structure. The kingdoms neighboring France provide good examples of the effective operations of companies, although these companies must not be allowed to degenerate into monopolies or to put an excessive price on merchandise.

Another speaker argues that psychological obstacles to trade must be overcome. One must offer incentives to encourage travel and alleviate ignorance of other countries, their languages, and their business practices. Merchants, no less than doctors and lawyers, must learn Latin and foreign languages. The young must be taught to value peace as much as the nobility has traditionally valued war. Despite their readiness to list reforms, these participants are confident that the French are poised to make great advances. Even now, they note, the French export more inventions than they import. Furthermore, France has a great deal to trade and the wherewithal to develop industry.

These conferences then indicate a great willingness on the part of participants to deal with the various aspects of commercial development, ranging from local security (which will allow localities to flourish) to revamping business organizations in order to diffuse risk and enhance profits. Participants recognize that the attitudes of French citizens about their role in the world must change, to allow them to develop concrete economic opportunities beyond local and national boundaries. Although they are divided over political issues, some deploring the shift in cultural values, they present much more of a consensus of opinion in discussing the economy.

The economic ideas expressed by Renaudot's conferees found their way into the works of English economic reformers of the 1640s. Samuel

Hartlib, for example, was eager to learn of the Bureau d'Adresse.[75] It is also significant that the state promoted public discussion of the economy in the sense that Jürgen Habermas uses to describe the public sphere.[76] Habermas argues that in the eighteenth century the development of the public sphere allowed individuals to critically assess the state. The growth of the Habermasian public sphere in the later eighteenth century resulted, in part, from the creation of a politicized public seeking new arenas in which to continue public discussions of state activities—a habit learned, ironically, with the state's encouragement. Because Richelieu asked conferees to address the issues of concern to the state, the conferences offer a compelling example of the crown's both organizing economic policies and seeking the advice of a Parisian group that might well be able to help cultivate the economy in the interest of the state. These conferences suggest that, in encouraging the group at the Bureau to critically assess the economy, the state, in Habermasian terms, fostered the development of the public sphere.

POLITICS IN THE DOMESTIC SPHERE

Political issues are integrally connected to social concerns and provide pervasive analogies for discussing them, but they are also extended into discussions of individual and personal relationships. Such discussions acknowledge in a disconcertingly forthright way that household relations are hierarchical and rooted in power relations, and as a result, the same political considerations should be brought to bear in discussing relationships between members of the household. A conference that raises the distinctly Machiavellian question of whether cruelty is an effective way to treat dependents and another that treats the concomitant question, derived from the popular saying "one has as many enemies as one has valets," demonstrate the thorough penetration of political issues into household dynamics.[77]

In the conference "Of the household,"[78] the first speaker notes that the household is the first and most ancient community. Perhaps because of its ancient history, participants find it appropriate, in a way uncommon in the conferences, to point to ancient citations about the household. The poet Hesiod said a household required no more than a house, a woman, and a cow, and according to Aristotle, those who were under the same roof constituted a household. Since a town is nothing more than an assembly of several households, whose members live in the same vicinity under the same laws for mutual assistance and defense from attackers, there is no great difference between a household and a state. Therefore each is master in his household as the king is sovereign in the state he governs. As far as this speaker is concerned, the same analogic relationships connect the household from "house, woman, cow" (all presumably property of the male) to the monarch. The second speaker suggests a more idyllic view, arguing, essentially, "happy family, happy state." Those who can govern their families are successful outside the household, although some, like Caesar Augustus, are successful outside the family and failures within. A speaker cites the inherent sociability of human beings, with the rare exception of misanthropes, like Timon of Athens, whom the Greek poets accurately berated as scoundrels. Those who are outside the community are seditious and lovers of trouble. Sociability is fundamental to the organization of human society and initially manifest in the household, for the sociable man "is pleased to live in company, which makes him first seek that of the woman, the most agreeable of all, from which the children come to be born, and the man acquires with the quality of husband that of father." Once the family is established, the other social relations follow; "they have need of servants and slaves for the convenience of life, as well as lodging and goods." Sociability also underlies and determines the nature of political structure; if there is justice there is no need for violence, and if amity no need for justice.

The final speaker takes a more pragmatic approach and considers what will be necessary for the well-being of the household. There should be commodious lodging, "the situation agreeable and the structure well regulated, food to eat and clothes to wear." He suggests that one should go beyond subsistence, but not as far as luxury. He adds an important caveat: "he should not consider this acquisition of goods as the end at which he should stop, thus do the merchants and other people who do not have any design other than to enrich themselves." Such activities are not valuable in themselves but serve man's end, viz to domesticate everything that serves his needs "from the fruits of the earth, the pastures, and from hunting, as the birds, fish, and savage beasts." It is interesting that the imperative to domesticate in these documents is not a scientific imperative but rather an economic one. Although this right to domestication does not extend beyond the animal kingdom to the subjugation of other human beings, nonetheless, "when civilized people war against Barbarians and savages who are born to obey and to serve, they are happier to be under reasonable treatment." Thus it is legitimate for a large-scale economy to acquire slaves, "just as one acquires goods for the comfort of his family in which servants or slaves, numbering among the possessions, are entirely submitted to the will of the chief of the house." Just as the father has control over his children, "to whom he is high priest or monarch," so too he has an absolute and despotic right over the slaves and "can dispose of them according to this will." The speaker does significantly distinguish a man's control over his wife from the absolute control he has over his children: "that which he has over his wife is only political or civil and comparable to the authority that a magistrate has over his citizen."

The conference "What is to be preferred, severity or gentleness toward one's own"[79] is interesting because participants construe it as a question about how one treats people in the state and the household, and thus it ultimately raises questions about legitimate political behavior. A speaker explains household relations through a variety of rather disconcerting political analogies. He begins with a dire warning that one must converse with valets as if one were a military captain and the valets were enemy soldiers. The first principle, one that seems quite Machiavellian, is that "just as kindness and familiarity engender scorn, so severity and gravity produce respect." When valets are equal to their masters, great disorder is produced. The pagans, he notes, were never more ridiculous than during the feast of Saturnalia, when valets became masters.[80] He then provides a catalog of misrule produced by insufficient severity. Claiming that majesty demands honor and service that kindness cannot elicit, he cites supporting historical examples: Germanicus was obeyed, whereas Nerva "weakened and enervated the Roman Republic"; and "no monarchy is so firmly established as that of the Ottomans, who owe all their grandeur to severity and rigor."

It is revealing that this speaker makes household relations analogous to the successful reigns of brutal emperors. Severity is desirable because household relations are a state of war, "because the misery, real or imagined, of inferiors, joined to their natural desire for liberty, carries them easily to felony, if fear and rigor do not tie their hands." Thus one must assume that valets are always poised for revolt and "can be kept in check only by fear of death." Such a law, he protests, "is not meant to endorse homicide, but rather to retain in these people a sense of their duty by apprehension of death." Reason, he notes, once obliged the Senate to put to death six hundred innocent slaves to serve as an example to others. Thus the discussions of the governance of the household lead participants directly into a discussion of the treatment of slaves in the Roman Republic. These arguments sanctioning despotic control and military tactics are deemed appropriate models for treating household dependents!

It is jarring that, in discussing politics or policies of the state, speakers insist that the practices of rulers be moderated by concern with the public good, but they allow unbridled license to the head of the household. Such remarks do not pass unchallenged. One participant contends that any security produced by severity has effects too violent to be durable. He does not question the legitimacy of despotic control over the household, only its efficacy. Rigor produces hatred, and it is better to be loved than hated. He continues, "we owe more to those who lack due to their birth and their fortune." Another also expresses understanding of the position of the servants: "The lowness and baseness of their fortune gives them enough cause for discontent without making them more miserable than they are." He is also concerned that the "laws which most authorize the severity of masters toward the slaves have little to guarantee against the final blows of their despair." He invokes the cries of Romans assassinated by their slaves, driven by despair and undeterred by severe punishment. To those who claim that kindness only produces familiarity, he responds, "it is in my opinion a great weakness, as if the empire and the majesty can not preserve one most agreeably in clemency." Severity is as inappropriate in government as it is in the household; it "is as ridiculous as it is odious."

The final speaker sits on the fence about which policy to pursue. Although kindness is more pleasant, he insists that leniency creates problems in the household; "the indulgence of good husbands toward their wives is the most apparent cause of the luxury, not to say worse, which reigns among this sex." Although he is concerned about excessive leniency, he sees the republic rather than monarchy or empire as the appropriate political analogy for the household. Acutely aware of the difficulties involved in determining when, how, or whether it is necessary to use kindness or severity, he develops a long medical analogy to gauge the appropriate response to specific situations. Just as certain temperaments respond well to one kind of treatment while others do not, so too certain individuals benefit by severe treatment and others by gentleness; extreme remedies should be reserved for extreme maladies. What is surprising about this conference is that political analogies are pervasive, particularly comparisons between Roman politics and the French household.

Another conference explores the validity of the contemporary maxim "One has as many enemies as valets."[81] A speaker argues that, although men are all similar at birth, fortune differentiates between them, making some inferior and others superior. An individual who acts as an equal to his valet only exacerbates the tension initially produced by fortune. The relationship between a valet and his master is rooted in the master's desire to make the valet do his will, which deprives the valet of what makes him a man, that is to say, the liberty to do what seems to him to be good. This speaker postulates, as do many other conferees, a desire for liberty as innate to man. However, he understands that fortune, which determines man's place in the hierarchy, frequently frustrates man's natural desire. Another speaker distinguishes the degree of control one can have over the three sorts of people one has the right to command—slaves, servants, and mercenaries. The first belong entirely to their masters, who can absolutely dispose of their bodies and goods; the second are not owned and owe nothing except obedience and fidelity in service; the third are obliged only to contribute their industry and their work, that is, to do the tasks for which they are employed. Although these relationships are based on power and the exercise of rights over certain individuals, nonetheless, one owes respect and *friendship* to those on whom one depends. The next speaker follows through on this conciliatory approach, noting that there is nothing so sweet as to command and nothing so contrary to man as to obey, especially to obey one who does not warrant respect. Inhumane treatment obliges servants to rebel against the tyranny of their masters, "which has passed to such excess that, not content to exercise over them all the cruelties imaginable, [it extends] even unto exposing them to ferocious beasts and poisoning them for light faults." (Many conferees express concern, in discussing very different topics, that although it is part of human nature to desire to command, command frequently degenerates into tyranny, and tyranny legitimately elicits revolt.)

A speaker, who argues for harshness based on the traditional authority of father over children, does not share this sympathy for the plight of servants. He claims that it is expedient to be rigorous toward servants; restraining them through fear is the only way to "contain these servile souls in their duty." If they escape those tasks, they may well turn the weapons they use against their masters against the state. Thus the loss of control over subservient people in the household can extend to lack of control in the state. He insists that masters have the same authority over servants that fathers have over children, whereby "they have the right to sell them up to three times and even to kill them without any justification." He bemoans the demise of obedience. Although fathers did not love their children any less in former times, there was more obedience than one sees now. Servants are so much less respectful toward their masters because masters do not have the right to chastise them as before and are thus constrained to suffer their insolence. As an added point (which seems quite self-serving and disingenuous), the speaker points to the more advantageous state of servants: "their condition, if they knew how to esteem it . . . would sometimes be more happy than that of their masters, being exempt from the anxieties that are inseparable from the conduct of a family." (Clearly no servant spoke at these conferences.) Another speaker blames the conduct of masters for servants who are enemies: "Servants become our enemies to the degree that they are treated, not as a father treats a child, but as a tyrant treats his subjects. We have as many enemies as servants, as we make enemies through our bad conduct."

These discussions of household relations definitely construe them in political terms but apply different political models to them. Some participants make the traditional argument about household relations the foundation for patriarchy, best exemplified by God's relationship to man and the king's relationship to his subjects. Some suggest that, if this relationship applies to the kingdom, it applies even more directly to the household itself. Others, while also considering the household in political terms, criticize the unwarranted exercise of political power in that context. This conference—like all those on household affairs, whether more or less authoritarian or more or less sympathetic to the plight of underlings—is conducted from the perspective of masters, providing further evidence of the relatively elite status of participants. (All discussions of behavior refer to *our* conduct and the conduct of *our* servants.)

📖

Because of optimism about their age, participants approach political issues with enviable confidence. They are explicitly activist, rejecting any calls to withdraw from the public forum. They assert that they are moderns and that the French are the most civilized of human beings, particularly as reflected in urban life. Their confidence derives largely from their understanding of the operations of nature—because they believe that nature's operations are always the same, there is little support for the idea that human nature or human society is in decline. Just as nature is governed by universal causes (which they consider themselves to be well positioned to understand), so too the forces of economic and political life will be revealed because of their efforts.[82]

Conferences like these assert the importance of economic and political discussion to the future of France. They are valuable because they were open, public, and critical, and (perhaps participants would have contended) "scientific." Because of their form, they illuminate areas of both topical concern and contestation. Because they avoid religious discussions, they suggest a secular ethos for the state, a concern well reflected in their reexamination of Renaissance ethical topics. Even though they are supposedly constrained from discussing political issues, conferees are clearly willing to discuss the nature of the state.

Several significant parameters shape the discussion of political issues. Participants are concerned to safeguard political liberty.[83] The notion of what this entails is limited and is perhaps more accurately described as protection against repression, as suggested by the discussion of censorship and the acknowledgment that certain conditions justify political revolt.[84] Participants are interested in moving beyond abstractions to deal realistically with human behavior and motivation. They are inclined to see the political philosophy of the ancients as impracticable idealism in part because they believe that human beings respond most effectively to negative reinforcement. Most importantly, because they are not, as a group, courtiers or directly subject to patronage,[85] participants are able to advance conflicting, critical, and independent views in this public setting, views that are then disseminated through print. Some suggest that France has become too luxury-loving, but most resist the inclination to write off the human race as too predisposed to evil, or contemporary society as irremediably corrupt.

While some participants defend a traditional, unchanging vision of the state, they are sharply challenged by others who assume that political change is equivalent to natural change and so can be known and studied scientifically. As a result, the state can use economic policy to foster its interests. Some historians of science—in their attempts to connect the scientific revolution to the development of the social sciences—assume that the advent of the mechanical sciences was an essential prerequisite that provided the means to rationalize the political. For example, Carolyn Merchant notes that mechanism coincided with the centralization of government power and contends that mechanism represents rational management in the natural sphere, which is then applied to society and economics.[86] As Descartes wrote to Mersenne in 1630, "God sets up mathematical laws in nature as a king sets up laws in his kingdom."[87] This connection between mechanism and absolutism is generally considered to characterize the scientific revolution—just as nature was subject to rational analysis, so too the state could be rationally assessed. Under the rationalizing tendencies emerging in the governments of strong nation-states such as France and England, nature came to be viewed as a resource to be subjected to control with human beings as her earthly managers.[88]

The conferences support a counter-analysis, however. The discussion of politics by Renaudot's group suggests that the state could be subject to rational analysis and control without adherence to mechanism. Conferees analyze the state and, at least in some speeches, suggest that a mathematical understanding of the state is ineffectual. For example, a speaker on the question of "Why there are more lawsuits in France now than in earlier times"[89] uses the question to address broader theoretical issues of justice and equity. He criticizes the notion that justice in public affairs is based on geometric proportion as "having no connection of the quantities between them." But a distribution of justice by geometric proportion fosters "a dangerous reflux in the body of the state" and as a result creates "the indignation of the nobles against the people, and the envy of people against the nobles." In contrast to these mathematical models, France has a harmonic relationship "by which the sovereign magistrate, using the law and equity, tempers the too great constraint of the first and the too great liberty of the other."

When they discuss the state, conferees are inevitably aware of the political ramifications that any state policy will have on their interests. They are inclined to see the state or the king as serving the interests of the people and to suggest changes that conform to these principles. They are much more conservative when discussing the household as opposed to the state and much less willing to sanction change in the household, which would almost inevitably erode authority over their dependents. Discussion of political topics both provokes dissension and elicits calls for reform. By turning to science or nature as a foundation for politics, participants can discuss politics unfettered by religious considerations, and (perhaps even more significant for their relationship to subsequent political discussion) they are able to weigh critically historical precedent.

Participants also shared and built upon the economic ideas of mercantilists.[90] Like other mercantilist writers, they offered economic advice that advocated the development of the economic potential of the nation and tried to assess the economy rationally. As a result, like other mercantilists, they too anticipate many of the positions of the laissez-faire economists of the eighteenth century, especially since they saw the economy as natural and the pursuit of economic goals as natural to human beings.[91]

Like later and more prominent seventeenth-century writers, conferees linked the notion of private interest to the pursuit of economic interest. The moral justification of commercial interest can readily be connected to subsequent developments in both economics and moral theory. The French conception of interest took into account the desire for recognition by others. For example, Jansenist moralists recognized this desire as part of the inherent human inclination to mask vices as virtues. Human beings, they noted, both seek the interests of others to gain a favorable reputation and pursue their own interests for social benefit. One of the most notable, Pierre Nicole, pointed out that greed had produced great benefits, perhaps more than charity had.[92] In general, the moral and political themes raised in the conferences resonate in later works, including the *Encyclopédie*.

ENCYCLOPEDIC THEMES

The *Encyclopédie*, edited by Denis Diderot and Jean d'Alembert, began in 1746 as a modest publishing venture, a plan to capitalize on the commercial success of Ephraim Chambers two-volume *Cyclopedia*. When it was completed in 1772, the *Encyclopédie* was a massive publication of thirty-eight volumes, and it stood as a monument of a new intellectual movement, the French Enlightenment. Like Renaudot's conferences it was a collective enterprise, written by approximately one hundred and fifty contributors. It too endeavored to present knowledge to a broad public. The contributions of encylopedists, as those who contributed were called, were more focused than Renaudot's proceedings. The editors had a more overtly polemical perspective than did Renaudot, and thus the encyclopedists' writings were more explicitly directed against the ancien régime. Their criticisms were shaped by the concentration of political power in the hands of the monarchy and the privileged and its abuses during the intervening time between the conferences and the publication of the *Encyclopédie*. Nonetheless, when the encyclopedists addressed political and economic issues, their arguments returned to positions taken by Renaudot's conferees. Because, I contend, conferees share more with the encyclopedists of the eighteenth century than with the writers of French classical culture of the later seventeenth century, it is worthwhile to explore briefly some of the affinities.

Like members of Renaudot's group, the encyclopedists were concerned about the impact of shifts in population. Montesquieu worried about depopulation, contending that the world is much less populated than in ancient times, whereas Damilaville asserted, in his article "Population," that the population of the world remains static.[93] *Encyclopédie* articles expressed dismay over the great inequities of wealth. As d'Alembert remarked in his article on "Fortune," "the means of enriching oneself can be morally criminal although permitted by law," as is the case in some countries that "nourish the scandalous luxury of a small number of citizens." This proclivity, he insists, is "against natural law and against humanity."[94] On the question of luxury, articles in the *Encyclopédie* reflect the same division of opinion that characterizes the conferences. In "Homme," Diderot argues in favor of reducing the number of men employed in luxury trades, and in "Population" Damilaville blames the pursuit of luxury for the decline of agriculture, with disastrous effects on the countryside. In the article "Luxe," Saint-Lambert tries to present a balanced view, insisting that luxury depends on the particular condition of the state and that it must be considered in terms of whether it works for or against the community. He cautions, as do many conferees, that the pursuit of luxury will exacerbate the problems of the poor.[95]

Like those who met at the Bureau, encyclopedists were concerned with solving the problems of poverty. Diderot, in his article "Hôpital," argues that "it should be much more important to work to prevent misery than to multiply the number of shelters for the miserable." Turgot expresses a concern that foundations established for the poor have in fact transformed industrious citizens into "mendicant vagabonds."[96] After stating in his article "Mendicant" that in a well-governed country there should be no poor except for those men who are born in poverty or fall into that state by accident, Jaucourt vigorously attacks the sturdy beggar. He would reserve hospitals for the sick and for those who were prevented by old age from working. As a physician and a humanitarian, he is horrified by the inadequacy of the provisions made for the sick, especially in light of the money he considers wasted on the undeserving poor.

Although conferees are ambivalent in their assessment of the changes taking place in French society, away from France's rural, feudal tradition, they are staunchly outspoken in their support for economic changes. Without exception, they look to the development of trade. Not all economic thinkers in the eighteenth century agreed; physiocrats wanted to foster agriculture as the source of economic development; but laissez-faire economists supported trade. This division is reflected in the *Encyclopédie* where the articles of laissez-faire economists take positions similar to those of Renaudot's group. Veron de Forbonnais, a staunch critic of the physiocrats, insists in his article "Commerce" that industry, too, is essential for prosperity, and in his article "Concurrence" he strongly advocates freedom of trade and economic competition. The philosophes engaged in a campaign to raise the level of the merchant, beginning with the sharp contrast Voltaire drew between the productive merchant and the unproductive courtier. Diderot in his article "Commissionnaire" and d'Alembert in his article "Fortune" connect economic development and political equality.[97] As we have seen, there are rudimentary formulations of all of these views in the conferences.

Encyclopedists and conferees share political ideas as well. For example, Jaucourt's article on "Sedition" claims that under some conditions it may be justified. He points to some of the same causes of sedition as conference participants do and suggests that to avoid sedition monarchs must follow injunctions spelled out by conferees.[98] Like some of them, he acknowledges that the cause of sedition is frequently the misdirected policies of a tyrannical government. Saint-Lambert, in his article on the legislator, insists, as do conferees, that whatever the form of government, it must be "based on the same principles," which are "the security of the state and the happiness of citizens." The lawgiver, by establishing "a rapport of goodwill" between himself and the people, must create public spirit so that the citizens will put the good of the community before their private interest. On the position of the nobility, the *Encyclopédie*, like the conferences, is ambiguous. A number of articles express hostility toward courtiers, an attitude that also characterizes the conferences. Diderot makes disparaging remarks about them in his articles "Cour," "Courtisan," and "Insinuant," and d'Holbach criticizes the court in some of his articles on peoples of other civilizations. Marmontel's article "Les Grands" praises the role of Richelieu in the destruction of the political pretensions of the feudal aristocracy.[99] Jaucourt, himself a member of a distinguished noble family, stresses the responsibilities of privilege, while Diderot's article on "Privilege" is a sweeping attack.[100] My claim here is not that the encyclopedists were directly indebted to Renaudot's conferences but rather that the conferences, more than one hundred years earlier, had raised many of the same issues and discussed them from the same "enlightened" perspective.

Although Renaudot's conferees share attitudes with eighteenth-century thinkers, they are somewhat out of step with other seventeenth-century political theorists. For example, they do not endorse a special morality for princes or *raison d'état* despite their general interest in fostering political culture. Instead, they suggest and practice the right of participants to analyze the government critically. Although participants uphold unchallenged the rights of individuals in households, they call into question those of the monarchs and suggest modifications and emphasize the monarch's responsibilities. This sense of both the nature of government and the role in it for men of talent dedicated to the community not only justified Richelieu's ministerial role but also empowered Renaudot. But an endorsement of political analysis by a group like Renaudot's does not presuppose that this analysis will remain privileged or secret. Because of this failure to align themselves with *raison d'état* and to restrict political analysis to councils of state, the conferences are out of step with most of the political writing produced under Louis XIII.

What do the conferences add to political writing of the early modern period? When historians look to this period in France, their discussion has most frequently been cast from the perspective of either the French Revolution or the development of seventeenth-century absolutism, the two political regimes that have decisively shaped our understanding of French political theory. Just as attempts to explain the revolution, in particular the totalitarian democracy of the Jacobins, have distorted understanding of the Enlightenment and its political theory, so too early seventeenth-century political theory is assumed to share the concerns of those who wrote under the much greater stringency of later absolutist culture. Political discussion by Renaudot's conferees raises questions about our understanding of seventeenth-century political analysis. Most striking, participants did not endorse absolutism. Although they do generally support monarchy, they endorse a republic as the ideal. Many speakers forthrightly extoll the republic as the form of government that allows the most accurate representation of the will of the people. They do not, as is generally assumed about seventeenth-century political discussions, abjure politics[101] or try to create clearly apolitical institutions to fill the void created by the impossibility of genuine discussion under an absolute monarchy. Political discussion in the conferences does not occur against a backdrop of hostility to political engagement as is characteristic of the reign of Louis XIV. Participants can be idealistic about what their discussion might accomplish without setting themselves in conscious opposition to the crown. Because their ideas are consistent with a republic or a benign monarch, they do not feel a need to set up the alternative institution of a republic of letters. Instead they consider it their obligation to critically assess the political order. They are critics, not opponents, of the status quo. Living under a centralizing but not yet absolute monarchy, participants espouse some of the same attitudes as the philosophes writing under a weakened monarchy. In other words, it was the relative weakness of the monarchy at the time of Louis XIII or Louis XV, as opposed to the greater strength under Louis XIV, that allowed the possibility of more concerted political opposition. Participants had the advantage over the philosophes—because they had not experienced full-blown absolutism—of being able still to invoke the image of a republic.

In some significant ways, participants in Renaudot's conferences might have been able to envision reform. As Daniel Gordon demonstrates, the philosophes could conceive of it largely because they could see the monarchy as separate from corporate privilege.[102] Because of their use of science as a perspective for social analysis, conferees could also assess the monarchy from a critical distance. Perhaps because they were neither historians nor legal scholars or perhaps because they did not present a systematic political philosophy, they were not at all concerned with corporate bodies. They wondered, based on what they understood of heredity, whether the position of the nobility was justified. Their concerns with science and nature allowed them to discount historical precedent and the corporate order and thus to critically assess the status quo and to envision reform.

Political discussion in the conferences reveals other points of affinity with Enlightenment political thought. For example, the conferences contribute to discussions of sociability as a foundation for political reform. Much of the later seventeenth-century political writing on sociability had to overcome the antisocial premises of Hobbes's *Leviathan*. (Conferees do not have Hobbes to respond to since Hobbes did not publish his political philosophy until *De Cive* in 1647.) Largely because of their emphasis on nature and on Aristotle's biological writings, they emphasize the inherent sociability of man. Their remarks generally begin with the notion that one of the fundamental distinctions between man and animals is that man is a social creature. According to Gordon, absolutist political theorists deemed sociability an impediment to be overcome or governed by law, whereas eighteenth-century philosophes identified sociability as a positive psychological motive.[103] But because they did not respond to Hobbes and because they were interested in a fundamentally physiological understanding of human beings, conferees could, like the later philosophes, make sociability apparent rather than latent. Science also gave participants a position from which to call hierarchy into question. When participants invoked hierarchy, their model was nature rather than history and tradition, which appeared more nearly to absolutize existing hierarchies. Appeals to science allowed some of them to overturn the traditional hierarchy, leaving open the possibility of further critiques of social hierarchy. It is important to emphasize the significance of the relationship between science and politics articulated by conferees because it is so strikingly at odds with the more conventional position. That approach, typified by Descartes, insisted (no doubt expediently) that science had no implications for politics. All these examples demonstrate that the period before the advent of Louis XIV allowed some of the same kinds of unfettered discussion as the mid–eighteenth century.

Despite the opportunities the conferences afforded for political discussion, the tenor of the political remarks made by conferees was frequently fundamentally conservative. Although they may have used new arguments and drawn evidence from nature and science to assess issues of perennial concern, they did not explicitly wield them as tools to destroy or dismantle the status quo. They analyzed and critiqued the old but were in no way radical reformers. This lack of an overt reformist agenda clearly distinguishes them from Enlightenment philosophes. However, they did legitimate evidentiary, scientific, and rhetorical tools of the Enlightenment. To the extent that they rationalized discussion of these issues and criticized the status quo insofar as it did not conform to reason, conferees also initiated Enlightenment methods, although without deploying them as effectively. Gordon distinguishes between the absolutists who emphasized the will of the sovereign and the philosophes who emphasized truth, which would come to light through discussion.[104] This fundamental premise—that public discussion will bring truth to light—shaped all discussion at the Bureau. Positions that will become central in the Enlightenment are just intimated in the conferences.

CHAPTER NINE

"The Extravagance of Women"

Science, Sex, and Gender

I

N A CONFERENCE ENTITLED "OF THE EXTRAVAGANCE OF WOMEN,"[1] PARTICI-
pants express a startling array of opinions about the nature of woman.
What is at issue is not whether women are capricious but how they
come to be so and to what degree this quality determines their behavior.
One speaker suggests that women's souls are ill-housed in their bodies.
Women are so tormented by such irregular motions that physicians are
unable to assign a true cause to these motions, and because their "spirits
are more agile and movable, they must have a less degree of wisdom."
A second speaker compares the capriciousness of women to Capricorn
the goat; women resemble goats by virtue of the similar conformation
of their brains, which, like those of goats, are full of sharp and biting
vapors. Just as goats hate olive trees, the symbols of peace, so too
women disrupt the peace. The third speaker begs to differ. Women, he
claims, more closely resemble mules because they are fearful, obstinate,
travel in company, and delight in finery (bells and muzzles in one case,
earrings and masks in the other). They are also both tractable most of
the time but occasionally unpredictable, delivering kicks or commit-

ting outrageous folly. The fourth speaker rises to defend mules as healthy, strong, and patient when hungry. (He does not extend his defense to women.) The final speaker asserts that God gave men wives to torment them.

Any compilation of seventeenth-century remarks about the nature, character, and abilities of women would be likely to feature notions of this sort. They fall well within the bounds of commonplaces in the *querelle des femmes,* the long-standing debate about women waged in literary texts since the fourteenth century.[2] The first half of the seventeenth century, an especially vigorously contested period in writings on women, produced an outpouring of both antifeminist writings and a concerted feminist response. The conferences contribute to this debate. The nature of the conferences themselves and the interests of their sponsor might lead the reader to expect that these conferences would embody an avant-garde or reformist perspective, even on such vexing questions as the nature of women. However, the range of remarks cited above demonstrates that it would be difficult to derive a progressive consensus from these disparate views. Insofar as they draw conclusions about women and their appropriate roles, the conferences are consistently less progressive than they are in other areas of discussion. However, they provide an interesting perspective from which to explore seventeenth-century attitudes toward women. In the context of this book, they allow one to revisit many of the themes previously discussed: science, nature, social values, and politics in particular. They represent so many divergent views that these conferences offer a much broader perspective than is available in most other texts. And as with other topics treated in this book, science offers participants a special focus for their discussions.

What is most striking in their treatment of the nature of women and their social roles is that science clearly offers conferees a much narrower perspective on these issues. When they treat other topics, participants draw on a range of theories, a great variety of perspectives, and an almost limitless fund of evidence. When they turn their attention to discussing women, Aristotle's biology reigns supreme; it clearly is *the* science that can be most effectively invoked. Those who would challenge it do not have other scientific perspectives to bring to bear, other than appeals to some kind of empirical evidence or experience. Because Aristotle's biology offered to participants a much narrower basis for scientific assessment than they had at their disposal for other topics, these conferences show a much great uniformity and consensus, and the social prescriptions deduced from science are also much more rigid. Although there are voices of opposition (as we shall see), participants are fundamentally limited in what science offers them for social analysis on these questions. Their discussion of women then affords a kind of reverse example of the effective use that participants made of multiple scientific views to assess other kinds of topics. Without a challenge to Aristotle's biology, even those who wished to were less able to develop progressive views sustained by science.

THE "WOMAN QUESTION"

The "woman question" is a topic of continual interest and debate in Western culture, and these conferences shed light on questions concerning the relationship between science and gender raised by recent scholarship: What role did women play in science, and how did they come to be excluded from it?[3] How was science used to define gender roles? Do gender issues taint our own "objective science," and if so, how would a feminist science be different?[4] In our own day as in other periods of contested opinion, science is frequently brought to bear on issues of gender. The right brain/left brain dichotomy is still invoked to describe the different abilities of men and women. Carol Gilligan's work objects to the traditional view that women are less capable of abstract thought by pointing out that men provide the template against which women are judged.[5]

It is perhaps surprising that contemporary discussions of gender roles, especially of the capacity of women for science, frequently return to the seventeenth century as a source of modern views. Evelyn Fox Keller sees in seventeenth-century science a battle between masculine and feminine, head versus heart, domination over versus merging with the object of study—a battle won by the masculine view that has defined the character of Western science ever since. Susan Bordo, using a primarily psychoanalytic study of Descartes's *Meditations,* argues that reason is masculinized over the course of the seventeenth-century as a flight from the feminine. Carolyn Merchant raises the question, Was the scientific revolution the imposition of a masculine science on a female nature? and answers it decisively in the affirmative.[6] Some scholars concentrate on the early modern period to further develop their argument that the scientific revolution brought about a crucial transition from an earlier female science to a masculine, technical, mechanical science. Others, following Michel Foucault, cite an epistemic break in the late eighteenth century that curtailed the opportunities for women to participate in science and used science to rigidly separate gender roles. For Londa Schiebinger, while the modern period excludes women from the scientific mainstream, the early modern period was more likely to include them.[7] These are but a few cursory citations that corroborate the importance of seventeenth-century science to gender in contemporary discussions.

When the *querelle des femmes* erupted in the seventeenth century, it drew on long-standing misogyny derived from many complementary strands in the Western tradition. Among the most significant sources are ancient Greek texts, particularly Aristotle and Plato. Religious texts from both Christian and Jewish traditions provide important background to early modern discussions of women, particularly the potent fusion of religious and classical strains of Western misogyny in the scholastic synthesis of Thomas Aquinas.

The Renaissance with its new urban, commercial revival suggested the possibility of new political and social roles. Changing social, economic, and political realities cast into flux previously held "eternal truths" about social and political organizations—immutable hierarchies, "natural" political forms, and God-given political systems. Due to these changing social realities and to the reinvigorated discussion of the nature and role of women in humanist writings, the "woman question" became quite prominent in intellectual discussions throughout the Renaissance. The rediscovery of ancient texts and the revival of new learning opened up new kinds of education that were not restricted to the clergy and even extended to some elite women.[8] Classical texts cast into high relief the "woman question," because they could be mobilized on both sides of the issue. For example, the neoplatonic revival produced a mixed legacy. Plato's *Timaeus* not only posited an original world without women but also specified that the penalty for a life that did not attain virtue through the diligent control of the passions was reincarnation as a woman, an inferior life form.[9] However, neoplatonism also contributed positive elements to the debate. Since neoplatonists appreciated love, including heterosexual love, as the fundamental source of generative power in the universe, a view largely derived from Plato's *Symposium,* women had a potentially central role in this understanding of the universe.[10]

While frequently invoking classical sources, examples, and modes of argumentation to address the "woman question," the Renaissance also added a number of new texts to the debate.[11] Giovanni Boccaccio's *De Mulieribus claris* provides a long list of exceptional classical women, reviving the practice of compiling such lists, perhaps best characterized by Plutarch's *Mulierum virtutes.* Building on Boccaccio's work, Christine de Pizan, the first woman to become involved in this debate, not only lists great women but also addresses the constraints that have kept women from achieving their potential. Agrippa von Nettesheim also argued for the superiority of women. In his *Book of the Courtier,* Baldassare Castiglione not only examined both sides of the argument by staging a debate on the question but also defined a civilizing role for women of the court, who moderate the male culture of the feudal warrior.[12]

The hermetic and alchemical tradition of the Renaissance added another, muddied legacy to both the biological understanding of women and the "woman question." Some historians of science have claimed that this tradition's depiction of nature as female and as the source of all life produced a greater veneration of both nature and women.[13] Paracelsus, a key figure in hermeticism, emphasized the fundamental harmony of nature, so much so that women were incorporated into his understanding of the Godhead, admittedly without any power or place in the Trinity but connected to "mystical female forces in stones and plants."[14] Yet this legacy is mixed. Paracelsus disassociated women from the generation of human beings. He contended that men provided the sole source of life; women were simply the generative soil. For him, one of the greatest secrets of alchemy was the generation of "beings like men or women," which he called "homunculi," without the assistance of the female organism.[15]

Renaissance neoplatonists did not simply rely on Platonic texts; they also made their own contributions to the debate on women. Some of them saw the soul as a female principle that sought a mystical marriage with God. According to Pico della Mirandola, the soul "purifies herself, and dressing in the golden vesture of the many sciences as in a nuptial gown, receives him, not as a guest merely, but as a spouse."[16] This analogy was extended to man's relationship to nature. Thus neoplatonists, like the hermeticists, understood nature as female, and creativity as the result of a union of masculine and feminine principles. Cambridge neoplatonists such as Henry More suggested a union of the female body with the male intellect as the solution to the vexing mind-body problem. The visual art of the period routinely represented both science and nature by female figures. The gendered portrayal of feminine science was especially characteristic of the Renaissance and remained common through the eighteenth century. Although the depictions of nature were invariably female, the scientist was portrayed as male. To carry the neoplatonic analogy into the realm of scientific practice, scientific knowledge would be attained by the masculine intellect in mystical union with female nature. This gendering of nature became even more pronounced with Francis Bacon's emphasis on a "masculine science," intent on wresting her secrets from a reluctant nature. In Bacon's imagery the relationship is one of human domination and control of nature.[17] The humanist rediscovery of hermetic texts combined with the Baconian ideal of "masculine science" makes questions of women and science unusually thorny in the early modern period.[18]

When the Renaissance moved into northern Europe in the sixteenth century, these issues and texts became part of the new tradition. In this new soil, the polemic raged with great heat but little light. The *querelle des femmes* as it was known in France and the *hic mulier et haec vir* controversy of the English Renaissance spilled much vituperative ink over the status of women.[19] Whether they take feminist or antifeminist positions, there is little originality in these texts; they incorporate wholesale the examples and arguments from earlier authors, feature endless lists of virtuous or wicked women or biographies of famous or infamous women to argue the superiority of one sex over the other. These texts are informed either by a fundamental belief in the inferiority of women or by an attempt to mitigate it.[20] As a result, most feminist texts are defensive; many of them begin with the negative remarks of the antifeminists and then use the same examples and the same Bible verses, but to assert a more positive view of women.[21] Although the arguments were not particularly original, some new dimensions were added to the conventional discussion, such as the issue of Salic law raised by the regencies of Catherine de Medici, Marie de Medici, and Anne of Austria.[22] The question of female education became more prominent as the possibility of its realization became more apparent, and questions of social and marital freedom for women were discussed with increasing vehemence.

In early seventeenth-century France, new, important ideas about women circulated, and women also came to occupy important cultural terrain.[23] Their increasing prominence may well explain the fervor of the debate. A new religious ideal for women, the *femme dévote*, prominent in France from 1590 to 1650 reflected the emphasis religious directors of the Catholic reformation like Francis de Sales and Vincent de Paul put on charitable activities for religious women in the public sphere, like teaching, nursing, and poor relief. The *honnête femme*, another contemporary ideal, was less overtly religious, but she embodied, at least in the hands of Jacques Du Bosc and François de Grenaille, chastity and piety. Although he believed in the remediability of human nature, Du Bosc was deeply concerned that luxury and effeminacy might vitiate the good of nature. He idealized the *honnête femme* in her housewifely role as a powerful force against luxury, which otherwise has debilitating effects on men.[24] *Honnêteté*, as its promoters defined it, was a term expressing appreciation for women but in a narrow, gender-prescribed sense, decreeing that "women were to foster elegance in dress, deportment and expression, thus promoting social grace and the smooth running of society."[25]

Although they took place in the period when these idealized depictions of women (as *femmes dévotes* or as *honnêtes femmes*) developed, the conferences did not reflect their concerns. Female piety was not a virtue extolled by conferees, and the aesthetic issues and values associated with the *honnête femme* were more characteristic of French classicism whose values are not really enshrined in the conferences. Although many participants express a desire to exclude women from political life, they do not hail the domestic life as a source of female virtue. Indeed, it is quite striking, given contemporary discussions of women, that no conference participants extol women for either piety or domestic virtues. When conferees address topics that relate to women, they bring the weight of Western thinking about women to bear, but they do not directly reflect these more recent French strands of that tradition.

There have been many recent studies about seventeenth-century gatherings in which women either participated or were discussed.[26] Many of these studies draw conclusions about these groups and their discussion of women from the writings of individual participants or from often sketchy biographical information; they thus extrapolate the interests of the group from the writings or biography of the most illustrious members. In many cases, I suspect, such extrapolations dress these groups in more modern garb than they wore. The conferences, on the other hand, offer an almost unique opportunity to explore what such a group actually said when they treated questions about women.

The "woman question," with all the attendant issues it implied, was not a subject of peripheral interest to Renaudot's group. The conventional issues and approaches evident in the *querelle des femmes* were indeed well represented in the conferences. Gender issues were among those most hotly contested; as one speaker noted, no one could remain indifferent to discussions of the merits of either sex.[27] The nature of women, their roles in society, the relationship between men and women, and related topics were the specified subjects for at least 45 of the 460 topics, and suppositions about gender roles frequently found their way into the discussions of scientific topics. This integral connection between science and gender characterized their discussions both because physicians were probable participants and because scientific thought was so influential to the cultural heritage within which women were defined and understood.

THE BIOLOGICAL BASIS FOR UNDERSTANDING WOMEN

In examining how conferees discuss women—their sexuality, their role in generation, their social roles—we shall see that Aristotelian biology had considerable power to shape the understanding of women's nature. Although Aristotle lost ground in cosmology and physics, he remains the most significant biological influence. Speakers use Aristotle but they do not cite him as an authority; instead they substantiate him by their own experience or simply take his biology as a given. Although some speakers moderate some of the most negative contemporary views of women, the treatment of these issues by conferees is ultimately less progressive than their treatment of other issues. Their treatment should provoke a reexamination of some recent historical work suggesting that the early modern period was a congenial one for women in science.

Conference discussions about women are set against a backdrop of scientific opinion that might best be considered an amalgam of Aristotelian biology and Galenic medicine. Aristotelian biology begins with the premise of female inferiority. Nature always seeks to create the perfect form, which, for Aristotle, is unquestionably male. Only when the operations of nature are impeded is a female produced. In *On the Generation of Animals* and *The History of Animals,* Aristotle develops a systematic science based on this premise.[28] According to his theories, heat is the crucial principle that leads to development—the greater the heat an animal generates the greater the development, and the greater the development the greater the perfection. Aristotle takes it as a given that women are colder and thus less perfect than men. In the humoral hierarchy, hot and dry are superior to cold and moist. When insufficient heat is brought to the process of generation, a female is produced.[31] As a result, women are by definition defects of nature.[29] Aristotle himself insists in the *Metaphysics* that women are individually mistakes of nature with inferior roles to play in generation, but they do not belong to a different species, and sexual difference is necessary for the preservation of the species.[30] Less heat imposes a number of physiological and psychological limits on women. Because they have less heat, women are smaller and weaker. Because their brains are also smaller, they have a host of undesirable personality traits; they are querulous, garrulous, inclined to be despondent, and shameless.

The conferences explicitly incorporate a great deal from this Aristotelian legacy and apply it directly to the questions they raised for discussion. One speaker on the question "Which is more noble, man or woman"[31] conveys the fundamentals of Aristotelian biology about women: "Woman is an imperfect animal, whom Plato wondered whether he should not rank among the irrational and whom Aristotle terms a monster; they who treat her most gently, style her a simple error of nature, which, through the deficiency of natural heat, could not attain to the making of a male." As defective males, women embody the less ethereal elements of earth and water and are thus wetter and colder than men, who embody air and fire. The emphasis placed on cold and wet also resonates within humoral medicine, which consigned to women the same humoral characteristics as children and criminals. Early feminist writers tried to turn their blighted legacy to positive account by arguing that this conjunction of humors was responsible for female chastity and constancy in love, and because of these humors, women were less prone to uncontrollable urges.[32]

Galen, who used Aristotle as the foundation of his medical thinking, was the other important figure in the biological understanding of women. His theories corroborated many points of Aristotelian biology but developed distinctive aspects of the polemic in ways that exacerbated tensions over gender issues. The Galenic tradition focused explicitly on genitalia as the crucial determinant of both life and sexual difference. According to Galen, women's genitalia remain interior, inferior copies of men's; they did not have sufficient heat to develop more fully into the male form. Galen also modified Aristotle's view that only the male seed contributed to generation. He believed that, because female genitalia were simply less developed male genitalia, they also produced semen but of a less developed kind. To produce a female embryo, a number of inferior elements had to combine, for example, semen from the left testes (the inferior side). But Galen expanded women's role in procreation, for female seed contributed both form and matter to the embryo. By emphasizing the necessity of female orgasm for procreation, Galen defined sexual pleasure as necessary, a belief that dominated medical literature until the nineteenth century.[33]

The Aristotelian/Galenic framework did not, however, constitute a straightforward, rigid, or comprehensive scientific system. It was flexible enough to incorporate Hippocratic notions of health and disease, which became topical again in the seventeenth century. As opposed to Aristotle, who provided both hierarchy and a comprehensive teleological system,[34] Hippocratic writings were less concerned to arrange polarities like hot/cold or large/small into hierarchies of values. Conferees, like other writers on medical topics, invoke a Hippocratic legacy when they emphasize the role of environmental causes in health and disease. They note, for example, that air, diet, exercise, the passions, or anything that adversely affects "goodness of temper" can impair fertility. The Hippocratic revival was also important to the contemporary understanding of female biology. Hippocrates, like Galen, believed that women did have semen, but that it was not as potent. Because both male and female contribute a seed, Hippocrates developed a whole range of possible characteristics, depending on whether the male or female seed dominated the mixture. This blurring of sexual distinction made sexual differences rather fluid and more problematic.[35] For example, in the case of hermaphrodites, Hippocrates claimed that *use* determined sex.[36] Because women were considered anatomically inverted men, Renaissance thinkers believed that with excessive heat the testes could descend and, as a result, women could become men. Montaigne presented the most compelling Renaissance discussion, and Pliny's *Natural History* provided classical examples.[37] These attested cases of ambiguous sexuality raised anxiety about sexual identity, sex roles, and other issues with social ramifications, such as inheritance rights. Hermaphrodites were understood not as midway between men and women but as unnatural creatures, the product of a critical imbalance in the blood, semen, and heat required for generation. Both Jean Fernel and Jean Riolan the Elder, influential seventeenth-century medical writers, asserted the role of malignant menses in the generation of such monstrous creatures.[38] A few authors in the period preceding the conferences emended the Aristotelian and Galenic medical theories, suggesting an appreciation of a distinct female phys-iology, especially the womb. Their physiological studies suggested that those colder, moister humans might have some distinctive physiolog-ical functions, such as the fat necessary for the production of milk.[39]

There were so many competing and generally complementary biological theories available, conferees could choose to emphasize specific strands of the tradition. These strands could be set in sharp opposition to each other, however, as they not only discussed biolog-ical issues but also set them in the context of gender roles and family relationships. Speakers drew on the entire heritage of biological knowl-edge, combined with their own experience, in order to explain the nature of women and the sex differences between men and women. For example, in a conference entitled "How are males and females engen-dered,"[40] the first speaker begins with the claim that male and female do not differ in essence but only in the parts that contribute to gener-ation. He cites as the most persuasive evidence of the greater genera-tive power of males the greater heat and vigor they demonstrate from the time they are in the uterus. In "Of resemblance,"[41] the first speaker brings several Aristotelian presuppositions to bear in discussing how children come to be of one sex or the other and how they come to resemble their relatives. He contends that the sex of the child is consid-ered the quintessence of "geniture." The process of generation is a meeting of male and female "genitures," but nature, inclined to perfec-tion, seeks to create a male offspring. A boy might resemble his grand-father when the generative virtue of the male ancestor is checked in the initial act of generation—by contrary female virtues or a cold wind—but the next generation allowed the male geniture to attain its proper dominance.

Participants consistently emphasize the importance of the father to the process of generation. In the conference "Whether the child derives more from the father or the mother,"[42] a speaker first cites the social customs that support the importance of the father. For example, names are patronymic because our forefathers wisely understood that the child derives more from the father than from the mother. The custom of tracing noble lineage through the father acknowledges the preeminence of the male as a creative force. These practices are fitting because they are rooted in nature: the male is perfect and rational, the female imperfect with impaired reason; the influence of the mother is merely comparable to that of a field, while that of the father is analogous to the all-important seed.[43] Although barrenness was generally attributed to women (presumably a defect of the field rather than the seed), one speaker refuses to assign responsibility for sterility to one sex or the other, noting that there are as many effeminate males as there are viragoes. In other words, there are as many men as women who deviate from the norm.[44] This remark reinforces the Galenic notion that distinctions between the sexes blur toward each other. But conferees, as is clear from the medical and scientific discussions, are not wedded to any particular system; they apply Aristotelian, Galenic, and Hippocratic ideas about generation rather indiscriminately. This does not reflect a lack of critical acumen but rather indicates the flexibility of early modern biological theory and the easy adaptability of theories of generation to the social construction of gender.

Most speakers invoke Aristotle, but his views do not go unchallenged. On rare occasions participants even refute Aristotle on the basis of biological arguments. For example, in a conference entitled "How are males and females engendered,"[45] a speaker insists we know nothing for certain about how to engender males. He does not find the Aristotelian emphasis on male heat and vigor at all persuasive, for "if it depended on heat and vigor, newlyweds would never have girls and old couples would never have boys." He is intent on proving that Aristotle's presupposition that women are mistakes of nature is false by drawing out the implications. If Aristotle were right, there would be a great many more males than females, since nature could not possibly make so many mistakes. To the contrary, he claims, the design of nature is entirely directed to the conservation of the species. If mistakes of nature were produced by an imperfect amount of heat, then nature, with too little heat, would produce an effeminate man and, with too abundant heat, a masculine woman. In his opinion, heat is too insignificant to alter nature's design, which is to conserve the species by producing both males and females.

Even if, despite this rare disclaimer, Aristotelian biology or some more eclectic form of it was a virtual given, it did not, in and of itself, necessarily entail a subordinate position for women. Dramatically different views of the significance of women could be derived from the same scientific presuppositions, especially since seventeenth-century science provided a very loose ideological framework for discussions of sex and gender. For example, the hot and dry (the male attributes) could entail negative connotations just as easily as the cold and wet, especially since so many diseases were considered the result of a deficiency of fluids and death was understood as desiccation.

Recent work in the history of science has explored the persistence of Aristotelian biology despite the accumulating evidence arrayed against it.[46] As the conferences demonstrate, in the case of Aristotelian support of traditional gender roles, consistency was clearly less important to participants than using science to maintain ideological notions of the proper position of women. This loose amalgam of Aristotelian biology, modified by Galen and Hippocrates, is readily extended into the social sphere to argue the support of nature and science for certain roles for women, almost invariably positions of inferiority. Thus the biological tradition sustains a prescriptive ideology of sex roles. From initial suppositions like "the law of nature, according to which the male as the most perfect is a head and master of the woman," far-reaching social implications can be drawn, such as "it is a monstrous thing for a body to have many heads, so it is for a woman to have many husbands. . . . Wherefore it is more expedient in a state whose chief strength consists in the number of men, that one husband have many wives, than one wife many husbands."[47]

SOCIAL ROLES FOR WOMEN

Although, in point of fact, elite women in the seventeenth century acted in central roles in many public situations as queens, regents, scholars, and patrons, nothing was more likely to provoke a vehement response in early modern texts than an assertion that women should fulfill such public roles.[48] Quotations from venerable ancients substituted for discussion: Cato, according to Plutarch's *Life of Cato*, bemoaned the control women exercised over their husbands. Once again, Aristotle was the key figure in applying biology to society. He criticized the Spartans for allowing women in public life; their lascivious nature made them unqualified for public office. Aristotle did maintain that women can practice virtues, but feminine virtues were more akin to feelings than to attributes of strong character. Woman's fundamental passivity made chastity, charity, and long-suffering her characteristic virtues, appropriate to the private sphere. These frequently cited virtues represent a deliberate selection within the classical tradition. Speakers could have cited, but generally did not, Plutarch's *Mulierum virtutes,* which claims that women and men practice the same virtues, or Plato's *Republic,* which assigns women equal roles in the public sphere.[49]

Humanist writers sometimes rehabilitated female character or mental ability but rarely endorsed a public role for them. Castiglione in *The Book of the Courtier* (1528) and Nicolas Faret in *L'Honnête Homme* (1630) emphasized the virtues of women and their role in court culture, but, because they were not interested in altering the social order, they did not sanction a public role for women outside the court. Within the court, women warranted respect and deference, but they were subservient to their husbands. Other humanists insisted that women had to be protected from the public sphere because their role in procreation circumscribed their social roles. Prominent humanist moral writers such as Erasmus and Vives saw society as divinely ordered and women's place within it prescribed accordingly. For neostoics such as Justus Lipsius, who distinguished between male and female in terms of strength and weakness, men and women practiced the same virtues, but differently, according to their different functions.[50] Bodin reflected on the orders of the realm: "I think it meet for them [women] to be kept far away from all magistracies, places of command, judgments, public assemblies, and counsels: so to be attentive only to their womanly and domestic business."[51]

When conferees assess the issue of public roles for women, they find analogies from nature as applied to society particularly persuasive. In the conference "Whether sterility is more commonly the fault of men or women,"[52] one speaker states, "For nature formed them [women] chiefly for propagation, as the conformation of their bodies seems to prove." Not only do bodies suggest reproductive roles, they are also linked to and alter the nature of fundamental organs like the brain.

Another speaker points out, "the parts serving to that purpose, as the womb and breasts, have direct communication not only between themselves, but also with the noblest parts of the body." Furthermore, nature's intentions are prescriptive: "woman, having been in nature's first intention designed for generation, must be also much more fit for it (because nature never fails of her end) than man, who being born for command, labor, contemplation, and other more sublime employments, is designed for generation, but in the more remote intention of nature."

This is but one of many discussions where consistency yields to maintain the dominant ideology of sex roles. Thus female sex organs restrict women to a role in procreation, and although the male sex organs give the male a dominant role in procreation, nature nonetheless directs men to a whole range of public roles as well. When the question concerns generation itself, conferees insist on the central role played by the male and the less significant role played by the female. But when questions treat the social roles assigned by sex, then participants argue that sex limits women to procreation. A few of them go so far as to assert that men and women should associate only as necessary to guarantee procreation. Men's other needs for association, to accomplish any other social functions, are better served by association with other men. In fact, association with women is assumed to impede other social functions. This understanding of male-female relations is deeply rooted in Greek philosophy, particularly Aristotle, and is well accepted by the Christian synthesizer Aquinas.[53]

Although arguments seem most persuasive when they move from the natural to the social, participants occasionally argue from the reverse perspective. Just as the ideal in politics and economics is diversity, so too, one speaker notes in "Whether husband and wife must be of the same humor,"[54] according to Aristotle the husband should be ten years older than his wife to heighten the diversity of temperament already attendant on sex differences. The age difference will have the added benefit of enhancing the desired social relationship, "to the end that both may keep their station, the one above, the other below, one commands, the other obeys." Furthermore, "since diversity of actions is necessary in a family, the office of the husband being other than that of the wife, it seems they ought to be as different in manners as they are in temper." In other words, because men and women are different by nature, the differences are appropriately reflected in different social functions. Some conferees suggest that nature would be even better served if social differences were made even more pointed and gender-specific.

In a conference on "Whether women should be learned,"[55] a speaker draws out some of the implications of arguing from nature to social issues in order to address the education of women. First, he asserts, women's bodies reveal that they are designed by nature for tasks other than learning, and in fact their bodies render them completely unfit for education. "The humidity of their brain, which is an enemy to science, and the weakness of their capricious spirit are sufficiently strong reasons to prohibit that sex the sciences, which require solidity of judgment, always found wanting in the writings of women." Second, judgment requires a different physiological constitution; it "depends upon a dry temper, contrary to that of a woman's brain, whose animal spirits are obscured by the clouds of humidity." This physiological character affects the quality of women's thought: "she hits well sometimes at the first assay, but not in second thoughts, which are always weaker than the first, a most sure mark of their weakness." On the contrary, he contends, the second thoughts of men prevail over the first, showing the strength of their ability to reason. Finally, women are emotional and therefore incapable of the dispassion required by reason.[56] "They are heady in their desires, and violent in their first passion, in which they ordinarily have neither measure nor moderation." Although these arguments are considered particularly telling by conferees, they are in essence simply applications of the logical deduction that if A is male and B is female, then A is better than B, no matter what quality is being considered. For example, there is little reason to favor dryness over humidity, or to argue that the dry should entail rationality and all the other positive qualities speakers identify with masculinity.

Participants assert a necessary connection between extant sex roles and the desire to maintain the traditional social order. For example, women should not attend comedies, not only because of the impressions these might make on their weak minds but also because "it is not expedient for the good of the household that this sex carry itself to curiosities." There should be no innovation that could disrupt the status quo. In fact, a husband has reason to fear an intelligent wife: "The too great capacity of his wife gives her authority over him [which] is contrary to the institution of marriage or makes her equal, which . . . is entirely the enemy of domestic repose." This speaker unleashes, in just a few sentences, a whole series of negative presuppositions about women. Their weak minds must stay focused so they do not stray from their appropriate sphere. Exposure to anything beyond the household will distort the hierarchical social order by making the woman equal or even superior in authority to her husband. These arguments assert the "naturalness" of the existing social order and sex roles and suggest that any change in sex roles is fraught with the dangers of social instability.

In principle, Aristotelian biology could be used just as easily to argue the superiority of women, although this would have been an unusual position to take. There are many examples within the conferences where speakers miss the opportunity to extend the logic of their arguments so as to reverse Aristotle's presuppositions about gender roles. One such missed opportunity occurred when a speaker, noting that there were fewer men than women, concludes that men must be more fruitful than women. He does not argue, as he might have, that because there were more women than men, they were nature's chosen sex, the stronger half of the species, or even that women were more essential to preserve the species.[57] Another such example occurs in a conference on wisdom, where a participant claims that cold and dry tempers allow the cultivation of wisdom but then does not credit women with greater wisdom than men, even though women were always considered colder than men.[58] Instead he simply concludes that men with colder temperaments are more inclined to wisdom. Furthermore, although Aristotle is used as the basis of arguments about nature and what is natural, these arguments are exceedingly loose and applied in an inconsistent fashion so as to result in the inevitably proper gender roles. In a conference entitled "Whether it be better that men have many wives or women many husbands,"[59] a speaker notes that, even though Christianity disallows polygamy, the laws of nature and of some nations nonetheless condone it.[60] Polyandry had been practiced in such remote times that it might well be considered part of the state of nature. Nonetheless, he concludes that to have many husbands is "something against the laws of nature." In this case, "nature" yields to traditional ideology. This example forcefully demonstrates that, for conferees, the ideology of traditional sex roles is readily adapted to incorporate conflicting arguments and to fit changing scientific paradigms.

There are, however, rare and interesting counter-examples. A speaker in the conference "Whether it be expedient for women to be learned"[61] demonstrates that Aristotle could effectively be used as the foundation for an argument about the superiority of women.[62] He asserts that "their memory, caused by the moist constitution of their brain and their sedentary and solitary life, is further favorable to study." Because of their natural, constitutional proclivity for scholarship ("constitution" is used here in the sense of physiological constitution), another speaker points out that "our ancient Gauls left to them the administration of the laws and other exercises of peace." Women, according to this reading of Aristotle's theory of physical constitution, were more fit for scholarship and government; men, on the other hand, should be restricted to military exploits. But—as Schiebinger notes, pointing out the difficulties involved in using traditional cosmologies to make feminist arguments—"however brilliantly they stood Aristotle on his head, he was easily set upright again."[63]

Some recent scholarship on gender and science asserts that Aristotelian biology and its attendant notions of gender roles actually offered more social possibilities for women than the science of the biological revolution (a position the preceding conference might tend to support). The claim made by these studies is that women, as defective males, were nonetheless part of the same "single-sex" continuum.[64] Thus, though defective, since they were still part of the same sex as men, they could be allowed to enjoy a wider range of social roles than could be condoned during the nineteenth century, when women were considered sexually distinct from men.[65] These recent studies have asserted that the dramatic decline in opportunities for and increase in negative perceptions of women were rooted in the shift in scientific treatment of sex and gender in the late eighteenth and early nineteenth centuries. This change was predicated on the notion of a decisive differ-ence between men and women, which focused specifically on the womb, and the ancillary argument that diseases of the womb such as hysteria mandated different social roles for women.

The discussion of women's nature and social roles in the conferences does not support these contentions. The notion of gender differences as rooted in distinct sex organs is clearly present in several of these mid-seventeenth-century conferences. Furthermore, any participant could well have drawn on the commonplace derived from Plato of the animality of the womb, a commonplace that enjoyed wide currency in the sixteenth and seventeenth centuries. In "Of the extravagance of women,"[66] a speaker claims that a woman's virtue or vice depends not on her sex but rather on the diseases that afflict the womb. "The irreg-ular motions of the organ, which distinguishes their sex and which is called an animal within an animal, many times have an influence in the business and increase the mobility of humors. Thus the health of their minds as well as that of their bodies many times suffers alteration." In "Whether sterility is more commonly the fault of men or women,"[67] a conferee claims that women are more subject to sterility because in woman the seed, the blood, and the womb must always be of the right "temper, conformation, or solution." Another proclaims that nature has designed women for fertility as their breasts and wombs prove. These arguments divide men and women into two distinct sexes with sharply differentiated gender roles determined by qualities or deficiencies asso-ciated with female sex organs.

Even if, as some recent historians have noted, Galen's emphasis on the comparability of men's and women's genitalia placed men and women on the same plane, women were nonetheless consigned to infe-rior places and sharply restricted roles because of their manifest defects. Even when men and women are understood as comparable and con-sidered part of a "single sex" (not the general understanding in the conferences), they are discussed in terms of antithetical physical charac-teristics.[68] For example, women's brains are more humid, their bodies more tender, their minds weaker. They have less vigor and less heat, but their passions are more violent.[69] The intellectual or moral attrib-utes of women are also defined in opposition to those of men. In a conference on "Whether man or woman is more inclined to love,"[70] a speaker equates love with passion and friendship with virtue. Because women have stronger fancies and weaker intellects, they love more but are less capable of friendship. This sense of women as embodying the antitheses of male qualities leads to some peculiar arguments. For example, since women are colder by nature and therefore less imaginative, they are constant in love. By contraposition then, inconstancy is a virtue, the sign of a good masculine spirit. In essence, women love more because they have less knowledge; men, who know more, love more lightly. This view is based in part on the underlying supposition that love and knowledge are antithetical, and as such, one must apply to men and the other to women. What might be considered a virtue, like constancy in love, becomes a defect because it is characteristic of women.

In many of the conferences, men and women not only embody antithetical physical characteristics and moral virtues but they are also presumed to be in direct competition. Conferences treat such hotly contested issues as to which sex is more virtuous, nobler, or loves more.[71] One conference details a specific contest.[72] In Rome, a widower survived twenty-two wives, and a widow outlived twenty-two husbands. When they married each other, all of Rome eagerly watched to see who would triumph in this battle of the sexes. When the wife preceded her husband in death, the men of Rome hailed this as a great victory. But a speaker questions whether this is the proper way to settle the issue. He suggests that, since there have always been more old women than old men, the real issue ought to be which sex has more dignity or inherent nobility than the other. He concludes that, since all family feuds are caused by the desire of women to command men instead of obeying them, obviously men are the more noble sex. Another speaker begs to differ; he notes that the courtship and eager pursuit of women by men attest to their value. Since woman was created after man and out of his rib rather than from dirt, she is obviously the more noble sex, an argument based on Agrippa's famous recasting of the creation account to the advantage of women.[73]

Such accounts do not long stand uncontested, however. A speaker counters with a veritable catalog of seventeenth-century misogyny. He too cites the creation account, but to serve different ends: God ordained that women should be subject to man; the fact that Eve was created from Adam's rib explains the hardheadedness of women; the only way Adam could be induced to marry Eve was to be put into a deep sleep. Men are addicted to women for the general good of the population even though it works to their individual disadvantage. Women are best classified as "necessary evils." This discourse, one of the most vehement in the entire collection, demonstrates that any argument challenging traditional gender roles provokes a sharp response.

The idea that the early modern period offered more possibilities for women than the modern period, specifically in the sciences, seems based on little more than wishful thinking. Proponents of an optimistic reading of the early modern period point to the careers of a few outstanding women scientists, or to the fact that in 1635 the Académie Française proposed three women as members, to suggest that women were not precluded from participation in science. [74] But despite the very real abilities of Gabrielle-Emilie du Châtelet, Margaret Cavendish, or Maria Winkelmann, the most prominent female scientists of the early modern period, these women do not form part of a scientific mainstream. Their institutional connections to science are either mediated by men or effected by their influence. Although some scholars have presumed that women did attend Renaudot's conferences, various remarks made by conferees suggest that women did not. For example, in a discussion of "Whether women should be learned,"[75] a speaker assumes that the Greeks in fact opened their academies to women but then says that this practice has no bearing on the present situation in France. Another prefaces his remarks with the phrase "if the ladies were here to defend themselves."[76] Attitudes like these, in a group that prides itself on progressiveness and liberality, do not suggest that the early modern period was conducive to the participation of women in science. The conferences for the most part highlight the vehemence of opinion against women's involvement in scientific culture and intellectual life.

The fact that the Académie Française was founded when the participants in the conferences were debating many issues concerning the roles, abilities, and nature of women makes the conferences a relevant source for discussing the exclusion of women from the new institutions of the seventeenth century. Although they do not represent the highest level of academic discourse, the conferences are perhaps more revealing of contemporary attitudes because they are less structured and less formal. Since it seems clear that women did not attend the conferences, these remarks do not have the artificial character of debates between women and men on these issues, such as that featured in the *Book of the Courtier,* or between men in front of an audience that is partially female or hosted by a woman, as in the context of the salon, for example.

The conferences were held during a period when natural philosophy was attempting to carve out for itself an institutional role within the cultural space opened by the demise of the influence of monasteries and universities and the rise of the academies. Whereas universities were generally closed to women, other social settings like the court, the salon, or the academy were not. In court culture, a woman had the status of her husband, thus noble women could exercise considerable influence over those of a lower social rank. As a result, women such as Marguerite of Navarre or Elisabetta Gonzaga at the court of Urbino (depicted in *The Book of the Courtier*) developed centers of intellectual culture in the courts.[77] And in the salons, women continued to exercise a powerful intellectual role.[78] But although *salonnières* could play a powerful role behind the scenes in selecting members of the Académie des Sciences, they could not attain membership themselves.

These limited roles for women in the culture of science were possible in part because of the nature of early modern science. There was no clear demarcation between professional and popular science. Women also had entrée into scientific networks by virtue of their social status, which was largely determined and sustained by a hierarchy of birth. Although it was perhaps not predestined that women would not have a place in the early academies, a general pattern emerged: as an academy became more influential, the participation of women declined. So, for example, the early academic precursors to the Académie Française, like Henry III's Palace Academy, had active women participants. Although women were initially proposed for membership in the Académie Française, when the general question of female membership was discussed, it was ultimately rejected. Women too were present in gatherings that were the forerunners to the Académie des Sciences, the scientific salons, and the Cartesian gatherings of Jacques de Rouhault. As the Académie des Sciences became more formalized with each position elected and salaried, it was closed to women. Given the character of the seventeenth-century debate about the nature and appropriate social roles of women, it is perhaps not surprising that the issue was decided against them.

MARRIAGE AND THE FAMILY

Closely connected to the discussions of roles for women were the conferences dedicated to a broad range of topics on marriage and the family. When participants address these topics, they work within a long-standing historical tradition and contribute to the early modern discussion of marriage, a discussion reopened by the Reformation. The Protestant Reformation had a significant influence on the Christian ideology of marriage. The fundamental Protestant tenet of the priesthood of all believers undermined a theological justification for a separate, celibate priesthood. Without the greater nobility of celibacy, marriage could no longer be simply the refuge, as Saint Paul would have it, of those without the strength to resist the lure of the flesh. Protestant reformers did not extol celibacy as a higher form of life than marriage and were thus inclined to view marriage favorably, to see it as intended by God for procreation, for the avoidance of fornication, and for companionship. While Protestant theologians replaced the Roman Catholic Church's vocation to the priesthood with an expanded concept of the vocations to which men were called by God, including any number of professions, marriage was considered *the* vocation of women. Catholic theologians responded to this newer acceptance of marriage among Protestants with their own marriage manuals. The topic of marriage had a new currency in the early modern period, which is well reflected in these conferences. But marriage cast in a positive light was something of a novelty.

Marriage from the Greeks to the seventeenth century was frequently discussed as a way to keep women in line. The Greeks believed both that marriage was a natural state and that, as an institution, it would effectively control women's animal passions. The *Oeconomicus* of Xenophon depicted the domesticated wife, restricted to the household and subject to the control of her husband. In classical texts, this natural state was reflected in the social order. The different natures of men and women prescribed their roles in society; man by nature was suited to the public sphere, and woman, less gifted in physical and mental strength, was appropriately restricted to the private sphere of the household. Despite Saint Paul's muted endorsement of marriage ("It is better to marry than to burn"), the Christian tradition endowed marriage with a sacramental character.[79] During the Renaissance, the Christian and the classical were fused in the texts of humanists such as Vives, Erasmus, and Agrippa.[80] These humanists imbued the household with the appropriate Christian virtues, such as chastity, submissiveness, and piety. Although works of Renaissance humanism elevated the status of Christian marriage and willingly attributed to women equal operations of the soul, they did not attempt to alter women's legal or marital status.[81]

Seventeenth-century France produced an intense discussion about marriage, in part because more critical feminist and antifeminist positions replaced the stalemated *querelle des femmes*. Feminist literature was inextricably bound to the subject of marriage; marriage was the state of most women, and discussions of marriage raised questions about the education of women and their social roles. These discussions rose sharply throughout the century until they fell off precipitously with the accession of Louis XIV. In the early part of the century, the literature focused on the traditional duties and obligations of women within marriage. Grenaille's *L'honneste mariage* and Claude Maillard's *Le bon mariage* are typical of the conventional discussion of marriage, which appraised the merits of celibacy versus marriage, examined the disadvantages of marriage and then offered an apology for it. But anti-marriage arguments, whether within or outside of a religious tradition, were part of a long-standing polemic. For example, Philippe Desportes's *Stance du mariage* of 1573 set forth the disadvantages of all women as wives.[82] Antifeminist texts, like Pierre Le Moyne's *La galerie des femmes fortes* and Jacques-Joseph Duguet's *Conduite d'une dame chrétienne,* argued that women must submit to all forms of authority because all authority was derived from God. Other antifeminists glorified marriage to keep women confined to the domestic sphere. Those who refused to marry and bear children were considered treasonous. Writers like Nicolas Boileau and Antoine Arnauld warned about the evils of theaters, assemblies, operas, and novels for women. These writers, as Lougee points out, associated any expansion of the roles of women with "illicit love, the reign of money, and the breakdown of traditional social stratification."[83] In response, some female writers, instead of chafing under the constraints on roles for women, counseled resignation.

Within the *libertin* tradition, writers employed traditional arguments about the physical and the psychological deficiency of women in order to castigate marriage. For example, Montaigne's essay "On some Lines of Virgil" indicted marriage as a prison.[84] Ultimately all prospective wives shared the inherent defects of women, which according to antifeminist writers were inconstancy, lustfulness, irrationality, and general perversity. These writers also focused on the undesirable aspects of marriage, including the restriction of the sexual experience of the husband. (There is no similar concern for deprivations of the wife!) One of Renaudot's conferees, who reflected this attitude, warned that marriage could lead to such dire effects as the spiritual disintegration of the husband or his domination by his wife.

Much of the discussion of marriage in the conferences reflects entirely conventional views, but there are some distinctive elements.[85] Most important of all, participants do not approach the topic from within the religious tradition. They do not, for example, extol celibacy or justify marriage as a curb to lust. Instead their discussions resonate within traditional secular disparagements of marriage, and to the limited degree that marriage or the roles of women within families are praised, the positive assessment is also cast in entirely secular terms.

Despite occasional progressive positions, conferees generally display a rather jaundiced view of marriage, quite in keeping with the ambivalence widely expressed in seventeenth-century moral tracts.[86] For example, at the beginning of a conference on "Whether men should marry,"[87] a speaker cites Cato, who, when urged to marry again after the death of his wife, replied that "once delivered from a shipwreck, he cared not to venture to sea again." (Other seventeenth-century texts also describe marriage as the shipwreck of life.)[88] The complaints of scholarly men are also heard: "Marriage adds to the misery of life by working against liberty and quiet." On the other side of the issue, one speaker says, "without marriage, men would be vagrants and stragglers like wild beasts." Another praises marriage as the only social relationship that produces "amity"; all others are based on "dissimulation and hypocrisy." The final speaker outlines a compromise position; marriage is either paradise or hell. But his final advice, since a wife is the one thing a man must keep all his life, is that "everyone ought to consult himself . . . [to determine] whether he believes he has virtue and constancy enough to suffer the defects of a woman, who may be commendable in some points, but at bottom is always a woman."

Scientific deliberations are brought to bear in discussing marriage. For example, humors and temperaments should be weighed in the decision to marry, and the correspondence between husband and wife should be sought in the heavens through astrology.[89] A speaker insists that marriage should replicate the natural hierarchy of female as subservient to male, because the male, as the most perfect thing, "has been put by nature as head and master of women." Thus polyandry violates nature by allowing "a monstrous thing," that is to say, a body with many heads.[90] While it is generally considered monstrous to have women rule men, polyandry extends the perversion of inverted hierarchy into the structure of the family itself. The conferences also demonstrate that science could be cited against the traditional authority of the church and in favor of the interests of the state on issues of sex, marriage, and the family. For example, one speaker in "Of chastity" argues that chastity is contrary to man's natural desire for immortality.[91] Participants frequently express dismay that the "law of grace" has ruled out divorce. Another, in a conference "Whether it is better to marry," speaks out against celibacy, saying that it has been publicly discounted and punished because nature has given men a desire to generate their like.[92] These conferences thus contribute to the contemporary rehabilitation of marriage, arguing that since it is unnatural, celibacy cannot be considered a better state than marriage.

Conferees take the interests of the state into consideration in discussions of sex and gender. For example, in a discussion of "Whether it be better that men have many wives or women many husbands," a participant notes that because prostitutes, who have sexual relations with many men, are barren, if women had many husbands, there would be fewer children. But, he continues, if husbands had many wives, there would be many more children, and so it is in the interest of the state that husbands have many wives. However, when a speaker points out that women should certainly not have many husbands because the husbands would not know which children were theirs, he is harshly rebuked by a speaker who suggests that the French should look to the Spartans; they rightly understood that children belong to the communities, *not* to their parents.[93] Another speaker in "On chastity" claims that chastity is not in the interest of the state; "marriage not only supplies laborers, artisans, soldiers, and citizens to the state, but kings and princes to the people, prelates and pastors to the church, and a nursery to paradise, which would not be peopled with virgins, did not the married give them being."[94] Conferees reflect concern with fertility and with establishing social patterns that would increase the population and recognize that marriage patterns have significant political ramifications.[95]

There are several examples in the conferences that reflect the more traditional repudiation of the flesh—for example, "the more we abstain from pleasure, the more pure we are"—but most speakers insist that fostering procreation is one of nature's fundamental interests. Whether one lacks this ability physically or by choosing chastity ("mental eunuchs," as speakers refer to the celibate), one has fundamentally violated nature. Nature ultimately disowns those who do not have the parts requisite for generation.[96]

Generation, construed as the crucial natural capability, also becomes the focus of discussions about relations between parents and children, which are the topic of five conferences. This becomes, as one might expect, a discussion of contested roles and competing authority within the family. The roles of father and mother within the family are explicitly discussed in terms of their contribution to generation, which obviously prejudices all remarks in favor of the father. Conferees both present the biological evidence for the predominance of father over mother in the process of generation and draw social ramifications from their understanding of physiology. They find this generational preeminence well reflected in social conventions, customs, and power relationships. Any contribution made by the "semen" of the mother, says one speaker, would be akin to much diluted wine. (Belief in female "semen" is Galenic, but this speaker does not put much credence in it.) Any resemblance between mother and child must be considered "a game of nature who pleases herself in diversity."[97] Another speaker in the same conference draws the following analogy: the mother is matter and the father is form, and the form is always more important than the matter. As a result of the father's biological importance, the Romans were right to give the power of life and death over children to the father and to give no rights to the mother.

Other participants refute claims for the preeminent influence of the father over the child on biological grounds. Armed with assertions of the importance of the mother to generation, they also call into question some of the roles that women have been assigned within the family and society. One speaker cites evidence from animal breeding to establish the significance of women to generation. Furthermore, after generation, the father has nothing to do with the embryo. Thus an infant born after the death of his father might well thrive, although a fetus taken from a dead mother rarely does well. The mother nurses the child, and the milk imprints her character. Those who are not nursed by their mothers take on the character of their wet-nurses instead.[98] (Well into the eighteenth century excessive maternal influence will be cited as an argument for wet-nursing.)[99] Because the mother contributes to generation, nourishes the child for nine months, and nurses it with milk from her body, the speaker finds it incredible that the fetus is not transformed completely into the nature of the mother.

The speeches that address the question of which sex contributes most to generation are sharply antithetical; they offer almost set pieces on the differences between the pro-masculine and the pro-feminine positions. One reason these issues are so hotly contested is that speakers assume that generation determines both the authority and the relative importance of mothers and fathers in the lives of their children. "Biology," or more accurately the generative legacy, is assumed to be absolutely crucial to discussing social structure; science is considered a critical determinant of the social order. As a speaker on the question "To which is one more obliged, the father or the mother,"[100] overtly argues, not only have the crucial physiological roles the mother plays after the generative act been undervalued, but this undervaluation has been used to restrict her social roles. To establish maternal significance, he notes the insignificance of the father's role after gestation, baldly stating that it is a matter of indifference to the embryo whether its father continues to live. And there can be no certitude about paternity as there clearly is about maternity. But men who make the laws have redressed their disadvantageous position with respect to their children by usurping the authority over children that women are entitled to by nature because for nine months they are one body. According to him, men violate the standards of nature through civil institutions. The extensive control, even beyond the obvious roles in generation, that nature has given mothers is demonstrated by the fact that the mother can imprint whatever marks on the child she pleases by her imagination alone. The relationship of child to father is much less fundamental; "if children are obliged to the father it is only for the goods of fortune." But even this economic role is not exclusive to fathers, as "there are found many women who are not only more capable than men of conserving these goods but also of acquiring them. And the goods of many families come through the maternal line."

This speaker indicates an unusual appreciation of the economic contribution of the mother to the well-being of the family. But this entire speech is quite unusual; it is much more common for speakers to argue that the preeminent social role of the father is established through his role in generation. The claims made for the social influence of fathers are extensive and at least partially argued through scientific analogy. For example, the conference "If a son can oblige his father"[101] suggests a great similarity between the relationship of son to father and slave to master, and those who would unequivocally assert the authority of the father over the son do so in terms of the father's generative role. The son has an almost overwhelming responsibility toward the father in recompense for the father's giving him life. (Interestingly, especially in light of claims made in the conference just discussed, no mention is made that children are similarly subject to the mother.) Another analogy suggests that the relationship between father and son is akin to that between God and individual, and thus the nature of the debt owed is commensurate. (One speaker does express concern that this incredible debt might provoke resentment on the part of sons.)

This conference begins with support for the claim of the father. A speaker declares that the father has the same role in the family that God has in the world and the sun has in the heavens, that is, as the efficient and formal cause in nature. Just as it would be impious to suggest that God has a competitor in the universe, so too only the ignorant fail to recognize that the sun is the father of light (a less than subtle attack on proponents of geocentrism). He does make the interesting disclaimer that, to compare father and mother, one would have to have comparable experiences and roles to compare not just as father and mother but also as male and female. "One would have to look at some hermaphrodites who have been father and mother to judge well." But despite this unusual caveat, he notes vehemently, "I find nothing in the feminine sex that can equal the affection and the offices of a father." Furthermore, he maintains, the affection of the mother is often deranged and resembles that of monkeys who suffocate their children. The labors of fathers to amass what is necessary to nourish, raise, clothe, and instruct their children reveals them as vigorous and powerful, whereas the indulgence of mothers exposes their impotence. Ultimately, the strength of the male and the weakness of the female define the responsibility of children toward their fathers.

Another speaker strongly disagrees; his remarks empathize with women, especially in the bearing and nurturing of infants.[102] He chides the husband, who, "not content with having violently and without any form of justice usurped command over the feminine sex," nonetheless exercises this authority "no less imperiously than if he had subjected her to right of arms." This tyranny goes so far as to deprive women of the only consolation "nature has left them for all the ills they suffer to be mother, which is the obligation and goodwill of their children." He argues against the position of the "naturalists" who claim that the woman is merely passive. He emphasizes the central role that women play in nurturing children and points out that experience shows a healthy child can be born to a leprous father and a healthy mother, but not to a leprous mother and a healthy father. So women must contribute more to the generation of children, and as a result, children have a greater obligation toward their mother than toward their father.

Furthermore, women endure labor and the dire effects of pregnancy on their health and beauty. The affection of mothers, so vividly reflected in their singing to and dancing with their infants when they cry, does not diminish as their children age. Thus the affection of mothers always surpasses that of fathers and consequently merits more recognition.

Another conference takes the question from the perspective of parental love by asking "Who loves their children more, the father or the mother."[103] The first speaker distinguishes between civil love, where one loves another for the profit or the pleasure one hopes to gain, from the natural love of parents for children. This pure love is drawn from both parents as the source of generation, but since the father is the active principle, he loves his child more perfectly than the mother, who is the passive principle. The second speaker disagrees. As the mother contributes more to the production of the child, she loves the child more than the father who simply disperses semen. (It is important to note that the issue has once again become focused on the contribution of each parent to the process of generation.) The "glory of generation" belongs to the woman who—imitating the earth, which heats and pushes the sap in its season—vivifies and animates the semen she receives in her womb and conserves it throughout her pregnancy. Thus she is more active in the generation than the father whose action is only momentary while hers is ongoing, and she continuously furnishes actual substance to the child. Mothers bear witness to the love of their children and they ought also to enjoy the glory of their greater love. Finally, he points out that Aristotle assures us in his *Morals* that children do not love their fathers until they have attained the age of understanding. (This example offers yet another case of the battling Aristotles.)[104] Another participant notes that the affection of parents toward their children is exempt from interest: the love of a father toward his children is similar to that of God toward men, but this purity of love is not extended to mothers.

In general, most conferees assert the importance of the father and support their claims by invoking Aristotelian biology. Some maintain the importance of the mother, by insisting on the crucial role of women in generation or by pointing to the nurturing role of women or the dynamic of their involvement in the family. But staunch defenses of the importance of women within the family provoke strenuous opposition, suggesting that women had little credibility even in terms of their maternal roles. However, within the context of the conferences, positive statements about women are made that are not restricted to reflections on maternity or the domestic sphere. A few participants suggest that these questions, formulated in terms of which sex is nobler, more courageous, or more virtuous are misbegotten because specific virtues are not tied to sex or gender but reflected in different individuals irrespective of sex.

Women and their value are defended on many different grounds. In "Who is the more noble, men or women,"[105] one speaker, probably taking his cue from Agrippa's defense of women, inverts the conventional impact of the creation account. He asserts that women are created of more noble material; they are created from Adam's rib rather than from dirt. He also claims that women can be identified with more "goods"; they have a greater quantity of the goods of the body (beauty), and they demonstrate greater goods of mind in that they mature earlier and demonstrate greater success in the practice of virtue. "They are acknowledged by all, to be more merciful, faithful, and charitable than men." Some speakers go further; they not only bemoan the limited roles men have allowed women but also endorse the expansion of women's social roles. The speaker who argues most strongly against assigning characteristics on the basis of sex points out that "many queens and empresses have manifested that women know how to command as well as men." Perhaps reflecting on the role of women in the new intellectual settings of the salons, a speaker in "Whether women's conversation is useful to men"[106] asserts the benefits of women's conversation for "sweetening the bitterness of their lives."

Perhaps the strongest statement in any of the discussions about women is made in response to the question "Whether it be expedient for women to be learned?"[107] A speaker not only answers in the affirmative but indicts in the harshest terms the imposition of the male control that has prevented women from learning and the disastrous effects for women of their limited intellectual opportunities. Men have acted as tyrants. While God "subjected the woman to the dominion of the man, man has attained absolute power through tyranny." As a result, "he has not only reserved to himself alone the authority of making laws (where women, not being called, have always had the worst) but has also appropriated the best things to himself, without admitting them [women] to partake of them."

It is interesting that, when discussing either women's roles or political issues, participants attack the illegitimate and punitive imposition of authority, which they denounce as self-serving, illegitimate, and tyrannical. Men have reduced women to economic servitude through marriage, and kept them from knowledge, and thus "unjustly deprive them of the greatest of all goods, to wit, that of the mind, whose fairest ornament is knowledge." A speaker insists that not only is understanding common to all human beings but women have the advantage of greater wit and greater curiosity. Only the prohibitions of men have kept women from the pursuits for which they were clearly designed by nature. "Their memory, caused by the moist constitution of their brain, and their sedentary and solitary life, is further favorable to study." Because they are not encouraged to follow their natural inclination, "their wits [are] like those good soils, which for want of better culture, run to weeds and briars." Only the tyranny of men has kept women from learning, the greatest human good and one for which they are naturally suited. According to him, the illegitimate exercise of male power has inverted the "natural" intellectual order.

Although science is usually invoked to argue the inferiority of women and to define for them limited and subservient social positions, the conferences contain enough strong and surprising statements in women's favor that some scholars have assumed women actually participated. For example, participants frequently claim that women have been limited in their accomplishments by the restricted roles they play in society or that laws and customs have had a negative effect on women.[108] One speaker claims that "if women had the making of the laws and histories, you would see more virtues exercised by women than by men."[109] Another strongly advocates the inclusion of women in science. "As for their science, their encyclopedia is a world that still has many unknown or less frequented parts. If women joined together with men in the discovery of those parts, who doubts but that a feminine curiosity would serve to sharpen the point of men's wits, distracted by extraneous affairs, and make marvelous progress, and discover various rare secrets, thus far unknown."[110] It is significant that women are included although the kind of science they offer is equally revealing; their science is the product of curiosity rather than wit, yields "rare secrets," and serves to sharpen men's wits.

Such staunch support for expanded social roles for women is striking but unusual. Perhaps more indicative of the conferences' mixed message on gender issues is the ambiguous discussion in a conference on "Whether it be better that men have many wives or women many husbands?"[111] where the question is answered on the basis of curious presuppositions about women. For example, a speaker claims that the laws, established by men, have allowed men to abuse their power over women and to secure their own advantage. As a result, men have more frequently allowed themselves to take many wives than they have permitted women to take many husbands. A more pragmatic participant wonders whether having more husbands, all of whom would act as tyrants, would really be in the interests of women. And polyandry would be socially disastrous; no man would be responsible for the education of a child if he could not be sure it was his.

Another speaker vehemently complains that this issue, as all others, has been resolved to the prejudice of women; women have not been heard and so have the right to complain.[112] He notes that the vehement and irregular appetite of women for men suggests that nature intended women to have more than one husband. He looks to ancient constitutions to find a historical precedent for polyandry. He rejects the example of Solon, who mandated that husbands visit their wives three times a month, and Cato, who visited his wife only when it rained.[113] But he praises Lycurgus, who said it was better to allow handsome young men to lie with the wives of old men, since they would take this liberty anyway and it would be better "to be quit of the blame." This speaker presents the strongest endorsement of the rights of women even though his defense focuses on the failure of the law to appreciate adequately the sexual appetites of women.[114] It is appropriate to end the discussion of the roles of women on this ambiguous note, especially since the conferences are less progressive on gender issues than on other topics.

Some recent literature suggests that the seventeenth century was a period when science was more sympathetic to women than the later modern era and more open to their participation in science.[115] The discussions at the Bureau on the nature of women and on the roles appropriate to them, and the ways in which science was used to sustain these arguments, cast doubt on any such claim. The notion that the early modern period was more amenable to the participation of women in science and more benign in depicting women, the conferences suggest, is simplistic. Instead of demonstrating a fundamental shift, they reveal that the use of science to comment on women and to define the roles appropriate to them was remarkably consistent. Perhaps a better case can be made that, in the last analysis, science sustained the predominant gender roles. In other words, writings from the late eighteenth century that explicitly emphasized sexual difference and argued against the inclusion of women in science did so in part because of the character of science at their disposal.[116] That is to say, in the modern period, scientific knowledge could be more consistently applied by scientists and physicians and counter-arguments less effectively made by independent intellectuals like those attending Renaudot's conferences. Thus the greater insistence on the scientific foundation of arguments about women in the late eighteenth century was rooted less in any change in the basic assumptions about the nature and roles of women and more in the credibility of science to assert such arguments. It is also important to acknowledge that the argument that science was less prescriptive in the early modern period than the modern rests on different kinds of sources. For the early modern period, historians cite groups like Renaudot's, but for the nineteenth century they use the writings of physicians seeking to extend the scope of their professional authority. These physicians were more adept and more dogmatic in the application of a more consistent science. They, like most of the conferees, intended to sustain arguments about the inferiority of women, but they had at their disposal a more developed professional stance with a more rigidly defined notion of medical science. More accurate information about female anatomy did not produce arguments broadening public roles for women, but instead, writers emphasized sex differences and used them to curtail the activities of women.

Even if the conferees' use of science on questions of sex and gender was not progressive, nonetheless, their approach to issues of gender resonates in many eighteenth- and nineteenth-century physiological and medical texts in which science was also used to connect sex and gender to the human sciences. Although not all claims to knowledge about gender were based on anatomy and physiology, these fields were central, and as a result medical language was pervasive.[117] The conferences appealed to empirical findings, particularly case studies. Such an approach became increasingly significant to the development of eighteenth- and nineteenth-century medicine and was applied more consistently to social and political theory. Conferees, like their eighteenth- and nineteenth-century descendents, used "nature" as a key term to discuss sexual differences, but as the conferences so vividly demonstrate, appeals to nature provide only the illusion of stability. The metaphorical constructions invoked by participants—such as the association of women with weak, superstitious minds, with political and social instability, and with overpowering lust—undergird the human sciences of the later period as well.[118] Like many more modern discussions, conferees tested their ideas about women and gender against a backdrop of discussion of the family. From the eighteenth century onward, in a development foreshadowed by the conferences, the facts of biology were increasingly used to justify cultural and political differences between the sexes. These differences, substantiated by biology, were increasingly the crucial determinants of both feminist and antifeminist arguments.

Although these conferences are full of entertaining anecdotes and quotable remarks about sex, gender, and the relationship between the sexes, their implications for contemporary scholarly treatments of the relationship of science and gender are somewhat less clear-cut. They do demonstrate that, although science was consistently used to sustain arguments about gender, the Aristotelian/Galenic/Hippocratic theses were loose and generally inconsistent. Thus when participants apply science to their discussions of sex or the nature of women and their roles, they frequently espouse contradictory positions. Science, although generally considered to sustain the subservience and inferiority of women, was sufficiently flexible and various in its evidence to be invoked on behalf of antithetical arguments. Participants present a considerable array of opinion on women and thus call into question any sense of a monolithic "ancient view" of women, which remained unassailed until the late eighteenth century. These conferences are nearly untouched by the new mechanical philosophy, yet the discussions of the relationship between science and gender show no trace whatsoever of what is often claimed as the pre-mechanical veneration of nature as female.[119] The most prevalent scientific understanding of women also does not suggest openness to the participation of women in academic or scientific life.[120] While some men speak on behalf of women, it is generally to argue against a vice that has been attributed to them.[121]

Participants use science as the basis of gender analysis, but this use is shaped and constrained by the premises of Aristotelian biology. The life sciences of the early seventeenth century offered only mild emendations to the dominant sway Aristotle held over the study of all living creatures. Although Aristotle's cosmology was under assault by the sixteenth century, his biology was not thoroughly undermined until the nineteenth century. Thus, although these documents offer some striking defenses of women, the tone of the conferences on this issue is more consistently conservative than on other topics. Because participants are so aware that any change in the status or roles of women is rife with social and political implications, discussing women provokes vehement responses.

The discussion of women and their roles at the Bureau might simply be considered a mere rehash of conventional rhetorical treatments of the "woman question." It demonstrates what Ian Maclean has characterized as ratiocination, that is to say, "imprecise generalizations about society, anatomy, and psychology, often facetious speculation on the relative importance of men and women, facile comparisons with nature."[122] Maclean and other scholars express frustration with such rhetoric in part because they look forward to the clear, Cartesian feminism of François Poullain de la Barre's *De l'égalité des deux sexes* (1673). This text uses Descartes's separation of body and mind to develop a forceful argument about the abilities of women, because, as Poullain de la Barre so memorably puts it, "the mind has no sex." Although the conferees rarely demonstrate such philosophical clarity, they nonetheless offer an integration of the scientific, medical, and philosophical material available on the topic of sex and gender and make full use of the classical and humanist traditions. As with all other topics, they apply to these social issues what appeared to be the relevant scientific information. But unlike in their discussion of human beings in general, science does not give them a standpoint from which to overturn conventions about gender. On other topics, science opens the way for a critique of society, but because gender roles are rooted in Aristotelian biology, so consistently negative in its view of women, it is very difficult to argue from science for any alteration of women's roles. Some participants, as we have seen, offer criticism and rebuttals of Aristotle, but they are unable to develop a consistent scientific viewpoint that would overturn conventional views of women.

Although participants make many arguments entirely in keeping with other seventeenth-century treatments of these topics, their approach is different in substance and tone in several important respects. The most striking is that they do not define their arguments in scriptural or theological terms. Thus the weight of Christian arguments generally directed against women is not brought to bear in the conferences, and pious arguments advanced as part of the *femme dévote* tradition have no place. Speakers rarely sentimentalize women. The *honnête femme* tradition, so common to literature of the time, finds little expression. There are very few adulatory statements about the civilizing or ameliorating roles women might exercise on male character—a theme more characteristic of court culture than of the less restrictive culture of the conferences.[123]

If these conferences do not strike any blows toward the development of early modern feminism, they nonetheless do raise issues that continued to dominate discussion of women from the seventeenth century into the Enlightenment. The argument made in the conferences (a conventional argument extending back at least to Christine de Pizan in the fourteenth century) that bad education is responsible for the intellectual failings of women gained greater currency in the course of the seventeenth century. Mademoiselle de Scudéry and Madame de Sévigné pleaded for a more thorough education for women. This advocacy bore fruit in some educational institutions for women, such as the Maison Royale de Saint-Louis (known as Saint-Cyr) under the direction of Madame de Maintenon, with a curriculum inspired by Fénelon's *De l'éducation des filles*.[124] The conference on "If women should be learned" addresses an issue prominent later in the century, most notably in Molière's plays *Les Précieuses Ridicules* (1659) and *Les Femmes Savantes* (1672). A number of other points raised by specific conference topics are debated well into the seventeenth century. For example, the *précieuses* make important claims for the intelligence and literary independence of women, although other important contemporaries such as Malebranche rebut these claims by arguing that women have no gift for science or abstract thought. Poullain de la Barre's argument that "the mind has no sex" eventually made Cartesian rationalism a basis from which women could define, as Harth puts it, their "versions and subversions" of the implications of Cartesianism for both men and women.[125]

In the period immediately after the conferences, several important intellectual movements emerged that were dominated by women, most notably the literary movement of the *précieuses* and the culture of the salon. Even if it remains conceivable that women attended certain conferences, these were clearly not designed or dominated by women or (given some of the speeches on topics pertaining to their roles and status) particularly receptive to them.[126] But the new movements, initiated and perpetuated by women, were quite unusual in encouraging the participation of women. Many of the *précieuses* rebelled against the restriction of women to domestic roles, and some of them rejected marriage. These avant-garde movements provoked hostility from antifeminists, who repudiated a public life for women and advocated domesticity. Although the conferences largely preceded these more profeminist movements, conferees did explore women's roles and the nature of marriage, and it is significant that even those who argued against a revised view of women or new roles for them, did not relegate them to domesticity or sentimentalize the domestic.

The discussions of gender issues in the conferences expose the explicit connection between science and social issues. They bring science and culture to bear on each other as they look at issues of sex and gender from perspectives not generally found in other more strictly scientific or literary texts. They frequently raise the social implications of a scientific understanding of women. Their method of presentation is more wide-ranging and perhaps slightly more anecdotal than literary texts or more conventional scientific writings (although the science of the period is generally quite anecdotal). These discussions certainly present a broader spectrum of opinion than literary or scientific texts by any single author. They are extremely eclectic but not merely so; the discussion crosses categories and juxtaposes issues in a way that is disconcertingly foreign to modern sensibilities but also often creative.

The conferences, then, typify in less rigid, less professionalized form the limits of the scientific or biological basis for the discussion of women. It is disheartening to see the ways in which this analysis is so much less productive on these issues than on other kinds of topics. But the limits of science as applied by conferees may be significant to understanding important things about a culture of science in the early modern period. The discussion of women tells us important things about how science is embedded in culture. These particular discussions are not remote from other discussions of women at the time. The conferences further suggest that there should be no sense of a rigid demarcation in the views of women into modern and early modern until Aristotelian biology had been effectively challenged, so that it did not set the terms for discussion of women. (While Poullain de la Barre makes an interesting point that will provoke some debate, Descartes, and by extension Cartesian mechanism, does not offer a definite challenge to Aristotle's biology.) Thus the conferences attest to the very limited ways in which participants could even envision a scientific challenge to Aristotle. In this case, appeals to empirical evidence would have been hard to distinguish in their conclusions from the traditional invocations of litanies of virtuous or wicked women that defined so much early modern writing on women. It is significant that participants do not consider such evidence relevant, but had they wished to do so, science would not have given them grounds to overturn traditional views. The question of whether they wished to do so is important, because as we saw with the politics of the family, it is indeed questionable whether these male participants would have been interested in challenging their own self-interest. The limits of these discussions ultimately raise questions about whether new science can readily overthrow deeply rooted cultural presuppositions, or whether these presuppositions—often focusing on relations between the sexes—prove particularly resistant to new social uses. Or whether, on these topics, new scientific findings are likely to be deployed to support a traditional social order. Despite their less than progressive use of science on issues of gender, conferees made a case for the paramount importance of science as the basis for understanding society and for the role of science in defining culture.

From a Culture of Science toward the Enlightenment

"A MODEL OF OUR CIVILIZATION AND A MIRROR OF HUMAN LIFE"—
so Charles Sorel expressed his appreciation of the comprehensive and
inclusive character of Renaudot's conferences. They provided a model
of civilization because of their open, accessible, and inclusive form of
intellectual exchange. They mirrored human life in the range of topics
they covered, from the natural to the political.

This conclusion begins then, as did this book, with the unique character of Renaudot's conferences. By Renaudot's deliberate design, there
can be no protagonists in this history. Because of his highly unusual
notion that the most appropriate way to convey knowledge is to have
anonymous speakers make presentations in a group as large as the room
could hold, the efforts of historians to attach concrete biographical data
to any of the participants or to provide a sociological analysis of the
group and its ideas have been thwarted.[1] We know no better at the end
of this study who attended the conferences than we did at the beginning. Even if more evidence ultimately comes to light about individual
participants, it would nonetheless remain impossible to assign specific
speeches to them. So this history is populated by the ideas of those who

attended. Those ideas are naked, without the robes of external authority. Only the intellectual antecedents so significant that they could be mentioned without violating the spirit of Renaudot's injunction against sustaining one's argument through the authority of others—Aristotle, Plato, Cicero, Montaigne, Ficino—appear in this history and then only as venerated shades. Participants did not embellish their remarks with extensive quotations, so even the intellectual context is more suggestive than concrete. The disembodied character of these conferences frustrates the historian's occupational proclivity to anchor ideas in a concrete context.

Despite the limits of the historical analysis one can bring to bear, these documents belong in our histories of the seventeenth century. They illuminate virtually every topic they address, from science to gender. Because they treat such a broad array of topics in such an undogmatic way, they better represent contemporary opinion than do elite academies. Because they took place in the 1630s and 1640s, crucial decades in the development of the new science and absolutism, they add important dimensions to our understanding of the early seventeenth century. But their import is even greater. They amplify—and in some cases provide counter-narratives to—conventional accounts of the history of France, its intellectual history, and particularly the history of early modern science.

The lacunae in our historical knowledge of this group were quite deliberately created: sociological knowledge was not as significant as what they discussed; it would only distract the reader from the ideas, precluding the ultimate recognition of and assent to truth. So, to our surprise, participants did not consider the experiments they performed worth publishing and recording, although such records would better integrate them into the history of science and would enhance their modern reputation. Instead it was important to publish multiple views on the questions raised. The participants produced an extensive record of their conversations to edify their contemporaries, to provide the service of comprehensive (by their lights) public knowledge so that truth would out. This truth would only be clouded by such extraneous information as the name, status, and reputation of the participants.

The conferences deliberately intended to treat a full range of questions, to present a veritable seventeenth-century encyclopedia. They frequently raise these issues as questions (often conventional questions within the *quodlibetal* tradition), and the knowledge presented is quite deliberately polyvalent. They do not mean to offer one, definitive answer, so their notion of an encyclopedia is somewhat different from that of the grand *Encyclopédie* of d'Alembert and Diderot. This encyclopedia stands as a monument to eighteenth-century thought—and indeed it would be unthinkable for historians to deny that role to the *Encyclopédie*. But in many ways Renaudot's conferences are better examples of encyclopedic knowledge and are perhaps even more revealing of their age, because of the great variety of views they present. Conference pieces were not written by carefully selected experts. They were not commissioned by the editors to offer a like-minded perspective or to present a single, authoritative view. Instead, Renaudot and his conferees were more interested in presenting an open view, unconstrained by any editor's proclivities or ideology. As we have repeatedly remarked, not even issues of the greatest interest to Renaudot (chemical medicine, for example) go unchallenged. The conferences encourage as free and open a presentation of opinions as could be elicited from the audience.

Despite their truly encyclopedic character, the conferences did not fulfill Renaudot's hopes that they would serve posterity, be useful, and stand as an encyclopedia of seventeenth-century knowledge. Although they do in many ways epitomize these hopes for modern historians seeking to understand the seventeenth century, they did not immediately serve posterity; they were not recognized by Renaudot's successors as having established an encyclopedic basis of knowledge nor did they have a pronounced effect on the next generation. Several short-lived groups, like that of Pierre Bourdelot, tried to replicate the form of the conferences, but they could not flourish without the kind of protection that Richelieu had afforded Renaudot. There are other, more compelling reasons that Renaudot's group did not exert much influence or have direct followers in the succeeding generations. The open, egalitarian notion of scientific discussion promoted by Renaudot was foreign to the world of state-sponsored science, like that of the Académie des Sciences. Renaudot's conception of public discourse, where ideas were presented without editorial comment and without crediting the speaker, was antithetical to the self-promotion and the jockeying for position and patronage necessary to succeed in the much more rigid, stratified society under Louis XIV. Renaudot's idealization of the anonymous presentation of ideas was out of step with the desire of scientists and philosophers to use their ideas to establish their reputations and then to use their reputations to gain patronage, position, and status.

Not only did the practice of science and its venues change dramatically from the period of Renaudot's conferences to that of the Académie des Sciences, the very nature of science changed. Cartesian mechanism swept Paris. It offered the features we more typically associate with the culture of science—the professionalized scientist, a mathematical understanding of nature, and the use of carefully measured experiments. Mechanism narrowed the scope of science to physics (although it was quickly applied to other areas like chemistry and medicine) and narrowed the method of science to mathematics.[2] The late seventeenth century responded to its crisis of knowledge by privileging mathematics, by rejecting the deductive and the empirical as only probable.[3] But these were the very kinds of inquiries most central to Renaudot's gatherings.

Perhaps most significant, the mathematization of science professionalized its practitioners. Science, as the stuff of sequestered academics competing for funding and for election to academies, became remote from the culture of the ordinary educated person. This newer culture of science combined with the culture of the court not only changed the nature of scientific discussion, it decisively separated science from culture at large—that is to say, science became more specialized and divorced from broader cultural issues. As Descartes forcefully insisted in the *Discourse on Method*, science was irrelevant to broader cultural concerns, especially the controversial subjects of religion, politics, and custom. Cartesian mechanism both privileged physics and separated science from the human sciences. Thus the science cultivated by Renaudot's group was too inclusive to be credible later in the century. The method practiced, if indeed one can be deduced from their very eclectic conversations, was too polymorphous, anecdotal, descriptive, and inconclusive. And science as understood by Renaudot's group was both essential and integral to social analysis. Their approach was rapidly superseded by a more rigid, hierarchical, state-controlled culture, which fostered a science clearly at odds with the conferees' understanding of science, especially its utility in social analysis. The conferences thus have no obvious intellectual heirs in the culture of absolutism and state-sponsored academic science.

It is ironic that, although mechanism divorced science from social concerns, it also made scientific prestige central to the culture and popularized science more accessible to the layman.[4] It fostered a new scientific culture in which scientists competed for what might be called the entertainment dollar of absolutist culture under Louis XIV and Louis XV—public experiments, demonstrations, and dissections could vie with plays and musical entertainments to attract seventeenth-century audiences.[5] These kinds of activities brought science to the layman, but in most cases the purpose was not to move the understanding but to delight the imagination. The scientific experiment was like the deus ex machina of classical theater; it defied expectations and provoked astonishment at the marvels of technology. Science, it can be argued, became not the common coin of discourse, as it was for Renaudot's conferees, but a method of demonstration.

The conventional recounting of the scientific revolution heralds the arrival of a mechanical science shaped by a rigorous method, produced by an increasingly professional group whose ways were too specialized for ordinary understanding. It is not surprising, then, that a group of conferees seeking to make knowledge public and accessible, to apply science as a method of rational analysis to all aspects of culture, and to break down, at least to some degree, social barriers to the acquisition of knowledge in the old regime would not be viewed as venerated ancestors by proponents of a new, narrower notion of scientific culture. The openness of Renaudot's group—with its implicit iconoclasm, both intellectual and social—makes it distinctive in the culture of the old regime. By the 1660s such iconoclasm would have been almost unimaginable in the meticulously hierarchical society of the court of Louis XIV. Both the organization and the mission of intellectual gatherings like Renaudot's are thus antithetical to the culture of absolutism. Although it had some modest and short-lived successors, Renaudot's group demonstrated a degree of intellectual independence that would not have been possible later. Its form—open, inclusive, unconstrained, egalitarian—could not be adapted to the dictates of classical style or to the social protocols of the court. The reformist agenda of Renaudot and the distinctive fusion of science and human science his group presented did not conform to the new science of the scientific revolution; the fluidity of its form did not correspond to the rigidity of culture in the court of Louis XIV.

Later in the seventeenth century, Renaudot's conferences could not have been as unconstrained in content as they were. To a degree unimaginable under Louis XIV, Renaudot's group avoided censorship or prohibition of the topics they discussed (though they themselves claimed to eschew religion and politics).[6] Their conversations were not stifled by a monarch like Louis XIV, who was both concerned with the expression of opinion and able to constrain opinion within the range he deemed acceptable. French intellectual life had not yet felt the chilling effect of the Fronde. That revolt, which took place from 1648 to 1653, began as a revolt by the parlementary judges of Paris but soon spread to involve the nobility and their troops. It made such an impression on the young Louis XIV that he removed his court to Versailles where he could both control the nobility and make royal patronage the source of most cultural productions. But because the conferences occurred in a less constrained environment, they could explore unconventional and even politically suspect ideas. Renaudot's group does not resemble the culture and science of the next generation and very likely would not have flourished or perhaps even survived in it.

Largely because his interests were so uncharacteristic of the culture of absolutism, Renaudot has only just begun to warrant mention in histories of the seventeenth century. Many use the period of Louis XIV as the standard for discussing the entire century. Most histories of philosophy in the seventeenth century take Descartes as a starting point, and histories of science move along the classic line from Galileo to Descartes to Newton.[7] The culture of the 1630s and 1640s, which

Renaudot's conferences show was quite rich and creative, is considered significant only as a forerunner to the culture of absolutism or mechanism. Renaudot's conferences suggest that this period should be reassessed to explore at greater length the connections between science and culture, precisely because this period was less constrained by absolutism or mechanism. Renaudot's conferences sustain a different reading of the connections between science and culture than is standard. This counter-reading suggests that the reign of Louis XIV with its espousal of mechanism, absolutism, and classicism should be seen as anomalous rather than characteristic of the early modern period. Just as Renaudot's conferences have greater affinity with the reactions against the culture of absolutism in the Enlightenment than with the period that immediately followed, so too the history of early modern France might better be understood as a period of cultural complexity, vitality, and critical acuity, interrupted by the long but unusual period of absolutism—the reign of Louis XIV.

Treating Louis XIV's reign as anomalous rather than as characteristic of early modern France can be productive in many respects. It allows us to focus on the great intellectual dynamism and the myriad forms of intellectual life that characterized France in the aftermath of the wars of religion, illuminating a rich embodiment of the republic of letters.[8] Such a reorientation also allows us to recognize the vitality of French scientific discussion. (The French academic tradition has not cultivated its own history of science and, with the significant exception of Descartes, the anglophone tradition has largely neglected it.) If absolutism is not considered the end point of early modern culture, we can see in the early seventeenth century concerted and productive social analysis and the application of a growing fascination with science to such analyses. If these analyses are not dismissed as unproductive because of subsequent absolutist constraints on such inquiries, they can be acknowledged as offering, at the very least, important antecedents of Enlightenment social science.

Renaudot's conferences sustain these arguments for the significance of the early seventeenth century in all these respects and in quite specific ways. The broad notion of science as the basis of a shared culture, both advocated and demonstrated by the conferences, most persuasively and logically ties them to the social sciences of these later periods. In these conferences, participants deploy scientific knowledge in new ways. They move beyond the Renaissance ethos and toward the Enlightenment, beyond the humanistic invocation of "nature" and toward the more definitive uses of nature as a foundation for understanding society.

Other connections can be productively drawn between Renaudot's group and the Enlightenment. Renaudot's group can reasonably be considered as an early forerunner of the culture of the republic of letters, and its members as antecedents to the philosophes of the French Enlightenment. This is not to say that the philosophes are directly indebted to Renaudot, but rather that his conferences suggest greater affinities between the early seventeenth and mid–eighteenth century than one might expect. Renaudot's conferences seem quite remote from the spirit and structure of classicism. The affinities between Renaudot's group and the philosophes should cause us to reflect on the supposed reliance of the Enlightenment on Newtonian science as a source of social criticism or the general belief that the mechanical sciences are the source or model of the social sciences. Many of the fundamental attitudes often identified with the Enlightenment are found in this very early group with only minimal exposure to the new mechanical philosophy—and of course no familiarity at all with Newton.

There are good reasons that Renaudot's group took positions akin to those taken later by Enlightenment philosophes. Philosophes reacted against the constraints of an established classicism and absolutism. Although their crusade was much more explicitly reformist and progressive, the greater openness they sought resembles that practiced by conferees. Like members of Renaudot's group, the philosophes could maneuver more effectively, better evade censors, and act with greater intellectual independence than intellectuals under Louis XIV. Despite their greater autonomy, they too chafed against a rigid social hierarchy and sought new audiences, appealing as Renaudot had done to a broadly inclusive understanding of the public.

The nature and character of science in the conferences has great affinity with sciences of the Enlightenment. Lorraine Daston's characterization of Enlightenment science suggests some very telling comparisons between Enlightenment science and the approach taken by Renaudot's conferees. Because Enlightenment science was so rich and diverse, she identifies certain expectations of science as the unifying ground on which these diverse manifestations can best be understood. Above all, the enlightened emphasized utility; they extolled science as the basis for material improvement and were "passionate for the moral and material improvement of the human estate." The Enlightenment was also, as Daston terms it, a veritable "echo chamber" of constant discussion of scientific topics in many venues.[9] These very attitudes are fundamental to Renaudot's conferences and perhaps most accurately describe their import as well. Both Renaudot's conferences and Enlightenment science were conducted with a concern to weigh ideas and information by the standards of utility and to disseminate them. Conferees thus pursued a goal of public enlightenment as well as offering, initially, a focused "echo chamber" of scientific and cultural discourse and then one broadly disseminated through print. Like the proponents of enlightened science, conferees were united more by shared values than by professional expertise, and they, like the philosophes, advocated the open dissemination of knowledge.

The Enlightenment has often been presented as the result of a more or less simplistic application of Newtonian science to the social sphere. But as the study of Enlightenment science has developed, it has become increasingly evident that this science was much more complex, diverse, and sophisticated than the conventional view suggests. When one probes beneath the surface, it is clear that Enlightenment science was extremely wide-ranging and diverse. It did not simply focus on the mathematical sciences but also became increasingly preoccupied with the earth sciences and the biological sciences, just as Renaudot's conferees had been. The annals of Enlightenment science record, although some histories of science do not much emphasize them, the works of Georges Buffon, Benoît de Maillet, and J.-B. Robinet. Enlightenment figures, like Renaudot's conferees, were students of nature, captivated by the study of natural phenomena. Although mechanism still retained a great hold over the scientific imagination and practice, it had also, by the first decades of the eighteenth century, begun to provoke some criticism as too narrow and too rigid.[10] Even such a devoted proponent of the "geometrical method" as Fontenelle recognized that "some room must be allowed for the empirical study of nature," and as early as 1753, Diderot bemoaned the tyranny of mathematics over the investigation of nature.[11]

Renaudot's group offers a well-developed, early modern manifestation of these more diverse interests, which will again occupy many eighteenth-century figures not only in France but also throughout Europe. Conferees discussed an array of natural phenomena and explored the sciences with a sense of nature's amplitude, incorporating natural history, geology, and chemistry. In other words, they looked to the actual world of nature, which mechanism tended to neglect. This is not to say that scientific discussion in the Enlightenment returned to as broad and diverse a theoretical base as Renaudot's conferees were willing to explore. But some of the areas that early eighteenth-century thinkers were most interested in were no more than slightly amenable to mechanism, and these were just the areas of investigation that Renaudot's group pursued: geology, physiology, the natural sciences, and medicine. But the continuing propensity of historians of science to privilege the physical sciences and to idealize a mathematical method has distorted the understanding of both early seventeenth-century science and the Enlightenment. Perhaps (as Renaudot's group suggests) the earth sciences, physiology, the natural sciences, and medicine should be recognized as of far greater significance to the development of social science and Enlightenment thought than historians generally concede.

Of course, science, as Renaudot's group uses it, is full of contradiction and competing theories in virtually every subdiscipline, and these competing theories offer useful explanatory devices extending far beyond conventional applications of science. For conferees, science—whatever model one held—could be used to comment effectively not only on scientific but also on social concerns. These conferences stand at a critical point of transition in the use of science as means of social analysis, demonstrating how the application of science to social topics could fundamentally alter the tenor of discussion. That analysis is neither as progressive as one might hope in a time of increasing absolutism, nor as focused and reform-minded as the analysis of the philosophes. Nonetheless, using science as a touchstone for discussing ethics, social practices, and political issues alters the character of discussion—religious arguments are excluded and arguments from authorities discouraged, so much so that the tenor of the conferences is strikingly distinct from that of other contemporary documents.

Many scholars have pointed to the greater secularism of the Enlightenment as a defining characteristic of the movement, especially in conjunction with an emphasis on science at the expense of theology. Whether or not it was the intention of Renaudot's group, their discussions serve to separate decisively religion from science, and (perhaps equally significant) religion from social analysis. This group was overtly opposed to religious explanations (though a few participants gave them), disinclined to credit tradition and authority, and inclined to favor instead the experiential, the pragmatic, and the demonstrable. Participants were acutely aware that science could both privilege arguments and give them a new authority to wield against old authorities. The "scientific perspective" was brought to bear on issues that would previously have been treated rhetorically, theologically, or metaphysically, and this produces a striking secular feel to these conferences. The cultivation of science per se was proclaimed as progressive and utilitarian. Like the philosophes, conferees recognized that unenlightened opinions could harden into prejudice.

The absence of appeals to religion in the conferences calls into question Paul Hazard's famous remark distinguishing the late seventeenth century from the Enlightenment. He described a revolutionary change of perspective: "One day the French people almost to a man were thinking like Bossuet. The day after they were thinking like Voltaire."[12] The conferences vividly demonstrate that, long before the advent of the Enlightenment, scarcely a single participant in Renaudot's conferences thought like Bossuet, and some shared attitudes that would later characterize the philosophes. The conferences also fostered attitudes essential to the development of the Enlightenment by eroding religious authority in specific ways. For example, a staunch reliance on the theory of temperaments undercut the significance of the soul in understanding human beings—an approach common among eighteenth-century physicians and physiologists. Like many Enlightenment figures, conferees demonstrated an appreciation for the relativity of customs and cultures. The model physician of the conferees—moderate, perhaps disinterested, and certainly not fanatical, immune to prejudice and thus able to evaluate evidence dispassionately, unfettered by religious or political restrictions, guided instead by empirical and pragmatic considerations—conjures up the philosophe.

Conferees and philosophes share similar epistemological positions. In some respects, the conferences prefigure Immanuel Kant's clarion call to Enlightenment, *sapere aude* (dare to know). Kant's first injunction to his contemporaries was to leave behind intellectual immaturity, which he defined as the incapacity to use one's mind without the guidance of others. Conferees, because of their willingness to cast aside the weight of the authorities of the past, demonstrate many of the same approaches to knowledge that the philosophes espouse. Both groups assume that nature can be known, that man should be placed in relationship to nature, and that nature prescribes the social.[13] D'Alembert rejects skepticism in favor of science, an attitude he shares with conferees, when he urges, "Therefore let us believe without wavering that in fact our sensations have the cause outside ourselves which we suppose them to have; because the effect which can result from the real existence of that cause could not differ in any way from the effect we experience."[14]

Although conferees effectively apply science to social analysis, such applications have impressed historians as strikingly progressive only when the analysis is based on the application of the "true science" of mechanism or Newtonianism. It has been easier for historians to discount the disconcertingly eclectic science of groups like Renaudot's than to recognize it as a significant, early modern application of science to society.

Much recent literature cites the Enlightenment as the source of the embryonic social sciences, although to avoid anachronism in talking about the origins of the social sciences, historians have used the term *human sciences* instead.[15] One can, for example, readily connect early eighteenth-century moralistic preoccupations with human nature to the origins of the social sciences. Those who developed the human sciences considered human nature and the nature and roles of women, tried to integrate man into nature, detached politics and ethics from tradition and religion—all with the aid of science. The early explorations of the "human sciences" during the eighteenth century return to points raised and concerns expressed by Renaudot's conferees.

Various Enlightenment authors proclaimed they were turning their attention, as none had done before, to the science of man. Ultimately, they are credited with the development of anthropology, sociology, psychology, and like sciences. Although it is certainly legitimate to point to the eighteenth century as the period when these issues became central intellectual concerns, this study makes clear that a century earlier Renaudot's group was preoccupied with the same issues. Their discussions can thus be used to trace further back into the early modern period the emergence of the social sciences.[16] It is perhaps peculiar, by our lights, that Renaudot's participants considered their rather inchoate understanding of science to be a sufficient basis for discussion of the human sciences. Even if they do not articulate as clear a social scientific agenda as the philosophes, they nonetheless consistently demonstrate their sense that science provides the best evidence and means of analysis of the social.

The conferences look ahead to the Enlightenment not only in content but also in form. The scientific community as defined by Renaudot has much in common with the later republic of letters. There are tantalizing connections suggested by the recent intense historiographical discussion of the phenomenon called the republic of letters. We are well aware of the appeals of the philosophes to a "republic of letters" during the eighteenth century as an idealized, fictional location where merit would prevail over privilege, equality over hierarchy, independence of mind over appeals to tradition. This eighteenth-century manifestation of the republic, unlike earlier incarnations, privileged the French language and thus French intellectuals.[17] This vision has elicited both contemporary and modern criticisms. Robert Darnton has highlighted the discontents of second-generation philosophes, like Mercier and Brissot, who could not gain admittance.[18] Others have pointed to the aristocratic composition of this reputed republic and questioned the intellectual independence of a republic whose members were funded by patronage. Regardless of its limitations, the notion allowed eighteenth-century men of letters to construct an idealized form of intellectual exchange and a community that challenged the more hide-bound and elitist institutions of the past.

This distinctive, eighteenth-century French manifestation of the republic of letters drew on earlier notions of the republic, which had developed chiefly in England and the Netherlands around the practitioners of print culture. As Anne Goldgar has demonstrated, this incarnation was characterized, as her title reinforces, by "impolite learning" and an emphasis on hierarchy within the new print culture.[19] (An even earlier French incarnation of the republic in the late seventeenth century was closely tied to court culture and could be considered neither independent nor egalitarian.)

It is the later development of the republic of letters among the philosophes that most emphatically illustrates just how much ahead of its time Renaudot's group was.[20] What explicitly connects Renaudot's group to later formulations of the republic of letters? The conferences demonstrate great openness, which Fontenelle contended was the identifying characteristic of the republic of letters. The conferences, like that republic, are rooted in the academic culture of Renaissance humanism. They appeal to the wider public both as audience and as potential adjudicator of opinion; they are offered without editorial comment, laying before their audience and readership a rich fare of scientific and cultural commentary. Renaudot's group did not simply pay lip service to egalitarianism; its forum was as universal, inclusive, and democratic as any in the early modern period, so much so that the gatherings offered no possible basis for hierarchy or the advancement of participants.

Although Renaudot defined the notion of an intellectual community in a strikingly original way for the seventeenth century, his definition becomes much more familiar if it is placed in a later context. His group probably included professionals, but its membership was not defined in terms of professional expertise, and even more significant, it was not defined by privilege. Its operating assumptions were more like those of an intellectual "republic" and thus antithetical to more formal academic institutions. The group emphasized consensus through the open presentation of multiple perspectives rather than individual endeavor. It was cooperative rather than competitive, anonymous rather than based on the credibility of participating members. It was open both in terms of its membership and its receptivity to eclectic ideas. In some ways these characteristics make it even more idealistic than any of the actual incarnations—and even conceptions—of the republic of letters. (This greater idealism might well have impeded the quest for professional success of members as intellectual figures, which was certainly a goal of many participants in later incarnations of the republic of letters.) The notion of intellectual community embodied by Renaudot's group might have been too inclusive even for the Enlightenment republic of letters; it suggests a model of science and medicine open to all educated men (and potentially women as well). It was not restricted to the traditional educated elites. It was iconoclastic and potentially subversive. Instead of suggesting, as scientists frequently did, that science transcended social and political concerns, this group provided a model of science as an effective means of social analysis.[21]

The progressive egalitarianism of the conferences suggests certain affinities between these anonymous individuals who gathered to discuss intellectual issues for nine years on one hand and the collective enterprise of the encyclopedists on the other. Conferees obviously share a sense of the pursuit of knowledge as a collective endeavor, perhaps fulfilling, as the English translator of the first two hundred conferences proclaimed, the agenda for science set by Francis Bacon—a claim d'Alembert more famously made later for the *Encyclopédie*. Because they attempted to break with their cultural antecedents or at least leave them unacknowledged and unspecified, they were able (as indeed were the philosophes) to claim science and the prospects it entailed as a new approach to social issues. Because they did not extensively cite their cultural antecedents, they could appeal to science as the new foundation for their analysis of culture; thus they had both a scientific agenda and a unifying platform. Like the encyclopedists, Renaudot's conferees understood knowledge to be progressive, but their expectations were less sanguine and less overtly positive. It is one thing to believe that knowledge is liberating and that the truth will out. It is another to believe that one already has the foundation for knowledge that will inevitably yield progress. In other words, conferees shared attitudes with the encyclopedists but did not express them with such self-assurance. They did not have as clear a definition of science or vision of what it could accomplish; nor did they have the experience of the mature absolutism of Louis XIV to give them a clear social and political agenda. Thus the social analysis of the conferees, while rooted in science like that of the Enlightenment, was less developed both because they were not united in concerted opposition to absolutism and because their sense of science provided a less uniform foundation.

This group's discussions offer a unique perspective for future research because participants critically reexamined received wisdom and thoughtfully employed scientific positions to comment on their culture. They provide ground on which it is possible to engage current historiographical debates on the new roles of intellectuals in the transformation of discourse in the public sphere, the relationship between intellectual and social history, and the relationship between science and gender. They raise issues of ethics, morals, and social values and shed light on broader perspectives such as the history of mentalities or moral economies. The conferences document that culture under Louis XIII has been understood too much in terms of the absolutism of Louis XIV. They show the earlier period's vibrancy and affinities to the Enlightenment's full-blown application of science to social issues.

The present study supports much larger contentions as well: that intellectual issues are crucial in constructing social reality for any modern social group, and that the intellectual issues of the early modern period are neither as static nor as uniform as the contours of traditional intellectual history suggest. It exposes the insufficiently explored congruencies of the history of science and intellectual history; it contests the remnant positivism that still adheres to some histories of science; it sheds light on the nature and character of science in the age of the scientific revolution. We must conclude, ultimately, that Renaudot's conferees did leave an important but neglected legacy. By discussing and weighing all the seventeenth-century sciences, they extended the sense of the relevance and the range of the application of science. They not only fostered a culture of science and the early development of the social sciences; they also created a set of expectations about the interpenetration of nature and culture that constitute the basis of modern civilization.

List of Conferences Cited

"Auquel on est plus obligé au père ou a la mère," 197, Tuesday, 3 May 1639, 4:45–49.

"Combien peut estre l'homme sans manger," 15.1, 28 November 1633, 1:117–21.

"Comment ceux qui sont mordus de la Tarantole guérissent par le son de quelque instrument Musical," 332, 19 May 1642, 5:167–70.

"Comment croissent les Mineraux?" 44.1, 19 June 1634, 1:353–57.

"Comment se fait l'accroissement," 131, 2 March 1637, 3:197–200.

"Comment s'engendrent les malles & les femelles," 185, 17 January 1639, 3:521–25.

"De Goust," 55.1, 4 December 1634, 2:41–43.

"De la Beauté," 26.2, 13 February 1634, 1:213–16.

"De la Cabbale," 37, 2 May 1634, 1:297–302.

"De la cause des Seditions," 337, 23 June 1642, 5:192–96.

"De la Chastété," 71.2, 27 March 1635, 2:173–76.

"De la Communauté des biens," 76.2, 7 May 1635, 2:213–17.

"De la Conference, & si c'est la plus instructive sorte d'enseigner," 285, 4 March 1641, 4:417–21.

"De la Coustume," 63.2, 29 January 1635, 2:108–12.

"De la Cure magnetique des maladies," 68.1, 5 March 1635, 2:145–49.

"De la danse," 66.2, 19 February 1635, 2:133–37.

"De la diversité des langues," 42, 7 June 1634, 1:341–44.

"De la fortune," 54.2, 27 November 1634, 2:36–40.

"De la generation des Metaux," 137, 20 April 1637, 3:221–24.

"De la goutte," 102, 18 February 1636, 3:17–22.

"De la Honte," 70.2, 19 March 1635, 2:165–68.

"De la Iolousie," 27.2, 20 February 1634, 1:221–24.

"De l'air," 7.1, 3 October 1633, 1:49–55.

"De la lépre, & pourquoi elle n'est pas si commune en ce siecle qu'aux precedens," 75.1, 30 April 1635, 2:201–5.

"De la Lethargie," 140, 11 May 1637, 3:233–37.

"De la Licorne," 248, 11 June 1640, 4:245–52.

"De la lumière," 59.1, 2 January 1635, 2:73–77.

"De la Mandragore," 222, 9 January 1640, 4:161–68.

"De la Matiere premiere," 4.1, 12 September 1633, 1:25–29.

"De la Métempsycose," 143, 8 June 1637, 3:245–49.

"De la methode," 1.1, 22 August 1633, 1:6–7.

"De l'amitié," 38.2, 8 May 1634, 1:309–12.

"De la Mort," 67.1, 25 February 1635, 2:137–43.

"De l'Antiperistaze," 340, 14 July 1642, 5:209–13.

"De la pathie des Stoïques," 251, 9 July 1640, 4:261–64.

"De la petite fille velüe qui se voit en cette ville," 11.2, 31 October 1633, 1:81–86.

"De la Physiognomie," 23.1, 23 January 1634, 1:185–88.

"De la Pierre Philosophale," 43.1, 12 June 1634, 1:345–49.

"De la Poudre de Sympathie," 342, 4 August 1642, 5:220–25.

"De l'apparition des Esprits ou Phantomes," 79.2, 4 June 1635, 2:235–40.

"De la purgation, & si on la peut faire en tout temps," 320, 24 January 1642, 5:107–12.

"De la quint'essence," 60.1, 8 January 1635, 2:81–85.

"De la Rage," 76.1, 7 May 1635, 2:209–13.

"De la Ressemblance," 5.1, 19 September 1633, 1:33–37.

"De l'art de Raimond Lulle," 204, 27 June 1639, 4:77–81.

"De la Saignée," 105.1, 10 March 1636, 3:41–45.

"De l'astrologie judiciaire," 22.1, 16 January 1634, 1:177–80.

"De la Sympathie & Antipathie," 32.1, 27 March 1634, 1:257–61.

"De la terre," 17 October 1633, 9.1, 1:65–69.

"De la Veuë," 58.1, 27 December 1634, 2:65–69.

"De la vie," 69.1, 12 March 1635, 2:153–57.

"De l'eau," 8.1, 10 October 1633, 1:57–61.

"De l'eloquence," 56.2, 11 December 1634, 2:53–56.

"De l'Envie," 73.2, 16 April 1635, 2:190–92.

"De l'epilepsie ou haut mal," 80.1, 12 June 1635, 2:241–45.

"De l'Harmonie," 57.2, 18 December 1634, 2:61–65.

"De L'Heur & du Mal-heur; & si les hommes sont heureux ou malheureux, pour ce qu'ils le sont, ou pour ce qu'ils le pensent estre," 135, 30 March 1637, 3:213–16.

"De l'intellect," 65.1, 12 February 1635, 2:121–25.

"De l'iyvrognerie," 66.1, 19 February 1635, 2:129–33.

"De l'Odorat," 56.1, 11 December 1634, 2:49–53.

"De l'origine des Pierres Précieuses," 136, 6 April 1637, 3:217–20.

"De l'origine des Fontaines," 20.1, 2 January 1634, 1:161–65.

"De l'Origine des Formes," 122, 29 December 1636, 3:161–64.

"De l'origine des montagnes," 188, 7 February 1639, 4:9–12.

"De l'Oüye," 57.1, 18 December 1634, 2:57–61.

"Des amuletes, & si l'on peut guérir les maladies par paroles, brevets, ou autres choses penduës au col, ou attachées aux corps des malades," 173, 17 May 1638, 3:465–68.

"Des Causes en general," 3.1, 5 September 1633, 1:17–20.

"Des causes de la petite Verole," 126, 26 January 1637, 3:177–80.

"Des Cométes," 41.1, 29 May 1634, 1:329–33.

"Des deux frères Monstrueux, vivans en un mesme corps, que se voyent à present en cette ville," 10.2, 24 October 1633, 1:78–80.

"Des diuers termes de l'accouchement des femmes, & pourquoi les enfans viuent plustost à sept mois qu'à huict," 303, 19 August 1641, 5:29–34.

"Des Eaux Minerales," 110.1, 21 April 1636, 3:82–85.

"Des Espéces visibles," 47.2, 10 July 1634, 1:381–84.

"Des Fables, & si elles apportent plus de mal que de bien," 283, 18 February 1641, 4:409–12.

"Des Incubes & Succubes & Si les Demons peuvent engendrer," 128, 9 February 1637, 3:185–88.

"Des inventions & de leurs causes & principes," 206, 11 July 1639, 4:85–89.

"Des masques, & s'il est permis de se déguiser," 282, 11 February 1641, 4:405–9.

"Des moyens de rendre quelque lieu peuplé," 75.2, 30 April 1635, 2:205–8.

"Des pâles-couleurs," 100.1, 4 February 1636, 2:413–15.

"Des principes & de la fin de toutes choses," 2.1, 29 August 1633, 1:9–13.

"Des principes de Chymie," 260, 3 September 1640, 4:305–8.

"Des Satyres," 250, 25 June 1640, 4:257–60.

"Des Somnambules," 33.1, 3 April 1634, 1:265–69.

"Des Sorciers," 77.1, 14 May 1635, 2:217–22.

"Des Taches & autres marques qui paroissent au visage," 335, 9 June 1642, 5:182–86.

"Des taches de la lune et du soliel," 93.1, 17 December 1635, 2:349–56.

"Des Talismans," 108.1, 7 April 1636, 3:65–70.

"Des Volcans," 109.1, 14 April 1636, 3:73–77.

"De trois Soleils," 12.1, 7 November 1633, 1:93–96.

"D'où viennent les bons & mauvais gestes, la bonne grace & les grimaces," 189, 21 February 1639, 4:13–17.

"D'où viennent les Crises des maladies," 168, 12 April 1638, 3:445–48.

"D'ou viennent les marques que les enfans apportent du ventre de leur mere," 120, 22 December 1636, 3:149–56.

"D'où vient la diversité des opinions," 158, 18 January 1638, 3:405–8.

"D'où vient le Présage que l'on tire de quelques animaux?" 40.1, 22 May 1634, 1:321–24.

"Du Bain," 83.1, 9 July 1635, 2:265–70.

"Du Bezoard," 256, 6 August 1640, 4:289–93.

"Du Caprice des Femmes," 46.2, 3 July 1634, 1:372–76.

"Du circuit ou accez des Fiévres," 38.1, 8 May 1634, 1:305–9.

"Du Courage," 48.2, 17 July 1634, 1:389–92.

"Du feu," 6.1, 26 September 1633, 1:41–46.

"Du flux & reflux de la mer," 19.1, 28 December 1633, 1:153–57.

"Du Menage," 345, 1 September 1642, 5:235–38.

"Du Mont de Pieté," 43.2, 12 June 1634, 1:348–52.

"Du mouvement ou repos de la Terre," 10.1, 24 October 1633, 1:73–78.

"Du Poinct d'Honneur," 19.2, 28 December 1633, 1:157–60.

"Duquel l'enfant tient-il le plus, du pere ou de la mere?" 287, 18 March 1641, 4:425–29.

"Du Réglement des Pauvres," 35.1, Wednesday, 19 April 1634, 1:284–8.

"Du Ris," 24.2, 30 January 1634, 1:197–200.

"Du Tact," 54.1, 27 November 1634, 2:33–36.

"Du tentement d'Oreille," 322, 10 March 1642, 5:117–21.

"Du Tremblement de Terre," 73.1, 16 April 1635, 2:185–90.

"Du Vuide," 46.1, 3 July 1634, 1:369–72.

"En quel temps l'ame raisonable est infuse," 142, 25 May 1637, 3:241–44.

"Est il plus expediant dans une Guerre Ciuile demeurer neutre que prendre party," 336, 16 June 1642, 5:187–91.

"Et du mouvement perpetuel," 4.2, 12 September 1633, 1:29–32.

"Et pourquoy chacun est jaloux de ses opinions, n'y eust-il aucun autre interest," 3.2, 5 September 1633, 1:20–24.

"Il faut escrire comme l'on pronounce, ou suivre l'ancienne & commune orthographe," 186, 24 January 1639, 4:1–5.

"Laquelle est à preférer de la mort naturelle ou

civile," 272, 26 November 1640, 4:357–60.

"Laquelle est la plus insuportable des offences de l'amie ou de l'ennemi," 196, 18 April 1639, 4:41–45.

"Le commerce deroge-t-il à la Noblesse?" 160, 1 February 1638, 3:413–16.

"Le courage est-il naturel ou aquis?" 155, 22 December 1637, 3:393–96.

"Lequel aimé le plus ses enfans du père ou de la mère," 331, 12 May 1642, 5:162–67.

"Lequel est à preferer de parler le premier ou le dernier," 294, 3 June 1641, 4:453–57.

"Lequel est à préferer la compagnie ou la solitude," 166, 22 March 1638, 3:437–40.

"Lequel est le plus en estime de la Science ou de la Vertu," 60.2, 8 January 1635, 2:85–89.

"Le quel est le plus necessaire à aquerir les disciplines, le grand esprit ou le grand travail," 193, 28 March 1639, 4:26–33.

"Lequel est le plus nuisible à un Estat, l'oisiveté ou le luxe," 270, 12 November 1640, 4:349–52.

"Lequel est le plus porté au vice, de l'ignorant ou du sçavant," 249, 18 June 1640, 4:253–57.

"Lequel est le plus propre à l'estude, le soir ou le matin," 191, 14 March 1639, 4:21–25.

"Lequel est le plus requis à la conversation, le jugement ou la memoire," 217, 28 November 1639, 4:141–45.

"Lequel vaudroit-il mieux sçavoir tout ce que sçavent les hommes, ou tout ce qu'ils ignorent?" 175, 7 June 1638, 3:473–76.

"Lequel vaut mieux se marier, ou ne se marier point," 141, 18 May 1637, 3:237–40.

"Lequel vaut mieux user de severité ou de douceur envers les siens," 93.2, 17 December 1635, 2:356–60.

"Pourquoi l'aiguille aimentée tire t'elle vers le Nord?" 205, 4 July 1639, 4:81–85.

"Pourquoi les hommes sont plustost enclins au Vice qu'à la Vertu," 21.2, 9 January 1634, 1:173–76.

"Pourquoi personne n'est-il content de sa condition?" 18.2, 19 December 1633, 1:149–52.

"Pourquoi tous aiment-ils mieux commander qu'obeir?" 40.2, 22 May 1634, 1:324–28.

"Pourquoi tous les hommes desirent naturellement sçavoir," 39.1, 15 May 1634, 1:315–17.

"Quel est le plus communicatif du bien ou du mal," 111.2, 28 April 1636, 3:94–96.

"Quel est le plus desirable de vivre peu ou longuement," 139, 4 May 1637, 3:229–32.

"Quel est le plus inclin à l'Amour de l'Homme ou de la Femme," 14.2, 21 November 1633, 1:114–16.

"Quel est le plus grand de tous les Vices," 36.2, 24 April 1634, 1:294–96.

"Quel est le plus noble de l'Homme ou de la Femme," 25.2, 6 February 1634, 1:204–8.

"Quel est le plus puissant de l'Amour ou de la Haine," 16.2, December 1633, 1:132–36.

"Quel est le plus sain de l'humide ou du sec," 92.1, 10 December 1635, 2:341–45.

"Quel est le plys propre pour acquerir la Sagesse, des richesses ou de la pauvreté," 102, 18 February 1636, 3:22–24.

"Quelle est la moins blasmable de l'Avarice, ou de la Prodigalité," 22.2, 16 January 1634, 1:181–84.

"Quelle est la plus forte de l'Esperance ou de la Crainte," 64.2, 5 February 1635, 2:117–20.

"Quelle est la plus grande Réjoüissance de l'homme?" 28.1, 27 February 1634, 1:228–32.

"Quelle est la plus necessaire à un Estat & la plus noble, la Medecine ou la Jurisprudence," 117, 24 November 1636, 3:137–40.

"Quelle science est la plus necessaire a un Estat," 286, 11 March 1641, 4:421–25.

"Quelle secte des Philosophes est la plus à suivre," 208, 25 July 1639, 4:97–100.

"Quelles sont les plus communes causes des procez: & pourquoy il y en a plus aujourdhui que les temps passe," 179, 15 November 1638, 3:497–500.

"Quels sont les plus ingenieux du monde," 194, 4 April 1639, 4:33–37.

"Qu'est-ce qu'a voulu entendre Paracelse par le livre de M★," 203, 20 June 1639, 4:73–76.

"Qu'est-ce qui donne le prix aux choses?" 261, 10 September 1640, 4:309–12.

"Qu'est-ce qui fait l'Homme sage," 9.2, 17 October 1633, 1:69–70.

"Qu'est-ce que Verite," 321, 3 March 1642, 5:112–16.

"Resultat des Assemblées tenües dans le Bureau d'Adresse, durant les vacations de la presente année 1638, touchant les moyens de establir le commerce," summer 1638, 3:489–96.

"Si de deux corps de difference peseanteur, l'un descend plus promptement que l'autre, & pourquoi," 269, 5 November 1640, 4:345–49.

"S'il faut plus Disner que Souper," 132, 9 March 1637, 3:201–4.

"Si la Beauté du corps est indice de la bonté et beauté de l'esprit," 293, 27 May 1641, 4:449–53.

"Si la Censure est necessaire en un Estat," 297, 1 July 1641, 5:5–8.

"Si la conversation des femmes est utile aux hommes," 307, 14 October 1641, 5:45–49.

"Si la langue Françoise est suffisante pour apprendre toutes les Sciences," 296, 24 June 1641, 5:1–5.

"Si l'amitié est plus durable entre égaux ou inégaux," 266, 15 October 1640, 4:329–33.

"Si la musique fait plus de mal que de bien," 176, 14 June 1638, 3:477–80.

"Si la Permutation est plus commode que l'achat & la vente," 39.2, 15 May 1634, 1:318–20.

"Si la poësie est utile," 55.2, 4 December 1634, 2:43–48.

"Si la sante peute communiquer," 313, 16 December 1641, 5:69–72.

"Si la sterilité vient plus communément des costé des hommes que des femmes, & au contraire," 177, 22 June 1638, 3:481–88.

"Si la vertu consiste en médiocrité," 170, 26 April 1638, 3:453–57.

"Si le courage vient de nature ou d'institution," 257, 13 August 1640, 4:293–97.

"Si le fer appliqué sur un tonneau empesche le tonnerre de corrompre le vin, & pourquoi," 289, 22 April 1641, 4:433–37.

"Si le Francois est leger et inconstant: et pourquoi," 146, 30 June 1637, 3:357–60.

"Si le Mari et la femme doivent estre de mesme humeur," 65.2, 12 February 1637, 2:125–29.

"Si le monde vieillit," 27.1, 20 February 1634, 1:217–21.

"Si le Pardon vaut mieux que la Vengeance," 41.2, 29 May 1634, 1:333–36.

"Si les changemens des Estats ont des causes naturelles," 150, 16 November 1637, 3:373–76.

"Si les cieux sont solides ou liquides," 45.1, 26 June 1634, 1:361–65.

"Si les couleurs sont reelles," 50.1, 31 July 1634, 1:401–5.

"Si les Ecroüelles se guerissent par l'attouchement d'un septiesme garçon, & pourquoi?" 328, 21 April 1642, 5:147–53.

"Si les especes ou les choses sont les objets des sens," 276, 24 December 1640, 4:381–85.

"Si les grosses testes ont plus d'esprit que les autres," 224, 23 January 1640, 4:173–77.

"Si les hommes se formeroient un langage n'en ayans point appris d'autre," 156, 4 January 1638, 3:397–400.

"Si les larmes viennent de foiblesse," 49, 24 July 1634, 1:397–401.

"Si les maigres sont plus sains, & de plus longue vie que les gras," 123, 5 January 1637, 3:165–68.

"Si les maladies se quérissent par leurs contraires ou par leurs semblables?" 262, 17 September 1640, 4:313–16.

"Si les maux de l'esprit sont plus grands que ceux du corps," 201, 30 May 1639, 4:65–69.

"Si l'esprit humain est borné en ses opérations, et pourquoi?" 209, 1 August 1639, 4:101–4.

"S'il est bon de se servir de remedes Chymiques," 107.1, Tuesday, 1 April 1636, 3:57–62.

"S'il est expédient aux femmes d'estre scavantes," 106.2, 17 March 1636, 3:32–37, 3:53–56.

"S'il est meilleur à un Estat d'avoir des Esclaves," 7.2, 3 October 1633, 1:54–57.

"S'il est permis de mourir pour son amy," 246, 30 April 1640, 4:237–41.

"S'il est permis de se loüer soy-meme," 26.1, 13 February 1634, 1:209–13.

"S'il est plus aisé de resister a la Volupté qu'à la Douleur," 11.2, 31 October 1633, 1:86–91.

"S'il est plus aisé de se faire obeïr par la douceur que par la crainte," 314, 30 December 1641, 5:73–76.

"S'il est venu plus de bien que de mal du partage des trois parties de la Medecine, en Medecins, Chirurgiens & Apotiquairies," 180, 22 November 1638, 3:501–4.

"S'il est vray qu'on a autant d'ennemis que de valets, & pourquoy," 324, 24 March 1642, 5:126–30.

"Si le tempérament le plus propre à la santé est aussi le plus propre à l'esprit," 315, 13 January 1642, 5:78–80.

"Si le vin aide ou empesche la digestion, & pourquoi," 152, 1 December 1637, 3:381–84.

"Si l'homme est le plus maladif de tous les animaux & pourquoy," 182, Tuesday, 7 December 1638, 3:509–12.

"Si l'Homme peut avoir trop de science," 305, 16 September 1641, 5:37–41.

"Si l'imagination peut produire & guérir des maladies," 171, 3 May 1638, 3:457–60.

"S'il n'y a rien dans l'intellect qui n'ait esté dans les sens," 210, 8 August 1639, 4:105–9.

"S'il vaut mieux bien parler que bien escrire," 50.2, 31 July 1634, 1:405–9.

"S'il vaut mieux citer les Autheurs que s'en abstenir," 310, 4 November 1641, 5:57–61.

"S'il vaut mieux estre sans passions, que les modérer," 31.2, 20 March 1634, 1:253–56.

"S'il vaut mieux garder sa frontière, que de porter la guerre chez l'ennemi," 157, 11 January 1638, 3:401–4.

"S'il vaut mieux que les hommes ayet plusiers femmes, ou les femmes plusiers maris," 130, 23 February 1637, 3:193–97.

"S'il vaut mieux scavoir de tout un petit, ou une seule chose solidement?" 44.2, 19 June 1634, 1:356–60.

"S'il vaut mieux se contenter d'un seul amy que d'en auoir plusiers," 316, 20 January 1642, 5:81–87.

"S'il vaut mieux suivre les opinions communes que les paradoxes," 308, 21 October 1641, 5:49–52.

"S'il y a des remédes spécifiques à chaque maladie," 49.1, 24 July 1634, 1:393–98.

"S'il y a eu de plus grands hommes en quelqu'un des siecles precédens qu'en cettui-ci," 144, 15 June 1637, 3:349–52.

"S'il y a quelque Art de deviner," 80.2, 12 June 1635, 2:245–48.

"S'il y a une Ambition loüable," 102.2, 18 February 1636, 3:164–68.

"Si quelques autres animaux que l'homme usent de raison," 52.2, 13 November 1634, 2:20–24.

"Si tout ce qui nourrit l'animal doit avoir eu vie," 48.1, 17 July 1634, 1:385–89.

"Si tout ce qui nourrit d'animal doit avoir eu vie," 48.1, 17 July 1634, 1:385.

"Si un fils peut obliger son père," 277, 7 January 1641, 4:385–89.

Notes

Please see the Bibliography for a list of five volumes of conferences, with their inclusive conference numbers. Each note reference will give the title, number, date, volume, and page number of the specific conference. I have retained the archaic spelling and accents of the original. For individual conferences, see the Appendix.

PREFACE

1. Solomon, *Public Welfare, Science, and Propaganda*, xiii.

2. Aristotle became the great scientific authority in the West when the scholastic theologian, Thomas Aquinas, synthesized his science with Christian teachings in the *Summa Theologica.*

3. There are 345 meetings. The first 115 meetings treated two topics per session.

4. Daston and Park make effective use of specific conferences on hermaphrodites and eunuchs in *Wonders and the Order of Nature,* 177–179, 199–204. Sutton singled out some conferences, specifically those topics most readily correlated to the Scientific Revolution, to demonstrate their lack of scientific perspicacity and scientific methodology, see *Science for a Polite Society,* 21–41 and "A Science for a Polite Society."

5. "Du Bain," 83.1, 9 July 1635, 2:265–70.

6. See Grieco, "The Body, Appearance and Sexuality," 48–51.

7. 83.1, 9 July 1635, "Du Bain," 2:265–270.

CHAPTER ONE

1. The epigraph is taken from "De la Conference, & si c'est la plus instructive sorte d'enseigner," 285, 4 March 1641, 4:417–21 (421).

2. Renaudot, "Preface sur la Conference des Beaux Esprits," 1:1–8 (2).

3. Participants generally stick to this intention. See Mazauric's study for a quantitative chart of number of references made and to whom in each volume, *Savoirs et philosophie,* 139.

4. Renaudot, "Preface," 1:4. Mazauric extensively studies the form of the conferences to ultimately conclude that little specific significance can be attached to their form. *Savoirs et philosophie,* 139–43.

5. See Greenblatt, *Renaissance Self-Fashioning.*

6. Renaudot, "Preface," 1:2–3.

7. Gatherings of *libertins,* or freethinkers, violated it. See Harth, *Cartesian Women;*

Pintard, *Le libertinage érudit;* Godard de Donville, *Le Libertin.*

8. See Robert, "Conference," *Dictionnaire alphabétique,* 362. The evolution of the term may well be a response to the *conference* as Renaudot used it.

9. Brown, *Scientific Organizations,* 23–24.

10. Mauret, "Introduction," in Renaudot, *Le Beveur d'Eau,* 21.

11. She does not develop this comparison further. Mazauric, *Savoirs et philosophie.*

12. Renaudot, *Le Beveur d'Eau,* 21.

13. There were hiatuses for holidays, and following feast days and holidays, conferences were convened on Tuesdays or even occasionally on Wednesdays.

14. Renaudot, "Preface," 1:6.

15. Hatin points to Renaudot's conferences as the beginning of collected memoirs of scholarly societies. *Théophraste Renaudot,* 137–39.

16. Mazauric, *Savoirs et philosophie,*107.

17. "De la Conference."

18. Renaudot, *Mercure de France,* 22:157.

19. Habermas, *The Structural Transformation of the Public Sphere.*

20. See, for example, Goodman, *The Republic of Letters.*

21. Although Renaudot's institutions carved out an influential niche in Parisian society, he does not seem to have been motivated by a desire for personal gain. Gohout estimates that the charitable consultations cost him two thousand livres of his personal money each year. *Théophraste Renaudot,* 47–48.

22. For Montpellier medicine, see the forthcoming study by Williams, *A Cultural History of Medical Vitalism.* The college was named for the patron saint of surgery, Saint Cosmos. His twin, Saint Damien, was the patron saint of physicians.

23. If the physicians had criticisms, they would surely have made them known since they subjected all of his other activities to unstinting criticism in pamphlets such as *La Défense de la Faculté de Médecine.*

24. Although this is a fictional depiction,

many scholars have accepted Furetière's gallant as the prototypical participant. Mazauric notes "on sait que les romanciers empruntent à la réalité" (one knows that novelists borrow from reality). *Savoirs et philosophie,* 106–107.

25. Tallemant des Reaux, *Historiettes,* 6:382. It is ironic that La Caprenède is disparaged for his association with Renaudot's conferences, since he was most interested in chronicling the exclusive society of the Hotel de Rambouillet. See Revel, "The Uses of Civility," 194. Harcourt Brown found reference to the conferences only in Furetière's *Roman bourgeois,* Sorel's *Discours sur l'Académie Françoise,* and Tallemant des Reaux's *Historiettes.* These literary references are somewhat derogatory, and the great writers of the seventeenth century do not mention the conferences. Brown, *Scientific Organizations,* 20.

26. Sorel, *Discours Sur l'Académie Françoise,* 135. Although Sorel had been an early critic, he was more laudatory in his *Discours;* see also Roy, *La Vie et les oeuvres de Charles Sorel.* This connection is explicit in the writings of Mathieu de Morgues, better known as the abbé de St. Germain. A member of the *dévot* party, Morgues favored the domestic interests of the queen mother and a foreign policy based on an alliance with the papacy. As a result, Richelieu was his nemesis, and he denounced Renaudot's group as Richelieu's claque. Mazauric, *Savoirs et philosophie,* 110.

27. Sorel, *Discours Sur l'Académie Françoise,* 175–76.

28. The rest of Sorel's quote further defends the conferences: "what end is attained in treating them [the conferences] with contempt because of the variety of affairs carried on there, such as the sale and distribution of the gazette, and the consultation there permitted of the registers of investments and houses for sale, and because of the valets found for hire there, the money loaned on security, the unredeemed goods for sale by auction, which sometimes made this house a real secondhand shop. That did not prevent it

appearing at other hours a school of philosophy; and one may say that its various uses were created to make it a model of our civilization, and a mirror of human life. As for its disputes or doctrinal discourses, although they were not performed with as much formality and order as they might have received in the houses of the nobility, yet they represented what a private person could achieve; and, in comparison with many others, this assembly had its excellence." Sorel, *Discours sur l'Académie Françoise,* 176–77 (my translation; unless otherwise noted, all translations from French are mine).

29. Mauret, "Introduction," in Renaudot, *Le Beveur d'Eau,* 21.

30. Brown, *Scientific Organizations,* 20.

31. Solomon, *Public Welfare, Science, and Propaganda,* 67

32. Jean Richesource, born in Renaudot's native town of Loudun in 1620, came to Paris before the demise of Renaudot's conferences and probably participated in them. He later organized a series of Conferences Académiques et Oratoires that began in 1653. In 1655, he followed Renaudot's model more directly, holding an assembly of savants at his home on Mondays. See M. Revillout, *Un Maître de conference.* Mazauric notes that, of the fourteen topics Richesource's group proposed to treat, six were virtually identical to those discussed by Renaudot's group. *Savoirs et philosophie,* 108–9.

33. Renaudot, *A General Collection,* 2:iv.

34. "De la methode, 1.1, 22 August 1633, 1:6–8 (8).

35. Mazauric, *Savoirs et philosophie,* 117–18.

36. Perhaps a scientific topic like "Of the origin of winds" was considered general in the sense that knowledge about the natural world was thought universal, whereas "Whether it is better to be without the passions than to moderate them" might be particular because it dealt with the human and thus the transitory.

37. "De la petite fille velüe qui se voit en cette ville," 11.2, 31 October 1633, 1:81–86; and "S'il vaut mieux que les hommes ayet

plusiers femmes, ou les femmes plusiers maris," 130, 23 February 1637, 3:193–97.

38. These claims are made without any citation and have become one of the conventional remarks scholars make about the conferences.

39. Sutton comments: "Solomon suggests that Jean-Baptiste Morin, Ismael Boulliau, and Marin Mersenne may have attended, but I do not find his circumstantial evidence convincing . . . there is not sufficient evidence to put a name to a single scientific speaker." "Science for a Polite Society," 31n. 15.

40. Brockliss and Jones, *The Medical World of early modern France,* 331; Headley, *Tommaso Campanella,* 122 and Mazauric, *Savoirs et philosophie,* 105.

41. So many conferences deal with gender issues that historians speculate perhaps women did participate in this unconventional academy. See, for example, Reynier, *La Femme au dix-septième siècle,* 142–49. But there is no real evidence on this point, as Solomon notes (69). The assumption that women participated is used by Schiebinger as an example of female participation in science and of the openness to women in the seventeenth-century. See *The Mind Has No Sex?* 21. Quite a few remarks suggest that women did not participate, among them, in "Si la Beauté du corps est indice de la bonté et beautée de l'esprit," 293, 27 May 1641, 4:449–53 (450), a speaker lists thirty qualities of female beauty but says that the qualities of men will have to be left to women to discuss, suggesting that there were no women present to comment. In "Quel est le plus noble de l'Homme ou de la Femme," 25.2, 6 February 1634, 1:206–7 (207), the third speaker notes that there are no women at the airing of this dispute.

42. They are so called most notably by the English translator of the first two hundred conferences. Renaudot, *A General Collection,* ed. G. Havers, iii.

43. Although he dismisses the science of the conferences, Sutton concedes that Renaudot's conferences were directed to the "middling sort" and thus they represent "popular literature, the reading matter of the

'cultured classes'." Sutton also recognizes that "in their pages one can learn what effect the great revolution in science going on around Renaudot's contemporaries had on the large intellectual community." *Science for a Polite Society,* 23.

44. Solomon, *Public Welfare, Science, and Propaganda,* 63.

45. Harth uses this exclusion to suggest that Renaudot's group was as socially exclusive as the academies. *Cartesian Women,* 18.

46. Solomon, *Public Welfare, Science, and Propaganda,* 72–74.

47. Sutton, "A Science for a Polite Society," 30–31.

48. Mazauric documents seven such cases. *Savoirs et philosophie,* 105.

49. Mazauric charts the number of speakers per conference. Ibid., 139.

50. See "The Great Cat Massacre" and "Peasants Tell Tales" in Darnton, *The Great Cat Massacre,* 75–143, 9–72.

51. Harth, *Cartesian Women,* 34.

52. Viala, *Naissance de l'écrivain,* 121–22.

53. An apt name for Renaudot's establishment, which was so intent on "crowing."

54. All quotations are from Renaudot, "Preface," 1:1–7.

55. Slawinski, "Rhetoric and Science."

56. Wilson distinguishes between the physical sciences, which are incorporated into the standard account, and the natural or proto-sciences. She also distinguishes between modern assumptions of why theories like corpuscularism were accepted and early modern reasons for their acceptance. Wilson, *Invisible World,* 3–38.

57. Many works of the new science presuppose that science will produce a moral regeneration. See, for example, Francis Bacon's *New Organon.*

58. *Absolutism* is the term regularly applied to the form of government under the ancien regime, although it, like most "isms," is a nineteenth-century term applied to an earlier era. *Absolutism* assumes greater centralization of government under the monarch, at the expense of provincial institutions and elites.

The apogee of this development is usually cited as the reign of Louis XIV. There is an extensive and long-standing debate among historians about how successful this centralization actually was, as opposed to the clearly effective government propaganda about the monarchy. Among historians who emphasize the actual centralization of power under the monarch are Mousnier, *La plume, la vaucille et le marteau;* Bercé, *History of Peasant Revolts;* Durand, *Les Fermiers généraux;* Bonney, *Political Change in France;* Major, *Representative Government.* Among historians who have questioned this development are Henshall, *The Myth of Absolutism;* Parker, *The Making of French Absolutism;* Collins, *The Fiscal Limits of Absolutism.* Kettering has a succinct summary of the historiography of this issue, in *French Society 1589–1715,* 84–94.

59. I am indebted to comments by Robert Schneider for this way to construe the relationship between Richelieu and Renaudot.

60. Blair, *The Theater of Nature.*

CHAPTER TWO

1. This understanding is a decisive element of the modern historical criticism of the policies of Louis XIV.

2. Brown, *Scientific Organizations,* 19.

3. On Italian academies see Field, *The Origins of the Platonic Academy.* In this chapter I am particularly indebted to the classic discussion of the French academic tradition in Yates, *The French Academies,* 19–20.

4. Botero, *The Reason of State,* 84.

5. Brown claims that, because these academies were creatures of their royal patrons, they mirrored their interests almost entirely. Charles IX's Académie Royale de Poésie et de Musique dealt primarily with poetry and music; under Henry III the academy reflected his concerns with ethics and morality. Brown, *Scientific Organizations,* 1–19. Yates distinguishes between the sixteenth-century Italian academies, with narrow philological interests, and their French counterparts, with more encyclopedic interests. *The French Academies,* 9, 22.

6. For a discussion of this academy, see Frémy, *Origines de l'Académie Française,* and Auge-Chiquet, *La Vie, les idées et l'oeuvre de Jean-Antoine de Baif.* Mersenne praised Baif's academy for its range of activities, which included mathematics, painting, and gymnastics. *Questions harmoniques.* Baif's academy provoked opposition because its critics knew well that behind the academic discussion of traditional rhetorical topics could lurk much more radical ideas and agendas. Yates, *The French Academies,* 11.

7. Yates, *The French Academies,* 235. The late sixteenth century also saw the rise of the salon, which, as Harth has noted, tended to be sexually mixed as it was run by women. Academies, on the other hand, tended to be all male groups, run by men, although some women attended less prestigious provincial academies. The salon, like the academy, was a much less structured institution in the sixteenth century than it would become in the seventeenth century. Of particular note was the salon of Madame de Rambouillet, which was devoted to the refinement of taste in speech. Harth explicitly compares the impact of Renaudot to that of Madame de Rambouillet, saying Renaudot "did for the conference what Madame de Rambouillet did for the salon in setting a precedent for discursive space." Harth, *Cartesian Women,* 16.

8. Yates, *The French Academies,* 276.

9. All quotations are from Flurance, *Le lecon faicte en la premiere ouverture de l'Académie Royale.* See also Yates's account of the first discourse in *The French Academies,* 278.

10. Sainte-Marthe, *Eloges des hommes illustres,* 47–48.

11. Montaigne, "Of the Art of Discussion," book 3, essay 8, 703–21. In French the title is "De L'art de Confère." Brown uses Montaigne's praise for the conference as the introduction to his study of academic culture in seventeenth-century France. *Scientific Organizations,* 1.

12. Ramus assumed that, once scholastic impediments were removed, greater knowledge of the liberal arts and their practical

implementation would ensue. Graves, *Peter Ramus,* 13–21, 85–110. This statement simply reflects a general sense of where participants are drawn from, not an explicit identification of the membership, their social class or professions.

13. Mandrou, *From Humanism to Science,* 183–86.

14. Yates, *The French Academies,* 277, 283.

15. In 1613 Mersenne became the disciple of Jacques Mauduit, the musician of Baif's academy. Ibid., 284.

16. Mersenne also insisted on the importance of music to a revival of learning. *Questions harmoniques.*

17. Yates, *The French Academies,* 287–90.

18. See Le Noble, *Mersenne ou la naissance du mécanisme,* and Dear, *Mersenne and the Learning of the Schools.*

19. Giard, "Remapping Knowledge, Reshaping Institutions," 39.

20. Brockliss has argued that French medical education and practice did not warrant their negative reputation although his defense applies primarily to the eighteenth century. See "Before the Clinic."

21. Gassendi has been the focus of recent work. See Joy, *Gassendi the Atomist;* Osler, *Divine Will and the Mechanical Philosophy;* and Sarasohn, *Gassendi's Ethics.* The standard work on Mersenne is Le Noble's *Mersenne ou la naissance du mécanisme.* See also Dear, *Mersenne and the Learning of the Schools.* On Peiresc, see Miller, *Peiresc's Europe.*

22. Cahen-Salvador, *Un Grand Humaniste.* The brothers Dupuy, who established the most durable of the private academies in Paris, were in touch with Peiresc. At this academy, Solomon notes, "the taste, or even better, the frenzy for books was supreme." *Public Welfare, Science, and Propaganda,* 190.

23. Harth, based on Pintard, claims that some members of the bourgeoisie attended. *Cartesian Women,* 60.

24. As Brown notes, "the membership was carefully selected, and in the letters of the Dupuy brothers one finds recorded cases of

exclusions and dismissal after admission," *Scientific Organizations,* 12. Miller points to the Cabinet Dupuy as representing an old form of French intellectual culture in the early seventeenth century. It was elite, serious, unfashionable, and deeply skeptical of involvement in political life. *Peiresc's Europe,* 68–69.

25. On Peiresc's patronage networks, see Sarasohn, "Nicholas-Claude Fabri de Peiresc." For Peiresc's role in the culture of the seventeenth-century, see Miller, *Peiresc's Europe.*

26. Cahen-Salvador, *Un Grand Humaniste,* 209.

27. Miller, *Peiresc's Europe,* 4–5.

28. Much of the reaction to Campanella's defense of Galileo within the scholarly community was negative: Mersenne was negative; in 1632 Robert Burton censured Campanella in his *Anatomy of Melancholy;* in 1658 Elias Ashmole attacked him. However, he was welcomed by Bishop John Amos Comenius and Bishop John Watkins who both praised him and were influenced by him. Campanella, *The Defense of Galileo of Thomas Campanella,* xli.

29. Hermes Trismegistus was believed to the author of works more ancient than those of the Greeks, which entered Renaissance literature as the newly translated *Corpus Hermeticus* (ca. 1460) and were subsequently discovered to be of much more recent origin. See Debus, *The Chemical Philosophy,* 2:425–51.

30. Headley, *Tommaso Campanella,* 117–26.

31. In his life of Peiresc, Gassendi, the chief proponent of mechanism in France, chronicled Peiresc's extensive involvement with Campanella, particularly his attempt to make Parisian connections for Campanella once the latter had evaded extradition to Spain. Gassendi, *The Mirrour of the True Nobility & Gentility,* 111.

32. Headley, *Tommaso Campanella,* 117–26

33. The conferences treated a series of occult topics between March and June of 1640, which Headley suggests was a way for the group to mark Campanella's death. For

Campanella's involvement in French politics, see ibid., 126–31.

34. Yates claims that Campanella expected Richelieu, as a representative of a mystical vision, to build the "City of the Sun." *The French Academies,* 292.

35. The reign of Louis XIV saw the full flowering of state sponsored academies: the Académie Française (1635), the Académie Royale de Peinture et de Sculpture (1648), the Académie de Danse (1661), the Académie des Inscriptions et Belles Lettres (1663), the Académie des Sciences (1666), the Académie Royale de Musique (1669), and the Académie d'Architecture (1671). Yates connects the rituals and practices of the early academy to the traditions of sixteenth-century academies, Ibid., 275, 292.

36. This development, Yates notes, "corresponds to the ossification of the later humanist tradition in Italy in which the study of 'words' was divorced from the study of 'things' or 'ideas.'" Ibid., 290.

37. In *Patronage and Royal Science,* Lux claims that the Fontenelle thesis for the history of science in France has distorted the study of the scientific academy in France.

38. Despite its name, the Royal Society was much more independent in both in research agenda and its funding. Without the competition of one heavily funded, state-sponsored institution, English science also saw the creation of many popular scientific groups.

39. Raynaud, *Les médecins au temps de Molière,* 260. Works written within the last twenty years are much more likely to mention Renaudot then those written previously.

40. There are other early modern, unconventional entrepreneurial spirits who united medical interest and reform. See, for example, Smith's study of Johann Joachim Becher, *The Business of Alchemy.*

41. Although Renaudot is rarely mentioned in studies of Richelieu, he is mentioned by Mousnier in *L'Homme rouge.* Hatin notes that Renaudot is a surprisingly forgotten figure. He is included neither in a three-volume history by Bazin of the reign of Louis XIII nor in a history of the mont-

de-piété by Ange-Blaize. The archives of Poitou and Loudun are silent on Renaudot. The histories of the provinces and collections of illustrious Poitevins are also silent, with the exception of Dreux du Radier, *Bibliothèque historique*, xi. Another biographer, Tourette, bemoans the fact that Renaudot has been subjected to "the greatest ingratitude" by historians. *Théophraste Renaudot*, 3.

42. Although Sutton cites Howard Solomon as his source on Renaudot and his career, the conclusions he draws from that source are almost entirely negative and quite out of keeping with the tenor of Solomon's remarks. At Sutton's hands, Renaudot is not only a royal ally but also a particularly venal individual. "A Science for a Polite Society," 25–30 (27).

43. Emery concludes that the education given Renaudot and his brothers supports an assumption that the paternal fortune was at least forty thousand livres. *Renaudot et l'introduction de la médication chemique*, 46. Bergin claims that Protestants exerted significant influence in Poitou. *The Rise of Richelieu*, 100–101.

44. Packard, *Guy Patin*.

45. Some biographers suggest that this period of travel was necessary because he was rather young (nineteen) to practice medicine. Emery, *Renaudot et l'introduction de la médication chemique*, 49.

46. The best evidence for the existence of one of these, the *Traité des Pauvres*, is an epigram found in the papers of Pierre, Scévole de Sainte-Marthe, thought to be a response to Renaudot's dedication of the treatise to him.

47. Tourette, *Théophraste Renaudot*, 15.

48. Tourette cites that moment as the formation of the triple alliance of Trembley-Richelieu-Renaudot. Ibid., 16. However, since Richelieu was out of favor as of 1617, this alliance seems to be a foreshadowing of later influence rather than an alliance with any real clout at the time.

49. Ibid., 27; Huxley, *The Devils of Loudun*.

50. This treatise, offered to his protector on 1 January 1623, is reputed to have existed in several private libraries in Loudun, but it has not been found.

51. Avenel, *Lettres*, I:27.

52. The climate of religious opinion became more contentious as disagreements escalated between Catholic factions, like those who supported the Jesuits versus those who identified with Père Joseph's newly established Capuchin community. Renaudot acted as a conciliator and mediator not only between Catholics and Protestants but also between various Catholic factions. One sign of Renaudot's great ability, as acknowledged by Père Joseph, was that he enjoyed the respect of both Catholics and Protestants. His ability to act as conciliator would have also been attractive to Richelieu, who in his initial episcopal address in 1608 had called upon all people, whether Huguenot or Catholic, to live in mutual affection.

53. Mousnier considers Renaudot's conversion in 1628 sincere because his oldest son received the tonsure, three of his five daughters became nuns, and after his wife died, he continued to have masses said for her soul. *L'Homme rouge*, 448.

54. The French court had to spend significant amounts of time in the west to shore up support. See Bergin, *The Rise of Richelieu*, 126–27.

55. This title was announced in a brevêt of 1612, confirmed by an *arrêt* of 1618, and followed by two arrêts of 28 February and 22 March 1624. On 14 October 1628, Renaudot became *médecin du roi* and was named *médecin ordinaire*, charged with general regulation of the poor. Levy-Valensi, *La Médecine*, 455. Packard notes the financial and professional attractions of the position of *médecin du roi*. These offices were highly sought after, sometimes sold at high prices, and sometimes awarded because of success in dealing with a royal patient or the influence of powerful advocates. *Guy Patin*, 59–62.

56. The Prévôt of Paris did not execute the declarations that sanctioned Renaudot's activities. No doubt there was some difficulty fostering the activities of an individual supported by Richelieu, who was then facing difficulties of his own. See Bergin, *The Rise of*

Richelieu, 173–213.

57. Renaudot is quoted from his pamphlet *Inventaire de addresses du Bureau d'adresse et rencontre*, reproduced by Hatin in *Théophraste Renaudot*, 31. There is only one known copy, in the Bibliothèque de Rouen.

58. Montaigne, *The Complete Essays*, book 1, essay 34, pp. 163–65.

59. Laffemas, *L'Histoire du commerce en France*, 102. *Mercure françois*, vol. 22:55–68, contains a long justification by Renaudot of the Bureau d'adresse.

60. Vives, *De l'assistance aux pauvres*, 98. Unlike Renaudot, Vives cites poverty as a gift of God that one should welcome (51–53).

61. On the Catholic reformation in France, see Bergin, *Cardinal de La Rochefoucauld;* Donnelly and Maher (eds.), *Confraternities and Catholic reform;* Phillips, *Church and Culture in Seventeenth-Century France*. On Vincent de Paul see the following collection of his writings, *Vincent de Paul and Louise de Marillac: Rules, Conferences, and Writings*.

62. Louis XIII, *Lettres patentes du roy en faveur des pauvres et particulièrement des malades*.

63. Louis XIII, *Déclaration du Roy Pour l'éstablissments des Bureaux d'adresse*.

64. *Mercure françois*, 22:55–68 (55).

65. Ibid., 62.

66. Ibid., 63.

67. Ibid., 54–55.

68. Denonain, "Les problèmes de l'honnête homme vers 1635," 236.

69. After the performance, the lyrics were printed under the title *Ballet du Bureau du rencontre donné au Louvres devant sa Majesté*. Hatin found and reproduced "vers du Ballet du Bureau d'adresse" although the ballet itself has not been found. *Théophraste Renaudot*, 72.

70. *Mercure françois*, 21:57 ff.

71. "Office of Intelligence" is essentially an English translation of Bureau d'Adresse.

72. Johann Michael Horn, who was in Paris, passed along the requested information about the Bureau. Turnbull, *Hartlib, Dury and Comenius*, 80. Arnold Boate claimed that Renaudot was shut down because of "gross

usurie," but another letter of the same year from Horn claimed that the Bureau was shut down after Richelieu's death because of "the envy of certain great people" but restored in 1647 with the support of Mazarin. Boate's claim may be colored by Renaudot's conversion, as is suggested by his remark "by revolting from us to Rome [he] procured for himself leave for erecting the office." *Arnold Boate Answers to Hartlib's Thirteen Queries about Renaudot's Bureau d'Adresse*, July 1648, as reproduced by Turnbull, in ibid., 123.

73. Hartlib makes the religious dimension clear: "A Brief discourse concerning the accomplishment of our Reformation, shewing that by an Office of Address in spirituell and temporall matters the glory of God and the happiness of this nation may be highly advanced." Ibid., 77. Brown asserts the direct influence of Renaudot on Hartlib in *Scientific Organizations*, 28.

74. Turnbull, *Hartlib, Dury and Comenius*, 76.

75. Comenius's remarks are undoubtedly, given their religious tenor, a direct response to Hartlib's *A Further Discoverie of the Office of Publick Addresse for Accommodations* (1648). Ibid., 424.

76. Robinson, *The Office of Addresses and Encounters*, 220–25.

77. Robinson, like Renaudot, had implemented low interest loans to the poor. Unlike Renaudot and perhaps reflective of his English context, Robinson argued for a fundamental fusion of free trade and political liberty and for a government based on a consolidation of landed and mercantile interests. W. K. Jordan, *Men of Substance*, 250–53.

78. Dalat, *Théophraste Renaudot*, 13.

79. The text of the lettres-patentes is reproduced in Hatin, *Théophraste Renaudot*, 14–15.

80. Renaudot, *Factum du procez d'entre Maistre Théophraste Renaudot*.

81. Renaudot, *Les Consultations charitables*, 248.

82. A late seventeenth-century source describes the operations of the *monts-de-piété*

in Italy: "In the time of Pope Paul the Third, there was a place appointed for the receiving of the pawns of poor peoples, and they called it the Mount of Piety and of Pawns. Here are received the pawns of all poor and indigent people whatsoever, and no, or, at least, no considerable use paid for the money given out upon them. The time allotted for redemption is eighteen months: if the pawns are not redeemed in that time, they are sold. The work is indeed a piece of very great charity, and extremely beneficial to the meaner sort of people." Theogorus Amydenus, *Pietas Romana,* 39–40.

83. Menning, *Charity and State in Late Renaissance Italy.*

84. Royal privilege permitted him to lend at a rate of "six deniers par livre" of the value of the item, which modern historians have considered the equivalent of approximately two and one half percent. Because an analysis of Renaudot's operation suggests that this would have been an inadequate amount, scholars generally assume that the difference between what he took in and what was necessary to operate the *monts-de-piété* came from Renaudot's own pocket. See Pierre Gohout, *Théophraste Renaudot.* In 1648 the Chevalier Balthazar Gerbier argued strongly for the creation of monts-de-piété. It may well have been designed to make his own case to reestablish the monts-de-piété, since Renaudot had lost royal authorization with the deaths of Louis XIII and Richelieu. Gerbier, *Justification particulière des intendants des monts-de-piété,* 227–31.

85. As Jones notes, Montpellier had a democratic tradition with powerful student control over faculty as compared to a magisterial institution like the University of Paris. "Medicalization of Eighteenth-Century France," 63.

86. Jean Riolan, the Younger (1577–1657), professor of anatomy and biology at the Collège Royale and physician to Marie de Medici, who betrayed her by spying on her for Richelieu, denied the circulation of blood but made important discoveries in anatomy, such as the appendices of the colon. He also named

the hepatic duct. Packard, *Guy Patin,* 167–68.

87. Patin was a firm believer in venesection—even in infancy and old age, which were usually considered risky times for such procedures. He may have run afoul of Renaudot on this point as well as on chemical remedies. When the polemic between Patin and Renaudot became personal, Renaudot responded by calling Patin "doctor three S's" because he relied primarily on bleeding (*la saignée*) syrup of roses, and senna. For an extensive discussion of Patin's polemical battle with Renaudot, see Packard, *Guy Patin,* 185–97.

88. Patin would have attacked Renaudot as a creature of Richelieu whom he hated because, as part of the Cinq Mars conspiracy, Richelieu had executed de Thou, son of the historian and a close friend of Patin. See Parker, *The Making of French Absolutism,* 4. For a discussion of Guy Patin's medical crusades, see Raynaud, *Les Médecins au temps de Molière,* 93–104.

89. Packard, *Guy Patin,* 49.

90. Renaudot argued in *Response . . . au libelle* that he had been offering consultations for ten years.

91. Renaudot, *Les Consultations charitables pour les Malades,* 251.

92. The proponents of chemical remedies did not finally prevail until the Faculty espoused treatment with antinomy in 1666.

93. Renaudot's Bureau was well known as a gathering place for doctors from Montpellier who considered it "leur maison commune." (their common house). Emery, *Renaudot et l'introduction de la médication chemique,* 38.

94. Renaudot, *Les Consultations charitables,* 9.

95. Renaudot, *La Présence des absens.*

96. Riolan, the Younger, *Curieuses recherches,* 3–4.

97. By 1640, Renaudot had drawn up plans for a new facility abutting the city ramparts in the tenement-packed Faubourg St. Antoine, housing all his medical facilities under one roof. The king had sweetened the project by granting Renaudot two hundred

thousand écus to implement it. Renaudot's permission was quite extraordinary, as property development on the ramparts was normally prohibited for reasons of town security. Town ramparts were also special, holy, and to remain eternally inviolate. Renaudot said that Louis XIII sent the letters-patent to Parlement in February 1643. They were opposed by the Duke of Uzes and his wife, who owned land adjacent to the proposed site. The letters were never registered. Louis XIII died on 14 May 1643, and the Maison des Consultations Charitables died with him. Solomon, *Public Welfare, Science, and Propaganda,* 171–73.

98. Renaudot, *Requeste presentée à la Reyne par Théophraste Renaudot.*

99. Hatin, *Théophraste Renaudot,* 154.

100. Montpellier physicians also had *urbi et orbi* privileges. Ibid., 147.

101. Faculty of Medicine, *Avertissement à l'examen de la Requeste.* The quotation is from Faculty of Medicine, *La Défense de la Faculté de Médecine de Paris contre son Calomniateur.*

102. The Faculty responded with the *Examen de la Requeste,* and Renaudot with a *Réponse à l'Examen de la Requeste.*

103. Faculty of Medicine, *Examen de la Requeste présentée à la Reine par le Gazettier,* 3, 4, 14, 22.

104. Renaudot, *Requeste presentée à la Reyne par Théophraste Renaudot.*

105. *Factum de l'instance,* 5, 6. This is Renaudot's history of the legal battle with the Faculty, and perhaps it is, as a result, a bit overstated.

106. Packard, *Guy Patin,* 245.

107. The tribunal of Châtelet not only forbade Renaudot and his adherents to practice medicine but also to have any conference, consultation, or assembly in the Bureau d'Adresse. Emery, *Renaudot et l'introduction de la médication chimique,* 115.

108. As historians have acknowledged, the process of 1644 was extremely partisan, but some of the charges have found their way into contemporary scholarship. For example, Chenvot, one of the most famous members of

the Paris bar, argued that Renaudot's monts-de-piété was usurious and called into question Renaudot's medical ability and commitment. See Raynaud, *Les Médecins au temps de Molière,* 267.

109. *Factum du procez d'entre Maistre Théophraste Renaudot,* 1–2.

110. Ibid., 2.

111. Père Joseph (b. 1579) became a Franciscan in 1599 and battled against the relaxation of monastic rule and the influence of Protestants, positions that later brought him into conflict with Richelieu.

112. This appointment would have placed him in position to rival physicians of the Faculty of Medicine.

113. Gouhot, *Théophraste Renaudot,* 31, 42. Louis XIII also called Renaudot to his bedside when he was sick in 1627.

114. Kettering, *Patrons, Brokers, and Clients,* 3.

115. Bergin, *The Rise of Richelieu,* 262. For a discussion of Richelieu's use of patronage, see Kettering, *Patrons, Brokers, and Clients,* 18–23, 157–61.

116. *Mercure françois,* 22:55–68.

117. See the *Lettres patentes du Roy en faveur des pauvres et particulièrement des malades* of 1640, in which Louis XIII endorses all of Renaudot's activities. The *Mercure françois* was the successor to the Pierre-Victor Palma-Cayet, *Chronologie septenaire,* which ceased publication in 1604.

118. Renaudot, "Preface au Lecteur," *Gazette de France Recueil,* 1631, 5.

119. Hatin, *Histoire . . . de la presse.* The *Gazette* has been discussed primarily in historical literature for its role in the evolution of the French press. Whether it is praised or scorned depends on how sympathetic one is to Renaudot or Richelieu and how much one is inclined to see the *Gazette* as simply a propaganda tool for the ancien régime.

120. Renaudot, *Mercure françois,* 22:55.

121. Solomon, *Public Welfare, Science, and Propaganda,* 57.

122. For Père Joseph, see Dalat, *Théophraste Renaudot,* 9. For Richelieu, see

Tourette, *Théophraste Renaudot,* 73.

123. Dalat, *Théophraste Renaudot,* 7–8.

124. Pamphlet literature of the period made fun of the propagandistic quality of the *Gazette.* See, for example, Richelieu, *Annotations plaisantes.* For an extensive treatment of seventeeth-century propaganda, see Sawyer, *Printed Poison.*

125. Moote, *Louis the Just,* 149. Louis XIII wrote an account of the negotiation between Richelieu and the Duke of Lorraine, which became the Treaty de Charmes. *Gazette* (1633):400–404. Louis wrote the account of Gaston's return to France in 1634. *Gazette* (1634):442–44, 458–60.

126. Tourette, *Théophraste Renaudot,* 72.

127. Renaudot wrote a pamphlet entitled *La Deplorable Mort de Charles I,* describing Charles I of England as heroic and his death as an act of unprecedented barbarism. Renaudot's support of the royal family during the Fronde and of French foreign policy in the *Gazette* produced particularly vicious attacks on him in contemporary pamphlet literature. To discredit these attacks on his defense of French foreign policy, Renaudot claimed they were actually written by the Spanish—a diversionary tactic that neither worked nor enhanced his reputation. *Résponse de Théophraste Renaudot . . . A l'Auteur des libelles intitulez Avis du Gazetier de Cologne.*

INTRODUCTION TO PART II

1. D'Alembert, *Preliminary Discourse,* 75, 78, 81, 84.

2. On French universities see Brockliss, *French Higher Education.* On the Académie des Sciences, see Hahn, *The Anatomy of a Scientific Institution,* and Paul, *Science and Immortality.* On the Royal Society see Sprat, *The History of the Royal Society;* Purver, *The Royal Society;* Miles, *Science, Religion and Belief;* Hall, *Science and Society;* and Hunter, *Establishing the New Science.*

3. D'Alembert, *Preliminary Discourse,* 74.

4. See especially the works of Schmitt et al., *The Cambridge History of Renaissance Philosophy;* Schmitt and Copenhaver, *Renais-*sance *Philosophy;* Schmitt, *The Aristotelian Tradition and Renaissance Universities;* Schmitt, *Aristotle and the Renaissance;* Schmitt, ed., *Reappraisals in Renaissance Thought.*

5. See Daston and Park, *Wonders and the Order of Nature;* Eamon, *Science and the Secrets of Nature;* Biagioli, *Galileo Courtier.*

6. Renaudot, "Preface," 1:2.

7. Solomon makes this claim without a citation; it has become the source of most information on Renaudot's group in subsequent discussions. *Public Welfare, Science, and Propaganda,* 68.

8. Demeulenaere-Douyère and Sturdy, "Image versus Reality," 190.

9. The word *house* suggests too limited a setting for all the activities that took place there.

10. Studies, like Hahn's study of the Académie des Sciences, which supports this thesis, or Lux's study of the Academy of Caen, which challenges it, demonstrate the advantages and disadvantages of state support.

11. Moss, *Novelties in the Heavens;* Pumfrey, Rossi, and Slawinski, eds., *Science, Culture, and Popular Belief in Renaissance Europe.*

12. Perhaps most disconcerting (as is the case in much early modern science), arguments that we might appreciate as "true" (such as heliocentricism) are made for reasons such as "it is fitting that the earth, which needs heat and light, should move to seek the sun," whereas subjects too bizarre to be credited nowadays as scientific (such as chiromancy or talismans) are addressed in a stringently empirical fashion.

13. My supposition works directly against that of Sutton who has used science in the conferences as the best exemplar of science before the advent of the scientific revolution's mechanical science. He takes it as a given that the science, which preceded the scientific revolution was Aristotelian, and that the scientific revolution occurred when a consistent Aristotelianism yielded paradigmatic place to mechanism.

14. Rappaport contrasts 1650s discussion

groups like those of Bourdelot, Justel, and Thevenot as modern as compared to Renaudot's conferences "whose meetings were chiefly devoted to speech making, each topic addressed by more than one speaker." *When Historians Were Geologists,* 27.

CHAPTER THREE

1. "Des Talismans," 108.1, 7 April 1636, 3:65–70. For an overview of the role of amulets in seventeenth-century medical practice, see Baldwin, "Toads and Plague."

2. In the seventeenth century, many people, Paracelsians in particular, believed that sympathy allowed the possibility for action at a distance, which could then explain magnetism and other natural phenomenon. One controversial application of sympathetic action was the belief in weapon-salve, a practice of treating the weapon rather than the wound. See Debus, "Robert Fludd." The weapon-salve issue became particularly controversial in the 1620s in Paris with the publication of van Helmont's *De Magnetica vulnerum curatione* in 1621. See Debus, *The French Paracelsians,* 102–15.

3. Speakers extrapolate specific examples from the historical record to provide concrete substantiation of specific points.

4. Although speakers do not treat religious topics, religion enters into other topics. In these cases, speakers are careful to distinguish between the religious ramifications of topics and those that could be explored without recourse to the inexplicable. For example, a speaker on the topics of amulets insists that it can be decided "in the ordinary course of natural things . . . without recourse to good or bad angels." "Des amuletes, & si l'on peut guérir les maladies par paroles, brevets, ou autres choses penduës au col, ou attachées aux corps des malades," 173, 17 May 1638, 3:465–68(465).

5. The word *occult* is not used by conferees as a term of opprobrium to discredit certain opinions. Topics with occult ramifications are treated in the same way as more orthodox topics, although they generally posed more

difficulty for discussion.

6. For a discussion of the centrality of occult phenomena, see Hutchison, "What Happened to Occult Qualities in the Scientific Revolution?" Hoppen demonstrated the degree to which leaders of the new science in England could use concepts and categories derived from the occult in "The Nature of the Early Royal Society." Other valuable sources on the importance of the occult in early modern science are Copenhaver, *Symphorien Champier,* and "Astrology and Magic"; Zambelli, *L'Ambigua natura della magia;* and Vickers, ed., *Occult and Scientific Mentalities in the Renaissance.*

7. This account is indebted to Allen Debus, who effectively integrates issues of occult science into the scientific revolution, especially in *Man and Nature in the Renaissance,* 1–33.

8. See Thomas, *Religion and the Decline of Magic.*

9. For example, Kepler was sufficiently concerned that his astronomy might be connected with that of Robert Fludd to differentiate explicitly his own use of mathematics from Fludd's mystical use. On the Kepler-Fludd polemic see Westman, "Nature, Art, and Psyche."

10. For a discussion of some of the historiographical implications of the scientific revolution see Lindberg and Westman, eds., *Reappraisals of the Scientific Revolution.*

11. See in particular Debus, *The French Paracelsians, Man and Nature in the Renaissance,* and *The Chemical Philosophy;* Dobbs, *Alchemical Death and Resurrection, The Foundations of Newton's Alchemy,* and *The Janus Faces of Genius;* and Principe, *The Aspiring Adept.*

12. Important sources on Paracelsus and van Helmont are Pagel, *Paracelsus,* "The Religious and Philosophical Aspects of van Helmont's Science," *Joan Baptista van Helmont,* and "Recent Paracelsian Studies"; Debus, *The English Paracelsians,* and "The Chemical Philosophers."

13. See Merchant, *The Death of Nature.*

14. "De la lumière," 59.1, 2 January 1635, 2:73–77(74).

15. "Des principes & de la fin de toutes choses," 2.1, 29 August 1633, 1:9–13(12).

16. "De la Terre," 9.1, 17 October 1633, 1:65–69(71).

17. "Comment croissent les Mineraux?" 44.1, 19 June 1634, 1:353–57(354).

18. For example, nature has given those animals that live by prey the most acute sense of smell. "De l'Odorat," 56.1, 11 December 1634, 2:49–53(52).

19. A speaker says that, because the earth is the most ponderous body, earthquakes must be caused by fire, the noblest element. "Du Tremblement de Terre," 73.1, 16 April 1635, 2:185–90(185).

20. "De la Pierre Philosophale," 43.1, 12 June 1634, 1:345–49(347).

21. "De l'Oüye," 57.1, 18 December 1634, 2:57–61(58).

22. For example, "as art can draw forth water by distillation and other ways taught by chemistry, so, by stronger reason, nature cannot fail to do the same." "De l'Harmonie," 57.2, 18 December 1634, 2:62.

23. "Si quelques autres animaux que l'homme usent de raison," 52.2, 13 November 1634, 2:20–24(21).

24. This relationship has theological implications, as a speaker insists that "God makes himself known to men by the marvelous effects of nature." "Si tout ce qui nourrit l'animal doit avoir eu vie," 48.1, 17 July 1634, 1:385–89(both quotes 385).

25. "S'il y a quelque Art de deviner," 80.2, 12 June 1635, 2:245–48.

26. D'Alembert, Preliminary Discourse, 46.

27. "Des Fables, & si elles apportent plus de mal que de bien," 283, 18 February 1641, 4:409–12.

28. "Des deux frères Monstrueux, vivans en un mesme corps, que se voyent à present en cette ville," 10.2, 24 October 1633, 1:78–80(68). While conferees are clear in their sense that they are remote from common culture, they do not indicate exactly how they are different. They share with their contemporaries an emphasis on social distinction, whereby old nobles emphasize distinctions

between themselves and new nobles, nobles emphatically note their differences with the bourgeoisie, and all are to be separated from the common people in terms of manners, practices, and beliefs. Flandrin, "Distinction through Taste," 302–3.

29. Daston and Park document the inclination to credit reports of strange phenomena from exotic locales from the Middle Ages, in Wonders and the Order of Nature, 25–39.

30. A speaker notes that "the particular nature . . . being sometimes hindered by some accident, which makes it bring forth monsters." "De L'Heur & du Mal-heur; & si les hommes sont heureux ou malheureux, pour ce qu'ils le sont, ou pour ce qu'ils le pensent estre," 135, 30 March 137, 3:213–16.

31. "Des Fables," 4:411. See Céard, La Nature et les prodiges; Daston and Park, "Unnatural Conceptions," and Wonders and the Order of Nature, 173–214.

32. "Des Incubes & Succubes & si les Demons peuvent engendrer," 128, 9 February 1637, 3:185–88(187).

33. "Si tout ce qui nourrit l' animal doit avoir eu vie," 1:385.

34. "Quel est le plus communicatif du bien ou du mal," 111.2, 28 April 1636, 3:94–96(96).

35. "De l'Origine des Formes," 122, 29 December 1636, 3:161–64(163).

36. The separation of matter by heat explains many diverse phenomena, including birthmarks. "D' ou viennent les marques que les enfans apportent du ventre de leur mere," 120, 22 December 1636, 3:149–56.

37. "De l' Heur & du Mal-heur," 3:214.

38. "Comment se fait l' accroissement," 131, 2 March 1637, 3:197–200(200).

39. To explain antiperistasis, one speaker claims that nature has imprinted in her creatures a strong inclination to preserve themselves "by fortifying them against the assault of their contraries." "De l'Antiperistaze," 340, 14 July 1642, 5:209–13(209). A speaker notes that "nature not contented to produce all things, has given them a desire of self-preservation," "Quel est le plus desirable de vivre

peu ou longuement," 139, 4 May 1637, 3:229–32(229).

40. "Des causes de la petite Verole," 126, 26 January 1637, 3:177–80(179).

41. "De l'Antiperistaze," 5:209.

42. Ibid.

43. "Quel est le plus desirable de vivre peu ou longuement," 3:230.

44. See Pumfrey, "The History of Science and the Renaissance Science of History," 51.

45. Speakers find it difficult to apply the definitions to specific phenomena. See, for example, "De la Sympathie & Antipathie," 32.1, 27 March 1634, 1:257–61(257).

46. "S' il y a quelque Art de deviner" 2:246–47.

47. "De la Sympathie & Antipathie," 1:258.

48. Johann Rudolf Glauber (1604–1670), a late Paracelsian, contributed much to the development of chemistry and understood chemistry as the foundation of a mystical explanation of nature. He combined mystical and pragmatic interests; he was interested in the establishment of Germany as "monarch of the world" and in chemistry as key to greater prosperity for farmers and as a more effective means of warfare. See Debus, *The Chemical Philosophy*, 2: 425–51.

49. "De l'Apparition des Esprits ou Phantomes," 79.2, 4 June 1635, 2:235–40(235).

50. See Popkin, *The History of Scepticism*, 129–56.

51. "Des Satyres," 250, 25 June 1640, 4:257–60(258).

52. "Des Incubes & Succubes."

53. "De la Mandragore," 222, 9 January 1640, 4:161–68(162).

54. "De la Licorne," 248, 11 June 1640, 4:245–52(246).

55. This speaker cites the importance of spirits to Aristotle and Plato. "De l'Apparition des Esprits ou Phantomes," 2:235.

56. "De la Licorne."

57. "Des Incubes & Succubes et si les Demons peuvent engendrer," 3:185–88(185).

58. He accepts coition with demons because of personal testaments and concludes that "we cannot deny without giving the lie to the infinite number of persons of all ages, sexes, and conditions, to whom the same happened." He also finds accounts form distant places, like the Island of Hispaniola, persuasive.

59. On the occult and Robert Boyle, see Hooykaas, *Robert Boyle,* and Wojcik, *Robert Boyle and the Limits of Reason.*

60. "De la Pierre Philosophale," 1:347.

61. "De la Sympathie & Antipathie," 1:259.

62. "Those that have most exactly examined the power of nature, find the mixture of these species impossible." "Des Satyres," 4:258.

63. "De la Mandragore."

64. These sorts of remarks hint at the kind of biological speculation that will prove so fruitful in the writings of philosophes such as Diderot.

65. For a discussion of how this distinction broke down in response to mathematics in the scientific revolution see Dear, *Discipline and Experience,* 151–79.

66. Daston and Park, *Wonders and the Order of Nature,* 264.

67. "Si le fer appliqué sur un tonneau empesche le tonnerre de corrompre le vin, & pourquoi," 289, 22 April 1641, 4:433–37.

68. "Et du mouvement perpetuel," 4.2, 12 September 1633, 1:29–32.

69. "De la Pierre Philosophale," 1:345.

70. "S' il y a quelque Art de deviner," 2:246.

71. This speaker notes that the devil rarely enriches one "either because he reserves his riches for Antichrist so as to seduce the nations; or because God does not allow it, lest men should forsake his service for that of devils, and the good should be too sorely afflicted by the wicked." Ibid.

72. Thomas, *Religion and the Decline of Magic.*

73. For a collection of seventeenth-century sources demonstrating these attitudes, see Kors and Peters, eds., *Witchcraft in Europe,*

311–73.

74. "Des deux frères Monstrueux."

75. Daston and Park, *Wonders and the Order of Nature*, 173–214.

76. "De la petite fille velüe qui se voit en cette ville." See Daston and Park's discussion of a hairy girl in *Wonders and the Order of Nature*, 192–94.

77. "De l'Astrologie judiciaire," 22.1, 16 January 1634, 1:177–80.

78. "D' où vient le Présage que l'on tire de quelques animaux?" 40.1, 22 May 1634, 1:321–24.

79. "Des Somnambules," 33.1 3 April 1634, 1:265–69.

80. "De la Cabbale," 35, 2 May 1634, 1:297–302.

81. Another speaker concurs, noting that the Church endorses this notion by using the name of Christ to cast out devils. Ibid. The tradition of demonic revelation as the source of black magic enters the Western tradition through the work of Augustine. For a discussion of the concern with the demonic in the scientific revolution, see Hutchison, "What happened to Occult Qualities in the Scientific Revolution?" 235–37, and Webster, *From Paracelsus to Newton*, 75–100.

82. Perhaps conscious of the violation of the spirit of the conferences, this speaker then refocuses discussion on more empirical grounds by comparing the cabala to numerology. (The sense that he has violated conference norms and retreats to a more acceptable treatment of this topic is simply personal conjecture.)

83. "Des Sorciers," 77.1, 14 May 1635, 2:217–21.

84. This speaker does allow the devil some real power: "The devil makes use of natural causes for such an effect . . . having lost no gifts of nature by sin, but only those of grace." Ibid., 2:217.

85. Ibid., 2:222. Although the Christian tradition may predispose some speakers to believe in the occult, the first speaker on the topic "On the existence of spirits and fantasms" cites many arguments for their exis-

tence derived from sources within the Western tradition—for example, Aristotle ("Aristotle has nine classes of spirits below the level of the First Mover"), and Hermes Trismegistus ("Trismegistus acknowledged only two, which hold the Arctic and Antarctic poles"). He also cites more orthodox arguments for the existence of spirits: some spirits are considered necessary for human preservation, like guardian angels; other spirits war with man constantly, like devils; other spirits animate bodies and separate from them at death. "De l'Apparition des Esprits ou Phantomes," 2:235.

86. "De la Métempsycose," 143, 8 June 1637, 3:245–49.

87. "Des Sayres."

88. "Qu'est-ce qu'a voulu entendre Paracelse par le livre de M★," 203, 20 June 1639, 4:73–76. The first speaker notes that the author is so committed to secrecy "that he conceals even the name of the books he studied" (73).

89. He distinguishes clearly between the kinds of knowledge available: "Now natural magic is the knowledge of the nature and properties of all things hidden to the vulgar, who take notice only of manifest qualities and reduce all to generalities, to avoid the pains of seeking the particular virtues of each thing. . . . Of this kind are many excellent secrets, whose effects seem miraculous, and much surpass those of ordinary remedies, whose virtues are collected only from their apparent qualities." This distinction is made by Porta, *Natural Magick*, 1.

90. He describes the talisman "M" this way, "as a Talismanic figure engraved in a seal, and employed by the Rosicrucians to understand one another; and called the Book M, because it represents an M crossed by some other letters, whose combination produces the mystery of the great work, designing its matter, vessel, fire and other circumstances; the first of which is dew, the true menstruum or dissolvers of the red dragon or gold." (75).

91. Daston and Park, *Wonders and the Order of Nature*.

92. Foucault, *The Order of Things*.

CHAPTER FOUR

1. "Si les cieux sont solides ou liquides," 45.1, 26 June 1634, 1:361–65.

2. Many of the topics that treat science are not included in this chapter, because they are discussed in the chapters on occult science or medicine. Other topics, which are rooted in Aristotelian biology but which center on gender and the family, are discussed in Chapter Nine.

3. A systematic study of Aristotelianism in the conferences remains to be done, and it might well make an intriguing case, extending some of the implications suggested by Schmitt's *Aristotle and the Renaissance* into the culture of the early seventeenth century. For Mazauric, in sharp distinction to Sutton, the conferences indicate great fidelity to Aristotle, *Savoirs et philosophie,* 199–207.

4. Sutton focused on these particular conferences to demonstrate what bad Aristotelians the participants were and, as a result, what bad science was done at the Bureau. *Science for a Polite Society,* 25–35.

5. "Des Causes en general," 3.1, 5 September 1633, 1:17–20.

6. "De la Matiere premiere," 4.1, 12 September 1633, 1:25–29. This kind of editorial presence is characteristic of only the first few conferences.

7. "Du feu," 6.1, 26 September 1633, 1:41–46.

8. Ibid., 44.

9. Sutton singles out the conference on fire as a particularly egregious example of a non-Aristotelian and thus misguided discussion. *Science for a Polite Society,* 90–101.

10. "De l'air," 7.1, 3 October 1633, 1:49–55.

11. "De l'eau," 8.1, 10 October 1633, 1:57–61.

12. "De la Terre."

13. "De la quint'essence," 60.1, 8 January 1635, 2:81–85.

14. The Aristotelian fifth element was an ether that filled the superlunar space and formed the substance of all heavenly bodies.

See Grant, *Physical Science in the Middle Ages,* 37.

15. Sutton, *Science for a Polite Society,* 40.

16. Even on method, as Sutton notes with exasperation, their discussion was particularly unmethodical. "A Science for a Polite Society," 30–36.

17. Ibid., 40.

18. Schmitt, *Aristotle and the Renaissance,* 115.

19. Renaudot, "Preface," 1:3.

20. Brown, *Scientific Organizations,* 25.

21. "S' il vaut mieux suivre les opinions communes que les paradoxes," 308, 21 October 1641, 5:49–52.

22. "Du mouvement ou repos de la Terre," 10.1, 24 October 1633, 1:73–78.

23. This speaker is heralded as prescient by Sutton in *Science for a Polite Society,* 35. But it is important to note that the kind of evidence he employs is not foreign to that presented by the speaker on the other side of the argument; they both argue for the position of the earth they support by invoking appropriateness, logic, analogy, and observation,

24. As Sutton notes, the condemnation came on 22 June 1633, some four months before the conference on the motion of the earth. Renaudot did not find out about the action of the Church until November, after this particular discussion and the publication of the proceedings. In fact, Renaudot's *Gazette* is the vehicle that made Galileo's condemnation and abjuration public. *Science for a Polite Society,* 37.

25. Descartes, *Discourse on Method.* Beaulieu, "Le Groupe de Mersenne," 24.

26. Solomon, *Public Welfare, Science, and Propaganda,* 73–74.

27. "Des Cométes," 41.1, 29 May 1634, 1:329–33.

28. As Sutton notes, only one speaker defends the perfection of the sublunary regions. *Science for a Polite Society,* 33.

29. Participants generally choose the more naturalistic approaches to comets from among the broad range of early modern possibilities. See Schechner, *Comets, Popular Culture, and*

the Birth of Modern Cosmology.

30. While many of the naturalistic explanations they offered of comets were problematic, participants used the same kinds of explanations to demystify the belief in the appearance of three suns in Normandy. "De trois Soleils," 12.1, 7 November 1633, 1:93–96.

31. "Des taches de la lune et du soleil," 93, 17 December, 1635, 2:349–56. Galileo's announcement of his discovery of sunspots in "The Starry Messenger" had led to his first official clash with the Church, for in that pamphlet he had advocated Copernican astronomy.

32. Sutton, *Science for a Polite Society,* 50. This seems to me to be a rather strong contention based on a very limited range of readings in the conferences.

33. As Sutton notes, the second participant presents Galileo's own argument from the *Dialogue Concerning the Two Chief World Systems.* See *Science for a Polite Society,* 52.

34. See Waard, *L'Experience barométrique.* Pascal, Descartes, and Mersennes were all preoccupied with this issue throughout the 1640s, see Beaulieu, "Un Moine passionné."

35. "Du Vuide," 46.1, 3 July 1634, 1:369–72.

36. He uses an experimental demonstration to support his claim: "For if you suck all the air out of a bottle, then stop it exactly, and, having put it under water with the mouth downwards, open it again, the water will immediately ascend to fill the vacuity left by the extraction of the air." Ibid.

37. "Si de deux corps de difference peseanteur, l'un descend plus promptement que l'autre, & pourquoi," 249, 5 November 1640, 4:345–49. Sutton claims that "The new mechanics of the late sixteenth and early seventeenth century eluded the Bureau; only five discussions confronted mechanical problems." "Science for a Polite Society," 45.

38. This year 1691 is conventionally cited as the date by which mechanism was accepted.

39. They include, for example, Galileo, *Dialogue concerning the Two Chief World Systems*

(1632), and *Discorsi* (1638); Descartes, *Discourse on Method* (1637), and *Meditations on First Philosophy* (1641); and Gassendi, *De Motu Impresso* (1642).

40. Some important sources treating this crisis are Pintard, *Le Libertinage érudit;* Popkin, *The History of Scepticism;* and Van Leeuwen, *The Problem of Certainty.*

41. "Quelle secte des Philosophes est la plus à suivre," 208, 25 July 1639, 4:97–100.

42. This conference is so long it goes into footnote type.

43. "D'où vient la diversite des opinions," 158, 18 January 1638, 3:405–8.

44. "Qu' est-ce que Verite," 321, 3 March 1642, 5:112–16.

45. "Si les especes ou les choses sont les objets des sens," 276, 24 December 1640, 4:381–85.

46. It is rather strange that participants are less skeptical about the role of internal senses than external ones.

47. "Du Tact," 54.1, 27 November 1634, 2:33–36(34).

48. "De la Veuë," 58.1, 27 December 1634, 2:65–69 (65).

49. "Du Tact," 2:35.

50. "De la Veuë," 2:67.

51. "De l'Oüye," 2:58.

52. "De l'Odorat," 2:49.

53. "De l'Oüye," 2:58.

54. "De Goust," 55.1, 4 December 1634, 2:41–43 (43).

55. "De l'Odorat," 2:53.

56. "De l'Oüye," 2:59.

57. "De la Veuë," 2:68.

58. "Des Espéces visibles, 47.2, 10 July 1634, 1:381–84.

59. The basilisk was a mythical serpent said to kill by a look. The same name was applied to several tropical American lizards.

60. "Si les couleurs sont reelles," 50.1, 31 July 1634, 1:401–5.

61. By the end of the seventeenth century, Fontenelle could praise "geometrical method" as being widely applied. However, as many of his contemporaries could acknowledge, "The

geometric mode being a method of proof, not a method of discovery, even its most dedicated proponents knew that some room must be allowed for the empirical study of nature." Rappaport, *When Historians Were Geologists*, 43, 51. Important sources on the early history of geology include Adams, *The Birth and Development of the Geological Sciences*, which is a particularly useful source for seventeenth-century geological discussions, such as the origin of fountains; Laudan, *From Mineralogy to Geology*, which argues the importance of earlier kinds of sciences like chemistry to the development of geology; Ellenberger, *Histoire de la géologie;* and Gohau, *Histoire de la géologie,* which presents an overview of geology from ancient times to the present, and his *Les Sciences de la terre,* which deals with the seventeenth and eighteenth centuries in much more depth. Rappaport puts geology into a broad context, in *When Historians Were Geologists*. I am grateful to Kenneth Taylor for bringing these sources to my attention.

62. "Comment croissent les Mineraux?"

63. Cardano, *De Subtilitate,* and Claves, *Paradoxes ou traitez philosophiques des pierres.*

64. "De la generation des Metaux," 137, 20 April 1637, 3:221–24.

65. Aristotle believed in the transmutation of minerals. *De Corruptione,* book 2.

66. For Thales, the force of water was the cause of earthquakes. For Anaxagoras, the clouds of vapors formed in the caverns of the earth in rapid collision became fire, which, when impeded, burst forth as an earthquake. Anaximenes saw the colliding of falling earth as the source. Archelaus maintained that when the air in underground caverns became too compressed it burst forth. Agricola, like Anaxagoras, considered the vapors in the earth to cause earthquakes but saw these vapors as produced by the action of a central fire on the moisture of the earth. Cardano specified that the fiery vapors of nitre, bitumen, and sulphur were the active agents of earthquakes. Adams, *The Birth and Development of the Geological Sciences,* 399–410.

67. "Du Tremblement de Terre.

68. "Des Volcans," 109.1, 14 April 1636, 3:73–77.

69. Alchemists not only believed that there was a great body of fire at the center of the earth but that this was proved by volcanoes. See Adams, *The Birth and Development of the Geological Sciences,* 279–83.

70. The conferences also reflect seventeenth-century interest in mining. This interest is provoked by religious concerns over the age of the world and the commercial prospects associated with the expansion of the world. One interesting contemporary text is Bertereau's *La Restitution de Pluton* (god of the underworld) on the mines and minerals of France, dedicated to Richelieu in hopes of persuading him that the treasures of the earth could be mobilized for the good of France.

71. "De l'origine des Pierres Précieuses," 136, 6 April 1637, 3:217–20.

72. Adams, *The Birth and Development of the Geological Sciences,* 90.

73. "De l'origine des montagnes," 188, 7 February 1639, 4:9–12.

74. "Pourquoi l'aiguille aimantie tire t'elle vers le Nord." 205, 4 July 1639, 4:81–85.

75. The speaker is accurately presenting Cardano's theory from *De Subtilitate* that minerals were analogous to plants and animals and thus had digestive organs.

76. D'Alembert, *Preliminary Discourse,* 23.

77. "Si le monde vieillit," 27.1, 20 February 1634, 1:217–21.

78. "Du flux & reflux de la mer," 19.1, 28 December 1633, 1:153–57.

79. See also Palissy, *Discours Admirable de la Nature des Eaux et fontaines.* "De l'origine des Fontaines," 20.1, 2 January 1634, 1:161–65.

80. Ward, *The Wonder of the Loadstone.*

81. Taylor, "La Genèse d'un naturaliste."

82. Laudan notes that from the sixteenth century through the eighteenth, the description of major mineral classes remained constant but the kinds of mineral within classes were "shuffled around," and as long as the Aristotelian theory of an eternal earth held sway, the history of the earth was of minimal changes in a stable system. *From Mineralogy to*

Geology, 20.

83. For the influence of Aristotle in the works of Galileo, see Wallace, *Galileo's Logic of Discovery and Proof.*

84. Schmitt, *Aristotle and the Renaissance.*

85. Schmitt, "Towards a Reassessment of Renaissance Aristotelianism," 177.

86. Schmitt, *Aristotle and the Renaissance,* 91.

87. Grant has contested the use of the term *Aristotelianism* as giving a false sense of coherence. See *The Foundations of Modern Science in the Middle Ages.*

88. Schmitt, "Towards a Reassessment of Renaissance Aristotelianism," 178.

89. Lux, citing the work of Charles Webster, Michael Hunter, Margaret Jacob, Simon Shaffer, and Steven Shapin, among others, asserts "the derivative nature of scientific activity," in "The Reorganization of Science, 1450–1700," 185. But Cunningham draws a sharp distinction between "precise science" and "imprecise science," to which Eamon responds that such a line makes an early modern history of science impossible. Wood, Cunningham, et al., "Making Knowledge," 44.

90. Dear traces the evolution of an emphasis on experience to one on experiment in *Discipline and Experience.*

91. Gaukroger's remarks in Gaukroger, Franklin, et al., "Seized by the Spirit of Modern Science," 5.

CHAPTER FIVE

1. By a narrow margin, medical topics dominate the conferences; there are sixty topics dedicated to them. The two conferences that have just one (presumably authoritative) speaker are on medical topics. Mazauric, *Savoirs et philosophie,* 162, 137.

2. Siraisi, *Medieval and Early Renaissance Medicine,* 4.

3. "De la Vie," 69.1, 12 March 1635, 2:153–57(153).

4. "De la Mort," 67. 1, 25 February 1635, 2:137–43(140).

5. Slack notes that, in early modern England, collections of medical recipes were best-sellers. Some authors of these texts were physicians but many were not. There was no clear professional demarcation in the content, and as a result much medical literature has the character of an almanac. See Slack, "Mirrors of Health." A wide variety of medical information was available in books, pamphlets, and magazines, directed both to medical practitioners and to the literate layman. Porter and Porter point out that, because medicine was an area open to public discourse, it created a dialogue between patient and physician. See Porter and Porter, *Patient's Progress,* 189–90, 197–200.

6. See Temkin, *Hippocrates in a World of Pagans and Christians.*

7. For a discussion of the prevalence of self-medication, see Porter and Porter, *Patient's Progress,* 33–53.

8. Brockliss and Jones, *The Medical World of Early Modern France,* 98–104.

9. Packard, *Guy Patin,* 33.

10. French medical education perpetuated the influence of the Faculty. After two years of study, if the scholar was twenty-two years old, he could take his examination for his bachelor's degree, which entailed three days of questions on his studies and a commentary on an aphorism of Hippocrates. If he passed his examinations, he took an oath that he would defend the decrees, practices, customs, and statutes of the Faculty. He promised to defend the Faculty against attacks on its privileges. He also had to produce first a certificate of good conduct from three physicians; to declare that he belonged to the Catholic Church; to swear on the Bible that he would be present at the masses said before the Faculty of Medicine. For an extensive discussion of seventeenth-century medical education, see Packard, *Guy Patin,* and Brockliss, *French Higher Education.*

11. Brockliss and Jones, *The Medical World of Early Modern France,* 91.

12. "Des Talismans."

13. "De la vie," 2:154. The second speaker says that the soul, being the principle of life,

can be described in terms of the three Aristotelian souls. The third amends the definition from a Platonic perspective.

14. "Si le vin aide ou empesche la digestion, & pourquoi," 152, 1 December 1637, 3:381–84. One speaker refers to "the opinion of a learned physician of the time, who published last year an elegant treatise on this subject" (382).

15. "De la vie"; "De la Mort."

16. "De la Saignée," 105.1, 10 March 1636, 3:41–45.

17. "Si le tempérament le plus propre à la santé est aussi le plus propre à l'esprit," 315, 13 January 1642, 5:78–80(79).

18. "De la Physiognomie," 23.1, 23 January 1634, 1:185–88(187–88).

19. "De la Cure magnetique des maladies," 68.1, 5 March 1635, 2:145–49 (148).

20. "De la Saignée," 3:41.

21. "Des Somnambules."

22. "De la Physiognomie," 1:186.

23. "Des Taches & autres marques qui paroissent au visage," 335, 9 June 1642, 5:182–86(185).

24. "S'il est bon de se servir de remedes Chymiques," 107.1, Tuesday, 1 April 1636, 3:57–62(57).

25. In medical terms, astrology meant that diseases could be avoided. Medical horoscopes or the macrocosm-microcosm analogy could ally the free will of the individual with the forces of nature so that health could be preserved. Chapman has traced the empowerment offered by astrology in "Astrological Medicine."

26. "Combien peut estre l'homme sans manger," 15.1, 28 November 1633, 1:117–21.

27. "Des Somnambules," 1:269.

28. "De la Physiognomie."

29. "S'il y a des remédes spécifiques à chaque maladie," 49.1, 24 July 1634, 1:393–98.

30. "Du tentement d'Oreille," 322, 10 March 1642, 5:117–21(117).

31. "Des diuers termes de l'accouchement des femmes, & pourquoi les enfans viuent plustost à sept mois qu'à huict," 303, 19 August 1641, 5:29–34.

32. Natural heat is considered particularly significant in determining whether an individual will recover from disease because it purges the body of impurities. See Hall, "Life, Death, and Radical Moisture."

33. "De la Lethargie," 140, 11 May 1637, 3:233–37(233).

34. "Si les maladies se guérissent par leurs contraires ou par leurs semblables?" 262, 17 September 1640, 4:313–16.

35. There is such unanimity on this point that dissent takes the form of warnings about excessive humidity.

36. "Quel est le plus sain de l'humide ou du sec," 92.1, 10 December 1635, 2:341–45.

37. "Si l'imagination peut produire & guérir des maladies," 171, 3 May 1638, 3:457–60.

38. Sacks, *The Man who Mistook His Hat for His Wife.*

39. "Si l'imagination peut produire & guérir des maladies."

40. "Si la sante peute communiquer," 313, 16 December 1641, 5:69–72(69).

41. Brockliss and Jones, *The Medical World of Early Modern France,* 112–13.

42. "De la lépre, & pourquoi elle n'est pas si commune en ce siecle qu'aux precedens, 75.1, 30 April 1635, 2:201–5; and "De la goutte," 102.1, 18 February 1636, 3:17–22.

43. "De l'epilepsie ou haut mal," 80.1, 12 June 1635, 2:241–45.

44. "De la goutte." This rather peculiar sense of disease is cited several times.

45. "D' où viennent les Crises des maladies," 168, 12 April 1638, 3:445–48.

46. Hippocrates compiled this information to determine the number of days from onset of the disease to its resolution or to trace recurrent fevers in diseases like malaria. This information was then combined with beliefs about the properties associated with specific numbers. See Siraisi, *Medieval and Early Renaissance Medicine,* 135.

47. "Du circuit ou accez des Fiévres,"

38.1, 8 May 1634, 1:305–9.

48. Brockliss and Jones, *The Medical World of Early Modern France*, 45.

49. "Des causes de la petite Verole."

50. See Quétal, *History of Syphilis*.

51. Fernel, *De naturali parte medicinae*, and *Universa Medicina*.

52. See Levy-Valensi, *La Médecine*.

53. "Des causes de la petite Verole."

54. "Comment ceux qui sont mordus de la Tarantole guérissent par le son de quelque instrument Musical," 332, 19 May 1642, 5:167–70.

55. "Si les Ecroüelles se guerissent par l'attouchement d'un septiesme garçon, & pourquoi?" 328, 21 April 1642, 5:147–53.

56. "Si l'homme est le plus maladif de tous les animaux & pourquoy," 182, Tuesday 7 December 1638, 3:509–12.

57. It is rather surprising that health conditions affecting only women are not generally mentioned except in questions of fertility and reproduction (see Chapter Nine), especially since, as one speaker puts it, "because of the parts that differentiate the sexes, the woman is still more sickly than man." Ibid., 3:509. Only a conference "Of the green-sickness" or lovesickness, because it ordinarily afflicts marriageable virgins, "Des Pâles-couleurs," 100.1, 4 February 1636, 2:413–15.

58. "De l'epilepsie ou haut mal."

59. "Des Eaux Minerales," 110.1, 21 April 1636, 3:82–85.

60. "De la goutte."

61. Galenism faced two other, more severe challenges in the second half of the seventeenth century, Harvey's circulatory system and the introduction of mechanism. No positive or negative mention of Harvey's theory appears in student theses before 1640. Brockliss and Jones, *The Medical World of Early Modern France*, 138.

62. "De la Poudre de Sympathie," 342, 4 August 1642, 5:220–25.

63. "Des principes de Chymie," 260, 3 September 1640, 4:305–8(305).

64. "S' il est bon de se servir de remedes Chymiques."

65. "Des principes de Chymie."

66. These comprehensive medical recommendations, which included diet, exercise, work, and travel, were intended to allow the patient to regain health by altering his physiological constitution. See Porter and Porter, *Patient's Progress*, 83–84.

67. Brockliss and Jones, *The Medical World of Early Modern France*, 114–15.

68. "S'il faut plus Disner que Souper," 132, 9 March 1637, 3:201–4.

69. Drugs became more significant in medical treatments after new drugs were available because of trade with the Far East and the New World, and Paracelsians relied heavily on chemicals and minerals. See Porter and Porter, *Patient's Progress*, 157–59.

70. Temperament, season, countries, exercises, diversity of food, custom, and in particular, the disposition of the organs all make a notable difference, as speakers remark in "Combien peut estre l'homme sans manger."

71. "Si le vin aide ou empesche la digestion, & pourquoy."

72. Brockliss and Jones, *The Medical World of Early Modern France*, 570.

73. "De l'iyvrognerie," 66.1, 19 February 1635, 2:129–33.

74. "De la Cure magnetique des maladies."

75. The following is the recipe given for the salve: "Take an ounce of the unctuous matter that sticks on the inside of the skull of one hanged and left in the air; let it be gathered when the moon waxes, and is in the sign either of Pisces, Taurus, or Libra, as near as may be to Venus, or mummy and man's blood yet warm, of each as much; of man's fat two ounces; of linseed oil, turpentine, and sole armeick, of each two drams; mingle altogether in a mortar, and keep the mixture in a long-necked glass well stopped. It must be made while the sun is in the sign Libra; and the weapon must be anointed with it, beginning from that part which did the mischief; from the point to the hilt, if it be a thrust; and from the edge, if it be a cut or blow." Ibid., 148.

76. Speakers recognize that therapy must be directed to both the body and the mind. See "De la Rage," 76.1, 7 May 1635, 2:209–13(209).

77. Brockliss and Jones, *The Medical World of Early Modern France*, 155.

78. "De la Saignée," 3:43.

79. "Combien peut estre l'homme sans manger," 1:118.

80. Brockliss and Jones, *The Medical World of Early Modern France*, 154–57.

81. "Des Cométes," 1:333.

82. "Du Bezoard," 256, 6 August 1640, 4:289–93.

83. Packard, *Guy Patin*, 147–48.

84. "Du Bezoard." Those who spoke against Bezoar might have been relying on Ambroise Paré's treatise on the uselessness of bezoar and unicorn's horn. Brockliss and Jones, *The Medical World of Early Modern France*, 148.

85. Packard, *Guy Patin*, 162–63.

86. For a discussion of the psychological value of diagnosis, see Slack, "Mirrors of Health," 237–73.

87. Brockliss and Jones, *The Medical World of Early Modern France*, 115–16.

88. Ibid., 81.

89. The appeal to social benefit is consistent with topics explored in other chapters of this study.

90. "Qu' elle est la plus necessaire à un Estat & la plus noble, la Medecine ou la Jurisprudence," 117, 24 November 1636, 3:137–40.

91. Brockliss and Jones, *The Medical World of Early Modern France*, 86.

92. "S'il est venu plus de bien que de mal du partage des trois parties de la Medecine, en Medecins, Chirurgiens & Apotiquairies," 180, 22 November 1638, 3:501–4.

93. To the degree that scholars discuss medicine in the conferences, they focus on the bitter dispute between Renaudot and the Faculty of Medicine over the issue of chemical remedies, especially antimony. For a thorough examination of this dispute, see Debus, *The French Paracelsians,* 46–100.

94. In her overview of a collection of essays on Enlightenment science, Daston highlights many of these same attitudes as the hallmarks of Enlightenment science. "Afterword: The Ethos of Enlightenment."

95. "Du circuit ou accez des Fiévres," 1:305.

96. "Combien peut estre l'homme sans manger," 1:120.

97. Porter cites Benjamin Rush, physician and signatory to the Declaration of Independence, and in Britain William Buchan, author of the best-selling domestic medicine (1769), as examples of this perspective, "Medical Science and Human Science in the Enlightenment." The phrase *recovery of nerve* is the title of the first chapter in Peter Gay, *The Science of Freedom.*

98. Lindemann notes that by the eighteenth century one can point to a less rigorous or blind adherence to theory and an increasing emphasis on observation and experience as signs of medical progress. See *Medicine and Socety in Early Modern Europe,* 91.

INTRODUCTION TO PART II

1. "Des Incubes & Succubes," 3:187.

2. "Quel est le plus communicatif du bien ou du mal," 3:94.

3. Shapin, *A Social History of Truth*.

4. "Si les maigres sont plus sains, & de plus longue vie que les gras," 123, 5 January 1637, 3:165–6 (167).

5. "Si les hommes se formeroient un langage n'en ayans point appris d'autre," 156, 4 January 1638, 3:391–400(398).

6. "Du Vuide," 1:371.

7. "Des principes & de la fin de toutes choses," 1:10.

8. Pourquoi tous aiment-ils mieux commander qu'obeir?" 40.2, 22 May 1634, 1:324–28. The sixth speaker presents the more orthodox opinion "that man having been created by God for command, as Holy Writ attests, he always retains the remembrance of his origin and would be master everywhere"

(327).

9. "S'il est meilleur à un Estat d'avoir des Esclaves," 7.2, 3 October 1633, 1:54–57(57).

10. "S'il y a eu de plus grands hommes en quelqu'un des siecles precédens qu'en cettui-ci," 144, 15 June 1637, 3:349–52.

11. Ibid., 3:351.

12. See Jacob, *The Cultural Meaning of the Scientific Revolution,* and Merchant, *The Death of Nature.*

13. D'Alembert, *Preliminary Discourse,* 61. The editor notes that d'Alembert reproduces Fontenelle's argument in favor of the moderns in his *Digression of the Ancients and the Moderns.*

14. Renaudot, "Preface."

15. Mandrou, *From Humanism to Science,* 56.

16. Hatin notes that Renaudot's conferences are the origin of the proceedings, collections, and memoirs of learned societies, a veritable "académie des sciences au petit pied." *Théophraste Renaudot,* 137–39.

CHAPTER SIX

1. "De l'intellect," 65.1, 12 February 1635, 2:121–25.

2. When participants cite the soul as the principle of movement, they reflect the influence of Aristotle's *De Anima,* II.1.412a. For a brief discussion of the use of Aristotle in the conferences, see Mazauric, *Savoirs et philosophie,* 203.

3. "En quel temps l'ame raisonable est infuse," 142, 25 May 1637, 3:241–44.

4. Aquinas, *Summa Theologica,* I.q84.a3–4; *Summa contra gentiles,* book 3, part 1, chapter 46.

5. "D' où viennent les bons & mauvais gestes, la bonne grace & les grimaces," 189, 21 February 1639, 4:13–17.

6. He gives a specific example: "a man of small stature has quick, brusque gestures, while the large and the melancholy have heavy and slow gestures."

7. "Si les maux de l'esprit sont plus grands que ceux du corps," 201, 30 May 1639,

4:65–69.

8. "Si la beauté du corps est indice de la bonté et beauté de l'esprit," 293, 27 May 1641, 4:449–53(452).

9. Aristotle said in chapter 6 of his physiognomy that the big head has less sense, and Avicenna praised the small head where one encounters the force and vigor of the formative virtue. See the discussion "Si les grosses testes ont plus d'esprit que les autres," 224, 23 January 1640, 4:173–77(173).

10. "S'il n'y a rien dans l'intellect qui n'ait esté dans les sens," 210, 8 August 1639, 4:105–9.

11. "Si l'esprit humain est borné en ses opérations, & pourquoi?" 209, 1 August 1639, 4:101–4.

12. Other speakers make remarks that even suggest—although this is, of course, a historical impossibility—a Cartesian refutation of John Locke's epistemology.

13. For example, in "Si les larmes viennent de foiblesse" (49, 24 July 1634, 1:397–401) a speaker connects the phenomena of tears to the way rain is produced, demonstrating that virtually any phenomenon can usefully and easily be correlated to natural phenomena (1:397).

14. "S'il esprit humain est borné en ses operation, et pourquoi?" 209, 1 August 1639, 101–4(101).

15. "De l'Amitié," 38.2, 8 May 1634, 1:309–12(311).

16. "S' il vaut mieux estre sans passions, que les modérer," 31.2, 20 March 1634, 1:253–56(254).

17. "Et pourquoy chacun est jaloux de ses opinions, n'y eust-il aucun autre interest," 3, 5 September 1633, 1:20–23(22).

18. "Pourquoi personne n'est-il content de sa condition?" 18.2, 19 December 1633, 1:149–52(149).

19. The discussion of the physiological process of laughter does not draw an analogy to a machine but does suggest that processes like the swelling and compression of solids and fluids is an important way to understand physiological processes. "Du Ris," 24.2, 30

January 1634, 1:197–200(198).

20. There is also a moral component of this question; man seeks to satisfy desires, but satisfaction of his desires is bad for him. "Pourquoi personne n'est-il content de sa condition?" 1:150.

21. "De la fortune," 54.2, 27 November 1634, 2:36–40(37).

22. "Pourquoi les hommes sont plustost enclins au Vice qu'à la Vertu," 21.2, 9 January 1634, 1:173–76(175).

23. "S' il est plus aisé de resister a la Volupté qu' à la Douleur," 11.2, 31 October 1633, 1:86–91(86).

24. "Quel est le plus puissant de l'Amour ou de la Haine," 16.2, December 1633, 1:132–36(132). La Mothe le Vayer, who is sometimes assumed to have attended the conferences, concurs that the passions "are natural emotions, which are formed in the sensual part where they have their seat." *Of Liberty and Servitude,* 849.

25. "De la Beauté." 26.2, 13 February 1634, 1:213–16.

26. For example, "in most sciences and arts, men have fancied to themselves proto-types and parallels, to serve instead as patterns and models, in policy, an accomplished commonwealth, such as Plato, Sir Thomas More . . . so they who have undertaken to speak of beauty have imagined a perfect one."

27. "Du Courage," 48.2, 17 July 1634, 1:389–92.

28. "Le courage est-il naturel ou aquis?" 155, 22 December 1637, 3:393–96. Courage is the only topic that merits two virtually identical topics.

29. "Si le courage vient de nature ou d'institution," 257, 13 August 1640, 4:293–97. This is one of the very few conferences that even repeat a theme, although "natural or acquired" has been sharpened into "from nature or from institutions."

30. For a discussion of the "wild girl" in eighteenth-century France, see Douthwaite, *Exotic Women.*

31. "Si la vertu consiste en médiocrité," 170, 26 April 1638, 3:453–57.

32. Participants might well have relied on Petrarch's *De remediis,* an influential humanist text on the passions and a discussion of stoic methods of healing the passions. For a discussion of this text, see Panizza, "Stoic Psychotherapy."

33. Gaubroger, *The Soft Underbelly of Reason,* 10. For an explication of this argument, see Harrison, "Reading the Passions," 50.

34. See Levi, *French Moralists.*

35. 3"S'il vaut mieux estre sans passions, que les modérer." 1:253.

36. Ibid., 1:253–56.

37. "De l'Apathie des Stoïques, 251, 9 July 1640, 4:261–64.

38. "Quelle est la plus forte de l'Esperance ou de la Crainte," 64.2, 5 February 1635, 2:117–20.

39. Ibid.

40. "S' il vaut mieux estre sans passions."

41. "De l'Envie," 73.2, 16 April 1635, 2:190–92.

42. Ibid.

43. "De la Honte," 70.2, 19 March 1635, 2:165–68; "De l'Envie," 2:190–92; "De la Rage."

44. "De la Honte."

45. "De la Iolousie," 27.2, 20 February 1634, 1:221–24.

46. "Quel est le plus grand de tous les Vices," 36.2, 24 April 1634, 1:294–96.

47. "Quelle est la plus grande Réjoüissance de l'homme?" 28.1, 27 February 1634, 1:228–32. This position is not developed with the radicalism inherent to French materialism until the medical writings of figures like La Mettrie, *Le Discours sur le bonheur.*

48. Keohane, *Philosophy and the State,* 112. See Montaigne, *Complete Essays,* 1:2, 77.

49. Given Descartes's inability to resolve questions about how the passions arising in the body affect the immaterial soul, it is unlikely that many of Renaudot's conferees would have found his account compelling. For a thorough exploration of Descartes on the passions, see Levi, *French Moralists.*

50. Keohane, *Philosophy and the State*, 140–43.

51. Charron, *Of Wisdom*, 11, 57–58.

52. "D'où vient la diversité des opinions."

53. These thinkers are cited as a fund of common knowledge.

54. Many historians who have studied the conferences have looked to the scientific topics and generally neglected the others, see Solomon, *Public Welfare, Science, and Propaganda,* and Sutton, *Science for a Polite Society.*

55. "Pourquoi tous les hommes desirent naturellement sçavoir," 39.1, 15 May 1634, 1:315–17.

56. "Si l'Homme peut avoir trop de science," 305, 16 September 1641, 5:37–41.

57. "Lequel est le plus porté au vice, de l'ignorant ou du sçavant," 249, 18 June 1640, 4:253–57.

58. "Des inventions & de leurs causes & principes," 206, 11 July 1639, 4:85–89.

59. "Lequel vaudroit-il mieux sçavoir tout ce que sçavent les hommes, ou tout ce qu'ils ignorent?" 175, 7 June 1638, 3:473–76.

60. "S' il vaut mieux scavoir de tout un petit, ou une seule chose solidement?" 44.2, 19 June 1634, 1:356–60.

61. "Si la Poësie est utile," 55.2. 4 December 1634, 2:43–48.

62. "Si la musique fait plus de mal que de bien," 176, 14 June 1638, 3:477–80.

63. "Le quel est le plus propre à l'estude, le soir ou le matin," 191, 14 March 1639, 4:21–25.

64. "Le quel est le plus necessaire à aquerir les disciplines, le grand esprit ou le grand travail," 193, 28 March 1639, 4:26–33.

65. "Quels sont les plus ingenieux du monde?" 194, 4 April 1639, 4:33–37.

66. "Sil vaut mieux bien parler que bien escrire," 50.2, 31 July 1634, 1:405–9.

67. On the primacy of hearing and oral culture in early modern culture, see Mandrou, *From Humanism to Science.*

68. Febvre and Martin, *The Coming of the Book;* Martin, *The History and the Power of the Writing.*

69. "De l'eloquence," 56.2, 11 December 1634, 2:53–56.

70. Nauert, ed., *Humanism and the Culture of Renaissance Europe;* Hill, ed., *Infinity, Faith, and Time.*

71. A number of conferences are dedicated to specific stylistic concerns, as conferees attempt to determine what rhetorical strategies or stylistic conventions will most effectively convey information and persuade listeners. See "S' il vaut mieux citer les Autheurs que s' en abstenir," 310, 4 November 1641, 5:57–61; "Lequel est le plus requis à la conversation, le jugement ou la memoire," 217, 28 November 1639, 4:141–45; "Lequel est à preferer de parler le premier ou le dernier," 294, 3 June 1641, 4:453–57.

72. "Si la langue Françoise est suffisante pour apprendre toutes les Sciences," 296, 24 June 1641, 5:1–5.

73. Mazauric, *Savoirs et philosophie,* 132–33.

74. Brunel, *Les philosophes et l'Académie française au dix-huitième siècle.*

75. "De la diversité des langues," 42, 7 June 1634, 1:341–44.

76. "Si les hommes se formeroient un langage."

77. This argument carries forth the medical notion that aging is a process of progressive drying.

78. "Il faut escrire comme l' on prononce, ou suivre l' ancienne & commune orthographe," 186, 24 January 1639, 4:1–5.

79. Bodin is cited so that the speaker can make a conservative argument about usage, because "letter" (by which he seems to mean literal letters) are the foundation.

80. Smith, *The Norton History of the Human Sciences;* McDonald, ed., *The Historic Turnin the Human Sciences;* French, Uehling, and Wettstein, eds., *The Philosophy of the Human Sciences.*

81. Montesquieu, *The Spirit of the Laws.* Jordanova develops this argument in "Sex and Gender," 162.

82. Smith, "The Languages of Human Nature," 100–101.

83. By the eighteenth century, as Jordanova has noted, the language of human nature signals an a priori notion of the human subject. *Sexual Visions*, 19–43.

CHAPTER SEVEN

1. "Quelle est la moins blasmable de l'Avarice, ou de la Prodigalité," 22.2, 16 January 1634, 1:181–84.

2. Some significant sources discussing this evolution are: MacIntyre, *After Virtue;* Hirschmann, *The Passions and the Interests;* and Stout, *Ethics after Babel; The Flight from Authority.*

3. "S'il est permis de se loüer soy-meme," 26.1, 13 February 1634, 209–13.

4. Kettering begins her overview of French society with a discussion of the contentious meeting of the Estates General of 1614, which so focused on issues of precedence that nothing was accomplished. *French Society*, 1–4.

5. "De l' Amitie," 1:309–12.

6. Participants recast discussions of friendship in terms of several scientific relationships, for example, as the union of form and matter or the phenomenon of like seeking like.

7. "S'il vaut mieux se contenter d'un seul amy que d'en auoir plusiers," 316, 20 January 1642, 5:81–87.

8. Note that relationships like friendship are discussed in quasi-commercial terms.

9. The reference to *honnêteté* is rare in the conferences, although it is common to the literature of the 1620s and 1630s. It defines a cultural ideal in conscious opposition to the decadence of the court. Chartier, *Passions of the Renaissance*, 192.

10. "Laquelle est la plus insupportable des offences de l'amie ou de l'ennemi," 196, 18 April 1639, 4:41–45.

11. Cicero, *De Amicitia;* Aristotle, *Aristotle's Ethics.*

12. "Si l'amitié est plus durable entre égaux ou inégaux," 266, 15 October 1640, 4:329–33.

13. An entire page of the conference is dedicated to the conditions that can produce inequalities between two friends who start out as equals. Ibid., 330.

14. Many discussions of equality assume that the issue is one of wealth rather than rank.

15. The poet is unidentified.

16. It is unusual in the context of early modern discussion of marriage to associate marriage with friendship.

17. Montaigne distinguished friendship from other relationships which are diluted by pleasure or profits, by public or private needs. See *Complete Essays*, I:28, 136.

18. "De la coustume," 63.2, 29 January 1635, 2:108–12.

19. He further distinguishes custom from law: "Approved by the tacit consent of the whole people; and therefore more grateful than law, which never equally pleases all; and, if of times formed in an instant, but custom, taking root by time, is not established except after long experience." Ibid., 109.

20. See, for example, the work of Casaubon, *A treatise concerning enthusiasme,* and *A treatise proving spirits, witches, and supernatural operations.*

21. Voltaire, "Essai sur les moeurs"; Montesquieu, *The Spirit of the Laws.*

22. See especially, La Mettrie, *Le Discours sur le bonheur*, 83–166; Denis Diderot, "Réfutation de l'ouvrage d'Helvétius intitulé de *L'Homme.*"

23. "De la danse," 66.2, 19 February 1635, 2:133–37.

24. "Des masques, & s' il est permis de se déguiser," 282, 11 February 1641, 4:405–9.

25. See Davis, *Society and Culture;* and Hotchkiss, *Clothes Make the Man.* The quotation is from Deuteronomy 1.

26. In their disparagement of makeup, participants reflect Renaissance moralists and a bourgeois return to simplicity. See Grieco, "Body, Appearance, and Sexuality," 57–63.

27. Dewald notes that these objections to masks gave way to an appreciation for the masked ball in the court of Louis XIV. By the late seventeenth century, he notes that there

was sufficient appreciation for elegance that it was common to look back at the early seventeenth century as a period of brutality and sexual license, *Aristocratic Experience*, 135.

28. These are suggested rather than confirmed, since we cannot determine who attended.

29. Dewald, *Aristocratic Experience*, 132. Jansenists were followers of Cornelius Jansen, who were prominent in seventeenth-century France. Perhaps their most prominent member was Blaise Pascal. They emphasized predestination and the human propensity toward evil. To remain within the Catholic Church, Jansenists had to repudiate several tenets of Jansen's thought.

30. "Des Fables."

31. See Knecht, *Richelieu*; Billaçois, *The Duel*.

32. "Du Poinct d'Honneur," 19.2, 28 December 1633, 1:157–60.

33. "S'il est permis de mourir pour son amy," 246, 30 April 1640, 4:237–41.

34. "Si le Pardon vaut mieux que la Vengeance," 41.2, 29 May 1634, 1:333–36. The question of pardon versus revenge brings to the fore a conflict betyween nature and civil culture. In general, speakers consider pardon to be better than revenge because it reflects reason, man's highest function, but they also acknowledge that revenge is given to man by nature, so it must serve a valuable purpose and ought not to be disparaged.

35. The interiorization of the moral life reflects Stoic *arete*, which invokes the notions of law to displace virtue. See MacIntyre, *After Virtue*, 157, 168.

36. "Lequel est à préferer la compagnie ou la solitude," 166, 22 March 1638, 3:437–40.

37. Lougee has noted that the pursuit of pleasure can be identified in its seventeenth-century context with the pursuit of luxury. *Le Paradis des Femmes*, 72–78.

38. Many historians resist associating changes in ethics with the rise of the bourgeoisie. Clearly the term *bourgeois*, as used in a Marxist sense to describe the middle classes created by industrial wealth, is anachronistic if applied to an earlier period. The resistance legitimately rests on a sense that changes are not class-based and that the bourgeoisie cannot be clearly identified in this period. See Hirschman, *The Passions and the Interests*, 9–11.

39. Ibid.

40. While it is usual to talk about an evolution from the heroic ideal of feudal times to the bourgeois ethic, Hirschman has considerably refined the picture by detailing a gradual transformation of the passions into something noble. The passions then become virtues, of benefit to the individual and the state. Ibid., 32, 48, 54.

41. The text explicitly discusses the interest one has in maintaining one's own opinion. "Et pourquoy chacun est jaloux de ses opinions."

42. Ibid., 1:22.

43. For example, a speaker contends that virtue and vice depend on one's nationality, noting that among the Spartans it was no crime to steal and that the northern nations are undecided about drunkenness. "Quel est le plus grand de tous les Vices," 1:295.

44. "Lequel est le plus en estime de la Science ou de la Vertu," 60.2, 8 January 1635, 2:85–89.

45. The argument that virtue endows one with moral worth but does not guarantee success is part of the Stoic tradition. MacIntyre, *After Virtue*, 157, 168. That sentiment does not shape this speaker's complaint.

46. "S' il y a une Ambition loüable," 20.2, 2 January 1634, 1:164–68. La Mothe le Vayer, who is often assumed to have attended the conferences, is more scathing than any conference participant about the deleterious effect of the court on liberty and morality. He claims that one must give up liberty for other desires; one can express no opinion; in essence the intellectual is prostituted by "flatterings so enormous and ridiculous, that one ever appears to have made bankrupt all manner of judgment," *Of Liberty and Servitude*, 28, 31, 32.

47. "S'il ya une Ambition loüable," 1:165.

48. Ambition emerged as a central value in

the memoirs of the nobility, whereas rural households were associated with vice, ignorance, and failure. See Dewald, *Aristocratic Experience,* 16–21. As Gordon noted, while Enlightenment social virtue melds selfishness and benevolence, it does not idealize self-interest or assume that order can result from avaricious pursuits. *Citizens without Sovereignty,* 70.

49. Du Jonc, *La Chimère ou fantôme de la mendicité* (Paris, 1607) in Denieul-Cormier, *Paris à l'aube du Grand Siècle,* 162–63.

50. Denieul-Cormier, *Paris à l'aube du Grand Siècle,* 165.

51. "Quel est le plys propre pour acquerir la Sagesse, des richesses ou de la pauvreté," 102.2, 18 February 1636, 3:22–24.

52. These sorts of observations underlie Montesquieu's *Spirit of the Laws.*

53. Vives, *De l'assistance aux pauvres,* 184.

54. Vives shares many approaches to poor relief both with those actually implemented under the aegis of the Bureau and those discussed by conference participants. However, he insists that poor relief must be administered with "care for the true good of the soul." Ibid., 191–217. Renaudot shares his concern with charity, but not with the care of the soul.

55. "Du Réglement des Pauvres," 35.1, Wednesday, 19 April 1634, 1:284–8.

56. "Du Mont de Pieté," 43.2, 12 June 1634, 1:348–52.

57. I have not modernized the language of the English translation of this text. For example, on the topic of education, Richelieu wrote, "Bee not lavish of your language, but rather sparing of speech. Let your words be such as carry with them their due authority and weight. And withall accustome yourself to passe diverse things under the great Seale of silence." *Emblema Anima,* 202–3.

58. "Policy may governe the World, nature policy, but religion both." Ibid., 10.

59. In his discourse 22, "Of ambition and pride," Richelieu claims that no vice is more heinous than ambition, because it can lead one "to violate the laws of reason and reli-gion." Ibid., 253-54.

60. Merchant, *The Death of Nature,* 214–15.

61. As Keohane notes, many of those who promulgated the ethic of strict separation on the side of the individual were scientists, philosophers, writers by profession, and thus bourgeois. *Philosophy and the State,* 120–36. On the class background of these authors, see Pintard, *Le Libertinage érudit,* 271–95; and J. S. Spink, *French Free Thought.*

62. The Huguenot political theoretician, Mayerne wrote a treatise, *De la monarchie aristo-democratique* (1611), in which he spoke directly for the interests of the new bourgeoisie and argued for the development of a social elite of men dedicated to the public welfare. See Keohane, *Philosophy and the State,* 128. Among the best studies of these theories are Levi, *French Moralists;* Krailsheimer, *Studies in Self-Interest;* Adam, *Histoire de la littérature française,* and *Les Libertins au XVIIe siècle.*

63. Gunn, in *Politics and Public Interest,* provides much useful information about the development of the notion of interest in the context of English politics where "interest" functioned as a realistic term describing the actual aspirations of princes. In France, the most important statement of the interest of the state was made by the Duke of Rohan who said "Princes rule people, and interest rules princes," *De l'interest des princes et des estats de la Chrestienete.*

64. MacIntyre suggests that philosophy in the early modern period provides an instrument of social analysis and criticism of the established order. *A Short History of Ethics,* 148.

65. Hirschman, *The Passions and the Interests,* 2–32.

66. Elias, *The Civilizing Process;* Arditi, *A Geneology of Manners.*

CHAPTER EIGHT

1. "Si la Censure est necessaire en un Estat," 297, 1 July 1641, 5:5–8.

2. Bodin made a similar point, warning

that certain cures were too dangerous to the state. *Six Bookes of a Commonweale,* 469. (This is the translation I refer to, although in English discussion of Bodin the translation is usually *Six Books of the Republic.*)

3. Renaudot, "Preface," 1:3. The dangers inherent to religious discussion by a group sponsored by a recent convert from Protestantism are obvious.

4. Richelieu restricted the content of remarks to a degree Renaudot's group did not accept, when he said of academic conversation that "Obscure sciences and great affairs must have a less share in their discourses than agreeableness and diversion." *The Art of pleasing in conversation,* 3, 161.

5. It should be clear that Renaudot does not seem to have controlled the discussion or to have imposed an agenda or particular point of view.

6. Keohane, *Philosophy and the State.* The following discussion of the political philosophy in seventeenth-century France is especially indebted to this work.

7. Just as the Anglo-American tradition has led to the neglect of political writings associated with absolutism, so too, the French Revolution and its problematic relationship to the Enlightenment has led historians to neglect the significance of the seventeenth century to the development of political theory.

8. The Estates General is the representative body of France. It is divided into three estates: the clergy, the nobility, and everyone else.

9. Duplessis-Mornay, *Vindiciae contra tyrannos.*

10. Because of this association, the arguments of French Huguenots effectively foreclosed some options in French political discussions. See Keohane, *Philosophy and the State,* 49.

11. Ibid., 9–43.

12. Absolutism has provoked a vehement division of opinion in response to Marxist analyses of economics under absolutism. Anderson maintains the persistence of feudalism under absolutism, in *Lineages of the Absolutist State.* Other scholars emphasize the connections between absolutism and capitalism. See Poulantzas, *Political Power and Social Classes,* and Wallerstein, *The Modern World-System,* Lublinskaya presents a critical analysis of all these views in *French Absolutism.* Since the demise of Marxist historiography, there has been little synthetic work done on seventeenth-century French politics.

13. Keohane, *Philosophy and the State,* 61–81.

14. Commynes, *Mémoires;* Seyssel, *La Monarchie de France.*

15. Keohane, *Philosophy and the State,* 29–33.

16. Sassoferrato, *Bartolus on the Conflict of Laws;* Emerton, *Humanism and Tyranny.*

17. Agrippa, *De occulta philosophia libri tres,* and *Declamation on the Nobility and Preeminence of the Female Sex.*

18. One speaker reveals a Machiavellian notion that the political theories of Plato and Aristotle might well be ideal, but they are impractical and, in fact, disastrous in their application. "De la Communauté des biens," 76.2, 7 May 1635, 2:213–17(215).

19. Montaigne, "Of Friendship," *The Complete Essays,* book 1, essay 28, pp. 135–45.

20. Lipsius, *Six Bookes of Politickes,* Book VI, 3.

21. La Mothe le Vayer, a figure sometimes identified with Renaudot, is an exception to this position among the *libertins;* he pursued a public career as a publicist and tutor to princes. He made important contributions to the development of theories of the public interest and *raison d'état* in France. See *Oeuvres.*

22. In "Laquelle est à preférer de la mort naturelle ou civile," 272, 26 November 1640, 4:357–60, the first speaker defines civil death as a banishment that prohibits a return to Rome, which generally functons as Paris in these discourses.

23. "Si le Francois est leger et inconstant: et pourquoi," 146, 30 June 1637, 3:357–60.

24. Most speakers support Machiavellian realpolitik in "S' il est plus aisé de se faire obeïr par la douceur que par la crainte," 314,

30 December 1641, 5:73–76. For an extensive discussion of the influence of Machiavelli on seventeenth-century political philosophy, see Thuau, *Raison d'état*, 54–101.

25. Bodin claims, "It is not at this day alone that French has been full of suits and contentions, the which cannot be altered and taken away, unless they decide to change the nature and disposition of the people, and it is much better to decide all controversies by law than by the sword." *The Six Bookes of a commonweale*, 559.

26. "Laquelle est à preférer de la mort naturelle ou civile." 272, 26 November 1640.

27. "Des principes & de la fin de toutes choses."

28. "Si le monde vieillit.

29. "S' il y a eu de plus grands hommes en quelqu' un des siecles precédens qu' en cettui-ci.

30. Bodin is once again a significant figure. He too was also concerned with change but construed it very broadly, citing a myriad of specific political causes, such as the failure of a prince to produce heirs, the quarrels of great men, the excessive riches of the few and the great poverty of the many, which produce changes of regime, *Six Books of a commonweale*, 412.

31. "Si les changemens des Estats ont des causes naturelles," 150, 16 November 1637, 3:373–76.

32. This argument reiterates that of the civic humanists, who asserted that republics allow the greatest human development. See for example, Bruni, *In libros Economicorum,* and Salutati, *Epistolario.*

33. He also provides historical examples to demonstrate that this is a reasonable question to raise, perhaps because none of the other speakers seems to consider it so. "De la Communauté des biens."

34. Campanella, *The City of the Sun,* 276–317.

35. "S' il est plus aisé de se faire obeïr par la douceur que par la crainte." Niccolò Machiavelli, *The Prince,* 59–62.

36. Bodin's seventh chapter—entitled, "Whether a Prince in civil factions ought to join himself to one of the parties, and whether a good subject ought to be constrained to take part with the one or the other faction"—warns that those who do not take a stand are a grave danger to the state. *Six Bookes of a commonweale,* 569.

37. Naudé, *Considérations politiques sur les coups d'estat,* 98, 110–11. See Pintard, *Le libertinage érudit,* 530–51. The Saint Bartholomew's Day Massacre was one of the bloodiest events of the French wars of religion. On August 24, 1572, the aristocracy of France were celebrating the marriage of Marguerite de Valois, the sister of the Catholic king of France Henry III, to one of the leaders of the Protestants, Henry IV. Although this marriage was intended to effect a truce between the factions, feelings ran so high that Catholic nobles turned on Protestant nobles, murdering them. The massacre soon included the people of Paris and also swept the provinces. Historians estimate that more than five thousand Protestants were murdered.

38. "De la cause des Seditions," 337, 23 June 1642, 5:192–96.

39. "Est il plus expediant dans une Guerre Ciuile demeurer neutre que prendre party," 336, 16 June 1642, 5:187–91.

40. This perspective is characteristic of the Stoics as in Lipsius, *Sixe Bookes of Politickes.* See Pintard for an extensive discussion of the political views of these seventeenth-century Stoics. *Le Libertinage érudit,* 530–49.

41. "Quelle science est la plus necessaire a un Estat," 286, 11 March 1641, 4:421–25(424). He concludes that the sciences are not useful to any group in the state: They impede the soldier, the laborer, and the artisan from doing what they should.

42. "Des moyens de rendre quelque lieu peuplé," 75.2, 30 April 1635, 2:205–8.

43. This speaker notes that before they adopted Christianity, the Romans permitted polygamy and divorce, authorized concubinate, and made natural children legitimate to foster propagation.

44. "S' il vaut mieux garder sa frontière, que de porter la guerre chez l' ennemi," 157,

11 January 1638, 3:401–4.

45. "Si la Permutation est plus commode que l' achat & la vente," 39.2, 15 May 1634, 1:318–20.

46. Laffemas pleads for the poor, specifically for the cultivation of industry as a solution to the problems of poverty, in *Recueil présenté an Roy,* 244–45.

47. Like other mercantilists, conferees recognize that the interests of the monarch and his subjects could be mutually enhanced through the fostering of vigorous commercial activity. See Wolfe, "French Views on Wealth and Taxes," 196. Heckscher, in *Mercantilism,* argues persuasively that the views of mercantilists and laissez-faire theorists were much the same on these dimensions.

48. Palm, "The Economic Policies of Richelieu."

49. Laffemas, *Histoire du commerce de France,* 412, 415–17.

50. Montchrétien, *Traicté,* 229, 232–33, 235, 243–44.

51. Ibid., 242–43, 247, 269.

52. If the contemplative life is fostered, "Les occupations civiles estant empesches et comme endormies dans le sein de la contemplation, il faudroit necessairement que la Republique tombast en ruine," (Civil occupations being impeded as if asleep within the breast of contemplation, the Republic must necessarily fall into ruin). Ibid., 18.

53. Ibid., xx.

54. Richelieu, *Political Testament.*

55. Knecht, *Richelieu,* 7.

56. The Assembly of Notables endorsed a number of Richelieu's proposals intended to maintain a navy, to tax imported goods, and to develop maritime commerce. Ibid., 154.

57. Ibid., 156.

58. Increased military expenditure was by far the most important factor. It fostered the ethos of French aristocratic military culture into the seventeenth century. Ibid., 10.

59. Parker, *The Making of French Absolutism,* 59–64.

60. "Lequel est le plus nuisible à un Estat, l'oisiveté ou le luxe," 270, 12 November 1640,

4:349–52.

61. Montchrétien, *Traicté,* 38–39.

62. Two key figures in the conflicting assessments are Elliott, who believes that the situations in France and Spain are comparable, in *Richelieu and Olivares;* and Shennan, who suggests stability from 1461 to 1661, in *Origins of the Early Modern State.*

63. Barthélemy de Laffemas, *Recueil présenté au Roi,* 220.

64. In his *Six livres de la republique,* Bodin disapproves of luxury because it drained off national resources to exotic lands. See particularly, *Six Bookes of a commonweale* bk. 6, chap. 2, 161.

65. Montchrétien, *Traicté,* 101–3.

66. "Le commerce deroge-t-il à la Noblesse?" 160, 1 February 1638, 3:413–16. Though participants address the role of the nobility in the political structure and are willing to make arguments to curtail its role, they take monarchy for granted and do not advance arguments about the relationship between the king and other powerful groups. To the degree that there is a specified understanding of absolutism, members of Renaudot's group are attuned to the progressive, economically advantageous aspects of absolutism.

67. Primogeniture is the inheritance pattern whereby the oldest son inherits the entire estate.

68. The speaker cites ancient examples of those who prohibited commerce, like "Lycurgus who forbade it altogether, Romulus who forbade it except *au bas peuple,* and Plato who founded his republic far from the sea so that it would not be corrupted by exposure to foreigners." Cicero claimed that the Carthaginians had learned fraud and lies as a result of the great babel of merchants. If French nobility remain restricted to warfare, "they will become more dextrous in its pursuit than they could be if their bodies and minds were divided by different occupations." Ibid., 415.

69. Laffemas, *Recueil présenté au Roy.* Montchrétien, too, believed that "wise nature" requires the aid of human authority to turn

the pursuit of profit to public advantage. He argues that such aid should come from a powerful government, operating according to the same principles as nature herself. The state should recognize the "bait of honor and the lure of profit" in human life and make sure that these motives are encouraged, given free scope, and properly rewarded. *Traicté,* 101–3.

70. "Qu' est-ce qui donne le prix aux choses?" 261, 10 September 1640, 4:309–12.

71. These three adjectives are also used to characterize friendship.

72. "Qu' est-ce qui donne le prix aux choses?" See also Findlen, "Jokes of Nature," 292–331.

73. "Resultat des Assemblées tenües dans le Bureau d'Adresse, durant les vacations de la presente anné 1638, touchant les moyens de establir le commerce," 3:489–96. These special sessions are collected in volume 3 of the conference proceedings, between conferences 179 and 180.

74. Ibid., 3:490.

75. Hartlib, *A Description of the famous Kingdom of Macaria.*

76. Habermas, *The Structural Transformation of the Public Sphere.*

77. There are other, anonymous, contemporary texts that respond to Machiavelli, such as Anon., *L'Hellebore,* and Molinier, *A Mirrour for Christian States.*

78. "Du Menage," 345, 1 September 1642, 5:235–38.

79. "Lequel vaut mieux user de Severité ou de douceur envers les siens," 93.2, 17 December 1635, 2:356–60.

80. This speaker avoids the more commonplace cases of social inversion in early modern France. See Davis, *Society and Culture.*

81. "S' il est vray qu' on a autant d' ennemis que de valets, & pourquoy," 324, 24 March 1642, 5:126–30.

82. "S' il y a eu de plus grands hommes en quelqu' un des siecles precédens qu' en cettui-ci."

83. La Mothe le Vayer, frequently cited as a presumed participant, argues for liberty and argues against slavery as a violation of natural liberty. *Of Liberty and Servitude,* 8–9.

84. "De la cause des Seditions," 5:192–96.

85. These participants do not suffer the loss of liberty described by many seventeenth-century thinkers as inherent to the position of courtier. La Mothe le Vayer, for example, claimed that the courtier can never enjoy philosophical liberty, "the pretensions of the Court being so eminent, and, as it were, almost infinite, obliges those that attain them unto extreme servitude." *Of Liberty and Servitude,* 32.

86. Merchant, *The Death of Nature,* 195.

87. But this, Margaret Jacob suggests, is a way to gain support of the one by invoking the other. *The Cultural Meaning of the Scientific Revolution.* It might be legitimate to consider that the power of laws could be extended to the state or that mechanism legitimates absolute monarchy and vice versa.

88. Merchant, *The Death of Nature,* 205.

89. "Quelles sont les plus communes causes des procez: & pourquoy il y en a plus aujourd' hui que les temps passe," 179, 15 November 1638, 3:497–500. But the real fault, the final speaker contends, is not France's system, which he admires for its freedom, but rather an excess of legal proceedings produced by "too great a knowledge of the law."

90. An important difference between mercantilism and laissez-faire was that mercantilism entailed a narrow and sometimes xenophobic identification with the national state. Mercantilists focused on the aggrandizement of national power and prosperity, understood as at the expense of the power and prosperity of other nations.

91. Wolfe, "French views on Wealth and Taxes," notes that mercantilists stressed the social utility of ambition. Akkerman in *Women's Vices, Public Benefits,* cites the seventeenth-century notion of interest as an important influence on the Enlightenment.

92. Akkerman develops this comparison in *Women's Vices, Public Benefits,* 15–16.

93. Diderot and d'Alembert, *Encyclopédie,* 13:91a.

94. "Les moyens de s'enrichir peuvent etre criminels en morale, quoique permis par les lois; il est contre le droit naturel et contre l'humanite que des millions d'hommes soient prives de necessaire, comme ils le sont dans certain pays, pour nourrir le luxe scandaleux d'un petit nombre de citoyens oisifs" (The means of enriching oneself can be morally criminal, although permitted by law; it is against natural law and humanity that millions of men are deprived of necessities, as they are in certain countries, to nourish the scandalous luxury of a small number of lazy citizens). Ibid., 7:206a.

95. Ibid., 9:786b.

96. Ibid., 8:294a, 7:73a.

97. Voltaire, *Philosophical Letters*. For Diderot and d'Alembert, see Wokler, "The Enlightenment Science of Politics," 310–31.

98. Diderot and d'Alembert, *Encyclopédie*, 14:887a.

99. See, for example, the article "Mether," in ibid., 10:445b. "Les Grands," ibid., 7:849b.

100. Note the difference between "Privilege (Gram.)," probably by Diderot, as opposed to "Privilege (Gouv. Comm. Polit.)," which is anonymous and much more cautious. Ibid., 12:389a.

101. As we have seen, a speaker occasionally suggests that such discussion is not appropriate.

102. Gordon, *Citizens without Sovereignty*, 23.

103. Ibid., 28.

104. Ibid., 200.

CHAPTER NINE

1. "Du Caprice des Femmes," 46.2, 3 July 1634, 1:372–76. "Of the Extravagance of Women" is the title in the English translation of the first two hundred conferences, *A General Collection*, 1:274–80. The traditional argument that woman was created to irritate men is long-standing. It is derived from many sources and is frequently embedded in creation accounts. See Tuana, *The Less Noble Sex*, 5–16.

2. This conference is more moderate than some contemporary sources in its denunciation of the fickleness of women both because remarks are brief and also because opposing opinions are presented.

3. Gilligan, *In a Different Voice;* Keller, *Reflections on Gender and Science;* Bordo, *Flight to Objectivity;* Harrington, *Medicine, Mind and the Double Brain.* For a discussion of the exclusion of women from American science, see Rossiter, *Women Scientists in America.* For a discussion of the exclusion of women from European academic science, see Schiebinger, *The Mind Has No Sex?*

4. This controversial question of science as gendered has been raised by Harding, *The Science Question in Feminism;* Harding and O'Barr, eds., *Sex and Scientific Inquiry;* and Harraway, *Primate Visions.* As Geertz put it, "Sexing science or even scientists makes everyone, even those most passionate to accomplish it, extremely nervous." "A Lab of One's Own," 19.

5. Gilligan, *In a Different Voice.*

6. Keller, *Reflections on Gender and Science;* Bonde, *Flight to Objectivity;* Merchant, *The Death of Nature.*

7. Laqueur argues in *Making Sex* that Aristotelian biology offered a one-sex view, which became rigidly divided into a two-sex theory in the late eighteenth century. Schiebinger in *The Mind Has No Sex?* sees science as more open to women before the late eighteenth century.

8. See in particular the work of King on Renaissance education for women, *Women of the Renaissance* and *Her Immaculate Hand.*

9. Plato, *Timaeus,* in *Collected Dialogues,* 1151–211.

10. Lougee sees neoplatonism as a significant antecedent to the salon movement because it both idealized women and allowed them a public sphere. *Le Paradis des femmes,* 34–36.

11. See Wiesner's chapter on ideas and laws regarding women, in *Women and Gender in Early Modern Europe,* 9–21.

12. Pizan, *The City of the Ladies;* Agrippa

von Nettesheim, *De nobilitate et praecellentia foeminei sexus;* Castiglione, *The Book of the Courtier,* 270–80.

13. See Merchant, *The Death of Nature.*

14. Maclean, *Woman Triumphant,* 22.

15. Tuana, *The Less Noble Sex,* 146.

16. Pico della Mirandola, *Oration on the Dignity of Man.*

17. Merchant sees in Bacon's views implications for the subsequent treatment of the earth and of women. *The Death of Nature,* 164–91.

18. Schiebinger, *The Mind Has No Sex?* 122.

19. The frontispiece *Hic Mulier, or the Man-Woman* shows an unnatural woman, with perverted sexual nature, a woman transformed into a man by cut of hair, a plumed hat, and a dagger. The book was published in the climactic phase of a long controversy over the impudence of women in copying men's dress. In 1620 James I urged the clergy to do something about this scandalous state of affairs. Trundle and Heber, *Hic Mulier or The Man-Woman.* For a discussion of *Hic Mulier,* see Borin, "Judging by Images," 229.

20. Maclean points to some softening of the antifeminists position, probably the influence of neoplatonism, in *Woman Triumphant,* 161–63.

21. An important text in this tradition is Gournay, *Egalité des Hommes et des Femmes.*

22. Richelieu defended the Salic law, asking "if this kingdom should fall into the feminine line . . . to what misery should we not be reduced?" *The Art of pleasing in conversation,* 166.

23. See Gibson, *Women in Seventeenth-Century France.*

24. This tradition emphasizes aesthetics and behavior appropriate to one's estate. See Du Bosc, *L'Honneste Femme (The Accomplished Woman),* 221, 215, 241.

25. Lougee, *Le Paradis des Femmes,* 21.

26. See the work of Harth, *Cartesian Women;* Lougee, *Le Paradis des Femmes;* Goldsmith, *Exclusive Conversations;* Goodman, *The Republic of Letters.*

27. "Quel est le plus noble de l'Homme ou de la Femme," 1:204.

28. Aristotle, *On the Generation of Animals* and *The History of Animals.*

29. Tuana has argued that Aristotle's presupposition that the perfect form is male determines the rest of his biology and creates an ideology of sexual inferiority that has infused Western science. *The Less Noble Sex,* ix, 18–28. An extreme conclusion drawn from the "defect of nature" argument is that women are in essence monsters. See, for example, Ambroise Paré's formulation, "chose outre le cours de Nature." Céard, *Des monstéres et prodiges,* 3.

30. Aristotle, *Metaphysics.* As Cadden notes, many of these ideas—such as an emphasis on balance, polarity, the crucial role of heat—are similar to the Hippocratic tradition, although for Hippocrates they did not entail a hierarchy of values. *Meanings of Sex Differences,* 17–19.

31. "Quel est le plus noble de l'Homme ou de la Femme," 1:204.

32. Maclean, *Woman Triumphant,* 6.

33. Grieco notes that the feminine "right to orgasm" was debated in confession manuals well into the eighteenth century, but the majority of theologians accepted the Galenist medical view that female satisfaction was crucial to conception. "The Body, Appearance and Sexuality," 73. This sense of the utility of the female orgasm survives in Anon., *Aristotle's Masterpiece,* a compilation of advice on procreation, pregnancy, and child rearing that survived into the nineteenth century.

34. For a discussion of this distinction, see Cadden, *Meanings of Sex Differences,* 15–26.

35. For a discussion of the Galenic modification of Aristotle's view of the relationship between male and female sexuality, see Maclean, *The Renaissance Notion of Woman,* 35; Tuana, *The Less Noble Sex,* 133–34.

36. See Maclean for a discussion of the hermaphrodite in Renaissance medical literature. *The Renaissance Notion of Woman,* 38. Daston and Park explore the hermaphrodite to illuminate Renaissance attitudes toward ambiguous sexuality. They argue that, because

Hippocrates made sexual preference in the hermaphrodite a feature of behavior rather than genitalia, the revival of Hippocrates in fact made questions of sexuality more ambiguous and thus more threatening to patterns of inheritance, civil order, and religious morality. "Hermaphrodites in Renaissance France."

37. Montaigne, *Complete Essays*, 1.2, 69; Pliny, *Natural History*, 7:4.

38. Fernel, *De naturali parte medicinae;* Riolan the Elder, *Ad libros Fernelli de abditis rerum causis*, 113–73.

39. Maclean sees a significant change in medical texts about 1600. *The Renaissance Notion of Woman*, 28–46. Two groups of doctors interpret female psychology to the advantage of woman. The first, inspired by the writings of Julius Scaliger, argues that men and women are of the same bodily temperature. The second group relates bodily temperature to function, that is, women must retain food and fat in order to be able to nourish the fetus. See ibid., 40–45.

40. "Comment s' engendrent les malles & les femelles," 185, 17 January 1639, 3:521–25.

41. "De La Ressemblance," 5.1, 19 September 1633, 1:33–37. By this accout, it would be difficult to explain resemblance to a female relative.

42. "Duqel l' enfant tient-il le plus, du pere ou de la mere?" 287, 18 March 1641, 4:425–29.

43. One speaker points to an experiment rooted in animal husbandry "that, if the right testicle be bound, males will be produced, as females will if it is the contrary." Ibid.

44. "Si la sterilité vient plus communément du costé des hommes que des femmes & au contraire," 177, 22 June 1638, 3:481–88

45. "Comment s'engendrent les malles & les femelles."

46. Laqueur shows how new scientific findings did not fundamentally alter Aristotelian presuppositions about gender. *Making Sex*, especially chap. 2.

47. "S' il vaut mieux que les hommes ayet plusiers femmes." See Maclean, *Woman Triumphant*, 22.

48. For a discussion of ancient commonplaces, see Maclean, *Woman Triumphant, 22.*

49. Maclean, *The Renaissance Notion of Woman*, 50–54.

50. Ibid., 55–58.

51. Bodin cited in Davis, "Women in Politics," 167.

52. "Si la sterilité vient plus communément du costé des hommes que des femmes."

53. Aquinas, "Whether Women should have been made in the first productions of things." *Summa Theologica* Ia.92.1.

54. "Si le Mari et la femme doivent estre de mesme humeur," 65.2, 12 February 1637, 3:125–29.

55. "S' il est expédient aux femmes d' estre scavantes," 106.2, 17 March 1636, 3:53–56.

56. Maclean notes that there is not as much commentary on women in the moral sphere as in medicine or law largely because they were not considered to have the active nature necessary for virtue. *Woman Triumphant*, 18–19.

57. "Si la sterilité . . .," 3:482.

58. "Qu' est-ce qui fait l'Homme sage," 9.2, 17 October 1633, 1:69–72.

59. "S' il vaut mieux que les hommes ayet plusiers femmes."

60. Because Renaissance commentators on ethics consider matrimony in relation to nature rather than to divine law, they are able to ask such questions as the relative naturalness of polygamy, polyandry, and the community of wives without incensing religious opinion. The disagreement of Plato and Aristotle over the question of the community of wives attracts much commentary. See Maclean, *The Renaissance Notion of Woman*, 57.

61. "S' il est expédient aux femmes d' estre scavantes." This is a perennial topic in writings about women from the fourteenth century, but it was particularly contentious in the seventeenth century. See Maclean, *Woman Triumphant*, 53–58.

62. Jordanova points to several examples in which the values of the polarity are reversed.

For example, in Mozart's opera *The Magic Flute,* superstition and women are valued over reason; and men and masculinity are associated with exploitation and inequality in the eighteenth-century French novel *Paul et Virginie.* See "Natural Facts," 42–43.

63. Schiebinger, *The Mind Has No Sex?* 170.

64. Laqueur, *Making Sex,* 1–113.

65. Schiebinger notes that precursors to the Academie Française, such as the Palace Academy of Henry III had active women participants, and that in 1635 the Academie Française proposed three women as members (although none of the three were accepted as members). *The Mind Has No Sex?* 11–24.

66. "Du Caprice des Femmes," 1:373.

67. "Si la sterilité vient plus communément du costé des hommes que des femmes."

68. Such a distinction relies on a long-standing and deeply rooted sense of polarity as the way to describe relations between men and women. See Lloyd, *Polarity and Analogy.* The texts of Peter Ramus revived interest in dichotomies in the sixteenth and seventeenth centuries.

69. These physical antitheses are largely Aristotelian, derived in particular from *The History of Animals* and *On the Generaton of Animals.* Although males and females are assigned antithetical characters and abilities, the polarities do not seem to correspond to those applied by anthropologists, such as culture versus nature or tame versus wild. Instead they are simply antithetical characteristics with the antithesis determined as the direct opposite of whatever positive quality is being assigned to men. For a discussion of anthropological polarities see MacCormack, "Nature, Culture and Gender." Jordanova has cautioned, quite rightly, that these oppositions, even the hardening of oppositions in the nineteenth century, have little to do with the real roles women played in everyday life. "Natural Facts," 42–44.

70. "Quel est le plus inclin à l' amour de l'Homme ou de la Femme," 14.2, 21 November 1633, 1:114–16. This is another example of a quality that might be considered a virtue but is turned to a failing because it characterizes women.

71. The treatment of these issues falls within the tradition of the *querelle des femmes.* See Maclean, *Woman Triumphant,* 25–64.

72. "Quel est le plus noble de l'Homme ou de la Femme."

73. The manner and order of the creation of women is important because the speaker assumes that they convey rank in the chain of being; since women were created after men they were more perfect creatures. Agrippa is a likely source for conference participants because of their interest in the Paracelsian and hermetic traditions.

74. Schiebinger, *The Mind Has No Sex?* 11.

75. "S' il est expedient aux femmes d' estre scavantes." The fourth speaker argues that "although the Greeks sometimes received women in their academies to carry out the functions of professors and regents, these examples still have no bearing on our century in which corruption is capable of changing virtues into vices."

76. "Quel est le plus noble de l'Homme ou de la Femme," 1:207.

77. See Castiglione, *The Book of the Courtier,* and Marguerite of Navarre, *Heptameron.*

78. See Lougee, *Le Paradis des Femmes,* and Goodmand, *The Republic of Letters.*

79. Saint Paul, 1 Corinthians 7:9.

80. Some important Renaissance texts on marriage are Erasmus, *Christiani matrimonii institutio;* Agrippa, *De nobilitate et praecellentia foeminei sexus;* and Vives, *De institutione foeminae Christianae.*

81. As Maclean notes, in the Renaissance there is no reason to challenge this notion of marriage, which so effectively integrates natural, social, and theological. *The Renaissance Notion of Woman,* 57–59. In France few writers were willing to challenge the Catholic position that marriage, as a sacrament, was stamped with an unassailable orthodoxy. Furthermore, marriage was in the interests of the state, and except for the life of the religious, celibacy was considered aberrant.

82. Maclean, *Woman Triumphant*, 118, 97.

83. Lougee, *Le Paradis des Femmes*, 90, 64.

84. Montaigne, "On Some Lines of Virgil," 3.8, 638–85.

85. In his study of the evolution of seventeenth-century French feminism, Maclean uses the conferences both to indicate early attitudes and to look at more progressive treatment of these issues that occurred in the 1630s. *Woman Triumphant*, 97–101.

86. See Malebranche, "Traité de morale"; Du Bosc, *L'Honneste Femme;* Charron, *De la Sagesse.*

87. "Lequel vaut mieux se marier, ou ne se marier point," 141, 18 May 1637, 3:237–40.

88. Olivier, *A Discourse of Women, shewing their imperfections alphabetically,* 13.

89. On the question "Si le Mari and la femme doivent estre de mesme humeur," the speaker argues that nature has already provided women with a different humor, which is fitting because they have different "offices" in the home.

90. "S' il vaut mieux que les hommes ayet plusiers femmes."

91. "De la Chastété," 71.2, 27 March 1635, 2:173–76.

92. "Lequel vaut mieux se marier," 3:237.

93. "S' il vaut mieux que les hommes ayet plusiers femmes."

94. "De la Chastété," 2:176.

95. "S' il vaut mieux que les hommes ayet plusiers femmes." A concern of the state with fertility is more often attributed to the Third Republic than to the ancien régime.

96. "Des Eunuques," 99.2, 28 January 1636, 2:407–10.

97. "Auquel on est plus obligé au père ou a la mère," 197, Tuesday 3 May 1639, 4:45–49(48). See also Findlen, "Jokes of Nature."

98. This speaker claims that the mother contributes more and draws his evidence from the animal kingdom where the mating of "un bouc & une brebis" produces a "brebis," or of "un mouton & une chevre" produces "une chevre."

99. See Moreau de St. Elier, *Traité de la communication des maladies et des passions.*

100. "Auquel on est plus obligé au père."

101. "Si un fils peut obliger son père." 277, 7 January 1641, 4:385–89.

102. The strong tenor of conferences like this one might have led some to believe that women might indeed have participated.

103. "Lequel aimé le plus ses enfans du père ou de la mère," 331, 12 May 1642, 5:162–67.

104. Aristotle's *Ethics* is sometimes invoked to argue for the importance of mother as set against his biology, which is consistently invoked to denigrate the significance of women to the process of generation but also to deny any role to women except in generation.

105. "Quel est le plus noble de l'Homme ou de la Femme."

106. "Si la conversation des femmes est utile aux hommes," 307, October 14, 1641 5:45–49.

107. "S'il est expedient aux femmes d'estre scavantes."

108. "Quel est le plus noble de l'Homme ou de la Femme."

109. "S'il est expedient aux femmes d'estre scavantes."

110. Ibid., 55.

111. "S' il vaut mieux que les hommes ayet plusiers femmes."

112. This citation also suggests it is unlikely that women were in fact heard in this forum.

113. This example comes from Plutarch's *Life of Cato,* 424.

114. One speaker cites Plato as a source for the notion that love is this union of indigence and plenty, and since women are needy "the woman desires the man, in the same manner that the first matter desires new forms, thus it is insatiable." "Quel est le plus inclin a l'Amour," 1:114. Maclean notes that the lubricious nature of women is one of the conventional themes of antifeminist writing of the seventeenth century. *Woman Triumphant,* 48–50.

115. See Laqueur, *Making Sex,* and Schiebinger, *The Mind Has No Sex?*

116. In the course of the professionalization of medicine, men increasingly encroached on the preserves of midwifery and medical cookery. Schiebinger, *The Mind Has No Sex?* 103–15.

117. As Jordanova points out, medicine "uniquely, could claim to root its knowledge about women in the anatomy and physiology of human beings and to have an area of practice that constantly generated new observations and findings." "Sex and Gender," 154–55.

118. Jordanova maintains that the association of women with luxury, with superstition, and with unreliable desires was significant to early modern human sciences. Ibid.,164–67, and "Naturalizing the Family."

119. If the conferences are influenced by a "new" philosophy, it is the medicine, chemistry, and philosophy of Paracelsus. There are specific conferences dedicated to such Paracelsian topics as the growth of metals and the Rosicrucians.

120. The discussion of women in the conference suggests that the individuals profiled by Schiebinger in *The Mind Has No Sex?* are notable exceptions rather than indications of an acceptance of women in science. For an extensive discussion of social roles for women in seventeenth-century France, see Gibson, *Women in Seventeenth-Century France,* 141–68.

121. Billon, *Le Fort inexpugnable de l'honneur du sexe feminin.*

122. Maclean, *Woman Triumphant,* 36.

123. This theme was much more pronounced later in the century, with Mademoiselle de Scudéry making the argument most compellingly, in *Choix de conversations.* One such example, extolling the benefits of female conversation for men, cites the salon as a positive influence on men. For a modern appreciation of the significance of these arguments, see Maclean, *Woman Triumphant,* 151–52. As Goldsmith points out, by midcentury manuals of civility advise seeking the conversation of women for its civilizing influence. *Exclusive Conversations,* 20. For a discussion of the significance of conversation, see Harth, *Cartesian Women,* 40–45.

124. See Lougee for a discussion of the eighteenth-century debate on the nature of female reason and its implications for female equality. *Le Paradis des Femmes,* 209–14.

125. Harth, *Cartesian Women: Versions and Subversions of Rational Discourse in the Old Regime.*

126. Maclean points to the *précieuses* as an important evolution from the *femme forte* literature of the regency and insists that the *précieuses* could not have occurred without advances of the 1630s and 1640s. *Woman Triumphant,* 122, 154.

CONCLUSION

1. One would like to have the wealth of specific informaton for Renaudot's conferees as was deployed by David Sturdy in *Académie des Sciences.*

2. See Dear, *Discipline and Experience.*

3. For a discussion of the implicatoins of this development on geology, see Rappaport, *When Historians Were Geologists,* 42.

4. This is the social implication that most conventional accounts of early modern science chose to emphasize in discussing the social ramifications of mechanism.

5. See Sutton, *Science for a Polite Society,* 103–43.

6. It is worth wondering, although impossible to know, how avant-garde Renaudot's group would have been, had they been free to discuss religion.

7. For example, the new *Cambridge History of Seventeenth-Century Philosophy,* edited by Garber and Ayers, begins with Descartes and treats the previous period only as background to Descartes.

8. Huppert argues in *The Style of Paris* that the late Renaissance has great affinity with the Enlightenment.

9. Daston, "Afterword."

10. See the physiologically based works of La Mettrie and Diderot, written in the 1740s:

La Mettrie, *L'Homme plante, L'Homme machine,* and *Le Systeme d'Epicure,* in *Oeuvres philosophiques;* Diderot, *Pensées philosophiques* and *Lettre sur les aveugles,* in *Oeuvres philosophiques.*

11. For Fontenelle, see Rappaport, *When Historians Were Geologists,* 43, 51. Diderot, *De l'Interprétation de la nature,* in *Oeuvres philosophiques.*

12. Hazard, *The European Mind,* 7.

13. The philosophes, like many writers from the Renaissance on and including the conferees, used "nature" as a prescriptive term. For just several of many examples, see d'Alembert's *Preliminary Discourses,* 11–12.

14. Ibid., 9.

15. See Fox's introduction to Fox, Porter, and Wokler, *Inventing Human Science,* 1–30; Moravia, "The Enlightenment and the Sciences of Man." *The History of the Human Sciences* 6 (1993) is an issue dedicated to the eighteenth-century development of the human sciences. See also Olson, *The Emergence of the Social Sciences.*

16. Eighteenth-century figures wanted to extend to the study of man the certainty and accuracy of the physical sciences. Major studies of the history of this correlation include Gusdorf, *Les Sciences humaines et la pensée occidentale;* Duchet and Blankaert, *Anthropologie et histoire au siècle des lumières;* and Baker's *Condorcet.*

17. Goodman, *The Republic of Letters.*

18. Darnton, *The Great Cat Massacre,* and *The Literary Underground of the Old Regime.*

19. Goldgar, *Impolite Learning.*

20. In the eighteenth-century republic of letters, there was little explicit discussion of what a "republic" meant even by those who considered themselves members. (Perhaps they saw it more clearly in terms of what it was not—the terms with which I began this discussion.) Members of Renaudot's group also offer only the vaguest of appreciation of a republic as a source of greater freedom, although in practice the group provides a compelling model of an intellectual community that was quite egalitarian.

21. Descartes's *Discourse on Method* is perhaps the most striking example of this claim, which Jacob has developed for many leading figures of the scientific revolution, in *The Cultural Meaning of the Scientific Revolution.*

Bibliography

PRIMARY SOURCES

Conferences by Théophraste Renaudot

Première Centurie des Questions traitées ez Conferences du Bureau d'adress, depuis le 22 jour d'Aoust 1633. Jusques au dernier Juillet 1634. Dédiée à monseigneur le Cardinal. Paris: Bureau d'Adresse, 1634. (Volume 1, conferences 1–50. In these early years, two conferences were held each afternoon. This volume includes Renaudot's "Preface sur la Conference des Beaux Esprits.")

Seconde Centurie des Questions traitées ez Conferences du Bureau, depuis le 3 novembre 1634. Jusques à l'11 fevrier 1636. Paris: Bureau d'Adresse, 1636. (Volume 2, conferences 51–100. In these early years, two conferences were held each afternoon.)

Troisième Centurie des Questions. Tractées aux Conferences du Bureau d'adresse, depuis le 18 Fevrier 1636. Jusques au 17. Janvier 1639. Paris: Au Bureau d'Adresse, 1639. (Volume 3, conferences 101–185.)

Quatrieme Centurie des Questions. Traitées aux Conferences du Bureau d'Adresse, depuis le 24 Janvier 1639 jusques au 10

Juin 1641. Paris: Au Bureau d'Adresse, 1641. (Volume 4, conferences 186–295.)

Recueil General des Questions Traitées es conferences du Bureau d'Adresse, sur toutes sortes de matières, Par les plus beaux Esprits de ce temps. Conferences depuis 24 juin 1641 jusqu'au 1 septembre 1642. Paris: Chez Jacques Le Gras, 1655. (Volume 5, conferences 296–348.)

A General Collection of Discourses of the Virtuosi of France upon all sorts of philosophy, and other Natural Knowledge. Made in the assembly of the Beaux Esprits at Paris by the most ingenius persons of that nation. Translated by G. Havers. 2 vols. London: T. Dring and J. Starkley, 1664–1665.

Le Beveur d'Eau de la Foire St-Germain par Theophraste Renaudot. Paris: Bureau d'adresse, 1640. Edited with a short introduction by Jeanne Mauret. Angers: Librairie Ancienne, 1931.

Other Works by Renaudot

Les Consultations charitables pour les Malades dédiées à Monseigneur de Noyers, Secrétaire d'estat. Paris: Au Bureau d'Adresse, 1640.

La Deplorable Mort de Charles I, Roy de Grande Bretagne. St. Germain en Laye, 18 March 1649.

Description d'un médicament appellé Polychreston, Dispensé publiquement par Jacques Boisse Maistre apotiquaire en la ville de Loudun, le 4 Decembre 1629. Avec le Harangue faite sur la subject par Theophraste Renaudot Docteur en Medecine. Loudun: Quentin Mareschal, 1619.

Eloge d'Armand-Jean du Plessis, cardinal de Richelieu. N.p., 1642.

Factum de l'instance de Theophraste Renaudot Docteur en Medecine de la Faculte de Montpellier & Medecin du Roy, defendeur au principal, appellant d'une sentence du Lieutenant civil, donnee par defaut, & demandeur en Lettres patentes au septieme Decembre Contre les Doyen & Docteurs de l'Ecole en Medecine de Paris intimez, defendeurs audites Lettre, & opposans a l'execution du committitur obtenu sur l'enterissement d'icelles. N.p., n.d.

Factum du Procez, d'entre Theophraste Renaudot, demandeur en rapport d'arrest: Et les Medecins de l'eschole de Paris deffendeurs. Paris, 1643.

Factum du procez d'entre Maistre Théophraste Renaudot, Docteur en Médecine de la Faculté de Montpellier, médecin du Roy, Commissaire général des pauvres malades & valides de ce Royaume, Maître & Intendant général des Bureaux d'Adresse de France demandeur en Requete présentée au conseil privé du Roi le 30 l'octobre 1640. Contre le Doyen & Docteurs en Médecine de la Faculté de Paris, déffendeurs: sans que les qualitez puissent préjudicier. Paris, n.d.

Funeral Oration de M. de Saint-Marthe decede. Loudun, 29 March 1624. Samur: B. Mignon, 1624.

Gazette de France, Recueil des Toutes les Gazette, Nouvelles. Relations et autres choses memoreables de toute l'Annee . . . Contenant le Recit des choses remarquables, avenues tout en ce Royaume qu'es pays estranges. Paris: Bureau d'Adresse, 1631–1653. (One volume per year.)

Inventaire des Adresses du Bureau de Rencontre, où chacun peut donner &

recevoir avis de toutes les necessitez & comoditez de la vie & société humaine. Par permission du Roy contenue en ses Brevets, Arrets de son conseil d'Estat, Déclaration, Privilege, Confirmation, Arret de Sa Cour de Parlement, Sentences & jugements donnez en consequence. Paris: A l'Enseigne du Coq rue de la Calnadre sortant au Marché neuf, ou l'un desdits Bureau est éstably, 1630.

La Présence des absens, ou facile moyen de rendre present au Médecin l'estat d'un malade absent. Dressé par les Docteurs en Médecine consultans charitablement a Paris pour les pauvres malades. Avec les figures du corps humain, et table servant a ce dessein: Ensemble l'instruction pour s'en servir mesmes par ceux qu ne scavent point escrire. Paris: Bureau d'Adresse, 1643.

Raisons convainquantes de la nécessité qu'il y a en France, d'establir les Vents à grâce et pures et simples, entérinant les Lettres patentes données au mois d'Octobre 1643. N.p, n.d.

La Renouvellement des Bureaux d'Adresse, a ce nouvel an MDCXLVII. Par Théophraste Renaudot Conseiller et Médecin du Roy, Historiographe de sa Majesté, Maistre et Intendant général des Bureaux d'Adresse de France. Paris: Bureau d'Adresse, 1647.

Requeste de Théophraste Renaudot, addressee au Conseil du Roy, pour que son proces contre la Faculté de Médecine du Paris ne soit pas porte devant le Parlement. N.p., 1640.

Requeste presentée à la Reyne par Théophraste Renaudot, en faveur des pauvres malades de ce Royaume. Paris: Bureau d'Adresse, 1643.

Response à l'Examen de la Requeste présentée à la Reine. Par Théophraste Renaudot. Paris, 1643.

Response de Théophraste Renaudot au libelle fait contre les consultations charitables pour les pauvres malades. Paris, 1641.

Response de Théophraste Renaudot conseiller et médecin du Roy, Maistre & Intendant Générales Bureaux d'adresse de France & Historiographe de Sa majesté. A l'Auteur des libelles intitulez *Avis du Gazetier de Cologne à celui de Paris: Résponse des peuples de Flandre au Donneu d'avis Francois & Refutation du correctif des ingrediens, etc.* Paris: Bureau d'Adresse, 1648.

Works by Other Authors

Agricola, Georgius. *De re metallica.* Translated by Herbert Clark Hooker and Lou Henry Hoover. New York: Dover Publications, 1950.

Agrippa von Nettesheim, Cornelius. *Declamation on the Nobility and Preeminence of the Female Sex.* Translated and edited by Albert Rabil Jr. Chicago: University of Chicago Press, 1996.

___. *De nobilitate et praecellentia foeminei sexus.* Antwerp: Michaelis Hillenius, 1529.

___. *De occulta philosophia libri tres.* Edited by V. Perrone Compagni. Leiden: E. J. Brill, 1992.

Alembert, Jean Le Rond d'. *Preliminary Discourse to the Encyclopedia of Diderot.* Translated by Richard N. Schwab. Indianapolis: Bobbs-Merrill, 1963.

Amydenus, Theogorus. *Pietas Romana et Parisiensis or a Faithful relation of the several sorts of charitable and pious works eminent in the cities of Rome and Paris.* Oxford, 1687.

Anon. *Aristotle's Masterpiece.* London, 1690.

___. *Arrest du conseil du Roy, Portant reglement a l'auenir de pouruoir en temps de necesite a la nourriture des pauures, auec deffences tant aux cours de parment qu'a tous autres officers, d'imposer des Ecclesiastiques pour raison de ce, a peine de nullite.* Paris, 1633.

___. *Arret du Conseils donnez en faveur des consultations charitables pour les pauvres malades entre M. Theophraste Renaudot & les autres Docteurs en Medecine Consultans avec lui d'une part & les Doyens & Docteurs de l'Eschole de Medecine de Paris.* Paris, n.d.

___. *Catolicon Francois ou Plainctes de Deux, Chasteaux, raportees par Renaudot,* *Maistres du Bureau d'adresse.* Paris, 1636.

___. *Le Cour d'etat de Louis XIII.* N.p., 1631.

___. *Extrait des registre du conseil Privé du Roy.* Paris, June 1641.

___. *L'Hellebore pour nos mal-contens cuelly au Iardin d'un Anti-Machiavel, Et mis en lumiere.* Paris, 1632.

___. *Justification particulière des intendants des monts-de-piété touchant les droits de trois deniers pour livre par mois que le rois et son conseil ont trouvé bon que les dits monts recoivent à l'ouverture de leur establissement, sur ce que les necessitaux y voudront porter volontairement, à l'example des donts establis en plusiers endroits de la Chrestianété par l'approbation des papes et conseils.* Paris, 1643. In *Archives Curieuses de l'Histoire de France Depuis Louis XI jusqu'à Louis XIII,* ed. F. Danjou, 227–31. 1704. Paris, 1838.

___. *Memoire concernant les pauvres que l'on appelle enfermez.* In *Archives curieuses de l'histoire de France,* ed. Cimber Dajou, 15:243–84. Paris: Beauvais, 1837.

___. *Le Roy du Roy contre le Cardinal Richelieu.* Paris, 1642.

Aquinas, Thomas. *Questions of the Soul.* Translated by J. H. Robb. Milwaukee: Marquette University Press, 1984.

___. *Summa contra gentiles.* 4 vols. Notre Dame: University of Notre Dame Press, 1975.

___. *Summa Theologica.* 5 vols. Westminster, Md.: Christian Classics, 1981.

Aristotle. *Aristotle's Ethics.* Introduced by J. L. Ackrill. London: Faber, 1973.

___. *The Basic Works of Aristotle.* Edited by Richard McKeon. New York: Random House, 1941.

___. *De Generatione Animalium (On the Generation of Animals).* In *Basic Works,* 665–88.

___. *De Generatione et Corruptione.* Translated by C. J. F. Williams. Oxford: Oxford University Press, 1982.

___. *Historia Animalium (The History of Animals).* In *Basic Works,* 633–42.

___. *Metaphysica (Metaphysics)*. In *Basic Works*, 689–934.

___. *Meteorologica*. Translated by H. D. P. Lee. Cambridge, Mass.: Harvard University Press, 1952.

___. *Physica (Physics)*. In *Basic Works*, 218–397.

Bacon, Francis. "The Masculine Birth of Science." In *The Works of Francis Bacon*, ed. James Spedding, Robert Ellis, and Douglas Health, 3:524–39. London, 1857–1874.

___. *The New Organon*. Edited by Lisa Jardine and Michael Silverthorne. Cambridge: Cambridge University Press, 2000.

Bertereau, Martine de. *La Restitution de Pluton: Des Mines & minieres de France, cachées & détenues jusques à present au ventre de la terre, par le moye desquelles les Finances de sa Majesté seront beaucoup plus grandes que celles de tous les Princes chréstiens, ses sujets plus heureux de tous les peuples*. Paris: H. du Mesnil, 1640.

Billon, François. *Le Fort inexpugnable de l'honneur du sexe feminin*. Paris: I. D'Allyer, 1555.

Boccaccio, Giovanni. *De Mulieribus claris*. Bern: Mathias Apiaripus, 1539.

Bodin, Jean. *Les six livres de la république*. Paris: Jacques du Pays, 1577. Published in English as *The Six Bookes of a commonweale*. London: G. Bishop, 1606. (Usually referred to as *Six Books of the Republic*.)

Botero, Giovanni. *An Historicall description of the most famous kingdomes and common-weales in the worlde*. London: John Jaggard, 1603.

___. *The Magnificencie and Greatness of Cities*. Norwood, N.J.: Theatrum Orbis Terrarum, 1979.

___. *On the Causes of the Greatness and Magnificence of Cities*. London, 1588.

___. *The Reason of State*. London, 1599.

Bruni, Leonardo. *In libros Economicorum*. Paris: Henrici Stephani, 1506.

Budé, Guillaume. *L'Institution du Prince*. In *Le Prince dans la France des XVI et XVIIe siècles*, ed. Claude Bontems, Léon Pierre Raybaud, and Jean-Pierre Brancourt, 1–108. Paris: Presses Universitaires de France, 1965.

Campanella, Tommaso. *The City of the Sun*. Washington, D.C.: Walter Dunne, 1901.

___. *The Defense of Galileo of Thomas Campanella*. Translated and edited by Grant McColley. *Smith College Studies in History* 22. April–July 1937.

___. *Delle virtu e dei vizi in particolare*. 3 vols. Rome: Centro Internazionale di Studi Umanistici, 1976–1980.

___. *Lettere a cura di Vincenzo Spampanaot*. Bari: Laterza, 1927.

Campolini, Fabricio. *Discours de la contrariété d'humeurs qui se trouve entre de certaines nations, et singulierement entre la françoise et l'espagnole*. Paris: Augustin Courée, 1647.

Cardano, Girolamo. *De Subtilitate*. Lyon: Philibert Rollet, 1554.

Casaubon, Meric. *A treatise concerning enthusiasme: as it is an effect of nature, but is mistaken by many for either Divine inspiration or diabolical possession*. London: R. Daniel, 1655.

___. *Treatise of Use and Customes*. London: John Legate, 1638.

___. *A treatise proving spirits, witches, and supernatural operations, by pregnant instances and evidences: together with other things worthy of note*. London: Brabagon Aylmer, 1672.

Castiglione, Baldasar. *The Book of the Courtier*. Translated by George Bull. London: Penguin, 1967.

Charron, Pierre. *De la Sagesse*, ed. A. Duval. 3 vols. Rapilly, 1827. Translated as *Of Wisdome*. London: Edward Blount and William Apley, 1612.

Cicero, Marcus. "De Amicitia." In *De Senectute, De Amicitia, De Divinatione*, trans. William Armistead Falconer, vol. 28. Cambridge, Mass.: Loeb Classical Library, 1964.

Claves, Etienne de. *Paradoxes ou traitez philosophiques des pierres, contre l'opinion vulgaire. Ausquels sont demonstrez la matière, la cause efficiente eterne, la* semence, la génération, la definition & la nutrition d'icelles. Paris, 1635.

Coeffeteau, Nicolas. *Tableau des passions humains*. Paris: Guillaume Loyson, 1632.

Comenius, John Amos. *A patterne of universall knowledge, in a plaine and true draught: or, A diatyposis, or model of the eminently learned, and pious promoter of science in generall*. London: T. Collins, 1651.

___. *A Reformation of the Schooles*. London, 1642.

Commynes, Philippe de. *Mémoires*. Edited by Joseph Calmette. 3 vols. Paris: Editions des Belles Lettres, 1925.

Descartes, René. *Discourse on Method*. In *Philosophical Writings*, 1:11–141.

___. *Meditations on First Philosophy*. In *Philosophical Writings*, 2:3–62.

___. *The Passions of the Soul*. In *Philosophical Writings*, 1:325–404.

___. *The Philosophical Writings of Descartes*. Edited by John Cottingham, Robert Stoothoff, and Dugald Murdoch. 2 vols. Cambridge: Cambridge University Press, 1984.

___. *The World or Treatise on Light*. In *Philosophical Writings*, 1:81–98.

Desportes, Philippe. *Stance du mariage*. In *Le mariage honni par Desportes: Louange par Blanchon, le Gaygnard Rouspeau*, ed. Hugues Vaganay, 1–32. Macon: Protat Frères, 1909.

Diderot, Denis. "Lettre sur les aveugles." In *Oeuvres philosophiques*, 81–149.

___. *Oeuvres complètes*. 20 vols. Paris: Garnier Frères, 1875–1877.

___. *Oeuvres philosophiques*. Edited by Pierre Vernière. Paris: Garnier Frères, 1964.

___. "Pensées philosophiques." In *Oeuvres philosophiques*, 9–79.

___. "Réfutation de l'ouvrage d'Helvétius intitulé de *L'Homme.*" In *Oeuvres complètes*, 10:267–456.

Diderot, Denis, and Jean Le Rond d'Alembert. *Encyclopédie; ou Dictionnaire raisonné des sciences, des arts et des métiers, par une société de gens de lettres. Mis en ordre & publié par m. Diderot . . . & quant à la partie mathématique, par m. d'Alembert . . .* 17 vols. Paris: Briasson, 1751–1765.

Dreux du Radier, Jean-François. *Bibliothèque historique et critique du Poitou*. Paris: Ganau, 1754.

Du Bosc, Jacques. *L'Honneste Femme*. Paris: Jean Jost, 1635.

Duguet, Jacques-Joseph. *Conduite d'une dame chrétienne*. Paris: Chez Jacques Vincent, 1725.

Duplessis-Mornay, Philippe. *Vindiciae contra tyrannos: sive, De Principes in populum, populique in principem legitima potestate*. Basel: P. Perna, 1580.

Erasmus, Desiderius. *Christiani matrimonii institutio*. In *Opera omnia*. Vol. 5. Leyden: Petri Vander Aa, 1703–1706.

Faculty of Medicine, University of Paris. *Avertissement à Théophraste Renaudot, contenant les Mémoires pour justifier les Anciens droicts et privilèges de la Faculté de Médecine de Paris*. Paris, 1641.

___. *La Défense de la Faculté de Médecine de Paris contre son Calomniateur. Dediée à Monsieur l'eminentissime Duc de Richelieu*. Paris: Pierre Ricolet, 1641.

___. *Examen de la Requeste présentée à la Reine par le Gazettier*. N.p., 1643.

___. *Requête présentée au prévôt de Paris par les Doyen et les Docteurs de la Faculté de Médecine de Paris contre Théophraste Renaudot*. Paris, 1643.

Fernel, Jean. *De naturali parte medicinae*. Paris, 1542.

___. *Universa Medicina*. Paris, 1554.

Flurance, David Rivault de. *Le dessein d'une Academie et de l'introduction d'icelle en la cour*. Paris: P. Le Court, 1612.

___. *Le lecon faicte en la premiere ouverture de l'Académie Royale. Au Louvre, le 6 May, 1612. Par le sieur Flurance Rivault, Gentilhomme ordinaire de la Chambre du Roy, second Précepteur de sa Majésté, & son Lecteur aux Mathématiques*. Paris: P. Le Court, 1612.

Fontenelle, Bernard de. *Fontenelle's Dialogues of the dead, in three parts: Dialogues of the antients; The antients with the moderns; The moderns. London: Jacob Tonson, 1708.

Furetière, Antoine. *Le Roman bourgeois*. Amsterdam: David Mortier, 1714.

Galilei, Galileo. *Dialogue Concerning the Two Chief World Systems*. Translated by Stillman Drake. Berkeley and Los Angeles: University of California Press, 1967.

___. *Les Nouvelles Pensées de Galilee mathématicien et ingénieur*. Translated into French by Mersenne, edited by Pierre Costabel. Paris: J. Vrin, 1973.

___. "The Starry Messenger." In *Discoveries and Opinions of Galileo,* translated with introduction and notes by Stillman Drake, 21–59. Garden City, N.Y.: Doubleday, 1957.

Gassendi, Pierre. *The Mirrour of the True Nobility & Gentility. Being the Life of the Renowned Nicolaus Claudius Fabricius, Lord of Peiresk, Senator of the Parlement at Aix. Written by the Learned Petrus Gassendus. Professor of the Mathematicks to the King of France.* London: J. Streater, 1657.

Gerbier, Balthasar. *Exposition du chevalier Balthazar Gerbier. A Messieurs le docteurs en Theologie de la Faculté à Paris sur l'éstablissement des monts-de-Piété.* Paris: N.p., 1644.

___. *Remonstrance très humble de Chevalier Balthazar Gerbier et ses associez, à Monseigneur l'illustrissime Archevesque de Paris touchant le Mont-de-piété et quelques Mauvais Bruits que nombre d'usuriers se ment contre de pieux, utile, et nécessaire establissement.* Paris, 1643. In *Archives Curieuses de l'Histoire de France Depuis Louis XI jusqu'à Louis XIII,* ed. F. Danjou. Paris: Beauvais, 1838.

Glanvill, Joseph. *Plus Ultra or the progress and advancement of knowledge since the days of Aristotle. In an account of some of the most remarkable late improvements of practical, useful learning to encourage philosophical endeavors occasioned by a conference by one of the notional way.* London: J. Collins, 1668.

Gournay, Marie Le Jars de. *Egalité des Hommes et des femmes.* N.p., 1622.

Grenaille, François. *L'honneste mariage.* Paris: Toussainct Quinet, 1640.

Hartlib, Samuel. *A Description of the famous Kingdom of Macaria; shewing its excellent government wherein the inhabitants live in great prosperity, health, and happiness; the king obeyed, the Nobles honoured; and all good men respected, vice punished, and vertue rewarded.* London: Francis Constable, 1641.

___. *A Further Discoverie of the office of Publick Addresse for Accommodations.* London, 1648.

Laffemas, Barthélemy de. *Le mérite du travail et labeur, dédié aux chefs de la police. Faict par B de L., valet de Chambre du Roi, natif de Beau-Semblant en Dauphiné.* Paris: Pierre Pautonnier, 1602.

___. *L'incredulité ou l'ignorance de ceux qui ne veulent cognoistre le bien & repos de l'estat & veoir renaistre la vie heureuse des François.* Paris: Chez Iamet et Pierre Mettayer, 1600.

___. *Recueil présenté au Roy de ce qui se passe en assemblée du commerce au Palais, à Paris, fait par Laffemas, controlleur-général dudict commerce.* Paris, 1604. In *Archives curieuses de l'histoire de France depuis Louis XI jusqu'à Louis XVIII,* ed. M. L. Cimber and F. Danjou. First series, 14:219–46. Paris: Bourgogne et Martinet, 1837.

___. *Le tesmoignage certain du profict & reuenu des soyes de France.* Paris: Pierre Pautonnier, 1602.

Laffemas, Isaac de. *L'Histoire du commerce en France, enrichie des plus notables antiquitez du traffic des pais estranges.* Paris: Toussaincts du Bray, 1606.

La Mettrie, Julien Offray de. *Oeuvres philosophiques.* 3 vols. Berlin, 1774.

___. *Le Discours sur le bonheur.* In *Oeuvres philosophiques,* 2:83–166.

La Mothe le Vayer, François. *Oeuvres.* Dresden: Michel Groell, 1756.

___. *Of Liberty and Servitude.* Translated by John Evelyn. London: M. Meighens and G. Bedell, 1649.

La Ramée, Pierre de (Peter Ramus). *Advertissement sur la reformation de l'Université de Paris.* Paris, 1562.

Le Moyne, Pierre. *La galerie des femmes fortes*. Paris: Antoine de Sommaville, 1647.

Lipsius, Justus. *Six Bookes of Politickes or Civil Doctrine*. Translated by William Jones. London: W. Ponsonby, 1594.

Louis XIII. *La Déclaration du Roi pour la Paix donnée au mais de Mars, et verifiéee en Parlement le premier d'avril 1649*. N.p., n.d.

_____. *Déclaration du Roy Pour l'éstablissments des Bureaux d'adresse et tables de rencontre, en tous les lieux de son obéissance*. N.p., n.d.

_____. *Lettres du Roy en forme de Chartre. Contenans le privilege octroye par Sa majesté à Théophraste Renaudot, l'un de ses Conseillers et médecins ordinaires, maistre et Intendant General des Bureaux d'Adresse de ce Royaume; et à ses enfans, successors, et ayans droit de lieu, de faire, imprimer, faire imprimer et vendre par qui et ou bon semblerea les Gazettes, Nouvelles, et Récits de tout ce qui s'est passe tant dedans que dehors le Royaume, Conference, prix courant des marchandises et autres impressions desdits Bureaux, a pepetutie et tant que les dires Gazettes, Nouvelles et autres impression auront cour en ce dit Royaume; et ce exclusivement a toutes autres personne: En suite des Déclarations, lettres et arrest de conseil, nagueres donnex sur le fait des dits impressions*. N.p., n.d.

_____. *Lettres patentes du Roy en faveur des pauvres et particulièrement des malades*. N.p., n.d.

Machiavelli, Niccolò. *The Prince*. New York: Bantam Books, 1985.

Maillard, Claude. *Le bon mariage, ou le moyen d'estre heureux*. Douai: Jean Serrurier, 1643.

Malebranche, Nicolas. "Traité de morale." In *Oeuvres complètes*, ed. M. Adam. Vol. 11. Vrin: Bibliothèque des Textes Philosophiques, 1962–1970.

Margues, Mathieu de. *Abrégé de la vie du Cardinal de Richelieu pour lui servir d'epitaphes*. Paris, 1643.

_____. *L'Ambassadeur chimerique ou le chercheur des Dupes du Cardinal de Richelieu*. N.p., 1643.

Mayerne, Louis Turquet de. *De la monarchie aristo-democratique*. Paris: Jean de Bouc, 1611.

Mercure françois. Le vingt-uniesme tome du Mercure François, ou suite de l'histoire de nostre temps, sous Le Règne du Très-Chrestien Roy de France et de Navarre, Louys XIII. Es années 1635 et 1636. Paris: Olivier de Varennes, 1639.

_____. *Le vingt-deuxieme tome du Mercure François, ou Suitte de l'histoire de nostre temps, sous le Regne du Tres-Chrestien Roy de France et de Navarr, Louys XIII. Es annees 1637 et 1638*. Paris: Olivier de Varennes, 1641.

_____. *Le vingt-troisiesme tome du Mercure François . . . Es années 1639 et 1640*. Paris: Olivier de Varennes, 1646.

_____. *Le vingt-quatriesme tome du Mercure François . . . Es années 1641, 1642, et 1643*. Paris: Olivier de Varennes, 1647.

Mersenne, Marin. *Correspondence*. Edited by D. de Waard and P. Tannery. Paris: G. Beauchesne, 1932.

_____. *Questiones Theologiques, Physiques, Morales et Mathematics*. Paris: H. Guenon, 1634.

_____. *Questions harmoniques dans lesquelles son contenues plusiers choses remarquable pour la physique, pour la morale, et pour les autres sciences*. Paris: Jacques Villery, 1634.

Molinier, E. *A Mirrour for Christian States: or a Table of Politick vertues considerable amongst Christians*. Translated by William Tyruhuit. London: T. Harper, 1635.

Montaigne, Michel de. *The Complete Essays*. Edited by Donald Frame. Stanford: Stanford University Press, 1965. (Three books in one volume.)

Montchrétien, Antoine de. *Traicté de l'oeconomie politique, dédié en 1615 au Roy et la Reine Mere du roy*. Introduction and notes by Theodore Funck-Brentano. Paris: Plon, 1889.

Montesquieu, Charles Secondat, Baron of. *The Spirit of the Laws*. Translated by Thomas Nugent. New York: Hafner Press, 1949.

Moreau de St. Elier, Louis. *Traité de la communication des maladies et des passions.* The Hague: Jean van Duren, 1738.

Mornay, Philippe de. *See* Duplessis-Mornay, Philippe.

Naudé, Gabriel. *Apologie pour tous les grands personnages qui ont esté faussement soupçonnez de Magie.* Paris: François Targa, 1625.

___. *Considérations politiques sur les coups d'estat.* Paris: Editions de Paris, 1988.

Navarre, Marguerite of. *Heptameron.* Paris: Garnier, 1967.

Olivier, Jacques. *A Discourse of Women, shewing their imperfections alphabetically.* London: Henry Brome, 1673.

Oudin, Antoine. *Curiositez françoises, pour supplement aux dictionnaires ou recueil de plusiers belles proprietez, avec une infinité de proverbes & quodlibets, pour l'explication de toutes sortes de livres.* Paris: Antoine de Sommaville, 1640.

Palissy, Bernard. *Discours Admirable de la Nature des Eaux et fontaines, Tant naturelles qu'artificielles, des metaux, des sels & salines, des pierres, des terres du feu des emaux.* Geneva: Flick, 1863.

Palma-Cayet, Pierre-Victor. *Chronologie septenaire de l'histoire de la paix entre les roys de France et d'Espagne. Contenant les choses plus memorables advenües en France, Espagne, Allemagne, Italie, Angleterre, Escois, Flanders, Hongrie, Pologne, Suede, Transsilvanie, & autre endroits de l'Europe; auec le succez de plusieurs navigations faictes aux Indes Orientales, Occidentales & Septentrionales, depuis le commencement de l'an 1598. iusques à la fin de l'an 1604.* Paris: I. Richer, 1609.

Paré, Ambroise. *Des monstres et prodiges.* 1573. Edited by Jean Céard. Geneva: Droz, 1971.

Pascal, Blaise. *Les Pensées.* Translated by A. J. Krailsheimer. London: Penguin, 1966.

Patin, Guy. *Lettres de Guy Patin.* Edited by J.-H. Reveille-Parise. 3 vols. Paris: Champion, 1846.

Paul, Vincent de, and Louise de Marillac. *Vincent de Paul and Louise de Marillac: Rules, Conferences, and Writings.* Edited by Frances Ryan and John E. Rybolt. New York: Paulist Press, 1995.

Peiresc, Nicholas-Claude. *Les Correspondants de Peiresc.* Agin: Philippe Tamizey de Larraque, 1899.

Pico della Mirandola, Giovanni. *Oration on the Dignity of Man.* Translated by Robert Caponigri. Chicago: University of Chicago Press, 1956.

Pizan, Christine de. *The City of the Ladies.* Translated by Earl Jeffrey Richards. New York: Persea Books, 1982.

Plato. *Plato: The Collected Dialogues.* Edited by Edith Hamilton and Huntington Cairns. Princeton: Princeton University Press, 1982.

Pliny. *Natural History: A Selection.* Translated by John Healy. London: Penguin, 1991.

Plutarch. *Life of Cato.* In *Plutarch: The Lives of the Noble Grecians and Romans,* trans. John Dryden, rev. Arthur Hugh Clough. 1864. New York: The Modern Library, 1992.

___. *Mulierum virtutes.* Brescia: Boninus de Boninis, 1485.

Porta, Giambattista della. *Natural Magick.* London: Thomas Young and Samuel Speed, 1588.

Ramus, Peter. *See* La Ramée, Pierre de.

Richelieu, Jean-Armand du Plessis, Cardinal. *Annotations plaisantes sur la Gazette de France.* Composée par le Cardinal de Richelieu. Paris, 1638.

___. *The Art of pleasing in conversation by Cardinal Richelieu. Translated out of the French.* London: R. Wellington, 1699.

___. *Emblema Anima or Morrall Discourses reflecting upon Humanite. Written by John Du Plessis now Cardinall of Richelieu.* Translated by J. Maxwell. London: Printed by Nic and Joh Okes, 1635.

___. *Les Papiers de Richelieu: Section politique intérieure correspondance et papiers d'état.* Edited by Pierre Grillon. Paris: Editions A. Pedone, 1975.

___. *Political Testament; The Significant Chapters and Supporting Selections.* Translated by Henry Bertram Hill. Madison: University of Wisconsin Press, 1961.

—— [attributed]. *La France Mourante piece contre le duc de Luynes. La Mort de la France ou la France en Croix avec la consolation au pauvre peuple afflige.* Paris [Amsterdam], 1638.

Richesource, Jean de Soudier de. *Conferences Academiques et Oratoires.* Paris, 1653.

Riolan, Jean, the Elder. "Ad libros Fernelli de abditis rerum causis." In *Opera Omnia,* 113–73. Paris: Hadrianum Perrier, 1610.

Riolan, Jean, the Younger. *Curieuses recherches sur les escholes en médecine de Paris et de Montpellier.* Paris: Gaspar Meturas, 1651.

Robinson, Henry. *The Office of Adresse and encounters: Where all people of each ranke and quality may receive direction and advice for the most cheap and speedy way of attaining whatsoever they can lawfully desire, etc.* London: Matthew Simmons, 1650.

Rohan, Henri, Duke of. *De l'interest des princes et des estats de la Chrestienete.* Paris [Amsterdam], 1638.

Sainte-Marthe, Pierre Scévole de. *Eloges des hommes illustres.* Paris, 1644.

Salutati, Coluccio. *Epistolario.* Edited by Francesco Novati. 4 vols. Rome, 1891.

Sassoferrato, Bartolo of. *Bartolus on the Conflict of Laws.* Translated by Joseph Henry Beale. Cambridge, Mass.: Harvard University Press, 1914.

Scott, Michael, Theobaldus Anguilbertus, et al. *The Philosophers' Banquet. Furnished and Decked forth with much variety of many several dishes, when the former services were neglected. Where now not only meats and drinks of all natures and kinds are served in, but the natures and kinds of all disputed of. As further, dilated by table conference, alteration and changes of states, diminution of the stature of man, Barreness*

of the earth, with the effects and causes thereof, physically and philosophically. London: Vavasour, 1633.

Scudéry, Madeline de. *Choix de conversations.* Edited by Philip J. Wolfe. Ravenna: Longo, 1977.

Senault, François. *De l'Usage des passions.* N.p., 1643.

Seyssel, Claude de. *La Monarchie de France.* Paris, 1515.

Sorel, Charles. *Discours sur l'Academie Françoise establie pour la correction & l'embellissement du Langage; Pour scauvoir si elle est de quelque utilite aux Particuliers & au Public.* Paris: Chez Guillaume de Luyne, 1654.

Sprat, Thomas. *The history of the Royal-Society of London for the Improving of Natural Knowledge.* London: Scot, Chiswell, Chapman and Sawbridge, 1702.

Tallemant des Reaux, Gideon. *Historiettes.* Edited by Antoine Adam. Paris: Gallimard, 1960–1961.

Trundle, John, and Richard Heber. *Hic Mulier, or The Man-Woman.* London: J. T., 1620.

Vives, Juan Luis. *De institutione foeminae Christianae.* Antwerp: Michaelis Hillenius, 1524.

___. *De l'assistance aux pauvres.* 1525. Translated by Ricard Aznar Casanova and Leopold Caby. Bruxelles: Editions Valero et Fils, 1943.

Voltaire, François Arouet de. *Essai sur les moeurs.* In *Oeuvres complètes de Voltaire,* vols. 11–13. 52 vols. Paris: Garnier Frères, 1877–1885.

___. *Philosophical Letters.* Translated by Ernest Dilworth. New York: Macmillan, 1961.

Ward, Samuel. *The Wonder of the Loadstone or the Loadstone newly reduct into a divine and morall Use.* London: Peter Cole, 1640.

SECONDARY SOURCES

Adam, Antoine. *Histoire de la littérature française au XVIIe siècle: L'époque de*

Henri IV et de Louis XIII. Paris: Domat, 1948.

___. Les Libertins au XVIIe siècle. Paris: Buchet-Chastel, 1964.

Adams, Frank D. The Birth and Development of the Geological Sciences. New York: Dover, 1938.

Akkerman, Tjitske. Women's Vices, Public Benefits: Women and Commerce in the French Enlightenment. Amsterdam: Het Spinhuis, 1992.

Anderson, Perry. Lineages of the Absolutist State. London: Verso, 1974.

Anis, Auguste-François. David Rivault de Fleurance et les autres précepteurs de Louis XIII. Paris: Alphonse Picard, 1893.

Arditi, Jorge. A Geneology of Manners: Transformations of Social Relations in France and England from the Fourteenth to the Eighteenth Centuries. Chicago: University of Chicago Press, 1998.

Ariès, Philippe, and Georges Duby, eds. A History of Private Life. Cambridge, Mass.: Belknap Press, 1986.

Armogathe, Jean-Robert. "Le Groupe de Mersenne et la vie académique parisienne." Dix-septième Siècle 174 (1992): 131–39.

Auge-Chiquet, Mathieu. La Vie, les idées et l'oeuvre de Jean-Antoine de Baif. Paris: Hachette, 1909.

Avenel, Denis-Louis, ed. Lettres, instructions, et papiers d'etat du Cardinal Richelieu. 8 vols. Paris: Imprimerie Nationale, 1853–1877.

Avenel, Georges d'. Richelieu et la monarchie absolue. 4 volumes. Paris: Plon, 1884–1890.

Baker, Keith. Condorcet: From Natural Philosophy to Social Mathematics. Chicago: University of Chicago Press, 1975.

Baldwin, Martha. "Toads and Plague: The Amulet Controversy in Seventeenth-Century Medicine." Bulletin of the History of Medicine 67 (1993): 227–47.

Barkan, Lawrence. Nature's Work of Art: The Human Body as Image of the World. New Haven, Conn.: Yale University Press, 1975.

Barker, Peter, and Ariew Roger, eds. Revolution and Continuity: Essays in the History of Early Modern Science. Washington, D.C.: Catholic University Press, 1991.

Beaulieu, Armand. "Le Groupe de Mersenne." In Geometrie atomismo nella Scuola Galileiania, ed. Massimo Bucciantini and Maurizio Torrini, 17–34. Florence: Leo Olschki, 1992.

___. "Un Moine passionné de musique, de sciences et d'amitié: Marin Mersenne." Dix-septième Siècle 163 (1989): 167–94.

Begue, Andre. Les consultations charitables de Théophraste Renaudot. Paris: J. B. Ballière, 1899.

Bercé, Yves-Marie. History of Peasant Revolts: The Social Origins of Rebellion in Early Modern France. Translated by Amanda Whitmore. Cambridge, England: Polity Press, 2000.

Bergin, Joseph. Cardinal de La Rochefoucauld: Leadership and Reform in the French Church. New Haven: Yale University Press, 1987.

___. The Rise of Richelieu. Manchester: Manchester University Press, 1991.

Berriot-Salvadore, Evelyne. Les Femmes dans la société française de la Renaissance. Geneva: Droz, 1990.

Biagioli, Mario. Galileo Courtier: The Practice of Science in the Culture of Absolutism. Chicago: University of Chicago Press, 1993.

Billaçois, François. The Duel: Its Rise and Fall in Early Modern France. Translated by Trista Selous. New Haven: Yale University Press, 1990.

Blair, Ann. The Theater of Nature: Jean Bodin and Renaissance Science. Princeton: Princeton University Press, 1997.

Blaize, A. Des Monts-de-piété et des banques de prêt sur gages en France et dans les divers états de l'Europe. Paris: Pagnerre, 1856.

Blanqui, Jerome-Adolphe. History of Political Economy in Europe. New York: G. P. Putnam, 1880.

Block, Maurice, and Jean Block. "Women and the Dialectic of Nature in Eighteenth-Century Thought." In MacCormack and Strathern, *Nature, Culture, and Gender*, 25–41.

Bonnefont, Gaston. *D'un Docteur d'Autrefois: Théophraste Renaudot, Créateur de la Presse, de la publicité, des dispensaires, du Mont-de-piété (1586–1653)*. Limoges: Ardant, 1899.

Bonney, Richard. *Political Change in France*. Oxford: Oxford University Press, 1978.

Bordo, Susan. *Flight to Objectivity: Essays in Cartesianism and Culture*. Albany: State University of New York, 1987.

Borin, Françoise. "Judging by Images." In *Renaissance and Enlightenment Paradoxes*, ed. Natalie Zemon Davis and Arlette Farge, 187–254. Vol. 3 of Duby and Perot, *A History of Women*.

Bouralière, M. de la. "Une Lettre inédite de Théophraste Renaudot." *Bulletin de la Société des Antiquaires de l'Ouest* (1884): 307–12.

Briggs, Robin. *Early Modern France*. Oxford: Oxford University Press, 1977.

Brockliss, L. W. B. "Before the Clinic: French Medical Teaching in the Eighteenth Century." In *Constructing Paris Medicine*, ed. Caroline Hannaway and Ann La Berge, 71–115. Amsterdam: Editions Rodopi, 1998.

———. *French Higher Education in the Seventeenth and Eighteenth Centuries: A Cultural History*. Oxford: Clarendon Press, 1987.

Brockliss, L. W. B., and Colin Jones. *The Medical World of Early Modern France*. Oxford: Clarendon Press, 1997.

Broman, Thomas. "The Habermasian Public Sphere." *History of Science* 36 (1998): 123–44.

Brown, Harcourt. *Scientific Organizations in Seventeenth-Century France, 1620–1680*. Baltimore: Wilkins and Wilkins, 1934.

Brunel, Lucien. *Les philosophes et l'Académie française au dix-huitième siècle*. Paris: Hachette, 1884.

Burke, Peter. *The Art of Conversation*. Ithaca: Cornell University Press, 1993.

———. *History and Social Theory*. Ithaca: Cornell University Press, 1993.

Butterfield, Herbert. *The Origins of Modern Science, 1300–1800*. London: Bell, 1949.

Cadden, Joan. *Meanings of Sex Differences in the Middle Ages: Medicine, Society, and Culture*. Cambridge: Cambridge University Press, 1994.

Cahen-Salvador, Georges. *Un Grand Humaniste, Peiresc, 1580–1637*. Paris: Albin Michel, 1951.

Caillet, Jules. *De l'administration en France sous le ministère du Cardinal de Richelieu*. Paris: Didot, 1857.

Carmona, Michel. *La France de Richelieu*. Paris: Fayard, 1984.

Céard, Jean. *Des monstres et prodiges*. Geneva: Droz, 1971.

———. *La Nature et les prodiges: L'Insolité au XVIe siècle en France*. Geneva: Librairie Droz, 1977.

Chalumeau, R. P. "L'Assistance aux malades pauvres au XVIIe siècle." *Dix-septième Siècle* 90 (1971): 75–86.

Chapman, Allan. "Astrological Medicine." In *Health, Medicine, and Morality*, ed. Charles Webster, 275–330. Cambridge: Cambridge University Press, 1979.

Chartier, Roger, ed. *Passions of the Renaissance*. Translated by Arthur Goldhammer. Vol. 3 of Ariès and Duby, *A History of Private Life*.

Clark, Henry. "Commerce, the Virtues, and the Public Sphere in Early Seventeenth-Century France." *French Historical Studies* 21 (1998): 415–40.

Cohen, H. Floris. *The Scientific Revolution*. Chicago: University of Chicago Press, 1994.

Collins, James. *The Fiscal Limits of Absolutism*. Berkeley and Los Angeles: University of California Press, 1988.

Cook, Harold J. "The Cutting Edge of a Revolution? Medicine and Natural History near the Shores of the North Sea." In *Renaissance and Revolution: Humanists, Scholars, Craftsmen and Natural Philosophers in Early Modern Europe*, ed. J. V. Field and Frank James, 44–61. Cambridge: Cambridge University Press, 1993.

Copenhaver, Brian. "Astrology and Magic." In *The Cambridge History of Renaissance Philosophy,* ed. C. B. Schmitt et al., 77–110. Cambridge: Cambridge University Press, 1988.

___. *Symphorien Champier and the Reception of the Occultist Tradition in Renaissance France.* The Hague: Mouton, 1978.

Coveney, P. J., ed. *France in Crisis.* Totowa, N.J.: Rowman and Littlefield, 1977.

Dalat, Jean. *Théophraste Renaudot, Chef du Cinqième Bureau de Sa Majesté Très Chrétienne Louis XIII. Discours prononcé par M. le Conseiller Jean Dalat. Cours d'appel de Poitiers. Audience solennelle de rentrée du 16 septembre 1959.* Poitiers: Université de Poitiers, 1959.

Darnton, Robert. *The Great Cat Massacre and Other Episodes in French Cultural History.* New York: Basic Books, 1984.

___. *The Literary Underground of the Old Regime.* Cambridge, Mass.: Harvard University Press, 1982.

Daston, Lorraine. "Afterword: The Ethos of Enlightenment." In *The Sciences in Enlightened Europe,* ed. William Clark, Jan Golinski, and Simon Schaffer, 495–504. Chicago: University of Chicago Press, 1999.

___. "The Ideal and Reality of the Republic of Letters in the Enlightenment." *Science in Context* 4.2 (1991): 367–86.

Daston, Lorraine, and Katharine Park. "Hermaphrodites in Renaissance France." *Critical Matrix* 1 (1985): 1–19.

___. "Unnatural Conceptions: The Study of Monsters in Sixteenth- and Seventeenth-Century France and England." *Past and Present* 92 (1981): 20–54.

___. *Wonders and the Order of Nature.* New York: Zone Books, 1998.

Davis, Natalie. *Society and Culture in Early Modern France: Eight Essays.* Stanford: Stanford University Press, 1975.

___. "Women in Politics." In *Renaissance and Enlightenment Paradoxes,* ed. Natalie Zemon Davis and Arlette Farge, 167–83. Vol. 3 of Duby and Perot, *A History of Women.*

Dear, Peter. *Discipline and Experience: The Mathematical Way in the Scientific Revolution.* Chicago: University of Chicago Press, 1995.

___. *Mersenne and the Learning of the Schools.* Ithaca: Cornell University Press, 1988.

Dear, Peter, ed. *The Literary Structure of Scientific Argument.* Philadelphia: University of Pennsylvania Press, 1991.

Debus, Allen G. "The Chemical Philosophers: Chemical Medicine from Paracelsus to van Helmont." *History of Science* 12 (1974): 235–59.

___. *The Chemical Philosophy: Paracelsian Science and Medicine in the Sixteenth and Seventeenth Centuries.* 2 vols. New York: Science History Publications, 1977.

___. *The English Paracelsians.* London: Oldbourne Press, 1965.

___. *The French Paracelsians: The Chemical Challenge to Medical and Scientific Tradition in Early Modern France.* Cambridge: Cambridge University Press, 1994.

___. *Man and Nature in the Renaissance.* Cambridge: Cambridge University Press, 1978.

___. "Robert Fludd and the Use of Gilbert's *De Magnete* in the Weapon-Salve Controversy." *Journal of the History of Medicine and Allied Sciences* 19 (1964): 389–417.

Demeulenaere-Douyère, Christiane, and David Sturdy. "Image versus Reality: The Archives of the French Académie des Sciences." In *Archives of the Scientific Revolution: The Formation and Exchange of Ideas in Seventeenth-Century Europe,* ed. Michael Hunter, 184–220. London: Boydell Press, 1998.

Denieul-Cormier, Anne. *Paris à l'aube du Grand Siècle.* Paris: Arthaud, 1971.

Denonain, J.-J. "Les Problèmes de l'honnête homme vers 1635: *Religio medici* et les *Conférences* au Bureau d'Adresse." *Etudes Anglaises* 18 (1965): 235–37.

Depaux, Jacques, "De la pauvrété à propos de la Sagesse de Pierre Charron: Question de définition." *Dix-septième Siècle* 170 (1991): 110–18.

Dewald, Jonathan. *Aristocratic Experience and the Origins of Early Modern Culture: France 1550–1715.* Berkeley and Los Angeles: University of California Press, 1993.

Dobbs, Betty Jo. *Alchemical Death and Resurrection: The Significance of Alchemy in the Age of Newton.* Washington, D.C.: Smithsonian Institution, 1988.

___. *The Foundations of Newton's Alchemy, or "The Hunting of the Greene Lyon."* Cambridge: Cambridge University Press, 1975.

___. *The Janus Faces of Genius: The Role of Alchemy in Newton's Thought.* Cambridge: Cambridge University Press, 1991.

Donnelly, John Patrick, and Michael W. Maher, eds. *Confraternities and Catholic Reform in Italy, France, and Spain.* Kirksville, Mo.: Thomas Jefferson University Press, 1999.

Douthwaite, Julia V. *Exotic Women: Literary Heroines and Cultural Strategies in Ancien Régime France.* Philadelphia: University of Pennsylvania Press, 1992.

Drevillon, Hervé. *Lire et écrire l'avenir: L'Astrologie dans la France du Grand Siècle, 1610–1715.* Seyssel: Champ Vallon, 1996.

Duby, Georges, and Michelle Perot, eds. *A History of Women.* Cambridge, Mass.: Belknap Press, 1999.

Duchet, Michèle, and Claude Blankaert. *Anthropologie et histoire au siècle des lumières.* Paris: A. Michel, 1995.

Du Jonc, C. *La chimère ou fantôme de la mendicité.* Paris, 1607. In Denieul-Cormier, *Paris à l'aube du Grand Siècle,* 162–63.

Du Long, Claude. *La Vie quotidienne des femmes au Grand Siècle.* Paris: Hachette, 1984.

Durand, Yves. *Les Fermiers généraux.* Paris: Presses Universitaires de France, 1971.

Eamon, William. "Author's Response." In Wood, Cunningham, et al., "'Making Knowledge': Review Symposium of *Science and the Secrets of Nature.*" *Metascience,* n.s., 6 (1994): 37–44.

___. *Science and the Secrets of Nature: Books of Secrets in Medieval and Early Modern Culture.* Princeton: Princeton University Press, 1994.

Ehrard, Jean. *L'Idée de la nature en France à l'aube des Lumières.* Paris: Flammarion, 1970.

Elias, Norbert. *The Civilizing Process: The History of Manners, and State Formation and Civilization.* Oxford: Basil Blackwell, 1994.

Ellenberger, François. *Histoire de la géologie.* 2 vols. Paris: Technique et Documentation Lavoisier, 1988.

Elliott, John H. *Richelieu and Olivares.* Cambridge: Cambridge University Press, 1984.

Emerton, Ephraim. *Humanism and Tyranny: Studies in the Italian Trecento.* Cambridge, Mass.: Harvard University Press, 1925.

Emery, Michel. *Renaudot et l'introduction de la médication chimique.* Montpellier: Hamelin Frères, 1888.

Febvre, Lucien, and Henri-Jean Martin. *The Coming of the Book: The Impact of Printing, 1450–1800.* Translated by David Gerard. London: Verso, 1976.

Field, Arthur. *The Origins of the Platonic Academy.* Princeton: Princeton University Press, 1988.

Figlio, Karl. "The Historiography of Scientific Medicine: An Invitation to Human Sciences." *Comparative Studies in Society and History* 19 (1977): 262–86.

___. "The Metaphor of Organization: An Historiographical Perspective on the Bio-Medical Sciences of the Early Nineteenth Century." *History of Science* 14 (1976): 17–53.

Findlen, Paula. "Jokes of Nature and Jokes of Knowledge: The Playfulness of Scientific Discourse in Early Modern Europe." *Renaissance Quarterly* 43 (1990): 292–331.

___. *Possessing Nature: Museums, Collecting, and Scientific Culture in Early Modern Italy.* Berkeley and Los Angeles: University of California Press, 1994.

Flandrin, Jean-Louis. "Distinction through Taste." In Chartier, *Passions of the Renaissance*, 265–307.

Foucault, Michel. *The Order of Things: The Archeology of the Human Sciences*. Translated by A. M. Sheridan-Smith. New York: Vintage Books, 1975.

Fox, Christopher, Roy Porter, and Robert Wokler, eds. *Inventing Human Science: Eighteenth-Century Domains*. Berkeley and Los Angeles: University of California Press, 1995.

France, Peter. *Politeness and Its Discontents: Problems in French Classical Culture*. Cambridge: Cambridge University Press, 1992.

Frémy, Edouard. *Origines de l'Académie Française: L'Académie des dernier Valois*. Paris: Ernst Le Roux, 1887.

French, Peter A., Theodore E. Uehling Jr., and Howard K. Wettstein, eds. *The Philosophy of the Human Sciences*. Notre Dame: University of Notre Dame Press, 1990.

Garber, Daniel, and Michael Ayers, eds. *Cambridge History of Seventeenth-Century Philosophy*. 2 vols. Cambridge: Cambridge University Press, 1998.

Gaukroger, Stephen, ed. *The Soft Underbelly of Reason: The Passions in the Seventeenth Century*. Introduction by Peter Harrison, 1–12. London: Routledge, 1998.

Gaukroger, Stephen, James Franklin, et al. "'Seized by the Spirit of Modern Science': A Review Symposium of Peter Dear, *Discipline and Experience*." *Metascience*, n.s., 9 (1996): 1–33.

Gay, Peter. *The Science of Freedom*. Vol. 2 of *The Enlightenment: An Interpretation*. New York: Knopf, 1969

Geertz, Clifford. "A Lab of One's Own." *New York Review of Books*, 8 November 1990, 19.

Giard, Luce. "Remapping Knowledge, Reshaping Institutions." In Pumfrey, Rossi, and Slawinski, *Science, Culture and Popular Belief in Renaissance Europe*, 19–47.

Gibson, Wendy. *Women in Seventeenth-Century France*. New York: St. Martin's Press, 1989.

Gilbert, Neal. *Renaissance Concepts of Method*. New York: Columbia University Press, 1960.

Gilligan, Carol. *In a Different Voice: Psychological Theory and Women's Development*. Cambridge, Mass.: Harvard University Press, 1982.

Godard de Donville, Louise. *Le Libertin des origines à 1665: Un produit des apologistes*. Seattle: Papers in Seventeenth-Century Literature, 1989.

Gohau, Gabriel. *Histoire de la géologie*. Paris: Editions La Découverte, 1987.

___. *Les Sciences de la terre aux XVIIe et XVIIIe siècles: Naissance de la géologie*. Paris: Albin Michel, 1990.

Gohout, Pierre. *Théophraste Renaudot ou médecin, philanthrope et gazetier*. Paris: La Pensée Universelle, 1974.

Goldgar, Anne. *Impolite Learning: Conduct and Community in the Republic of Letters, 1680–1750*. New Haven: Yale University Press, 1995.

Goldsmith, Elizabeth C. *Exclusive Conversations: The Art of Interaction in Seventeenth-Century France*. Philadelphia: University of Pennsylvania Press, 1988.

Goodman, Dena. *The Republic of Letters*. Ithaca: Cornell University Press, 1994.

Gordon, Daniel. *Citizens without Sovereignty: Equality and Sociability in French Thought, 1670–1789*. Princeton: Princeton University, 1994.

Grafton, Anthony, and Ann Blair. *The Transmission of Culture in Early Modern Europe*. Philadelphia: University of Pennsylvania Press, 1990.

Grant, Edward. *The Foundations of Modern Science in the Middle Ages: Their Religious, Institutional, and Intellectual Contexts*. Cambridge: Cambridge University Press, 1996.

___. *In Defense of the Earth's Centrality and Immobility: Scholastic Reaction to Copernicanism in the Seventeenth Century*. Philadelphia: American Philosophical Society, 1984.

___. *Physical Science in the Middle Ages*. Cambridge: Cambridge University Press, 1977.

Graves, Frank Pierpoint. *Peter Ramus and the Educational Reform of the Sixteenth Century*. New York: Macmillan, 1912.

Greenblatt, Stephen. *Renaissance Self-Fashioning: From More to Shakespeare*. Chicago: University of Chicago Press, 1980.

Grieco, Sara Matthews. "The Body, Appearance and Sexuality." In *Renaissance and Enlightenment Paradoxes*, ed. Natalie Zemon Davis and Arlette Farge, 46–100. Vol. 3 of Duby and Perot, *A History of Women*.

Gunn, J. A. W. *Politics and Public Interest in the Seventeenth Century*. Toronto: University of Toronto Press, 1969.

Gusdorf, Georges. *Les Sciences humaines et la pensée occidentale*. 6 vols. Paris: Payot, 1966–1973.

Habermas, Jürgen. *The Structural Transformation of the Public Sphere: An Inquiry into a Category of Bourgeois Society*. Translated by Thomas Burger. Cambridge, Mass.: MIT Press, 1993.

Hahn, Roger. *The Anatomy of a Scientific Institution: The Paris Academy of Sciences*. Berkeley and Los Angeles: University of California Press, 1971.

Hall, A. Rupert. *Science and Society: Historical Essays on the Relations of Science, Technology, and Medicine*. London: Variorum Reprints, 1994.

———. *The Scientific Revolution, 1500–1800*. London: Longman, 1954.

Hall, Thomas H. "Life, Death, and Radical Moisture: A Study of Thematic Patterns in Medical Theory." *Clio Medica* 6 (1960): 3–23.

Harding, Sandra. *The Science Question in Feminism*. Ithaca: Cornell University Press, 1986.

Harding, Sandra, and Jean F. O'Barr, eds. *Sex and Scientific Inquiry*. Chicago: University of Chicago Press, 1987.

Harraway, Donna. *Primate Visions: Gender, Race, and Nature in the World of Modern Science*. New York: Routledge and Kegan Paul, 1990.

Harrington, Anne. *Medicine, Mind and the Double Brain: A Study of Nineteenth-Century Thought*. Princeton: Princeton University Press, 1987.

Harrison, Peter. "Reading the Passions: The Fall, the Passions, and Dominion over Nature." In Gaukroger, *The Soft Underbelly of Reason*, 49–78.

Harth, Erica. *Cartesian Women: Versions and Subversions of Rational Discourse in the Old Regime*. Ithaca: Cornell University Press, 1992.

———. *Ideology and Culture in Seventeenth-Century France*. Ithaca: Cornell University Press, 1983.

Hatin, Eugene. *Histoire politique et litteraire de la presse en France*. Paris: Poulett-Malassis, 1859.

———. *Théophraste Renaudot et ses Innocentes Inventions*. Poitiers: Oudin, 1883.

Hausser, Henri. *La Pensée et l'action économique du Cardinal Richelieu*. Paris: Presses Universitaires de France, 1944.

Hazard, Paul. *The European Mind: The Critical Years, 1680–1715*. New Haven: Yale University Press, 1953.

Headley, John M. *Tommaso Campanella and the Transformation of the World*. Princeton: Princeton University Press, 1997.

Heckscher, Eli. *Mercantilism*. Translated by Mendel Shapiro. 2 vols. London: Allen and Unwin, 1955.

Henshall, Nicholas. *The Myth of Absolutism*. London: Longman, 1992.

Hill, John Spencer, ed. *Infinity, Faith, and Time: Christian Humanism and Renaissance Literature*. Montreal: McGill-Queen's University Press, 1997.

Hirschman, Albert. *The Passions and the Interests: Political Arguments for Capitalism before Its Triumph*. Princeton: Princeton University Press, 1977.

Hooykaas, Robert. *Robert Boyle: A Study in Science and Christian Belief*. Lanham, Md.: University Press of America, 1997.

Hoppen, K. Theodore. "The Nature of the Early Royal Society." *British Journal for the History of Science* 9 (1976): 1–24, 243–73.

Hotchkiss, Valerie. *Clothes Make the Man: Female Cross Dressing in Medieval Europe*. New York: Garland, 1996.

Hunter, Michael. *Establishing the New Science: The Experience of the Early Royal*

Society. Woodbridge, Suffolk: Boydell Press, 1989.

Huppert, George. *The Style of Paris: Renaissance Origins of the French Enlightenment.* Bloomington: University of Indiana Press, 1999.

Hutchison, Keith, "What Happened to Occult Qualities in the Scientific Revolution?" *ISIS* 73 (1982): 233–52.

Huxley, Aldous. *The Devils of Loudun.* New York: Harper and Row, 1952.

Jacob, Margaret. *The Cultural Meaning of the Scientific Revolution.* New York: Knopf, 1988.

Jones, Colin. "Montpellier Medical Studies and the Medicalization of Eighteenth-Century France." In *Problems and Methods in the History of Medicine,* ed. Roy Porter and Andrew Wear, 57–80. London: Croom Helm, 1982.

Jordan, W. K. *Men of Substance: A Study of the Thought of Two English Revolutionaries: Henry Parker and Henry Robinson.* Chicago: University of Chicago Press, 1942.

Jordanova, Ludmilla. "Natural Facts: A Historical Perspective on Science and Sexuality." In MacCormack and Strathern, *Nature, Culture and Gender,* 20–46.

___. "Naturalizing the Family: Literature and the Bio-Medical Sciences in the Late Eighteenth Century." In *Languages of Nature: Critical Essays on Science and Literature,* ed. Ludmilla Jordanova, 86–116. New Brunswick, N.J.: Rutgers University Press, 1986.

___. "Sex and Gender." In Fox, Porter, and Wokler, *Inventing Human Science,* 152–83.

___. *Sexual Visions: Images of Gender in Science and Medicine between the Eighteenth and Twentieth Centuries.* Madison: University of Wisconsin Press, 1989.

Joy, Lynn. *Gassendi the Atomist.* Cambridge: Cambridge University Press, 1987.

Keller, Evelyn Fox. *Reflections on Gender and Science.* Yale: Yale University Press, 1985.

Keohane, Nannerl O. *Philosophy and the State in France: The Renaissance to the Enlightenment.* Princeton: Princeton University Press, 1980.

Kettering, Sharon. *French Society, 1589–1715.* Essex: Pearson Education, 2001.

___. *Patrons, Brokers, and Clients in Seventeenth-Century France.* New York: Oxford University Press, 1986.

King, Margaret. *Women of the Renaissance.* Chicago: University of Chicago Press, 1991.

King, Margaret, ed. *Her Immaculate Hand: Selected Works by and about the Women Humanists of Quattrocento Italy.* Binghamton, N.Y.: Center for Medieval and Early Renaissance Studies, 1983.

Knecht, Robert. *Richelieu.* London: Longman, 1991.

Kors, Alan C., and Edward Peters, eds. *Witchcraft in Europe, 1100–1700: A Documentary History.* Philadelphia: University of Pennsylvania Press, 1972.

Krailsheimer, A. J. *Studies in Self-Interest from Descartes to La Bruyère.* Oxford: Oxford University Press, 1962.

Krajewsak, Barbara. *Du coeur à l'esprit: Mademoiselle de Scudéry et ses samedis.* Paris: Editions Kime, 1993.

Laqueur, Thomas. *Making Sex: The Making of the Modern Body.* Cambridge, Mass.: Harvard University Press, 1990.

Laudan, Rachel. *From Mineralogy to Geology: The Foundations of a Science, 1650–1830.* Chicago: University of Chicago Press, 1987.

Lazard, Madeleine. *Images littéraires de la femme à la Renaissance.* Paris: Presses Universitaires de France, 1985.

Le Noble, Robert. *Mersenne, ou la naissance du mécanisme.* Paris: Vrin, 1943.

Levi, Anthony. *Cardinal Richelieu and the Making of France.* New York: Carroll and Graf, 2000.

___. *French Moralists: The Theory of the Passions, 1585 to 1649.* Oxford: Clarendon Press, 1964.

Levy-Valensi, J. *La Médecine et les médecins français au XVII siècle.* Paris: J. B. Ballière et Fils, 1933.

Lindberg, David, and Robert Westman, eds. *Reappraisals of the Scientific Revolu-*

tion. Cambridge: Cambridge University Press, 1990.

Lindemann, Mary. *Medicine and Society in Early Modern Europe.* Cambridge: Cambridge University Press, 1999.

Lloyd, G. E. R. *Polarity and Analogy: Two Types of Argumentation in Early Greek Thought.* Cambridge: Cambridge University Press, 1971.

Lougee, Carolyn. *Le Paradis des femmes: Women, Salons, and Social Stratification in Seventeenth-Century France.* Princeton: Princeton University Press, 1976.

Lough, John. *The Encyclopédie.* New York: David McKay, 1971.

Lublinskaya, A. D. *French Absolutism: The Crucial Phase, 1620–1629.* Cambridge: Cambridge University Press, 1968.

Lux, David. *Patronage and Royal Science in Seventeenth-Century France: The Académie de Physique in Caen.* Ithaca: Cornell University Press, 1989.

___. "The Reorganization of Science, 1450–1700." In *Patronage and Institutions: Science, Technology and Medicine at the European Court, 1500–1700,* ed. Bruce Moran, 184–94. London: Boydell Press, 1991.

Lux, David, and Harold Cook. "Closed Circles or Open Networks? Communicating at a Distance during the Scientific Revolution." *History of Science* 36 (1988): 179–211.

MacCormack, Carol P. "Nature, Culture and Gender: A Critique." In MacCormack and Strathern, *Nature, Culture and Gender,* 1–24.

MacCormack, Carol P., and Marilyn Strathern, eds. *Nature, Culture and Gender.* Cambridge: Cambridge University Press, 1980.

MacIntyre, Alasdair. *After Virtue: A Study in Moral Theory.* Notre Dame: University of Notre Dame Press, 1981.

___. *A Short History of Ethics.* London: Routledge, 1998.

Maclean, Ian. *The Renaissance Notion of Woman: A Study in the Fortunes of Scholasticism and Medical Science in European Intellectual Life.* Cambridge: Cambridge University Press, 1980.

___. *Woman Triumphant: Feminism in French Literature, 1610–1652.* Oxford: Clarendon Press, 1977.

Magnusson, Lars. *Mercantilism: The Shaping of an Economic Language.* London: Routledge, 1994.

Magnusson, Lars, ed. *Mercantilist Economics.* Dordrecht: Kluwer Academic Publishers, 1993.

Major, J. Russell. *Representative Government.* New Haven: Yale University Press, 1980.

Mandrou, Robert. *From Humanism to Science, 1480–1700.* Translated by Brian Pearce. New York: Humanities Press, 1979.

Martin, Henri-Jean. *The History and the Power of the Writing.* Translated by Lydia G. Cochrane. Chicago: University of Chicago Press, 1988.

Mazauric, Simone. *Savoirs et philosophie à Paris dans la première moitié du XVIIe siècle.* Paris: Publications de la Sorbonne, 1997.

McDonald, Terrence J., ed. *The Historic Turn in the Human Sciences.* Ann Arbor: University of Michigan Press, 1996.

Menning, Carol Bresnahan. *Charity and State in Late Renaissance Italy: The Monte di Pietà.* Ithaca: Cornell University Press, 1993.

Merchant, Carolyn. *The Death of Nature: Women, Ecology and the Scientific Revolution.* New York: Harper and Row, 1980.

Miles, Rogers B. *Science, Religion and Belief: The Clerical Virtuosi of the Royal Society of London, 1663–1687.* New York: Peter Lang, 1992.

Millen, Ron. "The Manifestation of Occult Qualities." In *Religion, Science, and Worldview: Essays in Honor of Richard S. Westfall,* ed. Margaret J. Osler and Paul Lawrence Farber, 185–216. Cambridge: Cambridge University Press, 1995.

Miller, Peter. *Peiresc's Europe: Learning and Virtue in the Seventeenth Century.* New Haven: Yale University Press, 2000.

Moote, A. Lloyd. *Louis the Just.* Berkeley and Los Angeles: University of California Press, 1989.

Moran, Bruce. *Patronage and Institutions: Science, Technology and Medicine at the European Court, 1500–1700.* London: Boydell Press, 1991.

Moravia, Sergio. "The Enlightenment and the Sciences of Man." *History of Science* 18 (1980): 247–68.

Moss, Jean Dietz. *Novelties in the Heavens: Rhetoric and Science in the Copernican Controversy.* Chicago: University of Chicago Press, 1993.

Mousnier, Roland. *L'Homme rouge, ou la vie du Cardinal Richelieu.* Paris: Robert Laffont, 1992.

___. *La Plume, la faucille et le marteau.* Paris: Presses Universitaires de France, 1970.

___. *Les XVIe et XVIIe siècles.* Paris: Presses Universitaires de France, 1954.

Nauert, Charles G. Jr., ed. *Humanism and the Culture of Renaissance Europe.* Cambridge: Cambridge University Press, 1995.

Olson, Richard. *The Emergence of the Social Sciences, 1642–1792.* New York: Twayne Publishers, 1993.

Ong, Walter J., S.J. *Ramus, Method and the Decay of Dialogue: From the Art of Discourse to the Art of Reason.* Cambridge, Mass.: Harvard University Press, 1958.

Osler, Margaret, ed. *Atoms, Pneuma, and Tranquility: Epicurean and Stoic Themes in European Thought.* Cambridge: Cambridge University Press, 1991.

___. *Divine Will and the Mechanical Philosophy: Gassendi and Descartes on Contingency and Necessity in the Created World.* Cambridge: Cambridge University Press, 1994.

Packard, Francis. *Guy Patin and the Medical Profession in the Seventeenth Century.* New York: Paul Hoeber, 1925.

Pagel, Walter. *Joan Baptista van Helmont: Reformer of Science and Medicine.* Cambridge: Cambridge University Press, 1982.

___. *Paracelsus: An Introduction to Philosophical Medicine in the Era of the Renaissance.* Basel: S. Karger, 1958.

___. "Recent Paracelsian Studies." *History of Science* 12 (1974): 200–211.

___. "The Religious and Philosophical Aspects of van Helmont's Science." *Bulletin of the History of Medicine,* supplement no. 2. Baltimore: Johns Hopkins University Press, 1944.

Palm, Charles Franklin. "The Economic Policies of Richelieu." *University of Illinois Studies in the Social Sciences* 9.4 (1920).

Panizza, Letizia. "Stoic Psychotherapy in the Middle Ages and Renaissance: Petrarch's *De remediis.*" In Osler, *Atoms, Pneuma, and Tranquility,* 39–66.

Pannetier, Odette. *La Vie de Théophraste Renaudot.* Paris: Gallimard, 1929.

Parker, David. *The Making of French Absolutism.* New York: St. Martin's Press, 1983.

Paul, Harry B. *Science and Immortality: The Eloges of the Paris Academy of Sciences, 1699–1791.* Berkeley and Los Angeles: University of California Press, 1980.

Phillips, Henry. *Church and Culture in Seventeenth-Century France.* New York: Cambridge University Press, 1997.

Pintard, René. *Le Libertinage érudit dans la première moitié du XVIIe siècle.* Geneva: Slatkine Reprint Series, 1983.

___. *La Mothe le Vayer, Gassendi, Guy Patin: Etudes de bibliographie et de critique suivies de textes inédits de Guy Patin.* Paris: Biovin, 1943.

Popkin, Richard. *The History of Scepticism from Erasmus to Spinoza.* Berkeley and Los Angeles: University of California Press, 1977.

___. *The Third Force in Seventeenth-Century Thought.* Leiden: E. J. Brill, 1992.

Porter, Dorothy, and Roy Porter. *Patient's Progress: Doctors and Doctoring in Eighteenth-Century England.* Stanford: Stanford University Press, 1989.

Porter, Roy. "Medical Science and Human Science in the Enlightenment." In Fox, Porter, and Wokler, *Inventing Human Science,* 53–87.

Pottinger, David T. *The French Book Trade in the Ancien Regime, 1500–1791.*

Cambridge, Mass.: Harvard University Press, 1958.

Poulantzas, Nicos. *Political Power and Social Classes.* Translated by Timothy O'Hagan. London: Sheed and Ward, 1973.

Pribram, Jarl. *A History of Economic Reasoning.* Baltimore: Johns Hopkins University Press, 1983.

Principe, Lawrence. *The Aspiring Adept: Robert Boyle and His Alchemical Quest.* Baltimore: Johns Hopkins University Press, 1999.

Pumfrey, Stephen. "The History of Science and the Renaissance Science of History." In Pumfrey, Rossi, and Slawinski, *Science, Culture and Popular Belief in Renaissance Europe,* 48–70.

Pumfrey, Stephen, Paolo Rossi, and Maurice Slawinski, eds. *Science, Culture and Popular Belief in Renaissance Europe.* Manchester: Manchester University Press, 1991.

Purver, Margery. *The Royal Society: Concept and Creation.* London: Routledge and Kegan Paul, 1967.

Quétal, Claude. *History of Syphilis.* Oxford: Oxford University Press, 1990.

Ranum, Orest. *Paris in the Age of Absolutism.* Bloomington: University of Indiana Press, 1977.

___. *Richelieu and the Councillors of Louis XIII.* Oxford: Clarendon Press, 1963.

Rappaport, Rhoda. *When Historians Were Geologists, 1665–1750.* Ithaca: Cornell University Press, 1997.

Raynaud, Maurice. *Les Médecins au temps de Molière.* Paris: Didier, 1862.

Revel, Jacques. "The Uses of Civility." In Chartier, *Passions of the Renaissance,* 167–205.

Revillout, M. *Un Maître de conference au milieu du XVIIe siècle, Jean de Soudier de Richesource.* Montpellier: Boehm et Fils, 1881.

Reynier, Gustave. *La Femme au dix-septième siècle: Ses ennemis et ses défenseurs.* Paris: Editions J. Tallandier, 1929.

Rice, James. *Gabriel Naudé, 1600–1653.* Hopkins Studies in Romance Literature 35 (1939).

Robert, Paul. *Dictionnaire alphabetique et analogique de la langue française.* Paris: Société du Nouveau Littré, 1977.

Rossiter, Margaret. *Women Scientists in America: Struggles and Strategies to 1940.* Baltimore: Johns Hopkins University Press, 1982.

Rousselet, Albin. *Théophraste Renaudot, fondateur de policliniques.* Paris: Policlinique de Paris, 1819.

Roy, Emile. *La Vie et les oeuvres de Charles Sorel.* Paris: Hachette, 1891.

Sacks, Oliver W. *The Man Who Mistook His Hat for His Wife.* London: Duckworth, 1985.

Sarasohn, Lisa T. *Gassendi's Ethics: Freedom in a Mechanistic Universe.* Ithaca: Cornell University Press, 1996.

___. "Nicholas-Claude Fabri de Peiresc and the Patronage of the New Science in the Seventeenth Century." *ISIS* 84 (1993): 70–90.

Sawyer, Jeffrey. *Printed Poison: Pamplet Propaganda, Faction Politics, and the Public Sphere in Seventeenth-Century France.* Berkeley and Los Angeles: University of California Press, 1990.

Schechner, Sara. *Comets, Popular Culture, and the Birth of Modern Cosmology.* Princeton: Princeton University Press, 1997.

Schiebinger, Londa. *The Mind Has No Sex?* Cambridge, Mass.: Harvard University Press, 1989.

Schmitt, Charles. *The Aristotelian Tradition and Renaissance Universities.* London: Variorum Reprints, 1984.

___. *Aristotle and the Renaissance.* Cambridge, Mass.: for Oberlin College, by Harvard University Press, 1983.

___. "Towards a Reassessment of Renaissance Aristotelianism." *History of Science* 11, pt. 3 (September 1973): 169–83.

Schmitt, Charles, ed. *Reappraisals in Renaissance Thought.* London: Variorum Reprints, 1989.

Schmitt, Charles, and Brian P. Copenhaver. *Renaissance Philosophy.* Oxford: Oxford University Press, 1992.

Schmitt, Charles, Quentin Skinner, Eckhard Kessler, and Jill Kraye, eds. *The Cambridge History of Renaissance Philosophy*. Cambridge: Cambridge University Press, 1988.

Sealy, Robert. *The Palace Academy of Henry III*. Geneva: Droz, 1981.

Shapin, Steven. "Occultism and Reason." In *Philosophy, Its History and Historiography*, ed. A. J. Holland, 117–44. Dordrecht: D. Reidel, 1985.

___. *The Scientific Revolution*. Chicago: University of Chicago Press, 1996.

___. *A Social History of Truth: Civility and Science in Seventeenth-Century England*. Chicago: University of Chicago Press, 1994.

Shapin, Steven, and Simon Schaffer. *Leviathan and the Air Pump*. Princeton: Princeton University Press, 1985.

Shennan, J. H. *Origins of the Early Modern State*. London: Hutchinson, 1974.

Siraisi, Nancy. *Medieval and Early Renaissance Medicine*. Chicago: University of Chicago Press, 1990.

Slack, Paul. "Mirrors of Health." In *Health, Medicine, and Mortality in the Sixteenth Century*, ed. Charles Webster, 237–73. Cambridge: Cambridge University Press, 1979.

Slawinski, Maurice. "Rhetoric and Science/Rhetoric of Science/Rhetoric as Science." In Pumfrey, Rossi, and Slawinski, *Science, Culture and Popular Belief in Renaissance Europe*, 71–99.

Smith, Pamela. *The Business of Alchemy: Science and Culture in the Holy Roman Empire*. Princeton: Princeton University Press, 1994.

Smith, Roger. "The Languages of Human Nature." In Fox, Porter, and Wokler, *Inventing Human Science*, 83–111.

___. *The Norton History of the Human Sciences*. New York: W. W. Norton, 1997.

Solomon, Howard. *Public Welfare, Science, and Propaganda in Seventeenth-Century France: The Innovations of Théophraste Renaudot*. Princeton: Princeton University Press, 1972.

Spink, John S. *French Free Thought from Gassendi to Voltaire*. London: Athlone Press, 1960.

Stout, Jeffrey. *Ethics after Babel: The Languages of Morals and Their Discontents*. Boston: Beacon Press, 1988.

___. *The Flight from Authority: Religion, Morality and Quest for Autonomy*. Notre Dame: University of Notre Dame Press, 1981.

Sturdy, David. *Académie des Sciences, Science and Social Status: The Members of the Académie des Sciences, 1666–1750*. London: Boydell Press, 1995.

Sutton, Geoffrey. "A Science for a Polite Society: Cartesian Natural Philosophy in Paris during the Reigns of Louis XIII and XIV." Ph.D. dissertation, Princeton University, 1982.

___. *Science for a Polite Society: Gender, Culture and the Demonstration of Enlightenment*. Boulder, Co.: Westview Press, 1995.

Tapie, Victor L. *La France de Louis XII et de Richelieu*. Paris: Flammarion, 1967.

Taylor, Kenneth. "Earth and Heaven, 1750–1800: Enlightenment Ideas about the Relevance to Geology of Extraterrestrial Operations and Events." *Earth Sciences History* 17 (1998): 84–91.

___. "La Genèse d'un naturaliste: Desmarest, la lecture et la nature." In *De la géologie à son histoire: Essais présentés à François Ellenberger pour son 80ème anniversaire*, ed. Théodore Monod, Gabriel Gohau, and Goulven Laurent, 61–74. Paris: Comité des Travaux Historiques et Scientifiques, 1997.

___. "Volcanoes as Accidents: How `Natural' Were Volcanoes to Eighteenth-Century Naturalists?" In *Volcanoes and History*, ed. Nicoletta Morello, 595–618. Genoa: Brigati, 1998.

Temkin, Owsei. *Hippocrates in a World of Pagans and Christians*. Baltimore: Johns Hopkins University Press, 1991.

Thomas, Keith. *Religion and the Decline of Magic*. Cambridge: Cambridge University Press, 1971.

Thuau, Etienne. *Raison d'état et pensée politique à l'époque de Richelieu.* Paris: Armand Colin, 1966.

Tomaselli, Sylvana. "Political Economy: The Desire and Needs of Present and Future Generations." In Fox, Porter, and Wokler, *Inventing Human Science,* 292–322.

Tourette, Georges Gilles de la. *Théophraste Renaudot, d'après des documents inédits.* Paris: E. Plon Nourrit, 1884.

___. *La vie et les oeuvres de Théophraste Renaudot.* Paris: Edition du Comité, 1892.

Tuana, Nancy. *The Less Noble Sex: Scientific, Religious, and Philosophical Conceptions of Woman's Nature.* Bloomington: Indiana University Press, 1993.

Turnbull, George. *Hartlib, Dury and Comenius: Gleanings from Hartlib's Papers.* London: University Press of Liverpool, 1947.

___. *Samuel Hartlib: A Sketch of His Life and His Relation to J. A. Comenius.* London: Oxford University Press, 1920.

Van Kley, Dale. "Pierre Nicole, Jansenism, and the Morality of Enlightened Self-Interest." In *Anticipations of the Enlightenment in England, France, and Germany,* ed. Alan Charles Kors and Paul J. Korshin, 69–85. Philadelphia: University of Pennsylvania Press, 1987.

Van Leeuwen, Henry. *The Problem of Certainty in English Thought, 1630–1690.* The Hague: Nijhoff, 1963.

Varin-d'Ainvelle, M. *La Presse en France: Genèse et évolution de ses fonctions psychosociales.* Paris: Presses Universitaires de France, 1950.

Vartanian, Aram, "An Early French Treatise on Materialism." *Continuum* 3 (1991): 114–35.

Vernon, Richard. *Citizenship and Order: Studies in French Political Thought.* Toronto: University of Toronto Press, 1986.

Viala, Alain. *Naissance de l'écrivain: Sociologie de la littérature à l'âge classique.* Paris: Editions de Minuit, 1985.

Vickers, Brian. "Analogy versus Identity: The Rejection of Occult Symbolism, 1580–1680." In Vickers, *Occult and Scientific Mentalities,* 95–163.

Vickers, Brian, ed. *Occult and Scientific Mentalities in the Renaissance.* Cambridge: Cambridge University Press, 1984.

Waard, Christian de. *L'Expérience barométrique, ses antécédents et ses explications: Etude historique.* Thouars: Deux-Sèvres, 1993.

Wallace, William A. *Galileo's Logic of Discovery and Proof: The Background, Content, and Use of His Appropriated Treatises on Aristotle's "Posterior Analytics."* Boston Studies in the Philosophy of Science 137. Dordrecht and Boston: Kluwer Academic Publishers, 1992.

Wallerstein, Immanuel. *The Modern World-System.* New York: Academic Press, 1974.

Webster, Charles. *From Paracelsus to Newton: Magic and the Making of Modern Science.* Cambridge: Cambridge University Press, 1982.

Westman, Robert S. "Nature, Art, and Psyche: Jung, Pauli, and Kepler-Fludd Polemic." In Vickers, *Occult and Scientific Mentalities,* 177–229.

Wiesner, Merry. *Women and Gender in Early Modern Europe.* Cambridge: Cambridge University Press, 2000.

Williams, Elizabeth. *A Cultural History of Medical Vitalism in Enlightenment Montpellier.* Aldershot, England: Ashgate, 2003.

Wilson, Catherine. *Invisible World: Early Modern Philosophy and the Invention of the Microscope.* Princeton: Princeton University Press, 1995.

Wojcik, Jan W. *Robert Boyle and the Limits of Reason.* New York: Cambridge University Press, 1997.

Wokler, Robert. "The Enlightenment Science of Politics." In Fox, Porter, and Wokler, *Inventing Human Science,* 323–46.

Wolfe, Martin. "French Views on Wealth and Taxes from the Middle Ages to the Old Regime." In *Revisions in Mercantilism,* ed. D. C. Coleman, 190–210. London: Methuen, 1969.

Wood, Paul, Andrew Cunningham, et al. "'Making Knowledge': Review Symposium of *Science and the Secrets of Nature.*" *Metascience,* n.s., 6 (1994): 24–45.

Yates, Frances. *The French Academies of the Sixteenth Century.* Warburg Institute. London: University of London, 1947.

Zambelli, Paola. *L'Ambigua natura della magia: Filosophia, streghe, riti nel Rinascimento.* Milan: Il Saggiatore, 1991.

Index

107–17; Renaissance and, 116–17, 151

Arnauld, Antoine, 350

Assembly of Notables, 300

Astrologers, 167–68

Astrology, 72, 93–95, 102, 408n.25

Augustine, Saint, 263, 264

Augustinian, 213

Avicenna, 161

Bacon, Francis, 11, 59–60, 79, 85, 118, 151, 191, 330, 381; *New Atlantis,* 72

Baif, Jean-Antoine de, 25

Baroque, 5

"Beautiful curiosities," 10–11

Bezoard, 156, 184–85, 410n.84

Blair, Ann, 20

Bloodletting, 183–84

Boccaccio, Giovanni, 329

Bodin, Jean, 81, 279, 280, 284, 290, 291, 302, 303, 339, 418nn.25,30 *Six Books of the Republic,* 280

Boétie, Etienne de la, 252

Boileau, Nicolas, 350

Book of M, 99–102. *See also* Paracelsus, Theophrastus

Bordo, Susan, 327

Borromeo, Charles, Saint, 25

Bossuet, Jacques Bénigne, 377

Botero, Giovanni, 24

Boulliau, Ishmeal, 10

Bourdelot, Pierre, 12, 369; *Académie,* 65

Bourgeois, 263, 266, 415n.38

Bouteville, François, Count of, 259

Boyle, Robert, 18, 60, 64, 65, 73, 85, 103, 153

Brahe, Tycho, 121

Brissot, Jacques Pierre, 379

Brockliss, Laurence, 13, 159, 182, 194

Brown, Harcourt, 11, 118

Budé, Guillaume, 280

Buffon, Georges, 375

Bureau d'Adresse, 3–5, 7–8, 121; activities, 40–42; commerce and, 41; English interest in, 42; medicine and, 46–47; poor relief and, 38–44

Bureaux des charité, 43

Buridan, Jean, 121

Cabala, 94, 96

Cabinet Dupuy, 29–30

Caesar, Augustus, 310

Caesar, Julius, 239

Calvin, John, 263

Campanella, Tommaso, 13, 30–32, 62, 289; *The City of the Sun,* 32, 72, 289; defense of Galileo, 32, 394nn.28,32,33,34

Cardano, Girolamo, 8, 138, 141, 145, 146

Cartesian, 16, 232, 234, 348; dualism, 214, 216

Castiglione, Baldasare, 329, 339; *The Book of the Courtier,* 329, 339, 347

Cato, 225, 350, 359

Cattier, Isaac, 13

Cavendish, Margaret, 346

Censorship, 275–77, 372

Nerva, 311

Newton, Isaac, 18, 59–60, 61, 65, 73, 85, 153, 372, 374

Newtonian, 146, 150, 375

New World, 77, 136, 171, 269, 301

Nicole, Pierre, 318

Noblesse de la robe, 263

Non-naturals, Galenic, 165, 171, 221

Osma, Pietro de, 185

Palace Academy, 25, 347. *See also* Académie Royale de Poésie et de Musique

Palissy, Bernard, 148; *Discours Admirable de la Nature des Eaux et fountaines*, 148

Pansophia, 19, 20–21, 32

Paracelsians, 65, 99–102, 103, 104, 136, 177–79

Paracelsus, Theophrastus, 61, 69, 71, 73, 86, 99–102, 149, 153, 178, 190, 230, 329; Aristotle and, 71, 102, 112, 115; *Book of M★* and, 99–102; conferences and, 99–104; influence, 71–72. *See also* Medicine

Paré, Ambroise, 158

Park, Katharine, 101

Parlement of Paris, 47

Pascal, Blaise, 234

Pascalian, 213, 234

Passions, the, 222–29

Patin, Guy, 13, 46, 50, 159

Paul, Saint, 99, 251, 302, 349

Paul, Vincent de, 39

Paul III, 83

Peiresc, Nicholas-Claude, 29–30

Philosopher's stone, 63, 66, 70, 73, 75, 86, 88, 89, 206

Philosophes, 20, 76, 205, 324, 374, 378

Philosophy, natural, 18

Physiognomy, 163, 212–13

Pico della Mirandola, Giovanni, 24, 161, 330

Pizan, Christine de, 363

Plato, 24, 84, 113, 161, 219, 236, 280, 283, 328, 344, 368; *Republic*, 282, 283, 339; *Symposium*, 329; *Timaeus*, 329

Platonism, 29, 151

Pléiade, 24, 81

Pliny, 140, 142, 145; *Natural history*, 335

Plutarch, 167, 329; *Life of Cato*, 338; *Mulierum virtutes*, 329, 339

Point of honor, the, 259–61

Poitou, 35, 37–38

Politique, 261

Polychréton, 36

Poullain de la Barre, François, 362–63, 364, 365

Précieuses, 364

Principe, Lawrence, 73

Ptolemy, 119, 121, 124, 230

Public sphere, 7, 226

Puritanism, 257

Pythagoras, 149, 235

Pythagoreans, 142

Querelle des femmes, 326, 328, 330, 349

Ward, Samuel, 149
Wars of religion, 230, 279, 287
Weapon-salve, 72, 99, 182–83, 190; recipe, 409n.75
Willis, Thomas, 73
Winkelmann, Maria, 346

Witchcraft, 90

Xenophon, 348

Yates, Frances, 28, 393nn.7,8,9,14,17